P9-CFA-931

# ST. PAUL'S
# EPISTLE
## TO THE
# PHILIPPIANS

# ST. PAUL'S EPISTLE TO THE PHILIPPIANS

*A REVISED TEXT*
WITH
Introduction, Notes
and Dissertations

J. B. LIGHTFOOT, D.D., D.C.L., LL.D.

ZONDERVAN
PUBLISHING HOUSE
OF THE ZONDERVAN CORPORATION
GRAND RAPIDS, MICHIGAN 49506

*This 1953 edition of* ST. PAUL'S EPISTLE
TO THE PHILIPPIANS *is reprinted from the
original edition, published by Macmillan
& Company, London, 1913.*

First Zondervan printing  1953
Nineteenth printing  December 1980
ISBN 0-310-27650-0

PRINTED IN THE UNITED STATES OF AMERICA

TO

## THE REV. B. F. WESTCOTT, D.D.,

REGIUS PROFESSOR OF DIVINITY AT CAMBRIDGE,

IN AFFECTIONATE REMEMBRANCE

OF

MANY VALUABLE LESSONS LEARNT

FROM

AN INTIMATE PRIVATE FRIENDSHIP

AND FROM

ASSOCIATION IN A COMMON WORK

ΜΙΜΗΤΑΊ ΜΟΥ ΓΊΝΕϲΘΕ ΚΑΘΏϲ ΚἈΓΏ ΧΡΙϹΤΟΫ.

Παῦλος γενόμενος μέγιστος ὑπογραμμός.

CLEMENT.

Οὐχ ὡς Παῦλος διατάσσομαι ὑμῖν· ἐκεῖνος ἀπόστολος,
ἐγὼ κατάκριτος· ἐκεῖνος ἐλεύθερος, ἐγὼ δὲ μέχρ. νῦν δοῦλος.

IGNATIUS.

Οὔτε ἐγὼ οὔτε ἄλλος ὅμοιος ἐμοὶ δύναται κατακολουθῆσαι
τῇ σοφίᾳ τοῦ μακαρίου καὶ ἐνδόξου Παύλου.

POLYCARP.

# PREFACE TO THE FIRST EDITION.

The present volume is a second instalment of the commentary on St Paul's Epistles, of which I sketched a plan in the preface to my edition of the Galatians. At the same time it is intended, like its predecessor, to be complete in itself; so that the plan, as a whole, may be interrupted at any time without detriment to the parts.

Here again I have the pleasure of repeating my obligations to the standard works of reference, and to those commentators, both English and German, whose labours extend over both epistles and to whom I before acknowledged my debt of gratitude. The special commentaries on this epistle are neither so numerous nor so important, as on the former. The best, with which I am acquainted, are those of Van Hengel, of Rilliet, and of Eadie; but to these I am not conscious of any direct obligation which is not acknowledged in its proper place. I have also consulted from time to time several other more or less important works on this epistle, which it will be unnecessary to specify, as they either lay no claim to originality or for other reasons have furnished no material of which I could avail myself.

It is still a greater gratification to me to renew my thanks to personal friends, who have assisted me with their suggestions and corrections; and to one more especially whose aid has been freely given in correcting the proof-sheets of this volume throughout.

The Epistle to the Philippians presents an easier task to an editor than almost any of St Paul's Epistles. The readings are for the most part obvious; and only in a few passages does he meet with very serious difficulties of interpretation. I have taken advantage of this circumstance to introduce some investigations bearing on St Paul's Epistles and on Apostolic Christianity generally, by which this volume is perhaps swollen to an undue bulk, but which will proportionally relieve its successors. Thus the dissertation on the Christian ministry might well have been left for another occasion : but the mention of 'bishops and deacons' in the opening of this letter furnished a good text for the discussion ; and the Pastoral Epistles, which deal more directly with questions relating to the ministerial office, will demand so much space for the solution of other difficulties, that it seemed advisable to anticipate and dispose of this important subject.

In the dissertation on 'St Paul and the Three,' attached to the Epistle to the Galatians, I endeavoured to sketch the attitude of the Apostle towards Judaism and Judaic Christianity. In the present volume the discussion on St Paul and Seneca is offered as an attempt to trace the relations of the Gospel to a second form of religious thought—the most imposing system of heathen philosophy with which the Apostle was brought directly in contact. And on a later occasion, if this commentary should ever be extended to the Epistle to the Colossians, I hope to add yet a third chapter to this history in an essay on 'Christianity and Gnosis.' These may be considered the three most important types of dogmatic and systematized religion (whether within or without the pale of Christendom) with which St Paul was confronted.

As we lay down the Epistle to the Galatians and take up the Epistle to the Philippians, we cannot fail to be struck by the contrast. We have passed at once from the most dogmatic to the least dogmatic of the Apostle's letters, and the transition is instructive. If in the one the Gospel is presented in its opposition to an individual form of error, in the other it appears as it is in itself. The dogmatic element in the Galatians is due to special circumstances and bears a special character; while on the other hand the Philippian Epistle may be taken to exhibit the normal type of the Apostle's teaching, when not determined and limited by individual circumstances, and thus to present the essential substance of the Gospel. Dogmatic forms are the buttresses or the scaffold-poles of the building, not the building itself.

But, if the Epistle to the Philippians serves to correct one false conception of Christianity, it is equally impressive as a protest against another. In the natural reaction against excess of dogma, there is a tendency to lay the whole stress of the Gospel on its ethical precepts. For instance men will often tacitly assume, and even openly avow, that its kernel is contained in the Sermon on the Mount. This conception may perhaps seem more healthy in its impulse and more directly practical in its aim; but in fact it is not less dangerous even to morality than the other: for, when the sources of life are cut off, the stream will cease to flow. Certainly this is not St Paul's idea of the Gospel as it appears in the Epistle to the Philippians. If we would learn what he held to be its essence, we must ask ourselves what is the significance of such phrases as 'I desire you in the heart of Jesus Christ,' 'To me to live is Christ,' 'That I may know the power of Christ's resurrection,' 'I have all strength in Christ that giveth me power.' Though the Gospel is capable of doctrinal exposition, though it is eminently fertile in moral results, yet its substance is neither a dogmatic system nor an ethical code, but a Person and a Life.

Trinity College,
*July 1st,* 1868.

## PREFACE TO THE SIXTH EDITION.

The present edition is an exact reprint of the preceding one. This statement applies as well to the Essay on the Threefold Ministry, as to the rest of the work. I should not have thought it necessary to be thus explicit, had I not been informed of a rumour that I had found reason to abandon the main opinions expressed in that Essay. There is no foundation for any such report. The only point of importance on which I have modified my views, since the Essay was first written, is the authentic form of the letters of St Ignatius. Whereas in the earlier editions of this work I had accepted the three Curetonian letters, I have since been convinced (as stated in later editions) that the seven letters of the Short Greek are genuine. This divergence however does not materially affect the main point at issue, since even the Curetonian letters afford abundant evidence of the spread of episcopacy in the earliest years of the second century.

But on the other hand, while disclaiming any change in my opinions, I desire equally to disclaim the representations of those opinions which have been put forward in some quarters. The object of the Essay was an investigation into the origin of the Christian Ministry. The result has been a confirmation of the statement in the English Ordinal, 'It is evident unto all men diligently reading the Holy Scripture and ancient authors that from the Apostles' time there have been these orders of Ministers in Christ's Church, Bishops, Priests, and Deacons.' But I was scrupulously anxious not to overstate the evidence in any case; and it would seem that partial and qualifying statements, prompted by this anxiety, have assumed undue proportions in the minds of some readers, who have emphasized them to the neglect of the general drift of the Essay.

J. B. D.

_September 9, 1881._

## PREFACE TO THE TWELFTH EDITION.

*The following extracts from Bishop Lightfoot's works illustrate his
view of the Christian Ministry over and above the particular scope of
the Essay in his Commentary on the Philippians. He felt that unfair
use had been made of that special line of thought which he there
pursued, and soon after the close of the Lambeth Conference of* 1888
*he had this collection of passages printed.*

*It is felt by those who have the best means of knowing that he
would himself have wished the collection to stand together simply as
his reply to the constant imputation to him of opinions for which
writers wished to claim his support without any justification.*

1. Commentary on the Epistle to the Philippians (Essay on
the Christian Ministry, 1868).

(i) (See below, p. 201.)
'Unless we have recourse to a sweeping condemnation of received
documents, it seems vain to deny that early in the second century the
episcopal office was firmly and widely established. Thus during the last
three decades of the first century, and consequently during the lifetime of
the latest surviving Apostle, this change must have been brought about.'

(ii) (See below, p. 214.)
'The evidence for the early and wide extension of episcopacy throughout proconsular Asia, the scene of St John's latest labours, may be
considered irrefragable.'

(iii) (See below, p. 227.)
'But these notices, besides establishing the general prevalence of
episcopacy, also throw considerable light on its origin....Above all, they
establish this result clearly, that its maturer forms are seen first in those
regions where the latest surviving Apostles (more especially St John) fixed
their abode, and at a time when its prevalence cannot be dissociated from
their influence or their sanction.'

(iv) (See below, p. 234.)
'It has been seen that the institution of an episcopate must be
placed as far back as the closing years of the first century, and that
it cannot, without violence to historical testimony, be dissevered from the
name of St John.

(v) (See below, p. 267.)

'If the preceding investigation be substantially correct, the threefold ministry can be traced to Apostolic direction ; and short of an express statement we can possess no better assurance of a Divine appointment or at least a Divine sanction. If the facts do not allow us to unchurch other Christian communities differently organized, they may at least justify our jealous adhesion to a polity derived from this source.'

2. Commentary on the Epistle to the Philippians (Preface to the Sixth Edition), 1881. (See above, p. x.)

3. Sermon preached before the Representative Council of the Scottish Episcopal Church in St Mary's Church at Glasgow, October 10, 1882. ('Sermons preached on Special Occasions,' p. 182 sq.)

'When I spoke of unity as St Paul's charge to the Church of Corinth, the thoughts of all present must, I imagine, have fastened on one application of the Apostolic rule which closely concerns yourselves. Episcopal communities in Scotland outside the organization of the Scottish Episcopal Church—this is a spectacle which no one, I imagine, would view with satisfaction in itself, and which only a very urgent necessity could justify. Can such a necessity be pleaded ? " One body " as well as " one Spirit," this is the Apostolic rule. No natural interpretation can be put on these words which does not recognize the obligation of external, corporate union. Circumstances may prevent the realisation of the Apostle's conception, but the ideal must be ever present to our aspirations and our prayers. I have reason to believe that this matter lies very near to the hearts of all Scottish Episcopalians. May GOD grant you a speedy accomplishment of ¬our desire. You have the same doctrinal formularies : you acknowledge ,he same episcopal polity : you respect the same liturgical forms. "Sirs, ye are brethren." Do not strain the conditions of reunion too tightly. I cannot say, for I do not know, what faults or what misunderstandings there may have been on either side in the past. If there have been any faults, forget them. If there exist any misunderstandings, clear them up. " Let the dead past bury its dead."

\* \* \* \* \* \* \* \* \*

While you seek unity among yourselves, you will pray likewise that unity may be restored to your Presbyterian brothers. Not insensible to the special blessings which you yourselves enjoy, clinging tenaciously to the threefold ministry as the completeness of the Apostolic ordinance and the historical backbone of the Church, valuing highly all those sanctities of liturgical office and ecclesiastical season, which, modified from age to age, you have inherited from an almost immemorial past, thanking GOD, but not thanking Him in any Pharisaic spirit, that these so many and great privileges are continued to you which others have lost, you will nevertheless shrink, as from the venom of a serpent's fang, from any mean desire that their divisions may be perpetuated in the hope of profiting by their troubles. *Divide et impera* may be a shrewd worldly motto ; but coming in contact with spiritual things, it defiles them like pitch. *Pacifica et impera* is the true watchword of the Christian and the Churchman.'

4.  The Apostolic Fathers, Part ii., St Ignatius : St Polycarp, Vol. i. pp. 376, 377, 1885 (pp. 390, 391, 1889).

' The whole subject has been investigated by me in an Essay on " The Christian Ministry " ; and to this I venture to refer my readers for fuller information. It is there shown, if I mistake not, that though the New Testament itself contains as yet no direct and indisputable notices of a localized episcopate in the Gentile Churches, as distinguished from the moveable episcopate exercised by Timothy in Ephesus and by Titus in Crete, yet there is satisfactory evidence of its development in the later years of the Apostolic age ; that this development was not simultaneous and equal in all parts of Christendom ; that it is more especially connected with the name of St John ; and that in the early years of the second century the episcopate was widely spread and had taken firm root, more especially in Asia Minor and in Syria. If the evidence on which its extension in the regions east of the Ægean at this epoch be resisted, I am at a loss to understand what single fact relating to the history of the Christian Church during the first half of the second century can be regarded as established ; for the testimony in favour of this spread of the episcopate is more abundant and more varied than for any other institution or event during this period, so far as I recollect.'

5.  Sermon preached before the Church Congress at Wolverhampton, October 3, 1887. ('Sermons preached on Special Occasions,' p. 259 sq.)

'But if this charge fails, what shall we say of her isolation ? Is not this isolation, so far as it is true, much more her misfortune than her fault ? Is she to be blamed because she retained a form of Church government which had been handed down in unbroken continuity from the Apostolic times, and thus a line was drawn between her and the reformed Churches of other countries ? Is it a reproach to her that she asserted her liberty to cast off the accretions which had gathered about the Apostolic doctrine and practice through long ages, and for this act was repudiated by the Roman Church ? But this very position—call it isolation if you will—which was her reproach in the past, is her hope for the future. She was isolated because she could not consort with either extreme. She was isolated because she stood midway between the two. This central position is her vantage ground, which fits her to be a mediator, wheresoever an occasion of mediation may arise.

But this charge of isolation, if it had any appearance of truth seventy years ago, has lost its force now.'

6. Durham Diocesan Conference. Inaugural Address, October, 1887.

'When I speak of her religious position I refer alike to polity and to doctrine. In both respects the negative, as well as the positive, bearing of her position has to be considered. She has retained the form of Church government inherited from the Apostolic times, while she has shaken off a yoke, which even in medieval times our fathers found too heavy to bear, and which subsequent developments have rendered tenfold more oppressive. She has remained stedfast in the faith of Nicaea, but she has never compromised herself by any declaration which may entangle her in the meshes of science. The doctrinal inheritance of the past is hers, and the scientific hopes of the future are hers. She is intermediate and she may become mediatorial, when the opportunity occurs. It was this twofold inheritance of doctrine and polity which I had in view, when I spoke of the essentials which could under no circumstances be abandoned. Beyond this it seems to me that large concessions might be made. Unity is not uniformity......On the other hand it would be very short-sighted policy— even if it were not traitorous to the truth—to tamper with essentials and thus to imperil our mediatorial vantage ground, for the sake of snatching an immediate increase of numbers.'

7. Address on the Reopening of the Chapel, Auckland Castle, August 1st, 1888. (' Leaders in the Northern Church,' p. 145.)

' But, while we " lengthen our cords," we must " strengthen our stakes likewise. Indeed this strengthening of our stakes will alone enable us t lengthen our cords with safety, when the storms are howling around u We cannot afford to sacrifice any portion of the faith once delivered to th saints ; we cannot surrender for any immediate advantages the threefol ministry which we have inherited from Apostolic times, and which is th historic backbone of the Church. But neither can we on the other han return to the fables of medievalism or submit to a yoke which our father found too grievous to be borne—a yoke now rendered a hundredfold mor oppressive to the mind and conscience, weighted as it is by recent an unwarranted impositions of doctrine.'

# CONTENTS.

## DISSERTATIONS.

# I.

## ST PAUL IN ROME.

THE arrival of St Paul in the metropolis marks a new and important epoch in the history of the Christian Church. Hitherto he had come in contact with Roman institutions modified by local circumstances and administered by subordinate officers in the outlying provinces of the Empire. Now he was in the very centre and focus of Roman influence; and from this time forward neither the policy of the government nor the character of the reigning prince was altogether a matter of indifference to the welfare of Christianity. The change of scene had brought with it a change in the mutual relations between the Gospel and the Empire. They were now occupying the same ground, and a collision was inevitable. Up to this time the Apostle had found rather an ally than an enemy in a power which he had more than once successfully invoked against the malignity of his fellow-countrymen. This precarious alliance was henceforward exchanged for direct, though intermittent, antagonism. The Empire, which in one of his earlier epistles he would seem to have taken as the type of that restraining power which kept Antichrist in check[1], was itself now assuming the character of Antichrist. When St Paul appealed from the tribunal of the Jewish procurator to the court of Cæsar, he attracted the notice and challenged the hostility of the greatest power which the world had ever seen. The very emperor, to whom the appeal was made, bears the

---

[1] 2 Thess. ii. 6, 7.

The Neronian persecution a consequence.

ignominy of the first systematic persecution of the Christians; and thus commenced the long struggle, which raged for several centuries, and ended in establishing the Gospel on the ruins of the Roman Empire. It was doubtless the impulse given to the progress of Christianity by the presence of its greatest preacher in the metropolis, which raised the Church in Rome to a position of prominence, and made it a mark for the wanton attacks of the tyrant. Its very obscurity would have shielded it otherwise. The preaching of Paul was the necessary antecedent to the persecution of Nero.

St Paul's sense of the importance of this visit.

It is probable that the Apostle foresaw the importance of his decision, when he transferred his cause to the tribunal of Cæsar. There is a significant force in his declaration at an earlier date, that he '*must* see Rome[1].' It had long been his 'earnest desire[2]' to visit the imperial city, and he had been strengthened in this purpose by a heavenly vision[3]. To prepare the way for his visit he had addressed to the Roman Church a letter containing a more complete and systematic exposition of doctrine than he ever committed to writing before or after. And now, when the moment has arrived, the firm and undaunted resolution, with which in defiance of policy he makes his appeal, bears testimony to the strength of his conviction[4].

Its prominence in St Luke's narrative.

The sacred historian takes pains to emphasize this visit to Rome. He doubtless echoes the feeling of St Paul himself, when he closes his record with a notice of the Apostle's success in the metropolis, deeming this the fittest termination to his narrative, as the virtual and prospective realisation of our Lord's promise placed in its forefront, that the Apostles should be His witnesses to 'the uttermost part of the earth[5].'

Aspect of affairs when St Paul arrived.

It was probably in the early spring of the year 61, that St Paul arrived in Rome[6]. The glorious five years, which ushered in the reign of Nero amidst the acclamations of a

---

[1] Acts xix. 21.

[2] Rom. i. 10—16, xv. 22—24, 28, 29, 32, ἐπιποθῶ, ἐπιποθίαν ἔχων.

[3] Acts xxiii. 11 'So must thou bear witness also at Rome.'

[4] Acts xxv. 11.

[5] Acts i. 8. See Lekebusch *Apostelgeschichte* p. 227 sq.

[6] See Wieseler *Chronol.* p. 66 sq.

grateful people, and which later ages recalled with wistful regret, as an ideal of imperial rule[1], had now drawn to a close. The unnatural murder of Agrippina had at length revealed the true character of Nero. Burrus and Seneca, it is true, still lingered at the head of affairs: but their power was waning. Neither the blunt honesty of the soldier nor the calm moderation of the philosopher could hold their ground any longer against the influence of more subtle and less scrupulous counsellors.

At Rome the Apostle remained for 'two whole years,' preaching the Gospel without interruption, though preaching it in bonds. By specifying this period[2] St Luke seems to imply that at its close there was some change in the outward condition of the prisoner. This change can hardly have been any other than the approach of his long-deferred trial, which ended, as there is good ground for believing[3], in his acquittal and release. At all events he must have been liberated before July 64, if liberated at all. The great fire which then devastated Rome became the signal for an onslaught on the unoffending Christians; and one regarded as the ringleader of the hated sect could hardly have escaped the general massacre. *Length of his sojourn.*

It will appear strange that so long an interval was allowed to elapse before the trial came on. But while the defendant had no power to hasten the tardy course of justice, the accusers were interested in delaying it. They must have foreseen plainly enough the acquittal of a prisoner whom the provincial *Probable causes of the delay of his trial.*

[1] Aurel. Vict. *Cæs.* 5 'Uti merito Trajanus sæpius testaretur procul differre cunctos principes Neronis quinquennio.'

[2] Acts xxviii. 30, 31. The inference in the text will not hold, if, as some suppose, St Luke's narrative was accidentally broken off and terminates abruptly. From this view however I dissent for two reasons. (1) A comparison with the closing sentences of the Gospel shows a striking parallelism in the plan of the two narratives; they end alike, as they had begun alike. (2) The success of St Paul's preaching in Rome is a fitter termination to the history than any other incident which could have been chosen. It is the most striking realisation of that promise of the universal spread of the Gospel, which is the starting-point of the narrative.

[3] The discussion of this question is reserved for the introduction to the Pastoral Epistles.

governor himself had declared to be innocent[1]. If they wished to defer the issue, the collection of evidence was a sufficient plea to urge in order to obtain an extension of time[2]. St Paul was charged with stirring up sedition among 'all the Jews throughout the world[3].' From the whole area therefore, over which his labours had extended, witnesses must be summoned. In this way two years might easily run out before the prisoner appeared for judgment. But more potent probably, than any formal plea, was the indolence or the caprice of the emperor himself[4], who frequently postponed the hearing of causes indefinitely without any assignable reason, and certainly would not put himself out to do justice to a despised provincial, labouring under a perplexing charge connected with some 'foreign superstition.' If St Paul had lingered in close confinement for two years under Felix, he might well be content to remain under

*Indolence of Nero.*

---

[1] Acts xxv. 12, 25; comp. xxvi. 31,32.

[2] Two cases in point are quoted, as occurring about this time. Tac. *Ann.* xiii. 52 ' Silvanum magna vis accusatorum circumsteterat, poscebatque tempus evocandorum testium: reus illico defendi postulabat.' Silvanus had been proconsul of Africa. Also we are told of Suillius, who was accused of peculation in the government of Asia, *Ann.* xiii. 43 ' Quia inquisitionem annuam impetraverunt, brevius visum [sub-] urbana crimina incipi quorum obvii testes erant.' In both these cases the accusers petition for an extension of the period, while it is the interest of the defendant to be tried at once. In the second case a year is demanded and allowed for collecting evidence, though the crimes in question are confined to his tenure of office and to the single province of 'Asia.' On the whole subject see Wieseler, *Chronol.* 407 sq., who has fully discussed the possible causes of delay. Compare also Conybeare and Howson II. p. 462 sq. (2nd ed.).

[3] Acts xxiv. 5 πᾶσι τοῖς Ἰουδαίοις

τοῖς κατὰ τὴν οἰκουμένην.

[4] Josephus (*Ant.* xviii. 6. 5) says of Tiberius, whom he describes as μελλητὴς εἰ καί τις ἑτέρων βασιλέων ἢ τυράννων γενόμενος, that he deferred the trial of prisoners indefinitely in order to prolong their tortures. Nero seems to have been almost as dilatory, though more from recklessness and indolence than from deliberate purpose. The case of the priests accused by Felix (see below, p. 5, note 4) illustrates this. Felix ceased to be procurator in the year 60: yet they were still prisoners in 63 or 64, and were only then liberated at the intercession of Josephus. For the date see Clinton *Fasti Rom.* I. pp. 23, 45, 77. Geib *Geschichte des römischen Criminalprocesses etc.* p. 691, speaking of causes tried before the emperor, describes the practice of the early Cæsars as so ' unsteady and capricious in all respects,' that no definite rule can be laid down: ' Erst in der späteren Kaiser zeit,' he adds, 'ist dieses anders gewor den und zwar namentlich hinsichtlich des Appellationsverfahrens ' Similarly

less irksome restraints for an equal length of time, awaiting the pleasure of Cæsar.

Meanwhile events occurred at Rome which shook society to its foundations. The political horizon was growing every day darker[1]. Death deprived Nero of his most upright adviser in the person of Burrus the prefect of the prætorians. The office thus vacated was handed over to Tigellinus, with whom was associated as colleague the feeble and insignificant Rufus. By the death of Burrus the influence of Seneca was effectually broken[2]; and, though the emperor refused to consent to his retirement, his part in the direction of affairs was henceforth merely nominal. At the same time the guilty career of Nero culminated in the divorce and death of Octavia; and the cruel and shameless Poppæa became the emperor's consort in her stead. With a strange inconsistency of character, which would atone for profligate living by a fervour of religious devotion, and of which that age especially was fertile in examples, she had become a proselyte to Judaism[3], and more than once advocated the cause of her adopted race before the emperor with zeal and success[4].

*Stirring events in Rome,*

Laboulaye *Lois Criminelles des Romains* p. 444, 'Sous les premiers Césars tout se fit sans règle et sans mesure, et il ne faut pas chercher à cette époque de système régulier,' etc. There is no trace of a statutable limitation of time (præscriptio) applying to the imperial tribunal at this epoch.

[1] Tac. *Ann.* xiv. 51 'Gravescentibus indies publicis malis.'

[2] Tac. *Ann.* xiv. 52 'Mors Burri infregit Senecæ potentiam.'

[3] Joseph. *Antiq.* xx. 8. 11 θεοσεβὴς γὰρ ἦν, i.e. a worshipper of the true God, a proselytess. In connexion with this fact the notice of her burial is remarkable; Tac. *Ann.* xvi. 6 'Corpus non igni abolitum, ut Romanus mos; sed regum externorum consuetudine differtum odoribus conditur etc.' See Friedländer *Sittengeschichte Roms* i. p.

348 (2nd ed.).

[4] It is not irrelevant to relate two incidents which occurred at this time, as they illustrate the nature of the communication kept up between the Jews and the imperial court, and the sort of influence which Poppæa exerted on the affairs of this people.

(1) Felix, while procurator of Judæa, had brought a trivial charge against certain Jewish priests, and sent them to Rome to plead their cause before Cæsar. Here they were kept in a lingering captivity, living on the hardest fare, but remaining faithful in their allegiance to the God of their fathers. The historian Josephus, to whom these priests were known, then a young man, undertook a journey to Rome for the purpose of procuring their liberation. Like St Paul he was shipwrecked in

How far the personal condition of St Paul, or his prospects at the approaching trial, may have been affected by these two changes, I shall have to consider hereafter. At all events he cannot have been ignorant of such stirring incidents. His enforced companionship with the soldiers of the prætorian guard must have kept him informed of all changes in the administration of the camp. His intimacy with the members of Cæsar's household must have brought to his hearing the intrigues and crimes of the imperial court. It is strange therefore, that in the epistles written from Rome during this period there is not any, even the faintest, reference to events

so notorious in history. Strange at least at first sight. But the Apostle would not venture to risk his personal safety, or the cause which he advocated, by perilous allusions in letters which from their very nature must be made public. Nor indeed is it probable that he was under any temptation to allude to them. He did not breathe the atmosphere of political life; he was absorbed in higher interests and anxieties. With the care of all the churches daily pressing upon him, with a deep sense of the paramount importance of his personal mission,

---

the Adriatic, and like him he also landed at Puteoli. Arrived at Rome, he was introduced to Poppæa by a certain Jew, Aliturus by name, an actor of mimes, who was in great favour with Nero. The empress not only advocated the cause which he had at heart and procured the liberation of his friends, but sent him back to his native country laden with presents (Joseph. *Vit.* § 3). This took place in the year 63 or 64, and was therefore nearly, if not quite, coincident with St Paul's residence in Rome.

(2) The second incident almost certainly occurred while the Apostle was in the metropolis. The king's palace at Jerusalem stood in the immediate neighbourhood of the temple. Agrippa had recently built a lofty tower, which enabled him to overlook the sacred en-

closure and to witness the performance of the holy rites. This was an outrage on Jewish feeling, as well as a breach of immemorial custom, and was resented accordingly. The Jews erected a counterwall, which excluded all view from the royal residence. Festus the procurator took the side of the king and ordered the demolition of this wall; but afterwards yielded so far as to allow the Jews to refer the case to Nero. An embassy was accordingly sent to Rome, composed of twelve persons including Ismael the high-priest and Helcias the treasurer. Poppæa interested herself in the success of their mission, and in deference to her entreaties the emperor allowed the wall to stand (Joseph. *Ant.* xx. 8. 11).

It is suggested (Conybeare and Howson II. p. 462), that this embassy may

with a near and fervid anticipation of his own dissolution and
union with Christ, if not of the great and final crisis when
heaven and earth themselves shall pass away, it is not surprising that all minor events, all transitory interests, should be
merged in those more engrossing thoughts. His life—so he
himself writing from Rome describes the temper of the true
believer—his life was hidden with Christ in God[1].

The degree of restraint put upon a person labouring under
a criminal charge was determined by various circumstances; by
the nature of the charge itself, by the rank and reputation of
the accused, by the degree of guilt presumed to attach to him.
Those most leniently dealt with were handed over to their
friends, who thus became sureties for their appearance; the
worst offenders were thrown into prison and loaded with
chains[2]. The captivity of St Paul at Rome was neither the
severest nor the lightest possible.

By his appeal to Cæsar[3] he had placed himself at the
emperor's disposal. Accordingly on his arrival in Rome he is
delivered over to the commander of the imperial guards, the
prefect of the prætorians[4], under whose charge he appears to

*Character of his captivity.*

have been entrusted with the prosecu-
tion of St Paul. It seems at least
certain, that the ambassadors arrived
in Rome while the Apostle was still a
prisoner there; since Festus had ceased
to be procurator before the autumn of
62: but beyond the coincidence of date
all is conjecture. In any case the
friendly meeting of Festus and Agrippa,
related in the Acts, may have had reference to this dispute about Agrippa's
building: and if so, the incident links
together the accusation of St Paul and
the complaint against Agrippa.

[1] Col. iii. 3.

[2] On the different kinds of *custodia*,
roughly distinguished as *libera, publica*,
and *militaris*, but admitting various
modifications, see Geib p. 561 sq.,
Wieseler *Chronol.* p. 380 sq., 394 sq.

The custody of St Paul belongs to the
last of the three.

[3] In republican times a difference
was made between 'provocatio' and
'appellatio.' The former was a reference to the populus, the latter to the
tribunes. On the other hand, the appeal to the emperor was called indifferently 'provocatio' or 'appellatio'; for
he combined all functions in himself.
The latter term however seems to have
been the more common. On this subject consult Geib p. 675 sq., Rein *Das
Privatrecht etc.* p. 960. Krebs, *Opusc.*
p. 135 sq., has an essay *De provocatione
D. Pauli ad Cæsarem;* which however
does not contain any important matter.

[4] Acts xxviii. 16 παρέδωκεν τοὺς
δεσμίους τῷ στρατοπεδάρχῃ, i.e. to the
'præfectus prætorio' or 'præfectus præ-

He is in
bonds, but have remained throughout his captivity. He represents himself as strictly a prisoner : he speaks again and again of his
bonds[1]. At times he uses more precise language, mentioning the 'coupling-chain'[2]. According to Roman custom he was
bound by the hand to the soldier who guarded him, and was
never left alone day or night. As the soldiers would relieve
guard in constant succession, the prætorians one by one were
brought into communication with the 'prisoner of Jesus Christ,'

tori,' for both cases are found in inscriptions. From the use of the singular here it has been argued with much
probability that the officer in question
was Burrus. He held the prefecture
alone, whereas both before and after
his time the office was shared by two
persons: see Tac. *Ann.* xii. 42, xiv.
51. For the changes which this office
underwent at different times consult
Becker and Marquardt *Röm. Alterth.*
II. 3, p. 286. With the singular here
contrast the plural in Trajan's letter,
Plin. *Ep.* x. 65 ' Vinctus mitti ad præ-
fectos prætori mei debet,' and in Phi-
lostr. *Vit. Soph.* ii. 32 ἀνεπέμφθη εἰς
τὴν 'Ρώμην ὡς ἀπολογησόμενος τοῖς τῶν
στρατοπέδων ἡγεμόσιν: see Wieseler
*Chronol.* p. 88. The whole clause however is rejected by most recent editors,
as the balance of existing authorities is
very decidedly against it. On the other
hand the statement does not look like
an arbitrary fiction, and probably contains a genuine tradition, even if it was
no part of the original text.

[1] He calls himself δέσμος, Acts
xxviii. 17, Philem. 1, 9, Ephes. iii. 1,
iv. 1; his δεσμοί are mentioned Phil. i.
7, 13, 14, 17, Philem. 10, 13, Coloss.
iv. 18; comp. Coloss. iv. 3 δι' ὃ (or ὃν)
καὶ δέδεμαι.

[2] ἅλυσις, Ephes. vi. 20 ὑπὲρ οὗ πρεσ-
βεύω ἐν ἁλύσει, Acts xxviii. 20 τὴν
ἅλυσιν ταύτην περίκειμαι. The word
seems originally to differ from δεσμοί,
only as bringing out the idea of attach-

ment rather than *confinement*. Afterwards however it signifies especially
' hand-fetters ' (manicæ), as opposed to
πέδαι (pedicæ) ; Mark v. 4 πέδαις καὶ
ἁλύσεσιν δεδέσθαι, καὶ διεσπάσθαι ὑπ' αὐτοῦ τὰς ἁλύσεις καὶ τὰς πέδας συντετρίφθαι. Meyer indeed denies this distinction : but the words διεσπάσθαι,
συντετρίφθαι, if taken to denote the action of the hands and feet respectively,
are much more expressive; and the distinction of ἁλύσεις and πέδαι seems certainly to be observed elsewhere, e. g.
Polyb. iii. 82. 8, Dion. Hal. *Ant. Rom.*
vi. 26, 27: comp. Plut. *Mor.* p. 829 A
ταῖς χερσὶν ἁλύσεις. In Aristoph.*Fragm.*
(Meineke II. p. 1079), where both ἁλύσεις and πέδαι are mentioned as ladies'
ornaments, the former are perhaps
' bracelets ' or ' cuffs ': see also Nicostr.
*Fragm.* (ib. III. p. 289). Hence the
word is used especially of the 'coupling-
chain,' ' hand-cuff,' by which the prisoner was attached to his guard, as in
the case of Agrippa, Joseph. *Ant.* xviii.
6. 7, 10. Compare the metaphor in
Lucian, *Quom. hist. conscr.* § 55 ἐχόμε-
νον αὐτοῦ καὶ ἁλύσεως τρόπῳ (τρόπον?)
συνηρμοσμένον, with Senec. *Epist.* i. 5
' Quemadmodum eadem catena et cus-
todiam et militem copulat.' See a similar use in Plutarch, *Vit. Mar.* 27 ἦσαν
ὑπὲρ τοῦ μὴ διασπᾶσθαι τὴν τάξιν οἱ
πρόμαχοι μακραῖς ἁλύσεσι συνεχόμενοι.

When the confinement was very rigorous, the prisoner was bound to *two*
soldiers. This was the case with St

and thus he was able to affirm that his bonds had borne witness to the Gospel 'throughout the imperial regiments[1].'

On the other hand, the severity of his confinement was not so great as this circumstance standing alone might seem to imply. It is certain that all had free access to him, and that he was allowed to converse and write without restraint. He was not thrown into prison, but lived in rooms of his own. When he first arrived, he was taken to temporary lodgings; either to a house of public entertainment, or to the abode of some friend[2]. But afterwards he rented a dwelling of his own[3], and there he remained apparently till his release.

*enjoys compara- tive li- berty.*

A natural desire has been felt to determine a locality so fraught with interest as St Paul's abode in Rome. Some have imagined him a prisoner within the barracks attached to the imperial residence on the Palatine. Others have fixed his dwelling-place in the great camp, the head-quarters of the prætorians, without the walls to the north-east of the city. The former conjecture seems hardly consistent with the mention of his own hired house. The latter is less unlikely, for the camp

*St Paul's abode at Rome.*

---

Peter, Acts xii. 6 κοιμώμενος μεταξὺ δύο στρατιωτῶν δεδεμένος ἀλύσεσιν δυσίν. Such had also been St Paul's condition during the early days of his captivity at Jerusalem: Acts xxi. 33. A relaxation of the rigour of his earlier imprisonment is mentioned Acts xxiv. 23. On this whole subject see Wieseler *Chronol.* p. 380 sq. When Ignatius, *Rom.* 5, speaks of himself as ἐνδεδεμένος δέκα λεοπάρδοις ὅ ἐστιν στρατιωτικὸν τάγμα, we must understand that he was in charge of a company of ten, who successively relieved guard, so that he was attached to one at a time.

[1] Phil. i. 13 ἐν ὅλῳ τῷ πραιτωρίῳ.

[2] Acts xxviii. 23 εἰς τὴν ξενίαν. Suidas explains ξενίαν by καταγώγιον, κατάλυμα, and similarly Hesychius; comp. *Clem. Hom.* i. 15 ἐπιβάντος μου τῆς γῆς καὶ ξενίαν θηρωμένου, viii. 2, xii. 24, xiv. 1. 8. On the other hand Philem.

22 ἑτοίμαζέ μοι ξενίαν rather suggests a lodging in a friend's house: comp. Acts xxi. 16.

[3] Acts xxviii. 30 ἐνέμεινεν διετίαν ὅλην ἐν ἰδίῳ μισθώματι, where ἰδίῳ seems certainly to distinguish the μίσθωμα here from the ξενία above. The word μίσθωμα elsewhere signifies 'hire,' being used especially in a bad sense of shameful wages, e.g. Deut. xxiii. 18. Hence Philo *in Flacc.* p. 536 M μετὰ τὸν ἐπάρατον μισθόν, ἢ κυριώτερον εἰπεῖν, τὸ μίσθωμα: comp. Ælian *V. H.* iv. 12. The sense, which it has here, is not recognised by the Greek lexicographers, nor can I find any other instance. Wetstein indeed quotes ἐν μισθώματι οἰκεῖν as from Philo, but gives no reference, and I suspect there is a mistake. This exceptional meaning of μίσθωμα may perhaps be explained as a translation of the Latin 'conductum.'

was large and might have contained within its precincts lodgings
rented by prisoners under military custody.   Yet the reference
to the 'prætorium' does not require this, and the circumstances
seem naturally to point to a separate dwelling.   Within the
camp then his abode may have been, near to the camp it probably was, for in the choice of a locality the convenience of the
soldiers in relieving guard would naturally be consulted[1].

Thus mitigated, his captivity did not materially impede the
progress of his missionary work.   On the contrary he himself
regarded his bonds as a powerful agency in the spread of the
Gospel.   Beyond the dreary monotony of his situation, which
might well have crushed a spirit unsustained by his lofty hopes
and consolations, he was not very hardly treated.   It was at
least an alleviation, that no restriction was placed on the visits
of his friends.

Friends       Of these friends not a few names might be supplied by con-
resident in
Rome.       jecture from the long list of salutations in the Epistle to the
Romans.   Did he fall in once again with Aquila and Priscilla,
his fellow-artisans and fellow-sufferers, who 'for his life had
laid down their own necks'[2]?   Did he still find in Rome his
countrymen, perhaps his kinsmen, Andronicus and Junias and
Herodion[3]?   Did he experience once more the tender care of
the mother of Rufus, who in times past had treated him as her
own son[4]?   Did he renew his intimacy with those former friends
of whom he speaks with affectionate warmth, Epænetus his
well-beloved, Urbanus his helper in Christ, Mary who laboured
much for him, Amplias, Stachys, Persis[5]?

Of Roman residents however, beyond a general reference to
the members of Cæsar's household[6], he makes no mention in
his letters written from the metropolis.   They would probably
His perso-  be unknown to his distant correspondents.   But of occasional
nalcompa-
nions and  visitors in Rome, his converts or his colleagues in the Gospel, the

---

[1] See the detached notes on the
meaning of 'prætorium' in i. 13.

[2] Rom. xvi. 3.

[2] Rom. xvi. 7, 11.

[4] Rom. xvi. 13.

[5] Rom. xvi. 5, 6, 8, 9, 12.

[6] Phil. iv. 22.

companions of his travels and the delegates of foreign churches, other as-
not a few are named. His youthful disciple and associate sociates.
Timotheus, the best beloved of his spiritual sons, seems to have
been with him during the whole or nearly the whole of his
captivity[1]. Another friend also, who had shared with him the
perils of the voyage, Luke 'the beloved physician,' now his
fellow-labourer and perhaps his medical attendant, hereafter his
biographer, is constantly by his side[2]. His two favourite Macedonian churches are well represented among his companions :
Philippi despatches Epaphroditus with pecuniary aid, welcome
to him as a relief of his wants but doubly welcome as a token
of their devoted love[3]: Aristarchus is present from Thessalonica[4],
a tried associate, who some years before had imperilled his life
with St Paul at Ephesus[5] and now shared his captivity at Rome[6].
Delegates from the Asiatic churches too were with him : Tychicus[7], a native of the Roman province of Asia and probably of
Ephesus its capital[8], the Apostle's companion both in earlier
and later days[9]: and Epaphras the evangelist of his native
Colossæ, who came to consult St Paul on the dangerous heresies
then threatening this and the neighbouring churches over
which he watched with intense anxiety[10]. Besides these were

[1] His name appears in the opening
salutations of the Epistles to the Philippians, Colossians, and Philemon:
compare also Phil. ii. 19—23. It may
perhaps be inferred from St Luke's
silence, Acts xxvii. 2, that Timotheus
did not accompany St Paul on his journey to Rome, but joined him soon after
his arrival.

[2] Col. iv. 14, Philem. 24.

[3] Phil. ii. 25—30, iv. 14—18. See
below, p. 60.

[4] Col. iv. 10, Philem. 24. On the
notice of Aristarchus in Acts xxvii. 2,
see below, p. 34, note 2.

[5] Acts xix. 29.

[6] In Col. iv. 10, St Paul styles him
ὁ συναιχμάλωτός μου. Perhaps however
this may refer to the incident at Ephesus already alluded to (Acts xix. 29).

Or does it signify a spiritual subjection
(αἰχμαλωσία, Rom. vii. 23, 2 Cor. x. 5,
Ephes. iv. 8), so that it may be compared with σύνδουλος (Col. i. 7, iv. 7),
and συνστρατιώτης (Phil. ii. 25, Philem.
2)? St Paul uses the term συναιχμά-
λωτος also of Epaphras (Philem. 23),
and of his 'kinsmen' Andronicus and
Junias or Junia (Rom. xvi. 7). See
the note on Col. iv. 10.

[7] Ephes. vi. 21, Col. iv. 7.

[8] Acts xx. 4, 2 Tim. iv. 12. He is
mentioned together with Trophimus,
Acts l. c., and Trophimus was an Ephe-
sian, ib. xxi. 29.

[9] Acts xx. 4, 2 Tim. iv. 12: comp.
Tit. iii. 12. Perhaps also he is one of
the anonymous brethren in 2 Cor. viii.
18, 22.

[10] Col. i. 7, iv. 12.

other friends old and new : one pair especially, whose names are linked together by contrast ; John Mark who, having deserted in former years, has now returned to his post and is once more a loyal soldier of Christ[1]; and Demas, as yet faithful to his allegiance, who hereafter will turn renegade and desert the Apostle in his sorest need[2]. To these must be added a disciple of the Circumcision, whose surname 'the just'[3] proclaims his devotion to his former faith—one Jesus, to us a name only, but to St Paul much more than a name, for amidst the general defection of the Jewish converts he stood by the Apostle almost alone[4]. Lastly, there was Philemon's runaway slave Onesimus, 'not now a slave, but above a slave, a brother beloved,' whose career is the most touching episode in the apostolic history and the noblest monument of the moral power of the Gospel[5].

St Paul's correspondence with foreign Churches.    These friendships supported him under the ' care of all the churches,' which continued to press upon him in his captivity not less heavily than before. The epistles of this period bear testimony alike to the breadth and the intensity of his sympathy with others. The Church of Philippi which he had himself planted and watered, and the Church of Colossæ with which he had no personal acquaintance, alike claim and receive his fatherly advice. The temporal interest of the individual slave, and the spiritual well-being of the collective Churches of Asia[6], are equally the objects of his care. Yet these four epistles, which alone survive, must represent very inadequately the extent of the demands made upon his time and energies at this period. There is no notice here of Thessalonica, none of Corinth, none of the churches of Syria, of his own native Cilicia, of Lycaonia and Pisidia and Galatia. It is idle to speculate on the possibility of lost epistles : but, whether by his letters or by his delegates, we cannot doubt that these brotherhoods,

---

[1] Col. iv. 10, Philem. 24: comp. 2 Tim. iv. 11.

[2] Col. iv. 14, Philem. 24: comp. 2 Tim. iv. 10.

[3] See the note on Col. iv. 11.

[4] Col. iv. 11.

[5] Col. iv. 9, and Philem. 10 sq.

[6] The Epistle to the Ephesians seems to have been a circular letter to the Asiatic Churches.

which had a special claim upon him as their spiritual father, received their due share of attention from this 'prisoner of Jesus Christ.'

But it was on Rome especially that he would concentrate his energies: Rome, which for years past he had longed to see with an intense longing: the common sink of all the worst vices of humanity[1], and therefore the noblest sphere for evangelical zeal. Here he would find a wider field and a richer soil, than any which had hitherto attracted him. But the ground had not lain altogether fallow. There was already a large and flourishing Church, a mixed community of Jew and Gentile converts, founded, it would seem, partly by his own companions and disciples, partly by teachers commissioned directly from Palestine and imbued with the strongest prejudices of their race; a heterogeneous mass, with diverse feelings and sympathies, with no well-defined organization, with no other bond of union than the belief in a common Messiah; gathering, we may suppose, for purposes of worship in small knots here and there, as close neighbourhood or common nationality or sympathy or accident drew them together; but, as a body, lost in the vast masses of the heathen population, and only faintly discerned or contemptuously ignored even by the large community of Jewish residents.

*Existing state of the Roman Church.*

With the nucleus of a Christian Church thus ready to hand, but needing to be instructed and consolidated, with an enormous outlying population of unconverted Jews and Gentiles to be gathered into the fold, the Apostle entered upon his work. Writing to the Romans three years before, he had expressed his assurance that, when he visited them, he would 'come in the fulness of the blessing of Christ[2].' There is every reason to believe that this confidence was justified by the event. The notice, with which the narrative of St Luke closes, implies no small measure of success. The same may be inferred from

*Success of St Paul's labours in Rome.*

---

[1] Tac. *Ann.* xv. 44 'Quo cuncta undique atrocia aut pudenda confluunt celebranturque.' Tacitus is speaking of the spread of Christianity in Rome.

[2] Rom. xv. 29.

allusions in St Paul's own epistles and is confirmed by the
subsequent history of the Roman Church.

In considering the results of the Apostle's labours more in
detail, it will be necessary to view the Jewish and Gentile converts separately. In no Church are their antipathies and feuds
more strongly marked than in the Roman. Long after their
junction the two streams are distinctly traced, each with its own
colour, its own motion; and a generation at least elapses, before
they are inseparably united. In the history of St Paul they
flow almost wholly apart.

St Paul
addresses
himself
first to the
Jews,

1. Several thousands of Jews had been uprooted from their
native land and transplanted to Rome by Pompeius. In this
new soil they had spread rapidly, and now formed a very important element in the population of the metropolis. Living
unmolested in a quarter of their own beyond the Tiber, protected and fostered by the earlier Cæsars, receiving constant
accessions from home, they abounded everywhere, in the forum,
in the camp, even in the palace itself[1]. Their growing influence alarmed the moralists and politicians of Rome. 'The
vanquished,' said Seneca bitterly, 'have given laws to their
victors[2].' Immediately on his arrival the Apostle summoned to
his lodgings the more influential members of his race—probably
the rulers of the synagogues[3]. In seeking this interview he
seems to have had a double purpose. On the one hand he
was anxious to secure their good-will and thus to forestall the
calumnies of his enemies; on the other he paid respect to their
spiritual prerogative, by holding out to them the first offer of
the Gospel[4]. On their arrival he explained to them the cir-

---

[1] On the numbers and influence of
the Jews in Rome, see Merivale *History of the Romans* VI. p. 257 sq., Friedländer *Sittengesch.* III. p. 509 sq.

[2] Seneca quoted by St Augustine *De
Civ. Dei* vi. 11, 'Cum interim usque eo
sceleratissimæ gentis consuetudo con-
valuit, ut per omnes jam terras recep-
ta sit: victi victoribus leges dederunt.'

Compare also Pers. *Sat.* v. 180, Juv.
vi. 542. The mock excuse of Horace,
*Sat.* i. 9. 70. shows how wide was the
influence of this race in Rome, even a
generation earlier. See also Ovid *A. A.*
i. 76, and references in Merivale p. 259.

[3] Acts xxviii. 17 sq.

[4] He had declared this prerogative
of the Jews in writing to the Roman

cumstances which had brought him there.  To his personal ex- *but is coldly received.*
planations they replied, in real or affected ignorance, that they
had received no instructions from Palestine; they had heard no
harm of him and would gladly listen to his defence; only this
they knew, that the sect of which he professed himself an adherent, had a bad name everywhere[1].  For the exposition of his
teaching a later day was fixed.  When the time arrived, he ' expounded and testified the kingdom of God,' arguing from their
own scriptures ' from morning till evening.'  His success was not
greater than with his fellow-countrymen elsewhere.  He dismissed
them, denouncing their stubborn unbelief and declaring his intention of communicating to the Gentiles that offer which they had
spurned.  It is not probable that he made any further advances
in this direction.  He had broken ground and nothing more.

Yet it was not from any indisposition to hear of Messiah's *Their an-ticipation of Mes-siah.*
advent that they gave this cold reception to the new teacher.
The announcement in itself would have been heartily welcomed,
for it harmonised with their most cherished hopes.  For years
past Jewish society in Rome had been kept in a fever of excite-

---

Church, i. 16, ii. 9, 10, and would feel
bound to regard it, when he arrived in
the metropolis.

[1] It is maintained by Baur (*Paulus*
p. 368), Schwegler (*Nachapost. Zeit.* II.
p. 93), and Zeller (*Theolog. Jahrb.* 1849,
p. 571), that this portion of the narrative betrays the unhistorical character
of the Acts; that the language here
ascribed to the Jews ignores the existence of the Roman Church, and that
therefore the incident is irreconcileable
with the facts as gathered from the
Epistle to the Romans.  On the con-
rary, this language seems to me to be
quite natural under the circumstances,
as it was certainly most politic.  It is
not very likely that the leading Jews
would frankly recognise the facts of the
case.  They had been taught caution
by the troubles which the Messianic
buds had brought on their more im-
petuous fellow-countrymen : and they

would do wisely to shield themselves
under a prudent reserve.  Their best
policy was to ignore Christianity; to
enquire as little as possible about it,
and, when questioned, to understate
their knowledge.  In a large and popu-
lous city like Rome they might without
much difficulty shut their eyes to its
existence.  When its claims were directly pressed upon them by St Paul,
their character for fairness, perhaps
also some conscientious scruples, required them to give him at least a formal hearing.  At all events the writer
of the Acts is quite aware that there
was already a Christian Church in
Rome; for he represents the Apostle
as met on his way by two deputations
from it.  Indeed the two last chapters
of the narrative so clearly indicate the
presence of an eyewitness, that we can
hardly question the incidents, even if
we are at a loss how to interpret them.

ment by successive rumours of false Christs. On one occasion a tumult had broken out, and the emperor had issued a general edict of banishment against the race[1]. If this check had made them more careful and less demonstrative, it had certainly not smothered their yearnings after the advent of a Prince who was to set his foot on the neck of their Roman oppressors. But the Christ of their anticipations was not the Christ of St Paul's preaching. Grace, liberty, the abrogation of law, the supremacy of faith, the levelling of all religious and social castes— these were strange sounds in their ears; these were conditions which they might not and would not accept

Judaic Christianity in Rome.

But where he had failed, other teachers, who sympathized more fully with their prejudices and made larger concessions to their bigotry, might win a way. The proportion of Jewish converts saluted in the Epistle to the Romans[2], not less

---

[1] Sueton. *Claud.* 25 'Judæos impulsore Chresto assidue tumultuantes Roma expulit.' Suetonius here makes a double mistake: (1) He confuses the names Chrestus and Christus. This confusion was not unnatural, for the difference in pronunciation was hardly perceptible, and Chrestus, 'the good-natured,' was a frequent proper name, while Christus, 'the anointed,' would convey no idea at all to a heathen ignorant of the Old Testament and unacquainted with Hebrew customs. The mistake continued to be made long after Suetonius: comp. Justin *Apol.* i. p. 54 D ὅσον γε ἐκ τοῦ κατηγορουμένου ἡμῶν ὀνόματος, χρηστότατοι ὑπάρχομεν, Tertull. *Apol.* 3 'Cum perperam Chrestianus pronuntiatur a vobis,' *ad Nat.* i. 3, Theoph. *ad Autol.* i. 12 περὶ δὲ τοῦ καταγελᾶν μου καλοῦντά με Χριστιανόν, οὐκ οἶδας ὃ λέγεις· πρῶτον μὲν ὅτι τὸ χριστὸν ἡδὺ καὶ εὔχρηστον καὶ ἀκαταγέλαστόν ἐστιν; and even as late as Lactantius, *Inst. Div.* iv. 7 'Exponenda hujus nominis ratio est propter ignorantium errorem, qui eum immutata littera Chrestum *solent dicere.*' See also Boeckh *C. I.* 3857 p, App. The word 'Chrestianus' appears in an early inscription (Münter *Sinnbilder der alten Christen* I. p. 14, Orell. *Inscr.* 4426), where however it may be a proper name. At all events the designation 'Christian' would hardly be expected on a monument of this date; for other names in the inscription (Drusus, Antonia) point to the age of the earlier Cæsars. M. Renan (*Les Apôtres*, p. 234) is wrong in saying that the termination -anus betrays a Latin origin. Compare Σαρδιανός, Τραλλιανός. (2) It seems probable that the disturbances which Suetonius here attributes to the instigation of some one Chrestus (or Christus), understanding this as a proper name, were really caused by various conflicting rumours of claimants to the Messiahship. Yet even in this case we may fairly suppose that the true Christ held a prominent place in these reports; for He must have been not less known at this time than any of the false Christs.

[2] The only strictly Jewish name is Mary; but Aquila and Priscilla are

than the obvious motive and bearing of the letter itself, points
to the existence of a large, perhaps a preponderating, Jewish
element in the Church of the metropolis before St Paul's arrival.
These Christians of the Circumcision for the most part owed
no spiritual allegiance to the Apostle of the Gentiles : some of
them had confessed Christ before him[1]; many no doubt were
rigid in their adherence to the law. It would seem as though
St Paul had long ago been apprehensive of the attitude these
Jewish converts might assume towards him. The conciliatory
tone of the Epistle to the Romans—conciliatory and yet un-
compromising—seems intended to disarm possible opposition. Their opposition to St Paul.
Was it not this gloomy foreboding also which overclouded his
spirit when he first set foot on the Italian shore? He had
good reason to 'thank God and take courage,' when he was
met by one deputation of Roman Christians at the Forum
of Appius, by another at the Three Taverns[2]. It was a relief
to find that some members at least of the Roman Church were
favourably disposed towards him. At all events his fears were
not unfounded, as appeared from the sequel. His bold advocacy of the liberty of the Gospel provoked the determined
antagonism of the Judaizers. We can hardly doubt to what
class of teachers he alludes in the Epistle to the Philippians as
preaching Christ of envy and strife, in a factious spirit, only
for the purpose of thwarting him, only to increase his anguish
and to render his chains more galling[3]. An incidental notice
in another, probably a later epistle, written also from Rome,
reveals the virulence of this opposition still more clearly.
Of all the Jewish Christians in Rome the Apostle can name

known to have been Jews. St Paul's
kinsmen' also, Andronicus, Junia (Junias?), and Herodion, must have belonged to this race, whatever sense we
attach to the word 'kinsmen.' Apelles
too, though not a strictly Jewish name,
was frequently borne by Jews. If
moreover the Aristobulus mentioned in
ver. 10 belonged to the family of Herod,
as seems most probable (see p. 172 sq.),
then the members of ' his household'

also would in all likelihood be Jews.

[1] At the first day of Pentecost οἱ ἐπι-
δημοῦντες Ῥωμαῖοι, Ἰουδαῖοί τε καὶ προσ-
ήλυτοι, are mentioned among those present, Acts ii. 10. In the Epistle to the
Romans St Paul salutes certain Jewish
Christians, who were ' before him in
Christ,' xvi. 7.

[2] Acts xxviii. 15.

[3] Phil. i. 15—18.

three only as remaining stedfast in the general desertion; Aristarchus his own companion in travel and in captivity, Marcus the cousin of his former missionary colleague Barnabas, and Jesus surnamed the Just. 'In them,' he adds feelingly, 'I found comfort[1].'

Their zealous proselytism. But if these sectarians resolutely opposed St Paul, they were hardly less zealous in preaching Christ. The incentive of rivalry goaded them on to fresh exertions. Their gospel was dwarfed and mutilated; it ignored the principle of liberty which was a main feature of the true Gospel: but though their motives were thus unworthy and their doctrine distorted, still 'Christ was preached': and for this cause, smothering all personal feeling, the Apostle constrained himself to rejoice[2].

The Gentile Christians welcome St Paul. 2. Meanwhile among the Gentiles his preaching bore more abundant and healthier fruit. As he encountered in the existing Church of Rome the stubborn resistance of a compact body of Judaic antagonists, so also there were doubtless very many whose more liberal Christian training prepared them to welcome him as their leader and guide. If constant communication was kept up with Jerusalem, the facilities of intercourse with the cities which he himself had evangelized, with Corinth and Ephesus for instance, were even greater. The Syrian Orontes which washed the walls of Antioch the mother of Gentile Christendom, when it mingled its waters with the Tiber, assuredly bore thither some nobler freight than the scum and refuse of Oriental profligacy, the degraded religions and licentious morals of Asia[3]. Gentile Christianity was not less fairly represented in Rome than Judaic Christianity. If there were some who preached Christ of 'envy and strife,' there were others who preached Him of 'good-will.'

Thus aided and encouraged, the Apostle prosecuted his work among the Gentiles with signal and rapid success. In

---

[1] Col. iv. 10, 11 οἵτινες ἐγενήθησάν μοι παρηγορία. Compare the expression quoted above from Acts xxviii. 15 εὐχαριστήσας τῷ Θεῷ ἔλαβεν θάρσος.

[2] Phil. i. 18 ἀλλὰ καὶ χαρήσομαι.

[3] Juv. Sat. iii. 62 'Jam pridem Syrus in Tiberim defluxit Orontes etc.'

two quarters especially the results of his labours may be traced. *His success in the prætorium* The prætorian soldiers, drafted off successively to guard him and constrained while on duty to bear him close company, had opportunities of learning his doctrine and observing his manner of life, which were certainly not without fruit. He had not been in Rome very long, before he could boast that his bonds were not merely known but known in Christ throughout the prætorian guard[1]. In the palace of the Cæsars too his influence was felt. It seems not improbable that when he arrived in Rome he found among the members of the imperial household, *and the palace.* whether slaves or freedmen, some who had already embraced the new faith and eagerly welcomed his coming. His energy would be attracted to this important field of labour, where an opening was already made and he had secured valuable allies. At all events, writing from Rome to a distant church, he singles out from the general salutation the members of Cæsar's household[2], as a body both prominent enough to deserve a special salutation and so well known to his correspondents that no explanation was needed.

Occupying these two strongholds in the enemy's territory, he would not be slack to push his conquests farther. Of the social rank, of the race and religion from which his converts were chiefly drawn, we have no direct knowledge and can only hazard a conjecture. Yet we can hardly be wrong in assuming that the Church was not generally recruited from the higher classes of society and that the recruits were for the most part Greeks rather than Romans.

Of the fact that the primitive Church of the metropolis *Greek nationality of the Roman Church.* before and after St Paul's visit was chiefly Greek, there is satisfactory evidence[3]. The salutations in the Roman letter contain very few but Greek names, and even the exceptions hardly imply the Roman birth of their possessors. The Greek nation-

[1] Phil. i. 13. See the detached note.

[2] Phil. iv. 22.

[3] The Greek origin of the Roman Church is now generally allowed by the best writers. See for instance Westcott *History of the Canon* p. 244 sq., and Milman *Latin Christianity* I. p. 27 sqq. (1863).

ality of this church in the succeeding ages is still more clearly
seen.  Her early bishops for several generations with very few
exceptions bear Greek names.  All her literature for nearly
two centuries is Greek.  The first Latin version of the Scriptures was made not for Rome, but for the provinces, especially
for Africa.  Even later, the ill-spelt, ill-written inscriptions of
the catacombs, with their strange intermingling of Greek and
Latin characters, show that the church was not yet fully
nationalised.  Doubtless among St Paul's converts were many
who spoke Latin as their mother tongue : the soldiers of the
prætorian guard for instance would perhaps be more Italian
than Greek.  But these were neither the more numerous nor
the more influential members of the Church.  The Greeks were
the most energetic, as they were also the most intelligent and
enquiring, of the middle classes in Rome at this time.  The
successful tradesmen, the skilled artisans, the confidential servants and retainers of noble houses—almost all the activity and
enterprise of the common people whether for good or for evil—
were Greek[1].  Against the superior versatility of these foreign
intruders the native population was powerless, and a generation later the satirist complains indignantly that Rome is no
longer Roman[2].  From this rank in life, from the middle and
lower classes of society, it seems probable that the Church
drew her largest reinforcements.  The members of the Roman
Church saluted in St Paul's Epistle could assuredly boast no
aristocratic descent, whether from the proud patrician or the
equally proud plebeian families.  They bear upstart names,
mostly Greek, sometimes borrowed from natural objects, sometimes adopted from a pagan hero or divinity, sometimes de-
scriptive of personal qualities or advantages, here and there
the surnames of some noble family to which they were perhaps
attached as slaves or freedmen, but hardly in any case bearing
the stamp of high Roman antiquity[3].  Of Rome, not less than

*Social
rank of
the early
converts.*

---

[1] See especially Juv. *Sat.* iii. 73—
80. Comp. Friedländer *Sittengeschichte
Roms* I. p. 60 sq. (ed. 2).

[2] Juv. *Sat.* iii. 60 'Non possum ferre,
Quirites, Græcam urbem.'

[3] Examples of these different classes

of Corinth, it must have been true, that 'not many wise after the flesh, not many powerful, not many high-born' were called[1].

Not many, and yet perhaps a few. On what grounds and with what truth the great Stoic philosopher and statesman has been claimed as a signal triumph of the Gospel I shall have to consider hereafter. Report has swollen the list of Roman converts with other names scarcely less famous for their virtues or their vices. The poet Lucan, the philosopher Epictetus, the powerful freedmen Narcissus and Epaphroditus, the emperor's mistresses Acte and Poppæa[2], a strange medley of good and bad, have been swept by tradition or conjecture into that capacious drag-net which 'gathers of every kind.' For such conversions, highly improbable in themselves, there is not a shadow of evidence. Yet one illustrious convert at least seems to have been added to the Church about this time. Pomponia Græcina, the wife of Plautius the conqueror of Britain, was arraigned of 'foreign superstition.' Delivered over to a domestic tribunal according to ancient usage, she was tried by her husband in presence of her relations, and was pronounced by him innocent. Her grave and sad demeanour (for she never appeared but in a mourning garb) was observed by all. The untimely and cruel death of her friend Julia had drawn a cloud over her life, which was never dissipated[3]. Coupled with the charge already mentioned, this notice suggests that shunning society she had sought consolation under her deep sorrow in the duties and hopes of the Gospel[4]. At all events a generation later Christianity had worked its way even into the imperial family. Flavius Clemens and his wife Flavia Domi-

*Margin notes:* Converts from the higher classes. Pomponia Græcina.

---

of names among the Roman Christians are : Stachys; Hermes, Nereus; Epæ-netus, Ampliatus, Urbanus; Julia, Claudia (2 Tim. iv. 21).

[1] 1 Cor. i. 26.

[2] See Fleury *Saint Paul et Sénèque* II. p. 109, and the references there given.

[3] Tac. *Ann.* xiii. 32. The trial took place in the year 57 or 58, i.e. about the time when the Epistle to the Romans was written, and some three years before St Paul's arrival in Rome.

[4] The 'superstitio externa' of Tacitus in this passage has been explained by Lipsius and others after him as referring to Christianity. See especially Merivale's *History of the Romans* VI. p. 273.

Clemens
and Domi-
tilla.

tilla, both cousins of Domitian, were accused of 'atheism' and condemned by the emperor. Clemens had only just resigned office as consul; and his sons had been nominated successors to the empire. The husband was put to death; the wife banished to one of the islands. Allowing that the emperor sacrificed his kinsman on a 'most trivial charge,' the Roman biographer yet withholds his sympathy from the unoffending victim as a man of 'contemptible indolence[1].' One whose prejudice or ignorance

[1] Sueton. *Domit.* 15 'Flavium Clementem patruelem suum contemptissimæ inertiæ...repente ex tenuissima suspicione tantum non in ipso ejus consulatu interemit': Dion Cass. lxvii. 14 κἀν τῷ αὐτῷ ἔτει ἄλλους τε πολλοὺς καὶ τὸν Φλαουΐον Κλήμεντα ὑπατεύοντα, καίπερ ἀνεψιὸν ὄντα καὶ γυναῖκα καὶ αὐτὴν συγγενῆ ἑαυτοῦ Φλαουΐαν Δομιτίλλαν ἔχοντα, κατέσφαξεν ὁ Δομιτιανός· ἐπηνέχθη δὲ ἀμφοῖν ἔγκλημα ἀθεότητος, ὑφ' ἧς καὶ ἄλλοι ἐς τὰ Ἰουδαίων ἔθη ἐξοκέλλοντες πολλοὶ κατεδικάσθησαν, καὶ οἱ μὲν ἀπέθανον οἱ δὲ τῶν γοῦν οὐσιῶν ἐστερήθησαν· ἡ δὲ Δομιτίλλα ὑπερωρίσθη μόνον ἐς Πανδατερίαν. Atheism was the common charge brought against the early Christians. The relationship of this Domitilla to Domitian is not given by Dion Cassius. It appears however from other authorities that she was his sister's daughter; Quintil. *Inst.* iv. Prooem., Orelli-Henzen *Inscr.* 5422, 5423. Again Eusebius, *H. E.* iii. 18, refers to heathen historians as relating (with an exact notice of the date, the fifteenth year of Domitian) the persecution of the Christians, and more especially the banishment of Flavia Domitilla, the *niece* of Flavius Clemens (ἐξ ἀδελφῆς γεγονυῖαν Φλαουΐου Κλήμεντος) one of the actual consuls, to the island of *Pontia,* τῆς εἰς Χριστὸν μαρτυρίας ἕνεκεν. The heathen writer especially intended here is one Bruttius, as appears from another passage in Eusebius,*Chron.* p. 162 (Schöne) sub anno 95,'Scribit Bruttius plurimos

Christianorum sub Domitiano fecisse martyrium: inter quos et Flaviam Domitillam, Flavii Clementis consulis ex sorore neptem, in insulam Pontiam relegatam quia se Christianam esse testata est.' This Bruttius is not improbably the Præsens with whom the younger Pliny corresponds (*Epist.* vii. 3), Præsens being a cognomen of the Bruttii. For the various persons bearing this name see Lardner's *Testimonies of Ancient Heathens* xii. On the confirmation of this account derived from de Rossi's archæological researches, and on the possible connexion of Clement the writer of the Epistle with this Flavius Clemens, see *S. Clement of Rome Appendix* p. 257 sq.

It will be seen that the account of Bruttius (or Eusebius) differs from that of other authorities both in the place of exile and in the relationship of Domitilla to Clemens. Hence many writers have supposed that two Domitillas, aunt and niece, were banished by Domitian: so e. g. among recent writers, Imhof *Domitianus* p. 116, de Rossi *Bull. di Archeol. Crist.* 1865, p. 17 sq., 1875, p. 69 sq. The calendar also commemorates a Domitilla as a virgin and martyr, thus distinguishing her from the wife of Clemens: see Tillemont *Hist. Eccl.* ii. p. 124 sq. Yet it can hardly be doubtful that one and the same person is intended in these notices. Nor is it difficult to explain the two discrepancies. (1) The *locality.* Pontia (or Pontiæ, for it is a group of

allowed him to see in Christianity only a 'mischievous super-stition[1]' would not be very favourably impressed by a convert to the new faith, debarred by his principles from sharing the vicious amusements of his age, and perhaps also in the absorb-ing contemplation of his higher destinies too forgetful of the necessary forms of social and political life. There seems no reason to doubt that Clemens and Domitilla were converts to the Gospel[2].

It is impossible to close this notice of St Paul's captivity without casting a glance at the great catastrophe which over-whelmed the Roman Church soon after his release. The Nero-nian persecution, related on the authority of Tacitus and

The Nero-nian per-secution explained away.

islands) and Pandateria are close to each other; Strabo v. p. 233 Πανδα-τερία τε καὶ Ποντία οὐ πολὺ ἀπ' ἀλλήλων διέχουσαι. Hence they are constantly named together; e.g. Strabo ii. p. 123, Varro R. R. ii. 5, Suet. Calig. 15, Mela ii. 7. And both alike were con-stantly chosen as places of exile for members of the imperial family; Tac. Ann. xiv. 63, Suet. Tib. 53, 54, Calig. 15, Dion Cass. lv. 10, lix. 22. The cells, in which Domitilla was reported to have lived during her exile, were shown in Pontia in Jerome's time; Hieron. Ep. cviii. § 7 (I. p. 695). (2) The relationship. The divergence here may be explained very easily by the carelessness of Eusebius or some early transcriber. In the original text of Bruttius the words corresponding to 'Flavii Clementis' probably signified 'the wife of Flavius Clemens,' while those translated 'ex sorore neptem' described her relationship not to Cle-mens but to Domitian. G. Syncellus (p. 650, ed. Bonn.), copying the Chroni-con of Eusebius, says Φλαυία Δομετίλλα ἐξαδέλφη Κλήμηντος (sic) Φλαυίου ὑπα-τικοῦ ὡς Χριστιανὴ εἰς νῆσον Ποντίαν φυ-γαδεύεται. This expression suggests a very probable account of the error. If Bruttius (or some other authority)

wrote Φλαουία Δομετίλλα ἐξαδέλφη ἡ Φλαουίου Κλήμεντος, the accidental omission of ἡ would at once transfer the relationship from Domitian to Flavius Clemens. When Philostratus, Vit. Apoll. viii. 25, speaks of the wife of Clemens as the sister of the emperor, he confuses her with another Domitilla no longer living; unless indeed (as seems probable) the conjectural read-ing ἐξαδέλφην should be substituted for ἀδελφὴν in his text. The stemma of the Flavii, constructed by Momm-sen (Corp. Inscr. Lat. vi. p. 173), seems to me to have nothing to recommend it except the name of this truly great scholar. It contradicts Apollonius, Dion, Eusebius, and Quintilian alike; besides being open to other objections. See the criticism of de Rossi Bull. di Arch. Crist. 1875, p. 70 sq.

[1] Sueton. Nero 16 'superstitio nova ac malefica.'

[2] So even Gibbon, who says (c. xvi), 'The guilt imputed to their charge was that of Atheism and Jewish manners; a singular association of ideas, which cannot with any propriety be applied except to the Christians etc.' So too Baur Paulus p. 472. Early in the second century the Roman Christians are so influential that Ignatius fears

Suetonius and embodied as a cardinal article in the historic creed of the Church from the earliest times, has latterly shared the fate of all assumed facts and received dogmas. The historian of the 'Decline and Fall' was the first to question the truth of this persecution. 'The obscurity as well as the innocency of the Christians,' wrote Gibbon, 'should have shielded them from Nero's indignation and even from his notice.' Accordingly he supposed that the real sufferers were not Christians but Jews, not the disciples of the true Christ but the dupes of some false Christ, the followers not of Jesus the Nazarene but of Judas the Gaulonite. It might easily happen, so he argued, that Tacitus, writing a generation later when the Christians, now a numerous body, had been singled out as the objects of judicial investigation, should transfer to them 'the guilt and the sufferings which he might with far greater truth and justice have attributed to a sect whose odious memory was almost extinguished[1].' An able living writer also, the author of the 'History of the Romans under the Empire[2],' paying more deference to ancient authorities, yet feeling this difficulty, though in a less degree, suggests another solution. He supposes that the persecution was directed in the first instance against Jewish fanatics[3]; that the persons thus assailed strove to divert the popular fury by informing against the Christians; that the Christians confessed their allegiance to a King of their own in 'a sense which their judges did not care to discriminate'; that in consequence they were condemned and suffered; and finally, that later writers, having only an indistinct knowledge of the facts, confined the persecution directed against Jews and Christians alike to the latter, who nevertheless were not the principal victims. If I felt the difficulty which this suggestion is intended to remove, I should be disposed to accept the solution. But I do not feel justified in setting aside the authority of both Tacitus and Suetonius in a case like this, where the

*Testimony of Roman historians.*

---

lest their intercession may rob him of the crown of martyrdom.

[1] *Decline and Fall* c. xvi.

[2] vi. p. 280.

[3] A later notice however (Pseudo-Senec. *ad Paul.* Ep. 12) mentions the Jews also as sufferers.

incident recorded must have happened in their own life-time; an incident moreover not transacted within the recesses of the palace or by a few accomplices sworn to secrecy, but open and notorious, affecting the lives of many and gratifying the fanatical fury of a whole populace.

But besides the distinct testimony of the Roman historians, there is, I venture to think, strong though indirect evidence which has generally been overlooked. How otherwise is the imagery of the Apocalypse to be explained? Babylon, the great harlot, the woman seated on seven hills, 'drunken with the blood of the saints and with the blood of the martyrs of Jesus[1]'— what is the historical reference in these words, if the Neronian persecution be a figment of later date? It is plain that some great change has passed over the relations between the Gospel and the Empire, since the days when St Paul sought protection and obtained justice from the soldiers and the magistrates of Rome. The genial indolence of Gallio, the active interposition of Claudius Lysias, the cold impartiality of Festus, afford no explanation of such language. Roman justice or Roman indifference has been exchanged meanwhile for Roman oppression. *Allusion in the Apocalypse.*

And after all the sole ground for scepticism is the assumed insignificance of the Roman Church at this epoch, its obscure station and scanty numbers. But what are the facts of the case? Full six years before the Neronian outbreak the brethren of Rome are so numerous and so influential as to elicit from St Paul the largest and most important letter which he ever wrote. In this letter he salutes a far greater number of persons than in any other. Its tone shows that the Roman Church was beset by all the temptations intellectual and moral, to which only a large and various community is exposed. In the three years which elapsed before he arrived in the metropolis their numbers must in the natural course of events have increased largely. When he lands on the shores of *The Church of Rome not insignificant at this time.*

---

[1] Rev. xvii. 6. The argument in the text loses some of its force, if the later date be assigned to the Apocalypse; for the passage might then be supposed to refer to the persecution of Domitian.

Italy, he finds a Christian community established even at Puteoli[1]. For two whole years from this time the Gospel is preached with assiduous devotion by St Paul and his companions; while the zeal of the Judaizers, whetted by rivalry, is roused to unwonted activity in the same cause. If besides this we allow for the natural growth of the church in the year intervening after the Apostle's release, it will be no surprise that the Christian community had by this time attained sufficient prominence to provoke the indiscriminate revenge of a people unnerved by a recent catastrophe and suddenly awakened to the existence of a mysterious and rapidly increasing sect.

For it is in the very nature of a panic that it should take alarm at some vague peril of which it cannot estimate the character or dimensions. The first discovery of this strange community would be the most terrible shock to Roman feeling. How wide might not be its ramifications, how numerous its adherents? Once before in times past Roman society had been appalled by a similar revelation. At this crisis men would call to mind how their forefathers had stood aghast at the horrors of the Bacchanalian conspiracy; how the canker still unsuspected was gnawing at the heart of public morality, and the foundations of society were well-nigh sapped, when the discovery was accidentally made, so that only the promptest and most vigorous measures had saved the state[2]. And was not this a conspiracy of the same kind? These Christians were certainly atheists, for they rejected all the gods alike; they were traitors

*The Roman populace seized by a panic.*

---

[1] Acts xxviii. 14. The traffic with Alexandria and the East would draw to Puteoli a large number of Oriental sailors and merchants. The inscriptions bear testimony to the presence of Jews in these parts: see an article by Minervini in the *Bullett. Archeol. Napol.* Feb. 1855. For the reference to this article I am indebted to Friedländer *Sittengeschichte Roms* ii. p. 65. See also de Rossi *Bull. di Archeol.Crist.* 1864, p. 69 sq., on the Pompeian inscription.

[2] For the history of the Bacchanalian conspiracy detected in the year B.C. 186 see Livy xxxix. 8 sq. In reading this account it is impossible not to notice the resemblance of the crimes apparently proved against these Bacchanalians with the foul charges recklessly hurled at the Christians: see e.g. Justin *Apol.* i. 26, Tertull. *Apol.* 7, Minuc. Felix, 9, 28. [The passage in the text was written without any recollection that Gibbon had mentioned the Bacchanalian conspiracy in the same connexion.]

also, for they swore allegiance to another king besides Cæsar.
But there were mysterious whispers of darker horrors than
these; hideous orgies which rivalled the loathsome banquet of
Thyestes, shameless and nameless profligacies which recalled
the tragedy of the house of Laius[1]. To us, who know what the
Gospel has been and is, who are permitted to look back on the
past history of the Church and forward to her eternal destinies,
such infatuation may seem almost incredible; and yet this mode
of representation probably does no injustice to Roman feeling
at the time. The public mind paralysed by a great calamity has
not strength to reflect or to argue. An idea once seizing it
possesses it wholly. The grave and reserved demeanour of the
Christians would only increase the popular suspicion. The apparent innocence of the sect would seem but a cloak thrown over
their foul designs, which betrayed themselves occasionally by de-
nunciations of Roman life or by threats of a coming vengeance[2].

The general silence of the Roman satirists is indeed a signi- *Silence of
the Roman
satirists
explained.*
ficant fact, but it cannot fairly be urged to show the obscurity
of the Church at the date of the Neronian persecution. If no
mention is made of Christianity in the short poems of Persius,
it will be remembered that he died nearly two years before this
event. If Juvenal and Martial, who in the next generation
'have dashed in with such glaring colours Jews, Greeks, and
Egyptians[3],' banish the Christians to the far background of
their picture[4], the fact must not be explained by the comparative insignificance of the latter[5]. We may safely infer from

---

[1] See the letter of the Churches of
Lyons and Vienne in Euseb. *H. E.* v. 1.
§ 14 κατεψεύσαντο ἡμῶν Θυέστεια δεῖπνα
καὶ Οἰδιποδείους μίξεις καὶ ὅσα μήτε λα-
λεῖν μήτε νοεῖν θέμις ἡμῖν, Athenag.
*Legat.* 3 τρία ἐπιφημίζουσιν ἡμῖν ἐγκλή-
ματα, ἀθεότητα, Θυέστεια δεῖπνα, Οἰδιποδείους μίξεις, *ib.* 31, Theoph. *ad Aut.*
iii. 4, 15, Tertull. *ad Nat.* i. 7.

[2] See the suggestion of Dean Milman,
*History of Christianity* II. p. 456 (1863).
So also Pressensé *Trois Premiers
Siècles* II. p. 97.

[3] Merivale VI. p. 277.

[4] Mart. x. 25, Juv. i. 155, viii. 235.
Even in these passages the allusion is
doubtful.

[5] The following instance will show
how little dependence can be placed on
this line of argument. Dean Milman
(*History of Christianity*, III. p. 352)
writes: 'M. Beugnot has pointed out
one remarkable characteristic of Claudian's poetry and of the times—his extraordinary religious indifference. Here
is a poet writing at the actual crisis of

the narratives of Pliny and Tacitus that at this time they were at least as important and influential as the Jews. But in fact they offered very poor material for caricature. So far as they presented any salient features which the satirist might turn to ridicule, these were found in the Jews to a still greater degree. Where they differed, their distinctive characteristics would seem entirely negative to the superficial glance of the heathen. Even Lucian, who satirizes all things in heaven and earth, living at a time when Christians abounded everywhere, can say nothing worse of them than that they are good-natured charitable people, not overwise and easily duped by charlatans[1].

Reticence of the philosophers

But how did this vast religious movement escape the notice of philosophical writers, who, if they were blind to its spiritual import, must at least have recognised in it a striking moral phenomenon? If the Christians were so important, it is urged, how are they not mentioned by Seneca, 'though Seneca is full of the tenets of the philosophers[2]'? To this particular question it is perhaps sufficient to reply, that most of Seneca's works were written before the Christians on any showing had attracted public notice. But the enquiry may be pushed further, and a general answer will be suggested. How, we may well ask, are they not mentioned by Plutarch, though Plutarch discusses almost every possible question of philosophical or social interest, and flourished moreover at the very time, when by their large and increasing numbers, by their unflinching courage and steady principle, they had become so formidable, that the propraetor of Bithynia in utter perplexity applies to his imperial master for instructions how to deal with a sect thus passive and yet thus revolutionary? How is it again, that Marcus Aurelius, the philosophical emperor, dismisses them in his writings with one brief scornful allusion[3], though he had

the complete triumph of the new religion and the visible extinction of the old: if we may so speak, a strictly historical poet...Yet...no one would know the existence of Christianity at that period of the world by reading the works of Claudian.'

[1] Lucian *De Mort. Peregr.* § 11 sq.

[2] Merivale, l.c.

[3] M. Anton. xi. 3 μὴ κατὰ ψιλὴν παράταξιν (from mere obstinacy), ὡς ο Χριστιανοί, ἀλλὰ λελογισμένως καὶ σε

been flooded with apologies and memorials on their behalf, and though they served in large numbers in the very army which he commanded in person[1]? The silence of these later philoso- *assumed* phers at least cannot be ascribed to ignorance; and some other *for pru-dential* explanation must be sought. May we not fairly conclude *reasons.* that, like others under similar circumstances, they considered a contemptuous reticence the safest, if not the keenest, weapon to employ against a religious movement, which was working its way upwards from the lower grades of society, and which they viewed with alarm and misgiving not unmingled with secret respect[2]?

----

υνῶς καί, ὥστε καὶ ἄλλον πεῖσαι, ἀτρα-γῴδως.

[1] Thus much at least may be inferred from the story of the thundering legion: see especially Mosheim *De Rebus Christian.* sæc. 2. § xvii, and Lardner *Testimonies, etc.* xv. § 3.

[2] St Augustine *de Civ. Dei* vi. 11 says of Seneca, after mentioning this philosopher's account of the Jews, Christianos tamen, jam tunc Judæis inimicissimos, in neutram partem com-

memorare ausus est, ne vel laudaret contra suæ patriæ veterem consuetudinem vel reprehenderet contra propriam forsitan voluntatem.' Seneca indeed could hardly be expected to mention the Christians, for most of his works were perhaps written before the new sect had attracted the attention of his fellow-countrymen. But some such motive as Augustine here suggests must have sealed the lips of the later philosophers.

# II.

# ORDER OF THE EPISTLES OF THE CAPTIVITY.

ST PAUL remained in captivity between four and five years
(A.D. 58—63); the first half of this period being spent at
Cæsarea, the second at Rome.   While thus a prisoner he wrote
four epistles, to the Philippians, to the Colossians, to the Ephesians, to Philemon.   Though a few critics have assigned one or
more of these epistles to his confinement at Cæsarea[1], there are
serious objections to this view[2]; and the vast majority of writers

---

[1] The three epistles are assigned to
the Cæsarean captivity by Böttger
(*Beitr.* II. p. 47 sqq.), Thiersch (*Kirche
im apost. Zeit.* p. 176), Reuss (*Gesch.
der heil. Schriften* § 114), Meyer (*Ephes.
Einl.* § 2) and others : the Epistle to
the Philippians by Paulus (*Progr. Jen.*
1799, and *Heidelb. Jahrb.* 1825. H. 5,
referred to by Bleek), Böttger (l.c.), and
Thiersch (*ib.* p. 212), while Rilliet (in-
trod. § 11 and note on i. 13) speaks
doubtfully. The oldest tradition or conjecture dated all four epistles from
Rome : and this is the opinion of most
modern writers. Oeder alone (*Progr.
Onold.* 1731 : see Wolf *Cur. Phil.* III.
p. 168) dates the Philippians from Corinth during St Paul's first visit.

[2] Reasons for dating the three epistles from Cæsarea are given fully in
Meyer (*Ephes. Einl.* § 2). I cannot attach any weight to them. For the Epistle to the Philippians there is at least
this *prima facie* case, that the mention

of the prætorium in Phil. i. 13 would
then be explained by the statement in
Acts xxiii. 35, that St Paul was confined in 'the prætorium of Herod.' But
the expression 'throughout the prætorium' (ἐν ὅλῳ τῷ πραιτωρίῳ), while it
implies a wider space than the palace
or official residence of Herod, is easily
explained by the circumstances of St
Paul's connexion with the imperial
guards at Rome : see above, p. 9.   On
the other hand there are many serious
objections to Cæsarea as the place of
writing. (1) The notice of Cæsar's
household (Phil. iv. 22) cannot without
much straining of language and facts
be made to apply to Cæsarea. (2) St
Paul's account of his progress (i. 12
sq.) loses all its force on this supposition. He is obviously speaking of some
place of great consequence, where the
Gospel had received a new and remarkable development.   Cæsarea does not
satisfy these conditions.   It was after

agree in placing all four at a later date, after the Apostle had been removed thence to Rome.

Assuming then that they were all written from Rome, we have next to investigate their relative dates. And here again the question simplifies itself. It seems very clear, and is generally allowed, that the three epistles last mentioned were written and despatched at or about the same time, while the letter to the Philippians stands alone. Of the three thus connected the Epistle to the Colossians is the link between the other two. On the one hand its connexion with the Epistle to the Ephesians is established by a remarkable resemblance of style and matter, and by the fact of its being entrusted to the same messenger Tychicus[1]. On the other, it is shown to synchronize with the letter to Philemon by more than one coincidence: Onesimus accompanies both epistles[2]; in both salutations are sent to Archippus[3]; in both the same persons are mentioned as St Paul's companions at the time of writing[4].

The Philippian letter stands apart; the other three are linked together.

all not a very important place. It had been evangelized by the Apostles of the Circumcision. The first heathen convert Cornelius lived there. As a chief seaport town of Palestine, the great preachers of the Gospel were constantly passing to and fro through it. Altogether we may suppose it to have received more attention in proportion to its size than any other place; and the language of St Paul seems wholly inapplicable to a town with this antecedent history. (3) When this epistle is written, he is looking forward to his speedy release and purposes a visit to Macedonia (i. 26, ii. 24: compare Philem. 22). Now there is no reason to suppose that he expected this at Cæsarea. For what were the circumstances of the case? He had gone up to Jerusalem, intending immediately afterwards to visit Rome. While at Jerusalem he is apprehended on a frivolous charge and imprisoned. When at length he is brought to trial, he boldly appeals to

Cæsar. May we not infer that this had been his settled determination from the first? that he considered it more prudent to act thus than to stake his safety on the capricious justice of the provincial governor? that at all events he hoped thereby to secure the fulfilment of his long-cherished design of preaching the Gospel in the metropolis?

These considerations seem sufficient to turn the scale in favour of Rome, as against Cæsarea, in the case of the Epistle to the Philippians. As regards the other three, I shall endeavour to give reasons for placing them later than the Philippian letter: and if so, they also must date from Rome. At all events there is no sufficient ground for abandoning the common view.

[1] Col. iv. 7, Ephes. vi. 21.

[2] Col. iv. 9, Philem. 10—12.

[3] Col. iv. 17, Philem. 2. Hence it may be inferred that they went to the same place.

[4] Philem. 1, 23, 24, Col. i. 1, iv.

Was it written before or after the others?

The question then, which I propose to discuss in the following pages, is this: whether the Epistle to the Philippians should be placed early in the Roman captivity and the three epistles later; or whether conversely the three epistles were written first, and the Philippian letter afterwards. The latter is the prevailing view among the vast majority of recent writers, German and English, with one or two important exceptions[1]. I shall attempt to show that the arguments generally alleged in its favour will not support the conclusions: while on the other hand there are reasons for placing the Philippians early and the three epistles late, which in the absence of any decisive evidence on the other side must be regarded as weighty.

Arguments for its later date stated and examined.

The arguments in favour of the later date of the Philippian letter, as compared with the other three, are drawn from four considerations: (1) From the progress of Christianity in Rome, as exhibited in this epistle; (2) From a comparison of the names of St Paul's associates mentioned in the different epistles; (3) From the length of time required for the communications between Philippi and Rome; (4) From the circumstances of St Paul's imprisonment. These arguments will be considered in order.

1. Progress of the Roman Church.

1. It is evident that the Christians in Rome form a large and important body when the Epistle to the Philippians is written. The Gospel has effected a lodgment even in the imperial palace. The bonds of the Apostle have become known not only 'throughout the prætorium' but 'to all the rest.' There is a marvellous activity among the disciples of the new

---

7—14. The names common to both are Timotheus, Epaphras, Marcus, Aristarchus, Demas, Luke. Tychicus and Jesus the Just are mentioned in the Epistle to the Colossians alone.

[1] In Germany, De Wette, Schrader, Hemsen, Anger, Credner, Neander, Wieseler, Meyer, Wiesinger; in England, Davidson, Alford, Conybeare and Howson, Wordsworth, Ellicott, Eadie. The exceptions are Bleek (*Einl. in das*

*Neue Test.* pp. 430, 460) who considers the data insufficient to decide but treats the Philippians first in order; and Ewald (*Sendschreiben etc.* pp. 431 sq., 547), who however rejects the Epistle to the Ephesians, and supposes the remaining three to have been written about the same time. The older English critics for the most part (e.g. Ussher and Pearson) placed the Philippians first, without assigning reasons.

faith: 'In every way Christ is preached.' All this it is argued requires a very considerable lapse of time.

This argument has to a great extent been met already[1]. It is highly probable, as I have endeavoured to show, that St Paul found a flourishing though unorganized Church, when he arrived in Rome. The state of things exhibited in the Epistle to the Romans, the probable growth of Christianity in the interval, the fact of his finding a body of worshippers even at Puteoli, combine to support this inference. It has been suggested also (and reasons will be given hereafter for this suggestion) that the 'members of Cæsar's household' were, at least in some cases, not St Paul's converts after his arrival but older disciples already confessing Christ. And again, if when he wrote he could already count many followers among the prætorian soldiers, it is here especially that we might expect to see the earliest and most striking results of his preaching, for with these soldiers he was forced to hold close and uninterrupted intercourse day and night from the very first.

*Its condition before St Paul's coming.*

Nor must the expression that his 'bonds had become known to all the rest' of the Roman people be rigorously pressed. It is contrary to all sound rules of interpretation to look for statistical precision in words uttered in the fulness of gratitude and hope. The force of the expression must be measured by the Apostle's language elsewhere. In writing to the Thessalonians for instance, only a few months after they have heard the first tidings of the Gospel, he expresses his joy that 'from them has sounded forth the word of the Lord, not only in Macedonia and Achaia, but *in every place* their faith to Godward is spread abroad[2].'

*His language not to be pressed.*

Indeed this very passage in the Philippian letter, which has been taken to favour a later date because it announces the progress of the Gospel in Rome, appears much more natural, if written soon after his arrival. The condition of things which it describes is novel and exceptional. It is evidently the first awakening of dormant influences for good or

*The notice suggests an opposite inference.*

---

[1] See above, p. 25 sq.      [2] 1 Thess. i. 8.

evil, the stirring up of latent emotions of love, emulation, strife, godless jealousy and godly zeal, by the presence of the great Apostle among the Christians of Rome. This is hardly the language he would have used after he had spent two whole years in the metropolis, when the antagonism of enemies and the devotion of friends had settled down into a routine of hatred or of affection. Nor is the form of the announcement such as might be expected in a letter addressed so long after his arrival to correspondents with whom he had been in constant communication meanwhile.

2. St Paul's associates.

2. The argument drawn from the names of St Paul's associates is as follows. We learn from the Acts that the Apostle was accompanied on his voyage to Rome by Luke and Aristarchus[1]. Now their names occur in the salutations of the Epistles to the Colossians and to Philemon[2], but not in the Epistle to the Philippians. It seems probable therefore that the letter last mentioned was written later, his two companions having meanwhile separated from the Apostle.

General answer to this argument.

An argument from silence is always of questionable force. In order to be valid, it ought to apply to all these epistles alike. Yet in the Epistle to the Ephesians no mention is made of Aristarchus and Luke, and what is more remarkable, none of Timothy, though it was written at the same time with the letters to Colossæ and to Philemon. The omission in any particular case may be due to special reasons[3].

Nor is it difficult to account for this silence. In the Epistle to the Philippians St Paul throws his salutation into a general form; 'The brethren that are with me greet you.' In this expression it is plain that he refers to his own personal companions: for he adds immediately afterwards, 'All the brethren,'

---

[1] Acts xxvii. 2.

[2] Col. iv. 10, 14, Philem. 24.

[3] The doubtful force of such arguments from silence is illustrated by another case occurring in these epistles. Jesus Justus is mentioned in the Epistle to the Colossians (iv. 11), but not in the letter to Philemon. Of this omission no account can be given. There is the highest *a priori* probability that he would be mentioned either in both letters or in neither, for they both were sent to the same place and by the same messenger.

including the resident members of the Roman Church, 'but especially they of the household of Cæsar greet you[1].' If Aristarchus and Luke were with him, they might well be comprehended in this general salutation. Of Aristarchus the most probable account, I think, is, that he parted from St Paul at Myra, and therefore did not arrive in Rome with the Apostle but rejoined him there subsequently[2]. If this be the case, the absence of his name in the Philippian Epistle, so far as it deserves to be considered at all, makes rather for than against the earlier date. On the other hand St Luke certainly accompanied the Apostle to Rome: and his probable connexion with

*Aristarchus.*

*St Luke*

---

[1] Phil. iv. 21, 22.

[2] St Luke's account is this : 'Embarking on an Adramyttian vessel, intending to sail to (or along) the coasts of Asia (μέλλοντες πλεῖν τοὺς κατὰ τὴν Ἀσίαν τόπους) we put out to sea, Aristarchus a Macedonian of Thessalonica being with us (Acts xxvii. 2).' When they arrived at Myra, the centurion 'found an Alexandrian vessel sailing to Italy and put them (ἡμᾶς) on board.' Now it is generally (I believe, universally) assumed that Aristarchus accompanied St Paul and St Luke to Rome. But what are the probabilities of the case? The vessel in which they start belongs to Adramyttium a seaport of Mysia. If they had remained in this ship, as seems to have been their original intention, they would have hugged the coast of Asia, and at length (perhaps taking another vessel at Adramyttium) have reached Macedonia : and if they landed, as they probably would, at Neapolis, they would have taken the great Egnatian road through Philippi. Along this road they would have travelled to Dyrrhachium and thence have crossed the straits to Italy. Thus a long voyage in the open seas would have been avoided: a voyage peculiarly dangerous at this late season of the year, as the result proved. Such also, at least from Smyrna onwards, was

the route of Ignatius, who likewise was taken a prisoner to Rome and appears also to have made this journey late in the year. It was the accident of falling in at Myra with an Alexandrian ship sailing straight for Italy which induced the centurion to abandon his original design, for the sake, as would appear, of greater expedition. But the historian adds when mentioning this design, 'one Aristarchus a Macedonian of Thessalonica being with us.' Does he not, by inserting this notice in this particular place, intend his readers to understand (or at least understand himself) that Aristarchus accompanied them on the former part of their route, because he was *on his way home?* If so, when their plans were changed at Myra, he would part from them, continuing in the Adramyttian vessel, and so reach his destination.

I have hitherto given the received text, μέλλοντες πλεῖν, 'as we were to sail.' The greater number of the best authorities however read μέλλοντι πλεῖν 'as it (the vessel) was to sail.' If the latter be adopted, the passage is silent about the purpose of the centurion and his prisoners, but the probable destination of Aristarchus remains unaffected by the change. The copies which read μέλλοντι for the most part also insert

Philippi[1] suggests at least a presumption that he would be mentioned by name, if he were still with St Paul. Again, when in another passage[2] the Apostle declaring his intention of sending Timotheus to Philippi adds that he has 'no one like-minded who will naturally care for them, for all pursue their own' pleasures and interests, we cannot suppose that 'Luke the beloved physician' is included in this condemnation. It may reasonably be conjectured however that St Luke had left Italy to return thither at a later period, or that he was absent from Rome on some temporary mission, or at least that he was too busily occupied to undertake this journey to Philippi. Even if we assume Rome to have been the head-quarters of the evangelist during the whole of St Paul's stay, there must have been many churches in the neighbourhood and in more distant parts of Italy which needed constant supervision; and after Timotheus there was probably no one among the Apostle's companions to whom he could entrust any important mission with equal confidence.

**3. Journeys between Philippi and Rome.** 3. Again it is urged that the numerous communications between Philippi and Rome implied by the notices in this epistle in themselves demand a very considerable lapse of time after the Apostle's arrival.

**Four at most are required,** The narrative however requires at most two journeys from Rome to Philippi and two from Philippi to Rome; as follows.

(1) From Rome to Philippi. A messenger bears tidings to the Philippians of St Paul's arrival in Rome.

(2) From Philippi to Rome. The Philippians send contributions to St Paul by the hand of Epaphroditus[3].

(3) From Rome to Philippi. A messenger arrives at the latter place with tidings of Epaphroditus' illness.

---

εἰς before τοὺς κατὰ τὴν ᾿Ασίαν κ.τ.λ. It seems probable therefore that there has been a confusion between μέλλοντες and μέλλοντι εἰς. The best authorities are certainly in favour of the latter. On the other hand there would be a temptation to alter μέλλοντες in order to adapt it to subsequent facts.

[1] See below, pp. 53, 59.

[2] Phil. ii. 19—21.

[3] Phil. ii. 25, iv. 18.

(4) From Philippi to Rome. Epaphroditus is informed
that the news of his illness has reached the Philippians[1].

The return of Epaphroditus to Philippi cannot be reckoned
as a separate journey, for it seems clear that he was the bearer
of St Paul's letter[2].

I say four journeys at most; for the number may well be *and this*
halved without doing any violence to probability. As it has *number may be*
been already stated[3], St Luke's narrative seems to imply that *reduced.*
Aristarchus parted from the Apostle at Myra, coasted along
Asia Minor, and so returned to his native town Thessalonica
by the Egnatian road. On his way he would pass through
Philippi, and from him the Philippians would learn that the
Apostle had been removed from Cæsarea to Rome. Thus taking
into account the delay of several months occasioned by the ship-
wreck and the sojourn in Malta, Epaphroditus might well arrive
in Rome with the contributions from Philippi about the same
time with the Apostle himself; and this without any inconve-
nient hurry. On this supposition two of the four journeys
assumed to have taken place after St Paul's arrival may be dispensed with. Nor again does the expression 'he was grieved
because ye heard that he was sick' necessarily imply that Epaphroditus had received definite information that the tidings of
his illness had reached Philippi. He says nothing about the
manner in which the Philippians had received the news. The
Apostle's language seems to require nothing more than that
a messenger had been despatched to Philippi with the tidings in
question. This however is a matter of very little moment. On
any showing some months must have elapsed after St Paul's
arrival, before the letter to the Philippians was written. And
this interval allows ample time for all the incidents, consider-

---

[1] Phil. ii. 26 ἐπιποθῶν ἦν πάντας
ὑμᾶς [ἰδεῖν] καὶ ἀδημονῶν διότι ἠκούσατε
ὅτι ἠσθένησεν.

[2] Phil. ii. 25, 28, 29. The ἔπεμψα of
ver. 28 is an epistolary aorist: comp.

Philem. 11, 12, where ἀνέπεμψα is said
of Onesimus the bearer of the letter.
See the note on Gal. vi. 11.

[3] See above, p. 35, note 2.

ing that the communication between Rome and Philippi was constant and rapid[1].

4. St Paul's personal condition.

4. Lastly, it is urged that the general tone of the Epistle to the Philippians accords better with a later stage of the Apostle's captivity. The degree of restraint now imposed upon the

Contrast with the Acts,

prisoner appears to be inconsistent with the liberty implied in the narrative of the Acts: the spirit of anxiety and sadness which pervades the letter is thought to accord ill with a period of successful labour. For these reasons the epistle is supposed to have been written after those two years of unimpeded progress with which St Luke's record closes, the Apostle having been removed meanwhile from his own hired house to the precincts of the prætorium, and placed in more rigorous confinement.

and with

And the view thus suggested by the contrast which this

---

[1] A month would probably be a fair allowance of time for the journey between Rome and Philippi. The distance from Rome to Brundisium was 360 miles according to Strabo (vi. p. 283) or 358 according to the Antonine Itinerary (pp. 49, 51, 54, Parth. et Pind.). The distance from Dyrrhachium to Philippi was the same within a few miles; the journey from Dyrrhachium to Thessalonica being about 270 miles (267, Polybius in Strabo vii. p. 323; 269, *Itin. Anton.* p. 151; and 279, *Tab. Peuting.*), and from Thessalonica to Philippi 100 miles (*Itin. Anton.* pp. 152, 157). The present text of Pliny understates it at 325 miles, *H. N.* iv. 18. Ovid expects his books to reach Rome from Brundisium before the tenth day without hurrying (*Ep. Pont.* iv. 5. 8 'ut festinatum non faciatis iter'); while Horace moving very leisurely completes the distance in 16 days (*Sat.* i. 5). The voyage between Dyrrhachium and Brundisium ordinarily took a day: Cic. *ad Att.* iv. 1; comp. Appian I. p. 269 (ed. Bekker). The land transit on the Greek continent would probably not occupy much more time than on the Italian, the distances being the same. This calculation agrees with the notices in Cicero's letters. Cicero (if the dates can be trusted) leaves Brundisium on April 30th and arrives at Thessalonica on May 23rd (*ad Att.* iii. 8); but he travels leisurely and appears to have been delayed on the way. Again Atticus purposes starting from Rome on June 1st, and Cicero writing from Thessalonica on the 13th expects to see him 'propediem' (iii. 9). Again Cicero writing from Thessalonica on June 18th says that Atticus' letter has informed him of all that has happened at Rome up to May 25th (iii. 10). Lastly Cicero at Dyrrhachium receives on Nov. 27th a letter from Rome dated Nov. 12th (iii. 23). The sea route was more uncertain: but under favourable circumstances would be quicker than the journey by land, whether the course was by the gulf of Corinth or round the promontory of Malea. On the rate of sailing among the ancients see Friedländer *Sittengeschichte Roms* II. p. 12, to whom I owe some of the above references.

epistle offers to St Luke's narrative is further supported by a comparison with the other letters written during his captivity. As distinguished from the remaining three, the Epistle to the Philippians is thought to wear a gloomier aspect and to indicate severer restraints and less hopeful prospects[1].

At this point the aid of contemporary history is invoked. Have we not a sufficient account, it is asked, of the increased rigour of the Apostle's confinement in the appointment of the monster Tigellinus to succeed Burrus as commander of the imperial guards? Must not the well-known Jewish sympathies of Poppæa, now all-powerful as the emperor's consort, have darkened his prospects at the approaching trial?

The argument drawn from St Luke's narrative has been partially and incidently met already[2]. It seems highly probable that the prætorium does not denote any locality, whether the barracks on the Palatine or the camp without the city. Even if a local meaning be adopted, still it is neither stated nor implied that St Paul dwelt within the prætorium. If he did dwell there, he might nevertheless have occupied 'hired lodgings.' In the history, as in the letter, he is a prisoner in bonds. His external condition, as represented in the two writings, in no way differs. In tone, it is true, there is a strong contrast between St Luke's account and the language of St Paul himself: but this could hardly be otherwise. St Luke, as the historian of the Church, views events in the retrospect and deals chiefly with results, presenting the bright side of the picture, the triumph of the Church. St Paul, as the individual sufferer, writing at the moment and reflecting the agony of the struggle, paints the scene in darker colours, dwelling on his own sorrows. The Apostle's sufferings were in a great degree mental—the vexation of soul stirred up by unscrupulous opposition—the agony of suspense under his impending trial—his solicitude for the churches under his care—his sense of

---

[1] So Alford (*Prol.* § iii. 5). But Bengel, 'summa epistolæ, *gaudeo, gaudere*'; and Grotius, 'Epistola lætior alacriorque et blandior cæteris.'

[2] Above, p. 9, and on 'prætorium' in i. 13.

responsibility—his yearning desire to depart and be with Christ. It was impossible that the historian should reproduce this state of feeling : he has not done so in other cases[1].

Contrast with the other epistles considered.

And again : comparing the language of the Philippian letter with the other epistles, it is difficult to see anything more than those oscillations of feeling which must be experienced daily under trying circumstances of responsibility or danger. All these epistles alike reveal alternations of joy and sadness, moments of depression and moments of exaltation, successive waves of hope and fear. If the tone of one epistle is less cheerful than another, this is a very insecure foundation on which to build the hypothesis of an entire change in the prisoner's condition.

The argument neutralised by other passages.

Moreover arguments are sometimes alleged for the later date of the Philippian letter, which, though advanced for the same purpose, in reality neutralise those already considered. It is no longer to the prevailing gloom, but to the hopefulness of the Philippian letter, that the appeal is made. The Apostle is looking forward to his approaching trial and deliverance. He knows confidently that he shall abide and continue with the Philippians for their furtherance and joy of the faith : 'their rejoicing will abound by his coming to see them again[2]'; he 'trusts in the Lord that he shall visit them shortly[3].' Such passages are, I think, a complete answer to those who represent the sadness of this epistle as in strong contrast to the brighter tone of the other three. Yet considered in themselves they might seem to imply the near approach of his trial, and so to favour the comparatively late date of the epistle. But here again we must pause. These expressions, even if as strong, are not stronger than the language addressed to Philemon, when the Apostle bids his friend 'prepare him a lodging,' hoping that 'through their prayers he shall be given to them[4].' At many times doubtless during his long imprisonment, he expected his

---

[1] Compare for instance the agony of feeling expressed in the opening chapters of the Second Epistle to the Corinthians with the calm and unim- passioned account of the same period in St Luke.

[2] Phil. i. 25, 26.

[3] Phil. ii. 24.      [4] Philem. 22.

trial to come on. His life at this time was a succession of broken hopes and weary delays.

If this be so, we need not stop long to enquire how the political changes already noticed might possibly have affected St Paul's condition. A prisoner so mean in the eyes of the Roman world, a despised provincial, a religious fanatic—like Festus, they would see nothing more in him than this—was beneath the notice of a Tigellinus, intent on more ambitious and grander crimes. More plausible is the idea that Poppæa, instigated by the Jews, might have prejudiced the emperor against an offender whom they hated with a bitter hatred. Doubtless she might have done so. But, if she had interfered at all, why should she have been satisfied with delaying his trial or increasing his restraints, when she might have procured his condemnation and death ? The hand reeking with the noblest blood of Rome would hardly refuse at her bidding to strike down a poor foreigner, who was almost unknown and would certainly be unavenged. From whatever cause, whether from ignorance or caprice or indifference or disdain, her influence, we may safely conclude, was not exerted to the injury of the Apostle. *Political changes did not touch St Paul.*

Such are the grounds on which the Epistle to the Philippians has been assigned to a later date than the others written from Rome. So far from establishing this conclusion they seem to afford at most a very slight presumption in its favour. On the other hand certain considerations have been overlooked, which in the absence of direct evidence on the opposite side are entitled to a hearing. They are founded on a comparison of the style and matter of these epistles with the epistles of the preceding and the following groups—with the letters of the third Apostolic journey on the one side, and the Pastoral Epistles on the other. The inference from such a comparison, if I mistake not, is twofold; we are led to place the Epistle to the Philippians as early as possible, and the Epistles to the Colossians and Ephesians as late as possible, consistently with other known facts and probabilities. *The later date not established. Argument for the earlier date.*

1. The characteristic features of its group are less strongly *1. Reasons*

for placing
the Phi-
lippians
early. marked in the Epistle to the Philippians than in the others. Altogether in style and tone, as well as in its prominent ideas, it bears a much greater resemblance to the earlier letters, than

Resem-
blance to
the earlier
group, do the Epistles to the Colossians and Ephesians[1]. Thus it forms the link which connects these two epistles with those of the third apostolic journey. It represents an epoch of transition in the religious controversies of the age, or to speak more correctly, a momentary lull, a short breathing space, when one antagonistic error has been fought and overcome, and another is dimly foreseen in the future. The Apostle's great battle hitherto has been with Pharisaic Judaism; his great weapon the doctrine of grace. In the Epistle to the Philippians we have the spent wave of this controversy. In the third chapter the Apostle dwells with something like his former fulness on the contrast of faith and law, on the true and the false circumcision, on his own personal experiences as illustrating his theme. Henceforth when he touches on these topics, he will do so briefly and incidentally. Even now in his apostolic teaching, as in his inner life, he is 'forgetting those things which are behind and reaching forth unto those things which are before.' A new type of error is springing up—more speculative and less practical in its origin—which in one form or other mainly occupies his attention throughout the Epistles to the Colossians and Ephesians and the Pastoral Epistles; and which under the distinctive name of Gnosticism in its manifold and monstrous developments will disturb the peace of the Church for two centuries to come.

especially
to the
Romans. But of all the earlier letters it most nearly resembles the Epistle to the Romans, to which according to the view here maintained it stands next in chronological order. At least I do

---

[1] This fact is reflected in the opinions entertained respecting the genuineness of these epistles. While the authorship of the Epistle to the Philippians has been questioned only by the most extravagant criticism, more temperate writers have hesitated to accept the Colossians and Ephesians. This hesitation, though unwarranted, is instructive. The special characteristics of the main group (1, 2 Corinthians, Galatians, Romans) have been taken as the standard of the Apostle's style, when they rather indicate a particular phase in it. The Epistle to the Philippians has been spared because it reproduces these features more nearly than the other two.

not think that so many and so close parallels can be produced with any other epistle, as the following :

### PHILIPPIANS.

(1) i. 3, 4, 7, 8. I thank my God in every mention of you at all times in every request of mine ...as ye all are partakers with me in grace (τῆς χάριτος) : *for God is my witness*, how *I long for you all* in the bowels of Christ Jesus.

(2) i. 10. That ye may approve the things that are excellent.

(3) ii. 8, 9, 10, 11. He became obedient unto death...wherefore God also highly exalted Him... that in the name of Jesus every knee may bow of things in heaven and things on earth and things under the earth, and every tongue may confess that Jesus Christ is Lord, &c.

(4) ii. 2—4. That ye may have the same mind, having the same love, united in soul, having one mind : (Do) nothing in factiousness or vainglory,

but in humility holding one another superior to yourselves.

(5) iii. 3. For we are the circumcision,

who serve (λατρεύοντες) by the Spirit of God (θεοῦ v. l. θεῷ), and boast in Christ Jesus...

4, 5. If any other thinketh

### ROMANS.

i. 8—11. First I thank my God through Jesus Christ for you all...*for God is my witness*...how incessantly I make mention of you...at all times in my prayers making request...for *I long to see you*, that I may impart some spiritual grace (χάρισμα) to you.

ii. 18. Thou approvest the things that are excellent.

xiv. 9, 11. For hereunto Christ died and lived (i.e. rose again), that he may be Lord both of the dead and of the living...For it is written, I live, saith the Lord : for in me every knee shall bow and every tongue shall confess unto God (Is. xlv. 23, 24).

xii. 16—19. Having the same mind towards one another : not minding high things...Be not wise in your own conceits (φρόνιμοι παρ' ἑαυτοῖς)...having peace with all men : not avenging yourselves.

10. In honour holding one another in preference.

ii. 28. For the (circumcision) manifest in the flesh is not circumcision...but circumcision of the heart.

i. 9. God whom I serve (λατρεύω) in my spirit[1].

v. 11. Boasting in God through our Lord Jesus Christ.

xi. 1. For I also am an Is-

*Parallel passages.*

---

[1] The idea of the spiritual λατρεία appears again Rom. xii. 1, τὴν λογικὴν λατρείαν ὑμῶν, where this moral service of the Gospel is tacitly contrasted with the ritual service of the law as the living sacrifice to the dead victim. Compare also James i. 27 θρησκεία καθαρὰ καὶ ἀμίαντος κ.τ.λ. See the notes on Phil. iii. 3.

| PHILIPPIANS. | ROMANS. |
|---|---|
| to trust in the flesh, I more :... of the race of Israel, the tribe of Benjamin. | raelite, of the seed of Abraham, the tribe of Benjamin. |
| (6) iii. 9. Not having my own righteousness which is of law, but that which is through faith of Christ, the righteousness of God in faith... | x. 3. Ignorant of the righteousness of God, and seeking to establish their own (righteousness). ix. 31, 32. Pursuing a law of righteousness...not of faith, but as of works. |
| 10, 11. Being made conformable (συμμορφιζόμενος) unto His death, if by any means I may attain unto the resurrection from the dead : 21. That it may become conformable (σύμμορφον) to the body of His glory. | vi. 5. For if we have been planted (σύμφυτοι γεγόναμεν) in the likeness of His death, then shall we be also of His resurrection. viii. 29. He foreordained them conformable (συμμόρφους) to the image of His Son. |
| (7) iii. 19. Whose end is destruction, whose God is their belly. | vi. 21. For the end of those things is death. xvi. 18. They serve not our Lord Christ but their own belly. |
| (8) iv. 18. Having received from Epaphroditus the (gifts) from you, an odour of a sweet savour, a sacrifice acceptable, well-pleasing to God. | xii. 1. To present your bodies a living sacrifice, holy, well-pleasing to God. |

Some verbal coincidences besides might be pointed out, on which however no stress can be laid[1].

2. But if these resemblances suggest as early a date for

---

[1] I have observed the following words and expressions common to these two epistles and not occurring elsewhere in the New Testament; ἀποκαραδοκία, Rom. viii. 19, Phil. i. 20; ἄχρι τοῦ νῦν, Rom. viii. 22, Phil. i. 5; ἐξ ἐριθείας, Rom. ii. 8, Phil. i. 16; σύμμορφος, Rom. viii. 29, Phil. iii. 21; προσδέχεσθαι ἐν Κυρίῳ, Rom. xvi. 2, Phil. ii. 29; besides one or two which occur in the parallels quoted in the text. Compare also Rom. xiv. 14 οἶδα καὶ πέπεισμαι, with Phil. i. 25 τοῦτο πεποιθὼς οἶδα. The following are found in St Paul in these two epistles only, though occurring elsewhere in the New Testament; ἀκέραιος, Rom. xvi. 19, Phil. ii. 15 (comp. Matt. x. 16); ἐπιζητεῖν, Rom. xi. 7, Phil. iv. 17 (common elsewhere); λειτουργός, Rom. xiii. 6, xv. 16, Phil. ii. 25 (comp. Heb. i. 7, viii. 2); ὀκνηρός, Rom. xii. 11, Phil. iii. 1 (comp. Matt. xxv. 26); ὑπερέχειν, Rom. xiii. 1, Phil. ii. 3, iii. 8, iv. 7 (comp. 1 Pet. ii. 13); ὁμοίωμα, Rom. i. 23, v. 14, vi. 5, viii. 3, Phil. ii. 7 (comp. Rev. ix. 7); and perhaps μενοῦνγε, Rom. ix. 20, x. 18, Phil. iii. 8 (comp. Luke xi. 28).

the Epistle to the Philippians as circumstances will allow, there
are yet more cogent reasons for placing the others as late as
possible. The letters to the Colossians and Ephesians—the
latter more especially—exhibit an advanced stage in the development of the Church. The heresies, which the Apostle
here combats, are no longer the crude, materialistic errors of
the early childhood of Christianity, but the more subtle speculations of its maturer age. The doctrine which he preaches is
not now the 'milk for babes,' but the 'strong meat' for grown
men. He speaks to his converts no more 'as unto carnal' but
'as unto spiritual.' In the letter to the Ephesians especially
his teaching soars to the loftiest height, as he dwells on the
mystery of the Word and of the Church. Here too we find
the earliest reference to a Christian hymn[1], showing that the
devotion of the Church was at length finding expression in set
forms of words. In both ways these epistles bridge over the
gulf which separates the Pastoral letters from the Apostle's
earlier writings. The heresies of the Pastoral letters are the
heresies of the Colossians and Ephesians grown rank and corrupt. The solitary quotation already mentioned is the precursor
of the not infrequent references to Christian formularies in these
latest of the Apostle's writings. And in another respect also
the sequence is continuous, if this view of the relative dates be
accepted. The directions relating to ecclesiastical government,
which are scattered through the Pastoral Epistles, are the outward correlative, the practical sequel to the sublime doctrine of
the Church first set forth in its fulness in the Epistle to the
Ephesians. A few writers have questioned the genuineness of
the letters to the Colossians and Ephesians, many more of the
Pastoral Epistles. They have done so chiefly on the ground
that these writings present a later stage of Christian thought
and organization, than the universally acknowledged letters of
St Paul. External authority, supported by internal evidence
of various kinds, bids us stop short of this conclusion. But, if

2. Reasons for placing the other epistles late.

---

[1] Ephes. v. 14, διὸ λέγει

Ἔγειρε ὁ καθεύδων

Καὶ ἀνάστα ἐκ τῶν νεκρῶν

Καὶ ἐπιφαύσει σοι ὁ Χριστός.

we refuse to accept the inference, we can hardly fail to re-cognise the facts which suggested it. These facts are best met by placing the Epistles to the Colossians and Ephesians late in St Paul's first Roman captivity, so as to separate them as widely as possible from the earlier epistles, and by referring the Pastoral letters to a still later date towards the close of the Apostle's life.

## III.

## THE CHURCH OF PHILIPPI.

PHILIPPI[1] was founded by the great Macedonian king, whose name it bears, on or near the site of the ancient Crenides, 'Wells' or 'Fountains[2].' Its natural advantages were considerable. In the neighbourhood were gold and silver mines which had been worked in very early times by the Phœnicians and afterwards by the Thasians[3]. The plain moreover on which it was situated, washed by the Gangites a tributary of the Strymon, was and is remarkable for its fertility[4].

But the circumstance, to which even more than to its rich soil and mineral treasures Philippi owed its importance, was its

---

[1] On the geography and antiquities of Philippi, see Cousinéry *Voyage dans la Macédoine* II p. 1 sq. (1831); Leake *Northern Greece* III p. 214 sq. (1835); and more recently two short papers by Perrot in the *Revue Archéologique*(1860) I. p. 44 sq., p. 67 sq., entitled *Daton, Néopolis, les mines de Philippes*. A work of great importance was commenced under the auspices of the late French Emperor, *Mission Archéologique de Macédoine*, by MM. Heuzey and Daumet; of which the part relating to Philippi and the neighbourhood has appeared (1869). Besides several unpublished inscriptions it contains what appears to be a very careful map of the site of the town and district.

[2] Diod. Sic. xvi. 3, 8; Strabo vii. p. 331; Appian *Bell. Civ.* iv. p. 105

οἱ δὲ Φίλιπποι πόλις ἐστὶν ἣ Δᾶτος ὠνομάζετο πάλαι καὶ Κρηνίδες ἔτι πρὸ Δάτου, κρῆναι γάρ εἰσι περὶ τῷ λόφῳ ναμάτων πολλαί κ.τ.λ. Appian however is wrong in identifying Crenides and Philippi with Datos or Daton, though his statement is copied by more than one recent writer. The site of this last-mentioned place was near to Neapolis: see Leake p. 223 sq., Perrot p. 46, *Miss. Archéol.* p. 60 sq.

[3] On the mines of Philippi see Boeckh's *Public Economy of Athens* p. 8 (Engl. trans.), *Miss. Archéol.* p. 4, p. 55 sq.

[4] Cousinéry II. p. 5, 'Les produits seraient immenses si l'activité et l'industrie des habitans répondaient à la libéralité de la nature'; see also Perrot p. 49: comp. Athen. xv. p. 682 B, Appian iv. p. 105.

Its geogra-
phical im-
portance. geographical position, commanding the great high road between Europe and Asia. The almost continuous mountain barrier between the East and West is here depressed so as to form a gateway for this thoroughfare of the two continents[1]. It was this advantage of position which led Philip to fortify the site of the ancient Crenides. It was this which marked out the place as the battle-field where the destinies of the Empire were decided. It was this, lastly, which led the conqueror to plant a Roman colony on the scene of his triumph.

Neither to its productive soil nor to its precious metals can we trace any features which give a distinctive character to the early history of the Gospel at Philippi. Its fertility it shared Its mines
exhausted. with many other scenes of the Apostle's labours. Its mineral wealth appears at this time to have been almost, if not wholly, drained. The mines had passed successively into the hands of the three prerogative powers of civilised Europe, the Athenians, the Macedonians, and the Romans. Even before Philip founded his city, the works had been discontinued on account of the scanty yield. By his order they were reopened, and a large revenue was extracted from them[2]. But he seems to have taxed their productive power to the utmost; for during the Roman occupation we hear but little of them[3].

---

[1] Brutus and Cassius pitched their camps somewhere in the neighbourhood of the pass on two eminences which stand on either side of the road. Appian, iv. p. 106, describing their position says, τὸ δὲ μέσον τῶν λόφων, τὰ ὀκτὼ στάδια, δίοδος ἦν ἐς τὴν Ἀσίαν τε καὶ Εὐρώπην, καθάπερ πύλαι: see Miss. Archéol. p. 105 sq. The pass itself is formed by a depression in the ridge of Symbolum, so called because it bridges together the higher mountains on either side, Pangæum to the west and the continuation of Hæmus to the east. The ridge of Symbolum thus separates the plain of the Gangites from the sea-board, and must be crossed in visiting Philippi from Neapolis: Dion Cass.

xlvii. 35 Σύμβολον τὸ χωρίον ὀνομάζουσ. καθ' ὃ τὸ ὄρος ἐκεῖνο (i. e. Παγγαῖον ἑτέρῳ τινὶ ἐς μεσόγειαν ἀνατείνοντι συμ-βάλλει, καὶ ἔστι μεταξὺ Νέας πόλεως κα Φιλίππων· ἡ μὲν γὰρ πρὸς θαλάσσῃ κα ἀντιπέρας Θάσου ἦν, ἡ δὲ ἐντὸς τῶν ὁρῶ ἐπὶ τῷ πεδίῳ πεπόλισται; see Leak p. 217. The distance from Neapolis t Philippi is given by Appian (iv. 106) a 70 stadia, by the Jerus. Itin. (p. 321 Wess.) as 10 miles (not 9, as stated b MM. Heuzey and Daumet), and by th Antonin. Itin. (p. 603, Wess.) as 12 miles A recent measurement makes it fro 12 to 13 kilomètres (Mission Archéolo gique p. 19), i.e. about 9 Roman mile

[2] Diod. Sic. xvi. 8.

[3] On the working of the Macedonia

On the other hand the position of Philippi as a thorough- Its mixed
fare for the traffic of nations invests St Paul's preaching here tion.
with a peculiar interest. To this circumstance may be ascribed
the great variety of types among the first Philippian converts,
which is one of the most striking and most instructive features
in this portion of the narrative. We are standing at the con-
fluence of the streams of European and Asiatic life: we see
reflected in the evangelization of Philippi, as in a mirror, the
history of the passage of Christianity from the East to the
West.

It was in the course of his second missionary journey, St Paul's
about the year 52, that St Paul first visited Philippi. His first visit.
associates were Silas who had accompanied him from Jerusalem[1], Timotheus whom they had taken up at Lystra[2], and
Luke who had recently joined the party at Troas[3]. At this
last-mentioned place the Apostle's eyes were at length opened
to the import of those mysterious checks and impulses which
had brought him to a seaport lying opposite to the European
coast. 'A man of Macedonia' appeared in a night vision, and
revealed to him the work which the 'Spirit of Jesus[4]' had
designed for him. Forthwith he sets sail for Europe. His
zeal is seconded by wind and wave, and the voyage is made
with unwonted speed[5]. Landing at Neapolis he makes no
halt there, but presses forward to fulfil his mission. A
mountain range still lies between him and his work. Following the great Egnatian road he surmounts this barrier,
and the plain of Philippi, the first city in Macedonia, lies

---

mines generally under the Romans, see
Becker and Marquardt *Röm. Alterth.*
III. 2, p. 144. I have not found any
mention of those of Philippi after the
Christian era. The passages in ancient
writers referring to mining operations
are collected in J. and L. Sabatier
*Production de l'Or etc.* (St Petersburg,
1850) p. 5 sq.

[1] Acts xv. 40.

[2] Acts xvi. 1, 3.

[3] Compare Acts xvi. 8 κατέβησαν
εἰς Τρῳάδα, with xvi. 10 εὐθέως ἐζητή-
σαμεν ἐξελθεῖν εἰς τὴν Μακεδονίαν.

[4] Acts xvi. 7 τὸ πνεῦμα Ἰησοῦ, the
correct reading.

[5] Acts xvi. 11 εὐθυδρομήσαμεν εἰς
Σαμοθρᾴκην, τῇ δὲ ἐπιούσῃ εἰς Νεάπολιν.
On a later occasion the voyage from
Neapolis to Troas takes *five* days, Acts
xx. 5.

at his feet[1]. Here he establishes himself and delivers his message.

Two features in St Luke's account.

Before considering the circumstances and results of this mission, it will be necessary to direct attention to two features in the actual condition of Philippi which appear on the face of St Luke's narrative and are not without their influence on the progress of the Gospel—its political status and its resident Jewish population.

1. Philippi a Roman colony.

1. Appreciating its strategical importance of which he had had recent experience, Augustus founded at Philippi a Roman military colony with the high-sounding name 'Colonia Augusta

---

[1] This is the probable explanation of the expression in Acts xvi. 12, ἥτις ἐστὶν πρώτη τῆς μερίδος, Μακεδονίας πόλις, κολωνία, 'for this is the first place in the country (or district), a city of Macedonia, a colony.' The clause explains why the Apostle did not halt at Neapolis. Though the political frontier might not be constant, the natural boundary between Thrace and Macedonia was the mountain range already described: see p. 48, note 1. Thus, while Philippi is almost universally assigned to Macedonia, Neapolis is generally spoken of as a Thracian town, e.g. in Scylax (*Geog. Min.* I. p. 54, ed. Müller): see Rettig *Quæst. Philipp.* p. 10 sq. The reading of Acts xvi. 12, which I have given, seems the best supported, as well as the most expressive: the first τῆς (before μερίδος) ought probably to be retained, being omitted only by B, besides some copies which leave out μερίδος also; the second (before Μακεδονίας) to be rejected, as it is wanting in a majority of the best copies: but these variations do not affect the general sense of the passage. For the expression compare Polyb. ii. 16. 2 μέχρι πόλεως Πίσης, ἥ πρώτη κεῖται τῆς Τυρρηνίας ὡς πρὸς τὰς δυσμάς, and v. 80. 3 ἥ κεῖται μετὰ Ῥινοκόλουρα, πρώτη τῶν κατὰ κοίλην Συσίαν πόλεων,

κ.τ.λ., quoted by Rettig pp. 7, 8. For μερίς compare μεριδάρχης, Joseph. *Ant.* xii. 5. 5.

Thus πρώτη describes the *geographical position* of Philippi. All attempts to explain the epithet of its *political rank* have failed. In no sense was it a 'chief town.' So far as we know, Thessalonica was all along the general capital of Macedonia; and if this particular district had still a separate political existence, the centre of government was not Philippi but Amphipolis. Nor again can it be shown that πρώτη was ever assumed as a mere honorary title by any city in Greece or Macedonia, though common in Asia Minor. On this latter point Marquardt, in Becker *Röm. Alterth.* III. 1. p. 118, seems to be in error when he states that Thessalonica was styled πρώτη Μακεδόνων: he has misinterpreted the inscription mentioned in Boeckh no. 1967; see Leake III. pp. 214, 483, 486. The correction πρώτης μερίδος for πρώτη τῆς μερίδος might deserve some consideration, though unsupported by any external evidence, if it were at all probable that the original division of Macedonia by the Romans into *four* provinces was still recognised; but it seems to have been abandoned long before this date; see Leake III. p. 487.

Julia Philippensis[1].' At the same time he conferred upon it the special privilege of the 'jus Italicum[2].' A colony is described by an ancient writer as a miniature likeness of the great Roman people[3]; and this character is fully borne out by the account of Philippi in the apostolic narrative. The political atmosphere of the place is wholly Roman. The chief magistrates, more strictly designated duumvirs, arrogate to themselves the loftier title of prætors[4]. Their servants, like the attendant officers of the highest functionaries in Rome, bear the name of lictors[5]. The pride and privilege of Roman citizenship confront us at every turn. This is the sentiment

---

[1] Plin. *N. H.* iv. 18 'Intus Philippi colonia.' See the coins in Eckhel ii. p. 76, Mionnet i. p. 486; Orell. *Inscr.* 512. In one instance at least ' Victrix' seems to be added to this title, *Mission Archéologique* p. 17. According to Dion Cass. li. 4, Augustus ridded himself of troublesome neighbours by transplanting to Philippi and other colonies the inhabitants of those Italian towns which had espoused the cause of Antonius.

[2] Dig. L. 15. On the 'jus Italicum' see Becker and Marquardt *Röm. Alterth.* iii. i. p. 261 sq.

[3] Gell. xvi. 13 'Populi Romani, cujus istæ coloniæ quasi effigies parvæ simulacraque esse quædam videntur.'

[4] Acts xvi. 19, 22, 35, 36, 38. The same persons who are first designated generally ' the magistrates' (ἄρχοντες, ver. 19) are afterwards called by their distinctive title ' the prætors' (στρατηγοί). It is a mistake to suppose that the prisoners were handed over by the civil authorities (ἄρχοντες) to the military (στρατηγοί) to be tried. The chief magistrates of a colony were styled ' duumviri juri dicundo,' or ' duumviri' simply. On their functions see Savigny *Gesch. d. R. R.* i. p. 30 sq., with other references in Becker and Marquardt *Röm. Alterth.* iii. i. p. 352. A duumvir

of Philippi appears on an inscription, Orell. no. 3746 C. VIBIVS C. F. VOL. FLORVS . DEC . IIVIR . ET . MVNERARIVS . PHILIPPIS . FIL. CAR. C.; another on a monument at Neapolis, *Mission Archéologique* p. 15 [DECV] RIONATVS . ET . IIVIRALICIS . PONTIFEX . FLAMEN . DIVI CLAVDI . PHILIPPIS. See also a mutilated inscription, *ib.* p. 127 II[V]R. J[V]R . DIC . PHILIPPIS. The second must have been contemporary with St Paul. On the practice of assuming the title of ' prætor' see Cicero *de Leg. Agr.* ii. 34 'Vidi, quum venissem Capuam, coloniam deductam L. Considio et Sext. Saltio (quemadmodum ipsi loquebantur) prætoribus: ut intelligatis quantam locus ipse afferat superbiam...Nam primum, id quod dixi, quum ceteris in coloniis duumviri appellentur, hi se prætores appellari voluerunt.' This assumption however was by no means exceptional even in Italy (see Orell. *Inscr.* 3785, Hor. *Sat.* i. 5. 34, and notes); and where some Greek title was necessary, as at Philippi, στρατηγοί would naturally be adopted. See Cureton's *Anc. Syr. Doc.* p. 188. Another inscription (Orell. no. 4064) mentions a MAG. QVINQVENN. (quinquennalis), i.e. a censor, at Philippi.

[5] ῥαβδοῦχοι, Acts xvi. 35, 38.

which stimulates the blind loyalty of the people[1]: this is the power which obtains redress for the prisoners and forces an apology from the unwilling magistrates[2]. Nor is this feature entirely lost sight of, when we turn from St Luke's narrative to St Paul's epistle. Addressing a Roman colony from the Roman metropolis, writing as a citizen to citizens, he recurs to the political franchise as an apt symbol of the higher privileges of their heavenly calling, to the political life as a suggestive metaphor for the duties of their Christian profession[3].

2. The Jews of Philippi.

2. On this, as on all other occasions, the Gospel is first offered to the Jews. Their numbers at Philippi appear to have been very scanty. St Paul found no synagogue here, as at Thessalonica and Berœa. The members of the chosen race met together for worship every week at a 'place of prayer' outside the city gate on the banks of the Gangites[4]. The Apostle appears to have had no precise information of the spot[5], but the common practice of his countrymen would suggest the suburbs of the city, and the river-side especially, as a likely place for these religious gatherings[6]. Thither accordingly he repaired with his companions on the first sabbath day after their arrival. To the women assembled he delivered his mes-

---

[1] Acts xvi. 21 'And teach customs which it is not lawful for us to receive neither to observe, being Romans.'

[2] Acts xvi. 37—39.

[3] Phil. i. 27 μόνον ἀξίως τοῦ εὐαγγελίου τοῦ Χριστοῦ πολιτεύεσθε, iii. 20 ἡμῶν γὰρ τὸ πολίτευμα ἐν οὐρανοῖς ὑπάρχει.

[4] Acts xvi. 13 παρὰ ποταμόν. This river was the Gangas or Gangites (Appian iv. p. 106 ὃν Γάγγαν τινές, οἱ δὲ Γαγγίτην, λέγουσι) whose sources are near to Philippi and probably gave its name to Crenides. As this river is called by Herodotus, vii. 113, Ἀγγίτης, and now bears the name Anghista, it would appear that the initial consonant was not a decided G, but a guttural sound like the Shemitic Ayin which is sometimes omitted in Greek and some-

times represented by Γ. It is a great error to identify the stream mentioned by St Luke with the Strymon, which must be about 30 miles distant, and certainly would not be designated a river without the definite article.

[5] The correct reading seems to be, not οὗ ἐνομίζετο προσευχὴ εἶναι, but οὗ ἐνομίζομεν προσευχὴν εἶναι, 'where we supposed there was a place of prayer'; and may be explained in the way suggested in the text.

[6] Joseph. Ant. xiv. 10. 23 τὰς προσευχὰς ποιεῖσθαι πρὸς τῇ θαλάσσῃ κατὰ τὸ πάτριον ἔθος. So Tertullian speaks of the 'orationes littorales' of the Jews, adv. Nat. i. 13; comp. de Jejun. 16: see also Philo in Flacc. § 14, p. 535 M, and other references in Biscoe History of the Acts etc. p. 182 sq. (1840).

sage. Of strictly Hebrew converts the sacred record is silent ; but the baptism of a proselytess and her household is related as the first triumph of the Gospel at Philippi.

To the scanty numbers and feeble influence of the Jews we may perhaps in some degree ascribe the unswerving allegiance of this church to the person of the Apostle and to the true principles of the Gospel. In one passage indeed his grateful acknowledgment of the love and faith of his Philippian converts is suddenly interrupted by a stern denunciation of Judaism[1]. But we may well believe that in this warning he was thinking of Rome more than of Philippi ; and that his indignation was aroused rather by the vexatious antagonism which there thwarted him in his daily work, than by any actual errors already undermining the faith of his distant converts[2]. Yet even the Philippians were not safe from the intrusion of these dangerous teachers. At no great distance lay important Jewish settlements, the strongholds of this fanatical opposition. Even now there might be threatenings of an interference which would tamper with the allegiance and disturb the peace of his beloved church.

*No Judaic tendencies in the Philippian Church.*

The Apostle's first visit to Philippi is recorded with a minuteness which has not many parallels in St Luke's history. The narrator had joined St Paul shortly before he crossed over into Europe: he was with the Apostle during his sojourn at Philippi: he seems to have remained there for some time after his departure[3]. This exact personal knowledge of the writer, combining with the grandeur and variety of the incidents themselves, places the visit to Philippi among the most striking and instructive passages in the apostolic narrative.

*Character of St Luke's narrative.*

I have already referred to the varieties of type among the first disciples at Philippi, as a prominent feature in this portion of the history. The three converts, who are especially mentioned, stand in marked contrast each to the other in national

*Three different types in the Philippian converts.*

---

[1] Phil. iii. 2 sq.

[2] See below, p. 69 sq.

[3] The first person plural is dropped at Philippi (Acts xvii. 1, ἦλθον) and resumed at the same place (Acts xx. 5 ἔμενον ἡμᾶς) after a lapse of six or seven years. This coincidence suggests the inference in the text.

descent, in social rank, in religious education. They are representatives of three different races: the one an Asiatic, the other a Greek, the third a Roman. In the relations of everyday life they have nothing in common: the first is engaged in an important and lucrative branch of traffic: the second, treated by the law as a mere chattel without any social or political rights, is employed by her masters to trade upon the credulous superstition of the ignorant: the third, equally removed from both the one and the other, holds a subordinate office under government. In their religious training also they stand no less apart. In the one the speculative mystic temper of Oriental devotion has at length found deeper satisfaction in the revealed truths of the Old Testament. The second, bearing the name of the Pythian god the reputed source of Greek inspiration, represents an artistic and imaginative religion, though manifested here in a very low and degrading form[1]. While the third, if he preserved the characteristic features of his race, must have exhibited a type of worship essentially political in tone. The purple-dealer and proselytess of Thyatira—the native slave-girl with the divining spirit—the Roman gaoler—all alike acknowledge the supremacy of the new faith. In the history of the Gospel at Philippi, as in the history of the Church at large, is reflected the great maxim of Christianity, the central truth of the Apostle's preaching, that here 'is neither Jew nor Greek, neither bond nor free, neither male nor female, but all are one in Christ Jesus[2].'

Order of the conversions typical.

Again the order of these conversions is significant: first, the proselyte, next the Greek, lastly the Roman. Thus the incidents at Philippi in their sequence, not less than in their variety, symbolize the progress of Christianity throughout the world. Through the Israelite dispersion, through the proselytes whether of the covenant or of the gate, the message of the

---

[1] See Plut. *Mor.* p. 414 E, *Clem. Hom.* ix. 16. It has been conjectured that this girl with the ' Pytho-spirit ' was a ἱερό-δουλος attached to the famous oracle of Dionysus among the Satræ, a wild mountain tribe in the Hæmus chain: Herod. vii. 111. At all events the incident is illustrated by the religious temper of these half-barbarous mountaineers.

[2] Gal. iii. 28.

Gospel first reached the Greek. By the instrumentality of the Greek language and the diffusion of the Greek race it finally established itself in Rome, the citadel of power and civilisation, whence directly or indirectly it was destined to spread over the whole world.

These events however are only symbolical as all history—more especially scriptural history—is symbolical. The order of the conversions at Philippi was in itself the natural order. The sacred historian wrote down with truthful simplicity what he 'saw and heard.' The representative character of these several incidents can hardly have occurred to him. But from its geographical position Philippi, as a meeting-point of nations, would represent not unfairly the civilised world in miniature; and the phenomena of the progress of the Gospel in its wider sphere were thus anticipated on a smaller scale.

But while the conversions at Philippi had thus a typical character, as representing not only the universality of the Gospel but also the order of its diffusion, they seem to illustrate still more distinctly the two great social revolutions which it has effected. In most modern treatises on civilisation, from whatever point of view they are written, a prominent place is given to the amelioration of woman and the abolition of slavery, as the noblest social triumphs of Christianity. Now the woman and the slave are the principal figures in the scene of the Apostle's preaching at Philippi. Social influence of the Gospel symbolized in the case of

As regards the woman indeed it seems probable that the Apostle's work was made easier by the national feelings and usages of Macedonia. It may, I think, be gathered from St Luke's narrative, that her social position was higher in this country than in most parts of the civilised world. At Philippi, at Thessalonica, at Berœa, the women—in some cases certainly, in all probability, ladies of birth and rank—take an active part with the Apostle[1]. It forms moreover a striking coincidence, (1) The woman.

---

[1] At Philippi, xvi. 13 'We spoke to the *women* that were gathered together'; at Thessalonica, xvii. 4 'There were added to Paul and Silas...of the chief *women* not a few'; at Berœa, xvii. 12 'Many of them believed, and of the Greek *women* of rank (εὐσχημόνων) and men not a few.'

and surely an undesigned coincidence, between the history and the epistle, that while in the former the Gospel is related to have been first preached to women and the earliest converts specially mentioned are women, in the latter we find the peace of the Philippian Church endangered by the feuds of two ladies of influence, whose zealous aid in the spread of the Gospel the Apostle gratefully acknowledges[1]. Moreover the inference thus suggested by the narrative of St Luke and strengthened by the notice in St Paul's epistle is farther borne out, if I mistake not, by reference to other sources of information. The extant Macedonian inscriptions seem to assign to the sex a higher social influence than is common among the civilised nations of antiquity. In not a few instances a metronymic takes the place of the usual patronymic[2] and in other cases a prominence is given to women which can hardly be accidental[3]. But whether I am right or not in the conjecture that the work of the Gospel was in this respect

*Influence of the sex in Macedonia.*

---

[1] Euodia and Syntyche, Phil. iv. 2, αἵτινες ἐν τῷ εὐαγγελίῳ συνήθλησάν μοι.

[2] On the well-known inscription giving the names of the Thessalonian politarchs, Boeckh no. 1967, we read Σωσιπάτρου τοῦ Κλεοπάτρας and Ταύρου τοῦ·'Αμμίας; on a second at Beroea, 1957 f (add.) Πόρος 'Αμμίας; on a third not far from Beroea, 1957 g (add.) Μακέδων Εὐγείας; on a fourth near Thessalonica, 1967 b (add.) [ὁ δεῖνα] 'Αντιφίλης; on a fifth at Edessa, 1997 c (add.) 'Αλέξανδρος καὶ Εἰούλιος οἱ Μαρκίας, Ἕσπερο[s] Σεμέλης, [Εἰ]ούλ[ιο]s Καλλίστης. See Leake III. pp. 236, 277, 292.

[3] For instance one inscription (no. 1958) records how a wife erects a tomb 'for herself and her dear husband out of their common earnings (ἐκ τῶν κοινῶν καμάτων)': another (no. 1977) how a husband erects a tomb 'for his devoted and darling wife (τῇ φιλάνδρῳ καὶ γλυκυτάτῃ συνβίῳ) and himself,' in this case

also from their common savings (ἐκ τῶν κοινῶν κόπων). Again there are cases of monuments erected in honour of women by public bodies: e. g. no. 1997 d (add.) ἡ πόλις [κ]αὶ οἱ συνπρα[γ]ματε[υ]όμενο[ι] 'Ρωμαῖο[ι] Πετρωνίαν Λ. Πετρωνίου Βάσσο[υ] θυγατέρα Στρατύλλαν τιμῶντ[ε]s [Θε]οῖs, no. 1999 Μακεδόνων οἱ σύνεδροι Μαρκίαν 'Ακυλίαν Φαβρικιανοῦ Ἄπερος θυγατέρ[α] ἀνδρὸς ἀγαθοῦ, no. 1999 b (add.) τὸ κοινὸν τῶν Μακεδόνων Μαρλίαν Ποντελαν Λουκούλλαν Αὔλου Ποντίου Βήρου τοῦ λαμπροτάτου ἀνθυπάτου γυναῖκα ἀρετῆς ἕνεκεν. Again the deferential language used by the husband speaking of the wife is worthy of notice, e. g. no. 1965 Εὐτύχης Στρατονίκῃ τῇ συμβίῳ καὶ κυρίᾳ μνείας χάριν. These are the most striking but not the only instances in which an unusual prominence is given to women. The whole series of Macedonian inscriptions read continuously cannot fail, I think, to suggest the inference in the text.

aided by the social condition of Macedonia, the active zeal of the women in this country is a remarkable fact, without a parallel in the Apostle's history elsewhere and only to be compared with their prominence at an earlier date in the personal ministry of our Lord.

And as Christianity exerts its influence on the woman at Philippi, so does it also on the slave. The same person, whose conversion exemplifies the one maxim of the Gospel that in Christ is 'neither male nor female,' is made a living witness of the other social principle also that in Him is 'neither bond nor free.' It can hardly have happened that the Apostle's mission had never before crossed the path of the slave; yet it is a significant fact, illustrating the varied character and typical import of this chapter of sacred history, that the divining girl at Philippi is the earliest recorded instance, where his attention is directed to one of these 'live chattels[1].' *(2) The slave.*

But more than this: as the Gospel recognises the claims of the woman and the slave severally, so also it fulfils its noblest mission in hallowing the general relations of family life, which combines these and other elements. Here too the conversion of the Philippian Church retains its typical character. It has been observed[2], that this is the first recorded instance in St Paul's history where whole families are gathered into the fold. Lydia and her household—the gaoler and all belonging to him—are baptized into Christ. Henceforth the worship of households plays an important part in the divine economy of the Church. As in primeval days the patriarch was the recognised priest of his clan, so in the Christian Church the father of the house is the divinely appointed centre of religious life to his own family. The family religion is the true starting-point, the surest foundation, of the religion of cities and dioceses, of nations and empires. The church in the house of Philemon grows into the Church of Colossæ[3]; the church in the house of *Family religion exemplified.*

---

[1] Aristot. *Pol.* i. 4 ὁ δοῦλος κτῆμά τι ἔμψυχον. See *Colossians etc.* pp. 313, 319 sq.

[2] See Conybeare and Howson I. p. 348 (2nd edition).

[3] Philem. 2.

Nymphas becomes the Church of Laodicea[1]; the church in the house of Aquila and Priscilla loses itself in the Churches of Ephesus and Rome[2].

Grandeur of the incidents.   Altogether the history of St Paul's connexion with Philippi assumes a prominence quite out of proportion to the importance of the place itself.   In the incidents and the results alike of his preaching the grandeur of the epoch is brought out.   The persecutions which the Apostle here endured were more than usually severe, and impressed themselves deeply on his memory, for he alludes to them once and again[3].   The marvellous deliverance wrought for him is without a parallel in his history before or after.   The signal success which crowned his labours surpasses all his earlier or later achievements.

Loyalty of the Philippians.   On this last-mentioned feature it is especially refreshing to dwell.   The unwavering loyalty of his Philippian converts is the constant solace of the Apostle in his manifold trials, the one bright ray of happiness piercing the dark clouds which gather ever thicker about the evening of his life.   They are his 'joy and crown, his brethren beloved and eagerly desired[4].'   From them alone he consents to receive alms for the relief of his personal wants[5].   To them alone he writes in language unclouded by any shadow of displeasure or disappointment.

Their sufferings.   St Paul's first visit to Philippi closed abruptly amid the storm of persecution.   It was not to be expected that, where the life of the master had been so seriously endangered, the scholars would escape all penalties.   The Apostle left behind him a legacy of suffering to this newly born church.   This is not a mere conjecture: the afflictions of the Macedonian Christians, and of the Philippians especially, are more than once mentioned in St Paul's epistles[6].   If it was their privilege to believe in Christ,

---

[1] Col. iv. 15.

[2] 1 Cor. xvi. 19, Rom. xvi. 5.

[3] 1 Thess. ii. 2 'Though we had already suffered and been ignominiously treated (προπαθόντες καὶ ὑβρισθέντες), as ye know, at Philippi,' Phil. i. 30 'Having the same conflict which ye saw in me.'

[4] Phil. iv. 1.

[5] Phil. iv. 15.

[6] 2 Cor. viii. 2.   See the notes on Phil. i. 7, 28—30.

it was equally their privilege to suffer for Him[1]. To this refiner's fire may doubtless be ascribed in part the lustre and purity of their faith compared with other churches.

About five years elapsed between St Paul's first and second visit to Philippi: but meanwhile his communications with this church appear to have been frequent and intimate. It has been already mentioned that on the Apostle's departure St Luke seems to have remained at Philippi, where he was taken up after the lapse of several years and where perhaps he had spent some portion of the intervening period[2]. Again when in the year 57 St Paul, then residing at Ephesus, despatched Timotheus and Erastus to Macedonia[3], we may feel sure that the most loyal of all his converts were not overlooked in this general mission. When moreover about the same time, either through these or other messengers, he appealed to the Macedonian Christians to relieve the wants of their poorer brethren in Judæa, it may safely be assumed that his faithful Philippian Church was foremost in the promptness and cordiality of its response, where all alike in spite of abject poverty and sore persecution were lavish with their alms 'to their power, yea and beyond their power[4].' Nor is it probable that these notices exhaust all his communications with Philippi at this time. Lying on the high-road between Asia and Achaia, this city would be the natural halting-place for the Apostle's messengers[5], as they passed to and fro between the great centres of Gentile Christendom.

At length in the autumn of the year 57 the Apostle himself, released from his engagements in Asia, revisits his European churches. His first intention had been to sail direct to Achaia, in which case he would have called in Macedonia and returned

*Marginal note:* Later communications with Philippi.

---

[1] Phil. i. 29 ὑμῖν ἐχαρίσθη τὸ ὑπὲρ Χριστοῦ, οὐ μόνον τὸ εἰς αὐτὸν πιστεύειν ἀλλὰ καὶ τὸ ὑπὲρ αὐτοῦ πάσχειν.

[2] See above, p. 53, note 3.

[3] Acts xix. 22. Of Timotheus see also 1 Cor. iv. 17, xvi. 10, 2 Cor. i. 1. Putting together these notices we may infer that Timotheus did not proceed with Erastus to Corinth, but remained behind in Macedonia.

[4] 2 Cor. viii. 1—5.

[5] Titus and his companion for instance (2 Cor. ii. 13, vii. 6, xii. 18; comp. 1 Cor. xvi. 11, 12).

to Corinth.  But afterwards he altered his plan and travelled by land, so as to take Macedonia on the way[1].  Leaving Macedonia and visiting Corinth, he had purposed to take ship from this latter place direct to Palestine: but receiving information of a plot against his life, he changes his route and returns by land[2].  Thus owing to a combination of circumstances Macedonia receives a double visit.  On both occasions his affectionate relations with Philippi seem to attract and rivet him there.  On the former, seeking relief from the agony of suspense which oppresses him at Troas, he hurries across the sea to Macedonia, halting apparently at Philippi and there awaiting the arrival of Titus[3].  On the latter, unable to tear himself away, he despatches his companions to Asia in advance and lingers behind at Philippi himself, that he may keep the paschal feast with his beloved converts[4].  It is the last festival for some years to come, which he is free to celebrate as and where he wills.

Of the former visit St Luke records only the fact.  But the Second Epistle to the Corinthians certainly[5], the Epistle to the Galatians not improbably[6], were written from Macedonia on this occasion: and, though scarcely a single incident is directly related, they present a complete and vivid picture of the Apostle's inward life at this time.  Of his external relations thus much may be learnt: we find him busy with the collection of alms for Judæa, stimulating the Macedonian churches and gratefully acknowledging their liberal response[7]; we gather also from the mention of 'fightings without[8],' that the enemies whether Jewish or heathen, who had persecuted him in earlier years,

[1] 2 Cor. i. 15—17, comp. 1 Cor. xvi. 5, 6.

[2] Acts xix. 21, xx. 1—3.

[3] 2 Cor. ii. 12 sq., vii. 5, 6.

[4] Acts xx. 5, 6 'These going before waited for us at Troas: but we set sail from Philippi after the days of unleavened bread.'

[5] 2 Cor. ii. 13, vii. 5, viii. 1 sq., ix. 2, 4.  The subscription mentions Philippi as the place of writing, and this is probable, though the authority is almost worthless.

[6] See *Galatians*, p. 35 sq.

[7] 2 Cor. viii. 1—6, ix. 2.

[8] 2 Cor. vii. 5; comp. viii. 2. To this occasion also the Apostle may possibly refer in Phil. i. 30, τὸν αὐτὸν ἀγῶνα ἔχοντες οἷον εἴδετε ἐν ἐμοί.

made his reappearance in Macedonia a signal for the renewal of their attacks. Of the latter visit we know absolutely nothing, except the names of his companions and the fact already mentioned that he remained behind for the passover.

From this time forward we read no more of the Philippians till the period of St Paul's Roman captivity. When they heard of his destination, their slumbering affection for him revived. It was not the first time that they had been eager to offer and he willing to receive alms for the supply of his personal wants. After the close of his first visit, while he was still in Macedonia, they had more than once sent him timely assistance to Thessalonica[1]. When from Macedonia he passed on to Achaia, fresh supplies from Philippi reached him at Corinth[2]. Then there was a lull in their attentions. It was not that their affection had cooled, the Apostle believed, but that the opportunity was wanting. Now at length after a lapse of ten years their loyalty again took the same direction; and Epaphroditus was despatched to Rome with their gift[3].

*The Philippians send alms to St Paul.*

Their zealous attention was worthily seconded by the messenger whom they had chosen. Not content with placing this token of their love in St Paul's hands, Epaphroditus[4] devoted himself heart and soul to the ministry under the Apostle's guidance. But the strain of excessive exertion was too great for his physical powers. In his intense devotion to the work he lost his health and almost his life. At length the danger passed away: 'God had mercy,' says the Apostle, 'not on him only,

*Illness of Epaphroditus.*

[1] Phil. iv. 16.

[2] Phil. iv. 15 'When I left Macedonia, no church communicated with me in regard of giving and receiving but ye only'; 2 Cor. xi. 8, 9 'When I was present with you and wanted, I was not burdensome to any: for my want the brethren having come from Macedonia supplied.'

[3] Phil. ii. 25, 30, iv. 10—18.

[4] Epaphroditus is known to us only from the notices in this epistle. He is doubtless to be distinguished from Epaphras (Col. i. 7, iv. 12, Philem. 23); for, though the names are the same, the identity of the persons seems improbable for two reasons. (1) The one appears to have been a native of Philippi (Phil. ii. 25 sq.), the other of Colossæ (Col. iv. 12). (2) The longer form of the name is always used of the Philippian delegate, the shorter of the Colossian teacher. The name in fact is so extremely common in both forms, that the coincidence affords no presumption of the identity of persons.

but on myself also, that I might not have sorrow upon sorrow.' But his convalescence was succeeded by home-sickness. He was oppressed with the thought that the Philippians would have heard of his critical state. He was anxious to return that he might quiet their alarm[1].

The Epistle to the Philippians, A.D. 61 or 62? This purpose was warmly approved by St Paul. To contribute to their happiness in any way was to alleviate his own sorrows[2]. He would not therefore withhold Epaphroditus from them. So Epaphroditus returns to Philippi, bearing a letter from the Apostle, in which he pours out his heart in an overflow of gratitude and love.

Mission of Timothy. In this letter he expresses his intention of sending Timotheus to them immediately[3]. Whether this purpose was ever fulfilled we have no means of knowing. But in sending Timotheus he did not mean to withhold himself. He hoped before long to be released, and he would then visit them in person[4].

Later visits of St Paul. The delay indeed seems to have been greater than he then anticipated; but at length he was able to fulfil his promise. One visit at least, probably more than one, he paid to Philippi and his other Macedonian churches in the interval between his first and second captivities[5].

Ignatius at Philippi. The canonical writings record nothing more of Philippi. A whole generation passes away before its name is again mentioned. Early in the second century Ignatius, now on his way to Rome where he is condemned to suffer martyrdom, as he passes through Philippi is kindly entertained and escorted on

The name Epaphroditus or Epaphras is not specially characteristic of Macedonia, but occurs abundantly everywhere. On a Thessalonian inscription (Boeckh no. 1987) we meet with one Γάϊος Κλώδιος Ἐπαφρόδειτος. This concurrence of names is suggestive. The combination, which occurs once, might well occur again: and it is possible (though in the absence of evidence hardly probable) that Gaius the Macedonian of St Luke (Acts xix. 29) is the same person as Epaphroditus the Philippian of St Paul.

[1] Phil. ii. 25—30.
[2] Phil. ii. 28 'That having seen him ye may rejoice again, and I may be less sorrowful.'
[3] Phil. ii. 19.
[4] Phil. ii. 24.
[5] 1 Tim. i. 3. The notices in 2 Tim. iv. 13, 20 perhaps refer to a later date. If so, they point to a second visit of the Apostle after his release; for in going from Troas to Corinth he would naturally pass through Macedonia.

his way by the members of the church[1]. This circumstance seems to have given rise to communications with Polycarp, the youthful bishop of Smyrna and trusty friend of Ignatius, in which the Philippians invite him to address to them some words of advice and exhortation. Polycarp responds to this appeal. He congratulates them on their devotion to the martyrs 'bound in saintly fetters, the diadems of the truly elect.' He rejoices that 'the sturdy root of their faith, famous from the earliest days[2], still survives and bears fruit unto our Lord Jesus Christ.' He should not have ventured to address them, unless they had themselves solicited him. He, and such as he, cannot 'attain unto the wisdom of the blessed and glorious Paul,' who taught among them in person, and wrote to them when absent instructions which they would do well to study for their edification in the faith[3]. He offers many words of exhortation, more especially relating to the qualifications of widows, deacons, and presbyters[4]. He warns them against those who deny that Jesus Christ has come in the flesh, against those who reject the testimony of the cross, against those who say there is no resurrection or judgment[5]. He sets before them for imitation the example 'not only of the blessed Ignatius and Zosimus and Rufus, but also of others of their own church, and Paul himself and the other Apostles,' who have gone before to their rest[6].

There is however one cause for sorrow. Valens a presbyter

*(margin: Polycarp's letter.)*

*(margin: Commendation and warning.)*

---

[1] Martyr. Ignat. § 5; Polyc. *Phil.* 1 δεξαμένοις τὰ μιμήματα τῆς ἀληθοῦς ἀγάπης καὶ προπέμψασιν ὡς ἐπέβαλεν ὑμῖν, τοὺς ἐνειλημμένους [ἐνειλημένους?] τοῖς ἁγιοπρεπέσι δεσμοῖς ἅτινά ἐστι διαδήματα κ.τ.λ. The martyrs here alluded to are doubtlessIgnatiusandothersmentioned by name § 9. The letter of Polycarp was written after the death of Ignatius (§ 9); but the event was so recent that he asks the Philippians to send him information about Ignatius and his companions, § 13 'Et de ipso Ignatio et de his qui cum eo sunt (the present is doubtless due to the translator, where

the original was probably τῶν σὺν αὐτῷ) quod certius agnoveritis, significate.'

[2] § 1 ἐξ ἀρχαίων καταγγελλομένη χρόνων.

[3] § 3. On this passage see the detached note on iii. 1.

[4] §§ 4—6.

[5] § 7. It would not be a safe inference, that when Polycarp wrote the Philippian Church was in any special danger of these errors. The language is general and comprehensive, warning them against all the prevailing forms of heresy.

[6] § 9.

in the Philippian Church, and his wife whose name is not given, had brought scandal on the Gospel by their avarice[1]. From all participation in their crime Polycarp exonerates the great body of the church. He has neither known nor heard of any such vice in those Philippians among whom St Paul laboured, boasting of them in all the churches, at a time when his own Smyrna was not yet converted to Christ[2]. He trusts the offend-

[1] § 11. Polycarp after speaking of the crime of Valens adds, 'Moneo itaque vos ut abstineatis ab avaritia et sitis casti et veraces...Si quis non abstinuerit se ab avaritia, ab idololatria coinquinabitur.' The crime of Valens and his wife was doubtless avarice, not concupiscence, as the passage is frequently interpreted. In §§ 4, 6, 'avaritia' is the translation of φιλαργυρία; and this was probably the word used in the original here. But even if the Greek had πλεονεξία, it is a mistake to suppose that this word ever signifies 'unchastity' (see the note on Col. iii. 5); and the fact that both husband and wife were guilty of the crime in question points rather to avarice (as in the case of Ananias and Sapphira) than to impurity. The word 'casti' seems to have misled the commentators; but even if the original were ἁγνοί and not καθαροί, it might still apply to sordid and dishonest gain. This use of ἁγνὸς would not be unnatural even in a heathen writer (e.g. Pind. Ol. iii. 21 ἁγνὰ κρίσις); and the Apostle's denunciation of covetousness as idolatry (to which Polycarp refers in the context) makes it doubly appropriate here. 'Corruption' is a common synonyme for fraud. On the other hand 'veraces' is quite out of place, if concupiscence was intended.

The correct interpretation may be inferred also from other expressions in the letter. Polycarp seems to have had the crime of Valens in his thoughts when in an earlier passage, § 4, he declares that 'avarice is the beginning of

all troubles (ἀρχὴ πάντων χαλεπῶν φιλαργυρία),' and when again in enumerating the qualifications of presbyters (§ 6) he states that they must stand aloof from every form of avarice (μακρὰν ὄντες πάσης φιλαργυρίας). The Macedonian churches in St Paul's time were as liberal as they were poor (2 Cor. viii. 1—3). Greed of wealth was about the last crime that they could be charged with. There is no reason to suppose that their character had wholly changed within a single generation. But a notable exception had occurred at Philippi; and, though Polycarp distinctly treats it as an exception and acquits the Philippian church as a body (§ 11), yet it naturally leads him to dwell on the heinousness of this sin.

The name 'Valens' for some reason seems to have been frequent in Macedonia; perhaps because it had been borne by some local celebrity: see for instance Boeckh no. 1969 (at Thessalonica), where it occurs together with another common Macedonian name (Acts xx. 4), Οὐαλῆς καὶ Σεκοῦνδος. It is found also in another inscription at Drama (Drabescus?) in Perrot (Revue Archéol. 1860, ii. p. 73); and in a third and a fourth at Philippi itself, published in Cousinéry ii. p. 21, Miss. Archéol. p. 121.

[2] § 11 'In quibus laboravit beatus Paulus, qui estis in principio epistolæ ejus: de vobis etenim gloriatur in omnibus ecclesiis quæ Deum solæ tunc cognoverant, nos autem nondum noveramus.'

ers will be truly penitent: and he counsels the Philippians to treat them, not as enemies,- but as erring members. They are well versed in the scriptures[1], and will not need to be reminded how the duty of gentleness and forbearance is enforced therein.

At the conclusion, he refers to certain parting injunctions of Ignatius: he complies with their desire and sends copies of those letters of the martyr which are in his possession: he commends to their care Crescens, the bearer of the epistle, who will be accompanied by his sister. *Conclusion.*

With this notice the Philippian Church may be said to pass out of sight. From the time of Polycarp its name is very rarely mentioned; and scarcely a single fact is recorded which throws any light on its internal condition[2]. Here and there the name of a bishop appears in connexion with the records of an ecclesiastical council. On one occasion its prelate subscribes a decree as vicegerent of the metropolitan of Thessalonica[3]. But, though the see is said to exist even to the present day[4], the city itself has been long a wilderness. Of its destruction or decay no record is left; and among its ruins travellers have hitherto failed to find any Christian remains[5]. Of the church which stood foremost among all the apostolic communities in faith and love, it may literally be said that not one stone stands upon another. Its whole career is a signal monument of the inscrutable counsels of God. Born into the world with the brightest promise, the Church of Philippi has lived without a history and perished without a memorial. *Later history of Philippi.*

---

[1] § 12 'Confido enim vos bene exercitatos esse in sacris literis et nihil vos latet etc.'

[2] The rhetoric of Tertullian (*de Præscr.* 36, *adv. Marc.* iv. 5), who appeals among others to the Philippian Church as still maintaining the Apostle's doctrine and reading his epistle publicly, can hardly be considered evidence, though the fact itself need not be questioned.

When Hoog, *de Cœt. Christ. Philipp. tc.* p. 176 (1825), speaks of a council

held at Philippi,'imperantibus Constantini filiis,' he confuses Philippi with Philippopolis. See Socr. *H. E.* ii. 20, 22.

[3] Flavianus, who takes an active part at the C. of Ephesus, A.D. 431; Labb. *Conc.* III. 456 etc.

[4] Le Quien, *Or. Chr.* II. p. 70, gives the name of its bishop when he wrote (1740). Neale, *Holy Eastern Church* I. p. 92, mentions it among existing sees.

[5] I ought to except one or two inscriptions published since my first edition appeared, *Miss. Archéol.* pp. 96, 97.

## IV

## CHARACTER AND CONTENTS OF THE EPISTLE.

Motive of the epistle.

THE external circumstances, which suggested this epistle, have been already explained. It must be ascribed to the close personal relations existing between the Apostle and his converts. It was not written, like the Epistle to the Galatians, to counteract doctrinal errors, or, like the First to the Corinthians, to correct irregularities of practice. It enforces no direct lessons of Church government, though it makes casual allusion to Church officers. It lays down no dogmatic system, though incidentally it refers to the majesty and the humiliation of Christ, and to the contrast of law and grace. It is the spontaneous utterance of Christian love and gratitude, called forth by a recent token which the Philippians had given of their loyal affection. As the pure expression of personal feeling, not directly evoked by doctrinal or practical errors, it closely resembles the Apostle's letter to another leading church of Macedonia, which likewise held a large place in his affections, the First Epistle to the Thessalonians.

Affectionate relations with the Philippians.

But the Philippian Church was bound to the Apostle by closer ties than even the Thessalonian. His language in addressing the two has, it is true, very much in common; the absence of appeal to his apostolic authority, the pervading tone of satisfaction, even the individual expressions of love and praise. But in the Epistle to the Philippians the Apostle's commendation is more lavish, as his affection is deeper. He utters no misgivings of their loyalty, no suspicions of false play, no reproaches of disorderly living, no warnings against grosser sins. To the Philippians he had given the surest pledge of confidence which could be given by a high-minded and sensitive man, to whom it was of the highest importance for the sake of the great cause which he advocated to avoid the slightest breath of suspicion, and whose motives nevertheless were narrowly scanned and unscrupulously misrepresented. He had placed himself under pecuniary obligations to them. The alms sent from Philippi had relieved his wants even at Thessalonica.

Yet even at Philippi there was one drawback to his general satisfaction. A spirit of strife had sprung up in the church; if there were not open feuds and parties, there were at least disputes and rivalries. The differences related not to doctrinal but to social questions; and, while each eagerly asserted his own position, each severally claimed the Apostle's sympathies for himself. *Disputes and rivalries at Philippi.*

St Paul steps forward to check the growing tendency. This he does with characteristic delicacy, striking not less surely because he strikes for the most part indirectly. He begins by hinting to them that he is no partisan: he offers prayers and thanksgivings for *all*; he hopes well of *all*; he looks upon *all* as companions in grace; his heart yearns after *all* in Christ Jesus[1]. He entreats them later on, to be 'steadfast in one spirit,' to 'strive together with one mind for the faith of the Gospel[2].' He implores them by all their deepest Christian experiences, by all their truest natural impulses, to be of one mind,' to 'do nothing from party-spirit or from vainglory.' Having piled up phrase upon phrase[3] in the 'tautology of earnestness,' he holds out for their example the 'mind of Christ,' who, being higher than all, nevertheless did not assert His divine majesty, but became lowliest of the lowly. Towards the close of the epistle[4] he returns again to the sub- *St Paul rebukes this growing spirit.*

---

[1] See the studied repetition of πάντες the paragraph i. 3—8.
[2] i. 27.
[3] ii. 2, 3, 4.
[4] iv. 2 sq.

ject; and here his language becomes more definite. He mentions by name two ladies, Euodia and Syntyche, who had taken a prominent part in these dissensions; he asks them to be reconciled; and he invites the aid of others, of his true yoke-fellow, of Clement, of the rest of his fellow-labourers, in cementing this reconciliation. He urges the Philippians generally to exhibit to the world a spectacle of *forbearance*[1]. He reminds them of the peace of God, which surpasses all the thoughts of man. He entreats them lastly, by all that is noble and beautiful and good, to hear and to obey. If they do this, the God of peace will be with them.

**Indirect reference to doctrinal error.** Of errors in doctrine there is not the faintest trace in the Philippian Church. In one passage indeed, where the Apostle touches upon doctrinal subjects, he takes occasion to warn his converts against two antagonistic types of error—Judaic formalism on the one hand, and Antinomian license on the other. But while doing so he gives no hint that these dangerous tendencies were actually rife among them. The warning seems to have been suggested by circumstances external to the Philippian Church[2].

**Absence of plan in the epistle.** Of plan and arrangement there is even less than in St Paul's letters generally. The origin and motive of the epistle are hardly consistent with any systematic treatment. As in the Second Epistle to the Corinthians, the torrent of personal feeling is too strong to submit to any such restraint. Even the threefold division into the explanatory, doctrinal, and hortatory portions, which may generally be discerned in his epistles, is obliterated here.

**Structure of the epistle. i. 1—11.** At the same time the growth and structure of the epistle may be traced with tolerable clearness. After the opening salutation and thanksgiving, which in the intensity of his affection he prolongs to an unusual extent, the Apostle explains

---

[1] iv. 5 τὸ ἐπιεικὲς ὑμῶν γνωσθήτω κ.τ.λ. See the note there.

[2] Schinz, *die Christliche Gemeinde zu Philippi* (Zürich 1833), decides after a careful examination of the purport of this epistle, that the Philippian Church was not yet tainted by Judaism, and that the disputes were social rather than doctrinal. This result has been generally accepted by more recent writers.

his personal circumstances; the progress of the Gospel in i. 12—26.
Rome; the rivalry of his antagonists and the zeal of his adherents; his own hopes and fears. He then urges his con- i. 27—ii.
verts to unity in the strong reiterative language which has 16.
been already noticed. This leads him to dwell on the humility of Christ, as the great exemplar; and the reference is
followed up by a few general words of exhortation. Returning from this to personal matters, he relates his anticipation ii. 17—30.
of a speedy release; his purpose of sending Timothy; the
recent illness and immediate return of Epaphroditus.

Here the letter, as originally conceived, seems drawing to
a close. He commences what appears like a parting injunction: iii. 1.
'Finally, my brethren, farewell (rejoice) in the Lord.' 'To say
the same things,' he adds, 'for me is not irksome, while for you
it is safe.' He was intending, it would seem, after offering this
apology by way of preface, to refer once more to their dissensions, to say a few words in acknowledgment of their gift, and
then to close. Here however he seems to have been interrupted[1]. Circumstances occur, which recall him from these joy-
ful associations to the conflict which awaits him without and
which is the great trial and sorrow of his life. He is informed, Interrup-
we may suppose, of some fresh attempt of the Judaizers in the tion and
metropolis to thwart and annoy him. What, if they should portion.
interfere at Philippi as they were doing at Rome, and tamper

---

[1] Ewald, *die Sendschreiben etc.* p. 448
sq., has explained with characteristic
insight the sudden interruption and
subsequent lengthening of the letter.
I should be disposed however to make
the break not after ii. 30 with Ewald,
but after iii. 1 with Grotius. Moreover
I cannot agree with the former in referring iii. 17, 18, 19, still to Judaic formalism rather than to Antinomian excess. See the notes on the third chapter.

Le Moyne, *Var. Sacr.* II. pp. 332,
343, suggested that two letters were
combined in our Epistle to the Philippians, commenting on the plural in

Polycarp (§ 3, ὃς καὶ ἀπὼν ὑμῖν ἔγραψεν
ἐπιστολάς); and Heinrichs (*prol.* p. 31
sq.), carrying out the same idea, supposed i. 1—iii. 1 ἐν κυρίῳ to be written
to the Church generally, and iii. 2 τὰ
αὐτά—iv. 20 to the rulers, the concluding verses iv. 21—23 being the close
of the former letter. He was answered
by J. F. Krause *Dissert. Acad.* (Regiom.
1811). Paulus, *Heidelb. Jahrb.* P. 7, p.
702 (1812), adopted the theory of
Heinrichs, modifying it however by
making the close of the second letter
after iii. 9 instead of iii. 20. See Hoog
*de Cæt. Christ. Phil. etc.* p. 54 sq.

with the faith and loyalty of his converts?   With this thought
iii. 2—10. weighing on his spirit he resumes his letter.   He bids the Philippians beware of these dogs, these base artisans, these mutilators of the flesh.   This leads him to contrast his teaching with
theirs, the true circumcision with the false, the power of faith
with the inefficacy of works.   But a caution is needed here.
Warned off the abyss of formalism, might they not be swept
into the vortex of license?   There were those, who professed the
Apostle's doctrine but did not follow his example; who availed
themselves of his opposition of Judaism to justify the licentious-
ness of Heathenism; who held that, because 'all things were
lawful,' therefore 'all things were expedient'; who would even
iii. 12—21. 'continue in sin that grace might abound.'   The doctrine of
faith, he urges, does not support this inference; his own example does not countenance it.   Moral progress is the obligation
of the one and the rule of the other.   To a church planted in
the midst of a heathen population this peril was at least as
great as the former.   He had often raised his voice against it
iv. 1. before; and he must add a word of warning now.   He exhorts
the Philippians to be steadfast in Christ.

Subject re-    Thus the doctrinal portion, which has occupied the Apostle
sumed. since he resumed, is a parenthesis suggested by the circumstances of the moment.   At length he takes up the thread of
his subject, where he had dropped it when the letter was inter-
iv. 2, 3. rupted.   He refers again to their dissensions.   This was the
topic on which repetition needed no apology.   He mentions
by name those chiefly at fault, and he appeals directly to those
most able to heal the feuds.   And now once more he seems
iv. 4—7. drawing to a close: 'Farewell' (rejoice) in the Lord alway:
again I say, farewell (rejoice).'   Yet still he lingers: this farewell is prolonged into an exhortation and a blessing.   At length
iv. 8, 9. he gives his parting injunction: 'Finally, my brethren, whatsoever things are true, etc.'   But something still remains unsaid.
He has not yet thanked them for their gift by Epaphroditus,
v. 10—20. though he has alluded to it in passing.   With a graceful intermingling of manly independence and courteous delicacy he

acknowledges this token of their love, explaining his own circumstances and feelings at some length. At last the epistle closes with the salutations and the usual benediction. iv. 21—23.

The following then is an analysis of the epistle: Analysis of the epistle.

I.  i. 1, 2.  Opening salutation.
   i. 3—11.  Thanksgiving and prayer for his converts.
   i. 12—26.  Account of his personal circumstances and feelings; and of the progress of the Gospel in Rome.

II.  i. 27—ii. 4.  Exhortation to unity and self-negation.
   ii. 5—11.  Christ the great pattern of humility.
   ii. 12—16.  Practical following of His example.

III.  ii. 17—30.  Explanation of his intended movements; the purposed visit of Timothy; the illness, recovery, and mission of Epaphroditus.

IV.  iii. 1.  The Apostle begins his final injunctions; but is interrupted and breaks off suddenly.

[iii. 2—iv. 1.  He resumes; and warns them against two antagonistic errors:

*Judaism* (iii. 3—14).

He contrasts the doctrine of works with the doctrine of grace; his former life with his present. The doctrine of grace leads to a progressive morality. Thus he is brought to speak secondly of

*Antinomianism* (iii. 15—iv. 1).

He points to his own example; and warns his converts against diverging from the right path. He appeals to them as citizens of heaven.]

Here the digression ends; the main thread of the letter is recovered; and

iv. 2, 3.  The Apostle once more urges them to heal their dissensions, appealing to them by name.

iv. 4—9.  He exhorts them to joyfulness, to freedom from care, to the pursuit of all good aims.

V.  iv. 10—20.  He gratefully acknowledges their alms received through Epaphroditus, and invokes a blessing on their thoughtful love.

VI.  iv. 21—23.  Salutations from all and to all. The farewell benediction.

Thoughts
suggested
by the
epistle.
The Epistle to the Philippians is not only the noblest re-
flexion of St Paul's personal character and spiritual illumination,
his large sympathies, his womanly tenderness, his delicate courtesy, his frank independence, his entire devotion to the Master's
service; but as a monument of the power of the Gospel it yields
in importance to none of the apostolic writings. Scarcely thirty
years have passed since one Jesus was crucified as a malefactor
in a remote province of the empire; scarcely ten since one Paul
a Jew of Tarsus first told at Philippi the story of His cruel
death; and what is the result? Imagine one, to whom the
name of Christ had been hitherto a name only, led by circumstances to study this touching picture of the relations between
St Paul, his fellow-labourers, his converts; and pausing to ask
himself what unseen power had produced these marvellous results. Stronger than any associations of time or place, of race
or profession, stronger than the instinctive sympathies of common interest or the natural ties of blood-relationship, a mysterious bond unites St Paul, Epaphroditus, the Philippian converts; them to the Apostle, and him to them, and each to the
other. In this threefold cord of love the strands are so inter-
twined and knotted together, that the writer cannot conceive
of them as disentangled. The joy of one must be the joy of
all; the sorrow of one must be the sorrow of all.

The Apostle's language furnishes the reply to such a ques-
tioner. This unseen power is the 'power of Christ's resurrection[1].'
This mutual love is diffused from 'the heart of Christ Jesus[2],'
beating with His pulses and living by His life. When the contemporary heathen remarked how 'these Christians loved one
another,' he felt that he was confronted by an unsolved enigma.
The power which wrought the miracle was hidden from him.
It was no new commandment indeed, for it appealed to the
oldest and truest impulses of the human heart. And yet it was
a new commandment; for in Christ's life and death and resurrection it had found not only an example and a sanction, but
a power, a vitality, wholly unfelt and unknown before.

[1] Phil. iii. 10.　　　　　[2] Phil. i. 8.

To all ages of the Church—to our own especially—this Its great epistle reads a great lesson. While we are expending our lesson. strength on theological definitions or ecclesiastical rules, it recalls us from these distractions to the very heart and centre of the Gospel—the life of Christ and the life in Christ. Here is the meeting-point of all our differences, the healing of all our feuds, the true life alike of individuals and sects and churches: here doctrine and practice are wedded together; for here is the 'Creed of creeds' involved in and arising out of the Work of works.

## The Genuineness of the Epistle.

Internal evidence.

INTERNAL evidence will appear to most readers to place the genuineness of the Epistle to the Philippians beyond the reach of doubt. This evidence is of two kinds, positive and negative. On the one hand the epistle completely reflects St Paul's mind and character, even in their finest shades. On the other, it offers no motive which could have led to a forgery. Only as the natural outpouring of personal feeling, called forth by immediate circumstances, is it in any way conceivable. A forger would not have produced a work so aimless (for aimless in his case it must have been), and could not have produced one so inartificial.

Genuineness questioned.

Nevertheless its genuineness has been canvassed. Evanson (*Dissonance, etc.* p. 263) led the van of this adverse criticism. At a later date Schrader (*Der Apostel Paulus* v. p. 201 sq.) threw out suspicions with regard to different portions of the epistle. More recently it has been condemned as spurious by Baur (see especially his *Paulus* p. 458 sq.), who is followed as usual by Schwegler (*Nachap. Zeit.* II. p. 133 sq.) and one or two others. His objections, says Bleek (*Einl. ins N. T.* p. 433), rest sometimes on perverse interpretations of separate passages, sometimes on arbitrary historical assumptions, while in other cases it is hard to conceive that they were meant in earnest.

Objections need not be considered.

I cannot think that the mere fact of their having been brought forward by men of ability and learning is sufficient to entitle objections of this stamp to a serious refutation. They have not the suggestive character which sometimes marks even the more extravagant theories of this school, and serve only as a warning of the condemnation which unrestrained negative criticism pronounces upon itself. In this epistle surely, if anywhere, the two complementary aspects of St Paul's person and teaching—his strong individuality of character and his equally strong sense of absorption in Christ—the 'I' and the 'yet not I' of his great antithesis—both appear with a force and a definiteness which carry thorough conviction. Hilgenfeld, the present leader of the Tübingen school, refused from the first to subscribe to his master's view respecting this epistle and probably few in the present day would be found to maintain this opinion. The criticisms of Baur have been several times refuted: e. g. in the monographs of Lünemann *Pauli ad Phil. Epist. defend.*, Göttingen 1847, and B. B. Brückner *Epist. ad Phil. Paulo auctori vindic.*, Lips. 1848, and in the introductions to the commentaries of Wiesinger, Ladie, and others. See also more recently Hilgenfeld *Zeitschr. f. Wissensch. Theol.* 1871 p. 192 sq., 309 sq., 1873 p. 178 sq.

The quotations from this epistle in early Christian writers are not *Early quo-* so numerous, as they would probably have been, if it had contained more *tations.* matter which was directly doctrinal or ecclesiastical. Among the Apo- stolic fathers CLEMENT OF ROME (§ 47) uses the phrase 'in the beginning *Apostolic* of the Gospel' (Phil. iv. 15). Again he says, 'If we walk not worthily *fathers.* of Him' (μὴ ἀξίως αὐτοῦ πολιτευόμενοι, § 21; comp. Phil. i. 27). A third passage (§ 2), 'Ye were sincere and harmless and not mindful of injury one towards another,' resembles Phil. i. 10, ii. 15. And a fourth, in which he dwells upon the example of Christ's humility (§ 16), seems to reflect the familiar passage in Phil. ii. 5 sq. Though each resemblance in itself is indecisive, all combined suggest at least a probability that St Clement had seen this epistle. When IGNATIUS (*Rom.* 2) expresses his desire of being 'poured out as a libation (σπονδισθῆναι) to God, while yet the altar is ready,' this must be considered a reminiscence of Phil. ii. 17. In the Epistle to the Philadelphians also (§ 8) the words 'do nothing from party-spirit' (μηδὲν κατ' ἐριθείαν πράσσειν) are taken from Phil. ii. 3; for in an earlier passage of the same letter (§ 1) the writer reproduces the second member of St Paul's sentence, 'nor from vainglory' (οὐδὲ κατὰ κενο- δοξίαν). In the Epistle to the Smyrnæans again the words § 4 'I endure all things, while He strengtheneth me' are derived from Phil. iv. 13, and the words § 11 'Being perfect be ye also perfectly minded' from Phil. iii. 15. POLYCARP, addressing the Philippians, more than once directly mentions St Paul's writing to them (§ 3, 11): he commences the body of the letter with an expression taken from this epistle, 'I rejoiced with you greatly in the Lord' (συνεχάρην ὑμῖν μεγάλως ἐν Κυρίῳ, comp. Phil. iv. 10 ἐχάρην δὲ ἐν Κυρίῳ μεγάλως): and in other passages his words are a re- flexion of its language; e.g. § 2 'Unto whom all things were made subject that are in heaven and that are on the earth etc.,' of Phil. ii. 10; § 9 'I did not run in vain,' of Phil. ii. 16 (comp. Gal. ii. 2); § 10 'diligentes invicem, in veritate sociati, mansuetudinem Domini alterutri præstolantes,' of Phil. ii. 2—5; § 12 'inimicis crucis,' of Phil. iii. 18. The words ἐὰν πολιτευσώμεθα ἀξίως αὐτοῦ (§ 5) are perhaps taken from Clement of Rome (see above), though they resemble Phil. i. 27.

When HERMAS, *Vis.* i. 3, writes 'they shall be written into the books *Hermas* of life,' he probably refers rather to Rev. xx. 15, than to Phil. iv. 3. Other coincidences, as *Vis.* iii. 13 'If anything be wanting it shall be revealed to thee' (Phil. iii. 15), *Mand.* v. 2 'Concerning giving or receiving' (Phil. iv. 15), are not sufficient to establish a connexion.

In the TESTAMENTS OF THE TWELVE PATRIARCHS, a Jewish Christian *Test. xii* work probably dating early in the second century, a few expressions are *Patri-* borrowed from this epistle: *Levi* 4 'in the heart (ἐν σπλάγχνοις) of His *archs.* Son,' from Phil. i. 8; *Benj.* 10 'Worshipping the king of the heavens who appeared on earth in the form of man' (ἐν μορφῇ ἐνθρώπου, to which one text adds ταπεινώσεως, comp. Phil. iii. 21), and *Zab.* 9 'Ye shall see in the fashion of man etc.' (ὄψεσθε ἐν σχήματι ἀνθρώπου; it is doubtful whether or not θεὸν should follow, but the reference is plainly to Christ), from Phil. ii. 6—8; *Levi* 14 'Ye are the luminaries (οἱ φωστῆρες) of the heaven,' from Phil. ii. 15.

**Apologists.** The Apologists supply several references. In the EPISTLE TO DIOGNETUS occur the words 'their dwelling is on earth but their citizenship is in heaven' (ἐπὶ γῆς διατρίβουσιν ἀλλ' ἐν οὐρανῷ πολιτεύονται § 5): comp. Phil. iii. 20. JUSTIN MARTYR [?] *de Resurr.* (c. 7, p. 592 D) also speaks of 'our heavenly citizenship,' and in another place (c. 9, p. 594 E) writes, 'The Lord has said that our dwelling is in heaven (ἐν οὐρανῷ ὑπάρχειν).' In the second passage the reference is probably to such sayings as Joh. xiv. 2, 3; but the actual expression seems certainly to be borrowed from St Paul's language here. MELITO (*Fragm.* 6, p. 416, Otto) designates our Lord Θεὸς ἀληθὴς προαιώνιος ὑπάρχων, perhaps having in his mind Phil. ii. 6; and again he writes (*Fragm.* 14, p. 420, a passage preserved in Syriac) 'servus reputatus est' and 'servi speciem indutus,' obviously from the context of the same passage in our epistle. THEOPHILUS (*ad Autol.*) more than once adopts expressions from this epistle; i. 2 'approving the things that are excellent,' either from Phil. i. 10 or from Rom. ii. 18; ii. 17 'minding earthly things' (τὰ ἐπίγεια φρονούντων), from Phil. iii. 19; iii. 36 'these things are true and useful and just and lovely (προσφιλῆ),' apparently from Phil. iv. 8; and again, as quoted by Jerome *Epist.* 121 (ad Algasiam), he writes 'Quæ antea pro lucro fuerant, reputari in stercora' from Phil. iii. 8 (if the work quoted by Jerome may be accepted as genuine).

**Churches of Gaul.** In the EPISTLE OF THE CHURCHES OF VIENNE AND LYONS (A.D. 177) Euseb. *H. E.* v. 2, the text Phil. ii. 6 'who being in the form of God etc.' is quoted.

**Syriac Documents.** In ANCIENT SYRIAC DOCUMENTS (edited by Cureton) it is said of Christ (p. 14), 'He being God had appeared to them like men' (Phil. ii. 6, 7), and in another writing of the same collection (p. 56) these words occur; 'One of the doctors of the Church has said: The scars indeed of my body—that I may come to the resurrection from the dead'; a combination of Gal. vi. 17 and Phil. iii. 11.

**Heretics.** The SETHIANI, a very early heretical sect, are stated by Hippolytus (*Hæres.* v. p. 143, x. p. 318) to have interpreted the text Phil. ii. 6, 7, to explain their own doctrines. CASSIANUS a Valentinian (about 170) quotes Phil. iii. 20 (Clem. Alex. *Strom.* iii. 14, p. 554 Potter). And THEODOTUS (on the authority of the Excerpts published in the works of Clem. Alex., p. 966 Potter) has two distinct references to a passage in this epistle (Phil. ii. 7 in § 19 and § 35).

**Apocryphal Acts.** In the Apocryphal ACTS OF THOMAS § 27 we read 'The holy name of Christ which is above every name' (τὸ ὑπὲρ πᾶν ὄνομα), from Phil. ii. 9.

**Canons of Scripture.** The Epistle to the Philippians appears in all the CANONS OF SCRIPTURE during the second century: in the lists of the heretic Marcion and of the Muratorian fragment, as well as in the Old Latin and Peshito Syriac versions.

With the other Pauline Epistles of our Canon it is directly quoted and assigned to the Apostle by IRENÆUS, TERTULLIAN, and CLEMENT OF ALEX-ANDRIA. Tertullian more especially, in passages already quoted (p. 65, note 2), speaks of its having been read in the Philippian Church uninterruptedly to his own time. Though he may not say this from direct personal knowledge or precise information, yet the statement would not have been hazarded, unless the epistle had been universally received in the Church as far back as the traditions of his generation reached.

*Close of the 2nd century.*

# ΠΡΟΣ ΦΙΛΙΠΠΗΣΙΟΥΣ.

WE ALL ARE CHANGED INTO THE SAME IMAGE FROM
GLORY TO GLORY, AS OF THE LORD THE SPIRIT.

BUT THE FRUIT OF THE SPIRIT IS LOVE, JOY, PEACE.

---

*And so the Word had breath, and wrought*
*With human hands the creed of creeds*
*In loveliness of perfect deeds,*
*More strong than all poetic thought.*

# ΠΡΟΣ ΦΙΛΙΠΠΗΣΙΟΥΣ.

ΠΑΥΛΟΣ καὶ Τιμόθεος, δοῦλοι Χριστοῦ Ἰησοῦ,
πᾶσιν τοῖς ἁγίοις ἐν Χριστῷ Ἰησοῦ τοῖς οὖσιν

1. Παῦλος] The official title of
Apostle is omitted here, as in the
Epistles to the Thessalonians. In
writing to the Macedonian Churches,
with which his relations were so close
and affectionate, St Paul would feel an
appeal to his authority to be unnecessary. The same omission is found in
the letter to Philemon, and must be
similarly explained. He does not enforce a command as a superior, but
asks a favour as a friend (Philem. 8,
9, 14). In direct contrast to this
tone is the strong assertion of his
Apostleship in writing to the Galatian
Churches, where his authority and his
doctrine alike were endangered.

Τιμόθεος] The intercourse between
Timotheus and the Philippian Church
had been constant and intimate. He
had assisted the Apostle in its first
foundation (Acts xvi. 1, 13, and xvii.
14). He had visited Philippi twice
at least during the third missionary
journey (Acts xix. 22, comp. 2 Cor.
i. 1 ; and Acts xx. 3, 4, comp. Rom.
xvi. 21). He was there not improbably more than once during the
captivity at Cæsarea, when the Apostle himself was prevented from seeing them. And now again he was
on the eve of another visit, having
been chosen for this purpose, as one
whose solicitude for the Philippians
had become a second nature (γνησίως
μεριμνήσει ii. 20). In like manner his
name is associated with St Paul in
the letters to the other great church

of Macedonia (1 Thess. i. 1, 2 Thess.
i. 1).

But beyond the association of his
name in the salutation, Timotheus
takes no part in the letter. St Paul
starts with the singular (ver. 3) which
he maintains throughout ; and having
occasion to mention Timotheus speaks
of him in the third person, ii. 19.

πᾶσιν] see the note on ver. 4.

τοῖς ἁγίοις] 'the saints,' i.e. the
covenant people : a term transferred
from the old dispensation to the new.
The chosen race was a holy people
(λαὸς ἅγιος), the Israelites were saints
(ἅγιοι), by virtue of their consecration to Jehovah : see e.g. Exod. xix.
6, Deut. vii. 6, xiv. 2, 21, Dan. vii.
18, 22, 25, viii. 24. So 1 Macc. x. 39
τοῖς ἁγίοις τοῖς ἐν Ἱερουσαλήμ. The
Christian Church, having taken the
place of the Jewish race, has inherited all its titles and privileges ;
it is 'a chosen generation, a royal
priesthood, an holy nation (ἔθνος ἅγιον),
a peculiar people (1 Pet. ii. 9).' All who
have entered into the Christian covenant by baptism are 'saints' in the
language of the Apostles. Even the
irregularities and profligacies of the
Corinthian Church do not forfeit it
this title. Thus the main idea of the
term is *consecration*. But, though it
does not assert moral qualifications
as a fact in the persons so designated,
it implies them as a duty. And it
was probably because ἅγιος suggests
the moral idea, which is entirely want-

ἐν Φιλίπποις σὺν ἐπισκόποις καὶ διακόνοις. ²χάρις ὑμῖν
καὶ εἰρήνη ἀπὸ Θεοῦ πατρὸς ἡμῶν καὶ κυρίου Ἰησοῦ
Χριστοῦ.

³Εὐχαριστῶ τῷ Θεῷ μου ἐπὶ πάσῃ τῇ μνείᾳ ὑμῶν

ing to ἱερός, that the former was adopted by the LXX translators as the common rendering of קֹדֶשׁ, while the latter
is very rarely used by them in any
sense: see esp. Lev. xi. 44 ἁγιασθή-
σεσθε καὶ ἅγιοι ἔσεσθε ὅτι ἅγιός εἰμι
ἐγώ.

ἐν Χριστῷ Ἰησοῦ] to be connected
with ἁγίοις. For the omission of the
article see the notes on 1 Thess. i. 1.

ἐπισκόποις καὶ διακόνοις] 'the presbyters and deacons.' The contributions were probably sent to St Paul in
the name of the officers, as well as of
the church generally: comp. Acts xv.
23. Hence St Paul mentions them in
reply. It seems hardly probable that
this mention was intended, as some
have thought, to strengthen the hands
of the presbyters and deacons, their
authority being endangered. The dissensions in the Philippian Church do
not appear to have touched the officers. On ἐπίσκοπος and πρεσβύτερος,
as interchangeable terms, see the
detached note, p. 95.

2. χάρις ὑμῖν κ.τ.λ.] On the form
of salutation see the note on 1 Thess.
i. 1.

3. The thanksgiving in this epistle
is more than usually earnest. The
Apostle dwells long and fondly on the
subject. He repeats words and accumulates clauses in the intensity of his
feeling. As before in the omission of
his official title, so here in the fulness
of his thanksgiving, the letters to the
Thessalonians present the nearest parallel to the language of this epistle:
see introduction p. 66.

3—5. 'I thank my God for you
all at all times, as I think of you,
whensoever I pray for you (and these
prayers I offer with joy), for that you
have co-operated with me to the fur-

therance of the Gospel from the day
when you first heard of it to the present moment.'

The arrangement of the clauses in
these verses is doubtful. They may
be connected in various ways, and the
punctuation will differ accordingly.
On the whole however the words
πάντοτε ἐν πάσῃ δεήσει μου ὑπὲρ πάντων
ὑμῶν seem naturally to run together;
and if so, we have the alternative of
attaching them to the foregoing or to
the following words. I have preferred
the former for two reasons. (1) The
structure of the passage is dislocated
and its force weakened, by disconnect-
ing clauses pointed out so obviously
as correlative by the repetition of the
same word πάσῃ, πάντοτε, πάσῃ, πάντων; see Lobeck Paral. p. 56. (2)
The words μετὰ χαρᾶς τὴν δέησιν ποιούμενος seem to stand apart, as an explanatory clause defining the character of the foregoing πάσῃ δεήσει; for
there would be great awkwardness in
making one sentence of the two, ἐν
πάσῃ δεήσει τὴν δέησιν ποιούμενος. For
the connexion εὐχαριστεῖν πάντοτε (in
most cases with περὶ or ὑπὲρ ὑμῶν) see
1 Cor. i. 4, 1 Thess. i. 2, 2 Thess. i. 3,
ii. 13, Ephes. v. 20, and perhaps also
Col. i. 3, Philem. 4: comp. also Ephes.
i. 16 οὐ παύομαι εὐχαριστῶν.

τῷ Θεῷ μου] 'my God.' The singular expresses strongly the sense of a
close personal relationship: comp. Acts
xxvii. 23 'whose I am and whom I
serve': see also the note on Gal. ii. 20,
and comp. iii. 8.

ἐπὶ πάσῃ τῇ μνείᾳ] 'in all my remembrance,' not 'on every remembrance (ἐπὶ πάσῃ μνείᾳ),' which would
point rather to isolated, intermittent
acts. On μνεία and εὐχαριστῶ see the
notes 1 Thess. i. 2.

⁴πάντοτε ἐν πάσῃ δεήσει μου ὑπὲρ πάντων ὑμῶν, μετὰ
χαρᾶς τὴν δέησιν ποιούμενος, ⁵ἐπὶ τῇ κοινωνίᾳ ὑμῶν εἰς
τὸ εὐαγγέλιον ἀπὸ [τῆς] πρώτης ἡμέρας ἄχρι τοῦ νῦν·

4. ὑπὲρ πάντων ὑμῶν] should be connected rather with εὐχαριστῶ than with ἐν πάσῃ δεήσει, for the following reasons. (1) The words are more naturally taken as independent and co-ordinate with all the preceding clauses, ἐπὶ πάσῃ τῇ μνείᾳ, πάντοτε, ἐν πάσῃ δεήσει, than as dependent on any one singly. (2) The stress of the Apostle's statement is rather on the *thanksgiving* for all than the *prayer* for all, as he is dwelling on their good deeds. (3) In the parallel passages already quoted the common connexion is εὐχαριστεῖν ὑπὲρ (or περὶ) ὑμῶν.

There is a studied repetition of the word 'all' in this epistle, when the Philippian Church is mentioned : see i. 2, 7 (ὑπὲρ πάντων ὑμῶν, πάντας ὑμᾶς), 8, 25, ii. 17, iv. 21. It is impossible not to connect this recurrence of the word with the strong and repeated exhortations to unity which the epistle contains (i. 27, ii. 1—4, iv. 2, 3, 5, 7, 9). The Apostle seems to say, 'I make no difference between man and man, or between party and party : my heart is open to all; my prayers, my thanksgivings, my hopes, my obligations, extend to all.' See the introduction, p. 67.

μετὰ χαρᾶς κ.τ.λ.] 'Summa epistolae,' says Bengel, '*gaudeo gaudete*': comp. i. 18, 25, ii. 2, 17, 18, 28, 29, iii. 1, iv. 1, 4, 10. The article before δέησιν refers it back to the previous δεήσει.

5. ἐπὶ τῇ κοινωνίᾳ κ.τ.λ.] The previous clause μετὰ χαρᾶς τὴν δέησιν ποιούμενος being a parenthesis, these words are connected with εὐχαριστῶ. For εὐχαριστεῖν ἐπὶ see 1 Cor. i. 4. The words signify not 'your participation in the Gospel' (τοῦ εὐαγγελίου, comp. ii. 1, iii. 10), but 'your cooperation towards, in aid of the Gospel' (εἰς τὸ εὐαγγέλιον). For the construction see 2 Cor. ix. 13 ἀπλότητι τῆς κοινωνίας εἰς αὐτούς, Rom. xv. 26 κοινωνίαν τινὰ ποιήσασθαι εἰς τοὺς πτωχούς. In the passages just quoted κοινωνία has a restricted meaning, ' contributions, almsgiving' (as also in 2 Cor. viii. 4, Hebr. xiii. 16; so κοινωνεῖν, Rom. xii. 13; κοινωνικός, 1 Tim. vi. 18; see Fritzsche *Rom.* III. p. 81); but here, as the context shows, it denotes co-operation in the widest sense, their participation with the Apostle whether in sympathy or in suffering or in active labour or in any other way. At the same time their almsgiving was a signal instance of this cooperation, and seems to have been foremost in the Apostle's mind. In this particular way they had cooperated from the very first (ἀπὸ τῆς πρώτης ἡμέρας) when on his departure from Philippi they sent contributions to Thessalonica and to Corinth (iv. 15, 16 ἐν ἀρχῇ τοῦ εὐαγγελίου), and up to the present time (ἄχρι τοῦ νῦν) when again they had despatched supplies to Rome by the hands of Epaphroditus (iv. 10 ἤδη ποτέ).

πρώτης] '*the first.*' The article is frequently omitted, because the numeral is sufficiently definite in itself: comp. Mark xii. 28—30, xvi. 9, Acts xii. 10, xvi. 12, xx. 18, Ephes. vi 2. Here some of the oldest MSS read τῆς πρώτης, but the article might perhaps be suspected, as a likely addition of some transcriber for the sake of greater precision.

6, 7. 'I have much ground for thanksgiving; thanksgiving for past experience, and thanksgiving for future hope. I am sure, that as God has inaugurated a good work in you, so He will complete the same, that it may be prepared to stand the test in the day of Christ's advent. I have every reason to think thus favourably of you *all*; for the remembrance is ever in

⁶πεποιθὼς αὐτὸ τοῦτο, ὅτι ὁ ἐναρξάμενος ἐν ὑμῖν ἔργον
ἀγαθὸν ἐπιτελέσει ἄχρι[ς] ἡμέρας Ἰησοῦ Χριστοῦ, ⁷καθ-
ώς ἐστιν δίκαιον ἐμοὶ τοῦτο φρονεῖν ὑπὲρ πάντων ὑμῶν,
διὰ τὸ ἔχειν με ἐν τῇ καρδίᾳ ὑμᾶς ἔν τε τοῖς δεσμοῖς

6.  ἡμέρας Χριστοῦ Ἰησοῦ.

my heart, how you—yes, *all* of you—
have tendered me your aid and love,
whether in bearing the sorrows of my
captivity or in actively defending and
promoting the Gospel : a manifest token that ye *all* are partakers with me
of the grace of God.'

6.  πεποιθὼς αὐτὸ τοῦτο] '*since I
have this very confidence.*' This assurance, built on the experience of
the past, enables the Apostle to anticipate matter for thankfulness. For
αὐτὸ τοῦτο comp. Gal. ii. 10, 2 Cor. ii.
3, 2 Pet. i. 5 (with a v. l.). The order
alone seems sufficient to exclude another proposed rendering of αὐτὸ τοῦτο, 'on this very account,' i. e. 'by reason of your past cooperation.'

ὁ ἐναρξάμενος] The words ἐνάρχεσθαι,
ἐπιτελεῖν, possibly contain a sacrificial
metaphor : see the notes on Gal. iii. 3,
and compare ii. 17 εἰ καὶ σπένδομαι ἐπὶ
τῇ θυσίᾳ. For the omission of Θεὸς
before ὁ ἐναρξάμενος compare Gal. i. 6,
15 (notes).

ἔργον ἀγαθόν] By this 'good work'
is meant their cooperation with and
affection for the Apostle. By the
workers of this work St Paul doubtless means the Philippians themselves.
Nevertheless it is God's doing from
beginning to end : He inaugurates
and He completes. This paradox of
all true religion is still more broadly
stated in ii. 12, 13, 'Work out *your own*
salvation, for it is *God* that *worketh
in you* both to will and to work etc.'

ἄχρις ἡμέρας Ἰησοῦ] refers to the
foregoing notes of time, ἀπὸ πρώτης
ἡμέρας and ἄχρι τοῦ νῦν ; but the expression implies something more than
a temporal limit. The idea of a *testing* is prominent : 'God will advance
you in grace, so that you may be pre-

pared to meet the day of trial.' On
the meaning of ἡμέρα and on the absence of the definite article see the
notes on 1 Thess. v. 2.

As 'the day of Christ' is thus a
more appropriate limit than 'the day
of your death,' it must not be hastily
inferred from this expression that St
Paul confidently expected the Lord's
advent during the lifetime of his Philippian converts.  On the other hand,
some anticipation of its near approach
seems to underlie ἄχρις here, as it is
implied in St Paul's language elsewhere, e. g. in ἡμεῖς οἱ ζῶντες 1 Thess.
iv. 17, and in πάντες οὐ κοιμηθησόμεθα
(probably the correct reading) 1 Cor.
xv. 51.

7. This confidence is justified by
their past cooperation, which is indeli-
bly stamped on the Apostle's memory.
The stress of the reason (διά), which
is the foundation of this assurance,
rests not on ἔχειν ἐν τῇ καρδίᾳ but on
συνκοινωνούς τῆς χάριτος, not on the
act of remembering but on the thing
remembered.

καθώς] See the note Gal. iii. 6.

τοῦτο φρονεῖν κ.τ.λ.] '*to entertain
this opinion concerning you all.*' On
the difference between ὑπὲρ and περὶ
see the note on Gal. i. 4, and comp.
Winer § xlvii. p. 466.

διὰ τὸ ἔχειν με κ.τ.λ.] '*because I have
you*'; not, as it is sometimes taken,
'because you have me.'  The order of
the words points to this as the correct
rendering ; and the appeal which follows, 'for God is my witness,' requires it.

ἔν τε τοῖς δεσμοῖς κ.τ.λ.] Are these
words to be taken with the foregoing
or with the following clause ? According as they are attached to the

μου καὶ ἐν τῇ ἀπολογίᾳ καὶ βεβαιώσει τοῦ εὐαγγελίου
συνκοινωνούς μου τῆς χάριτος πάντας ὑμᾶς ὄντας· ⁸μάρ-
τυς γάρ μου ὁ Θεός, ὡς ἐπιποθῶ πάντας ὑμᾶς ἐν σπλάγ-

one or the other, their meaning will be different. (1) If we connect them with what precedes, ἐν will be temporal, and the sense will then be, 'I bear this in mind, both when I am in bonds and when I am pleading my cause in court.' But even if there were ground for supposing that the trial had already begun, the clause is thus rendered almost meaningless. (2) On the other hand, if they are attached to the following words, the sense is easy: 'participators with me both in my bonds and in my defence and maintenance of the Gospel,' i.e. 'If I have suffered, so have you; if I have laboured actively for the Gospel, so have you': comp. vv. 29, 30.

τῇ ἀπολογίᾳ κ.τ.λ.] The two words, being connected by the same article, combine to form one idea. As ἀπολογία implies the negative or defensive side of the Apostle's preaching, the preparatory process of removing obstacles and prejudices, so βεβαίωσις denotes the positive or aggressive side, the direct advancement and establishment of the Gospel. The two together will thus comprise all modes of preaching and extending the truth. For ἀπολογία see ver. 16; for βεβαίωσις 1 Cor. i. 6.

συνκοινωνούς μου κ.τ.λ.] 'partakers with me in grace.' The genitives are best treated as separate and independent, so e.g. ii. 30: comp. Winer § xxx. p. 239. In this case ἡ χάρις with the definite article stands absolutely for 'the Divine grace,' as frequently: e.g. Acts xviii. 27, 2 Cor. iv. 15, Gal. v. 4, Ephes. ii. 8. 'Grace' applies equally to the 'bonds,' and to the 'defence and confirmation of the Gospel.' If it is a privilege to preach Christ, it is not less a privilege to suffer for Him: comp. ver. 29 ὑμῖν ἐχαρίσθη τὸ ὑπὲρ Χριστοῦ, οὐ μόνον τὸ εἰς

αὐτὸν πιστεύειν ἀλλὰ καὶ τὸ ὑπὲρ αὐτοῦ πάσχειν. A more special rendering of the passage is sometimes adopted, 'joint-contributors to the gift which I have received': see e.g. Paley's Hor. Paul. vii. 1. But though χάρις sometimes refers specially to almsgiving (e.g. 1 Cor. xvi. 3, 2 Cor. viii. 4), such a restriction here seems to sever this clause from the context and to destroy the whole force of the passage.

ὑμᾶς] repeated: comp. Col. ii. 13 (the correct reading), and see Winer § xxii. p. 184.

8. 'I call God to witness that I did not exaggerate, when I spoke of having you all in my heart.' The same form of attestation occurs in Rom. i. 9: see also 2 Cor. i. 23, 1 Thess. ii. 5, 10.

ἐπιποθῶ] 'I yearn after.' The preposition in itself signifies merely direction; but the idea of straining after the object being thereby suggested, it gets to imply eagerness: comp. Diod. Sic. xvii. 101 παρόντι μὲν οὐ χρησάμενος ἀπόντα δὲ ἐπιποθήσας. It is a significant fact, pointing to the greater intensity of the language, that, while the simple words πόθος, ποθεῖν, etc. are never found in the New Testament, the compounds ἐπιποθεῖν, ἐπιποθία, ἐπιπόθησις, ἐπιπόθητος, occur with tolerable frequency.

ἐν σπλάγχνοις κ.τ.λ.] 'Did I speak of having you in my own heart? I should rather have said that in the heart of Christ Jesus I long for you.' A powerful metaphor describing perfect union. The believer has no yearnings apart from his Lord; his pulse beats with the pulse of Christ; his heart throbs with the heart of Christ. 'In Paulo non Paulus vivit,' says Bengel, 'sed Jesus Christus'; see the note on Gal. ii. 20. Comp. Test. xii. Patr. Levi 4 ἐν σπλάγχνοις υἱοῦ αὐτοῦ. Theophilus

χνοις Χριστοῦ Ἰησοῦ· ⁹καὶ τοῦτο προσεύχομαι, ἵνα ἡ ἀγάπη ὑμῶν ἔτι μᾶλλον καὶ μᾶλλον περισσεύῃ ἐν ἐπιγνώσει καὶ πάσῃ αἰσθήσει, ¹⁰εἰς τὸ δοκιμάζειν ὑμᾶς τὰ διαφέροντα, ἵνα ἦτε εἰλικρινεῖς καὶ ἀπρόσκοποι εἰς ἡμέραν

9.   μᾶλλον περισσεύσῃ.

(ad *Autol.* ii. 10, 22) uses σπλάγχνα and καρδία as convertible terms, speaking of the Word in one passage as ἐνδιάθετον ἐν τοῖς ἰδίοις σπλάγχνοις (τοῦ Θεοῦ), in another as ἐνδιάθετον ἐν καρδίᾳ Θεοῦ.

The σπλάγχνα are properly the nobler viscera, the heart, lungs, liver etc., as distinguished from the ἔντερα, the lower viscera, the intestines: e.g. Æsch. *Agam.* 1221 σὺν ἐντέροις τε σπλάγχνα. The σπλάγχνα alone seem to be regarded by the Greeks as the seat of the affections, whether anger, love, pity, or jealousy. On the other hand no such distinction is observed in Hebrew. The words רחמים, מעים, and even קרב, which occur commonly in this metaphorical sense, seem to correspond rather to ἔντερα than to σπλάγχνα: whence even κοιλία and ἔγκατα are so used in the LXX. The verb σπλαγχνίζεσθαι seems not to be classical, and was perhaps a coinage of the Jewish dispersion, the metaphor being much more common in Hebrew than in Greek.

9. 'I spoke of praying for you (ver. 4). This then is the purport of my prayer ⟨τοῦτο προσεύχομαι⟩, that your love may ever grow and grow, in the attainment of perfect knowledge and universal discernment.'

ἵνα] introduces the clause which describes the *purport* of τοῦτο. For this connexion of τοῦτο ἵνα compare 1 Joh. iv. 17: see also 3 Joh. 4 μειζοτέραν τούτων οὐκ ἔχω χαρὰν ἵνα ἀκούω κ.τ.λ., Joh. xv. 13 μείζονα ταύτης ἀγάπην οὐδεὶς ἔχει ἵνα τις τὴν ψυχὴν αὐτοῦ θῇ κ.τ.λ. For such later usages of ἵνα, which in older classical Greek always denotes *motive* or *design*, see the notes on 1 Thess. ii. 16, v. 4, Gal. v. 17.

ἡ ἀγάπη] '*love*,' neither towards the Apostle alone nor towards one another alone, but love absolutely, the inward state of the soul.

ἔτι μᾶλλον κ.τ.λ.] An accumulation of words to denote superabundance, as below ver. 23. The present (περισσεύῃ), perhaps better supported than the aorist (περισσεύσῃ), is certainly more in place, as expressing the *continuous* growth.

ἐπιγνώσει] '*advanced, perfect knowledge.*' The intensive preposition (ἐπί) before γνώσει answers to the adjective before αἰσθήσει. Comp. 1 Cor. xiii. 12 ἄρτι γινώσκω ἐκ μέρους τότε δὲ ἐπιγνώσομαι: see also the distinction of γνῶσις and ἐπίγνωσις in Justin *Dial.* p 220 D. The substantive, which appears in St Paul in the Epistle to the Romans (i. 28, x. 2) for the first time, is found several times in the letters of the captivity and afterwards. Its more frequent occurrence thus corresponds to the more contemplative aspect of the Gospel presented in these later epistles. See Col. i. 9 (note).

πάσῃ αἰσθήσει] '*all perception.*' Love imparts a sensitiveness of touch, gives a keen edge to the discriminating faculty, in things moral and spiritual. While ἐπίγνωσις deals with general principles, αἴσθησις is concerned with practical applications. The latter word does not occur elsewhere in the New Testament, but αἰσθητήρια is used similarly to denote the organs of *moral* sense, Hebr. v. 14 τῶν διὰ τὴν ἕξιν τὰ αἰσθητήρια γεγυμνασμένα ἐχόντων πρὸς διάκρισιν καλοῦ τε καὶ κακοῦ: comp. Jer. iv. 19 τὰ αἰσθητήρια τῆς καρδίας.

10. τὰ διαφέροντα] not 'things which are opposed,' as good and bad (so for instance Fritzsche *Rom.* I. p. 129)— for it requires no keen moral sense to discriminate between these—but

Χριστοῦ, ¹¹πεπληρωμένοι καρπὸν δικαιοσύνης τὸν διὰ
Ἰησοῦ Χριστοῦ εἰς δόξαν καὶ ἔπαινον Θεοῦ.

¹²Γινώσκειν δὲ ὑμᾶς βούλομαι, ἀδελφοί, ὅτι τὰ κατ᾽
ἐμὲ μᾶλλον εἰς προκοπὴν τοῦ εὐαγγελίου ἐλήλυθεν,

'things that transcend,' 'ex bonis me-
liora' in Bengel's words. The phrase
δοκιμάζειν τὰ διαφέροντα occurs also
Rom. ii. 18.

εἰλικρινεῖς] signifies properly 'distinct, unmixed,' and hence 'pure, un-
sullied.' The probable derivation and
first meaning of the word (a strategical term, εἴλη, εἰληδόν, 'gregatim,'
comp. φυλοκρινεῖν) are suggested by
Xen. *Cyrop.* viii. 5. 14 καὶ διὰ τὸ εἰλι-
κρινῆ ἕκαστα εἶναι [τὰ φῦλα], πολὺ μάλ-
λον ἦν δῆλα, καὶ ὁπότε τις εὐτακτοίη καὶ
εἴ τις μὴ πράττοι τὸ προσταττόμενον. A
different account of the word however
(deriving it from εἴλη, 'sunlight') is
generally received.

ἀπρόσκοποι] might be either in-
transitive, 'without stumbling,' as Acts
xxiv. 16 ἀπρόσκοπον συνείδησιν ἔχειν
πρὸς τὸν Θεόν, or transitive, 'not causing offence,' as 1 Cor. x. 32 ἀπρόσκοποι
καὶ Ἰουδαίοις γίνεσθε καὶ Ἕλλησιν. If
the former sense be taken, εἰλικρινεῖς
and ἀπρόσκοποι will be related to each
other as the positive and the negative:
if the latter, they will denote respectively the relation to God (εἰλικρινεῖς)
and the relation to men (ἀπρόσκοποι).
The former is to be preferred; for it
is a question solely of the fitness of the
Philippians to appear before the tribunal of Christ, and any reference to
their influence on others would be out
of place. Comp. Jude 24, 25, τῷ δὲ δυναμένῳ φυλάξαι ὑμᾶς ἀπταίστους καὶ
στῆσαι κατενώπιον τῆς δόξης αὐτοῦ ἀμώ-
μους κ.τ.λ.

εἰς ἡμέραν Χριστοῦ] not '*until*,' but
'*for the day of Christ*'; comp. ii. 16,
and see also i. 6.

11. καρπὸν δικαιοσύνης] The expression is taken from the Old Testament,
e.g. Prov. xi. 30, Amos vi. 12, and occurs also James iii. 18. For the ac-

cusative after πληροῦσθαι comp. Col.
i. 9: similarly Luke xi. 46 φορτίζετε
τοὺς ἀνθρώπους φορτία δυσβάστακτα.
See Winer § xxxii. p. 287.

τὸν διὰ Ἰησοῦ] added to guard against
misunderstanding. The Apostle means
'righteousness in Christ,' as contrasted
with 'righteousness by law': comp. iii.
9. Only so far as the life of the believer
is absorbed in the life of Christ, does
the righteousness of Christ become
his own. Thus righteousness by faith
is intimately bound up with the life in
Christ: it must in its very nature be
fruitful; it is indeed the condition of
bearing fruit. Comp. John xv. 4 'As
the branch cannot bear fruit of itself,
except it abide in the vine, no more
can ye, except ye abide in me.'

εἰς δόξαν κ.τ.λ.] The only true aim
of all human endeavours: comp. ii. 11.
'The glory,' the manifestation of His
power and grace; 'the praise,' the recognition of these divine attributes by
men: comp. Ephes. i. 6 εἰς ἔπαινον δόξης τῆς χάριτος αὐτοῦ, ib. i. 12, 14.

12. 'Lest you should be misinform-
ed, I would have you know that my
sufferings and restraints, so far from
being prejudicial to the Gospel, have
served to advance it. My bonds have
borne witness to Christ, not only among
the soldiers of the imperial guard, but
in a far wider circle. The same bonds
too have through my example inspired
most of the brethren with boldness,
so that trusting in the Lord they are
more zealous than ever, and preach
the word of God courageously and un-
flinchingly.'

τὰ κατ᾽ ἐμέ] '*my circumstances*,' as
Col. iv. 7, Ephes. vi. 21: comp. Tobit
x. 8, 1 Esdr. i. 22.

μᾶλλον] '*rather*' than the reverse,
as might have been anticipated.

¹³ὥστε τοὺς δεσμούς μου φανεροὺς ἐν Χριστῷ γενέσθαι
ἐν ὅλῳ τῷ πραιτωρίῳ καὶ τοῖς λοιποῖς πᾶσιν, ¹⁴καὶ τοὺς
πλείονας τῶν ἀδελφῶν ἐν Κυρίῳ πεποιθότας τοῖς δεσμοῖς
μου περισσοτέρως τολμᾶν ἀφόβως τὸν λόγον τοῦ Θεοῦ

προκοπήν] The verb προκόπτειν is strictly classical; not so the substantive, which is condemned in Phrynichus (Lobeck, p. 85). It is however common in writers of this age.

13. φανεροὺς κ.τ.λ.] 'have become manifest in Christ,' i.e. 'have been seen in their relation to Christ, have borne testimony to the Gospel.'

ἐν ὅλῳ τῷ πραιτωρίῳ] 'throughout the prætorian guard,' i.e. the soldiers composing the imperial regiments. This seems to be the best supported meaning of πραιτώριον. If a local sense is assigned to it, it will probably signify the 'prætorian camp,' but clear examples of this sense are wanting : see the detached note, p. 99. On St Paul's intercourse with the prætorian soldiers see the introduction, pp. 7 19.

τοῖς λοιποῖς πᾶσιν] ' to all the rest ': comp. 2 Cor. xiii. 2; a comprehensive expression, which must not be rigorously interpreted: see the introduction, p. 32 sq. The translation of the Authorised Version, 'in all other places,' will not stand.

14. τοὺς πλείονας] 'the greater number.' St Paul excepts a minority, who through cowardice or indifference held back.

ἐν Κυρίῳ] to be taken with πεποιθότας τοῖς δεσμοῖς μου. Similarly Gal. v. 10 πέποιθα εἰς ὑμᾶς ἐν Κυρίῳ, 2 Thess. iii. 4 πεποίθαμεν δὲ ἐν Κυρίῳ ἐφ' ὑμᾶς. Comp. also below ii. 24, Rom. xiv. 14. The words ἐν Κυρίῳ are thus emphatic by their position. They cannot well be attached to τῶν ἀδελφῶν, as τῶν ἀδελφῶν alone designates the Christian brotherhood, and the addition would be unmeaning. The instances quoted in favour of this connexion (Col. i. 2, iv. 7, Ephes. vi. 21) are no correct pa-

rallels; for in none of these passages does the preposition depend directly on ἀδελφός. For πέποιθα, with a dative of the thing in which the confidence reposes (τοῖς δεσμοῖς), see Philem. 21.

περισσοτέρως] This word seems never to lose its comparative force : see the note on Gal. i. 14. Here it denotes the increased zeal of the brethren, when stimulated by St Paul's endurance. The Apostle accumulates words expressive of courage, πεποιθότας, περισσοτέρως, τολμᾶν ἀφόβως, as above in ver. 9 (see the note).

τοῦ Θεοῦ] These words, which are wanting in the received reading, have a decided preponderance of authority in their favour, and should probably stand in the text: comp. Acts iv. 31 ἐλάλουν τὸν λόγον τοῦ Θεοῦ μετὰ παρρησίας.

15—17. 'But though all alike are active, all are not influenced by the same motives. Some preach Christ to gratify an envious and quarrelsome spirit: others to manifest their goodwill. The latter work from love, acknowledging that I am appointed to plead for the Gospel : the former proclaim Christ from headstrong partisanship and with impure motives, having no other aim than to render my bonds more galling.'

These antagonists can be none other than the Judaizing party, who call down the Apostle's rebuke in a later passage of this letter (iii. 2 sq.) and whose opposition is indirectly implied in another epistle written also from Rome (Col. iv. 11): see above, pp. 17, 18. They preach Christ indeed, but their motives are not single. Their real object is to gain adherents to the law. The main-spring of their activity

λαλεῖν· ¹⁵τινὲς μὲν καὶ διὰ φθόνον καὶ ἔριν, τινὲς δὲ καὶ δι᾽
εὐδοκίαν τὸν Χριστὸν κηρύσσουσιν· ¹⁶οἱ μὲν ἐξ ἀγάπης,
εἰδότες ὅτι εἰς ἀπολογίαν τοῦ εὐαγγελίου κεῖμαι, ¹⁷οἱ

is a factious opposition to the Apostle, a jealousy of his influence. They value success, not as a triumph over heathendom, but as a triumph over St Paul. It enhances their satisfaction to think that his sufferings will be made more poignant by their progress.

But how, it has been asked, can St Paul rejoice in the success of such teachers? Is not this satisfaction inconsistent with his principles? Does he not in the Epistle to the Galatians for instance wholly repudiate their doctrine, and even maintain that for those who hold it Christ has died in vain? This apparent incongruity has led some writers to deny any reference to the Judaizers here; while to others it has furnished an argument against the genuineness of the whole epistle. But the two cases are entirely different. In the one, where the alternative is between the liberty of the Gospel and the bondage of ritualism, he unsparingly denounces his Galatian converts for abandoning the former and adopting the latter. Here on the other hand the choice is between an imperfect Christianity and an unconverted state; the former, however inadequate, must be a gain upon the latter, and therefore must give joy to a high-minded servant of Christ. In Rome there was room enough for him and for them. He was content therefore that each should work on independently. It was a step in advance to know Christ, even though He were known only 'after the flesh.'

καὶ διὰ φθόνον] 'even from envy,' monstrous as this will seem. For διὰ φθόνον see Matt. xxvii. 18, Mark xv. 10. Philemon the comic poet (Meineke, IV. p. 55), πολλά με διδάσκεις ἀφθόνως διὰ φθόνον, has been quoted in illustration of this passage.

καὶ δι᾽ εὐδοκίαν] 'also out of good-will'; this second καὶ must be differently translated from the former. The substantive εὐδοκία may mean either (1) 'purpose, design, desire,' Ecclus. xi. 17 ἡ εὐδοκία αὐτοῦ εἰς τὸν αἰῶνα εὐοδωθήσεται, Rom. x. 1 ἡ εὐδοκία τῆς ἐμῆς καρδίας καὶ ἡ δέησις πρὸς τὸν Θεόν; or (2) 'satisfaction, contentment, happiness,' Ecclus. xxxv. 14 οἱ ὀρθρίζοντες εὑρήσουσιν εὐδοκίαν, 2 Thess. i. 11 πᾶσαν εὐδοκίαν ἀγαθωσύνης; or (3) 'benevolence, goodwill,' Ps. l 20 ἀγάθυνον, Κύριε, ἐν τῇ εὐδοκίᾳ σου τὴν Σιών, cv. 4, and perhaps Luke ii. 14. These different significations arise out of the object to which εὐδοκία is directed. In the first case it refers to things future, in the second to things present, in the third to persons. Fritzsche (Rom. II. p. 371) has separated the different meanings of this word, but is not happy in his examples. In the present passage the opposition to διὰ φθόνον καὶ ἔριν seems to require the third meaning.

16, 17. The order of the clauses is reversed by the figure called chiasm, so that the subject last introduced is discussed first; as e.g. Gal. iv. 4, 5. In the received text the verses are transposed, with a view to remedying this supposed irregularity.

ἐξ ἀγάπης] 'the one preach Christ out of love'; and ἐξ ἐριθείας must be similarly taken. Others connect οἱ ἐξ ἐριθείας, οἱ ἐξ ἀγάπης, 'the factious,' 'the loving,' comparing Rom. ii. 8 τοῖς δὲ ἐξ ἐριθείας (see also iii. 26, Gal. iii. 7, 9); but the order in the second clause is very awkward with this arrangement, which makes τὸν Χριστὸν καταγγέλλουσιν unduly emphatic.

κεῖμαι] 'I am appointed,' as Luke ii. 34 οὗτος κεῖται εἰς πτῶσιν καὶ ἀνάστασιν πολλῶν, 1 Thess. iii. 3 αὐτοὶ γὰρ

δὲ ἐξ ἐριθείας [τὸν] Χριστὸν καταγγέλλουσιν οὐχ ἁγ-
νῶς, οἰόμενοι θλίψιν ἐγείρειν τοῖς δεσμοῖς μου. ¹⁸τί
γάρ; πλὴν ὅτι παντὶ τρόπῳ, εἴτε προφάσει εἴτε ἀληθείᾳ, Χριστὸς καταγγέλλεται, καὶ ἐν τούτῳ χαίρω·
ἀλλὰ καὶ χαρήσομαι· ¹⁹οἶδα γὰρ ὅτι τοῦτό μοι ἀπο-

19.   οἶδα δὲ ὅτι.

οἴδατε ὅτι εἰς τοῦτο κείμεθα: comp.
Josh. iv. 6. The idea of *prostration*,
if implied at all, can only be subordinate.

17.   ἐξ ἐριθείας] The interests of
party were predominant with the Judaizers: their missionary zeal took the
form of a political canvass. For the proper meaning of ἐριθεία, 'partisanship,'
see the note on Gal. v. 20. The words
τὸν Χριστὸν καταγγέλλουσιν seem to be
added to bring out the contrast between the character of their motives
and the subject of their preaching;
for there is a moral contradiction between ἐριθεία and Χριστός.

οὐχ ἁγνῶς] '*with mixed, impure motives,*' explained afterwards by προφάσει. The insincere, selfish, and even
sordid motives of the Judaizers are
denounced in other passages also :
2 Cor. xi. 13, 20, Gal. vi. 12.

θλίψιν ἐγείρειν] '*to make my chains
gall me,*' where the metaphor in θλίψις
is clearly seen. This word, though extremely common in the LXX, occurs
very rarely in classical writers even of
a late date, and in these few passages
has its literal meaning. The same
want in the religious vocabulary, which
gave currency to θλίψις, also created
'tribulatio' as its Latin equivalent.
On the accent of θλίψις see Lipsius
*Gramm. Unters.* p. 35. The reading
ἐγείρειν, besides being better supported, carries out the metaphor better
than ἐπιφέρειν of the received text.
The gathering opposition to the Apostle's doctrine of liberty, the forming
of a compact party in the Church
bound to the observance of the law,
were the means by which they sought

to annoy and wound him.

18.   τί γάρ;] '*What then,*' as Xen.
*Mem.* ii. 6. 2, 3, iii. 3. 6, and commonly
in classical writers: comp. also LXX,
Job xvi. 3, xxi. 4.

πλὴν ὅτι] '*only that,*' as Acts xx.
23; comp. Plut. *Mor.* p. 780 A, Plato
*Phæd.* p. 57 B, *Theæt.* p. 183 A. This
seems on the whole the most probable
reading. Some texts have πλὴν alone,
others ὅτι alone; both which readings
appear like attempts to smooth the
construction. The latter however,
which is supported by one excellent
authority, may possibly be correct.

προφάσει] 'as a cloke for other designs,' i.e. using the name of Christ to
promote the interests of their party
and to gain proselytes to the law.
On πρόφασις, 'an ostensible purpose,'
generally but not necessarily implying
insincerity, see the note on 1 Thess. ii.
5. The opposition of πρόφασις and
ἀλήθεια is illustrated by numerous examples in Wetstein and Raphel.

ἐν τούτῳ] '*herein,*' i.e. ἐν τῷ καταγ-
γέλλεσθαι Χριστόν.

ἀλλὰ καὶ χαρήσομαι] '*yea and I shall
rejoice.*' The abruptness reflects the
conflict in the Apostle's mind : he
crushes the feeling of personal annoy-
ance, which rises up at the thought of
this unscrupulous antagonist. The
A. V. however, 'I *will* rejoice,' brings
out the idea of *determination* more
strongly than the original justifies.

19, 20.   'Is not my joy reasonable?
For I know that all my present trials
and sufferings will lead only to my
salvation, and that in answer to your
prayers the Spirit of Christ will be
shed abundantly upon me. Thus will be

βήσεται εἰς σωτηρίαν διὰ τῆς ὑμῶν δεήσεως καὶ ἐπιχορ-
ηγίας τοῦ πνεύματος Ἰησοῦ Χριστοῦ, ²⁰κατὰ τὴν ἀπο-
καραδοκίαν καὶ ἐλπίδα μου, ὅτι ἐν οὐδενὶ αἰσχυνθήσομαι,
ἀλλ' ἐν πάσῃ παρρησίᾳ ὡς πάντοτε καὶ νῦν μεγαλυνθήσεται Χριστὸς ἐν τῷ σώματί μου, εἴτε διὰ ζωῆς εἴτε διὰ

fulfilled my earnest longing and hope,
that I may never hang back through
shame, but at this crisis, as always,
may speak and act courageously; so
that, whether I die a martyr for His
name or live to labour in His service,
He may be glorified in my body.'

19. τοῦτο] 'this state of things,' these
perplexities and annoyances. It is unconnected with the preceding ἐν τούτῳ,
ver. 18.

σωτηρίαν] 'salvation,' in the highest
sense. These trials will develope the
spiritual life in the Apostle, will be a
pathway to the glories of heaven. His
personal safety cannot be intended
here, as some have thought; for the
σωτηρία, of which he speaks, will be
gained equally whether he lives or
dies (ver. 20).

τῆς ὑμῶν δεήσεως κ.τ.λ.] The two
clauses are fitly connected by the same
article; for the supply of the Spirit is
the answer to their prayer.

ἐπιχορηγίας] 'bountiful supply'; see
the note on Gal. iii. 5. But must the
following genitive τοῦ πνεύματος be
considered subjective or objective? Is
the Spirit the giver or the gift? Ought
we not to say in answer to this question, that the language of the original
suggests no limitation, that it will bear
both meanings equally well, and that
therefore any such restriction is arbitrary? 'The Spirit of Jesus' is both
the giver and the gift. For the expression τὸ πνεῦμα Ἰησοῦ Χριστοῦ compare Rom. viii. 9, Gal. iv. 6, and Acts
xvi. 7 (the correct reading).

20. ἀποκαραδοκίαν] 'earnest desire.'
The substantive occurs once again in
the New Testament, Rom. viii. 19.
The verb is not uncommon in Polybius

and later writers. The idea of eagerness conveyed by the simple word
καραδοκεῖν is further intensified by the
preposition, which implies abstraction,
absorption, as in ἀποβλέπειν, ἀπεκδέ-
χεσθαι, etc.: comp. Joseph. B. J. iii.
7. 26 τοῖς μὲν οὖν καθ' ἕτερα προσφέρουσι τὰς κλίμακας οὐ προσεῖχεν, ἀπε-
καραδόκει δὲ τὴν ὁρμὴν τῶν βελῶν, i.e.
his attention was drawn off and concentrated on the missiles; a passage
quoted by C. F. A. Fritzsche, whose account of the word however (Fritzsch.
Opusc. I. p. 150) is not altogether
satisfactory.

αἰσχυνθήσομαι κ.τ.λ.] αἰσχύνη and
παρρησία are opposed, Prov. xiii. 5
ἀσεβὴς δὲ αἰσχύνεται καὶ οὐχ ἕξει παρρησίαν, 1 Joh. ii. 28 σχῶμεν παρρησίαν
καὶ μὴ αἰσχυνθῶμεν ἀπ' αὐτοῦ. This
right of free speech (παρρησία) is the
badge, the privilege, of the servant of
Christ: see esp. 2 Cor. iii. 12.

καὶ νῦν] 'so now.' For καὶ νῦν (καὶ
ἄρτι) corresponding to ὡς (καθώς) comp.
1 Joh. ii. 18, Gal. i. 9.

μεγαλυνθήσεται] After ἐν πάσῃ παρρησίᾳ the first person might naturally
be expected: but with sensitive reverence the Apostle shrinks from any
mention of his own agency, lest he
should seem to glorify himself. It is
not μεγαλυνθήσομαι, not even μεγα-
λυνῶ τὸν Χριστόν, but μεγαλυνθήσεται
Χριστὸς ἐν τῷ σώματί μου. For the
thought compare 2 Cor. iv. 10 πάντοτε τὴν νέκρωσιν τοῦ Ἰησοῦ ἐν τῷ σώματι περιφέροντες, ἵνα καὶ ἡ ζωὴ τοῦ
Ἰησοῦ ἐν τῷ σώματι ἡμῶν φανερωθῇ,
1 Cor. vi. 20 δοξάσατε δὴ τὸν Θεὸν ἐν
τῷ σώματι ὑμῶν.

21—26. 'Others may make choice
between life and death. I gladly

θανάτου. ²¹ἐμοὶ γὰρ τὸ ζῆν Χριστὸς καὶ τὸ ἀποθανεῖν
κέρδος· ²²εἰ δὲ τὸ ζῆν ἐν σαρκὶ τοῦτό μοι καρπὸς ἔργου—

accept either alternative. If I live, my life is one with Christ: if I die, my death is gain to me. Yet when I incline to prefer death, I hesitate: for may not my life—this present existence which men call life—may not my life be fruitful through my labours? Nay, I know not how to choose. I am hemmed in, as it were, a wall on this side and a wall on that. If I consulted my own longing, I should desire to dissolve this earthly tabernacle, and to go home to Christ; for this is very far better. If I consulted your interests, I should wish to live and labour still: for this your needs require. And a voice within assures me, that so it will be. I shall continue here and abide with you all; that I may promote your advance in the faith and your joy in believing: and that you on your part may have in me fresh cause for boasting in Christ, when you see me present among you once more.'

21. ἐμοί] '*to me*,' whatever it may be to others: so ἡμῶν, iii. 20.

τὸ ζῆν Χριστός] '*life is Christ*.' 'I live only to serve Him, only to commune with Him; I have no conception of life apart from Him.' 'Quicquid vivo,' is Bengel's paraphrase, 'Christum vivo': comp. Gal. ii. 20 ζῶ δὲ οὐκέτι ἐγώ, ζῇ δὲ ἐν ἐμοὶ Χριστός, and Col. iii. 3, 4.

τὸ ἀποθανεῖν κέρδος] '*death is gain,* for then my union with Christ will be more completely realised.' The tense denotes not the act of dying but the consequence of dying, the state after death: comp. 2 Cor. vii. 3 εἰς τὸ συναποθανεῖν καὶ συνζῆν, 'to be with you in death and in life.' The proper opposition to ζῆν is not ἀποθνήσκειν, but ἀποθανεῖν or τεθνάναι, e.g. Plato *Leg.* p. 958 E, *Gorg.* p. 483 B, *Phæd.* 62 A. The difference is marked in Plato *Phæd.* 64 A οὐδὲν ἄλλο ἐπιτηδεύ-

ουσιν ἢ ἀποθνήσκειν τε καὶ τεθνάναι.

22. The grammar of the passage reflects the conflict of feeling in the Apostle's mind. He is tossed to and fro between the desire to labour for Christ in life, and the desire to be united with Christ by death. The abrupt and disjointed sentences express this hesitation.

εἰ δὲ τὸ ζῆν κ.τ.λ.] Of several interpretations that have been suggested, two only seem to deserve consideration: (1) 'But if my living in the flesh will be fruitful through a laborious career, then what to choose I know not.' In this case καί will introduce the apodosis. The only passage at all analogous in the New Testament is 2 Cor. ii. 2 εἰ γὰρ ἐγὼ λυπῶ ὑμᾶς, καὶ τίς ἐ εὐφραίνων με; comp. *Clem. Hom.* ii. 44 εἰ δὲ τὸ πίον ὄρος ἐπιθυμεῖ, καὶ τίνος τὰ πάντα; εἰ ψεύδεται, καὶ τίς ἀληθεύει; κ.τ.λ. But the parallel is not exact, for in these instances καί introduces a direct interrogative. Passages indeed are given in Hartung (I. pp. 130, 131) where καί ushers in the apodosis after εἰ, but these are all poetical. And even if this use of καί be admissible, the sentence still runs awkwardly. (2) 'But if (it be my lot) to live in the flesh, then my labour will be productive of fruit. And so what to choose I know not.' Thus the sentence εἰ δὲ τὸ ζῆν κ.τ.λ. is treated as elliptical, the predicate being suppressed. But, though ellipses are very frequent in St Paul (comp. e.g. Rom. iv. 9, v. 18, ix. 16, 1 Cor. iv. 6, xi. 24, 2 Cor. i. 6, Gal. ii. 9, v. 13, etc.), yet the present instance would be extremely harsh. Of the two explanations already considered the first seems preferable; but may not a third be hazarded? (3) 'But what if my living in the flesh will bear fruit, etc.? In fact what to choose I know not.' In this case εἰ implies an interrogation,

καὶ τί αἱρήσομαι οὐ γνωρίζω· ²³συνέχομαι δὲ ἐκ τῶν
δύο, τὴν ἐπιθυμίαν ἔχων εἰς τὸ ἀναλῦσαι καὶ σὺν Χρισ-

the apodosis being suppressed ; as in Rom. ix. 22, Acts xxiii. 9 (where the received text adds μὴ θεομαχῶμεν). On this and similar uses of εἰ see Winer § lvii. p. 639, § lxiv. p. 750, A. Buttmann pp. 214, 215. I do not know whether this interpretation has ever been suggested ; but it seems to be in keeping with the abruptness of the context, and to present less difficulty than those generally adopted.

τὸ ζῆν ἐν σαρκί] St Paul had before spoken of the natural life as τὸ ζῆν simply; but the mention of the gain of death has meanwhile suggested the thought of the higher life. Thus the word ζῆν requires to be qualified by the addition of ἐν σαρκί. After all death is true life. The sublime guess of Euripides, τίς οἶδεν εἰ τὸ ζῆν μέν ἐστι κατθανεῖν τὸ κατθανεῖν δὲ ζῆν, which was greeted with ignoble ridicule by the comic poets, has become an assured truth in Christ.

καρπὸς ἔργου] Comp. Rom. i. 13 ἵνα τινὰ καρπὸν σχῶ καὶ ἐν ὑμῖν. For the metaphor see 1 Cor. iii. 6 sq.

οὐ γνωρίζω] 'I do not perceive.' Γνωρίζειν has two distinct senses ; (1) 'To understand, know'; (2) 'To declare, make known.' In classical Greek the former seems to be the more common, even at a late date, though the latter occurs not infrequently. On the other hand in biblical Greek the latter is the usual meaning (e.g. below, iv. 6), the exceptions being very few, as here and Job iv. 16 (Symm.), xxxiv. 25 (LXX): comp. Test. xii. Patr. Dan 2 φίλον οὐ γνωρίζει.

23. συνέχομαι ἐκ τῶν δύο] 'I am hemmed in on both sides, I am prevented from inclining one way or the other.' The preposition seems to denote direction, as in ἐκ δεξιᾶς, ἐκ θαλάσσης, etc. The δύο are the two horns of the dilemma, stated in verses 21, 22.

τὴν ἐπιθυμίαν κ.τ.λ.] 'my own desire tends towards.' Comp. Gal. vi. 4.

τὸ ἀναλῦσαι] 'to break up, depart, comp. ἀνάλυσις 2 Tim. iv. 6. The metaphor is drawn from breaking up an encampment, e.g. Polyb. v. 28. 8 αὖθις εἰς παραχειμασίαν ἀνέλυσε, 2 Macc. ix. 1 ἀναλελυκὼς ἀκόσμως. The camp-life of the Israelites in the wilderness, as commemorated by the annual feast of Tabernacles, was a ready and appropriate symbol of man's transitory life on earth : while the land of promise with its settled abodes, the land flowing with milk and honey, typified the eternal inheritance of the redeemed : Hebr. iv. 1 sq. See especially 2 Cor. v. 1 ἐὰν ἡ ἐπίγειος ἡμῶν οἰκία τοῦ σκήνους καταλυθῇ, οἰκοδομὴν ἐκ Θεοῦ ἔχομεν, οἰκίαν ἀχειροποίητον αἰώνιον ἐν τοῖς οὐρανοῖς, and ver. 4. Compare also the metaphor in Plut. Mor. 76 D οὐ μονὰς ποιοῦσιν ἢ ἐποχὰς ὥσπερ ἐν ὁδῷ τῆς προκοπῆς ἀλλ' ἀναλύσεις.

σὺν Χριστῷ εἶναι] The faithful immediately after death are similarly represented as in the presence and keeping of the Lord also in 2 Cor. v. 6, 8 ἐνδημοῦντες ἐν τῷ σώματι ἐκδημοῦμεν ἀπὸ τοῦ Κυρίου κ.τ.λ., Acts vii. 59 ; comp. Clem. Rom. § 5 ἐπορεύθη εἰς τὸν ὀφειλόμενον τόπον τῆς δόξης of St Peter and εἰς τὸν ἅγιον τόπον ἐπορεύθη of St Paul, Polyc. Phil. § 9 εἰς τὸν ὀφειλόμενον αὐτοῖς τόπον εἰσὶ παρὰ τῷ Κυρίῳ. On the other hand their state after death is elsewhere described as a sleep from which they will arise, 1 Cor. xv. 51, 52, 1 Thess. iv. 14, 16. The one mode of representation must be qualified by the other.

πολλῷ μᾶλλον κρεῖσσον] For the triple comparative see Isocr. Archid. § 83 πολὺ γὰρ κρεῖττον...τελευτῆσαι τὸν βίον μᾶλλον ἢ ζῆν κ.τ.λ. and other references in Wetstein: comp. Winer § xxxv. p. 254. The insertion of γὰρ is supported by most of the best MSS ; and yet a reading which comes to the

τῷ εἶναι· πολλῷ [γὰρ] μᾶλλον κρεῖσσον· ²⁴τὸ δὲ ἐπιμένειν [ἐν] τῇ σαρκὶ ἀναγκαιότερον δι' ὑμᾶς. ²⁵καὶ τοῦτο
πεποιθὼς οἶδα, ὅτι μενῶ καὶ παραμενῶ πᾶσιν ὑμῖν εἰς
τὴν ὑμῶν προκοπὴν καὶ χαρὰν τῆς πίστεως, ²⁶ἵνα τὸ
καύχημα ὑμῶν περισσεύῃ ἐν Χριστῷ Ἰησοῦ ἐν ἐμοὶ διὰ
τῆς ἐμῆς παρουσίας πάλιν πρὸς ὑμᾶς.

relief of a disjointed syntax must be regarded with suspicion.

24. ἐπιμένειν τῇ σαρκί] not 'to abide *in*,' but 'to abide *by* the flesh,' to cling to this present life, to take it with all its inconveniences. This is the common construction of ἐπιμένειν in St Paul, Rom. vi. 1, xi. 22, 23, Col i. 23, 1 Tim. iv. 16. The insertion of ἐν weakens the force of the expression; besides that this preposition is not found with ἐπιμένειν elsewhere in St Paul, except in 1 Cor. xvi. 8 ἐπιμενῶ ἐν Ἐφέσῳ which is no parallel.

ἀναγκαιότερον] The comparative corresponds to the foregoing κρεῖσσον. Either alternative is in a manner necessary, as either is advantageous. But the balance of necessity (of obligation) is on one side, the balance of advantage on the other.

25. τοῦτο πεποιθὼς οἶδα] '*of this I am confidently persuaded, that etc.*'; comp. Rom. xiv. 14 οἶδα καὶ πέπεισμαι ...ὅτι κ.τ.λ., and Ephes. v. 5 τοῦτο γὰρ ἴστε γινώσκοντες ὅτι πᾶς πόρνος κ.τ.λ. The words are commonly taken, 'being persuaded of this (that my life will be advantageous to you), I know that etc.'

οἶδα] not a prophetic inspiration, but a personal conviction: comp. ii. 24. The same word οἶδα is used Acts xx. 25, where he expresses his belief that he shall not see his Asiatic converts again. Viewed as infallible presentiments, the two are hardly reconcilable; for the one assumes, the other negatives, his release. The assurance here recorded was fulfilled (1 Tim. i. 3); while the presentiment there expressed was overruled by events (1 Tim. i. 3, 2 Tim. i. 15, 18, iv. 20).

παραμενῶ] is relative, while μενῶ is absolute. It denotes continuance in a certain place or with certain persons or in certain relations. Very frequently, as here, it takes a dative of the person, e.g. Plat. *Apol.* p. 39 E, *Phæd.* 115 D οὐκέτι ὑμῖν παραμενῶ, etc. The reading of the received text συμπαραμενῶ may be dismissed, as insufficiently supported. μενῶ καὶ παραμενῶ may be translated 'bide and abide.'

τῆς πίστεως] to be taken with both substantives. For χαρὰν τῆς πίστεως comp. Rom. xv. 13 πληρῶσαι ὑμᾶς πάσης χαρᾶς καὶ εἰρήνης ἐν τῷ πιστεύειν. On joyfulness, as the key-note of this epistle, see the notes, i. 4, iv. 4.

26. ἵνα τὸ καύχημα κ.τ.λ.] 'that you may have more matter for boasting in me,' not 'that I may have more matter for boasting in you,' as it is sometimes taken. Either would accord with the Apostle's language elsewhere, 2 Cor. i. 14 ὅτι καύχημα ὑμῶν ἐσμὲν καθάπερ καὶ ὑμεῖς ἡμῶν ἐν τῇ ἡμέρᾳ τοῦ Κυρίου Ἰησοῦ (comp. v. 12); but the former is the simpler interpretation of the words here. The words καυχᾶσθαι, καύχησις, καύχημα, link this epistle with the preceding group, where they occur very abundantly (see the introduction, p. 42 sq.). In the later epistles only one instance is found, Ephes. ii. 9. On the difference between καύχημα, καύχησις, see the note Gal. vi. 4.

ἐν] repeated. The first denotes the sphere in which their pride lives; the second the object on which it rests. Compare Col. ii. 7 περισσεύοντες ἐν αὐτῇ ἐν εὐχαριστίᾳ.

παρουσίας πάλιν] For the position of πάλιν see the note on Gal. i. 13.

*The synonymes 'bishop' and 'presbyter.'*

IT is a fact now generally recognised by theologians of all shades of opinion, that in the language of the New Testament the same officer in the Church is called indifferently 'bishop' (ἐπίσκοπος) and 'elder' or 'presbyter' (πρεσβύτερος). The bearing of this fact on the origin and authority of the 'episcopate,' as the term was understood later and as it is understood in the present day, will be considered in a dissertation at the end of this volume. At present it will be sufficient to establish the fact itself; but before doing so, it may be useful to trace the previous history of the two words. *The two words synonymes.*

*Episcopus*, 'bishop,' 'overseer,' was an official title among the Greeks. In Athenian language it was used especially to designate commissioners appointed to regulate a new colony or acquisition, so that the Attic 'bishop' corresponded to the Spartan 'harmost¹.' Thus the impostor, who intrudes upon the colonists in Aristophanes (*Av.* 1022), says ἐπίσκοπος ἥκω δεῦρο τῷ κυάμῳ λαχών. These officers are mentioned also in an inscription, Boeckh no. 73. The title however is not confined to Attic usage; it is the designation for instance of the inspectors whose business it was to report to the Indian kings (Arrian *Ind.* xii. 5); of the commissioner appointed by Mithridates to settle affairs in Ephesus (Appian *Mithr.* 48); of magistrates who regulated the sale of provisions under the Romans (Charisius in the *Dig.* l. 4. 18); and of certain officers in Rhodes whose functions are unknown (Ross. *Inscr. Grœc. Ined.* fasc. III. nos. 275, 276)². *Meaning of 'bishop' in heathen writers*

In the LXX the word is common. In some places it signifies 'inspectors, superintendents, taskmasters,' as 2 Kings xi. 19, 2 Chron. xxxiv. 12, 17, Is. lx. 17; in others it is a higher title. 'captains' or 'presidents,' Neh. xi. 9, *and in the LXX.*

---

¹ Harpocration s. v. (ed. Dindorf. p.129) quotes from Theophrastus,πολλῷ γὰρ κάλλιον κατά γε τὴν τοῦ ὀνόματος θέσιν, ὡς οἱ Λάκωνες ἁρμοστὰς φάσκοντες εἰς τὰς πόλεις πέμπειν, οὐκ ἐπισκόπους οὐδὲ φύλακας, ὡς 'Αθηναῖοι. See also Schol. on Arist. Av. l. c. οἱ παρ' 'Αθηναίων εἰς τὰς ἐπηκόους πόλεις ἐπισκέψασθαι τὰ παρ' ἑκάστοις πεμπόμενοι ἐπίσκοποι καὶ φύλακες ἐκαλοῦντο οὕς οἱ Λάκωνες ἁρμοστὰς ἔλεγον.

² In these instances the ἐπίσκοποι seem to hold some office in connexion with a temple. In another inscription (Ross. *Inscr. Grœc. Ined.* fasc. II. no. 198), found at Thera, the word again occurs; Δεδόχθαι· ἁ[ποδε]ξαμένος τὴν ἐπαγγελίαν τὸ μ[ὲν ἀρ]γύριον ἐγδανεῖσαι τὸς ἐπισκό[πος] Δίωνα καὶ Μελέϊππον, where among other dialectic forms the accusative plural in ος occurs. M.Wesch-

er in an article in the *Revue Archéologique*, p. 246 (Avril 1866), supposes the ἐπίσκοποι here to be officers of a club or confraternity (ἔρανος or θίασος), in which he is followed by Renan *Les Apôtres* p. 353. If their opinion be correct, this inscription presents a closer analogy to the Christian use of the term, than the instances given in the text. The context of the inscription however is not decisive, though this interpretation seems fairly probable: see below p. 194. There can be no reasonable doubt I imagine about the reading ἐπισκόπος; though Ross himself suggested ἐπισσόφος, because he found the word in another Theræan inscription (Boeckh no. 2448). In this latter inscription ἐπισσόφος is probably a mason's blunder for ἐπισκόπος.

14, 22. Of Antiochus Epiphanes we are told that when he determined to overthrow the worship of the one true God, he 'appointed commissioners (ἐπισκόπους, bishops) over all the people,' to see that his orders were obeyed (1 Macc. i. 51: comp. Joseph. *Ant.* xii. 5. 4; in 2 Macc. v. 22 the word is ἐπιστάτας). The feminine ἐπισκοπή, which is not a classical word, occurs very frequently in the LXX, denoting sometimes the *work*, sometimes the *office*, of an ἐπίσκοπος. Hence it passed into the language of the New Testament and of the Christian Church.

*ἐπισκοπή.*

Thus beyond the fundamental idea of *inspection*, which lies at the root of the word 'bishop,' its usage suggests two subsidiary notions also; (1) Responsibility to a superior power; (2) The introduction of a new order of things.

The earlier history of the word *presbyterus* (elder, presbyter, or priest) is much more closely connected with its Christian sense. If the analogies of the 'bishop' are to be sought chiefly among heathen nations, the name and office of the 'presbyter' are essentially Jewish. Illustrations indeed might be found in almost all nations ancient or modern, in the γερουσία of Sparta for instance, in the 'senatus' of Rome, in the 'signoria' of Florence, or in the 'aldermen' of our own country and time, where the deliberative body originally took its name from the advanced age of its members. But among the chosen people we meet at every turn with presbyters or elders in Church and State from the earliest to the latest times. In the lifetime of the lawgiver, in the days of the judges, throughout the monarchy, during the captivity, after the return, and under the Roman domination, the 'elders' appear as an integral part of the governing body of the country. But it is rather in a special religious development of the office, than in these national and civil presbyteries, that we are to look for the prototype of the Christian minister. Over every Jewish synagogue, whether at home or abroad, a council of 'elders' presided[1]. It was not unnatural therefore that, when the Christian synagogue took its place by the side of the Jewish, a similar organization should be adopted with such modifications as circumstances required; and thus the name familiar under the old dispensation was retained under the new.

The term presbyter or elder

transferred from the Synagogue to the Church.

Of the identity of the 'bishop' and 'presbyter' in the language of the apostolic age, the following evidence seems conclusive.

(1) In the opening of this epistle St Paul salutes the 'bishops' and 'deacons[2].' Now it is incredible that he should recognise only the first

Identity of the two in the apostolic writings

---

[1] See especially Vitringa *de Synag. Vet.* III. I. c. 1, p. 613 sq.

[2] It may be worth while correcting a mistake which runs through the critical editions of the Greek Testament. Chrysostom is quoted as reading συνεπισκόποις in one word. His editors no doubt make him read so, but of this reading there is no trace in the context. After explaining that the terms deacon, presbyter, bishop, were originally convertible (οἱ πρεσβύτεροι τὸ παλαιὸν ἐκαλοῦντο ἐπίσκοποι καὶ διάκονοι Χριστοῦ καὶ

οἱ ἐπίσκοποι πρεσβύτεροι), he illustrates this by the fact that even in his own day bishops often addressed a presbyter as a fellow-presbyter, a deacon as a fellow-deacon (ὅθεν καὶ νῦν πολλοὶ συμπρεσβυτέρῳ ἐπίσκοποι γράφουσι καὶ συνδιακόνῳ): but his language nowhere implies that he read συνεπισκόποις. The comment of Theodore of Mopsuestia again has been understood (see Tischendorf) as referring to and combating the reading συνεπισκόποις. This also is an error. After explaining the identity of

and third order and pass over the second, though the second was absolutely essential to the existence of a church and formed the staple of its ministry. It seems therefore to follow of necessity that the 'bishops' are identical with the 'presbyters.' Whether or not the Philippian Church at this time possessed also a 'bishop' in the later sense of the term, is a question which must be reserved for the present.

(2) In the Acts (xx. 17) St Paul is represented as summoning to Miletus the 'elders' or 'presbyters' of the Church of Ephesus. Yet in addressing them immediately after he appeals to them as 'bishops' or 'overseers' of the church (xx. 28).

(3) Similarly St Peter, appealing to the 'presbyters' of the churches addressed by him, in the same breath urges them to 'fulfil the office of bishops' (ἐπισκοποῦντες) with disinterested zeal (1 Pet. v. 1, 2).

(4) Again in the First Epistle to Timothy St Paul, after describing the qualifications for the office of a 'bishop' (iii. 1—7), goes on at once to say what is required of 'deacons' (iii. 8—13). He makes no mention of presbyters. The term 'presbyter' however is not unknown to him; for having occasion in a later passage to speak of Christian ministers he calls these officers no longer 'bishops,' but 'presbyters' (v. 17—19).

(5) The same identification appears still more plainly from the Apostle's directions to Titus (i. 5—7); 'That thou shouldest set in order the things that are wanting and ordain *elders* in every city, as I appointed thee; if any one be *blameless*, the husband of one wife, having believing children who are not charged with riotousness or unruly; for a *bishop* (τὸν ἐπίσκοπον)[1] must be *blameless* etc.[2]'

(6) Nor is it only in the apostolic writings that this identity is found. and in Clement of Rome.

---

bishops and presbyters Theodore adds, προσεκτέον ὅτι τὸ σὺν ἐπισκόποις λέγει, οὐχ ὥς τινες ἐνόμισαν ὥσπερ ἡμεῖς σὺν πρεσβυτέροις γράφειν εἰώθαμεν· οὐ γὰρ πρὸς τὸ ἑαυτοῦ πρόσωπον εἶπεν τὸ σύν, ἵνα ᾖ σὺν ἐπισκόποις ἡμῶν· ἀλλὰ πρὸς τὸ πᾶσι τοῖς ἐν Φιλίπποις ἁγίοις, σὺν τοῖς αὐτόθι ἐπισκόποις τε καὶ διακόνοις: 'It must be observed that when he says *with the bishops*, it is not, as some have thought, a parallel to our practice of writing 'together with the elders' (i.e. of associating the elders with themselves in the superscription, as for instance Polycarp does in writing to the Philippians): 'for he does not use the word *with* in reference to himself, meaning *with our bishops*, but in reference to *all the saints that are at Philippi*, i.e. with the bishops and deacons that are *there*.' Here I have substituted σὺν πρεσβυτέροις for συμπρεσβυτέροις, as the context seems to require, and corrected the corrupt ᾖ ἰσὴν into ᾖ σὺν with the Latin. The Latin version of Theodore

however (Raban. Maur. VI. p. 479, ed. Migne) mistakes and confuses his meaning. The interpretation which Theodore is combating appears in the Ambrosian Hilary; '*Cum episcopis et diaconibus:* hoc est, cum Paulo et Timotheo, qui utique episcopi erant: simul significavit et diaconos qui ministrabant ei. Ad plebem enim scribit: nam si episcopis scriberet et diaconibus, ad personas eorum scriberet; et loci ipsius episcopo scribendum erat, non duobus vel tribus, sicut ad Titum et Timotheum.' See below, p. 230.

[1] In τὸν ἐπίσκοπον the definite article denotes the type, as in 2 Cor. xii. 12 τὰ σημεῖα τοῦ ἀποστολοῦ, Joh. x. 11 ὁ ποιμὴν ὁ καλός: see the notes on Gal. iii. 20.

[2] The identity of the two titles in the New Testament is recognised by the Peshito Syriac Version, which commonly translates ἐπίσκοπος by kashisho, i.e. presbyter or elder: see Wichelhaus *de Vers. Syr. Ant.* p. 209.

St Clement of Rome wrote probably in the last decade of the first century and in his language the terms are still convertible. Speaking of the Apostles he says that 'preaching in every country and city (κατὰ χώρας καὶ κατὰ πόλεις) they appointed their first-fruits, having tested them by the Spirit, to be *bishops* and *deacons* of them that should believe (μελλόντων πιστεύειν)' § 42. A little later, referring to the disorganised state of the Corinthian Church, he adds, 'Our Apostles knew through our Lord Jesus Christ that there would be strife concerning the authority (ἐπὶ τοῦ ὀνόματος) of the *bishopric*'...'We shall incur no slight guilt if we eject from the *bishopric* those who have presented the offerings (δῶρα) unblameably and holily. Blessed are the *presbyters* who have gone before, whose departure was crowned with fruit and mature (οἵτινες ἔγκαρπον καὶ τελείαν ἔσχον τὴν ἀνάλυσιν)' § 44.

Different usage in Ignatius and Polycarp.
This is the last instance of identification. With the opening of a second century a new phraseology begins. In the epistles of Ignatius the terms are used in their more modern sense. In his letter to Polycarp (§ 6) he writes: 'Give heed to the bishop, that God also may give heed to you. I am devoted (ἀντίψυχον ἐγώ) to those who are obedient to the bishop, to presbyters, to deacons (τῷ ἐπισκόπῳ, πρεσβυτέροις, διακόνοις).' The bishop is always singled out by this writer, as the chief officer of the Church[1]. So about the same time Polycarp, writing to the Philippians, gives directions to the *deacons* (§ 5) and the *presbyters* (§ 6). He also begins his letter, 'Polycarp and the *presbyters* that are with him.' With this form of address may be coupled the fact that the writer is distinctly called '*bishop* of Smyrna' by Ignatius (*Polyc.* init.).

Towards the close of the second century the original application of the term 'bishop' seems to have passed not only out of use, but almost out of memory. So perhaps we may account for the explanation which Irenæus gives of the incident at Miletus (Acts xx. 17, 28). 'Having called together the *bishops and presbyters* who were from Ephesus and *the other neighbouring cities*[2].' But in the fourth century, when the fathers of the Church began to examine the apostolic records with a more critical eye, they at once detected the fact. No one states it more clearly than Jerome. 'Among the ancients,' he says, 'bishops and presbyters are the same, for the one is a term of dignity, the other of age[3].' 'The Apostle plainly shows,' he writes in another place, 'that presbyters are the same as bishops...It is proved most clearly that bishops and presbyters are the same[4].' Again in a third passage he says 'If any one thinks the opinion

The identity proved by Jerome,

---

[1] Besides the passages quoted in the text see *Polyc.* 5, *Ephes.* 2. All these passages are found in the Syriac. The shorter Greek teems with references to the bishop as chief officer of the Church.

[2] Iren. iii. 14. 2. His explanation of the incident has been charged with dishonesty, but I know of nothing to justify such a charge. It would appear a very natural solution of a difficulty, if the writer had only an indistinct knowledge of the altered value of the term. At all events the same account has been given by writers who lived in a more critical age; e.g. Potter, *Church Government* c. iii. p. 118.

[3] *Epist.* lxix (I. p. 414 sq., ed. Vallarsi).

[4] *Epist.* cxlvi (I. p. 1081) 'Quum Apostolus *perspicue doceat* eosdem esse presbyteros quos episcopos'...'*manifestissime comprobatur* eundem esse episcopum atque presbyterum.'

that the bishops and presbyters are the same, to be not the view of the Scriptures but my own, let him study the words of the apostle to the Philippians,' and in support of his view he alleges the scriptural proofs at great length[1]. But, though more full than other writers, he is hardly more explicit. Of his predecessors the Ambrosian Hilary had discerned the same truth[2]. Of his contemporaries and successors, Chrysostom, Pelagius, Theodore of Mopsuestia, Theodoret, all acknowledge it[3]. Thus in every one of the extant commentaries on the epistles containing the crucial passages, whether Greek or Latin, before the close of the fifth century, this identity is affirmed. In the succeeding ages bishops and popes accept the verdict of St Jerome without question. Even late in the mediæval period, and at the era of the reformation, the justice of his criticism or the sanction of his name carries the general suffrages of theologians[4]. *and recognised by earlier and later writers.*

## *The meaning of 'prætorium' in i. 13.*

The word 'prætorium' signifies properly (1) 'The general's tent,' 'the head-quarters in a camp.' From this it gets other derived meanings: (2) 'The residence of a governor or prince,' e.g. Acts xxiii. 35 ἐν τῷ πραιτωρίῳ τοῦ Ἡρώδου (A.V. 'judgment hall'), Mark xv. 16 ἀπήγαγον αὐτὸν ἔσω τῆς αὐλῆς ὅ ἐστιν πραιτώριον, *Acta Thomæ* § 3 πραιτώρια βασιλικά, Juv. *Sat.* x. 161 'sedet ad prætoria regis,' Tertull. *ad Scap.* § 3 'solus in prætorio suo etc.' (3) 'Any spacious villa or palace'; Juv. *Sat.* i. 75 'criminibus debent hortos prætoria mensas,' Sueton. *Tiber.* 39 'juxta Terracinam in prætorio cui speluncæ nomen erat incœnante eo' (comp. *Octav.* 72, *Calig.* 37), Epict. *Diss.* iii. 22. 47 οὐ πραιτωρίδιον ἀλλὰ γῆ μόνον κ.τ.λ. *Common meanings of the word.*

So much for the word generally. It remains to enquire, what sense it would probably bear, when used by a person writing from Rome and speaking of the cause which he advocated as becoming known 'in the whole of the prætorium.' Several answers have been given to this question. *Explanations of the word in St Paul.*

(1) 'The imperial residence on the Palatine.' So our English Version, following the Greek commentators. Thus Chrysostom, 'They still (τέως) called the palace by this name.' Similarly Theodore of Mopsuestia[5], *(1) The palace.*

---

[1] *Ad Tit.* i. 5 (VII. p. 695).

[2] On Ephes. iv. 11. But he is hardly consistent with himself. On 1 Tim. iii. 8 he recognises the identity less distinctly; on Phil. i. 1 (see above, p. 97, note) he ignores it; while on Tit. i. 7 he passes over the subject without a word.

[3] Chrysostom on Phil. i. 1 (on 1 Tim. iii. 8, Tit. i. 7, he is not so clear); Pelagius on Phil. i. 1, 1 Tim. iii. 12, Tit. i. 7;

Theodore of Mopsuestia on Phil. i. 1, Tit. i. 7, and especially on 1 Tim. iii. (where the matter is fully discussed); Theodoret on Phil. i. 1, 1 Tim. iii. 1 sq., Tit. i. 7, following closely in the steps of Theodore. See also Ammonius on Acts xx. 28 in Cramer's *Catena*, p. 337.

[4] Later authorities are given in Gieseler *Kirchengesch.* I. pp. 105, 106.

[5] In Raban. Maur. *Op.* VI. p. 482 A.

'What we are in the habit of calling the palace, he calls the prætorium. Theodoret giving the same meaning adds, 'It is probable that the palace was so called at that time[1].' This interpretation, which has the advantage of illustrating the reference to 'Cæsar's household' at the close of the epistle, is thus ably advocated by Dean Merivale[2]; "In the provinces the emperor was known, not as Princeps, but as Imperator. In Judæa, governed more immediately by him through the imperial procurators, he would be more exclusively regarded as a military chief. The soldier, to whom the Apostle was attached with a chain, would speak of him as his general.. When Paul asked the centurion in charge of him, 'Where shall I be confined at Rome?', the answer would be, 'In the prætorium' or the quarters of the general. When led, as perhaps he was, before the emperor's tribunal, if he asked the attending guard, 'Where am I?', again they would reply, 'In the prætorium.' The emperor was protected in his palace by a body-guard, lodged in its courts and standing sentry at its gates; and accordingly they received the name of prætorians."

**Objection to this meaning.** It is hardly probable however that in the early ages of the empire the feelings of Roman citizens would be thus outraged by the adoption of a term which implied that they were under a military despotism. In the days of the republic the consuls were required to lay down their 'imperium' without the walls and to appear in the city as civilians. And under the early Cæsars the fiction of the republic was carefully guarded, though the reality had ceased to exist. If it be urged that the name was confined to the soldiers (as Dean Merivale seems to suggest), it is difficult to conceive why St Paul after several months' residence at least in Rome, during which he must have mixed with various classes of men, should have singled out this exceptional term, especially when writing to distant correspondents.

**No instance of this sense.** But whatever may be said of the *a priori* probability, it is a fatal objection that not a single instance of this usage has been produced. The language of the Greek fathers quoted above shows that though they *assumed* the word must have had this meaning at an earlier date, it was certainly not so when they wrote. While 'prætorium' is a frequent designation of splendid villas, whether of the emperors or others, away from Rome, the imperial residence on the Palatine is not once so called[3]. Indeed the word seems to have suggested to a Roman the idea of a *country* seat. Thus when Tacitus and Suetonius are relating the same event, the one uses 'villa,' the other 'prætorium,' to describe the scene of the occurrence[4]. Hence Forcellini with right appreciation defines the word, 'ædes elegantiores ornatioresque *in agris* exstructæ et villa quæque

---

[1] His words are τὰ βασίλεια γὰρ πραιτώριον προσηγόρευσεν· εἰκὸς δὲ ὅτι καὶ οὕτως κατ' ἐκεῖνον ὠνομάζετο τὸν καιρόν· ἀρχὴν γὰρ εἶχεν ἡ ῥωμαϊκὴ δυναστεία.

[2] *History of the Romans* VI. p. 268.

[3] In Phlegon *de Longæv.* § 4 ἐκ Σαβίνων ἀπὸ πραιτωρίου παλλαντιανοῦ, a palace of the emperor in the Sabine territory is meant. Παλλαντιανὸς here is explained 'imperial' 'Cæsarean' by Perizonius *de Prætor.* p. 252, as if connected with παλάτιον (comp. Dion Cass. liii. 16 quoted above in the text); but, like *horti Pallantiani*, the name is doubtless derived from its former owner Pallas; see Friedländer *Sittengesch. Roms* I. p. 98.

[4] Tac. *Ann.* iv. 59, Suet. *Tiber.* 39.

minime rustica vel villæ pars nobilior et cultior ubi domini, *rusticari cum libet*, morantur.' In Rome itself a 'prætorium' would not have been tolerated[1].

(2) The 'prætorium' is not the imperial palace itself, but the prætorian barracks attached thereto. This interpretation is open to many of the objections urged against the former. Moreover it is equally destitute of authority. In a passage of Dion Cassius indeed (liii. 16) there seems to be mention of a 'prætorium' on the Palatine; καλεῖται δὲ τὰ βασίλεια παλάτιον...ὅτι ἔν τε τῷ παλατίῳ ὁ Καῖσαρ ᾤκει καὶ ἐκεῖ τὸ στρατήγιον εἶχε. Here στρατήγιον is doubtless a rendering of the Latin 'prætorium'; but the sense is hardly local. As this passage stands alone, the words would appear to mean simply that the emperor was surrounded by his body-guards and kept state as a military commander. This language, though it would probably have been avoided by a contemporary, was not in itself inappropriate when applied to Augustus, of whom Dion is speaking, before the prætorian camp was built, and when the barracks attached to the palace were still the head-quarters of the prætorian guards[2]. At all events, if 'prætorium' ever had this sense, it can hardly have been meant by St Paul here; for the expression ' *throughout* the prætorium,' in connexion with the context, would be wholly out of place in reference to a space so limited.

(3) The great camp of the prætorian soldiers is so designated. Tiberius concentrated the cohorts previously scattered up and down the city (Tac. *Ann.* iv. 2) and established them outside the Colline gate at the North East of the city in a permanent camp, whose ramparts can be traced at the present day, being embedded in the later walls of Aurelian. If 'prætorium' here has a local sense, no other place could be so fitly designated; for as this camp was without the walls, the term so applied would give no offence. But this meaning again lacks external support. It might indeed be argued that as the Greek equivalent to 'præfectus prætorio' is στρατοπεδάρχης, 'the commander of the camp,' the camp itself would be designated 'prætorium'; but, as a question of fact, no decisive instance of this sense is produced. The camp is sometimes called 'castra prætoria' (Plin. *N. H.* iii. 9), sometimes 'castra prætorianorum' (Tac. *Hist.* i. 3), once at least 'castra prætori' (i.e. prætorii, Orell. *Inscr.* 21); but never 'prætorium.'

As all attempts to give a local sense to 'prætorium' thus fail for want of evidence, it remains to discover some other suitable meaning, which is not open to this objection.

(4) Prætorium signifies not a place, but a body of men. It is used for instance of a council of war, the officers who met in the general's tent: e.g. Liv. xxvi. 15, xxx. 5. But more frequently it denotes the prætorian

*Side notes:*
(2) The barracks on the Palatine.

(3) The Prætorian camp.

(4) The Prætorian guards.

---

[1] On the other hand away from Rome the residence of the emperor's representative is frequently so called; e.g. at Cologne (Orell. 3297), at Munda (*ib.* 3303).

[2] See Perizonius p. 230. It must be remembered that Dion Cassius wrote about two centuries after the event. For this sense of στρατήγιον comp. Tac. *Ann.* iii. 33 'duorum egressus coli, duo esse prætoria,' where a complaint is made of the pomp maintained by the wives of provincial governors.

regiments, the imperial guards. This in fact is the common use of the term. It is found in 'castra prætorii' already quoted and probably also in 'præfectus prætorio.' It occurs also in such phrases as 'veteranus ex prætorio' (Tac. *Hist.* ii. 11, Suet. *Nero* 9, Orell. *Inscr.* 123), 'missus ex prætorio' (Orell. no. 1644, note), 'lectus in prætorio' (Orell. no. 941; comp. nos. 3589, 6806, 6817). A guardsman was said to serve 'in prætorio,' a soldier of the line 'in legione' (Orell. nos. 3547, 5286, 5291). If St Paul seeing a new face among his guards asked how he came to be there, the answer would be 'I have been promoted to the prætorium'; if he enquired after an old face which he missed, he might be told 'He has been discharged from the prætorium.' In this sense and this alone can it be safely affirmed that he would hear the word 'prætorium' used daily. The following passages will further illustrate this meaning: Plin. *N. H.* xxv. 2 'Nuper cujusdam militantis in prætorio mater vidit in quiete...in Lacetania res gerebatur, Hispaniæ proxima parte': Tac. *Hist.* i. 20 'Exauctorati per eos dies tribuni, e prætorio Antonius Taurus et Antonius Naso, ex urbanis cohortibus Æmilius Pacensis, e vigiliis Julius Fronto'; *ib.* iv. 46 'Militiam et stipendia orant...igitur in prætorium accepti': Joseph. *Ant.* xix. 3. 1 οἱ περὶ τὸ στρατηγικὸν καλούμενον ὅπερ ἐστὶ τῆς στρατιᾶς καθαρώτατον, i.e. 'the prætorium, which is the flower of the army': Dosith. *Hadr. Sent.* § 2 αἰτοῦντός τινος ἵνα στρατεύηται, Ἀνδριανὸς εἶπεν· Ποῦ θέλεις στρατεύεσθαι; ἐκείνου λέγοντος Εἰς τὸ π ρ α ι τ ώ ρ ι ο ν, Ἀδριανὸς ἐξήτασεν Ποῖον μῆκος ἔχεις; λέγοντος ἐκείνου Πέντε πόδας καὶ ἥμισυ, Ἀδριανὸς εἶπεν Ἐν τοσούτῳ εἰς τὴν πολιτικὴν στρατεύου, καὶ ἐὰν καλὸς στρατιώτης ἔσῃ τρίτῳ ὀψωνίῳ δυνήσῃ εἰς τὸ π ρ α ι τ ώ ρ ι ο ν μεταβῆναι'; *Mission Archéol. de Macédoine* no. 130 (p. 325) Τι. Κλαύδιον οὐετρανὸν στρατευσάμενον ἐν π ρ α ι τ ω ρ ί ῳ, no. 131 (p. 326) Τι. Κλαύδιος Ῥοῦφος οὐετρανὸς ἐκ π ρ α ι τ ω ρ ί ο υ.

This sense to be adopted.   This sense is in all respects appropriate. It forms a fit introduction to the words καὶ τοῖς λοιποῖς πᾶσιν which follow. It is explained by St Paul's position as an imperial prisoner in charge of the prefect of the prætorians. And lastly it avoids any conflict with St Luke's statement that the Apostle dwelt in 'his own hired house[2]': for it is silent about the locality.

---

[1] See also Plin. *N. H.* vii. 19, Orell. no. 3477. On the meaning of the word prætorium see especially 'Perizonii cum Hubero *Disquisitio de Prætorio*, etc. (Franeq. 1690),' a 12mo volume containing more than 900 pages. Huber maintained that by 'prætorium' in Phil. i. 13 must be understood the palace or the audience-chamber therein. Perizonius, whose refutation of his adversary is complete, explained it of the prætorian cohorts or the prætorian camp. If he had omitted this second alternative, his work would in my judgment have been entirely satisfactory: though I must confess to having once taken it to mean the camp; *Journal of Class. and Sacr. Phil.* no. x. p. 58. Al-

most all recent commentators on the Philippians occupy themselves in discussing the possible *local* senses of 'prætorium,' barely, if at all, alluding to the only meaning which is really well supported and meets all the requirements of the case. Of recent writers on St Paul two only, so far as I have noticed, Bleek (*Einl. in das N. T.* p. 433) and apparently Ewald (*Sendschreiben etc.* p. 441), take what seems to be the correct view, but even they do not explain their reasons. On this account I have entered into the question more fully than its absolute importance deserves.

[2] This difficulty indeed is very slight, if it be interpreted of the camp; for the camp was large and might perhaps have

The following account, relating to a contemporary of St Paul, who Account of<br>Agrippa. also spent some time in Rome under military custody, is abridged from Josephus (*Ant.* xviii. 6. 5 sq.). As throwing light on the condition of a prisoner under such circumstances, it may fitly close this investigation.

Herod Agrippa, then a young man and resident in Rome, contracted an intimate friendship with Caius. On one occasion, when the two were driving together, Agrippa was overheard praying that Tiberius would resign the empire to make way for his friend who was 'in all respects more worthy.' Some time after, the charioteer, having been dismissed by Agrippa and bearing a grudge against him, reported his words to Tiberius. So Agrippa was consigned to Macro, the prefect of the prætorians, to be His con-<br>finement. put in chains. Hereupon Antonia, the sister-in-law of Tiberius, who had a kindly feeling for the Jewish prince as a friend of her grandson Caius,

contained houses or rooms rented by prisoners: see above, p. 9 sq. But if the palace or the Palatine barracks were meant, St Luke's statement would not be so easily explained. Wieseler indeed (*Chronol.* p. 403, note 3), who pronounces in favour of the Palatine barracks, adduces the instances of Drusus and Agrippa in support of his view. But both cases break down on examination. (1) Drusus, it is true, was imprisoned in the palace; Tac. *Ann.* vi. 23, Suet. *Tiber.* 54. But this is no parallel to the case of St Paul. Drusus, as a member of the imperial family, would naturally be confined within the precincts of the imperial residence. Moreover, as Tiberius had designs on his nephew's life, secresy was absolutely necessary for his plans. Nor indeed could one, who might at any moment become the focus of a revolution, be safely entrusted to the keeping of the camp away from the emperor's personal cognisance. (2) Wieseler misunderstands the incidents relating to Agrippa, whose imprisonment is wholly unconnected with the Palatine. When Tiberius ordered him to be put under arrest, he was at the emperor's Tusculan villa (§ 6). From thence he was conveyed to the camp, where we find him still confined at the accession of Caius, which led to his removal and release (§ 10). Wieseler's mistake is twofold. *First;* he explains τοῦ βασιλείου as referring to the palace *at Rome;* though Josephus lays the scene of the arrest at Tusculanum (Τιβέριος ἐκ τῶν Καπρεῶν εἰς Τουσκουλανὸν παραγί-νεται). For the existence of such palaces

at Tusculum see Strabo v. p. 239 δεχό-μενος βασιλείων κατασκευὰς ἐκπρεπεστά-τας. Secondly; he boldly translates στρα-τόπεδον by 'prætorium,' understanding thereby the Palatine barracks; though these barracks were in no sense a camp and were never so called. Building upon these two false suppositions, he makes the Palatine the scene of both his arrest and his imprisonment. Caractacus also, like Agrippa, appears to have been imprisoned in the prætorian camp, Tac. *Ann.* xii. 36. And, if these royal captives were not retained on the Palatine, it is very improbable that an exception should be made in the case of a humble prisoner like St Paul, whose case would not appear to differ from many hundreds likewise awaiting the decision of Cæsar.

It will appear from the account relating to Agrippa, given in the text, that this prince was confined in the camp during the reign of Tiberius; but that on the accession of Caius he was removed to *a house of his own,* though *still under military custody.* The notices in the Acts suggest that St Paul's captivity resembled this latter condition of Agrippa, and that he did not reside actually within the camp. A Roman tradition is perhaps preserved in the notice of the Roman Hilary (Ambrosiaster) in his prologue to the Ephesians; 'In custodia sub fidejussore intelligitur degisse manens *extra castra in conductu suo.*' In Acts xxviii. 16 some MSS (Greek and Latin) read ἔξω τῆς παρεμβολῆς, 'extra castra.'

grieving at his misfortune, and yet not daring to intercede with the emperor, spoke to Macro on his behalf. Her entreaties prevailed. The prefect took care that the soldiers appointed to guard him should not be over severe, and that the centurion to whom he was bound should be a man of humane disposition. He was permitted to take a bath every day ; free access was granted to his freedmen and his friends; and other indulgences were allowed him. Accordingly his friend Silas and his freedmen, Marsyas and Stœcheus, were constant in their attendance: they brought him food that was palatable to him; they smuggled in clothes under pretence of selling them; they made his bed every night with the aid of the soldiers, who had received orders to this effect from Macro.

**Death of Tiberius.** In this way six months rolled by and Tiberius died. On hearing of the emperor's death, Marsyas ran in hot haste to Agrippa to tell him the good news. He found the prince on the threshold, going out to the baths, and making signs to him said in Hebrew, 'The lion's dead.' The centurion in command noticed the hurry of the messenger and the satisfaction with which his words were received. His curiosity was excited. At first an evasive answer was returned to his question; but as the man had been friendly disposed, Agrippa at length told him. The centurion shared his prisoner's joy, unfastened his chain, and served up dinner to him. But while they sat at table, and the wine was flowing freely, contrary tidings arrived. Tiberius was alive and would return to Rome in a few days. The centurion who had committed himself so grievously was furious at this announcement. He rudely pushed Agrippa off the couch, and threatened him with the loss of his head, as a penalty for his lying report. Agrippa was again put in chains, and the rigour of his confinement increased. So he passed the night in great discomfort. But the next day the report of the emperor's death was confirmed. And soon after a letter arrived from Caius to Piso the prefect of the city, directing the removal of Agrippa from the camp to the house where he had lived before he was imprisoned.

**Release of Agrippa.** This relieved and reassured him. Though he was still guarded and watched, yet less restraint was put upon his movements (φυλακὴ μὲν καὶ τήρησις ἦν, μετὰ μέντοι ἀνέσεως τῆς εἰς τὴν δίαιταν). When the new emperor arrived in Rome, his first impulse was to release Agrippa at once: but Antonia represented to him that this indecent haste would be regarded as an outrage on his predecessor's memory. So after waiting a few days to save appearances, he sent for Agrippa, placed the royal diadem on his head, gave him the tetrarchies of Philip and Lysanias, and removing his iron fetter (ἀλύσει) invested him with a golden chain of the same weight.

²⁷Μόνον ἀξίως τοῦ εὐαγγελίου τοῦ Χριστοῦ πολιτεύεσθε, ἵνα εἴτε ἐλθὼν καὶ ἰδὼν ὑμᾶς εἴτε ἀπὼν ἀκούω
τὰ περὶ ὑμῶν ὅτι στήκετε ἐν ἑνὶ πνεύματι, μιᾷ ψυχῇ

27. ἀπὼν ἀκούσω τὰ περὶ ὑμῶν.

27—30. 'But under all circumstances do your duty as good citizens of a heavenly kingdom; act worthily of the Gospel of Christ. So that whether I come among you and see with my own eyes, or stay away and obtain tidings from others, I may learn that you maintain your ground bravely and resolutely, acting by one inspiration; that with united aims and interests you are fighting all in the ranks of the Faith on the side of the Gospel; and that no assault of your antagonists makes you waver: for this will be a sure omen to them of utter defeat, to you of life and safety: an omen, I say, sent by God Himself; for it is His grace, His privilege bestowed upon you, that for Christ—yea, that ye should not only believe on Him, but also should suffer for Him. For ye have entered the same lists, ye are engaged in the same struggle, in which you saw me contending then at Philippi, in which you hear of my contending now in Rome.'

27. Μόνον] 'Only,' i.e. 'whatever may happen, whether I visit you again or visit you not': see Gal. ii. 10, v. 13, vi. 12, 2 Thess. ii. 7.

πολιτεύεσθε] 'perform your duties as citizens.' The metaphor of the heavenly citizenship occurs again, iii. 20 ἡμῶν τὸ πολίτευμα ἐν οὐρανοῖς ὑπάρχει, and Ephes. ii. 19 συνπολῖται τῶν ἁγίων. See the note on iii. 20. It was natural that, dwelling in the metropolis of the empire, St Paul should use this illustration. The metaphor moreover would speak forcibly to his correspondents; for Philippi was a Roman colony, and the Apostle had himself obtained satisfaction, while in this place, by declaring himself a Roman citizen: Acts xvi. 12, 37, 38. Though the word

πολιτεύεσθαι is used very loosely at a later date, at this time it seems always to refer to public duties devolving on a man as a member of a body: so Acts xxiii. 1 πάσῃ συνειδήσει ἀγαθῇ πεπολίτευμαι τῷ Θεῷ κ.τ.λ., where St Paul had been accused of violating the laws and customs of the people and so subverting the theocratic constitution; Joseph. Vit. § 2 ἠρξάμην πολιτεύεσθαι τῇ Φαρισαίων αἱρέσει κατακολουθῶν, for the Pharisees were a political as well as a religious party. The opposite to πολιτεύεσθαι is ἰδιωτεύειν, e.g. Æschin. Timarch. p. 27.

The phrase ἀξίως πολιτεύεσθαι is adopted in Clem. Rom. § 21. Polycarp also, writing to these same Philippians (§ 5), combines it very happily with another expression in St Paul (2 Tim. ii. 12), ἐὰν πολιτευσώμεθα ἀξίως αὐτοῦ, καὶ συμβασιλεύσομεν αὐτῷ, 'If we perform our duties under Him as simple citizens, He will promote us to a share of His sovereignty.'

ἵνα εἴτε ἐλθὼν κ.τ.λ.] The sentence is somewhat irregular. It would have run more smoothly ἵνα, εἴτε ἐλθὼν καὶ ἰδών, εἴτε ἀπὼν καὶ ἀκούων, μάθω τὰ περὶ ὑμῶν. For εἴτε, εἴτε, with participles, comp. e.g. 2 Cor. v. 9 εἴτε ἐνδημοῦντες εἴτε ἐκδημοῦντες. On this plan the sentence is begun: but in the second clause the symmetry is lost and the participle (ἀκούων) exchanged for a finite verb (ἀκούω), so that in place of a general word applying to both participial clauses (e.g. μάθω) is substituted a special one (ἀκούω) referring to the second clause only.

στήκετε] 'stand firm,' 'hold your ground.' For the metaphor see Ephes. vi. 13 ἵνα δυνηθῆτε ἀντιστῆναι ἐν τῇ ἡμέρᾳ τῇ πονηρᾷ, καὶ ἅπαντα κατεργασάμενοι στῆναι. στῆτε οὖν, περιζωσά

συναθλοῦντες τῇ πίστει τοῦ εὐαγγελίου, ²⁸καὶ μὴ πτυρόμενοι ἐν μηδενὶ ὑπὸ τῶν ἀντικειμένων· ἥτις ἐστὶν αὐτοῖς ἔνδειξις ἀπωλείας, ὑμῶν δὲ σωτηρίας, καὶ τοῦτο
ἀπὸ Θεοῦ· ²⁹ὅτι ὑμῖν ἐχαρίσθη τὸ ὑπὲρ Χριστοῦ, οὐ

μενοι κ.τ.λ. In the form στήκω the
idea of *firmness* or *uprightness* is
prominent : see the note on Gal. v. 1.
In a later passage the Apostle compares the Christian life to the Greek
stadium (iii. 14). Here the metaphor
seems to be drawn rather from the
combats of the Roman amphitheatre.
Like criminals or captives, the believers are condemned to fight for their
lives : against them are arrayed the
ranks of worldliness and sin : only unflinching courage and steady combination can win the victory against such
odds: comp. 1 Cor. iv. 9 ὁ Θεὸς ἡμᾶς
τοὺς ἀποστόλους ἐσχάτους ἀπέδειξεν ὡς
ἐπιθανατίους, ὅτι θέατρον ἐγενήθημεν
τῷ κόσμῳ κ.τ.λ.
ἐνὶ πνεύματι] differs from μιᾷ ψυχῇ.
The spirit, the principle of the higher
life, is distinguished from the soul, the
seat of the affections, passions, etc.
For this distinction of πνεῦμα and
ψυχή see the notes on 1 Thess. v. 23.
For ἐν πνεῦμα comp. Ephes. iv. 4,
Clem. Rom. 46, Hermas *Sim.* ix. 13.
συναθλοῦντες τῇ πίστει] '*striving in
concert with the faith.*' Comp. *Mart.
Ign.* § 3 παρεκάλει συναθλεῖν τῇ αὐτοῦ
προθέσει, Ignat. *Polyc.* § 6 συγκοπιᾶτε
ἀλλήλοις, συναθλεῖτε. Thus ἡ πίστις is
here objective, 'the faith,' 'the teaching of the Gospel'; see the notes on
Gal. iii. 23. For this idea of association
with the faith, thus personified and
regarded as a moral agent, compare
1 Cor. xiii. 6 συγχαίρει δὲ τῇ ἀληθείᾳ,
2 Tim. i. 8 συγκακοπάθησον τῷ εὐαγγελίῳ, 3 Joh. 8 συνεργοὶ γινώμεθα τῇ ἀληθείᾳ. The other construction, which de-
taches τῇ πίστει from the preposition in
συναθλοῦντες and translates it '*for* the
faith,' seems harsh and improbable.
28.   μὴ πτυρόμενοι] '*not blenching,*'

'*not startled*': comp. *Clem. Hom.* ii.
39 πτύραντες ἀμαθεῖς ὄχλους, M. Anton.
viii. 45, Polycr. in Euseb. *H. E.* v. 24.
The metaphor is from a timid horse
(πτοεῖν); comp. Plut. *Mor.* p. 800 ο
μήτε ὄψει μήτε φωνῇ πτυρόμενος ὥσπερ
θηρίον ὕποπτον, *Vit. Fab.* 3 ἐντρόμου τοῦ
ἵππου γενομένου καὶ πτυρέντος. Though
apparently not an Attic word, it seems
to have been used in other dialects
from the earliest times, e.g. Hippocr.
*de Morb. Mul.* 1. p. 600 ἢ δεδίσσηται
καὶ πτύρηται.
ἥτις] '*seeing that it,*' i.e. 'your fear-
lessness when menaced with persecution'; by attraction with ἔνδειξις : comp.
Ephes. iii. 13 αἰτοῦμαι μὴ ἐγκακεῖν ἐν
ταῖς θλίψεσίν μου ὑπὲρ ὑμῶν ἥ τις ἐστὶν
δόξα ὑμῶν, and see Winer § xxiv. p.
209. St Paul uses very similar language in writing to the other great
church of Macedonia, 2 Thess. i. 47.
In this sentence the received text
presents two variations: (1) For ἐστὶν
αὐτοῖς it reads αὐτοῖς μέν ἐστιν : (2)
For ὑμῶν it has ὑμῖν. These are obviously corrections for the sake of
balancing the clauses and bringing out
the contrast.
τοῦτο ἀπὸ Θεοῦ] referring to ἔνδειξις.
It is a direct indication from God.
The Christian gladiator does not anxi-
ously await the signal of life or death
from the fickle crowd (Juv. *Sat.* iii.
36 'Munera nunc edunt et verso pollice
vulgi quem libet occidunt populariter').
The great ἀγωνοθέτης Himself has
given him a sure token of deliverance.
29.   ἐχαρίσθη] 'God has granted you
the high privilege of suffering for
Christ; this is the surest sign, that
He looks upon you with favour.' See
the note on i. 7.
τὸ ὑπὲρ Χριστοῦ] i.e. πάσχειν. The

μόνον τὸ εἰς αὐτὸν πιστεύειν, ἀλλὰ καὶ τὸ ὑπὲρ αὐτοῦ
πάσχειν· ³⁰τὸν αὐτὸν ἀγῶνα ἔχοντες οἷον εἴδετε ἐν ἐμοὶ
καὶ νῦν ἀκούετε ἐν ἐμοί.

II.    ¹Εἴ τις οὖν παράκλησις ἐν Χριστῷ, εἴ τι παρα-

sentence is suspended by the insertion
of the after-thought οὐ μόνον τὸ εἰς
αὐτὸν πιστεύειν, and resumed in τὸ
ὑπὲρ αὐτοῦ πάσχειν.

30. ἀγῶνα] 'a gladiatorial or athletic contest,' as 1 Tim. vi. 12, 2 Tim.
iv. 7 ; compare συναθλοῦντες, ver. 27.

ἔχοντες] It is difficult to say whether
this word should be taken (1) with
στήκετε συναθλοῦντες καὶ μὴ πτυρόμενοι,
the intermediate words being a parenthesis ; or (2) with ὑμῖν ἐχαρίσθη κ.τ.λ.
as an irregular nominative, of which
many instances occur in St Paul, e.g.
Col. iii. 16, Ephes. iii. 18, iv. 2 : see
Winer § lxiii. p. 716. As στήκετε is
so far distant, the latter construction
seems more probable.

εἴδετε] 'ye saw'; for the Apostle
suffered persecution at Philippi itself;
see Acts xvi. 19 sq., 1 Thess. ii. 2,
in which latter passage he uses the
same word as here, ἐν πολλῷ ἀγῶνι.
See the introduction, pp. 58, 60.

II. 1. 'If then your experiences in
Christ appeal to you with any force, if
love exerts any persuasive power upon
you, if your fellowship in the Spirit is
a living reality, if you have any affectionate yearnings of heart, any tender
feelings of compassion, listen and obey.
You have given me joy hitherto. Now
fill my cup of gladness to overflowing.
Live in unity among yourselves, animated by an equal and mutual love,
knit together in all your sympathies
and affections, united in all your
thoughts and aims. Do nothing to
promote the ends of party faction, nothing to gratify your own personal
vanity : but be humble-minded and
esteem your neighbours more highly
than yourselves. Let not every man regard his own wants, his own interests; but let him consult also the

interests and the wants of others.'

The Apostle here appeals to the
Philippians, by all their deepest experiences as Christians and all their
noblest impulses as men, to preserve
peace and concord. Of the four grounds
of appeal, the first and third (παρά
κλησις ἐν Χριστῷ, κοινωνία πνεύματος)
are objective, the external principles of
love and harmony ; while the second
and fourth (παραμύθιον ἀγάπης, σπλάγ
χνα καὶ οἰκτιρμοί) are subjective, the inward feelings inspired thereby. The
form of the appeal has been illustrated from Virgil Æn. i. 603 'Si qua
pios respectant numina, si quid usquam justitiæ est, et mens sibi conscia
recti, etc.'

παράκλησις ἐν Χριστῷ] i.e. 'If your
life in Christ, your knowledge of Christ,
speaks to your hearts with a persuasive eloquence.' The subject of the
sentence, the exhortation to unity, requires that παράκλησις should be taken
here to mean not 'consolation' but
'exhortation.' See the next note.

παραμύθιον] 'incentive, encouragement,' not 'comfort,' as the word more
commonly means. For this sense of
παραμύθιον, 'a motive of persuasion or
dissuasion,' see Plat. Legg. vi. p. 773 E,
ix. p. 880 A ἐὰν μέν τις τοιούτοις παρα
μυθίοις εὐπειθὴς γίγνηται, εὐήνιος ἂν εἴη,
Euthyd. p. 272 B. This, which is the
original meaning of the word, appears
still more frequently in παραμυθία, πα
ραμυθεῖσθαι. For the conjunction of
παράκλησις, παραμύθιον, in the sense in
which they are here used, see 1 Thess.
ii. 11 παρακαλοῦντες ὑμᾶς καὶ παραμυ
θούμενοι καὶ μαρτυρόμενοι (with the
note), and perhaps 1 Cor. xiv. 3.

εἴ τις κοινωνία κ.τ.λ.] 'If communion
with the Spirit of love is not a mere
idle name, but a real thing.' Com

μύθιον ἀγάπης, εἴ τις κοινωνία πνεύματος, εἴ τις σπλάγχνα καὶ οἰκτιρμοί, ²πληρώσατέ μου τὴν χαράν, ἵνα τὸ
αὐτὸ φρονῆτε, τὴν αὐτὴν ἀγάπην ἔχοντες, σύνψυχοι,
τὸ ἓν φρονοῦντες· ³μηδὲν κατ᾽ ἐριθείαν μηδὲ κατὰ κενο-

pare the benediction in 2 Cor. xiii. 13.

εἴ τις σπλάγχνα κ.τ.λ.] The ancient copies are unanimous in favour of this reading (the only important exception being Clem. Alex. Strom. vi. p. 604 Potter, where τινα is perhaps a later correction); and we cannot therefore look upon τινα as anything more than an arbitrary, though very obvious, emendation in the later MSS where it occurs. Nevertheless it seems hardly possible that St Paul could have intended so to write. If τις is retained, it can only be explained by the eager impetuosity with which the Apostle dictated the letter, the εἴ τις of the preceding clause being repeated, and then by a sudden impulse σπλάγχνα καὶ οἰκτιρμοὶ being substituted for some possible masculine or feminine substantive. Some few MSS of no great authority read in like manner εἴ τις παραμύθιον. But it seems more probable that εἴ τις is an error of some early transcriber, perhaps of the original amanuensis himself, for εἴ τινα or εἴ τι. If εἴ τι were intended, the error would be nothing more than an accidental repetition of the first letter in σπλάγχνα. Under any circumstances, the reading εἴ τις is a valuable testimony to the scrupulous fidelity of the early transcribers, who copied the text as they found it, even when it contained readings so manifestly difficult. See the note on ἦλθεν in Gal. ii. 12.

σπλάγχνα] See the note on i. 8. By σπλάγχνα is signified the abode of tender feelings, by οἰκτιρμοὶ the manifestation of these in compassionate yearnings and actions: comp. Col. iii. 12 σπλάγχνα οἰκτιρμοῦ.

2. πληρώσατε] 'complete, as you have begun.' He has already express-

ed his joy at their faith and love, i. 4, 9. Compare Joh. iii. 29 αὕτη οὖν ἡ χαρὰ ἡ ἐμὴ πεπλήρωται.

ἵνα] 'so as to,' see the note on i. 9.

τὸ αὐτὸ φρονῆτε] a general expression of accordance, which is defined and enforced by the three following clauses. It is the concord not of a common hatred, but of a common love (τὴν αὐτὴν ἀγάπην ἔχοντες). It manifests itself in a complete harmony of the feelings and affections (σύνψυχοι). It produces an entire unison of thought and directs it to one end (τὸ ἓν φρονοῦντες). The redundancy of expression is a measure of the Apostle's earnestness: βαβαί, says Chrysostom, ποσάκις τὸ αὐτὸ λέγει ἀπὸ διαθέσεως πολλῆς. See the introduction, p. 67.

τὸ ἓν φρονοῦντες] a stronger expression than the foregoing τὸ αὐτὸ φρονῆτε, from which it does not otherwise differ. The two are sometimes combined, e.g. Aristid. de Conc. Rhod. p. 569, ἓν καὶ ταὐτὸν φρονοῦντες, comp. Polyb. v. 104. 1 λέγοντες ἓν καὶ ταὐτὸ πάντες καὶ συμπλέκοντες τὰς χεῖρας, quoted by Wetstein. So too the Latin 'unum atque idem sentire.' The definite article before ἓν gives additional strength to the expression.

3. μηδέν] 'do nothing.' The verb is suppressed, as is very frequently the case in imperative sentences after μή, e.g. Gal. v. 13 (see the note there): comp. Klotz on Devar. II. p. 669. This construction is more natural and more forcible than the understanding φρονοῦντες with μηδὲν from the preceding clause.

κατ᾽ ἐριθείαν] So Ignat. Philad. 8 μηδὲν κατ᾽ ἐριθείαν πράσσειν. See the introduction, p. 75. On the meaning of ἐριθεία, 'factiousness, party-spirit,' see the note on Gal. v. 20. The two

δοξίαν, ἀλλὰ τῇ ταπεινοφροσύνῃ ἀλλήλους ἡγούμενοι
ὑπερέχοντας ἑαυτῶν, ⁴μὴ τὰ ἑαυτῶν ἕκαστοι σκοποῦντες, ἀλλὰ καὶ τὰ ἑτέρων ἕκαστοι.

4, 5.   μὴ τὰ ἑαυτῶν ἕκαστος σκοποῦντες ἀλλὰ καὶ τὰ ἑτέρων. ῞Εκαστοι τοῦτο
φρονεῖτε κ.τ.λ.

impediments to an universal, diffusive, unconditional charity are the exaltation of party and the exaltation of self. Both these are condemned here; the first in κατ' ἐριθείαν, the second in κατὰ κενοδοξίαν. The μηδὲ κατὰ κενοδοξίαν of the older MSS distinguishes and emphasizes the two false motives more strongly than the ἢ κενοδοξίαν of the received text.

κενοδοξίαν] 'vain-glory, personal vanity.' See the note on Gal. v. 26.

τῇ ταπεινοφροσύνῃ] 'your lowliness of mind.' Though a common word in the New Testament, ταπεινοφροσύνη seems not to occur earlier. Even the adjective ταπεινόφρων and the verb ταπεινοφρονεῖν, though occurring once each in the LXX (Prov. xxix. 23, Ps. cxxx. 2), appear not to be found in classical Greek before the Christian era. In heathen writers indeed ταπεινὸς has almost always a bad meaning, 'grovelling,' 'abject.' In Aristotle (?) for instance (Eth. Eudem. iii. 3) ταπεινὸς is associated with ἀνδραποδώδης; in Plato (Legg. iv. p. 774 c) with ἀνελεύθερος; in Arrian (Epict. i. 3) with ἀγεννής. To this however some few exceptions are found, especially in Plato and the Platonists; see Neander Church Hist. I. p. 26 (Eng. Tr.). On the other hand, St Paul once uses ταπεινοφροσύνη in disparagement, Col. ii. 18. It was one great result of the life of Christ (on which St Paul dwells here) to raise 'humility' to its proper level; and, if not fresh coined for this purpose, the word ταπεινοφροσύνη now first became current through the influence of Christian ethics. On its moral and religious significance see Neander Planting I. p. 483 (Eng. Tr.).

ἀλλήλους κ.τ.λ.] i.e. 'each thinking

the other better.' See esp. Rom. xii. 10 τῇ τιμῇ ἀλλήλους προηγούμενοι.

4, 5. These verses exhibit several various readings. The received text has σκοπεῖτε for σκοποῦντες, and φρονείσθω for φρονεῖτε, also inserting γὰρ after τοῦτο. All these variations may be at once dismissed, as they have not sufficient support and are evident alterations to relieve the grammar of the sentence. But others still remain, where it is more difficult to decide. In ver. 4, at the first occurrence of the word, there is about equal authority for ἕκαστος and ἕκαστοι; at its second occurrence, the weight of evidence is very decidedly in favour of ἕκαστοι as against ἕκαστος. On the grammar it should be remarked; (1) That the plural of ἕκαστος, though common elsewhere, does not occur again either in the New Testament (for in Rev. vi. 11 it is certainly a false reading) or, as would appear, in the LXX. (2) That we should expect either τὰ ἑαυτῶν ἕκαστοι or τὰ ἑαυτοῦ ἕκαστος; but this consideration is not very weighty, for irregularities sometimes occur; and as τὰ ἑαυτῶν precedes ἕκαστος, the latter might be looked upon as an afterthought inserted parenthetically. (3) That St Paul can hardly have written ἕκαστος in the first clause and ἕκαστοι in the second, intending the clauses as correlative; and therefore if we retain ἕκαστος in the first case, it will be necessary to detach the following ἕκαστοι, and join it on with the next sentence. This view seems to have been taken by some older expositors and translators; and I have given it as an alternative reading. Whether the probabilities (independently of the evidence) are in favour of ἕκαστος or ἕκα-

⁵Τοῦτο φρονεῖτε ἐν ὑμῖν, ὃ καὶ ἐν Χριστῷ Ἰησοῦ,
⁶ὃς ἐν μορφῇ Θεοῦ ὑπάρχων οὐχ ἁρπαγμὸν ἡγήσατο τὸ

στοι in the first case, it is difficult to
say. The plural ἕκαστοι would mean
'each *and all.*'

σκοποῦντες] '*regarding as your aim*
(σκοπός).' For this sense of σκοπεῖν
τὸ ἑαυτοῦ, 'to consult one's own interests,' comp. Eur. *El.* 1114, Thuc. vi.
12, and other passages quoted by Wetstein. For other instances of participles used where imperatives might
have been expected, see Rom. xii. 9,
Heb. xiii. 5.

ἀλλὰ καί] '*but also,*' i.e. let them
look *beyond* their own interests to those
of others.

ἕκαστοι] for the repetition of the
word compare 1 Cor. vii. 17.

5—11. 'Reflect in your own minds
the mind of Christ Jesus. Be humble,
as He also was humble. Though existing before the worlds in the Eternal
Godhead, yet He did not cling with
avidity to the prerogatives of His
divine majesty, did not ambitiously
display His equality with God; but divested Himself of the glories of heaven,
and took upon Him the nature of a
servant, assuming the likeness of men.
Nor was this all. Having thus appeared among men in the fashion of a
man, He humbled Himself yet more,
and carried out His obedience even to
dying. Nor did He die by a common
death: He was crucified, as the lowest
malefactor is crucified. But as was
His humility, so also was His exaltation. God raised Him to a preeminent height, and gave Him a title and
a dignity far above all dignities and
titles else. For to the name and majesty of Jesus all created things in
heaven and earth and hell shall pay
homage on bended knee; and every
tongue with praise and thanksgiving
shall declare that Jesus Christ is Lord,
and in and for Him shall glorify God
the Father.'

ς. ἐν ὑμῖν] '*in yourselves,*' i.e. 'in

your hearts,' as Matt. iii. 9 μὴ δόξητε
λέγειν ἐν ἑαυτοῖς, ix. 3 εἶπαν ἐν ἑαυτοῖς
(explained by ἐν ταῖς καρδίαις ὑμῶν
which follows), ix. 21 etc. For ὑμῖν,
where the New Testament writers
generally have ἑαυτοῖς and classical
authors ὑμῖν αὐτοῖς, compare Matt. vi.
19 μὴ θησαυρίζετε ὑμῖν θησαυρούς; and
see A. Buttmann, p. 97. These slight
difficulties, together with the irregularity of construction mentioned in the
next note, have doubtless led to the
substitution of φρονείσθω for φρονεῖτε
in the received text.

ὃ καὶ κ.τ.λ.] sc. ἐφρονεῖτο. The regular construction would have been ὃ
καὶ Χριστὸς Ἰησοῦς ἐφρόνει ἐν ἑαυτῷ.

6. ἐν μορφῇ Θεοῦ] '*in the form of
God.*' On the meaning of μορφή and
its distinction from σχῆμα see the detached note at the end of this chapter.
Though μορφή is not the same as φύ
σις or οὐσία, yet the possession of the
μορφή involves participation in the οὐ
σία also: for μορφή implies not the external accidents but the essential attributes. Similar to this, though not so
decisive, are the expressions used
elsewhere of the divinity of the Son,
εἰκὼν τοῦ Θεοῦ 2 Cor. iv. 4, Col. i. 15,
and χαρακτὴρ τῆς ὑποστάσεως τοῦ Θεοῦ
Heb. i. 3. Similar also is the term
which St John has adopted to express
this truth, ὁ Λόγος τοῦ Θεοῦ.

ὑπάρχων] The word denotes 'prior
existence,' but not necessarily 'eternal
existence.' The latter idea however
follows in the present instance from
the conception of the divinity of Christ
which the context supposes. The
phrase ἐν μορφῇ Θεοῦ ὑπάρχων is
thus an exact counterpart to ἐν ἀρχῇ
ἦν ὁ Λόγος καὶ ὁ Λόγος ἦν πρὸς τὸν Θεὸν
κ.τ.λ., John i. 1. The idea corresponding to ὑπάρχων is expressed in other
terms elsewhere; Col. i. 15, 17 πρωτό
τοκος πάσης κτίσεως, αὐτός ἐστιν πρὸ
πάντων, Heb. i. 8, 10, John viii. 58,

εἶναι ἴσα Θεῷ, ⁷ἀλλὰ ἑαυτὸν ἐκένωσεν μορφὴν δούλου

xvii. 24, and Apoc. i. 17, iii. 14.
οὐχ ἁρπαγμὸν ἡγήσατο] 'yet *did not
regard it as a prize*, a treasure to be
clutched and retained at all hazards.'
The more usual form of the word is
ἅρπαγμα, which properly signifies simply 'a piece of plunder,' but especially
with such verbs as ἡγεῖσθαι, ποιεῖσθαι,
νομίζειν, etc., is employed like ἕρμαιον,
εὕρημα, to denote 'a highly-prized possession, an unexpected gain': as Plut.
*Mor.* p. 330 D οὐδὲ ὥσπερ ἅρπαγμα καὶ
λάφυρον εὐτυχίας ἀνελπίστου σπαράξαι
καὶ ἀνασύρασθαι διανοηθείς, Heliod. vii.
20 οὐχ ἅρπαγμα οὐδὲ ἕρμαιον ἡγεῖται τὸ
πρᾶγμα, *ib.* viii. 7 ἅρπαγμα τὸ ῥηθὲν
ἐποιήσατο ἡ 'Αρσάκη, Titus Bostr. *c.
Manich.* i. 2 ἅρπαγμα ψευδῶς τὸ ἀναγκαῖον τῆς φύσεως ἡγεῖται, Euseb. *H. E.*
viii. 12 τὸν θάνατον ἅρπαγμα θέμενοι, *Vit.
Const.* ii. 31 οἷον ἅρπαγμά τι τὴν ἐπάνοδον ποιησάμενοι.

It appears then from these instances that ἅρπαγμα ἡγεῖσθαι frequently signifies nothing more than
'to clutch greedily,' 'prize highly,' 'to
set store by;' the idea of plunder or
robbery having passed out of sight.
The form ἁρπαγμὸς however presents
greater difficulty; for neither analogy
nor usage is decisive as to its meaning : (1) The termination -μὸς indeed
denotes primarily the *process*, so that
ἁρπαγμὸς would be 'an act of plundering.' But as a matter of fact substantives in -μὸς are frequently used to
describe a concrete thing, e. g. θεσμός,
χρησμός, φραγμός, etc. (see Buttmann,
*Ausf. Sprachl.* § 119. 23 (II. p. 399);
with which compare the English
'seizure, capture,' and the like): so
that the form is no impediment to
the sense adopted above. (2) And
again the particular word ἁρπαγμὸς
occurs so rarely that usage cannot
be considered decisive. In Plut. *Mor.*
p. 12 A τὸν ἐκ Κρήτης καλούμενον
ἁρπαγμόν, the only instance of its occurrence in any classical writer (for

though it appears as a various reading for ἁρπαγὴ in Pausan. i. 20. 2, the
authority is too slight to deserve
consideration), it seems certainly to
denote the act. On the other hand
in Euseb. *Comm. in Luc.* vi. (Mai,
*Nov. Patr. Bibl.* IV. p. 165) ὁ Πέτρος
δὲ ἁρπαγμὸν τὸν διὰ σταυροῦ θάνατον
ἐποιεῖτο διὰ τὰς σωτηρίους ἐλπίδας (a
reference which I owe to a friend), in
Cyril. Alex. *de Ador.* I. p. 25 (ed. Aubert.) οὐχ ἁρπαγμὸν τὴν παραίτησιν ὡς
ἐξ ἀδρανοῦς καὶ ὑδαρεστέρας ἐποιεῖτο
φρενός (speaking of Lot's importunity
when the angels declined his offer of
hospitality), and in a late anonymous
writer in the *Catena Possini* on Mark
x. 42 τῷ δεῖξαι ὅτι οὐκ ἔστιν ἁρπαγμὸς
ἡ τιμή, τῶν ἐθνῶν γὰρ τὸ τοιοῦτον, it is
equivalent to ἅρπαγμα. Under these
circumstances we may, in choosing
between the two senses of ἁρπαγμός,
fairly assign to it here the one which
best suits the context.

The meaning adopted above satisfies this condition : '*Though* He preexisted in the form of God, *yet* He
did not look upon equality with God
as a prize which must not slip from
His grasp, *but* He emptied Himself,
divested Himself, taking upon
Him the form of a slave.' The idea
is the same as in 2 Cor. viii. 9 δι'
ὑμᾶς ἐπτώχευσεν πλούσιος ὤν. The
other rendering (adopted by the A.V.),
'thought it not *robbery* to be equal
with God,' disconnects this clause from
its context. The objections to this
latter interpretation will be considered
more at length in the detached note at
the end of the chapter.

τὸ εἶναι ἴσα Θεῷ] '*to be on an
equality with God.*' For this use of
ἴσα as a predicate, comp. Job xi. 12
βροτὸς δὲ γεννητὸς γυναικὸς ἴσα ὄνῳ
ἐρημίτῃ. So ὅμοια in Thucyd. i. 25 δυνάμει ὄντες...ὅμοια τοῖς Ἑλλήνων πλουσιωτάτοις : see Jelf, *Gramm.* § 382.
The examples of the mere adverbial

λαβών, ἐν ὁμοιώματι ἀνθρώπων γενόμενος, ⁸καὶ σχήματι
εὑρεθεὶς ὡς ἄνθρωπος ἐταπείνωσεν ἑαυτόν, γενόμενος

use of ἴσα accumulated by commentators do not throw much light on the meaning here. Between the two expressions ἴσος εἶναι and ἴσα εἶναι no other distinction can be drawn, except that the former refers rather to the *person*, the latter to the *attributes*. In the present instance ἴσα Θεῷ expresses better the Catholic doctrine of the Person of Christ, than ἴσος Θεῷ ; for the latter would seem to divide the Godhead. It is not the statement either of the Lord Himself or of the evangelist, but the complaint of the Jews, that He 'made Himself ἴσον τῷ Θεῷ (John v. 18).'

In the letter of the synod of Ancyra, directed against the Sabellianism of Marcellus, attention is called to the absence of the article with Θεὸς here and above (ἐν μορφῇ Θεοῦ) ; καθὸ Θεὸς ὢν οὔτε μορφῇ [οὔτ' ἐν μορφῇ ?] ἐστι τοῦ Θεοῦ ἀλλὰ Θεοῦ, οὔτε ἴσα ἐστὶ τῷ Θεῷ ἀλλὰ Θεῷ, οὔτε αὐθεντικῶς ὡς ὁ πατήρ (Epiphan. *Hær.* lxxiii. 9, p. 855 Petav.). The object of this comment, whether right or wrong, is apparently to distinguish between Θεὸς God absolutely and ὁ Θεὸς God the Father ; but the editors generally after Petau substitute ἀλλὰ Θεός, ἀλλὰ Θεός, for ἀλλὰ Θεοῦ, ἀλλὰ Θεῷ, thus disregarding the MS and confusing the sense.

7. ἀλλὰ ἑαυτόν] 'So far from this ; He divested Himself,' not of His divine nature, for this was impossible, but 'of the glories, the prerogatives, of Deity. This He did by taking upon Him the form of a servant.' The emphatic position of ἑαυτὸν points to the humiliation of our Lord as *voluntary, self-imposed.*

ἐκένωσεν] '*emptied*, stripped *Himself*' of the insignia of majesty.

μορφὴν δούλου λαβών] '*by taking the form of a slave.*' The action of λαβὼν is coincident in time with the action of ἐκένωσεν, as e.g. Ephes.

i. 9 : comp. Plat. *Men.* p. 92 ο εὐεργέτησον φράσας, and see Hermann *on Viger* no. 224, Bernhardy *Griech. Synt.* p. 383. By 'form' is meant not the external semblance only (σχῆμα of the following verse), but the characteristic attributes, as in ver. 6. For ἄνθρωπος the stronger word δοῦλος is substituted : He, who is Master(κύριος) of all, became the slave of all. Comp. Matt. xx. 27, 28, Mark x. 44, 45.

This text was made the starting-point of certain mystic speculations by the early sect of the Sethians ; Hippol. *Hær.* v. 19, x. 11.

ἐν ὁμοιώματι] Unlike μορφή, this word does not imply the reality of our Lord's humanity : see Trench *N. T. Syn.* § xv. '*Forma* (μορφή) dicit quiddam absolutum ; *similitudo* (ὁμοίωμα) dicit relationem ad alia ejusdem conditionis ; *habitus* (σχῆμα) refertur ad aspectum et sensum,' is Bengel's distinction. Thus ὁμοίωμα stands midway between μορφὴ and σχῆμα. The plural ἀνθρώπων is used ; for Christ, as the second Adam, represents not the individual man, but the human race ; Rom. v. 15, 1 Cor. xv. 45—47.

γενόμενος] like λαβὼν is opposed to the foregoing ὑπάρχων (ver. 6), and marks the assumption of the new upon the old.

8. 'Nor was this His lowest degradation. He not only became a man, but He was treated as the meanest of men. He died the death of a criminal slave.'

σχήματι κ.τ.λ.] The former verse dwells on the contrast between what He *was from the beginning* and what He *became afterwards :* hence λαβὼν (not ἔχων), ὁμοίωμα (not μορφή), γενόμενος (not ὤν), all words expressive of *change.* In the present the opposition is between what He *is* in Himself, and what He *appeared* in the eyes of men ;

ὑπήκοος μέχρι θανάτου, θανάτου δὲ σταυροῦ· ⁹ διὸ καὶ ὁ
Θεὸς αὐτὸν ὑπερύψωσεν καὶ ἐχαρίσατο αὐτῷ τὸ ὄνομα

hence σχήματι (for ὁμοιώματι or μορφῇ), εὑρεθείς (for γενόμενος or ὑπάρχων), ὡς ἄνθρωπος (for ἄνθρωπος), all expressions implying *external semblance*. 'He hath no form nor comeliness: there is no beauty that we should desire him: he was despised and we esteemed him not' (Is. liii. 2, 3). For σχήματι εὑρεθεὶς κ.τ.λ. compare *Test. xii Patr.* Zab. 9 ὄψεσθε Θεὸν ἐν σχήματι ἀνθρώπου, Benj. 10 ἐπὶ γῆς φανέντα ἐν μορφῇ ἀνθρώπου [ταπεινώσεως].

ὑπήκοος] sc. τῷ Θεῷ : comp. ver. 9, διὸ καὶ ὁ Θεὸς κ.τ.λ. On the ὑπακοὴ of Christ comp. Rom. v. 19, Hebr. v. 8.

θανάτου δὲ σταυροῦ] 'I said death, but it was no common death. It was a death which involved not intense suffering only but intense shame also : a death reserved for malefactors and slaves: a death on which the Mosaic law has uttered a curse (Deut. xxi. 23), and which even Gentiles consider the most foul and cruel of all punishments (Cic. *Verr.* v. 64); which has been ever after to the Jews a stumblingblock and to the Greeks foolishness.' Compare Heb. xii. 2 ὑπέμεινεν σταυρὸν αἰσχύνης καταφρονήσας, and see *Galatians* p. 152 sq. The contrast of his own position must have deepened St Paul's sense of his Master's humiliation. As a Roman citizen he could under no circumstances suffer such degradation ; and accordingly, if we may accept the tradition, while St Peter died on the cross, he himself was executed by the sword : see Tertull. *Scorp.* 15, and comp. *Ep. Gall.* in Euseb. *H. E.* v. 1, § 12.

9. διό] In consequence of this voluntary humiliation, in fulfilment of the divine law which He Himself enunciated, ὁ ταπεινῶν ἑαυτὸν ὑψωθήσεται (Luke xiv. 11, xviii. 14).

διὸ καί] is a frequent collocation of particles in the New Testament with various shades of meaning. Here the καί implies reciprocation.

ὑπερύψωσεν] The word is found several times in the LXX, but apparently does not occur in classical writers.

ἐχαρίσατο αὐτῷ] '*gave to Him*, the Son of Man.' Ὑπερύψωσεν and ἐχαρίσατο are used in reference to the subordinate position voluntarily assumed by the Son of God.

τὸ ὄνομα] '*the name*, i.e. the title and dignity,' comp. Ephes. i. 21 ὑπεράνω πάσης ἀρχῆς καὶ ἐξουσίας καὶ δυνάμεως καὶ κυριότητος καὶ παντὸς ὀνόματος ὀνομαζομένου, Heb. i. 4 ὅσῳ διαφορώτερον παρ' αὐτοὺς κεκληρονόμηκεν ὄνομα. If St Paul were referring to any one term, Κύριος would best explain the reference ; for it occurs in the context ὅτι Κύριος Ἰησοῦς Χριστός, ver. 11. But here, as in the passages quoted, we should probably look to a very common Hebrew sense of 'name,' not meaning a definite appellation but denoting office, rank, dignity. In this case the use of the ' Name of God ' in the Old Testament to denote the Divine Presence or the Divine Majesty, more especially as the object of adoration and praise, will suggest the true meaning: since the context dwells on the honour and worship henceforth offered to Him on whom ' *the* name ' has been conferred. ' To praise *the name*, to bless *the name*, to fear *the name*, of God ' are frequent expressions in the Old Testament. See especially Gesenius *Thesaur.* p. 1432, s. v. שֵׁם, where he defines ' the name of God,' ' Deus quatenus ab hominibus invocatur, celebratur.' Philo in a remarkable passage (among other titles assigned to our Lord in the Apostolic writings) gives ' the Name of God ' as a designation of the ' Word ': καὶ ἂν μηδέπω μέντοι τυγχάνῃ τις ἀξιόχρεως ὢν υἱὸς Θεοῦ προσαγορεύεσθαι, σπουδαζέτω κοσμεῖσθαι κατὰ τὸν πρωτόγονον αὐτοῦ

τὸ ὑπὲρ πᾶν ὄνομα, ¹⁰ἵνα ἐν τῷ ὀνόματι Ἰησοῦ πᾶν
γόνυ κάμψῃ ἐπουρανίων καὶ ἐπιγείων καὶ καταχθο-

λόγον, τὸν ἄγγελον πρεσβύτατον, ὡς ἀρχάγγελον πολυώνυμον ὑπάρχοντα καὶ γὰρ ἀρχὴ καὶ ὄνομα Θεοῦ καὶ λόγος καὶ ὁ κατ᾽ εἰκόνα ἄνθρωπος καὶ ὁρῶν Ἰσραὴλ προσαγορεύεται (de Conf. Ling. § 28, p. 427 M). St Paul's idea here seems to be the same; for the parallel remains unaffected by the fact that the Word was not revealed to Philo as an incarnate Person. Somewhat different in expression, though similar in meaning, is St John's language, Rev. xix. 13. The reading τὸ ὄνομα (for which the received text has ὄνομα without the article) is unquestionably correct, both as having the support of the oldest MSS, and as giving a much fuller meaning. For other instances where τὸ ὄνομα is used absolutely, comp. Acts v. 41 κατηξιώθησαν ὑπὲρ τοῦ ὀνόματος ἀτιμασθῆναι, Ignat. Eph. 3 δέδεμαι ἐν τῷ ὀνόματι, Philad. 10 δοξάσαι τὸ ὄνομα. In all these cases transcribers or translators have stumbled at the expression and interpolated words to explain it. The same motive will account for the omission of the article here.

10. This passage is modelled on Isaiah xlv. 23 ὅτι ἐμοὶ κάμψει πᾶν γόνυ καὶ ἐξομολογήσεται πᾶσα γλῶσσα τῷ Θεῷ (so Alex., but Vat. has καὶ ὀμεῖται π. γλ. τὸν Θεόν, and Sin. καὶ ὀμνιταἰ π. γλ. τὸν Κύριον), the text being modified to suit St Paul's application to the Son. In Rom. xiv. 10, 11, on the other hand, the same text is directly quoted: πάντες γὰρ παραστησόμεθα τῷ βήματι τοῦ Θεοῦ (v. l. τοῦ Χριστοῦ)· γέγραπται γάρ, Ζῶ ἐγώ, λέγει Κύριος, ὅτι ἐμοὶ κάμψει κ.τ.λ.; the introductory words however, Ζῶ ἐγώ, λέγει Κύριος, being substituted for κατ᾽ ἐμαυτοῦ ὀμνύω of the prophet. In the passage in the Romans then, if the reading τοῦ Χριστοῦ were adopted, Κύριος would refer naturally to our Lord, and thus it would serve to illustrate the application of the text here; but the balance of authority is de-

cidedly in favour of τοῦ Θεοῦ, which is doubtless correct; the other reading having been introduced from 2 Cor. v. 10, where the words τὸ βῆμα τοῦ Χριστοῦ occur.

Yet even without the countenance which would thus have been obtained from Rom. xiv. 11, it seems clear from the context that ' the name of Jesus ' is not only the medium but the object of adoration. The motive of the passage (as shown by the last verse) is to declare the honour paid to Jesus; and that the individual expressions suggest this interpretation will appear from the following note.

ἐν τῷ ὀνόματι] 'in the name,' i.e. the majesty, the manifestation to man, as an object of worship and praise. It is not ' the name Jesus,' but 'the name of Jesus.' The name here must be the same with the name in the preceding verse. And the personal name Jesus cannot there be meant; for the bestowal of the name is represented as following upon the humiliation and death of the Son of Man. If such had been the meaning, the words should have run, not ' He bestowed on Him the name etc.,' but ' He exalted the name borne by Him'); for, though eminently significant in His case and thus prophetic of His glorious office (Matt. i. 21), it was the personal name of many others besides. That the bending of the knee is an act of reverence to Jesus, and not only to God through Him, will appear from the following considerations; (1) The parallel clause describes an act of reverence paid directly to the Son as its object, the ultimate aim however being the glory of the Father, πᾶσα γλῶσσα ἐξομολογήσεται ὅτι Κύριος Ἰησοῦς κ.τ.λ. (2) The construction ἐν τῷ ὀνόματι Ἰησοῦ πᾶν γόνυ κάμψῃ in this sense is supported by many analogous instances where direct adoration is meant: e. g. Ps. lxiii.

νίων, ¹¹καὶ πᾶϲα γλῶϲϲα ἐξομολογήϲεται ὅτι Κύριος
Ἰησοῦς Χριστὸς εἰς δόξαν Θεοῦ πατρός.

¹²″Ὥστε, ἀγαπητοί μου, καθὼς πάντοτε ὑπηκούσατε,

5 ἐν τῷ ὀνόματί σου ἀρῶ τὰς χεῖράς μου,
Ps. xliv. 10 ἐν τῷ ὀνόματί σου ἐξομο-
λογησόμεθα, Ps. cv. 3 ἐπαινεῖσθε ἐν τῷ
ὀνόματι τῷ ἁγίῳ αὐτοῦ, 1 Kings viii. 44
προσεύξονται ἐν ὀνόματι Κυρίου, besides
the very frequent expression ἐπικαλεῖ-
σθαι ἐν ὀνόματι Κυρίου (or Θεοῦ) 1 Kings
xviii. 24, 25, 26, 2 Kings v. 11, Ps. xx.
8, cxvi. 17, 2 Chron. xxviii. 15.

τῶν ἐπουρανίων κ.τ.λ.] 'all creation,
all things whatsoever and wheresoever
they be.' The whole universe, whether
animate or inanimate, bends the knee
in homage and raises its voice in
praise: see especially Rev. v. 13 καὶ
πᾶν κτίσμα ὃ ἐν τῷ οὐρανῷ καὶ ἐπὶ τῆς
γῆς καὶ ὑποκάτω τῆς γῆς καὶ ἐπὶ τῆς θαλάσσης [ἃ] ἐστιν καὶ τὰ ἐν αὐτοῖς πάντα,
καὶ ἤκουσα λέγοντας τῷ καθημένῳ κ.τ.λ.:
and comp. Ephes. i. 20—22. So in
like manner St Paul represents 'all
creation' as awaiting the redemption
of Christ, Rom. viii. 22. Compare
Ignat. Trall. 9 βλεπόντων τῶν ἐπουρανίων καὶ ἐπιγείων καὶ ὑποχθονίων,
Polyc. Phil. 2 ᾧ ὑπετάγη τὰ πάντα ἐπου-
ράνια καὶ ἐπίγεια. It would seem therefore that the adjectives here are neuter; and any limitation to intelligent
beings, while it detracts from the universality of the homage, is not required by the expressions. The personification of universal nature offering its
praise and homage to its Creator in
the 148th Psalm will serve to illustrate St Paul's meaning here. If this
view be correct, all endeavours to
explain the three words of different
classe of intelligent beings; as Christians, Jews, heathens; angels, men,
devils; the angels, the living, the dead;
souls of the blessed, men on earth, souls
in purgatory, etc., are out of place.

11. ἐξομολογήσεται] 'proclaim with
thanksgiving.' In itself ἐξομολογεῖ-
σθαι is simply 'to declare or confess
openly or plainly.' But as its second-

ary sense 'to offer praise or thanksgiving' has almost entirely supplanted
its primary meaning in the LXX, where
it is of frequent occurrence, and as
moreover it has this secondary sense in
the very passage of Isaiah which St Paul
adapts, the idea of praise or thanksgiving ought probably not to be excluded here. Compare the construction ἐξομολογοῦμαί σοι πάτερ ὅτι, Matt.
xi. 25, Luke x. 21. The authorities
are divided between ἐξομολογήσηται
and ἐξομολογήσεται. In a doubtful
case I have given the preference to
the latter, as transcribers would be
tempted to substitute the conjunctive
to conform to κάμψῃ. The future is
justified by such passages as Rev. xxii.
14 ἵνα ἔσται...καὶ εἰσέλθωσιν ; see
Winer § xli. p. 360 sq.

Κύριος Ἰησοῦς] See Acts ii. 36 καὶ
Κύριον αὐτὸν καὶ Χριστὸν ὁ Θεὸς ἐποίη-
σεν, τοῦτον τὸν Ἰησοῦν ὃν ὑμεῖς ἐσταυ-
ρώσατε, Rom. x. 9 ἐὰν ὁμολογήσῃς ἐν
τῷ στόματί σου Κύριον Ἰησοῦν, i.e. 'confess Jesus to be Lord,' where the
other reading ὅτι Κύριος Ἰησοῦς is a
paraphrase; comp. 1 Cor. xii. 3.

12, 13. 'Therefore, my beloved,
having the example of Christ's humility to guide you, the example of
Christ's exaltation to encourage you,
as ye have always been obedient
hitherto, so continue. Do not look to
my presence to stimulate you. Labour
earnestly not only at times when I am
with you, but now when I am far away.
With a nervous and trembling anxiety
work out your salvation for yourselves.
For yourselves, did I say? Nay, ye
are not alone. It is God working in
you from first to last: God that inspires the earliest impulse, and God
that directs the final achievement: for
such is His good pleasure.'

ὑπηκούσατε 'were obedient,' i.e. to
God, not to St Paul himself. Ὑπακοὴ

μὴ ὡς ἐν τῇ παρουσίᾳ μου μόνον, ἀλλὰ νῦν πολλῷ μᾶλλον ἐν τῇ ἀπουσίᾳ μου, μετὰ φόβου καὶ τρόμου τὴν
ἑαυτῶν σωτηρίαν κατεργάζεσθε· ¹³ Θεὸς γάρ ἐστιν ὁ
ἐνεργῶν ἐν ὑμῖν καὶ τὸ θέλειν καὶ τὸ ἐνεργεῖν ὑπὲρ τῆς

is most frequently so used in the New Testament of submission to the Gospel, e.g. Rom. i. 5, xv. 18, xvi. 19, 26, 2 Cor. vii. 15, x. 5, 6. It here refers back to the example of Christ, who Himself 'showed obedience' (ὑπήκοος γενόμενος ver. 8).

μὴ ὡς ἐν τῇ κ.τ.λ.] 'do not, as though my presence prompted you, work out in my presence only etc.' The sentence is a fusion of two ideas, μὴ ὡς ἐν τῇ παρουσίᾳ μου κατεργάζεσθε, and μὴ ἐν τῇ παρουσίᾳ μου μόνον κατεργάζεσθε, 'do not be energetic because I am present,' and 'do not be energetic only when I am present.' The pleonastic ὡς lays stress on the sentiment or motive of the agent: compare Rom. ix. 32, 2 Cor. ii. 17, Philem. 14.

φόβου καὶ τρόμου] i.e. a nervous and trembling anxiety to do right. Such at least seems to be the meaning of the phrase in St Paul, 2 Cor. vii. 15, Ephes. vi. 5: comp. 1 Cor. ii. 3. The words occur together frequently in the LXX, where however they have a sterner import: Gen. ix. 2, Exod. xv. 16, Deut. ii. 25, xi. 25, Ps. liv. 5, Is. xix. 16.

ἑαυτῶν] The word is emphatic in reference both to what goes before and to what follows. 'Do not depend on me, but on yourselves,' 'When you depend on yourselves, you depend on God.'

κατεργάζεσθε] 'work out,' as e.g. Xen. Mem. iv. 2.7 πλειόνων περὶ ταῦτα πραγματευομένων ἐλάττους οἱ κατεργαζόμενοι γίγνονται. It is a common word in St Paul.

13. γάρ] This verse supplies at once the stimulus to and the corrective of the precept in the preceding: 'Work, for God works with you': and 'The good is not your own doing, but God's.'

ἐνεργῶν] 'works mightily, works effectively.' The preposition of the compound is unconnected with the ἐν of ἐν ὑμῖν ('in your hearts'). See the notes on Gal. ii. 8.

καὶ τὸ θέλειν κ.τ.λ.] 'not less the will, the first impulse, than the work, the actual performance.' 'Nos ergo volumus, sed Deus in nobis operatur et velle; nos ergo operamur, sed Deus in nobis operatur et operari,' Augustin. de Don. Persev. 33 (x. p. 838, ed. Ben.). It was not sufficient to say Θεός ἐστιν ὁ ἐνεργῶν, lest he should seem to limit the part of God to the actual working: this activity of God comprises τὸ θέλειν as well as τὸ ἐνεργεῖν. The θέλειν and the ἐνεργεῖν correspond respectively to the 'gratia praeveniens' and the 'gratia cooperans' of a later theology.

ὑπὲρ τῆς κ.τ.λ.] 'in fulfilment of His benevolent purpose'; for God 'will have all men to be saved' (1 Tim. ii. 4). The words should therefore be connected with Θεός ἐστιν ὁ ἐνεργῶν, not with καὶ τὸ θέλειν κ.τ.λ.; for this latter connexion would introduce an idea alien to the context. On εὐδοκία see the note i. 15.

14—16. 'Be ye not like Israel of old. Never give way to discontent and murmuring, to questioning and unbelief. So live that you call forth no censure from others, that you keep your own consciences single and pure. Show yourselves blameless children of God amidst a crooked and perverse generation. For you are set in this world as luminaries in the firmament. Hold out to others the word of life. That so, when Christ shall come to judge all our works, I may be able to boast of your faith, and to show

εὐδοκίας. ¹⁴πάντα ποιεῖτε χωρὶς γογγυσμῶν καὶ δια-
λογισμῶν, ¹⁵ἵνα γένησθε ἄμεμπτοι καὶ ἀκέραιοι, τέκνα
Θεοῦ ἄμωμα μέσον γενεᾶς σκολιᾶς καὶ διεστραμ-
μένης, ἐν οἷς φαίνεσθε ὡς φωστῆρες ἐν κόσμῳ, ¹⁶λόγον

that my race has not been run in vain,
that my struggles have indeed been
crowned with success.'

14. γογγυσμῶν] 'murmurings.' The
word is constantly used in the LXX
of Israel in the wilderness : compare
1 Cor. x. 10 μηδὲ γογγύζετε καθάπερ τινὲς
αὐτῶν ἐγόγγυσαν. The same reference
to the Israelites, which is directly expressed in the passage just quoted,
seems to have been present to the
Apostle's mind here; for in the next
verse he quotes from the song of
Moses. For γογγυσμὸς the Athenians
used τονθορυσμός : the former however
occurs in the oldest Ionic writers (see
Lobeck Phryn. p. 358). This is one
of many instances of the exceptional
character of the Attic dialect : see
above on πτυρόμενοι i. 28 and Galatians vi. 6, and p. 92 sq.

διαλογισμῶν] This word in the New
Testament means sometimes 'inward
questionings,' sometimes 'disputes, discussion' ; for there is no sufficient
ground for denying it this second
meaning: see 1 Tim. ii. 8. Here it
seems to have the former sense. As
γογγυσμὸς is the moral, so διαλογισμὸς
is the intellectual rebellion against God.

15. γένησθε] 'may approve yourselves' : better supported than the
other reading ἦτε.

ἀκέραιοι] 'pure, sincere,' literally
'unmixed,' 'unadulterated' (from κε-
ράννυμι); for the word is used of pure
wine (Athen. ii. 45 E), of unalloyed
metal (Plut. Mor. 1154 B), and the
like. Comp. Philo Leg. ad Cai. § 42,
p. 594 M τὴν χάριν διδοὺς ἔδωκεν οὐκ
ἀκέραιον ἀλλ' ἀναμίξας αὐτῇ δέος ἀργα-
λεώτερον. The stress laid in the New
Testament on simplicity of character
appears in this as in many other words :

ἁπλοῦς, εἰλικρινής, δίψυχος etc. Of the
two words here used, the former (ἄ-
μεμπτοι) relates to the judgment of
others, while the latter (ἀκέραιοι) describes the intrinsic character.

τέκνα Θεοῦ κ.τ.λ.] A direct contrast
to the Israelites in the desert, who in
the song of Moses are described as οὐκ
αὐτῷ τέκνα (i.e. no children of God)
μωμητά, γενεὰ σκολιὰ καὶ διεστραμμένη
(Deut. xxxii. 5, LXX): comp. Luke ix. 41.

ἄμωμα] Both forms ἄμωμος and ἀμώ-
μητος are equally common. Here the
weight of evidence is in favour of the
former, though there is some authority
for the latter : in 2 Pet. iii. 14 on the
other hand, ἀμώμητοι has much stronger
support than ἄμωμοι.

μέσον] For this adverbial use see
Steph. Thes. (ed. Hase and Dindorf),
s. v. p. 824. The received text substi-
tutes ἐν μέσῳ.

διεστραμμένης] 'distorted,' a stronger
word than σκολιᾶς: comp. Arrian Epict.
iii. 6. 8 οἱ μὴ παντάπασι διεστραμμένοι
τῶν ἀνθρώπων (comp. i. 29. 3). It corresponds to a strong, reduplicated
form in the Hebrew פְּתַלְתֹּל.

φαίνεσθε] 'ye appear,' not 'ye shine'
(φαίνετε) as the A. V. The same error
is made in Matt. xxiv. 27, Rev. xviii.
23. On the other hand in Matt. ii. 7
τοῦ φαινομένου ἀστέρος, it is correctly
rendered 'appeared.' φαίνεσθε here
should be taken as an indicative, not
an imperative.

ὡς φωστῆρες] 'as luminaries.'
The word is used almost exclusively
of the heavenly bodies (except when
it is metaphorical (as e.g. Gen. i. 14,
16 (where it is a rendering of מָאוֹר),
Ecclus. xliii. 7, Orac. Sibyll. ii. 186,
200, iii. 88, etc. Comp. Dan. xii. 3
(LXX) φανοῦσιν ὡς φωστῆρες τοῦ οὐρα-

ζωῆς ἐπέχοντες, εἰς καύχημα ἐμοὶ εἰς ἡμέραν Χριστοῦ,
ὅτι οὐκ εἰς κενὸν ἔδραμον οὐδὲ εἰς κενὸν ἐκοπίασα.
¹⁷ἀλλὰ εἰ καὶ σπένδομαι ἐπὶ τῇ θυσίᾳ καὶ λειτουργίᾳ

νοῦ, Wisd. xiii. 2 φωστῆρας οὐρανοῦ πρυτάνεις κόσμου. The word occurs only
once again in the N. T., Rev. xxi. 11,
where also it should be translated
'luminary.'

ἐν κόσμῳ] To be taken not with
φωστῆρες alone (as the passage of Wisdom just quoted might suggest), but
with φαίνεσθε ὡς φωστῆρες. For in
the former case κόσμῳ must signify
the material world as *distinguished
from* the moral world. But this is
hardly possible in the language of the
New Testament: for though κόσμος
sometimes refers to external nature,
yet as it much more frequently has a
moral significance, it cannot well, unless so defined by the context, signify
the former to the exclusion of the latter.
It is therefore used here in the same
sense as in John iii. 19 τὸ φῶς ἐλήλυθεν εἰς τὸν κόσμον καὶ ἠγάπησαν οἱ ἄν-
θρωποι μᾶλλον τὸ σκότος κ.τ.λ.: comp.
i. 9, 10, ix. 5, xii. 46, etc.

16. ἐπέχοντες] The foregoing clause
ἐν οἷς φαίνεσθε ὡς φωστῆρες ἐν κόσμῳ
should probably be taken as paren-
thetical, so that ἐπέχοντες is attached
to ἵνα γένησθε κ.τ.λ. For this sense of
ἐπέχειν 'to hold out' see Hom. *Il.* ix.
489, xxii. 494, Ar. *Nub.* 1382, etc. (οἶνον,
κοτύλην), Pausan. i. 33. 7, Plut. *Mor.*
265 A, 268 F (μαστόν, θηλήν, γάλα). If
therefore we are to look for any metaphor in ἐπέχοντες, it would most naturally be that of offering food or wine.
At all events it seems wholly unconnected with the preceding image in
φωστῆρες.

εἰς ἡμέραν Χριστοῦ] '*against the
day of Christ*,' as i. 10; comp. i. 6.
'The day of Christ' is a phrase peculiar to this epistle. More commonly
it is 'the day of the Lord.' For this
reference to the great judgment in
connexion with his ministerial labours

compare 1 Cor. iii. 12, 13, iv. 3—5, and
esp. 2 Cor. i. 14.
εἰς κενὸν ἔδραμον] as Gal. ii. 2. This
passage is quoted Polyc. *Phil.* § 9
οὗτοι πάντες οὐκ εἰς κενὸν ἔδραμον: compare 2 Tim. iv. 7.
ἐκοπίασα] Probably a continuation
of the same metaphor, referring to the
training for the athletic games: compare 1 Cor. ix. 24—27. At least κο-
πιᾶν is elsewhere associated with τρέ-
χειν in the same way: Anthol. III. p.
166 πῖνε καὶ εὐφραίνου· τί γὰρ αὔριον, ἢ
τί τὸ μέλλον, οὐδεὶς γινώσκει· μὴ τρέχε,
μὴ κοπία, 1 gnat. *Polyc.* 6 συγκοπιᾶτε
ἀλλήλοις, συναθλεῖτε, συντρέχετε.

17, 18. 'I spoke of my severe labours for the Gospel. I am ready *even
to die* in the same cause. If I am required to pour out my life-blood as a
libation over the sacrificial offering of
your faith, I rejoice myself and I congratulate you all therein. Yea in like
manner I ask you also to rejoice and
to congratulate me.'

Thus the particles ἀλλὰ εἰ καὶ will
refer to the preceding ἔδραμον, ἐκοπίασα. Most recent commentators explain the connexion in a very harsh
and artificial way. Assuming that St
Paul had before mentioned his anticipation of living till the advent of Christ
εἰς ἡμέραν Χριστοῦ (ver. 16), they suppose that he now suggests the alternative of his dying before. But in fact
no such anticipation was expressed:
for his work would be equally tested
at 'the day of Christ,' whether he
were alive or dead when that day came.
The faint expectation, which in i. 6,
10 (where the same phrase occurs) is
suggested by the context, finds no expression here. On εἰ καὶ as distinguished from καὶ εἰ see the note on Gal. i. 8

σπένδομαι] As his death actually
approaches, he says ἐγὼ γὰρ ἤδη σπέν

τῆς πίστεως ὑμῶν, χαίρω καὶ συγχαίρω πᾶσιν ὑμῖν·
¹⁸τὸ δὲ αὐτὸ καὶ ὑμεῖς χαίρετε καὶ συγχαίρετέ μοι.

δομαι 2 Tim. iv. 6. Comp. Ignat. *Rom.*
2 πλέον μοι μὴ παράσχησθε τοῦ σπονδισθῆναι Θεῷ, ὡς ἔτι θυσιαστήριον ἕτοιμόν
ἐστιν, uttered under similar circumstances. It is a striking coincidence,
that St Paul's great heathen contemporary Seneca, whose name tradition
has linked with his own, is reported to
have used a similar metaphor when on
the point of death : Tac. *Ann.* xv. 64
'respergens proximos servorum, addita
voce libare se liquorem illum Jovi libe-
ratori': compare the account of Thrasea, *Ann.* xvi. 35. The present tense
σπένδομαι places the hypothesis vividly
before the eyes : but it does not, as
generally explained, refer to present
dangers, as though the process were
actually begun : comp. e.g. Matt. xii.
26, xviii. 8, 9, etc.

ἐπὶ τῇ θυσίᾳ] The general import
of the metaphor is clear ; but it has
been questioned whether the reference
is to heathen libations or to Jewish
drink-offerings. The preposition (ἐπί)
seems hardly conclusive. Even if it be
true that the drink-offerings of the
Jews were always poured around and
not upon the altar (Joseph. *Ant.* iii. 9.
4 σπένδουσι περὶ τὸν βωμὸν τὸν οἶνον;
see Ewald *Alterth.* p. 37 sq. 2te ausg.),
yet the LXX certainly uses the preposition 'upon' to describe them : Levit.
v. 11 οὐκ ἐπιχεεῖ ἐπ' αὐτὸ ἔλαιον, Num.
xxviii. 24 ἐπὶ τοῦ ὁλοκαυτώματος τοῦ διὰ
παντὸς ποιήσεις τὴν σπονδὴν αὐτοῦ. Nor
need ἐπὶ with the dative necessarily
be translated 'upon,' but may mean
'accompanying.' On the other hand,
as St Paul is writing to converted heathens, a reference to heathen sacrifice
is more appropriate (comp. 2 Cor. ii.
14); while owing to the greater prominence of the libation in heathen rites
the metaphor would be more expressive. For the appropriateness of the
preposition in this case see Hom. *Il.*
xi. 775 σπένδων αἴθοπα οἶνον ἐπ' αἰθομέ-

νοις ἱεροῖσιν, Arrian *Alex.* vi. 19 σπεί-
σας ἐπὶ τῇ θυσίᾳ τὴν φιάλην κ.τ.λ., and
the common word ἐπισπένδειν. The
'sacrifice' (θυσία) here is the victim,
not the act.

λειτουργίᾳ] This word has passed
through the following meanings : (1)
A civil service, a state-burden, especially in the technical language of
Athenian law : (2) A function or office
of any kind, as of the bodily organs,
e.g. the mouth, Arist. *Part. An.* ii. 3 :
(3) Sacerdotal ministration especially,
whether among the Jews (as Heb. viii.
6, ix. 21, and commonly in the LXX),
or among heathen nations (as Diod.
Sic. i. 21, where it is used of the Egyptian priesthood): (4) The eucharistic
services ; and thence more generally
(5) Set forms of divine worship. As
the word is applied most frequently in
the Bible to sacerdotal functions, it
should probably be taken here as sup-
plementing the idea of θυσία. Thus
St Paul's language expresses the fundamental idea of the Christian Church,
in which an universal priesthood has
supplanted the exclusive ministrations
of a select tribe or class : see 1 Pet. ii.
5 ἱεράτευμα ἅγιον ἀνενέγκαι πνευματικὰς
θυσίας. The Philippians are the priests;
their faith (or their good works springing from their faith) is the sacrifice :
St Paul's life-blood the accompanying
libation. Commentators have much
confused the image by representing
St Paul himself as the sacrificer.

συγχαίρω] 'I congratulate,' not 'I
rejoice with.' As joy is enjoined on
the Philippians in the second clause,
it must not be assumed on their part
in the first. For this sense of συγχαί-
ρειν 'to congratulate,' where reciprocation on the part of the person appealed to is not so much presupposed
as invited, see e.g. Plut. *Mor.* 231 B
συγχαίρω τῇ πόλει τριακοσίους κρείττο-
νάς μου πολίτας ἐχούσῃ, Polyb. xxix. 7. 4,

¹⁹Ἐλπίζω δὲ ἐν Κυρίῳ Ἰησοῦ Τιμόθεον ταχέως πέμψαι ὑμῖν, ἵνα κἀγὼ εὐψυχῶ γνοὺς τὰ περὶ ὑμῶν. ²⁰οὐδένα γὰρ ἔχω ἰσόψυχον, ὅστις γνησίως τὰ περὶ ὑμῶν μεριμνήσει· ²¹οἱ πάντες γὰρ τὰ ἑαυτῶν ζητοῦσιν, οὐ τὰ

Barnab. I μᾶλλον συγχαίρω ἐμαυτῷ, etc.

18. τὸ δὴ αὐτό]'in the same way,' i.e. τὴν αὐτὴν χαρὰν χαίρετε; as Matt. xxvii. 44 τὸ δ' αὐτὸ καὶ οἱ λῃσταὶ...ὠνείδιζον αὐτόν. The accusative defines the character rather than the object of the action, so that ταὐτὰ χαίρειν (Demosth. de Cor. p. 323) is 'to have the same joys.' For the poetical use of χαίρειν and similar words with an accusative of the object see Valcknaer on Eur. Hipp. 1338.

καὶ ὑμεῖς χαίρετε] We are reminded of the messenger who brought the tidings of the battle of Marathon, expiring on the first threshold with these words on his lips, χαίρετε καὶ χαίρομεν, Plut. Mor. p. 347 c. See the note on iv. 4.

19—24. 'But though absent myself, I hope in the Lord to send Timotheus shortly to you. This I purpose not for your sakes only but for my own also; that hearing how you fare, I may take heart. I have chosen him, for I have no other messenger at hand who can compare with him, none other who will show the same lively and instinctive interest in your welfare. For all pursue their own selfish aims, reckless of the will of Christ. But the credentials of Timotheus are before you: you know how he has been tested by long experience, how as a son with a father he has laboured with me in the service of the Gospel. Him therefore I hope to send without delay, when I see what turn my affairs will take. At the same time I trust in the Lord, that I shall visit you before long in person.'

19. Ἐλπίζω δέ] This is connected in thought with ver. 12. 'I urged the duty of self-reliance during my absence. Yet I do not intend to leave

you without guidance. I purpose sending Timotheus directly, and I hope to visit you myself before long.' Recent commentators seem to agree in taking ἐλπίζω δέ as oppositive to the fear expressed in the foregoing εἰ καὶ σπένδομαι; but the possibility of his own death and the intention of sending Timotheus do not stand in any sort of opposition.

ἐν Κυρίῳ Ἰησοῦ] So above i. 14 and below ii. 24. The same idea is expressed still more explicitly i. 8 ἐν σπλάγχνοις Χριστοῦ Ἰησοῦ. The Christian is a part of Christ, a member of His body. His every thought and word and deed proceeds from Christ, as the centre of volition. Thus he loves in the Lord, he hopes in the Lord, he boasts in the Lord, he labours in the Lord, etc. He has one guiding principle in acting and in forbearing to act, μόνον ἐν Κυρίῳ (1 Cor. vii. 39).

κἀγὼ εὐψυχῶ] 'I also may take courage.' Comp. ver. 27 οὐκ αὐτὸν δὲ μόνον ἀλλὰ καὶ ἐμέ. The guidance of the Philippians was one object of Timothy's mission; St Paul's comfort was another. While εὔψυχος, εὐψυχία, are not uncommon, the verb εὐψυχεῖν seems not to occur in classical writers, though the imperative εὐψύχει appears frequently on epitaphs: see Jacobs Anthol. XII. p. 304. In Pollux iii. 28 εὐψυχεῖν is given as a synonyme for θαρσεῖν. Comp. Hermas Vis. i. 2.

20. οὐδένα γάρ] This condemnation must be limited to the persons available for such a mission. See the introduction, p. 36.

ἰσόψυχον] 'like-minded,' not with St Paul himself, as it is generally taken, but with Timotheus. Otherwise the words would have been οὐδένα γὰρ

Ἰησοῦ Χριστοῦ. ²²τὴν δὲ δοκιμὴν αὐτοῦ γινώσκετε, ὅτι
ὡς πατρὶ τέκνον σὺν ἐμοὶ ἐδούλευσεν εἰς τὸ εὐαγγέλιον.
²³τοῦτον μὲν οὖν ἐλπίζω πέμψαι, ὡς ἂν ἀφίδω τὰ περὶ

21.  οὐ τὰ Χριστοῦ Ἰησοῦ.

ἄλλον or οὐδένα γὰρ πλὴν τούτου. The
word ἰσόψυχος is extremely rare. It
occurs in Æsch. *Agam.* 1470 (1446)
where it has much the same sense as
here. In Ps. liv. 14 ἄνθρωπε ἰσόψυχε
it is a rendering of כְּעֶרְכִּי 'as my
price,' i. e. 'quem mihi æquiparabam,
quem diligebam ut me ipsum'(Gesen.),
being thus equivalent to ἀντίψυχε.
ὅστις] '*such that he.*' See Gal. iv.
24 (note), 26, v. 19.
γνησίως] i. e. as a birth-right, as
an instinct derived from his spiritual
parentage : see esp. [Demosth.] *c.
Neær.* p. 1353 τοὺς φύοει πολίτας καὶ
γνησίως μετέχοντας τῆς πόλεως, *Epi-
taph.* p. 1390 τοὺς μὲν...πολίτας προσ-
αγορευομένους ὁμοίους εἶναι τοῖς εἰσποιη-
τοῖς τῶν παίδων, τούτους δὲ γνησίους
γόνῳ τῆς πατρίδος πολίτας εἶναι. Timotheus was neither a supposititious
(νόθος) nor an adopted (εἰσποιητος) son,
but, as St Paul calls him elsewhere,
γνήσιον τέκνον ἐν πίστει (1 Tim. i. 2,
comp. Tit. i. 4); comp. Hippol. *Hær.*vi.
20 Ἰσίδωρος ὁ Βασιλείδου παῖς γνήσιος 'his father's own son.' He recognised this filial relationship (ὡς πατρὶ
τέκνον ver. 22); he inherited all the
interests and affections of his spiritual
father. This, I suppose, is Chrysostom's meaning, when he explains it
τουτέστι πατρικῶς (compare πατρικὴ
φιλία, ἔχθρα etc.). Comp. Heb. xii. 8
ἄρα νόθοι καὶ οὐχ υἱοί ἐστε.
21. οἱ πάντες] '*one and all,*' 'all
without exception.' For the force of
the article with πάντες, πάντα, see Bernhardy vi. p. 320, Jelf § 454.
22. δοκιμήν] 'approved character,'
as in 2 Cor. ii. 9, ix. 13, and probably
Rom. v. 4. See Fritzsche *Rom.* I. p. 259.
γινώσκετε] '*ye recognise,*' 'ye remember and acknowledge.' Timotheus
was personally well known to the

Philippians ; see the note i. 1.
ὡς πατρὶ τέκνον] This is often explained by understanding σὺν with
πατρὶ from the following clause σὺν
ἐμοί; see Jelf § 650. Instances of such
omissions however occur chiefly though
not always in poetry, and are found
mostly in clauses connected by con-
junctions (ἤ, καί, etc.). The preposition
is omitted here, because the exact form
of the sentence was not yet decided
in the writer's mind when the first
words were written; see Winer § 1. p.
525, § lxiii. p. 722. For this testimony
to Timotheus compare 1 Cor. iv. 17 ὅς
ἐστίν μου τέκνον ἀγαπητὸν καὶ πιστὸν ἐν
Κυρίῳ, xvi. 10 τὸ γὰρ ἔργον Κυρίου ἐρ-
γάζεται ὡς κἀγώ.
23. τοῦτον μὲν οὖν] '*him then,*' the
clause being answered by πέποιθα δὲ
ὅτι καὶ αὐτὸς ἐλεύσομαι (ver. 24),
while ἐξαυτῆς is matched by ταχέως.
ὡς ἄν...ἐξαυτῆς] '*at once when.*' For
ὡς ἄν temporal comp. Rom. xv. 24,
1 Cor. xi. 34.
ἀφίδω] So ἀφορῶντες Heb. xii. 2.
If any weight is to be attached to the
agreement of the older MSS, the as-
pirated form (ἀφίδω for ἀπίδω) must
be read here. In Acts ii. 7 (οὐχ or
οὐχὶ ἰδοὺ) and in Acts iv. 29 (ἔφιδε)
they are divided. In the three principal MSS of the LXX, so far as I have
noticed, the following instances of
aspirates in compounds of εἶδον occur:
Gen. xvi. 13, εφιδων A ; Gen. xxxi. 49,
εφιδοι A ; Ps. xxx. 8, εφειδες A ; Ps.
xci. 12, εφιδεν A ; Ps. cxi. 8, εφιδη א ;
Jer. xxxi. 19, εφιδε א : Jonah iv. 5,
αφειδη א ; 1 Mac. iii. 59, εφιδειν א A ;
1 Macc. i. 27, εφειδε (for επιδε imper.) A;
2 Macc. viii. 2, εφιδειν (εφιδι) A ; Deut.
xxvi. 15, καθιδε B ; Judith vi. 19,
καθειδε (for κατιδε) A. It must be remembered that in the Vatican MS

ἐμέ, ἐξαυτῆς· <sup>24</sup>πέποιθα δὲ ἐν Κυρίῳ ὅτι καὶ αὐτὸς ταχέως ἐλεύσομαι [πρὸς ὑμᾶς]. <sup>25</sup>ἀναγκαῖον δὲ ἡγησάμην
Ἐπαφρόδιτον τὸν ἀδελφὸν καὶ συνεργὸν καὶ συνστρα-
τιώτην μου, ὑμῶν δὲ ἀπόστολον καὶ λειτουργὸν τῆς

almost all the book of Genesis is lost
and that the Sinaitic contains less
than half of the Old Testament. The
collations of other MSS in Holmes' and
Parsons' LXX supply many additional
examples both in these and other passages. Similarly ἐλπὶς is sometimes
preceded by an aspirate (ἀφελπίζοντες
Luke vi. 35, ἐφ' ἐλπίδι, Rom. viii. 20,
1 Cor. ix. 10, ἀφελπικῶς Hermas *Vis.*
iii. 12); when naturalised in Coptic it
is always so written, and we frequently
find *Helpis* is a proper name in Latin.
In both cases the anomaly is supported by inscriptions: ΕΦΕΙΔΕ Boeckh
no. 3333; ΗΕΛΠΙΔΑ no. 170; the latter being as old as the 5th century B.C.
The aspirates are doubtless to be explained as remnants of the digamma,
which both these words possessed:
see Curtius *Griech. Etym.* pp. 217, 238
(2nd ed.). It is less easy to account
for οὐχ ὄψεσθε Luke xvii. 22, οὐχ
ὀλίγος Acts xii. 18 (in which passages
however the aspirate is not well supported), though there are some indications that ὄπτομαι had a digamma.
On οὐχ Ἰουδαικῶς, Gal. ii. 14, see the
note there.

24. With St Paul's language here
compare 1 Cor. iv. 17, 19, ἔπεμψα
ὑμῖν Τιμόθεον ὅς ἐστίν μου τέκνον κ.τ.λ.
ἐλεύσομαι δὲ ταχέως πρὸς ὑμᾶς ἐὰν ὁ
Κύριος θελήσῃ.

ταχέως] If the view taken in the
introduction (p. 31 sq.) of the date of
this epistle be correct, St Paul's
release was delayed longer than he at
this time expected. We have a choice
between supposing him disappointed
in the anticipation expressed here
or in the anticipation implied in the
injunction to Philemon (ver. 22).

25—30. 'Meanwhile, though I purpose sending Timotheus shortly, though

I trust myself to visit you before very
long, I have thought it necessary
to despatch Epaphroditus to you at
once; Epaphroditus, whom *you* commissioned as your delegate to minister
to my needs, in whom *I* have found a
brother and a fellow-labourer and a
comrade in arms. I have sent him,
because he longed earnestly to see
you and was very anxious and troubled
that you had heard of his illness. Nor
was the report unfounded. He was
indeed so ill that we despaired of his
life But God spared him in His
mercy; mercy not to him only but to
myself also, that I might not be
weighed down by a fresh burden of
sorrow. For this reason I have been
the more eager to send him, that
your cheerfulness may be restored by
seeing him in health, and that my
sorrow may be lightened by sympathy
with your joy. Receive him therefore
in the Lord with all gladness, and
hold such men in honour; for in his
devotion to *the work*, he was brought
to death's door, hazarding his life,
that he might make up by his zeal
and diligence the lack of your personal
services to supplement your charitable
gift.'

25. ἀναγκαῖον κ.τ.λ.] The same expression occurs 2 Cor. ix. 5. ἡγησάμην is here the epistolary aorist, like
ἔπεμψα (ver. 28); for Epaphroditus
seems to have been the bearer of the
letter. See the introduction p. 37 and
the note on Gal. vi. 11.

Ἐπαφρόδιτον] On Epaphroditus see
the introduction p. 61 sq. He is not
mentioned except in this epistle. The
name (corresponding in meaning to the
Latin 'venustus') was extremely common in the Roman period. It was as
sumed by the dictator Sylla himself in

χρείας μου, πέμψαι πρὸς ὑμᾶς, ²⁶ἐπειδὴ ἐπιποθῶν ἦν
πάντας ὑμᾶς, καὶ ἀδημονῶν, διότι ἠκούσατε ὅτι ἠσθένησεν. ²⁷καὶ γὰρ ἠσθένησεν παραπλήσιον θανάτῳ· ἀλλὰ

writing to the Greeks (Λεύκιος Κορνήλιος
Σύλλας Ἐπαφρόδιτος, Plut. *Syll.* 34;
comp. Appian. *Civ.* i. 97). It was
borne by a freedman of Augustus
(Dion Cass. li. 11, 13); by a favourite
of Nero, likewise a freedman (Tac.
*Ann* xv. 55 etc.); by a grammarian
of Chæroneia residing at Rome during
this last emperor's reign (Suidas s. v.);
by a patron of literature (possibly the
same with one of those already mentioned) who encouraged Josephus
(*Antiq.* procem. 2, *Vit.* 76). The name
occurs very frequently in inscriptions
both Greek and Latin, whether at full
length Epaphroditus, or in its contracted form Epaphras.

ἀδελφὸν κ.τ.λ.] The three words
are arranged in an ascending scale;
common sympathy, common work,
common danger and toil and suffering.
Συνστρατιώτης occurs again Philem. 2.
The metaphor is naturally very common: see esp. 2 Cor. x. 3, 4, 1 Tim. i.
18, 2 Tim. ii. 3, 4.

ὑμῶν δέ] This prominent position is
given to ὑμῶν, both to contrast it with
the immediately preceding μου, and to
bind together the words following;
for ἀπόστολον καὶ λειτουργὸν τῆς χρείας
μου form one idea, 'a messenger sent
to minister to my need.' Epaphroditus was the bearer of the contributions
from Philippi (iv. 18), which just below
are designated λειτουργία (ver. 30):
comp. Rom. xv. 27 ἐν τοῖς σαρκικοῖς
λειτουργῆσαι αὐτοῖς. For this sense of
ἀπόστολος, 'a delegate or messenger of
a church,' see 2 Cor. viii. 23 ἀπόστολοι
ἐκκλησιῶν. The interpretation which
makes Epaphroditus an apostle or
bishop of Philippi will be considered
in the Dissertation on the Christian
Ministry.

τῆς χρείας μου] as iv. 16; comp.
Acts xx. 34, Rom. xii. 13.

26. ἐπιποθῶν] 'eagerly longing after': see the note on i. 8. Here the
expression is still further intensified
by the substitution of ἐπιποθῶν ἦν for
ἐπεπόθει. While the external evidence
for and against ἰδεῖν is very evenly
balanced, the language seems to gain
in force by the omission. It may have
been added because ἐπιποθεῖν ἰδεῖν
was a well-remembered expression in
St Paul; Rom. i. 11, 1 Thess. iii. 6,
2 Tim. i. 4.

ἀδημονῶν] 'distressed.' The word is
used in connexion with ἀπορεῖν, ἰλιγ-
γιᾶν (Plato *Theæt.* p. 175 D), with ξενο-
παθεῖν (Plut. *Mor.* 601 c), and the like.
It describes the confused, restless,
half-distracted state, which is produced by physical derangement, or by
mental distress, as grief, shame, disappointment, etc. For its sense here
comp. Dion. Hal. *A. R.* i. 56 ἀδημο-
νοῦντι τῷ ἀνδρὶ καὶ παρεικότι τὸ σῶμα
ὑπὸ λύπης. The derivation of ἀδη-
μονεῖν suggested by Buttmann (*Lexil.*
p. 29), from ἄδημος 'away from home'
and so 'beside oneself' (in which however he seems not to have been aware
that he was anticipated by Photius
*Lex.* p. 9: see Steph. *Thes.* s. v.), is
almost universally accepted. But to
say nothing else, the form of the word
is a serious obstacle; and Lobeck,
*Pathol.* pp. 160, 238, is probably right
in returning to the older derivation
ἀδήμων, ἀδῆσαι. In this case the primary idea of the word will be loath-
ing and discontent. The word occurs in Symmachus, Ps. cxv. 2 (ἐν τῇ
ἐκστάσει LXX), Ps. lx. 2 (ἀκηδιάσαι
LXX), Eccl. vii. 16 (ἐκπλαγῆς LXX); and
in Aquila, Job xviii. 20 (ἐστέναξαν
LXX).

27. καὶ γάρ] 'for indeed.' The
καὶ implies that the previous ἠσθένησεν understates the case.

ὁ Θεὸς ἠλέησεν αὐτόν, οὐκ αὐτὸν δὲ μόνον, ἀλλὰ καὶ
ἐμέ, ἵνα μὴ λύπην ἐπὶ λύπην σχῶ. ²⁸σπουδαιοτέρως οὖν
ἔπεμψα αὐτόν, ἵνα ἰδόντες αὐτὸν πάλιν χαρῆτε, κἀγὼ
ἀλυπότερος ὦ. ²⁹προσδέχεσθε οὖν αὐτὸν ἐν Κυρίῳ μετὰ
πάσης χαρᾶς, καὶ τοὺς τοιούτους ἐντίμους ἔχετε, ³⁰ὅτι

ἐπὶ λύπην] So all the best copies,
while the received text reads ἐπὶ λύπῃ.
In such cases the dative is more common in classical authors, but the accusative is supported by several passages in the LXX, e. g. Ezech. vii. 26
ἀγγελία ἐπὶ ἀγγελίαν, Ps. lxviii. 28
ἀνομίαν ἐπὶ τὴν ἀνομίαν, Is. xxviii. 10
(where both constructions are combined) θλίψιν ἐπὶ θλίψιν, ἐλπίδα ἐπ᾽
ἐλπίδι. Comp. Matt. xxiv. 2, and see
A. Buttmann p. 291.

28. σπουδαιοτέρως] 'with increased
eagerness' on account of this circumstance: see for the comparative Winer
§ xxxv. p. 304, and compare the note
on περισσοτέρως i. 14.

ἔπεμψα] i. e. with the letter, as in
Ephes. vi. 22, Col. iv. 8, Philem. 11,
and perhaps also 2 Cor. ix. 3. On this
aorist see above, ver. 25.

πάλιν χαρῆτε] 'may recover your
cheerfulness,' which had been marred
by the news of Epaphroditus' illness:
for the order suggests the connexion
of πάλιν with χαρῆτε rather than with
ἰδόντες.

ἀλυπότερος ὦ] 'my sorrow may be
lessened.' The expression is purposely substituted for πάλιν χαρῶ, for a
prior sorrow will still remain unremov-
ed; comp. ver. 27 λύπην ἐπὶ λύπην.

29. προσδέχεσθε κ.τ.λ.] Comp. Rom.
xvi. 2.

30. τὸ ἔργον] Comp. Acts xv. 38
Παῦλος δὲ ἠξίου τὸν ἀποστάντα ἀπ᾽
αὐτῶν ἀπὸ Παμφυλίας καὶ μὴ συνελ-
θόντα αὐτοῖς εἰς τὸ ἔργον, μὴ συν-
παραλαμβάνειν τοῦτον, where we seem
to have St Paul's very words. So too
Ignat. Ephes. 14 οὐ γὰρ ἐπαγγελίας τὸ
γον, Rom. 3 οὐ πεισμονῆς τὸ ἔργον
ἀλλὰ μεγέθους ἐστὶν ὁ χριστιανισμός.

Thus τὸ ἔργον is used absolutely, like
ἡ ὁδός, τὸ θέλημα, τὸ ὄνομα (see on
ver. 9), etc. Though one only of the
oldest MSS has τὸ ἔργον alone, this
must be the correct reading. The
others add Κυρίου, Χριστοῦ, τοῦ Κυρίου,
τοῦ Χριστοῦ, or τοῦ Θεοῦ, of which the
two first are highly supported; but the
authorities, being very evenly divided,
neutralise each other. All alike are
insertions to explain τὸ ἔργον.

παραβολευσάμενος] 'having gambled
with his life.' From παραβάλλεσθαι,
to throw down a stake, to make a
venture (e. g. Polyb. ii. 94. 4 οὐδαμῶς
κρίνων ἐκκυβεύειν οὐδὲ παραβάλλεσθαι
τοῖς ὅλοις) comes παράβολος, 'gambling,
rash, reckless,' whence παραβολεύεσθαι
'to play the gambler,' formed on the
analogy of ἀσωτεύεσθαι, διαλεκτικεύ-
εσθαι, περπερεύεσθαι, πονηρεύεσθαι, 'to
play the spendthrift, quibbler, brag-
gart, scoundrel, etc.' : see Lobeck
Phryn. p. 67. With the use here
compare the ecclesiastical sense of
parabolani, brotherhoods who at the
risk of their lives nursed the sick and
buried the dead. For the expression
compare Diod. Sic. iii. 35 ἔκριναν
παραβαλέσθαι ταῖς ψυχαῖς, Hom. Il.
ix. 322 αἰεὶ ἐμὴν ψυχὴν παραβαλλό-
μενος. While παραβάλλεσθαι takes
either an accusative or a dative of the
thing staked, παραβολεύεσθαι from its
nature can have only the latter. The
original meaning of the English word
'hazard' is the same, 'a game of
chance': see for the derivation Diez
Etymol. Worterb. der Rom. Spr. p.
33 s. v. azzardo, E. Müller Etym.
Worterb. der Eng. Spr. s. v. No one
who has felt the nervous vigour of St
Paul's style will hesitate between παρα-

διὰ τὸ ἔργον μέχρι θανάτου ἤγγισεν παραβολευσάμε-
νος τῇ ψυχῇ, ἵνα ἀναπληρώσῃ τὸ ὑμῶν ὑστέρημα τῆς
πρός με λειτουργίας.

III.    ¹Τὸ λοιπόν, ἀδελφοί μου, χαίρετε ἐν Κυρίῳ·

βολευσάμενος and παραβουλευσάμενος. The latter, which would mean 'having consulted amiss,' stands in the received text: but the evidence is strongly in favour of the former. Both words alike are very rare.

ἀναπληρώσῃ κ.τ.λ.] as in 1 Cor. xvi. 17 χαίρω ἐπὶ τῇ παρουσίᾳ Στεφανᾶ κ.τ.λ. ὅτι τὸ ὑμέτεοον ὑστέρημα αὐτοὶ ἀνεπλήρωσαν: comp. Clem. Rom. § 38 δι' οὗ ἀναπληρωθῇ αὐτοῦ τὸ ὑστέρημα. So also ἀνταναπληροῦν in Col. i. 24 and προσαναπληροῦν in 2 Cor. xi. 9.

τὸ ὑμῶν ὑστέρημα κ.τ.λ.] i. e. 'what your services towards me lacked to be complete,' in other words 'your personal ministrations,' as in 1 Cor. xvi. 17 just quoted. It seems plain from this expression that Epaphroditus illness was the consequence not of persecution but of over-exertion.

III. 1. 'And now, my brethren, I must wish you farewell. Rejoice in the Lord. Forgive me, if I speak once more on an old topic. It is not irksome to me to speak, and it is safe for you to hear.'

τὸ λοιπόν] 'for the rest,' i.e. 'finally, in conclusion.' With λοιπὸν or τὸ λοιπὸν St Paul frequently ushers in the concluding portion of his letters containing the practical exhortations; 1 Thess. iv. 1, 2 Thess. iii. 1, 2 Cor. xiii. 11, Ephes. vi. 10 (where however τοῦ λοιποῦ should probably be read). Sometimes this concluding portion is prolonged, as in the First Epistle to the Thessalonians, where it extends over two chapters. In the present instance the letter is interrupted, a fresh subject is introduced, the conclusion is for a time forgotten, and St Paul resumes his farewell injunctions later at iv. 8 τὸ λοιπόν, ἀδελφοὶ κ.τ.λ. See the introduction, p. 69 sq.

In other passages λοιπὸν and τὸ λοιπὸν occur in reference to the approaching end of all things; as 1 Cor. vii. 29 ὁ καιρὸς συνεσταλμένος ἐστίν, τὸ λοιπὸν ἵνα κ.τ.λ., Ign. Ephes. 11, Smyrn. 9.

χαίρετε] 'farewell.' At the same time the word conveys an injunction to rejoice; see ii. 18, iv. 4, and the note on the latter passage.

τὰ αὐτά] 'the same things.' But to what does St Paul refer? To his own personal intercourse with the Philippians? To messages delivered by his delegates? To previous letters not now extant? To some topic contained in this present epistle? The expression itself τὰ αὐτὰ γράφειν seems to limit the range of choice to written communications. The theory of an earlier letter or letters, which seems to be supported by an expression of Polycarp (§ 3 ἀπὼν ὑμῖν ἔγραψεν ἐπιστολάς), will be considered in the detached note. At present it is sufficient to say that if the epistle itself supplies the requisite allusion, it is much more naturally sought here than elsewhere. On what subject then does this epistle dwell repeatedly?

Two answers will suggest themselves. (1) The duty of rejoicing. This topic is very prominent in the epistle: see the note on i. 4. It has occurred more than once already. It has the advantage also of appearing in the immediate context, χαίρετε ἐν Κυρίῳ. Nevertheless it seems inadequate to explain St Paul's language here. Such an injunction has no very direct bearing on the safety of the Philippians; its repetition could hardly be suspected of being irksome to the Apostle. The words seem obviously to refer to some actual or threatened evil, against which a reiterated warn-

Τὰ αὐτὰ γράφειν ὑμῖν ἐμοὶ μὲν οὐκ ὀκνηρόν, ὑμῖν δὲ
ἀσφαλές.

ing was necessary. (2) Such an evil existed in the *dissensions* among the Philippians. This topic either directly or indirectly has occupied a very considerable portion of the letter hitherto; and it appears again more than once before the close: see the introduction p. 67 sq. It is the Apostle's practice to conclude with a warning against the prevailing danger of his correspondents. The Corinthians are again reminded that 'the Lord cometh' (1 Cor. xvi. 22); the Galatians are told once more that 'circumcision is nothing and uncircumcision is

nothing' (Gal. vi. 15); the Thessalonians receive a parting injunction against the spirit of restlessness and disorder spreading among them (1 Thess. v. 14, 2 Thess. iii. 14). The Apostle therefore would naturally lay stress on this point here, intending, as he appears to have done, to bring his letter to a speedy close. See the note on iii. 2.

ὀκνηρόν] '*irksome, tedious.*' The word generally signifies 'dilatory, sluggish,' as in the LXX frequently; but here it is active, 'causing ὄκνος,' as in Soph. *Œd. T.* 834 ἡμῖν μέν, ὦναξ, ταῦτ᾽ ὀκνηρά.

## The synonymes μορφή and σχῆμα[1].

The word σχῆμα corresponds exactly in derivation, though but partially Classical in meaning, to the old English 'haviour.' In its first sense it denotes the sense of figure, shape, fashion, of a thing. Thence it gathers several derived mean- σχῆμα ings. It gets to signify, like the corresponding Latin 'habitus,' sometimes the dress or costume (as Aristoph. *Eq.* 1331 τεττιγοφόρας ἀρχαίῳ σχήματι λαμπρός), sometimes the attitude or demeanour (as Eur. *Ion* 238 τρόπων τεκμήριον τὸ σχῆμ' ἔχεις τόδε). It is used also for a 'figure of speech,' as the dress in which the sense clothes itself or the posture which the language assumes. It signifies moreover pomp, display, outward circumstance (as Soph. *Ant.* 1169 τύραννον σχῆμ' ἔχων), and frequently semblance, pretence, as opposed to reality, truth (as Plat. *Epin.* p. 989 c οὐ σχήμασι τεχνάζοντας ἀλλὰ ἀληθείᾳ τιμῶντας ἀρετήν, Plut. *Vit. Galb.* 15 ἀρνήσεως σχῆμα τὴν ἀναβολὴν εἶναι φάσκοντες, Eur. *Fragm. Æol.* 18 οὐδὲν ἄλλο πλὴν ὄχλος καὶ σχῆμα). Altogether it suggests the idea of something changeable, fleeting, unsubstantial.

Μορφή, like σχῆμα, originally refers to the organs of sense[2]. If σχῆμα and of may be rendered by 'figure,' 'fashion,' μορφή corresponds to 'form.' It μορφή. comprises all those sensible qualities, which striking the eye lead to the conviction that we see such and such a thing. The conviction indeed may be false, for the form may be a phantom; but to the senses at all events the representation of the object conceived is complete. The word has not and cannot have any of those secondary senses which attach to σχῆμα, as gesture or dress or parade or pretext. In many cases indeed the words are used convertibly, because the sense is sufficiently lax to include either. But the difference between the two is tested by the fact that the μορφὴ of a definite thing as such, for instance of a lion or a tree, is one only, while its σχῆμα may change every minute. Thus we often find μορφῆς σχῆμα, as in Latin 'figura formæ[3],' but rarely, if ever, σχήματος μορφή (Eur. *Iph. Taur.* 292 οὐ ταὐτὰ μορφῆς σχήματα, *Ion* 992 ποῖόν τι μορφῆς σχῆμα;). The σχῆμα is often an accident of the μορφή.

[1] The following note is founded on some remarks which appeared several years ago (in the *Journal of Class. and Sacr. Philol.* no. VII. p. 113 sq., 121), enlarged and modified. The distinction of μορφὴ and σχῆμα has since been drawn out by Archbishop Trench (*N. T. Syn.* § lxx) in his pointed and instructive manner.

[2] I have purposely avoided the question of its derivation, feeling that I have no right to an opinion on the subject. Benfey, *Wurzel-lex.* II. p. 309, connects it with the Sanscrit 'varpas,' 'form.'

[3] As e.g. Lucr. iv. 69 'formai servare figuram.' Compare the account of 'forma' and 'figura' given by Döderlein, *Lat. Syn.* III. p. 25 sq. (referred to by Trench, l. c. p. 93). His distinction corresponds to that which is here given of μορφὴ and σχῆμα. 'The form (Gestalt),' he says, 'so far as it has definite outlines is *figura*; so far as it is the visible impression and the stamp of the inner being and corresponds thereto, it is *forma*.'

From the primary popular sense of μορφή we pass to its secondary philosophical meaning. And here the older philosophers do not render much assistance. In Parmenides indeed (μορφὰς γὰρ κατέθεντο δύο, ver. 112 Karsten) the word signifies 'natures,' 'essences,' for he is speaking of two elemental principles of the universe. But without the light thrown upon its use here by the phraseology of later thinkers, no inference could safely be drawn from this solitary instance.

In Plato we first meet with a clear example of its philosophical sense. In the Phædo (p. 103 E, 104 A) Socrates, eliciting the doctrine of ideas by question and answer after his wont, concludes that 'not only is the same name always claimed for the εἶδος[1] itself, but also for something else which is not the εἶδος and yet has its μορφή always whenever it exists.' And in illustration of his meaning he adduces the example of the odd and the number three, the latter being always called odd and being inseparable from oddness, though not the odd itself. Thus in Plato's language the μορφή is the impress of the idea on the individual, or in other words the specific character. It need not therefore denote any material sensible quality, as in the instance quoted it does not. In Plato however the philosophical sense of μορφή is very rare. On the other hand Aristotle uses it commonly.

But its relation to εἶδος has undergone a change, corresponding to the difference in his metaphysical views. As he discards Plato's doctrine of ideas wholly, as he recognises no eternal self-existent archetype distinct from the specific character exhibited in the individuals, it follows as a matter of course that with him εἶδος and μορφή are identical. There are, according to his teaching, two elements or principles or causes of things; the matter, the substratum supporting the qualities, and the form, the aggregate of the qualities[2]. The form he calls indifferently εἶδος or μορφή[3]. He moreover designates it by various synonymes. It is sometimes 'the abstract conception realised' (τὸ τί ἦν εἶναι[4]), sometimes 'the essence corresponding to the definition' (ἡ οὐσία ἡ κατὰ τὸν λόγον),

---

[1] Here the εἶδος is plainly the ἰδέα. Plato seems to have used both words alike to denote the eternal archetype, as for instance in the passages in Trendelenburg, *Platon. de ideis doctr.* p. 33 sqq. Where however especial accuracy was aimed at, ἰδέα would naturally be preferred to εἶδος: see Thompson's note on Archer Butler's *Lectures* II. p. 128.

[2] A large number of passages is collected by Waitz, *Organon* II. p. 401 sq. See also Heyder *Aristot. u. Hegel. Dialektik* p. 182 sq., and especially Ritter and Preller *Hist. Phil.* p. 324 sq. (ed. 2). In other places Aristotle speaks of four causes, the efficient, the material, the formal, and the final. The final and the efficient causes however may be conceived as involved in the formal: see esp. G. Schneider, *De Causa*

*Finali Aristotelea* (Berol. 1865), p. 15 sq.

[3] See Waitz *Organon* II. p. 405. There are exceptional cases where either word is used in its popular rather than its philosophical sense, referring directly to the organs of *vision*: but Biese, *die Philosophie des Aristoteles* I. p. 439, is not justified in his general distinction that μορφή is 'die aüsserliche sichtbare Form der Dinge,' and εἶδος 'das die Dinge von innen heraus Gestaltende.' This distinction may suit one passage, but it is contradicted by twenty others. The same remark applies to the attempt made by the old commentators on Aristotle to distinguish μορφή and εἶδος.

[4] On this term see Trendelenburg *Rhein. Mus.* II. p. 457 sq., esp. pp. 469, 481 (1828); comp. his note on *de Anima* i. 1, 2, p. 192 sq.

sometimes 'the definition of the essence' (ὁ λόγος τῆς οὐσίας), sometimes 'the definition alone, sometimes 'the essence' alone. He calls it also 'the actuality' (ἐνέργεια) or 'the perfection' (ἐντελέχεια)[1], matter being designated 'the potentiality' (δύναμις). 'So rich in wealth and titles,' said a later writer of a rival school half in irony, 'is the εἶδος with Aristotle[2].' The significance of his μορφή or εἶδος will appear also from the fact that he elsewhere identifies it with the final cause (τέλος or οὗ ἕνεκα)[3], because the end or purpose is implicitly contained in the qualities. It is still more evident from the intimate connexion which he conceives to exist between the form and the nature. 'The term nature,' he says, 'is used to signify three things; sometimes it is equivalent to the matter, sometimes to the form, sometimes to both combined. Of the nature according to matter and the nature according to form, the latter is the more influential (κυριωτέρα)[4],' i.e. it has a more important function in making the thing what it is.

It will appear moreover from this account, that the term μορφή, though originally derived from the organs of sense like εἶδος, and referring to external conformation, has in the language of Aristotle a much wider application, being not only applied to physical qualities generally, but also extended to immaterial objects. Thus he says in one passage that skin, vein, membrane, and all such things, belong to the same μορφή[5]; in another, that courage and justice and prudence have the same μορφή in a state as in an individual[6]; in a third, that science and health may be called the μορφή and εἶδος of the scientific and the healthy respectively[7]; while in a fourth, criticising the saying of Democritus that 'anybody could see what was the form (μορφή) of a man,' meaning that he might be known by his shape and colour, he replies that 'a corpse has the form (μορφή) of the human shape (σχήματος) and yet nevertheless is not a man[8].' The form of a man therefore in Aristotle's conception was something more than his sensible appearance.

This sense of μορφή, as the specific character, was naturally transmitted Later from these great original thinkers to the philosophers of later ages. It is philoso- found for instance in Plutarch[9]. It appears very definitely in the Neopla- phers.

---

[1] On the form regarded as the ἐνέργεια and the ἐντελέχεια see Trendelenburg de Anima ii. 1, p. 295 sq.

[2] A Platonist in Stobæus Ecl. i. c. 13 οὕτως αὐτῷ πλούσιόν τε καὶ πολυώνυμόν ἐστι τὸ εἶδος.

[3] See Schneider de Caus. Fin. Aristot. p. 10 sq. and the passages quoted p. 12.

[4] Phys. Ausc. ii. 1, p. 192 A (Bekker), de Part. An. i. 1, p. 640 B. See below, note 8.

[5] de Anim. Gen. ii. 3, p. 737 B.

[6] Polit. vii. 1, p. 1323 B.

[7] de Anima ii. 2, p. 414 A.

[8] de Part. An. i. 1, p. 640 B, ἡ γὰρ κατὰ τὴν μορφὴν φύσις κυριωτέρα τῆς ὑλικῆς φύσεως. εἰ μὲν οὖν τῷ σχήματι

καὶ τῷ χρώματι ἕκαστόν ἐστι τῶν τε ζῴων καὶ τῶν μορίων, ὀρθῶς ἂν Δημόκριτος λέγοι· φαίνεται γὰρ οὕτως ὑπολαβεῖν. φησὶ γοῦν παντὶ δῆλον εἶναι οἷόν τι τὴν μορφήν ἐστιν ὁ ἄνθρωπος, ὡς ὄντος αὐτοῦ τῷ τε σχήματι καὶ τῷ χρώματι γνωρίμου. καίτοι καὶ ὁ τεθνεὼς ἔχει τὴν αὐτὴν τοῦ σχήματος μορφήν, ἀλλ' ὅμως οὐκ ἔστιν ἄνθρωπος (i.e. the corpse has the μορφή of the human σχῆμα, but it has not the μορφή of a man).

[9] Mor. p. 1013 C αὐτός τε γὰρ ὁ κόσμος οὗτος καὶ τῶν μερῶν ἕκαστον αὐτοῦ συνέστηκεν ἔκ τε σωματικῆς οὐσίας καὶ νοητῆς, ὧν ἡ μὲν ὕλην καὶ ὑποκείμενον, ἡ δὲ μορφὴν καὶ εἶδος τῷ γενομένῳ παρέσχε κ.τ.λ. Comp. p. 1022 E. For these references and the passage in the

tonists[1]. And what is more to our purpose, it is recognised by Philo, the chief representative of Alexandrian Judaism[2].

Popular language. Nor can it have been wholly without influence on the language of everyday life. Terms, like ideas, gradually permeate society till they reach its lower strata. Words stamped in the mint of the philosopher pass into general currency, losing their sharpness of outline meanwhile, but in the main retaining their impress and value. The exclusive technicalities of the scholastic logic are the common property of shopmen and artisans in our own day.

New Testament usage

Do we then find in the New Testament any distinction between μορφή and σχῆμα corresponding to that which appears to have held roughly in the common language of the Greeks and to have been still further developed in the technical systems of philosophers?

of σχῆμα

A review of the passages where σχῆμα and its derivatives are used will not, I think, leave any doubt on the mind that this word retains the notion of 'instability, changeableness,' quite as strongly as in classical Greek. Thus 'the fashion of this world,' which 'passeth away,' is τὸ σχῆμα τοῦ κόσμου τούτου (1 Cor. vii. 31). 'To fall in with the fashion of this world' is συνσχηματίζεσθαι τῷ αἰῶνι τούτῳ (Rom. xii. 2). 'To follow the capricious guidance of the passions' is συνσχηματίζεσθαι ταῖς ἐπιθυμίαις (1 Pet. i. 14). The fictitious illusory transformation whereby evil assumes the mask of good—the false apostles appearing as the true, the prince of darkness as an angel of light, the ministers of Satan as ministers of righteousness—is described by the thrice repeated word μετασχηματίζεσθαι (2 Cor. xi. 13, 14, 15). The significance of σχῆμα will be felt at once, if in any of these passages we attempt to substitute μορφή in its stead[3].

and μορφή

On the other hand the great and entire change of the inner life, otherwise described as being born again, being created anew, is spoken of as a conversion of μορφή always, of σχῆμα never. Thus 'He fore-ordained them conformable (συμμόρφους) to the image of His Son' (Rom. viii. 29); 'Being made conformable (συμμορφιζόμενος) to His death' (Phil. iii. 10); 'We are transformed (μεταμορφούμεθα) into the same image' (2 Cor. iii. 18); 'To be transformed by the renewal of the mind' (Rom. xii. 2); 'Until Christ be formed (μορφωθῇ) in you' (Gal. iv. 19). In these passages again, if any one doubts whether μορφή has any special force, let him substitute σχῆμα and try the effect. In some cases indeed, where the organs of sense are concerned and where the appeal lies to popular usage, either word might be used. Yet I think it will be felt at once that in the account of the transfiguration μετα-

next note I am indebted to Wyttenbach's note on Plato, Phæd. p. 103 E.

[1] See e.g. Plotin. Ennead. i. 6, p. 52 A, especially the expression οὐκ ἀνασχομένης τῆς ὕλης τὸ πάντη κατὰ τὸ εἶδος μορφοῦσθαι.

[2] de Vict. Off. § 13, p. 261 M, τὸ τεθλασμένον ἀφῄρηται τὴν ποιότητα καὶ τὸ εἶδος καὶ οὐδὲν ἕτερόν ἐστιν ἢ κυρίως εἰπεῖν ἄμορφος ὕλη, and lower down,

ταῖς ἀσωμάτοις δυνάμεσιν, ὧν ἔτυμον ὄνομα αἱ ἰδέαι, κατεχρήσατο πρὸς τὸ γένος ἕκαστον τὴν ἁρμόττουσαν λαβεῖν μορφήν. For other references see Dähne Jüdisch-Alex. Religionsphilosophie I. p. 185.

[3] In 1 Cor. iv. 6 ταῦτα μετεσχημάτισα εἰς ἐμαυτὸν κ.τ.λ. the word refers to a rhetorical σχῆμα, and here μετεμόρφωσα would of course be out of place.

σχηματίζεσθαι would have been out of place and that μεταμορφοῦσθαι alone is adequate to express the completeness and significance of the change (Matt. xvii. 2, Mark ix. 2). Even in the later addition to St Mark's Gospel where our Lord is described as appearing to the two disciples ἐν ἑτέρᾳ μορφῇ, though μορφὴ here has no peculiar force, yet σχῆμα would perhaps be avoided instinctively, as it might imply an illusion or an imposture. It will be observed also that in two passages where St Paul speaks of an appearance which is superficial and unreal, though not using σχῆμα, he still avoids μορφὴ as inappropriate and adopts μόρφωσις instead (Rom. ii. 20 τὴν μόρφωσιν τῆς γνώσεως καὶ τῆς ἀληθείας, 2 Tim. iii. 5 μόρφωσιν εὐσεβείας). Here the termination denotes the aiming after or affecting the μορφή.

And the distinction, which has thus appeared from the review of each word separately, will be seen still more clearly from those passages where they occur together. In Rom. xii. 2 μὴ συνσχηματίζεσθαι τῷ αἰῶνι τούτῳ ἀλλὰ μεταμορφοῦσθαι τῇ ἀνακαινώσει τοῦ νοὸς the form of the sentence calls attention to the contrast, and the appropriateness of each word in its own connexion is obvious : 'Not to follow the fleeting *fashion* of this world, but to undergo a complete change, assume a new *form*, in the renewal of the mind.' On the other hand in Phil. iii. 21 μετασχηματίσει τὸ σῶμα τῆς ταπεινώσεως ἡμῶν σύμμορφον τῷ σώματι τῆς δόξης αὐτοῦ, the difference is not obvious at first sight. The meaning however seems to be, 'will *change* the *fashion* of the body of our humiliation and *fix* it in the *form* of the body of His glory.' Here I think it will be clear that a compound of σχῆμα could not be substituted for σύμμορφον without serious detriment to the sense : while on the other hand μεταμορφώσει might possibly have stood for μετασχηματίσει[1].

*Concurrence of the two words.*

I now come to the passage in the Epistle to the Philippians out of which this investigation has arisen. But before attempting to discover what is implied by μορφὴ Θεοῦ, it will be necessary to clear the way by disposing of a preliminary question. Does the expression ἐν μορφῇ Θεοῦ ὑπάρχων refer to the pre-incarnate or the incarnate Christ? Those who adopt the latter view for the most part explain the words of the supernatural or divine power and grace manifested by our Lord during His earthly ministry. Thus in ancient times the Ambrosian Hilary, 'Deus apparet, dum mortuos excitat, surdis reddit auditum, leprosos mundat, et alia' : thus in a later age Erasmus, 'Ipsis factis se Deum esse declararet etc.'; and Luther, 'Dass göttliche Gestalt nichts anderes sei denn sich erzeigen mit Worten und Werken gegen andere als ein Herr und Gott[2].' Against this view De Wette, though himself referring the expression to Christ incarnate, urges with justice that the point of time marked by ὑπάρχων is evidently prior to our Lord's actual ministry,

*Phil. ii. 6, 7.*

*The pre-incarnate Christ is meant.*

---

[1] Of the two words μετασχηματίζειν would refer to the transient condition *from* which, μεταμορφοῦν to the permanent state *to* which, the change takes place. Archbishop Trench however supposes that μετασχηματίζειν is here preferred to μεταμορφοῦν as expressing

'transition but no absolute solution of continuity,' the spiritual body being developed from the natural, as the butterfly from the caterpillar; *N. T. Syn.* 2nd ser. p. 91.

[2] *Postill. ad. Epist. Domin. Palm.*(XII. p. 630 ed. Hall.), quoted by De Wette.

the period of this ministry itself being a period of humiliation. He therefore explains it as describing the glory dwelling *potentially* in Christ, at the moment when He commenced His ministry. The meaning of St Paul, he thinks, is best illustrated by the account of the temptation (Matt. iv. 8), where our Lord rejects Satan's offer of 'all the kingdoms of the world and their glory.' At that moment and in that act of renunciation it might be said of Him that ἐν μορφῇ Θεοῦ ὑπάρχων οὐχ ἁρπαγμὸν ἡγήσατο τὸ εἶναι ἴσα Θεῷ ἀλλὰ ἑαυτὸν ἐκένωσεν. But this is quite as unsatisfactory as the explanation which he rejects. The point of time is clearly prior not only to our Lord's open ministry, but also to His becoming man. Even if the words μορφὴν δούλου λαβὼν did not directly refer to the incarnation, as they appear to do, nothing else can be understood by ἐν ὁμοιώματι ἀνθρώπων γενόμενος. We cannot suppose St Paul to have meant, that our Lord was not in the likeness of men before His baptism and ministry, and became so then for the first time. On the contrary all accounts alike agree in representing this (so far as regards His earthly life) as the turning-point when He began to 'manifest forth His *glory* (John ii. 11).' It was an exaggeration indeed when certain early heretics represented His baptism as the moment of His first assumption of *Deity*: but only by a direct reversal of the accounts in the Gospel could it be regarded in any sense as the commencement of His *humanity*. The whole context in St Paul clearly implies that the being born as man was the first step in His humiliation, as the death on the Cross was the last. In other words, it requires that ἐν μορφῇ Θεοῦ ὑπάρχων be referred to a point of time prior to the incarnation.

Thus μορφή refers to the divine attributes. This being so, what meaning must we attach to 'the form of God' in which our Lord pre-existed? In the Clementine Homilies St Peter is represented as insisting upon the anthropomorphic passages in the Scriptures and maintaining therefrom that God has a sensible form (μορφή). To the objection of his opponent that if God has a form (μορφή), He must have a figure, a shape (σχῆμα) also, the Apostle is made to reply by accepting the inference : 'God has a σχῆμα; He has eyes and hands and feet like a man; nevertheless He has no need to use them[1].' Not such was St Paul's conception of God. Not in this sense could he speak of the μορφή, not in any sense could he speak of the σχῆμα, of Him who is ' King of kings and Lord of lords, who only hath immortality, who dwelleth in light unapproachable, whom no man hath seen or can see (1 Tim. vi. 15, 16).' It remains then that μορφή must apply to the attributes of the Godhead. In other words, it is used in a sense substantially the same which it bears in Greek philosophy[2]. It suggests the same idea which is otherwise expressed in

---

[1] *Clem. Hom.* xvii. 3, 7, 8.

[2] A passage in Justin Martyr (*Apol.* i. 9) fairly illustrates the distinction of μορφή and σχῆμα in St Paul. He says that Christians do not believe the idols formed by men's hands to have the form (μορφήν) of God; they have only the names and the shapes (σχήματα) of demons; the form of God is not of this kind (οὐ τοιαύτην ἔχειν τὴν μορφήν) His glory and form are ineffable (ἄρρητο. δόξαν καὶ μορφὴν ἔχων). He thus appears to contrast the visible σχήματα ο demons with the insensible immateria μορφή of God. A corresponding dis tinction also seems to hold in the *Pisti*

St John by ὁ Λόγος τοῦ Θεοῦ, in Christian writers of succeeding ages by
υἰὸς Θεοῦ ὢν Θεός, and in the Nicene Creed by Θεὸς ἐκ Θεοῦ.

In accepting this conclusion we need not assume that St Paul con- St Paul's
sciously derived his use of the term from any philosophical nomenclature. usage ac-
There was sufficient definiteness even in its popular usage to suggest this for.
meaning when it was transferrred from the objects of sense to the conceptions of the mind. Yet if St John adopted λόγος, if St Paul himself adopted
εἰκὼν, πρωτοτοκος, and the like, from the language of existing theological
schools, it seems very far from improbable that the closely analogous expression μορφὴ Θεοῦ should have been derived from a similar source. The
speculations of Alexandrian and Gnostic Judaism formed a ready channel,
by which the philosophical terms of ancient Greece were brought within
reach of the Apostles of Christ.

Thus in the passage under consideration the μορφὴ is contrasted with General
the σχῆμα, as that which is intrinsic and essential with that which is acci- result.
dental and outward. And the three clauses imply respectively the true
divine nature of our Lord (μορφὴ Θεοῦ), the true human nature (μορφὴ δούλου), and the externals of the human nature (σχήματι ὡς ἄνθρωπος)[1].

## Different interpretations of οὐχ ἁρπαγμὸν ἡγήσατο.

It will appear from the notes, that two principal interpretations of οὐχ Two inter-
ἁρπαγμὸν ἡγήσατο have been proposed, depending on the different senses pretations
assigned to ἁρπαγμός. In the one the prominent idea is the assertion, in
the other the surrender, of privileges. The one lays stress on the majesty,
the other on the humility, of our Lord. These two interpretations may
conveniently be considered side by side and discussed at greater length.

1. If ἁρπαγμὸς 'plundering' is taken to mean 'robbery,' 'usurpation,' (1) ἁρ-
then the expression asserts that the equality with God was the natural παγμὸς
possession, the inherent right, of our Lord. This interpretation suits the robbery.

Sophia, where both words occur several
times, pp. 38, 184, 226, 246, 253, 272,
273, 274, 277; the former especially in
the phrase ἀλήθεια μορφῆς opposed to
similitude or copy (παράδειγμα, see p.
253), the latter in connexion with τύποι
and παραδείγματα (see esp. 272 sq.).
[1] In the controversies of the fourth
and fifth centuries great stress was laid
by Catholic writers on the force of
μορφὴ here. See for instance Hilary of
Poitiers de Trin. viii. 45 (II. p. 245),
Psalm cxxxviii. (I. p. 569), Ambrose
Epist. 46 (II. p. 986), Greg. Nyss.
Eunom. iv. p. 566 (ἡ δὲ μορφὴ τοῦ Θεοῦ

ταὐτὸν τῇ οὐσίᾳ πάντως ἐστίν), and the
commentators Victorinus, Ambrosiaster, Chrysostom, and Theodoret, on this
passage. St Chrysostom especially discusses the matter at some length. It is
not surprising that they should have
taken this view, but they could hardly
have insisted with such confidence on
the identity of μορφὴ and οὐσία, unless
they had at least a reasonable case
on their side. I trust the investigation in the text will show that their
view was not groundless, though their
language might be at times over-
strained.

words themselves well enough, when isolated from their context, and so far is free from objection. But it takes no account of the clauses which

The context lost sight of.

immediately precede and follow. (1) It neglects the foregoing words. For the Apostle is there enforcing the duty of humility, and when he adds 'Have the mind which was in Jesus Christ,' we expect this appeal to our great Example to be followed immediately by a reference, not to the right which He *claimed*, but to the dignity which He *renounced*. The dislocation of thought caused by this interpretation is apparent; 'Be ye humble and like-minded with Christ, who partaking of the divine nature claimed equality with God.' The mention of our Lord's condescension is thus postponed too late in the sentence. (2) And again this interpretation wholly disregards the connexion with the words following. For in the expression οὐχ ἁρπαγμὸν ἡγήσατο κ.τ.λ. ἀλλὰ ἑαυτὸν ἐκένωσεν, the particles οὐχ and ἀλλὰ obviously correspond, 'not the one *but* the other'; so that ἐκένωσει ἑαυτὸν must contain the idea which directly contrasts with ἁρπαγμὸν ἡγήσατο. On the other hand the interpretation in question renders ἀλλὰ as equivalent to ἀλλ' ὅμως. Besides being unnatural in itself after οὐχ, this rendering fails entirely to explain the emphatic position of ἁρπαγμόν.

Influence of the Latin fathers.

This sense, which is adopted in our own English Version and has been extensively received in modern times, may probably be traced to the influence of the Latin fathers, who interpreted the rendering of the Latin Version without reference to the original. The Latin phrase 'rapinam arbitrari' did not convey the secondary meaning which was at once suggested by ἁρπαγμὸν (ἅρπαγμα) ἡγεῖσθαι; nor perhaps would the Latin particles 'non...sed' bring out the idea of contrast so strongly as οὐχ...ἀλλά. At all events it should be noticed, that while this interpretation is most common (though not universal) among Latin writers, it is unsupported by a single Greek father, unless possibly at a very late date.

Such is the interpretation of TERTULLIAN *de Resurr. Carn.* 6, *adv. Prax.* 7, *adv. Marc.* v. 20; of the AMBROSIAN HILARY here; of ST AMBROSE *de Fid.* ii. 8 (II. p. 483 ed. Bened.) 'Quod enim quis non habet, rapere conatur; ergo non quasi rapinam habebat aequalitatem cum Patre etc.'; of PRIMASIUS here; and above all of ST AUGUSTINE who again and again quotes and explains the passage in his *Sermons*, 92 (v. p. 500 ed. Bened.), 118 (p. 587), 183 (p. 875), 186 (p. 885), 213 (p. 937), 244 (p. 1019), 264 (p. 1075), 292 (p. 1170), 304 (p. 1235); comp. *in Psalm.* xc (IV. p. 972). The distinctness with which this interpretation was enunciated by the greatest teacher of the Western Church would necessarily secure for it a wide reception.

(2) ἁρπαγμὸς 'a prize.'

2. If on the other hand ἁρπαγμὸν ἡγεῖσθαι is considered equivalent to the common phrase ἅρπαγμα ἡγεῖσθαι, so that ἁρπαγμὸς will signify 'a prize, a treasure,' then the logical connexion with the context before and after is strictly preserved: 'Be humble as Christ was humble: He, though existing before the worlds in the form of God, did not treat His equality with God as a prize, a treasure to be greedily clutched and ostentatiously displayed: on the contrary He resigned the glories of heaven.' The only objection to this rendering, the form ἁρπαγμὸς in place of ἅρπαγμα, has been considered in the notes.

*External Evidence*

This is the common and indeed almost universal interpretation of the Greek fathers, who would have the most lively sense of the requirements of the language. So it is evidently taken in the earliest passage where it is quoted, in the Epistle of the Churches of Gaul (Euseb. *H. E.* v. 2), where praising the humility of the martyrs they say ἐπὶ τοσοῦτον ζηλωταὶ καὶ μιμηταὶ Χριστοῦ ἐγένοντο, ὃς ἐν μορφῇ Θεοῦ ὑπάρχων οὐχ ἁρπαγμὸν ἡγήσατο τὸ εἶναι ἴσα Θεῷ, evidently thinking this clause to contain in itself a statement of His condescension. So Origen clearly takes it; *in Joann.* vi. § 37 (IV. p. 156 D) μέχρι θανάτου καταβαίνειν ὑπὲρ ἀσεβῶν, οὐχ ἁρπαγμὸν ἡγούμενον τὸ εἶναι ἴσα Θεῷ, καὶ κενοῦν ἑαυτὸν κ.τ.λ.; *in Matth. Comm. Ser.* (III. p. 916 c) 'Vere Jesus non rapinam arbitratus est esse se æqualem Deo, et non semel sed frequenter pro omnibus seipsum humiliavit'; *in Rom.* v. § 2 (IV. p. 553 A) 'Nec rapinam ducit esse se æqualem Deo, hoc est, non sibi magni aliquid deputat quod ipse quidem æqualis Deo et unum cum patre sit'; *ib.* x. § 7 (IV. p. 672 c) 'Christus non sibi placens nec rapinam arbitrans esse se æqualem Deo semetipsum exinanivit.' So too Methodius; *Fragm.* p. 105 (Jahn) αὐτὸς ὁ Κύριος, ὁ υἱὸς τοῦ Θεοῦ, τιμῶν αὐτὸ [τὸ μαρτύριον] ἐμαρτύρησεν, οὐχ ἁρπαγμὸν ἡγησάμενος τὸ εἶναι ἴσα Θεῷ, ἵνα καὶ τούτῳ τὸν ἄνθρωπον τῷ χαρίσματι εἰς ὃν κατέβη στέψῃ. So again Eusebius unmistakeably; *Eccl. Proph.* iii. 4 ἐγενήθη πένης, οὐχ ἁρπαγμὸν ἡγούμενος τὸ εἶναι ἴσα Θεῷ ἀλλ' ἑαυτὸν ταπεινῶν κ.τ.λ.; *Eccles. Theol.* i. 13 (p. 57) προϋπάρχων, θεότητι πατρικῆς δόξης τετιμημένος· οὐ μὴν ἁρπαγμὸν ἡγούμενος τὸ εἶναι ἴσα Θεῷ ἑαυτὸν δ' οὖν κενώσας κ.τ.λ.; comp. *ib.* i. 20 (p. 94). So also Theodore of Mopsuestia (Raban. Maur. *Op.* VI. p. 488 B ed. Migne) 'Non magnam reputavit illam quæ ad Deum est æqualitatem et elatus in sua permansit dignitate, sed magis pro aliorum utilitate præelegit humiliora etc.'; and after him Theodoret, interpreting the passage, τὴν πρὸς τὸν πατέρα ἰσότητα ἔχων οὐ μέγα τοῦτο ὑπέλαβε. So moreover the Pseudo-Athanasius *Hom. de Sem.* (Athan. *Op.* II. p. 49 ed. Bened.) χρισθεὶς δὲ ὁ Δανεὶδ εἰς βασιλέα οὐχ ἅμα ἥρπασε τὴν βασιλείαν ἀλλ' ἠνείχετο πολλοῖς χρόνοις δουλεύων τῷ Σαούλ· καὶ ὁ σωτὴρ ἡμῶν γεννηθεὶς βασιλεὺς πρὸ τῶν αἰώνων...ἠνείχετο, οὐχ ἁρπαγμὸν ἡγήσατο τὸ εἶναι ἴσα Θεῷ κ.τ.λ. So in like manner Isidore of Pelusium *Epist.* iv. 22 εἰ ἕρμαιον ἡγήσατο τὸ εἶναι ἴσον οὐκ ἂν ἑαυτὸν ἐταπείνωσεν...δοῦλος μὲν γὰρ καὶ ἐλευθερωθεὶς καὶ υἱοθεσίᾳ τιμηθεὶς ἅτε ἅρπαγμα ἢ εὕρημα τὴν ἀξίαν ἡγησάμενος οὐδ' ἂν ὑποσταίη οἰκετικὸν ἔργον ἀνύσαι· ὁ δὲ γνήσιος υἱὸς κ.τ.λ.; and Cyril of Alexandria *c. Jul.* vi (VI. p. 195 ed. Aubert.) ὁ μὲν γὰρ τῶν ὅλων σωτὴρ καὶ Κύριος, καίτοι μετὸν αὐτῷ τὸ ἐν μορφῇ καὶ ἰσότητι τῇ κατὰ πᾶν ὁτιοῦν ὁρᾶσθαι πρὸς τὸν πατέρα καὶ τοῖς τῆς θεότητος ἐναβρύνεσθαι θάκοις, οὐχ ἁρπαγμὸν ἡγήσατο κ.τ.λ. (where the καίτοι is decisive). In addition to this positive testimony it should be noticed, that throughout the important controversies of the fourth and fifth centuries it does not seem once to have occurred to any Greek father to put forward the other explanation of the passage, though so eminently favourable to the orthodox belief[1].

*Margin notes:* The sense adopted by the Greek fathers. Churches of Gaul. Origen. Methodius. Eusebius. Theodore. Theodoret. Pseudo-Athanasius. Isidore of Pelusium. Cyril of Alexandria.

---

[1] It is not clear what interpretation was adopted by Didymus of Alexandria *de Trin.* i. 26 (p. 73), Τί τῆς ἰσότητος ταύτης εὑρίσκεται ἄνισον; οὐχ ἥρπασε γάρ, φησίν, οὐκ ἔλαβε τὸ ἴσον εἶναι τῇ φύσει τῷ Θεῷ καὶ πατρί· καὶ δὴ ὁ μὴ ὑπ' ἄλλου κενωθεὶς ἑαυτὸν δὲ κενώσας αὐθέντην δεσπότην ὁμοῦ καὶ

Nor is the interpretation thus generally adopted by Greek writers confined to them alone. Some of the most acute and learned of the Latin
fathers explain it in the same way. Thus perhaps HILARY OF POITIERS *de Trin.* viii. 45 (II. p. 246 ed.
Bened.) 'Non sibi rapiens esse se æqualem Deo, ad susceptionem se formæ
servilis per obedientiam exinanivit...non tamen æqualem se Deo per rapinam existimaus quamvis in forma Dei et æqualis Deo per Deum Deus sig-
natus exstaret[1]'; and more clearly JEROME *ad Hedib. Q.* 9 (*Epist.* 120, 1.
p. 837) 'Pro quibus non rapinam arbitratus est se esse æqualem Deo sed
semetipsum exinanivit'; see also his notes on Gal. iv. 12, v. 14².

In comparing these two interpretations, it will be seen that while the
former makes οὐχ ἁρπαγμὸν ἡγήσατο a continuation and expansion of the
idea already contained in ἐν μορφῇ Θεοῦ ὑπάρχων, 'He existed in the form
of God *and so* did not think it usurpation to be equal with God'; the
latter treats the words as involving a contrast to this idea, 'He existed
in the form of God *but nevertheless* did not eagerly assert His equality
with God.' In short the two interpretations of the clause, as I have said
before, are directly opposed, inasmuch as the one expresses our Lord's *assertion*, the other His *cession*, of the rights pertaining to His divine majesty.

And between these two explanations—the one which interprets ἁρπαγμὸν by ἀδικίαν, and the other which interprets it by ἕρμαιον—our choice
must be made. A middle interpretation however was maintained by
St Chrysostom, and has been adopted with more or less distinctness by
others, especially in recent times. It agrees very nearly with the first in
the sense assigned to ἁρπαγμός, and yet approaches to the second in the
general drift of the clause. 'Being in the form of God, He did not consider that He was plundering, when He claimed equality with God. He
did not therefore look upon His divine prerogatives as a booty of which
He feared to be deprived and which therefore it was necessary to guard
jealously. He reigned not as a tyrant but as a lawful sovereign. He could
therefore divest himself of the outward splendours of His rank without
fear³.'

As an indirect doctrinal inference from the passage, this account is
admissible; but as a direct explanation of its bearing, it is faulty because
it *understands too much*, requiring links to be supplied which the connexion does not suggest and which interrupt the sequence of thought.

---

ἀτδιον ἑαυτὸν ἀπέδειξεν. comp. *ib.* iii. 17
(p. 377). The expression οὐχ ἥρπασε
however seems to point to an intermediate interpretation like the one adopted
by Chrysostom, as given in the text.
Nothing can be inferred from the language of St Basil *adv. Eunom.* iv.
(I. p. 294 E, 295 A), or from *Liturg.
S. Bas.* p. 158 (Neale).

¹ Yet in another passage *c. Const.
Imper.* § 19 (II. p. 577) he says, 'Non ra-
pit quod erat Christus,' which points to
the other sense of ἁρπαγμός. Perhaps
he, like Chrysostom, adopted a middle

interpretation combining features of
both.

² This is probably the view also of
Victorinus in his commentary on the
passage, 'Ergo nunc Paulus, Non, inquit, Christus rapinam credidit, id est,
hoc sibi vindicavit, tantum habere
voluit ut forma Dei esset, sed etiam se
ipsum exinanivit etc.'; but his language is not distinct. See again his
treatise *c. Arium* i. 9, Galland *Bibl.
Vet. Patr.* VIII. p. 155.

³ *Op.* XI. p. 245. I have abridged
his explanation.

All similar attempts to mediate between the two opposing explanations fail in the same way and tend only to confuse the interpretation of the passage. Of the two explanations then, between which our choice lies, the context, as I have shown, seems imperatively to require the second; and if authority count for anything, the list of names, by which it is maintained, sufficiently refutes the charge of being 'liable to grave suspicion on theological grounds.' We should do wisely however to consider its doctrinal bearing, without reference to authority.

Now while the other explanation directly asserts our Lord's divinity, this confessedly does not. Yet on the other hand the theological difference is only apparent. For, though we miss the direct assertion in this particular clause, the doctrine still remains. It is involved in the preceding words, for the 'pre-existence in the form of God,' as will appear I think from the last note, means substantially this. It is indirectly implied moreover in this very clause taken in connexion with the context. For how could it be a sign of humility in our Lord not to assert His equality with God, if He were not divine? How could such a claim be considered otherwise than arrogant and blasphemous, if He were only a man? If St Chrysostom's interpretation must be rejected as faulty and confused, his argument at least is valid; 'No one wishing to exhort to humility says, Be humble and think less of yourself than of your compeers (ἔλαττον φρόνει τῶν ὁμοτίμων), for such and such a person being a slave did not set himself up against his master; therefore imitate him. Nay, one might reply, here is a question not of humility, but of infatuation (ἀπονοίας)'; 'It is no humility for the inferior not to set himself up against his superior'; 'If being a man, He washed the feet of men, He did not empty, did not humble Himself; if being a man, He did not grasp at equality with God, He deserves no praise[1].'

Theological bearing of the interpretation adopted.

One who refuses to claim some enviable privilege may be influenced by either of two motives, by a feeling of humility or by a sense of justice, according as he has or has not a right to this privilege. Those who hold humanitarian views of the Person of Christ necessarily take the latter view of the motive in this instance. The equality with God, they argue, was not asserted, because it would have been an act of usurpation to do so. To this view it may fairly be objected, that it overlooks the true significance of ἁρπαγμὸν (ἅρπαγμα) ἡγεῖσθαι, which as a recognised phrase is equivalent to ἕρμαιον ἡγεῖσθαι and therefore refers to the desirableness of the possession or acquisition. But its fatal condemnation is this, that it treats the clause as isolated and takes no account of the context. The act expressed by οὐχ ἁρπαγμὸν ἡγήσατο is brought forward as an example of humility, and can only be regarded as such, if the expression τὸ εἶναι ἴσα Θεῷ refers to rights which it was an act of condescension to waive[2].

It does not favour humanitarian views.

---

[1] Op. xi. pp. 236, 237, 247.

[2] One other interpretation put forward by recent commentators deserves attention. Meyer (followed by Dean Alford), desirous of giving ἁρπαγμὸν the active sense which its termination suggests, translates the words, 'Did not

look upon His being on an equality with God, as a means of self-enrichment.' In answer to the mechanical objection urged against this sense, that a state (τὸ εἶναι) cannot be regarded as an action (ἁρπαγμὸν), he justly appeals to 1 Tim. vi. 5 νομιζόντων πορισμὸν εἶναι

## Lost Epistles to the Philippians?

It has been maintained by some, that a passage in the Epistle to the Philippians implies a more or less sustained correspondence between St Paul and his converts, so that the extant letter is only a single link in a long chain. 'To write the same things,' says St Paul, 'to me is not irksome, while for you it is safe.' The reference, it is urged, cannot be explained from the epistle itself, since it does not supply any topic which satisfies the two conditions, of occurring in the immediate context, and of being repeated elsewhere in the course of the letter.

Moreover the inference thus suggested is thought to be confirmed by an allusion in the Epistle of Polycarp. Writing to these same Philippians, he says (§ 3); 'Neither I nor another like me can attain to the wisdom of the blessed and glorious Paul; who coming among you taught the word of truth accurately and surely before the men of that day; who also when absent wrote letters (ἐπιστολάς) to you, into which if ye search ye can be builded up unto the faith given to you.'

Against this view no objection can be taken from the probabilities of the case. On the contrary it is only reasonable to suppose, that during the ten or eleven years which elapsed between the epoch of their conversion and the date of this epistle, the Apostle, ever overflowing with love and ever prompt to seize the passing opportunity, would have written not once or twice only to converts with whom his relations were so close and affectionate. And—to consider the broader question—if we extend our range of view beyond the Philippians to the many churches of his founding, if we take into account not these ten years only but the whole period of his missionary life, we can hardly resist the conclusion that in the epistles of our Canon we have only a part—perhaps not a very large part—of the whole correspondence of the Apostle either with churches or with individuals.

But, if there be any reluctance to allow that the letter of an inspired Apostle could have been permitted to perish, a moment's thought will dissipate the scruple. Any theory of inspiration, which would be consistent with historical fact, must find a place for this supposition. It is true of Him who 'spake as never man spake,' that if all His words had been preserved, 'the world itself could not contain the books that should be written.' Yet His recorded sayings may be read through in a very few hours. And

τὴν εὐσέβειαν, which presents an exact parallel in this respect. This interpretation suits the context very fairly, but it seems to me to be somewhat strained; and the fact that ἅρπαγμα ἡγεῖσθαι (ποιεῖσθαι) is a common phrase meaning 'to prize highly, to welcome eagerly,' and that ἁρπαγμὸν ἡγεῖσθαι (ποιεῖσθαι), wherever else it occurs, has also this sense, would appear to be decisive. Meyer indeed attempts to force his own

meaning on ἁρπαγμὸν in the passage of Cyril, de Ador. i. p. 25, quoted above (in the notes, p. 111); but when this writer, speaking of Lot's renewal of the offer of hospitality when declined by the angels, describes this importunity by οὐχ ἁρπαγμὸν τὴν παραίτησιν ἐποιεῖτο it is difficult to conceive that the phrase can mean anything else but 'did not eagerly close with, did not gladly welcome their refusal.'

on the ground of inspiration we cannot assuredly claim for the letters of the Apostle an immunity from the ravages of time, which was denied to the words of the Saviour Himself. The 'litera scripta' indeed has a firmer hold on life. But the difficulty of multiplying copies, the strife of parties within the Church, and the perils assailing the brotherhood from without, are sufficient to explain the loss of any documents in the earlier ages. And from the nature of the case the letters of the Apostles could not have been so highly prized by their contemporaries, as by later generations. History confirms the suggestion which reason makes, that the writings of the first teachers of the Gospel grew in importance, as the echo of their voice died away. A letter from a dear friend is a poor substitute for the free interchange of conversation. But when he is taken from us, we know not how to value his correspondence highly enough[1].

At all events indications are not wanting of other letters besides those which have been preserved for the instruction of the Church. The two short Epistles to the Thessalonians stand alone in a period which extends over at least twenty years before and after[2]. Yet in one of these the Apostle calls attention to his mode of signature, as a guarantee of genuineness, which occurred 'in every epistle' written by him[3]. Such an expression would be conclusive, even if unsupported by other allusions, which suggest at least the suspicion that several letters may have passed between St Paul and his Thessalonian converts[4]. Again, his written communications with the Corinthians seem to have extended beyond the two extant epistles. In a passage in the First Epistle, according to the most probable interpretation, he directly alludes to a previous letter addressed to them[5]: and the acknowledgment of the Corinthians, which he elsewhere mentions, that his 'letters are weighty and powerful,' together with his own reply 'Such as we are by letters when absent etc.[6],' cannot be ex-

*Indications of other lost letters. Thessalonica.*

*Corinth.*

---

[1] Prof. Jowett, *Epistles of St Paul* I. p. 195 (2nd ed.), has an instructive essay on the probability of many epistles having been lost. With some of his special criticisms however I venture to disagree. He supposes for instance that 1 Cor. v. 9 refers to the First Epistle to the Corinthians itself, and that Col. iv. 16 does not refer to the Epistle to the Ephesians.

[2] Fourteen years at least, probably seventeen (see notes Gal. ii. 1), elapsed between St Paul's conversion and the third visit to Jerusalem (A.D. 51). The Epistles to the Corinthians, which probably follow next in order after the Epistles to the Thessalonians, were not written till A.D. 57, 58. Thus the whole period will be 20 or 23 years, according to the reckoning adopted.

[3] 2 Thess. iii. 17.

[4] 2 Thess. ii. 2, 15.

[5] 1 Cor. v. 9 ἔγραψα ὑμῖν ἐν τῇ ἐπιστολῇ μὴ συναναμίγνυσθαι πόρνοις. The real difficulty in referring this allusion to the First Epistle itself lies not in ἔγραψα, which might be explained as an epistolary aorist, but in ἐν τῇ ἐπιστολῇ 'in my letter,' which is thus rendered meaningless: see *Journal of Class. and Sacr. Phil.* II. p. 196 (note). Two independent reasons have probably conspired to promote the unnatural explanation by which it is referred to the First Epistle. (1) On *theological* grounds commentators have been unwilling to admit that an epistle of St Paul could have perished: while (2) they have been misled *critically* by the context, ver. 11 νῦν δὲ ἔγραψα κ.τ.λ., taking νῦν in its primary temporal sense, whereas it appears to mean, 'under these circumstances,' 'the world being what it is.'

[6] 2 Cor. x. 10, 11.

plained quite satisfactorily (though the explanation might pass) by the single extant epistle written before this date. On the other hand the 'letter from Laodicea,' which the Apostle directs the Colossians to procure and read[1], must not be classed among these lost letters, as there is very good reason for supposing that he there refers to the circular letter to the Asiatic Churches, sent to Laodicea as one of the great centres and thence communicated to the neighbouring town of Colossæ, but circulated in the Church at large through the metropolis of Asia and therefore generally known as the Epistle to the Ephesians. Whether to these lost letters to Thessalonica and to Corinth we are required to add one or more addressed to the Philippians, I propose now to consider. The general question has only been introduced to prepare the way for this investigation.

1. The passage in the Epistle to the Philippians itself has been variously explained. Some have interpreted it 'to repeat in writing the same injunctions which I gave you myself by word of mouth,' or 'which I charged you by my messengers.' But such amplifications receive no encouragement from the words themselves, which mean simply 'to write the same things again and again.' To written communications therefore our attention must be confined.

Even with this limitation, three solutions are offered. Either (1) The extant epistle itself consists of two separate letters welded together; or (2) A lost letter must be assumed in which the same subject was introduced; or (3) The often repeated topic must be discovered in the extant letter. The first of these solutions has been already considered and set aside[2]; nor indeed does it contribute anything towards the interpretation of this passage (though it would explain the plural in Polycarp), for no new topic is introduced by the disintegration of the existing letter. The second might very fairly be accepted in default of a better : but there is nothing in the words which suggests a reference to any incident external to the letter itself, and it is therefore simpler not to look elsewhere for the allusion. The third view then seems preferable, if any topic can be found which satisfies the conditions. And in the notes on the passage I have attempted to show that such a topic is not wanting.

2. But the reference in the Epistle of Polycarp still remains to be explained. What account must be given of the 'letters,' which St Paul wrote to the Philippians ? Does Polycarp, as some have thought, include the Thessalonian Epistles, which as being addressed to a neighbouring Church would be known and read at Philippi also ? This is possible ; but a simpler solution offers itself. Notwithstanding the plural ἐπιστολαί, the reference may be satisfied by the one extant Epistle to the Philippians. Of this usage of the plural ἐπιστολαί, applying to a single letter[3], there can be no doubt. This will appear plainly from Thucyd. viii. 51 ὅσον οὐ παροῦσαν ἀπὸ τοῦ Ἀλκιβιάδου περὶ τούτων ἐπιστολήν, compared with αἱ δὲ παρὰ τοῦ Ἀλκιβιάδου ἐπιστολαὶ οὐ πολὺ ὕστερον ἧκον ; from Joseph. Ant. xii. 4. 10

---

[1] Col. iv. 16. I hope to consider the question of the 'epistle from Laodicea' in the introduction to the Epistle to the Ephesians: see also *Colossians* p. 274 sq.

[2] See the introduction, page 69 note.

[3] Thom. Mag. p. 354 καὶ ἐπιστολὴ καὶ ἐπιστολαὶ πληθυντικῶς· ῥητορικόν.

ὁ Λακεδαιμονίων βασιλεὺς Ἄρειος πρεσβείαν τε ἔπεμπε καὶ ἐπιστολὰς ὧν τὸ ἀντίγραφόν ἐστι τοιοῦτον, compared with ἡ μὲν οὖν ἐπιστολὴ ἡ πεμφθεῖσα παρὰ τοῦ Λακεδαιμονίων βασιλέως τοῦτον περιεῖχε τὸν τρόπον[1]: and from Alciphron *Epist.* ii. 4 ὡς διεπέμψω μου τοῦ βασιλέως τὰς ἐπιστολάς, εὐθὺς ἀνέγνων, compared with σοβοῦσα ταῖς χερσὶν ἐμαυτῆς τὴν ἐπιστολὴν σὺν αὐτῇ τῇ βασιλικῇ σφραγῖδι; the singular in each case standing in the immediate neighbourhood of the plural and referring to the same writing.

I have placed these instances side by side, because the context in all three cases determines the sense, and because being taken from writers of different epochs they show that the usage was not confined to any one period. The following references also, which might be multiplied many times, serve to illustrate its occurrence in classical writers at different stages of the language: Eur. *Iph. Taur.* 589, 767, *Iph. Aul.* 111, 314, Thucyd. i. 132, iv. 50, Polyb. v. 43. 5, Lucian. *Amor.* 47 (II. p. 450), Julian. *Epist.* 73 (comp. *Epist.* 44)[2]. Nor is this usage confined to classical Greek. In Esth. iii. 14 ἐπιστολαί is a translation of a singular substantive (נשתן); while in 1 Macc. v. 14, x. 3, 7, xi. 29, xii. 5 etc., it plainly refers to a single document. And in ecclesiastical writers of a later date examples are found. Eusebius (*H. E.* vi. 1) for instance, like the authors first quoted, uses ἐπιστολή and ἐπιστολαί in the same context when speaking of one and the same letter[3].

If therefore we find that in another place Polycarp, referring again to the Epistle to the Philippians, uses the singular (ἐπιστολή)[4], this circumstance will present no difficulty; for we have seen similar variations of usage in the passages of Thucydides and Alciphron, of Josephus and Eusebius, where the anomaly is rendered more striking by the fact that in these authors the singular and plural occur in close proximity. — Singular and plural interchanged.

But a later passage of this same father has been quoted to show that he carefully distinguishes between the singular and the plural of this word. 'The letters (ἐπιστολάς) of Ignatius,' he writes, 'which were sent to us by him, and such others as we had by us, we have sent to you, as ye commanded; all which (αἵτινες) are appended to this letter (ἐπιστολῇ); from which ye may derive great advantage' (§ 13). The plural here has been explained as referring to the two letters, the one to the Smyrnæans, the other to Polycarp, contained in the short Greek recension. This explanation, it will be seen, supposes either the genuineness of the short Greek recension of the Ignatian letters or the spuriousness of this portion of Polycarp's epistle. Into these questions it would be beside the purpose to enter here. I would only say that here again the ἐπιστολαί may very well be used of a single letter, and that on this supposition there is a certain propriety in the — Polycarp's usage elsewhere considered.

[1] Comp. also *Antiq.* xiii. 4. 8.
[2] I owe a few of these references to Rettig *Quæst. Phil.* p. 38.
[3] Comp. also *H. E.* vi. 43, quoted by Cotelier on Polyc. *Phil.* 3. The plural 'epistolæ' in Latin is used in the same way; Justin xi. 8, 12, Plin. *N. H.* xxxiii. 12, quoted by Fabric. *Bibl. Græc.* IV. p. 804 (ed. Harles).

[4] Polyc. *Phil.* 11 'qui estis in principio epistolæ ejus,' where some word like 'laudati' should perhaps be supplied. Others however suppose the original Greek to have been οἱ ὄντες ἐν ἀρχῇ ἐπιστολαὶ αὐτοῦ, comparing for ἐν ἀρχῇ. Phil. iv. 15, and for ἐπιστολαὶ αὐτοῦ 2 Cor. iii. 2, 3.

change from the plural to the singular, when the writer has occasion to speak of himself. For the plural ἐπιστολαί, which signifies properly 'directions, injunctions,' whenever it occurs in prose of a single epistle, seems to denote a missive of importance, such as a king's mandate or a bishop's pastoral; and its employment by Polycarp to designate his own letter would have jarred strangely with his pervading tone of humility, though it would fitly describe the communications of the blessed Apostle Paul (§ 3) or the holy martyr Ignatius (§ 13)[1].

He does not refer to a lost letter.   On the whole then it would appear probable that Polycarp refers solely to the extant Epistle to the Philippians; for though the existence of other letters was seen to be in itself antecedently probable, yet it seems very unlikely that an epistle of St Paul, which had survived the opening of the second century and was then known to the Churches of Smyrna and Philippi, should so soon afterwards have passed wholly out of memory. Irenæus, the pupil of Polycarp, is evidently acquainted with only one Epistle of St Paul to the Philippians[2].

[1] By a curious coincidence Maximus uses the plural of Polycarp's own epistle: Dion. Areop. *Op.* II. p. 93 (ed. Corder.), ἔχει δὲ καὶ ἐπιστολὰς ὁ αὐτὸς θεῖος Πολύκαρπος πρὸς Φιλιππησίους.

[2] Georgius Syncellus indeed (*Chron.* I. p. 651 ed. Dind., a passage which I owe to Rettig *Quæst. Phil.* p. 38) speaking of St Clement of Rome writes, τούτου καὶ ὁ ἀπόστολος ἐν τῇ πρὸς Φιλιππησίους μέμνηται πρώτῃ ἐπιστολῇ εἰπών,

Μετὰ καὶ Κλήμεντος κ.τ.λ.: but it seems wholly incredible that Syncellus himself, and very unlikely that any authority quoted by him, should have been acquainted with more than one Epistle to the Philippians: and I can only account for the reading by supposing that a superfluous α crept into the text and was afterwards written out in full πρώτῃ.

²Βλέπετε τοὺς κύνας,    βλέπετε τοὺς κακοὺς ἐρ-

III. 2—6. 'Be on your guard. Shun these shameless dogs, these workers of mischief, these mutilators of the flesh. I call it *mutilation*, for we are the true circumcision, we offer the genuine service ; we—you and I— Gentile and Jew alike—who serve by the Spirit of God, who place our boast in Christ Jesus and put no trust in the flesh. And yet, whatever be the value of this confidence in the flesh, I assert it as well. If any other man claims to put trust in the flesh, my claim is greater. I was circumcised on the eighth day, a child of believing parents. I am descended of an old Israelite stock. I belong to the loyal and renowned tribe of Benjamin. I am of a lineage which has never conformed to foreign usages, but has preserved throughout the language and the customs of the fathers. Thus much for my inherited privileges ; and now for my personal career. Do they speak of law ? I belong to the Pharisees, the strictest of all sects. Of zeal ? I persecuted the Church. This surely is enough ! Of righteousness ? In such righteousness as consists in obedience to law, I have never been found a defaulter.'

2. A probable account of the abrupt introduction of this new topic is given in the introduction p. 69. As the Apostle is on the point of referring once more to the divisions in the Philippian Church before concluding, he is interrupted. Whether the interruption was momentary, or whether some hours or even days elapsed before the letter was resumed, it is vain to conjecture. But it has diverted, or at least modified, the current of his thoughts. He speaks no longer of the social dissensions actually prevalent among the Philippians ; but he warns them against a much more serious though hitherto distant peril —the infection of Judaism. It seems probable therefore that he had mean-

while been apprised of some fresh outbreak or reminded of some old antagonism on the part of his Judaizing opponents in Rome ; see p. 17.

The thrice repeated ' mark ye,' together with the recurrence of the definite article in the three clauses—*the* dogs, *the* evil workers, *the* concision— shows that St Paul is alluding to a well-known and well-marked party in or out of the Church.

Βλέπετε] ' *look to*, be on your guard against, mark and watch.' Comp. Mark iv. 24 βλέπετε τί ἀκούετε, 2 Joh. 8 βλέπετε ἑαυτούς : so frequently βλέπετε ἀπό (e.g. Mark viii. 15) and βλέπετε μή (e.g. Luke xxi. 8).

τοὺς κύνας] St Paul retorts upon the Judaizers the term of reproach, by which they stigmatized the Gentiles as impure. In the Mosaic law the word is used to denounce the foul moral profligacies of heathen worship (Deut. xxiii. 19 οὐ προσοίσεις μίσθωμα πόρνης οὐδὲ ἄλλαγμα κυνός). Among the Jews of the Christian era it was a common designation of the Gentiles, involving chiefly the idea of ceremonial impurity ; see esp. *Clem. Hom* ii. 19 εἶπεν Οὐκ ἔξεστιν ἰᾶσθαι τὰ ἔθνη ἐοικότα κυσὶν διὰ τὸ διαφόροις χρῆσθαι τροφαῖς καὶ πράξεσιν, ἀποδεδομένης τῆς κατὰ τὴν βασιλείαν τραπέζης τοῖς υἱοῖς 'Ισραήλ· ἡ δὲ τοῦτο ἀκούσασα, καὶ τῆς αὐτῆς τραπέζης ὡς κύων ψιχίων ἀποπιπτόντων συμμεταλαμβάνειν [δεομένη], μεταθεμένη ὅπερ ἦν, τῷ ὁμοίως διαιτᾶσθαι τοῖς τῆς βασιλείας υἱοῖς τῆς εἰς τὴν θυγατέρα, ὡς ἠξίωσεν, ἔτυχεν ἰάσεως. The writer thus interprets from a Judaizing point of view the incident in Matt. xv. 22 sq., where our Lord uses the Jewish phraseology of the day to test the faith of the Canaanite woman. See the rabbinical quotations in Schöttgen I. p. 1145. St John applies the term to those whose moral impurity excludes them from the new Jerusalem, the spiritual Israel, Apoc. xxii. 15. As a term of reproach the

γάτας, βλέπετε τὴν κατατομήν. ³ἡμεῖς γάρ ἐσμεν ἡ
περιτομή, οἱ πνεύματι Θεοῦ λατρεύοντες καὶ καυχώμενοι

word on the lips of a Jew signified chiefly 'impurity'; of a Greek, 'impudence.' The herds of dogs which prowl about eastern cities, without a home and without an owner, feeding on the refuse and filth of the streets, quarrelling among themselves, and attacking the passer-by, explain both applications of the image. To the Jew more especially the comparison of the heathen to a dog would commend itself, as describing his indiscriminate use of meats whether clean or not. Thus St Paul's language here is strikingly significant: 'They speak of themselves as God's children; they boast of eating at God's table ; they reproach us as dogs, as foul and unclean, as outcasts from the covenant, because forsooth we eat meat bought at the shambles, because we do not observe the washing of cups and platters. I reverse the image. *We* are the children, for we banquet on the spiritual feast which God has spread before us : *they* are the dogs, for they greedily devour the garbage of carnal ordinances, the very refuse of God's table.' See the note on σκύβαλα ver. 8.

κακοὺς ἐργάτας] So again he says of the Judaizing teachers 2 Cor. xi. 13 οἱ τοιοῦτοι ψευδαπόστολοι, ἐργάται δόλιοι. The proselytizing zeal of the party has been already noticed by St Paul, i. 15, 16. There he contemplates it as exerted upon heathendom, and with very mixed feelings he constrains himself to rejoice: here on the other hand he apprehends its assaults on a more liberal Christianity, and an unqualified condemnation is pronounced upon it. The Pharisaic party (Acts xv. 5) which 'compassed sea and land to make one proselyte' (Matt. xxiii. 15) had carried its old leaven into the Christian Church. There was the same zealous activity in the pursuit of its aims (ἐργάτας), and there were

the same pernicious consequences in the attainment (κακούς).

τὴν κατατομήν] ' the concision, the mutilation.' The corresponding verb κατατέμνειν is used in the LXX only of mutilations and incisions forbidden by the Mosaic law; Levit. xxi. 5 ἐπὶ τὰς σάρκας αὐτῶν οὐ κατατεμοῦσιν ἐντομίδας, 1 Kings xviii. 28 κατατέμνοντο κατὰ τὸν ἐθισμὸν αὐτῶν, Is. xv. 2, Hos. xvii. 14. Hence the appropriateness here: 'This circumcision, which they vaunt, is in Christ only as the gashings and mutilations of the idolatrous heathen': comp. Gal. v. 12 ὄφελον καὶ ἀποκόψονται, with the note. Thus it carries out the idea of κύνας. For the paronomasia of κατατομή, περιτομή, compare 2 Thess. iii. 11 μηδὲν ἐργαζομένους ἀλλὰ περιεργαζομένους, Rom. xii. 3 μὴ ὑπερφρονεῖν παρ' ὃ δεῖ φρονεῖν ἀλλὰ φρονεῖν εἰς τὸ σωφρονεῖν : see Winer § lxviii. p. 793 sq. See the monograph by J. F. Böttcher *de Paron. etc. Paulo freq.* (Lips. 1823) ; and for instances in the Old Testament Glass. *Phil. Sacr.* v. ii. 2, p. 926. But, though especially frequent in the Bible, they are naturally common everywhere. The saying of Diogenes, that the school of Euclides was not σχολὴ but χολὴ and the discourse of Plato not διατριβὴ but κατατριβή (Diog. Laert. vi. 24), may be matched in English by the ambassador's complaint that he had been sent not to Spain but to Pain or Leicester's report of the English troops in the Netherlands that the Queen's 'poor subjects were no better than abjects,' or Coleridge's description of French philosophy as 'psilosophy,' or again in Latin by the taunt of pope against antipope that he was not 'consecratus' but 'execratus,' or the common proverb 'compendia dispendia.' See also Farrar's *Chapter on Language* p. 265 sq.

3. ἡμεῖς κ.τ.λ.] ' We are the tru

ἐν Χριστῷ Ἰησοῦ καὶ οὐκ ἐν σαρκὶ πεποιθότες. ⁴καίπερ
ἐγὼ ἔχων πεποίθησιν καὶ ἐν σαρκί· εἴ τις δοκεῖ ἄλλος

*circumcision;* we, who have put off
the impurity of the heart and have
put on Christ, whether belonging to
the outward circumcision, as I, or to
the outward uncircumcision, as you.'

ἡ περιτομή] The contrast of the
material and the spiritual circumcision occurs more than once elsewhere in St Paul: Rom. ii. 25—29,
Col. ii. 11, comp. Ephes. ii. 11 οἱ λεγό-
μενοι ἀκροβυστία ὑπὸ τῆς λεγομένης
περιτομῆς ἐν σαρκὶ χειροποιήτου. In
this respect, as in so many others, St
Stephen's speech contains an anticipation of St Paul: Acts vii. 51 ἀπερίτμη-
τοι καρδίαις καὶ τοῖς ὠσίν. The use
made of the image of circumcision, as
a metaphor for purity, in the Old Testament had prepared the way for the
Apostle's application : e.g. the circumcision of the heart, Levit. xxvi. 41,
Deut. x. 16, xxx. 6, Ezek. xliv. 7 ; of
the ear, Jer. vi. 10 ; of the lips, Exod.
vi. 12, 30; comp. Jer. ix. 25, 26. Thus
too Philo discusses at some length the
significance of this rite, as a symbol of
moral purgation, *de Circum.* ii. p. 211
M, comp. *de Vict. Off.* ii. p. 258 M.
So too Justin. *Dial.* 12, p. 229 C δευ-
τέρας ἤδη χρεία περιτομῆς, καὶ ὑμεῖς
ἐπὶ τῇ σαρκὶ μέγα φρονεῖτε (comp. § 19,
p. 236 C), § 43, p. 261 C οὐ ταύτην τὴν
κατὰ σάρκα περιλάβομεν περιτομὴν
ἀλλὰ πνευματικήν, Barnab. § 9.

πνεύματι Θεοῦ] '*by the Spirit of
God,*' and not with the ordinances
and traditions of men. Thus Θεοῦ,
besides being the better supported
reading, is also more emphatic than
Θεῷ. The latter however presents a
closer parallel to Rom. i. 9 ὁ Θεὸς ᾧ
λατρεύω ἐν τῷ πνεύματί μου. See the
next note.

λατρεύοντες] The terms λατρεία,
λατρεύειν, had got to be used in a very
special sense to denote the service
rendered to Jehovah by the Israelite
race, as His peculiar people: see especially Rom. ix. 4 ὧν ἡ υἱοθεσία κ.τ.λ.

καὶ ἡ λατρεία καὶ αἱ ἐπαγγελίαι,
Acts xxvi. 7 εἰς ἣν τὸ δωδεκάφυλον
ἡμῶν ἐν ἐκτενείᾳ νύκτα καὶ ἡμέραν λα-
τρεῦον κ.τ.λ. ; comp. Heb. ix. 1, 6.
Hence the significance of St Paul's
words here; '*We possess the true
περιτομή*, the circumcision not of the
flesh but of the heart, and we also offer
the true λατρεία, the service not of external rites but of a spiritual worship':
comp. Joh. iv. 23, 24. The same opposition between the external and the
spiritual λατρεία is implied again in
Rom. xii. 1 παραστῆσαι τὰ σώματα
ὑμῶν θυσίαν ζῶσαν ἁγίαν εὐάρεστον τῷ
Θεῷ, τὴν λογικὴν λατρείαν ὑμῶν,
besides Rom. i. 9 quoted in the previous note. Compare Athenag. *Leg.*
13 προσφέρειν δέον ἀναίμακτον θυσίαν
καὶ τὴν λογικὴν προσάγειν λατρείαν,
and see the note on iv. 18. This definite sense of λατρεύειν explains how it
is used absolutely without any case of
the object following, as in Luke ii. 37,
Acts xxvi. 7. The substitution of
Θεῷ for Θεοῦ here was probably an
attempt to relieve the apparent awkwardness of this absolute use.

καυχώμενοι κ.τ.λ.] in accordance
with the precept in Jer. ix. 23, 24,
twice quoted in a condensed form by
St Paul, 1 Cor. i. 31, 2 Cor. x. 17, ὁ
καυχώμενος ἐν Κυρίῳ καυχάσθω.

οὐκ ἐν σαρκί] Comp. 2 Cor. xi. 18,
Gal. vi. 13, 14. The expression ἐν
σαρκὶ extends beyond περιτομὴ to all
external privileges.

4. καίπερ ἐγὼ κ.τ.λ.] '*though having myself confidence.*' The Apostle
for the moment places himself on the
same standing ground with the Judaizers and, adopting their language,
speaks of himself as having that which
in fact he had renounced : comp. 2 Cor.
xi. 18 ἐπεὶ πολλοὶ καυχῶνται κατὰ [τὴν]
σάρκα, κἀγὼ καυχήσομαι. The proper
force of ἔχων πεποίθησιν must not be
explained away. The καίπερ ἐγὼ
singles out the Apostle (comp. 1 Thess.

πεποιθέται ἐν σαρκί, ἐγὼ μᾶλλον· ⁵περιτομῇ ὀκταή-
μερος, ἐκ γένους Ἰσραήλ, φυλῆς Βενιαμείν, Ἑβραῖος ἐξ

ii. 18), for the Philippians did not
likewise possess these claims.

καὶ ἐν σαρκί] '*in the flesh as well*
as in Christ; as if forsooth this one
topic did not cover the whole field of
boasting.'

δοκεῖ πεποιθέναι] '*thinks to have
confidence*'; 'seems to himself' rather
than 'seems to others'; for the former,
besides being the more common meaning in St Paul (1 Cor. iii. 18, vii. 40, x.
12, xi. 16 etc.), is also more forcible.
With ἐγὼ μᾶλλον we must understand
δοκῶ πεποιθέναι in the same sense;
'If they arrogate to themselves these
carnal privileges, I also arrogate them
to myself.' St Paul is using an *argu-
mentum ad hominem;* in his own
language, he is for the moment 'speaking foolishly,' is 'speaking not after
the Lord,' 2 Cor. xi. 17. See the preceding note.

5. This passage has a close parallel
in 2 Cor. xi. 21; and the comparison
is instructive. With the same depth
of feeling and the same general purport, the form of expression in the
two passages differs widely. The tu-
multuous eagerness of the Apostle's
earlier style, which appears in the
letter to the Corinthians, is replaced
here by a more subdued, though not
less earnest, tone of remonstrance.
Compare also Rom. ix. 3—5, xi. 1.

The four clauses at the beginning
of the fifth verse, which describe the
privileges inherited by the Apostle
apart from his own act or will, are
arranged in an ascending scale. (1)
The due performance of the rite of
circumcision shows that his parents
were neither heathens nor sons of
Ishmael. (2) But as this is consistent with their being proselytes, he
specifies his direct Israelite descent.
(3) Again, his ancestors might have
been descendants of Israel and yet
have belonged to a renegade tribe.
Against this possibility he guards by

naming the faithful tribe of Benjamin.
(4) Lastly, many of those, whose descent was unimpeachable and who inherited the faith of the Mosaic law,
yet as living among heathens adopted
the language and conformed to the
customs of the people around them.
Not such were the forefathers of Saul
of Tarsus. There had been no Hellenist among them; they were all strict
Hebrews from first to last.

περιτομῇ ὀκταήμερος] Converts to
Judaism would be circumcised in
mature age; Ishmaelites in their thirteenth year. Concerning the latter
see Joseph. *Ant.* i. 12. 2. For the
dative περιτομῇ 'in respect of circumcision' comp. ii. 7 σχήματι εὑρεθείς,
and see Winer § xxxi. p. 270. The
nominative περιτομή, read in some
texts, is hardly translatable. For ὀκ-
ταήμερος 'eight days old' compare
τριήμερος (M. Anton. iv. 50), τετραήμε-
ρος (Arist. *Pol.* iii. 15), πενθήμερος
(Xen. *Hell.* vii. 1. 14), δεχήμερος
(Thucyd. v. 26, 32), etc. The passages
quoted show that the words denote
properly not *interval* but *duration*,
so that 'on the eighth day' is not a
very accurate translation. The broken
days at the beginning and end are of
course counted in to make up the eight.

ἐκ γένους Ἰσραήλ] i. e. his parents
were not grafted into the covenant
people, but descended from the original stock. On the significance of
'Israel, Israelite,' as implying the
privileges of the theocratic covenant,
see the note on Gal. vi. 16.

φυλῆς Βενιαμείν] As Benjamin gave
to the Israelites their first king, as
Benjamin alone was faithful to Judah
at the disruption, so also this tribe
had from the earliest times held the
post of honour in the armies of the
nation. 'After thee, O Benjamin' was
a battle-cry of Israel; Judges v. 14,
Hos. v. 8. The glory of the Benjamite
however did not end here. He re-

Ἑβραίων, κατὰ νόμον Φαρισαῖος, <sup>6</sup>κατὰ ζῆλος διώκων
τὴν ἐκκλησίαν, κατὰ δικαιοσύνην τὴν ἐν νόμῳ γενόμενος

membered with pride that his forefather alone of the twelve patriarchs was born in the land of promise (see the words put into the mouth of Mordecai in *Megill.* Esth. iii. 4, quoted by Wetstein). He would also recal the great national deliverance wrought by means of a Benjamite, which was commemorated in the yearly festival of Purim. St Paul mentions his descent from Benjamin again Rom. xi. 1. He doubtless derived his name 'Saul' directly or indirectly from the Benjamite king, to whom he himself refers with marked emphasis (Acts xiii. 21). At a very early date the prediction in Jacob's blessing of Benjamin (Gen. xlix. 27), 'In the morning he shall devour the prey and at night he shall divide the spoil,' was applied to the persecuting zeal and later conversion of St Paul; *Test. xii Patr.* Benj. 11, Tertull. *adv. Marc.* v. 1, Hippol. *Fragm.* 50 (p. 140 Lagarde), Ephr. Syr. iv. pp. 114, 193, (comp. p. 288); see *Galatians* p. 321. On the character of Saul of Tarsus in connexion with the character of the tribe see Stanley *Jewish Church* ii. p. 40.

Ἑβραῖος ἐξ Ἑβραίων] As Ἰουδαῖος is opposed to Ἕλλην in the New Testament (e.g. Rom. i. 16), so is Ἑβραῖος to Ἑλληνιστής (Acts vi. 1). In other words, while the former pair of terms expresses a contrast of race and religion, the latter implies difference of language and manners. Within the pale of the Jewish Church a man was Ἰουδαῖος, who traced his descent from Jacob and conformed to the religion of his fathers, but he was not Ἑβραῖος also, unless he spoke the Hebrew tongue and retained Hebrew customs: see Trench *N. T. Syn.* § xxxix. p. 129. Hence here, as in 2 Cor. xi. 22, 'Hebrew' implies something which is not expressed in 'Israelite.' Though St Paul was born in Tarsus, he was yet

brought up under a great Hebrew teacher in the Hebrew metropolis (Acts xxii. 3); he spoke the 'Hebrew' language fluently (xxi. 40, xxii. 2); he quotes frequently from the Hebrew Scriptures which he translates for himself, thus contrasting with his contemporaries the Jewish Philo and the Christian writer of the Epistle to the Hebrews, who commonly use the Hellenistic version of the Seventy. The tradition mentioned by Jerome on Philem. 23 (vii. p. 762, ed. Vallarsi), that St Paul's parents lived in the Galilean town of Gischala and were driven thence by the Roman invasion, contains its own refutation in a manifest anachronism; but it seems to illustrate St Paul's statement here, for it may rest on a reminiscence of the long residence of his family in those parts. For the form of expression Ἑβραῖος ἐξ Ἑβραίων, 'a Hebrew and of Hebrew ancestry', comp. Herod. ii. 143 πίρωμιν ἐκ πιρώμιος, Demosth. *Andr.* p. 614 δούλους ἐκ δούλων καλῶν ἑαυτοῦ βελτίους καὶ ἐκ βελτιόνων, Polyb. ii. 59. 1 οὐ μόνον γεγονέναι τύραννον ἀλλὰ καὶ ἐκ τυράννων πεφυκέναι, with other passages collected in Wetstein and Kypke.

Having thus enumerated his inherited privileges, the Apostle goes on to speak of matters which depended on his own personal choice. Here are three topics of boasting. (1) As regards *law*, he attached himself to the sect which was strictest in its ritual observance. (2) As regards *zeal*, he had been as energetic as any of his countrymen in persecuting the Church. (3) As regards *righteousness*, he had left nothing undone which the law required.

νόμον] 'law,' not 'the law'; for though the Mosaic law is meant, yet it is here regarded in the abstract, as a principle of action, being coordinated with ζῆλος and δικαιοσύνην. For the

ἄμεμπτος. ⁷[ἀλλὰ] ἄτινα ἦν μοι κέρδη, ταῦτα ἥγημαι
διὰ τὸν Χριστὸν ζημίαν. ⁸ἀλλὰ μὲν οὖν [καὶ] ἡγοῦμαι
πάντα ζημίαν εἶναι διὰ τὸ ὑπερέχον τῆς γνώσεως Χρισ-

7.  ἄτινά μοι ἦν κέρδη.        8.  ἀλλὰ μενοῦνγε [καὶ] ἡγοῦμαι.

distinction of νόμος and ὁ νόμος see
the notes on Gal. ii. 19, iv. 4, 5 21,
v. 18, vi. 13.

Φαρισαῖος] Acts xxiii. 6 ἐγὼ Φαρι-
σαῖός εἰμι υἱὸς Φαρισαίων (where υἱὸς
Φαρισαίων perhaps refers rather to his
teachers than to his ancestors, being
a Hebraism like ' the sons of the prophets'; comp. Amos vii. 14), xxvi. 5
κατὰ τὴν ἀκριβεστάτην αἵρεσιν τῆς ἡμε-
τέρας θρησκείας ἔζησα Φαρισαῖος, xxii.
3 πεπαιδευμένος κατὰ ἀκρίβειαν τοῦ
πατρῴου νόμου. Similarly St Paul calls
himself ζηλωτὴς τῶν πατρικῶν παρα-
δόσεων in Gal. i. 14: see the note there.

6.  κατὰ ζῆλος κ.τ.λ.] An expression
of intense irony, condemning while he
seems to exalt his former self: 'I was
zealous above them all ; I asserted my
principles with fire and sword; I persecuted, imprisoned, slew these infatuat-
ed Christians; this was my great claim
to God's favour.' This condensed irony
is more common in the earlier epistles: e.g. 1 Cor. iv. 8, 2 Cor. xi. 1, 7,
19. The correct reading is ζῆλος (not
ζῆλον), for which form see Winer
§ ix. p. 76, A. Buttmann p. 20. In
Clem. Rom. §§ 3, 4, 5, 6, where the
word occurs frequently, the masculine
and neuter seem to be interchanged
without any law.

διώκων] The references to his persecution of the Church are frequent in
St Paul : see the note on Gal. i. 13 καθ'
ὑπερβολὴν ἐδίωκον τὴν ἐκκλησίαν τοῦ
Θεοῦ.

τὴν ἐν νόμῳ] added to qualify and
explain δικαιοσύνην; 'Such righteousness as consists in law, in obedience to
formal precepts', but not the true
righteousness : see ver. 9. Here ἐν
νόμῳ is used without the article for
the same reason as in ver. 5.

γενόμενος ἄμεμπτος] 'showing my-

self blameless', i.e. 'I omitted no observance however trivial', for μέμφεσ-
θαι applies to sins of omission.

ἄτινα κ.τ.λ.] 'All such things which
I used to count up as distinct items
with a miserly greed and reckon to my
credit—these I have massed together
under one general head as loss'. This
paraphrase is intended to bring out,
though with a necessary exaggeration,
the idea faintly expressed by the
change from the plural (κέρδη) to the
singular (ζημίαν). Otherwise there
would be a natural tendency to make
both plural or both singular : comp.
Menand. Mon. 301 (Meineke iv. p. 348)
κέρδος πονηρὸν ζημίαν ἀεὶ φέρει with
ib. 496 (p. 354) τὰ μικρὰ κέρδη ζημίας
μεγάλας φέρει. For ἄτινα, denoting
'the class of things', see the notes on
Gal. iv. 24, v. 19.

διὰ τὸν Χριστόν] 'for Christ', i.e. as
it is explained below (ver. 8), ἵνα Χριστὸν κερδήσω. To this end it was necessary first to renounce all other
claims to righteousness: see especially
Gal. v. 4.

8.  ἀλλὰ μὲν οὖν κ.τ.λ.] 'nay moreover I do count all things etc.'; see
Winer § liii. p. 552. This combination of particles introduces the
present statement as an amendment
and extension of the former. The
advance consists in two points; (1) The
substitution of the present for the
perfect (ἡγοῦμαι for ἥγημαι); (2) The
expansion of ταῦτα into πάντα.

διὰ τὸ ὑπερέχον κ.τ.λ.] The preposition may mean either 'for the sake
of' (as in διὰ τὸν Χριστὸν above and
δι' ὃν below); or, as the sense of
ὑπερέχον suggests, 'by reason of', signifying that the surpassing worth of
this knowledge eclipses and annihi-
lates all other gains in comparison;

τοῦ Ἰησοῦ τοῦ Κυρίου μου, δι᾽ ὃν τὰ πάντα ἐζημιώθην
καὶ ἡγοῦμαι σκύβαλα, ἵνα Χριστὸν κερδήσω ⁹καὶ εὑρεθῶ
ἐν αὐτῷ μὴ ἔχων ἐμὴν δικαιοσύνην τὴν ἐκ νόμου, ἀλλὰ

as 2 Cor. iii. 10 οὐ δεδόξασται τὸ δεδο-
ξασμένον ἐν τούτῳ τῷ μέρει εἵνεκεν
τῆς ὑπερβαλλούσης δόξης.
τοῦ Κυρίου μου] See the note on
i. 3.
τὰ πάντα ἐζημιώθην] 'I suffered the
confiscation, was mulcted, of all things
together.' For τὰ πάντα, which is
somewhat stronger than πάντα, comp.
Rom. viii. 32, xi. 36, 1 Cor. viii. 6, etc.

σκύβαλα] The word seems to signify generally 'refuse', being applied
most frequently in one sense or other
to food, as in Plut. Mor. p. 352 D περίτ-
τωμα δὲ τροφῆς καὶ σκύβαλον οὐδὲν ἁγνὸν
οὐδὲ καθαρόν ἐστι· ἐκ δὲ τῶν περιττω-
μάτων ἔρια καὶ λάχναι καὶ τρίχες καὶ
ὄνυχες ἀναφύονται. The two significations most common are : (1) 'Excre-
ment,' the portion of food rejected by
the body, as not possessing nutritive
qualities: e.g. Joseph. B. J. v. 13. 7.
This sense is frequent in medical writers. (2) 'The refuse or leavings of
a feast,' the food thrown away from
the table: e.g. Leon. Alex. 30 (Anthol.
II. p. 196) ὡς ἀποδειπνιδίου γευσόμενος
σκυβάλου, Aristo 2 (ib. II. p. 258) δεῖπνον
συχνὸν ἀπὸ σκυβάλων, Adesp. 13 (ib. iii.
p.253) ἐρρίφθω ξηροῖς φυρόμενον σκυβά-
λοις, Q. Maec. 8 (ib. II. p. 238), Adesp.
386 (ib. III. p. 233); and metaphori-
cally Heges. 4 (ib. I. p. 254) ἐξ ἁλὸς
ἡμίβρωτον ἀνηνέγκαντο σαγηνεῖς ἄνδρα
πολύκλαυτον ναυτιλίης σκύβαλον. So
again σκυβάλισμα, Pseudo-Phocyl. 144
μηδ᾽ ἄλλου παρὰ δαιτὸς ἔδης σκυλβά-
λισμα τραπέζης.
As regards derivation, it is now
generally connected with σκῶρ, σκατός
(Benfey Wurzel. I. p. 628, II. p. 172,
Lobeck Pathol. p. 92). This derivation countenances the former of the
two senses given above; but Suidas
explains the word, τὸ τοῖς κυσὶ βαλλό-
μενον κυσίβαλόν τι ὄν (comp. Etym.

Mag. p. 719, 53); and so Pott, Etym.
Forsch. II. p. 295, taking σκυ- to represent ἐς κύνας and comparing σκορα-
κίζειν. This account of the word seems
at least as probable as the other; but
whether correct or not, it would appear to have been the popular derivation, and from this circumstance the
second of the two meanings would
become more prominent than the
first.
At all events this meaning, which is
well supported by the passages quoted,
is especially appropriate here. The
Judaizers spoke of themselves as
banqueters seated at the Father's
table, of Gentile Christians as dogs
greedily snatching up the refuse meat
which fell therefrom. St Paul has
reversed the image. The Judaizers
are themselves the dogs (ver. 2); the
meats served to the sons of God are
spiritual meats; the ordinances, which
the formalists value so highly, are the
mere refuse of the feast.
The earnest reiteration of St Paul's
language here expresses the intensity
of his desire to produce conviction:
κέρδη, κερδήσω—ἥγημαι, ἡγοῦμαι, ἡγοῦμαι—ζημίαν, ζημίαν, ἐζημιώθην—διά, διά,
διά—πάντα, τὰ πάντα—Χριστόν, Χριστοῦ, Χριστόν; see above i. 9, 14, 27,
ii. 2.

9. εὑρεθῶ] 'may be found'; perhaps at the great day of revelation
(2 Cor. v. 3), perhaps more generally
(1 Cor. iv. 2). For the frequent use
of this word in Aramaised Greek see
the note on Gal. ii. 17.
ἐν αὐτῷ] 'in Christ', as part of
Christ, as a member of His body. It
is only by becoming one with Christ,
that Christ's righteousness can become
our righteousness.
ἐμὴν δικαιοσύνην] 'Any righteousness that I may have or not have.'

τὴν διὰ πίστεως Χριστοῦ, τὴν ἐκ Θεοῦ δικαιοσύνην ἐπὶ
τῇ πίστει, ¹⁰τοῦ γνῶναι αὐτὸν καὶ τὴν δύναμιν τῆς ἀναστάσεως αὐτοῦ καὶ κοινωνίαν [τῶν] παθημάτων αὐτοῦ,

It is ἐμήν, not τὴν ἐμήν; for the latter
would seem to assume the existence
of such personal righteousness. Comp.
Rom. x. 3 ἀγνοοῦντες γὰρ τὴν τοῦ Θεοῦ
δικαιοσύνην καὶ τὴν ἰδίαν [δικαιοσύνην]
ζητοῦντες στῆσαι τῇ δικαιοσύνῃ τοῦ
Θεοῦ οὐχ ὑπετάγησαν. St Paul is applying and extending the language of
the Old Testament: comp. Ps. lxxi. 16,
Is. lxiv. 6.

τὴν ἐκ νόμου] See above ver. 6;
comp. Gal. ii. 16—21, iii. 10—12, 21,
Rom. iii. 21—31, iv. 13, 14, ix. 30—32,
x. 4, 5.

ἀλλὰ κ.τ.λ.] Here διὰ πίστεως Χριστοῦ is opposed to ἐκ νόμου, and ἐκ
Θεοῦ to ἐμήν, of the preceding clause.

διὰ πίστεως Χριστοῦ] 'through faith
in Christ.' The ἐκ of the former
clause is changed into διὰ here, because faith is only the means, not
the source, of justification: see the
note on Gal. ii. 16.

ἐπὶ τῇ πίστει] 'on the condition of
faith'; as Acts iii. 16. The article (τῇ
πίστει) is used here, because πίστεως
has gone before; 'the faith thus supposed'.

10. 'That I may know Him. And
when I speak of knowing Him, I mean,
that I may feel the power of His resurrection; but to feel this, it is first
necessary that I should share His sufferings.' The essence of knowing Christ
consists in knowing the power of His
resurrection; hence the words καὶ τὴν
δύναμιν τῆς ἀναστάσεως αὐτοῦ are added
by way of explanation. But these words
again suggest another thought; no
one can participate in His resurrection,
who has not first participated in His
death. Hence a further addition καὶ
κοινωνίαν τῶν παθημάτων αὐτοῦ, which
logically precedes τὴν δύναμιν κ.τ.λ.,
as appears from the explanation following, συμμορφιζόμενος τῷ θανάτῳ
αὐτοῦ, εἴ πως κ.τ.λ.

τοῦ γνῶναι] not simply 'know', but
'recognise, feel, appropriate'. On γινώσκειν see the notes to Gal. iii. 7, iv. 9.
This intense sense of γινώσκειν, and
even of εἰδέναι (e.g. 1 Thess. v. 12), is
the more common in Biblical Greek,
because both words are used in the
LXX as renderings of ידע which frequently has this sense.

τὴν δύναμιν κ.τ.λ.] 'the power of
His resurrection'; as the assurance
of immortality (Rom. viii. 11, 1 Cor.
xv. 14 sq.), as the triumph over sin
and the pledge of justification (Rom.
iv. 24, 25), as asserting the dignity and
enforcing the claims of the human body
(1 Cor. vi. 13—15, Phil. iii. 21); thus
quickening and stimulating the whole
moral and spiritual being (Rom. vi. 4
sq., Gal. ii. 20, Ephes. ii. 5, Col. ii. 12).
On this see Westcott's *Gospel of the
Resurrection* ii. § 31 sq.

καὶ κοινωνίαν κ.τ.λ.] The participation in Christ's sufferings partly follows upon and partly precedes the
power of His resurrection. It follows,
as the practical result on our life;
it precedes, as leading up to the full and
final appreciation of this power. In
this latter aspect it is taken up in
the explanatory clause which comes
immediately after, συμμορφιζόμενος
κ.τ.λ. For the expression τὴν κοινωνίαν κ.τ.λ. comp. 2 Cor. i. 5 περρισσεύει
τὰ παθήματα τοῦ Χριστοῦ εἰς ἡμᾶς κ.τ.λ.,
1 Pet. iv. 13 κοινωνεῖτε τοῖς τοῦ Χριστοῦ
παθήμασιν, Col. i. 24, Polyc. *Phil.* 9
παρὰ τῷ Κυρίῳ ᾧ καὶ συνέπαθον. See
also for the idea the passages quoted in
the next note. The τὴν before κοινωνίαν
in the received text, besides being
deficient in authority, severs the close
connexion between 'the power of His
resurrection' and 'the participation
in His sufferings.'

συμμορφιζόμενος κ.τ.λ.] See Rom.
vi. 5 εἰ γὰρ σύμφυτοι γεγόναμεν τῷ

συμμορφιζόμενος τῷ θανάτῳ αὐτοῦ, ¹¹εἴ πως καταντήσω εἰς τὴν ἐξανάστασιν τὴν ἐκ νεκρῶν.　¹²οὐχ ὅτι ἤδη

ὁμοιώματι τοῦ θανάτου αὐτοῦ, ἀλλὰ καὶ
τῆς ἀναστάσεως ἐσόμεθα, 2 Cor. iv. 10
πάντοτε τὴν νέκρωσιν τοῦ Ἰησοῦ ἐν τῷ
σώματι περιφέροντες, ἵνα καὶ ἡ ζωὴ τοῦ
Ἰησοῦ φανερωθῇ ἐν τῇ θνητῇ σαρκὶ ἡμῶν
κ.τ.λ.; comp. Rom. viii. 17, 2 Tim. ii. 11,
12. The conformity with the sufferings
of Christ implies not only the endurance
of persecution for His name, but all
pangs and all afflictions undergone in
the struggle against sin either within
or without. The agony of Gethsemane,
not less than the agony of Calvary,
will be reproduced however faintly in
the faithful servant of Christ. For
συμμορφιζόμενος see the detached note
on μορφή and σχῆμα above p. 130.

εἴ πως καταντήσω] 'if so be I may
attain.' The Apostle states not a
positive assurance but a modest hope.
For εἴ πως see Acts xxvii. 12 (optat.),
Rom. i. 10 (fut.), xi. 14 (fut. or conj.).
Here καταντήσω is probably the conjunctive, as εἰ καὶ καταλάβω follows
immediately. The conjunctive with εἰ,
barely tolerated in Attic prose (though
less rare in poetry), is hardly more
common in the Greek Testament.
The only decisive instance seems to
be εἰ καὶ καταλάβω below, ver. 12.
In other passages (as Luke ix. 13,
1 Cor. ix. 11, xiv. 5, 1 Thess. v. 10,
Rev. xi. 5) the possibility of error or
the existence of various readings renders it more or less doubtful.

τὴν ἐξανάστασιν κ.τ.λ.] The 'resurrection from the dead' is the final
resurrection of the righteous to a
new and glorified life. This meaning,
which the context requires, is implied
by the form of expression. The general
resurrection of the dead, whether
good or bad, is ἡ ἀνάστασις τῶν νεκρῶν
(e.g. 1 Cor. xv. 42); on the other hand
the resurrection of Christ and of those
who rise with Christ is generally
[ἡ] ἀνάστασις [ἡ] ἐκ νεκρῶν (Luke xx.
35, Acts iv. 2, 1 Pet. i. 3). The former

includes both the ἀνάστασις ζωῆς and
the ἀνάστασις κρίσεως (Joh. v. 29); the
latter is confined to the ἀνάστασις
ζωῆς. The received reading τῶν νεκρῶν
for τὴν ἐκ νεκρῶν, besides being feebly
supported, disregards this distinction.
Here the expression is further intensified by the substitution of ἐξ-
ανάστασις for ἀνάστασις, the word not
occurring elsewhere in the New Testament.

12. In the following verses, though
St Paul speaks of himself, his language
seems really to be directed against the
antinomian spirit, which in its rebound
from Jewish formalism perverted
liberty into license. It is necessary to
supply a corrective to such false inferences drawn from the doctrine of grace
broadly stated. This he does by pointing to his own spiritual insecurity, his
own earnest strivings, his own onward
progress. 'To continue in sin that grace
may abound' gains no countenance
either from his doctrine or from his
example. Having thus prepared the
way, he in the 18th verse directly
condemns those professed followers
who thus dragged his teaching in the
dust. See the introduction p. 70.

12—16. 'Do not mistake me, I
hold the language of hope, not of
assurance. I have not yet reached
the goal; I am not yet made perfect.
But I press forward in the race, eager
to grasp the prize, forasmuch as Christ
also has grasped me. My brothers,
let other men vaunt their security.
Such is not my language. I do not
consider that I have the prize already
in my grasp. This, and this only, is
my rule. Forgetting the landmarks
already passed and straining every
nerve and muscle in the onward race,
I press forward ever towards the
goal, that I may win the prize of my
heavenly rest whereunto God has called me in Christ Jesus. Let us therefore,

ἔλαβον ἢ ἤδη τετελείωμαι, διώκω δὲ εἰ καὶ καταλάβω,
ἐφ᾿ ᾧ καὶ κατελήμφθην ὑπὸ Χριστοῦ. ¹³ἀδελφοί, ἐγὼ
ἐμαυτὸν οὐ λογίζομαι κατειληφέναι· ¹⁴ἓν δέ, τὰ μὲν ὀπίσω ἐπιλανθανόμενος τοῖς δὲ ἔμπροσθεν ἐπεκτεινόμενος

who have put away childish things, who boast that we are men in Christ, so resolve. Then, if in any matter we lose our way, God will at length reveal this also to us. Only let us remember one thing. Our footsteps must not swerve from the line in which we have hitherto trodden.'

12. οὐχ ὅτι κ.τ.λ.] The change of tense is not accidental. The aorist ἔλαβον points to a past epoch, to which ἐζημιώθην, κατελήμφθην, also refer ; 'not as though by my conversion I did at once attain'. The perfect τετελείωμαι describes his present state; 'not as though I were now already perfected.' For οὐχ ὅτι compare 2 Cor. iii. 5, vii. 9, 2 Thess. iii. 9, and below iv. 11, 17.

διώκω κ.τ.λ.] For the connexion of διώκειν and καταλαμβάνειν see Herod. ix. 58 διωκτέοι εἰσὶ εἰς ὁ καταλαμφθέντες κ.τ.λ., Lucian Hermot. 77 ὠκύτεροι παραπολὺ διώκοντες οὐ κατέλαβον: compare LXX Exod. xv. 9, Eccles. xi. 10. For the meaning of these two words see the note on ἐπεκτεινόμενος ver. 14 ; for the conjunctive καταλάβω, the note on καταντήσω ver. 10.

ἐφ᾿ ᾧ] may mean either (1) 'Wherefore, whereunto,' thus fulfilling God's purpose; or (2) 'Because,' thus fulfilling his own duty. In this second sense ἐφ᾿ ᾧ is apparently used Rom. v. 12, 2 Cor. v. 4. The former meaning seems more appropriate here, though the latter is better supported by St Paul's usage elsewhere. On the different senses of ἐφ᾿ ᾧ see Fritzsche on Rom. I. p. 299. Others, as the English Version, understand an antecedent, καταλάβω ἐκεῖνο ἐφ᾿ ᾧ (comp. Luke v. 25); but καταλάβω, like κατειληφέναι below, seems to be used absolutely, as ἔλαβον and διώκω also are used.

13. ἀδελφοί] 'my brothers,' with a view of arresting attention ; see the notes on Gal. iii. 15, vi. 1, 18.

ἐγὼ ἐμαυτόν] 'Facile hoc alii de Paulo existimare possent,' says Bengel. This however seems hardly to be the point of the expression. St Paul is not contrasting his own estimate of himself with other people's estimate of him, but his estimate of himself with others' estimate of themselves. He is in fact protesting against the false security, the antinomian reckless-ness, which others deduced from the doctrine of faith : see the notes on τέλειοι ver. 15, and on vv. 12, 19, and the introduction p. 70.

14. ἓν δέ] This usage may be illustrated by the classical expression δυοῖν θάτερον. It is difficult to say whether ἓν is a nominative or an accusative. If (with Winer § lxvi. p. 774) we may compare 2 Cor. vi. 13, it is the latter.

τὰ ὀπίσω] i.e. the portion of the course already traversed. Compare Lucian Calumn. 12 οἷόν τι καὶ ἐπὶ τοῖς γυμνικοῖς ἀγῶσιν ὑπὸ τῶν δρομέων γίγνεται· κἀκεῖ γὰρ ὁ μὲν ἀγαθὸς δρομεὺς τῆς ὕσπληγος εὐθὺς καταπεσούσης, μόνον τοῦ πρόσω ἐφιέμενος καὶ τὴν διάνοιαν ἀποτείνας πρὸς τὸ τέρμα κ.τ.λ.

ἐπεκτεινόμενος] 'superextensus: oculus manum, manus pedem prævertit et trahit,' is Bengel's paraphrase. The metaphor may possibly be derived from the chariot races in the Circus, as the epistle was written from Rome. On this supposition the meaning of ἐπεκτεινόμενος has been aptly illustrated by Virgil's 'Instant verbere torto Et proni dant lora' (Georg. iii. 106). To this view διώκω lends some support, for it is frequently said of charioteers (e.g. Soph. El. 738); but all the terms

κατὰ σκοπὸν διώκω εἰς τὸ βραβεῖον τῆς ἄνω κλήσεως
τοῦ Θεοῦ ἐν Χριστῷ Ἰησοῦ. ¹⁵ὅσοι οὖν τέλειοι, τοῦτο
φρονῶμεν· καὶ εἴ τι ἑτέρως φρονεῖτε, καὶ τοῦτο ὁ Θεὸς

15.  τοῦτο φρονοῦμεν.

used are equally appropriate to the
foot-race, and there seems no reason
for departing from St Paul's usual
metaphor. Moreover the not looking
back, which showed a right temper
in a runner (Lucian l. c.), would be
fatal to the charioteer; see Themist.
*Orat.* xv. p. 196 B ἀνδρὶ δὲ ἡνιοχοῦν-
τι...ἀνάγκη...τὰ μὲν πρόσω μὴ πάνυ ὁρᾶν
ὀπίσω δὲ ἀεὶ τετράφθαι τῇ γνώμῃ πρὸς
τοὺς διώκοντας κ.τ.λ. The word occurs
Iren. i. 11. 3 (comp. i. 2. 2).

εἰς τὸ βραβεῖον] '*unto the prize*';
comp. 1 Cor. ix. 24. This preposition
is used, because the prize marks the
position of the goal. The ἐπὶ of the
common text is an obvious substitution
for a more difficult reading.

τῆς ἄνω κλήσεως] '*our heavenward
calling*'; so Philo *Plant.* § 6 p. 333 M
πρὸς γὰρ τὸ θεῖον ἄνω καλεῖσθαι θέμις
τοὺς ὑπ' αὐτοῦ καταπνευσθέντας, comp.
Heb. iii. 1. The words ἐν Χριστῷ Ἰησοῦ
must be taken with κλήσεως; see
1 Cor. vii. 22, 1 Pet. v. 10.

15.  ὅσοι οὖν τέλειοι] The τέλειοι
are 'grown men' as opposed to children;
e.g. 1 Cor. xiv. 20, Ephes. iv. 13, Heb.
v. 14. They are therefore those who
have passed out of the rudimentary
discipline of ordinances (Gal. iv. 3, 4),
who have put away childish things
(1 Cor. xiii. 10—12), who have assumed
the Apostle's ground respecting the
law. The τέλειοι in fact are the same
with the πνευματικοί: comp. 1 Cor.
ii. 6 with iii. 1. But these men, who
were proud of their manhood, who
boasted their spiritual discernment,
were often regardless of the scruples
of others and even lax in their own
lives. Hence the stress which St
Paul here lays on the duty of moral
and spiritual progress, as enforced by
his own example. Thus in ὅσοι τέλειοι,
'all we who attained our manhood, our

independence, in Christ', there is the
same reproachful irony as in 1 Cor.
viii. 1 οἴδαμεν ὅτι πάντες γνῶσιν ἔχομεν,
in Rom. xv. 1 ἡμεῖς οἱ δυνατοί, and
possibly also in Gal. vi. 1 ὑμεῖς οἱ
πνευματικοί. The epithet τέλειοι seems
to have been especially affected by
the party both at this time and later ;
comp. Barnab. 4 γενώμεθα πνευματικοί,
γενώμεθα ναὸς τέλειος τῷ Θεῷ, Iren.
i. 6. 4 ἑαυτοὺς δὲ ὑπερυψοῦσι, τελείους
ἀποκαλοῦντες καὶ σπέρματα ἐκλογῆς
(comp. § 3, where οἱ τελειότατοι is said
in irony, and see also i. 13. 5, i. 18. 1, iii.
13. 5), Clem. Alex. *Pæd.* i. 6 (p. 128 Potter) ἐμοὶ δὲ καὶ θαυμάζειν ἔπεισιν ὅπως
σφᾶς τελείους τινὲς τολμῶσι καλεῖν καὶ
γνωστικούς, ὑπὲρ τὸν ἀπόστολον φρονοῦντες, φυσιούμενοί τε καὶ φρυαττόμενοι
κ.τ.λ., Hippol. *Hær.* v. 8 οὐδεὶς τούτων
τῶν μυστηρίων ἀκροατὴς γέγονεν εἰ μὴ
μόνοι οἱ γνωστικοὶ τέλειοι, not without
a reference to the secondary sense of
the word, 'instructed in the mysteries.'
See *Clem. Hom.* iii. 29 τελείως ἐκφαί-
νειν τὸν μυστικὸν λόγον ... τοῖς ἤδη
τελείοις ἔφη.

τοῦτο φρονῶμεν] '*let us have this
mind*', i.e. let us make it our rule to
forget the past and press ever forward.

καὶ εἴ τι ἑτέρως κ.τ.λ.] '*Then*, if only
you hold this fundamental principle,
if progress is indeed your rule ; *though
you are at fault on any subject, God
will reveal this also to you*'; comp.
Joh. vii. 17 ἐάν τις θέλῃ τὸ θέλημα
αὐτοῦ ποιεῖν, γνώσεται περὶ τῆς διδαχῆς
πότερον ἐκ τοῦ Θεοῦ ἐστὶν κ.τ.λ. Here
ἑτέρως seems to have the meaning
'amiss' : see the note on Gal. i. 6. It
may however be 'otherwise,' in reference to τοῦτο φρονῶμεν; in which case
εἴτι will mean 'in any minor point': 'If
you are sound at the core, God will
remove the superficial blemishes.'

ὑμῖν ἀποκαλύψει· ¹⁶πλὴν εἰς ὃ ἐφθάσαμεν, τῷ αὐτῷ
στοιχεῖν.
¹⁷Συνμιμηταί μου γίνεσθε, ἀδελφοί, καὶ σκοπεῖτε

Comp. Herm. *Vis.* iii. 13 ἐάν τι δὲ
δέῃ, ἀποκαλυφθήσεταί σοι.
16. πλὴν εἰς ὃ κ.τ.λ.] ‘*only we must
walk by the same rule whereunto we
attained.*’ What is meant by this same
rule ? Is it (1) The rule of moral
progress ? or (2) The rule of faith as
opposed to works ? In the former case,
the words would simply enforce the
preceding τοῦτο φρονῶμεν; in the latter,
they are added as a parting caution
against ‘the dogs, the base workers,
the concision.’ The latter seems preferable, as on the whole the reference
to the Judaizers is the more probable,
both because St Paul's earnestness
would naturally prompt him to recur
to this subject, and because the
phrase is elsewhere used in the
same connexion; Gal. vi. 16 ὅσοι τῷ
κανόνι τούτῳ στοιχήσουσιν, comp. v. 25.
The words after στοιχεῖν in the received text (κανόνι, τὸ αὐτὸ φρονεῖν)
are interpolated from Gal. vi 16,
Phil. ii. 2. Of these κανόνι is a correct
gloss, while τὸ αὐτὸ φρονεῖν expresses
an idea alien to the context. Though
πλὴν is now generally connected with
πλέον, πλεῖν, as if it signiffed ‘more
than, beyond’ (e. g. Klotz *Devar.* II.
p. 724, Curtius *Griech. Etym.* p. 253),
the etymology which connects it with
πέλας seems to offer a better explanation of its usage. It will then signify
‘besides,’ and hence, in passages like
the present, ‘apart from this,’ ‘setting
this aside’; so that it is conveniently
translated ‘only’: comp. i. 18, iv. 14.
In this case it has an accusatival form,
like δίκην, ἐπίκλην, or the Latin ‘clam,’
‘palam,’ etc. For the dative of the
rule or direction (τῷ αὐτῷ) see the
notes on Gal. v. 16, 25, vi. 16. The
infinitive στοιχεῖν is equivalent to an
emphatic imperative; see Fritzsche
*Rom.* III. p. 85, and Winer § xliii.
p. 398. For φθάνειν εἰς, ‘to reach

to’ see Dan. iv. 19, Rom. ix. 31.
17—21. ‘My brethren, vie with each
other in imitating me, and observe
those whose walk of life is fashioned
after our example. This is the only
safe test. For there are many, of
whom I told you often and now tell
you again even in tears, who professing our doctrine walk not in our
footsteps. They are foes to the cross
of Christ; they are doomed to per-
dition; they make their appetites their
god; they glory in their shame; they
are absorbed in earthly things. Not
such is *our* life. In heaven we have even
now our country, our home; and from
heaven hereafter we look in patient
hope for a deliverer, even the Lord
Jesus Christ, who shall change the
fleeting fashion of these bodies—the
bodies of our earthly humiliation—so
that they shall take the abiding form
of His own body—the body of His
risen glory: for such is the working
of the mighty power whereby He is
able to subdue all things alike unto
Himself.’
17. Συνμιμηταί μου] i.e. ‘Vie with
each other in imitating me,’ ‘one and
all of you imitate me’: so συμμιμεῖσθαι
Plat. *Polit.* p. 274 D. Compare 1 Cor.
iv. 16, xi. 1, 1 Thess. i. 6, 2 Thess. iii.
7, 9, ἵνα ἑαυτοὺς τύπον δῶμεν ὑμῖν εἰς τὸ
μιμεῖσθαι ἡμᾶς. In 1 Cor. xi. 1 the
injunction μιμηταί μου γίνεσθε is addressed, as here, to the party of reaction against Judaism.
σκοπεῖτε] ‘*mark* and follow,’ not as
generally ‘*mark* and avoid’, e.g. Rom.
xvi. 17. Under ἡμᾶς are included
Timotheus, Epaphroditus, and other
faithful companions known to the
Philippians. Shrinking from the ego-
tism of dwelling on his own personal example, St Paul passes at once from the
singular (μου) to the plural (ἡμᾶς).
18. πολλοὶ γάρ] If the view which

τοὺς οὕτω περιπατοῦντας καθὼς ἔχετε τύπον ἡμᾶς.
¹⁸πολλοὶ γὰρ περιπατοῦσιν, οὓς πολλάκις ἔλεγον ὑμῖν,
νῦν δὲ καὶ κλαίων λέγω, τοὺς ἐχθροὺς τοῦ σταυροῦ τοῦ

I have taken be correct, the persons here denounced are not the Judaizing teachers, but the antinomian reactionists. This view is borne out by the parallel expression, Rom. xvi. 18 τῷ Κυρίῳ ἡμῶν Χριστῷ οὐ δουλεύουσιν ἀλλὰ τῇ ἑαυτῶν κοιλίᾳ, where the same persons seem to be intended; for they are described as creating divisions and offences (ver. 17), as holding plausible language (ver. 18), as professing to be wise beyond others (ver. 19) and yet not innocent in their wisdom; this last reproach being implied in the words θέλω δὲ ὑμᾶς σοφοὺς εἶναι εἰς τὸ ἀγαθὸν ἀκεραίους δὲ εἰς τὸ κακόν. They appear therefore to belong to the same party to which the passages vi. 1—23, xiv. 1—xv. 6, of that epistle are chiefly addressed. For the profession of 'wisdom' in these faithless disciples of St Paul see 1 Cor. i. 17 sq., iv. 18 sq., viii. 1 sq., x. 15. Compare the note on τέλειοι above.

περιπατοῦσιν] An adverbial clause, such as οὐκ ὀρθῶς, might have been expected: but in the earnestness of expression the sentence is uninterrupted, the qualifying idea being for the moment dropped. It reappears in a different form in the words τοὺς ἐχθροὺς κ.τ.λ. attached to the dependent sentence οὓς πολλάκις ἔλεγον κ.τ.λ.

νῦν δὲ] 'but now', for the evil has grown meanwhile.

καὶ κλαίων] The stress of St Paul's grief would lie in the fact, that they degraded the true doctrine of liberty, so as to minister to their profligate and worldly living. They made use of his name, but did not follow his example.

τοὺς ἐχθροὺς τοῦ σταυροῦ] See Polyc. Phil. § 12. These words do not in themselves decide what persons are

here denounced; for the enemies of the cross may be twofold; (1) D. ctrinal. The Judaizers, who deny the efficacy of the cross and substitute obedience to a formal code in its place; comp. Gal. v. 11, vi. 12, 14. (2) Practical. The Antinomians, who refuse to conform to the cross (iii. 10, 2 Cor. i. 5, 6) and live a life of self-indulgence; comp. 1 Cor. i. 17. If the view, which I have adopted and which the context seems to require, is correct, the latter are here meant; see the last note. In the passages, Polyc. Phil. 7 ὃς ἂν μὴ ὁμολογῇ τὸ μαρτύριον τοῦ σταυροῦ, Ignat. Trall. 11 ἐφαίνοντο ἂν κλάδοι τοῦ σταυροῦ, the reference is apparently to docetism, as denying the reality of the passion. But belonging to a later generation, these passages throw no light on St Paul's meaning here.

19. τὸ τέλος ἀπώλεια] Comp. Rom. vi. 21 τὸ τέλος ἐκείνων θάνατος: see also 2 Cor. xi. 15, Hebr. vi. 8.

ὁ θεὸς ἡ κοιλία] See Rom. xvi. 18 already quoted: comp. Seneca de Benef. vii. 26 'Alius abdomini servit', Eur. Cycl. 335 θύω...τῇ μεγίστῃ γαστρὶ τῇδε δαιμόνων· ὡς τοὐμπιεῖν γε καὶ φαγεῖν τοὐφ' ἡμέραν Ζεὺς οὗτος ἀνθρώποισι τοῖσι σώφροσιν. So in attacks on Epicurean ethics 'venter' commonly appears as the type of sensual appetites generally, e. g. Cic. Nat. Deor. i. 40, Senec. Vit. Beat. ix. 4, xiv. 3. The Apostle elsewhere reminds these lax brethren, that 'the kingdom of God is not eating and drinking,' Rom. xiv. 17; comp. 1 Cor. viii. 8. The self-indulgence, which wounds the tender conscience of others and turns liberty into license, is here condemned.

ἡ δόξα κ.τ.λ.] The unfettered liberty, of which they boast, thus perverted becomes their deepest degradation.

Χριστοῦ, ¹⁹ ὧν τὸ τέλος ἀπώλεια, ὧν ὁ θεὸς ἡ κοιλία,
καὶ ἡ δόξα ἐν τῇ αἰσχύνῃ αὐτῶν, οἱ τὰ ἐπίγεια φρονοῦντες. ²⁰ ἡμῶν γὰρ τὸ πολίτευμα ἐν οὐρανοῖς ὑπάρχει, ἐξ οὗ καὶ σωτῆρα ἀπεκδεχόμεθα Κύριον Ἰησοῦν Χρισ-

20.  ἡμῶν δὲ τὸ πολίτευμα.

Comp. Hosea vii. 8 τὴν δόξαν αὐτῶν
εἰς ἀτιμίαν θήσω.
οἱ τὰ ἐπίγεια κ.τ.λ.] 'Men whose
minds are set on earthly things'! For
the abrupt nominative occurring without any grammatical connexion and
expressing amazement, comp. Mark
xii. 38—40; see Winer § xxix. p. 228.
20.  ἡμῶν γὰρ κ.τ.λ.] 'Their souls
are mundane and grovelling. They
have no fellowship with *us*; for *we*
are citizens of a heavenly commonwealth '. The emphatic position of
ἡμῶν contrasts the false adherents of
St Paul with the true. About the connecting particle there is some difficulty.
While the earliest MSS all read γάρ, the
earliest citations (with several versions)
have persistently δέ. I have therefore given δέ as a possible alternative ;
although it is probably a substitution
for γάρ, of which the connexion was
not very obvious.
τὸ πολίτευμα] This may mean
either (1) ' The state, the constitution,
to which as citizens we belong', e.g.
Philo *de Jos.* ii. p. 51 M ἐγγραφῆς τῆς
ἐν τῷ μεγίστῳ καὶ ἀρίστῳ πολιτεύματι
τοῦδε τοῦ κόσμου, *de Confus.* i. p.
421 M ἐγγράφονται τῷ τῆς προτέρας
πολιτεύματι, 2 Macc. xii. 7 τὸ σύμπαν
τῶν Ἰοππιτῶν πολίτευμα ; or (2) ' The
functions which as citizens we perform', e.g. Demosth. *de Cor.* p. 262
πάντα τὰ τοιαῦτα προηρούμην πολιτεύ-
ματα κ.τ.λ., Lucian *Prom.* 15 ἐπὶ τῷ
πολιτεύματι τούτῳ, Tatian *ad Græc.*
19. The singular points to the former
meaning, which is also more frequent.
In either case ἐξ οὗ ' whence' will refer
not to πολίτευμα, but to οὐρανοῖς. On
the metaphor see above i. 27. Compare
also Philo *de Confus.* i. p. 416 M πατρί-
δα μὲν τὸν οὐράνιον χῶρον ἐν ᾧ πολιτεύ-

ονται ξένον δὲ τὸν περίγειον ἐν ᾧ παρῴ-
κησαν νομίζουσαι, *Epist. ad Diogn.*
§ 5 ἐπὶ γῆς διατρίβουσιν ἀλλ᾽ ἐν οὐρανῷ
πολιτεύονται, *Clem. Hom.* i. 16 αὕτη σε
ἡ ἀλήθεια ξένον ὄντα τῆς ἰδίας πόλεως
καταστήσει πολίτην. See also M. Anton.
iii. 11 πολίτην ὄντα πόλεως τῆς ἀνωτάτης
ἧς αἱ λοιπαὶ πόλεις ὥσπερ οἰκίαι εἰσίν.
It was a favourite metaphor with the
Stoics, Clem. Alex. *Strom.* iv. 26 (p.
642 Potter) λέγουσι γὰρ καὶ οἱ Στωϊκοὶ
τὸν μὲν οὐρανὸν κυρίως πόλιν τὰ δὲ ἐπὶ
γῆς ἐνταῦθα οὐκ ἔτι πόλεις, λέγεσθαι μὲν
γάρ, οὐκ εἶναι δέ κ.τ.λ. ; see below, p.
303 sq. Somewhat similarly Plato says
of his ideal state (*Resp.* ix. p. 592 B)
ἐν οὐρανῷ ἴσως παράδειγμα [τῆς πόλεως]
ἀνάκειται τῷ βουλομένῳ ὁρᾶν καὶ ὁρῶντι
ἑαυτὸν κατοικίζειν. But the reply of
Anaxagoras (Diog. Laert. ii. 7) to one
who reproached him with indifference
to his countrymen, εὐφήμει, ἐμοὶ γὰρ
καὶ σφόδρα μέλει τῆς πατρίδος (δείξας
τὸν οὐρανόν), ought not to be quoted
in illustration, as it refers to his astro-
nomical studies.
ὑπάρχει] '*is even now*', for the
kingdom of heaven is a present kingdom; so Ephes. ii. 19 οὐκέτι ἐστὲ
ξένοι καὶ πάροικοι ἀλλὰ ἐστὲ συνπολῖται τῶν ἁγίων κ.τ.λ. (comp. ver. 6).
σωτῆρα ἀπεκδεχόμεθα] '*we eagerly
await as a saviour*'. On ἀπεκδέ-
χεσθαι see Gal. v. 5, together with
the note on ἀποκαραδοκία above, i. 20.
21. μετασχηματίσει] '*will change
the fashion*'. For μετασχηματίσει and
σύμμορφον see the detached note on
μορφή and σχῆμα, p. 130.
τῆς ταπεινώσεως ἡμῶν] '*of our humiliation*', i. e. the body which we
bear in our present low estate, which
is exposed to all the passions, sufferings, and indignities of this life. The

τόν, ²¹ ὃς μετασχηματίσει τὸ σῶμα τῆς ταπεινώσεως
ἡμῶν σύμμορφον τῷ σώματι τῆς δόξης αὐτοῦ, κατὰ τὴν
ἐνέργειαν τοῦ δύνασθαι αὐτὸν καὶ ὑποτάξαι αὐτῷ τὰ
πάντα. IV. ¹ ὥστε, ἀδελφοί μου ἀγαπητοὶ καὶ ἐπι-

English translation, 'our vile body', seems to countenance the Stoic contempt of the body, of which there is no tinge in the original.

σύμμορφον] 'so as to be conformable', see Winer § lxvi. p. 779. The words εἰς τὸ γενέσθαι αὐτὸ, occurring before σύμμορφον in the received text, must be struck out as a gloss, though a correct one. This transformation is described at greater length and in other language, 1 Cor. xv. 35—53.

τῆς δόξης αὐτοῦ] i.e. with which He is clothed in His glorified estate.

τὴν ἐνέργειαν τοῦ δύνασθαι] 'The exercise of the power which He possesses.' This expression involves the common antithesis of δύναμις and ἐνέργεια; comp. Ephes. i. 19. 'Potentia arbor, efficacia fructus,' says Calvin. Comp. Herm. Mand. vi. I τίνα δύναμιν ἔχει καὶ ἐνέργειαν.

καὶ ὑποτάξαι] 'also to subject'; for this power of subjugating the human body is only one manifestation of the universal sovereignty of Christ. On the subjection of all things to the Son see 1 Cor. xv. 25—27. For τὰ πάντα with the article see the note above ver. 8.

αὐτῷ] i.e. τῷ Χριστῷ, referring to the subject of the principal verb, as e.g. in Acts xxv. 21, Ephes. i. 4. In such connexions the reflexive pronoun ἑαυτοῦ would be required in Classical Greek. In the later language however we find αὐτοῦ etc. in place of ἑαυτοῦ etc. in almost every case, except where it stands as the direct object, the immediate accusative of the verb. See the excellent account of the usage of αὐτὸς and ἑαυτοῦ in A. Buttmann p. 97. In this passage there is not sufficient authority for the reading ἑαυτῷ. The forms αὐτοῦ, αὐτῷ, αὐτόν,

have no place in the Greek Testament, as is clearly shown by A. Buttmann l.c. Winer, § xxii. p. 188 sq., speaks hesitatingly.

IV. 1. ὥστε] 'therefore.' 'Bearing these things in mind, living as citizens of a heavenly polity, having this hope of a coming Saviour.'

ἐπιπόθητοι] This adjective does not occur elsewhere in the New Testament : comp. Clem. Rom. 59, Appian. Hisp. 43. The Apostle's love finds expression in the accumulation and repetition of words. In the final ἀγαπητοὶ he seems to linger over this theme, as if unable to break away from it.

χαρὰ καὶ στέφανός μου] He uses the same language in addressing the other great Macedonian church, 1 Thess. ii. 19. The word στέφανος 'a chaplet' must be carefully . distinguished from διάδημα 'a regal or priestly diadem'. To the references given in Trench N. T. Syn. § xxiii, p. 74, add Is. lxii. 3 στέφανος κάλλους ...καὶ διάδημα βασιλείας, Test. xii Patr. Levi 8 ὁ ἕκτος στέφανόν μοι τῇ κεφαλῇ περιέθηκεν, ὁ ἕβδομος διάδημα τῇ κεφαλῇ μοι ἱερατείας περιέθηκε, Diod. Sic. xx. 54 διάδημα μὲν οὐκ ἔκρινεν ἔχειν, ἐφόρει γὰρ ἀεὶ στέφανον. Thus the idea conveyed by στέφανος is not dominion, but either (1) victory, or (2) merriment, as the wreath was worn equally by the conqueror and by the holidaymaker. Without excluding the latter notion, the former seems to be prominent in this and in the parallel passage ; for there, as here, the Apostle refers in the context to the Lord's coming. His converts will then be his wreath of victory, for it will appear that he οὐκ εἰς κενὸν ἔδραμεν (ii. 16), and he will receive the successful athlete's reward ; comp. 1 Cor. ix. 25

πόθητοι, χαρὰ καὶ στέφανός μου, οὕτως στήκετε ἐν
Κυρίῳ, ἀγαπητοί. ² Εὐοδίαν παρακαλῶ καὶ Συντύχην παρακαλῶ τὸ
αὐτὸ φρονεῖν ἐν Κυρίῳ. ³ ναὶ ἐρωτῶ καὶ σέ, γνήσιε σύν-

οὕτως στήκετε] 'stand fast so, as you are guided by my precept and my example, as becomes citizens of a heavenly kingdom.' On στήκετε see the notes, i. 27, Gal. v. 1.

2. The Apostle at length returns from his long digression (see the notes on iii. 1, 2) to the subject of the dissensions at Philippi. His injunctions here take the form of a direct personal appeal to those chiefly at fault; and two ladies especially are mentioned by name.

2, 3. 'I appeal to Euodia, and I appeal to Syntyche, to give up their differences and live at peace in the Lord. Yes I ask you, my faithful and true yokefellow, who are now by my side, who will deliver this letter to the Philippians, to reconcile them again: for I cannot forget how zealously they seconded my efforts on behalf of the Gospel. I invite Clement also, with the rest of my fellow-labourers, whose names are enrolled in the book of life, the register of God's faithful people, to aid in this work of reconciliation.'

Εὐοδίαν κ.τ.λ.] Both these names occur in the inscriptions : Euhodia or Euodia for instance in Gruter p. 695, 4, p. 789. 5, Muratori p. 107. 9, p. 932. 5, p. 1161. 4, p. 1185. 7, p. 1340. 8, p. 1362. 2, p. 1671. 3, 5 (comp. Tertull. ad Scap. 4); Syntyche, Suntyche, or Syntiche, in Gruter p. 890. 7, p. 987. 8, Muratori, p. 857. 7, p. 972. 5, p. 1315. 17, p. 1569. 4, p. 1664. 4. The English Version treats the first as a man's name; and others have in like manner interpreted the second. No instance however of either ' Euodias' or ' Syntyches' has been found in the inscriptions. The former indeed might be considered a contraction of Euodianus which occurs occasionally : but the masculine form of the latter is Syntychus, a very rare name (Gruter p. 372. 5). But, though it were possible to treat the words in themselves as masculine, two female names are clearly required here, as there is nothing else in the sentence to which αὐταῖς can be referred. Euodia and Syntyche appear to have been ladies of rank, or possibly (like Phœbe, Rom. xvi. 1) deaconesses in the Philippian church. On the position of women in Macedonia and on their prominence in the history of the Gospel there, see the introduction, p. 55 sq.

παρακαλῶ] St Paul repeats the word as if, says Bengel, ' coram adhortans seorsum utramvis.'

3. ναί] 'yea,' introducing an affectionate appeal, as Philem. 20 ναί, ἀδελφέ, ἐγώ σου ὀναίμην. The καὶ of the received text must be considered a misprint, or a miswriting of a few late MSS.

ἐρωτῶ] 'I ask'; a late use of the word which in the classical language signifies not ' rogo' generally, but 'interrogo' specially. In this late sense of 'requesting,' ἐρωτῶ differs from αἰτῶ, as ' rogo' from ' peto'; the two former being used towards an equal, the two latter towards a superior; see Trench N. T. Syn. § xl. p. 135.

γνήσιε σύνζυγε] 'true yoke-fellow,' comp. Æsch. Ag. 842; so 2 Cor. vi. 14 ἑτεροζυγοῦντες. It is doubtful whom the Apostle thus addresses. On the whole however it seems most probable that Epaphroditus, the bearer of the letter, is intended; for in his case alone there would be no risk of making the reference unintelligible by the suppression of the name. Different commentators have explained it of Barnabas, of Luke, of Silas, of Timotheus, of

ζύγε, συλλαμβάνου αὐταῖς, αἵτινες ἐν τῷ εὐαγγελίῳ
συνήθλησάν μοι, μετὰ καὶ Κλήμεντος καὶ τῶν λοιπῶν
συνεργῶν μου, ὧν τὰ ὀνόματα ἐν βίβλῳ ζωῆς.
⁴Χαίρετε ἐν Κυρίῳ πάντοτε· πάλιν ἐρῶ, χαίρετε.

the chief presbyter or bishop of Philippi. Others again have taken Σύνζυγος itself as a proper name, explaining γνήσιε 'truly called.' The case
for this interpretation is well stated
by Laurent *Neutest. Stud.* p. 134. It
would be plausible, if Σύνζυγος occurred commonly, or occurred at all, in
the inscriptions. The passage would
then present a parallel to the play on
the name Onesimus in Philem. 11.
Less can be said in favour of another
expedient which makes Γνήσιος the
proper name. A very ancient interpretation again (Clem. Alex. *Strom.*
iii. p. 535 Potter, Orig. *Rom.* I. p. 461
Delarue) takes 'yokefellow' to mean
St Paul's wife; but the Apostle would
doubtless have written γνησία in this
case, and it seems clear moreover from
1 Cor. vii. 8 that he was either unmarried or a widower. The grammatical
objection applies equally to Renan's
suggestion (*St Paul* p. 148) that Lydia
is meant. For γνήσιε comp. Ecclus. vii.
18, and see the note on γνησίως ii. 20.

συλλαμβάνου, κ.τ.λ.] '*assist them,*
Euodia and Syntyche, *since they laboured with me etc.*' They may have
belonged to the company of women to
whom the Gospel was first preached
at Philippi, Acts xvi. 13 ταῖς συνελθού-
σαις γυναιξίν. For αἵτινες, '*inasmuch
as they,*' comp. e.g. Acts x. 41, 47,
Rom. ii. 15, vi. 2, etc. While ὅς simply
marks the individual, ὅστις places him
in a class, and thus calls attention to
certain characteristic features; hence
the meaning 'quippe qui.' On the
distinction of ὅς and ὅστις see the
notes on Gal. iv. 24, 26, v. 19. The
rendering adopted by the English version, 'Help those women who laboured
etc.' is obviously incorrect, and would
require ἐκείναις αἱ συνήθλησαν.

μετὰ καὶ Κλήμεντος κ.τ.λ.] '*with
Clement also.*' These words ought
perhaps to be connected rather with
συλλαμβάνου αὐταῖς than with συνήθλησάν μοι. The Apostle is anxious to
engage *all* in the work of conciliation.
On the Clement here meant see the
detached note p. 168. The καὶ before
Κλήμεντος seems to be retrospective
(referring to γνήσιε σύνζυγε) rather
than prospective (referring to καὶ τῶν
λοιπῶν συνεργῶν μου); as in John ii. 2.
For its position comp. Clem. Rom. § 59
σὺν καὶ Φορτουνάτῳ.

ὧν τὰ ὀνόματα κ.τ.λ.] '*whose names,*
though not mentioned by the Apostle,
are nevertheless *in the book of life.*'
The 'book of life' in the figurative
language of the Old Testament is the
register of the covenant people : comp.
Is. iv. 3 οἱ γραφέντες εἰς ζωὴν ἐν Ἱερουσαλήμ, Ezek. xiii. 9 ἐν παιδείᾳ τοῦ λαοῦ
μου οὐκ ἔσονται οὐδὲ ἐν γραφῇ οἴκου
Ἰσραὴλ οὐ γραφήσονται. Hence 'to
be blotted out of the book of the living' means 'to forfeit the privileges
of the theocracy,' 'to be shut out from
God's favour,' Ps. lxix. 28 ; comp. Exod.
xxxii. 32. But the expression, though
perhaps confined originally to temporal blessings, was in itself a witness
to higher hopes; and in the book of
Daniel first (xii. 1 sq.) it distinctly refers to a blessed immortality. In the
Revelation τὸ βιβλίον τῆς ζωῆς is a
phrase of constant recurrence, iii. 5,
xiii. 8, xvii. 8, xx. 12, 15, xxi. 27, xxii.
19 ; comp. Hermas *Vis.* i. 3. See also
Luke x. 20, Heb. xii. 23. It is clear
from the expression 'blotting out of
the book' (Rev. iii. 5), that the image
suggested no idea of absolute predes-
tination. For the use of the phrase
in rabbinical writers see Wetstein here.

4. χαίρετε] This word combines a

⁵τὸ ἐπιεικὲς ὑμῶν γνωσθήτω πᾶσιν ἀνθρώποις. ὁ Κύριος ἐγγύς. ⁶μηδὲν μεριμνᾶτε, ἀλλ᾽ ἐν παντὶ τῇ προσευχῇ καὶ τῇ δεήσει μετ᾽ εὐχαριστίας τὰ αἰτήματα ὑμῶν
γνωριζέσθω πρὸς τὸν Θεόν. ⁷καὶ ἡ εἰρήνη τοῦ Θεοῦ ἡ

parting benediction with an exhortation to cheerfulness. It is neither
'farewell' alone, nor 'rejoice' alone.
Compare for this same combination of
senses the dying words of the Greek
messenger χαίρετε καὶ χαίρομεν quoted
above on ii. 18; see the notes on ii. 18,
iii. 1.

πάλιν ἐρῶ] 'again I will say'; for
ἐρῶ seems to be always a future in the
New Testament as in Attic Greek.
Compare Æsch. Eum. 1014 χαίρετε,
χαίρετε δ᾽ αὖθις, ἐπανδιπλοίζω. See the
notes on i. 4.

5—7. 'Let your gentle and forbearing spirit be recognised by all
men. The judgment is drawing near.
Entertain no anxious cares, but throw
them all upon God. By your prayer
and your supplication with thanksgiving make your every want known
to Him. If you do this, then the
peace of God, far more effective than
any forethought or contrivance of
man, will keep watch over your hearts
and your thoughts in Christ Jesus.'

5. τὸ ἐπιεικὲς ὑμῶν] 'your forbearance,' the opposite to a spirit of
contention and self-seeking. The ἐπι-
εικής stands in contrast to the ἀκριβο-
δίκαιος, as being satisfied with less
than his due, Arist. Eth. Nic. v. 10.
The word is connected with ἄμαχος,
πᾶσαν ἐνδεικνύμενος πραΰτητα (Tit. iii. 2,
comp. 1 Tim. iii. 3), with εἰρηνικός, εὐ-
πειθής, μεστὸς ἐλέους κ.τ.λ. (James iii.
17), with χρηστός, πολυέλεος (Ps. lxxxv.
5), with ἀγαθός ('kind', 1 Pet. ii. 18),
with φιλάνθρωπος (2 Macc. ix. 27). This
quality of ἐπιείκεια was signally manifested in our blessed Lord Himself
(2 Cor. x. 1).

ὁ Κύριος ἐγγύς] The nearness of
the Lord's advent is assigned as a reason for patient forbearance. So simi-

larly in St James v. 8, μακροθυμήσατε
καὶ ὑμεῖς...ὅτι ἡ παρουσία τοῦ Κυρίου ἤγ-
γικεν κ.τ.λ. The expression ὁ Κύριος
ἐγγὺς is the Apostle's watchword. In
1 Cor. xvi. 22 an Aramaic equivalent is
given, Μαρὰν ἀθά, whence we may infer
that it was a familiar form of mutual
recognition and warning in the early
Church. Compare Barnab. § 21 ἐγγὺς
ἡ ἡμέρα ἐν ᾗ συναπολεῖται πάντα τῷ πο-
νηρῷ, ἐγγὺς ὁ Κύριος καὶ ὁ μισθὸς αὐτοῦ.
See also Luke xxi. 31, 1 Pet. iv. 7.
Thus we may paraphrase St Paul's language here: 'To what purpose is this
rivalry, this self-assertion? The end
is nigh, when you will have to resign all. Bear with others now, that
God may bear with you then.' On the
other hand a different interpretation
is suggested by such passages as Ps.
cxix. 151 ἐγγὺς εἶ Κύριε, cxlv. 18 ἐγγὺς
Κύριος πᾶσι τοῖς ἐπικαλουμένοις αὐτόν
(comp. xxxiv. 18), Clem. Rom. § 21
ἴδωμεν πῶς ἐγγύς ἐστιν κ.τ.λ. (comp.
Hermas Vis. ii. 3; Clem. Alex. Quis
div. 41, p. 958); but this is neither
so natural nor so appropriate here.

6. μηδὲν μεριμνᾶτε] 'have no anxieties'; for μέριμνα is anxious harassing
care. See Trench, On the Authorized
Version p. 13 sq. (on Matt. vi. 25):
and comp. 1 Pet. v. 7, where μέριμνα
is used of human anxieties, μέλει of
God's providential care.

τῇ προσευχῇ κ.τ.λ.] While προσευχὴ
is the general offering up of the wishes
and desires to God, δέησις implies special petition for the supply of wants.
Thus προσευχὴ points to the frame of
mind in the petitioner, δέησις to the
act of solicitation. The two occur together also in Ephes. vi. 18, 1 Tim. ii. 1,
v. 5. In αἰτήματα again the several
objects of δέησις are implied. More on
the distinction of these words may be

ὑπερέχουσα πάντα νοῦν φρουρήσει τὰς καρδίας ὑμῶν καὶ
τὰ νοήματα ὑμῶν ἐν Χριστῷ Ἰησοῦ.

⁸Τὸ λοιπόν, ἀδελφοί, ὅσα ἐστὶν ἀληθῆ, ὅσα σεμνά,
ὅσα δίκαια, ὅσα ἁγνά, ὅσα προσφιλῆ, ὅσα εὔφημα, εἴ

seen in Trench, *N. T. Syn.* § li. p.
177 sq.

πρὸς τὸν Θεόν] '*before God,*' 'to
Godward,' not simply τῷ Θεῷ.

μετ' εὐχαριστίας] Since thankfulness
for past blessings is a necessary condition of acceptance in preferring new
petitions. Great stress is laid on the
duty of εὐχαριστία by St Paul; e.g.
Rom. i. 21, xiv. 6, 2 Cor. i. 11, iv. 15,
ix. 11, 12, Ephes. v. 20, Col. ii. 7, iii. 17,
1 Thess. v. 18, 1 Tim. ii. 1. All his own
letters addressed to churches, with the
sole exception of the Epistle to the
Galatians, commence with an emphatic thanksgiving. In this epistle
the injunction is in harmony with the
repeated exhortations to cheerfulness
(χαρά) which it contains; see the note
on i. 4.

7. καὶ ἡ εἰρήνη κ.τ.λ.] '*then the
peace of God*'; again an indirect allusion to their dissensions. So too in
ver. 9 ὁ Θεὸς τῆς εἰρήνης. Compare 2
Thess. iii. 16 αὐτὸς δὲ ὁ Κύριος τῆς εἰρήνης δῴη ὑμῖν τὴν εἰρήνην κ.τ.λ.

ὑπερέχουσα κ. τ. λ.] '*surpassing
every device* or *counsel*' of man, i. e.
which is far better, which produces
a higher satisfaction, than all puncti-
lious self-assertion, all anxious forethought. This sense seems better
adapted to the context, than the meaning frequently assigned to the words,
surpassing all intelligence, transcend-
ing all power of conception.' In favour
of the latter however may be quoted
Ephes. iii. 20 τῷ δυναμένῳ ὑπὲρ πάντα
ποιῆσαι ὑπερεκπερισσοῦ ὧν αἰτούμεθα ἢ
νοοῦμεν.

φρουρήσει κ.τ.λ.] A verbal paradox, for φρουρεῖν is a warrior's duty;
'God's peace shall stand sentry, shall
keep guard over your hearts.' Compare
1 Thess. iv. 11 φιλοτιμεῖσθαι ἡσυχάζειν

for a similar instance. The νοήματα
reside in and issue from the καρδίαι
(comp. 2 Cor. iii. 14, 15); for in the
Apostle's language καρδία is the seat
of thought as well as of feeling.

8. Τὸ λοιπόν] '*Finally.*' Again the
Apostle attempts to conclude; see the
note on τὸ λοιπὸν iii. 1, and the introduction, p. 69 sq.

ὅσα ἐστὶν ἀληθῆ κ.τ.λ.] Speaking
roughly, the words may be said to be
arranged in a descending scale. The
first four describe the character of the
actions themselves, the two former
ἀληθῆ, σεμνά, being absolute, the two
latter δίκαια, ἁγνά, relative; the fifth
and sixth προσφιλῆ, εὔφημα, point to
the moral approbation which they conciliate; while the seventh and eighth
ἀρετή, ἔπαινος, in which the form of
expression is changed (εἴτις for ὅσα),
are thrown in as an afterthought, that
no motive may be omitted.

ἀληθῆ] not 'veracious,' but 'true'
in the widest sense. So St Chrysostom, ταῦτα ὄντως ἀληθῆ ἡ ἀρετή, ψεῦδος
δὲ ἡ κακία. In like manner the most
comprehensive meaning must be given
to δίκαια ('righteous,' not simply
'just'), and to ἁγνά ('pure, stainless'
not simply 'chaste'): comp. Cic. *Fin.*
iii. 4 'Una virtus, unum istud, quod
honestum appellas, rectum, laudabile,
decorum, erit enim notius quale sit,
pluribus notatum vocabulis idem de-
clarantibus.'

προσφιλῆ] '*amiable, lovely*'; see
Ecclus. iv. 7, xx. 13. It does not occur elsewhere in the New Testament.
Comp. Cic. *Læl.* 28 'Nihil est amabi-
lius virtute, nihil quod magis alliciat
ad diligendum.'

εὔφημα] not 'well-spoken of, well-
reputed,' for the word seems never to
have this passive meaning; but with

τις ἀρετὴ καὶ εἴ τις ἔπαινος, ταῦτα λογίζεσθε· ⁹ἃ καὶ
ἐμάθετε καὶ παρελάβετε καὶ ἠκούσατε καὶ εἴδετε ἐν
ἐμοί, ταῦτα πράσσετε, καὶ ὁ Θεὸς τῆς εἰρήνης ἔσται
μεθ᾽ ὑμῶν.

¹⁰Ἐχάρην δὲ ἐν Κυρίῳ μεγάλως, ὅτι ἤδη ποτὲ ἀνε-

its usual active sense, '*fair-speaking*,'
and so 'winning, attractive.' Compare Plut. *Vit. Thes.* 20 ἃ δὲ εὐφημό-
τατα τῶν μυθολογουμένων, *Mor.* 84 D
τιμὴν εὔφημον, Lucian *Prom.* 3 πρὸς τὸ
εὐφημότατον ἐξηγούμενος τὸ εἰρημένον,
i. e. putting the most favourable construction on the account.

εἴ τις ἀρετή] St Paul seems studiously to avoid this common heathen
term for moral excellence, for it occurs
in this passage only. Neither is it
found elsewhere in the New Testament, except in 1 Pet. ii. 9, 2 Pet. i.
3, 5, in all which passages it seems to
have some special sense. In the Old
Testament it always signifies 'glory,
praise' (as in 1 Pet. ii. 9); though in the
Apocrypha (e. g. Wisd. iv. 1) it has its
ordinary classical sense. Its force here
is doubtful. Some treat εἴ τις ἀρετή,
εἴ τις ἔπαινος, as comprehensive expressions, recapitulating the previous
subjects under two general heads, the
intrinsic character and the subjective
estimation. The strangeness of the
word however, combined with the
change of expression εἴ τις, will suggest another explanation; 'Whatever
value may reside in your old heathen
conception of virtue, whatever consideration is due to the praise of men';
as if the Apostle were anxious not to
omit any possible ground of appeal.
Thus Beza's remark on ἀρετή seems to
be just; 'Verbum nimis humile, si
cum donis Spiritus Sancti comparetur.'
With this single occurrence of ἀρετή,
compare the solitary use of τὸ θεῖον in
the address on the Areopagus, Acts
xvii. 29.

9. In the former verse the proper
subjects of meditation (λογίζεσθε) have
been enumerated; in the present the

proper line of action (πράσσετε) is indicated. The Philippians must obey
the Apostle's precepts (ἃ ἐμάθετε καὶ
παρελάβετε) and follow his example (ἃ
ἠκούσατε καὶ εἴδετε ἐν ἐμοί).

καὶ ἐμάθετε κ.τ.λ.] The verbs should
probably be connected together in
pairs, so that the καὶ before ἐμάθετε is
answered by the καὶ before ἠκούσατε.
With ἐμάθετε καὶ παρελάβετε we may
understand παρ᾽ ἐμοῦ from the ἐν ἐμοὶ
of the next clause. The word παρελάβετε adds little to ἐμάθετε, except the
reference to the person communicating the instruction: comp. Plat. *Theæt.*
p. 198 B παραλαμβάνοντα δὲ μανθάνειν.

ἐν ἐμοί] to be attached to ἠκούσατε,
as well as to εἴδετε; 'heard when I was
away, and saw when I was with you':
comp. i. 30 οἷον εἴδετε ἐν ἐμοὶ καὶ νῦν
ἀκούετε ἐν ἐμοί.

10—19. 'It was a matter of great
and holy joy to me that after so long
an interval your care on my behalf
revived and flourished again. I do
not mean that you ever relaxed your
*care*, but the *opportunity* was wanting. Do not suppose, that in saying
this I am complaining of want; for I
have learnt to be content with my
lot, whatever it may be. I know how
to bear humiliation, and I know also
how to bear abundance. Under all circumstances and in every case, in plenty
and in hunger, in abundance and in
want, I have been initiated in the
never-failing mystery, I possess the
true secret of life. I can do and
bear all things in Christ who inspires
me with strength. But, though I am
thus indifferent to my own wants, I
commend you for your sympathy and
aid in my affliction. I need not re-
mind you, my Philippian friends; you

θάλετε τὸ ὑπὲρ ἐμοῦ φρονεῖν· ἐφ᾽ ᾧ καὶ ἐφρονεῖτε, ἠκαι-
ρεῖσθε δέ. ¹¹οὐχ ὅτι καθ᾽ ὑστέρησιν λέγω· ἐγὼ γὰρ
ἔμαθον ἐν οἷς εἰμὶ αὐτάρκης εἶναι. ¹²οἶδα καὶ ταπει-
νοῦσθαι, οἶδα καὶ περισσεύειν. ἐν παντὶ καὶ ἐν πᾶσιν

yourselves will remember; that in the
first days of the Gospel, when I left
Macedonia, though I would not receive contributions of money from
any other Church, I made an exception in your case. Nay, even before
I left, when I was still at Thessalonica, you sent more than once to supply my wants. Again I say, I do not
desire the gift, but I *do* desire that
the fruits of your benevolence should
redound to your account. For myself, I have now enough and more
than enough of all things. The presents which you sent by Epaphroditus have fully supplied my needs.
I welcome them, as the sweet savour
of a burnt-offering, as a sacrifice accepted by and well-pleasing to God.
And I am confident that God on my
behalf will recompense *you* and supply all *your* wants with the prodigal
wealth which He only can command,
in the kingdom of His glory, in Christ
Jesus.'

10. ἐχάρην δὲ κ.τ.λ.] So Polycarp
writing to these same Philippians begins (§ 1) συνεχάρην ὑμῖν μεγάλως ἐν
Κυρίῳ ἡμῶν Ἰησοῦ Χριστῷ κ.τ.λ. The δὲ
arrests a subject which is in danger of
escaping: see Gal. iv. 20. It is as if
the Apostle said: 'I must not forget
to thank you for your gift.'

ἤδη ποτὲ ἀνεθάλετε κ.τ.λ.] '*at
length ye revived your interest in
me.*' For ἤδη ποτέ 'at length' (not
necessarily referring to present time)
see Rom. i. 10, with the passages
quoted in illustration by Kypke. For
this construction of ἀναθάλλειν, 'to
put forth new shoots,' with an accusative of the thing germinated, compare Ezek. xvii. 24 (ξύλον ξηρόν),
Ecclus. i. 18 (εἰρήνην, ὑγίειαν), xi. 22
(εὐλογίαν), l. 10 (καρπούς). As the

two expressions ἤδη ποτέ and ἀνεθάλετε combined might seem to convey
a rebuke, the Apostle hastens to remove the impression by the words
which follow, ἐφ᾽ ᾧ καὶ ἐφρονεῖτε and
οὐχ ὅτι καθ᾽ ὑστέρησιν λέγω.

ἐφ᾽ ᾧ κ.τ.λ.] '*in which ye did indeed interest yourselves.*' The antecedent to ᾧ is 'my wants, my interests,' being involved in, though not
identical with, τὸ ὑπὲρ ἐμοῦ φρονεῖν.
Such grammatical irregularities are
characteristic of St Paul's style: compare for instance ii. 5. To obviate
the fancied difficulty, it has been proposed to explain the previous clause
[ὥστε] φρονεῖν τὸ ὑπὲρ ἐμοῦ, in which
case τὸ ὑπὲρ ἐμοῦ would form a strict
antecedent to ᾧ. But the separation
of τὸ ὑπὲρ ἐμοῦ from φρονεῖν is harsh
and unnatural.

ἠκαιρεῖσθε] '*ye had no opportunity*'; a late and rare word. The
active ἀκαιρεῖν is found in Diod. Sic.
*Exc.* p. 30 (Mai).

11. οὐχ ὅτι] 'It is *not* that I speak,
etc.' For οὐχ ὅτι comp. iii. 12, iv. 17:
see A. Buttmann p. 319. For καθ᾽
ὑστέρησιν, 'in language dictated by
want,' comp. Rom. x. 2 κατ᾽ ἐπίγνωσιν,
Acts iii. 17 κατὰ ἄγνοιαν, etc: see
Winer § xlix. p. 501 sq.

ἐν οἷς εἰμὶ κ.τ.λ.] '*in the position
in which I am placed.*' The idea of
αὐτάρκεια is 'independence of external
circumstances.' Compare 2 Cor. ix.
8 ἐν παντὶ πάντοτε πᾶσαν αὐτάρκειαν
ἔχοντες, 1 Tim. vi. 6. Socrates, when
asked 'Who was the wealthiest,' replied, 'He that is content with least,
for αὐτάρκεια is nature's wealth' (Stob.
*Flor.* v. 43). The Stoics especially laid
great stress on this virtue: see Senec.
*Ep. Mor.* 9 (passim). So M. Anton. i.
16 τὸ αὔταρκες ἐν παντί, where also an-

μεμύημαι, καὶ χορτάζεσθαι καὶ πεινᾶν, καὶ περισσεύειν
καὶ ὑστερεῖσθαι. ¹³πάντα ἰσχύω ἐν τῷ ἐνδυναμοῦντί με.
¹⁴πλὴν καλῶς ἐποιήσατε συνκοινωνήσαντές μου τῇ θλί-

other phrase found in St Paul (2 Tim.
iv. 5) occurs in the context, νῆφον ἐν
πᾶσι. See the notes on πολίτευμα iii.
20, and on ἀπέχειν iv. 18, and the dissertation on 'St Paul and Seneca.'

12. καὶ ταπεινοῦσθαι] This clause
seems to be shaped in anticipation of
the καὶ περισσεύειν which follows, so
that the one καὶ would answer the
other, 'both to be abased and to
abound'; but the connexion is afterwards interrupted by the repetition
of οἶδα for the sake of emphasis. So
too perhaps 1 Cor. xv. 29, 30 τί καὶ
βαπτίζονται...τί καὶ ἡμεῖς κ.τ.λ.; comp.
Rom. i. 13.

ἐν παντὶ καὶ ἐν πᾶσιν] A general
expression corresponding to the English 'all and every'; ἐν παντὶ 'in
every case' singly, ἐν πᾶσιν 'in all
cases' collectively: comp. 2 Cor. xi. 6
ἐν παντὶ φανερώσαντες ἐν πᾶσιν εἰς ὑμᾶς.

μεμύημαι] 'I have been initiated,
I possess the secret,' as Plut. Mor. p.
795 E τὰ μὲν πρῶτα μανθάνων ἔτι πολιτεύεσθαι καὶ μυούμενος, τὰ δὲ ἔσχατα
διδάσκων καὶ μυσταγωγῶν, Alciphr.
Epist. ii. 4 πρωρατεύειν μυηθήσομαι.
The same metaphor is employed by
St Paul in μυστήρια applied to revealed truths, and perhaps also in σφρα-
γίζεσθαι (Eph. i. 13). And St Ignatius also addresses the Ephesians (§ 12)
as Παύλου συμμύσται τοῦ ἡγιασμένου,
thus taking up the Apostle's own
metaphor.

χορτάζεσθαι] The word χορτάζειν,
properly 'to give fodder to animals,'
is in the first instance only applied to
men as a depreciatory term, e. g.
Plat. Resp. ix. p. 586 A βοσκημάτων
δίκην...χορταζόμενοι. Hence the earlier examples of this application are
found chiefly in the Comic poets, as
in the passages quoted by Athenæus,
iii. p. 99 sq., where the word is dis-

cussed. In the later language however χορτάζεσθαι has lost the sense of
caricature, and become a serious equivalent to κορέννυσθαι, being applied
commonly to men and directly opposed
to πεινᾶν, e. g. Matt. v. 6. On χορτάζειν see Sturz de Dial. Mac. p. 200.
A parallel instance of a word casting
off all mean associations in the later
language is ψωμίζειν, 1 Cor. xiii. 3.

πεινᾶν] On this form see A. Buttmann p. 38, Lobeck Phryn. p. 61.

13. τῷ ἐνδυναμοῦντί με] 'in Him
that infuses strength into me,' i. e.
Christ: comp. 1 Tim. i. 12. The word
occurs several times in St Paul.

14. πλήν] 'nevertheless, though I
could have dispensed with your contributions.'

συνκοινωνήσαντες κ.τ.λ.] i. e. 'by
making common cause with my affliction, by your readiness to share
the burden of my troubles.' It was
not the actual pecuniary relief, so
much as the sympathy and companionship in his sorrow, that the Apostle valued. On the construction of
κοινωνεῖν see the note on Gal. vi. 6.

15. The object of this allusion
seems to be not so much to stimulate
them by recalling their former zeal
in contributing to his needs, as to
show his willingness to receive such
contributions at their hands. 'Do
not mistake my meaning,' he seems to
say, 'do not imagine that I receive
your gifts coldly, that I consider them
intrusive. You yourselves will recollect that, though it was my rule not
to receive such contributions, I made
an exception in your case.'

καὶ ὑμεῖς] 'ye too, ye yourselves,
without my reminding you': comp. 1
Thess. ii. 1 αὐτοὶ γὰρ οἴδατε, ἀδελφοί.

Φιλιππήσιοι] Stephanus Byzant. says,
'Ο πολίτης Φιλιππεύς, Φιλιππηνὸς δὲ

ψει. ¹⁵οἴδατε δὲ καὶ ὑμεῖς, Φιλιππήσιοι, ὅτι ἐν ἀρχῇ τοῦ
εὐαγγελίου, ὅτε ἐξῆλθον ἀπὸ Μακεδονίας, οὐδεμία μοι
ἐκκλησία ἐκοινώνησεν εἰς λόγον δόσεως καὶ λήμψεως,

παρὰ Πολυβίῳ. The passage of Polybius to which he refers is not extant.
Though Stephanus does not mention
the form Φιλιππήσιος, it occurs in the
heading of Polycarp's letter (Iren. iii.
3. 4) as well as of this epistle. Φιλιππεύς is found three times in a Bœotian
inscription in Keil p. 172 (see Dindorf's
Steph. Thes. s. v.).

ἐν ἀρχῇ τοῦ εὐαγγελίου] 'in the earliest days of the Gospel,' especially in
reference to Macedonia. Similarly,
writing to the Thessalonians soon
after his first visit, St Paul says (2
Thess. ii. 13) εἵλατο ὑμᾶς ὁ Θεὸς ἀπαρ-
χὴν (v. l. ἀπ' ἀρχῆς) εἰς σωτηρίαν. The
expression occurs in Clem. Rom. § 47
τί πρῶτον ὑμῖν ἐν ἀρχῇ τοῦ εὐαγγελίου
ἔγραψεν, and possibly this is the meaning of Polycarp § 11 'qui estis in
principio epistolæ ejus': see above,
p. 141, note 4.

ὅτε ἐξῆλθον ἀπὸ Μακεδονίας] 'when
I departed from Macedonia' may
mean either (1) 'at the moment of
my departure,' or (2) 'after my departure.' This latter meaning is justified by the pluperfect sense which
the aorist frequently has (see Winer
§ xl. p. 343); though in fact this is
no peculiarity of Greek, but a loose-
ness of expression common to all languages. If this meaning be adopted,
the allusion is explained by the contributions sent from Macedonia to
Corinth (2 Cor. xi. 8, 9). If on the
other hand the former sense were
rigorously pressed (though this is un-
reasonable), contributions might well
have been conveyed to him through
'the brethren' who escorted him from
Macedonia to Athens, Acts xvii. 14,
15. The 'undesigned coincidence' between the history and the epistles in
the matter of these contributions is
well put by Paley (Hor. Paul. vii. no. 1).

εἰς λόγον κ.τ.λ.] 'as regards'; literally 'to the account or score of';
comp. Thuc. iii. 46 ἐς χρημάτων λόγον
ἰσχυούσαις, Demosth. F. L. p. 385 εἰς
ἀρετῆς λόγον καὶ δόξης ἣν οὗτοι χρημάτων ἀπέδοντο, Polyb. xi. 28. 8 εἰς ἀργυ-
ρίου λόγον ἀδικεῖσθαι. In the passages
quoted, as here, the original application to a money transaction is kept
more or less distinctly in view; but
this is not always the case, e.g. Polyb.
v. 89. 6 ξύλα εἰς σφηκίσκων λόγον.
With the expression here compare
Cic. Lœl. 16 'ratio acceptorum et da-
torum.'

δόσεως καὶ λήμψεως] 'giving and
taking,' 'credit and debit,' a general
expression for pecuniary transactions,
derived from the two sides of the
ledger: see Ecclus. xlii. 7 καὶ δόσις καὶ
λῆμψις·παντὶ ἐν γραφῇ, xli. 19 ἀπὸ σκο-
ρακισμοῦ λήμψεως καὶ δόσεως, Arrian.
Epict. ii. 9 τὸν φιλάργυρον [ἐπαύξου-
σιν] αἱ ἀκατάλληλοι λήψεις καὶ δόσεις,
Hermas Mand. v. 2 περὶ δόσεως ἢ λήψεως ἢ περὶ τοιούτων μωρῶν πραγμάτων.
The phrase refers solely to the passing of money between the two. The
explanation given by St Chrysostom
and followed by many later writers,
εἰς λόγον δόσεως τῶν σαρκικῶν καὶ
λήψεως τῶν πνευματικῶν (the Philippians paying worldly goods and receiving spiritual), is plainly inappropriate; for the intermingling of different
things destroys the whole force of the
clause εἰς λόγον δόσεως καὶ λήμψεως,
which is added to define the kind of
contributions intended.

εἰ μὴ ὑμεῖς μόνοι] So, speaking of
this same period, he asks the Corinthians whether he did them a wrong
in taking no contributions from them
and preaching the Gospel to them
gratuitously (2 Cor. xi. 7). The limitation ἐν ἀρχῇ τοῦ εὐαγγελίου perhaps

εἰ μὴ ὑμεῖς μόνοι, ¹⁶ὅτι καὶ ἐν Θεσσαλονίκῃ καὶ ἅπαξ
καὶ δὶς [εἰς] τὴν χρείαν μοι ἐπέμψατε. ¹⁷οὐχ ὅτι ἐπιζητῶ τὸ δόμα, ἀλλὰ ἐπιζητῶ τὸν καρπὸν τὸν πλεο-
νάζοντα εἰς λόγον ὑμῶν. ¹⁸ἀπέχω δὲ πάντα καὶ περισσεύω, πεπλήρωμαι δεξάμενος παρὰ Ἐπαφροδίτου τὰ
παρ᾽ ὑμῶν, ὀσμὴν εὐωδίας, θυσίαν δεκτήν εὐάρεστον τῷ
Θεῷ. ¹⁹ὁ δὲ Θεός μου πληρώσει πᾶσαν χρείαν ὑμῶν
κατὰ τὸ πλοῦτος αὐτοῦ ἐν δόξῃ ἐν Χριστῷ Ἰησοῦ.

implies that he relaxed his rule later,
when he became better known and
understood.

16. ὅτι καὶ κ.τ.λ.] '*for* not only
did you contribute to my wants after
my departure from Macedonia, but
*also in Thessalonica,* before I left etc.'
So St Paul himself reminds the Thessalonians (1 Thess. ii. 5, 2 Thess. iii. 8)
that he did not burden them at all.
At the same time it appears from
those passages, that his bodily wants
were supplied mainly by the labours
of his own hands. Thus it would seem
that the gifts of the Philippians were
only occasional, and the same may be
gathered from the words καὶ ἅπαξ καὶ
δὶς here. On the abbreviated expression ἐν Θεσσαλονίκῃ 'when I was in
Thessalonica' see Winer § 1. p. 515;
comp. below, ver. 19.

καὶ ἅπαξ καὶ δὶς] '*more than once*':
comp. 1 Thess. ii. 18. The double καὶ
is common in such cases, e.g. καὶ δὶς
καὶ τρίς, Plat. *Phæd.* p. 63 D.

εἰς τὴν χρείαν] '*to relieve my want,*'
the preposition indicating the object;
see Winer § xlix. p. 495. The omission
of εἰς in some old copies is probably
due to the similar ending of the preceding word. Otherwise the reading
might claim to be adopted, though in
this sense the plural τὰς χρείας would
be more natural.

17. Again the Apostle's nervous
anxiety to clear himself interposes.
By thus enlarging on the past liber-
ality of the Philippians, he might be

thought to covet their gifts. This
possible misapprehension he at once
corrects.

οὐχ ὅτι ἐπιζητῶ] For οὐχ ὅτι see
the notes on ver. 11 and on iii. 12 ;
for the indirectly intensive force of the
preposition in ἐπιζητῶ, the note on
ἐπιποθῶ i. 8. The repetition of ἐπιζητῶ is emphatic ; 'I do *not* want
the gift, I *do* want the fruit etc.'
Compare the repetition of παρακαλῶ
ver. 2, and of οἶδα ver. 12.

τὸν καρπὸν κ.τ.λ.] 'i.e. the recompense which is placed to your account
and increases with each fresh demonstration of your love.'

18. ἀπέχω κ.τ.λ.] ' *I have all
things to the full,*' as Matt. vi. 2, 5,
16, Luke vi. 24. For the phrase ἀπέχειν πάντα compare Arrian. *Epict.* iii.
2. 13 ἀπέχεις ἅπαντα, iii. 24. 17 τὸ γὰρ
εὐδαιμονοῦν ἀπέχειν δεῖ πάντα ἃ θέλει
πεπληρωμένῳ τινὶ ἐοικέναι: comp. Diog.
Laert. vii. 100 καλὸν δὲ λέγουσι τὸ
τέλειον ἀγαθὸν παρὰ τὸ πάντας ἀπέχειν
τοὺς ἐπιζητουμένους ἀριθμοὺς ὑπὸ τῆς
φύσεως κ.τ.λ. See also Gataker on
M. Anton. iv. 49. Like αὐτάρκεια, it
seems to have been a favourite Stoic
word: see the note on ver. 11. As in
ἀπολαμβάνειν (see Gal. iv. 5), the idea of
ἀπό in this compound is *correspondence* i.e. of the contents to the capacity,
of the possession to the desire, etc., so
that it denotes the *full* complement.
The following word περισσεύω expresses an advance on ἀπέχω; 'not
only full, but overflowing.'

²⁰τῷ δὲ Θεῷ καὶ πατρὶ ἡμῶν ἡ δόξα εἰς τοὺς αἰῶνας τῶν
αἰώνων, ἀμήν.
²¹Ἀσπάσασθε πάντα ἅγιον ἐν Χριστῷ Ἰησοῦ. ἀ-
σπάζονται ὑμᾶς οἱ σὺν ἐμοὶ ἀδελφοί. ²²ἀσπάζονται
ὑμᾶς πάντες οἱ ἅγιοι, μάλιστα δὲ οἱ ἐκ τῆς Καίσαρος
οἰκίας.   ²³Ἡ χάρις τοῦ Κυρίου Ἰησοῦ Χριστοῦ μετὰ τοῦ
πνεύματος ὑμῶν. [ἀμήν.]

παρὰ Ἐπαφροδίτου κ.τ.λ.] 'at the
hands of Epaphroditus the gifts transmitted from you.' On the preposition παρὰ see the note Gal. i. 12.

ὀσμὴν εὐωδίας] A very frequent expression in the LXX for the smell of
sacrifices and offerings, being a rendering of ריח ניחח (e.g. Gen. viii. 21,
Exod. xxix. 18, etc.). St Paul employs
it as a metaphor likewise in Ephes. v.
2; comp. 2 Cor. ii. 15, 16. So too
*Test. xii Patr.* Levi 3 προσφέρουσι
Κυρίῳ ὀσμὴν εὐωδίας λογικὴν καὶ θυσίαν
ἀναίμακτον.

θυσίαν δεκτὴν κ.τ.λ.] So Rom. xii. 1
παραστῆσαι τὰ σώματα ὑμῶν θυσίαν
ζῶσαν ἁγίαν εὐάρεστον τῷ Θεῷ κ.τ.λ.
comp. 1 Pet. ii. 5, Heb. xiii. 16. The
expression εὐάρεστος τῷ Θεῷ occurs
Wisd. iv. 10 (comp. Clem. Rom. 49,
Ign. *Smyrn.* 8), and εὐαρεστεῖν τῷ Θεῷ
is common in the LXX.

19. ὁ Θεός μου] 'my God': comp.
i. 3. The pronoun is especially expressive here: 'You have supplied all
*my* wants (vv. 16, 18), God *on my
behalf* shall supply all *yours*.'

ἐν δόξῃ] These words show that
the needs here contemplated are
not merely temporary. Πληρώσει ἐν
δόξῃ seems to be a pregnant phrase,
signifying 'shall supply by placing you
in glory'; comp. ver. 16 ἐν Θεσσαλονίκῃ.
This is still further explained by ἐν
Χριστῷ Ἰησοῦ, 'through your union
with, incorporation in, Christ Jesus.'

20. ἡ δόξα. See the notes Gal. i. 5.

ἡμῶν] It is no longer μου, for the
reference is not now to himself as distinguished from the Philippians, but
as united with them.

21. ἐν Χριστῷ Ἰησοῦ] probably to
be taken with ἀσπάσασθε; comp. Rom.
xvi. 22, 1 Cor. xvi. 19.

οἱ σὺν ἐμοὶ ἀδελφοί] Apparently
the Apostle's personal companions
and fellow-travellers are meant, as
distinguished from the Christians resident in Rome who are described in
the following verse: see the note on
Gal. i. 2. On St Paul's companions
during or about this time see the introduction p. 11.

22. πάντες οἱ ἅγιοι] All the Christians in Rome, not his personal at-
tendants only.

οἱ ἐκ τῆς Καίσαρος οἰκίας] ' The
members of Cæsar's household,' probably slaves and freedmen attached
to the palace: see the detached note
p. 171, and the introduction pp. 14, 19.
The expression οἰκία Καίσαρος corresponds to 'familia' or 'domus Cæsaris'
(Tac. *Hist.* ii. 92) and might include
equally the highest functionaries and
the lowest menials. Compare Philo
*Flacc.* p. 522 M εἰ δὴ μὴ βασιλεὺς ἦν
ἀλλά τις τῶν ἐκ τῆς Καίσαρος οἰκίας,
οὐκ ὤφειλε προνομίαν τινὰ καὶ τιμὴν
ἔχειν; Hippol. *Hær.* ix. 12 οἰκέτης
ἐτύγχανε Καρποφόρου τινὸς ἀνδρὸς
πιστοῦ ὄντος ἐκ τῆς Καίσαρος οἰκίας.
See *St Clement of Rome, Appendix*,
p. 256 sq.

## ‘ Clement my fellow-labourer.’

Identical
with Cle-
ment of
Rome?

WE have seen the Christians of Philippi honourably associated with
two Apostolic Fathers, Ignatius and Polycarp[1]. But were they even
more intimately connected with the third name of the triad? Is there
sufficient ground for identifying Clement St Paul's fellow-labourer, saluted
in this epistle, with Clement the writer of the letter to the Corinthians,
the early bishop of Rome, the central figure in the Church of the succeeding generation?

Authori-
ties for the
identifica-
tion.

Of the Roman bishop Irenæus says, that he ‘had seen the blessed
Apostles and conversed with them and had the preaching of the Apostles still ringing in his ears and their tradition before his eyes[2].’ From
his silence about St Paul it may perhaps be inferred that he did not
see any direct mention of the Roman Clement in the epistles of this
Apostle. Origen however very distinctly identifies the author of the Corinthian letter with the person saluted in the Epistle to the Philippians[3].
And, starting from Origen, this view was transmitted through Eusebius
to later writers[4]. Nor does the supposition do any violence to character.
The epistle of the Roman Clement was written to heal a feud in a distant
but friendly Church: and in like manner St Paul's fellow-labourer is here
invoked to aid in a work of reconciliation.

Difficulties
of place

Nevertheless the notices of place and time are opposed to the identification of the two. For (1) the author of the letter to Corinth was a
leading member of the Roman Church, while St Paul's fellow-labourer
seems clearly to be represented as resident at Philippi[5]. And again (2)

and date.

the date interposes a serious though not insuperable difficulty. Historical
evidence[6] and internal probability[7] alike point to the later years of Domitian (about A.D. 96), as the time when the Epistle of Clement was
written. If Eusebius is correct, the author died soon after, in the
third year of Trajan, A.D. 100[8]. But in the list of the early bishops of
Rome, where even the order is uncertain, the dates may fairly be considered conjectural or capricious; and there is some ground for supposing
that he may have lived even longer than this. If the received chronology
be only approximately true, the Shepherd of Hermas can hardly have
been written much earlier than A.D. 140[9]. Yet the author there represents

---

[1] See the introduction, p. 62 sq.

[2] Iren. iii. 3. 3.

[3] *In Joann.* i. 29 (IV. p. 153, Delarue).

[4] Euseb. *H. E.* iii. 4, 15, Epiphan.
*Hær.* xxvii. 6 (where however by a slip
of memory the Epistle to the Romans is
mentioned), Hieron. *Vir. Ill.* 15, *adv.
Jovin.* i. 11; comp. *Apost. Const.* vi. 8.

[5] The name VALERIVS . CLEMENS occurs in a Philippian inscription, *Corp.*

*Inscr. Lat.* III. p. 121.

[6] Hegesippus in Euseb. *H.E.* iii. 16
comp. iv. 22.

[7] See *St Clement of Rome* p. 4, with
the references.

[8] Euseb. *H.E.* iii. 34. The date in the
*Chronicon* of the same writer is A.D. 95

[9] The statements in the text are
founded on two data; (1) The assertion
in the Muratorian Fragment (Westcott *Canon* p. 480, 2nd ed.), ‘Pastorem

himself as divinely commissioned to deliver the book to Clement[1]. It
is true we may place the imaginary date of the vision many years before the actual writing and publication of the Shepherd: yet even then
the difficulty does not altogether vanish; for the author describes himself as a married man with a family of children grown or growing up[2]
at the time when Clement is living. On these grounds it would appear
that we cannot well place the death of Clement earlier than A.D. 110
i.e. nearly 50 years after the date of the Epistle to the Philippians. And
it is not likely, though far from impossible, that St Paul's fellow-labourer
should still be living and active after the lapse of half a century.

Another objection also has been urged against the identity. Early
tradition almost uniformly represents St Clement of Rome as a disciple
not of St Paul but of St Peter[3]. On this however I cannot lay any
stress. The tradition may be traced to the influence of the Clementine
Homilies and Recognitions: and it belongs to the general plan of these
Judaic writings to transfer to St Peter, as the true Apostle of the Gentiles, the companionships and achievements of St Paul[4]. On the other
hand St Clement's letter itself, though it shows a knowledge of the First
Epistle of St Peter, bears yet stronger traces of St Paul's influence. It
is at least possible that St Clement knew both Apostles, as he quotes the
writings of both and mentions both by name[5].

All these difficulties however might be set aside, if Clement were a
rare name. But this is far from being the case. Lipsius enumerates
five Clements mentioned by Tacitus alone[6]: and extant inscriptions would
supply still more convincing proofs of its frequency[7]. Though common
enough before, its popularity was doubtless much increased under the
Flavian dynasty, when it was borne by members of the reigning house.

A strange destiny has pursued the name of Clement of Rome. The
romance of story, which gathered about it in the earliest ages of the
Church, has been even surpassed by the romance of criticism of which

vero nuperrime temporibus nostris in
urbe Roma Hermas conscripsit, sedente
cathedra urbis Romæ ecclesiæ Pio episcopo fratre ejus'; (2) The received date
of the episcopate of Pius (A.D. 142—157,
Euseb. *H.E.* iii. 15, 34; A.D. 138—152,
Euseb. *Chron.*). But on the other hand
it must be said (1) That as the Muratorian Fragment is obviously a translation from the Greek, we cannot feel
any certainty that the original stated
the book to have been written *during*
the episcopate of Pius, though the Latin
*sedente* seems to imply this ; and (2) That
no confidence can be placed in the dates
of the early Roman bishops; for while
Eusebius himself has two different lists,
the catalogues of other writers differ
from both. Hermas may have written
*before* his brother's episcopate, or Pius

may have become bishop at an earlier
date than Eusebius supposes. If either
or both these suppositions be true, the
interval between the death of Clement
and the writing of the Shepherd may be
considerably diminished, and the chronological difficulty which I have suggested in the text vanishes. See *St
Clement of Rome*, p. 315 sq.

[1] Hermas *Vis.* ii. 4.

[2] *Vis.* i. 3, ii. 3.

[3] See especially Tertull. *Præscr.
Hær.* 32, Origen *Philoc.* 22 : and consult Lipsius *de Clem. Rom.* p. 172 sq.

[4] See *Galatians*, p. 329.

[5] Clem. Rom. § 5. See *Galatians*,
pp. 338, 358.

[6] Lipsius, p. 168.

[7] See *St Clement of Rome*, p. 264 sq.

it has been the subject in these latest days. Its occurrence in the Epistle to the Philippians has been made the signal for an attack on the genuineness of this letter. The theory of Baur[1] is as follows. The conversion of Flavius Clemens, the kinsman of Domitian, is the sole foundation in fact, upon which the story of Clement the Roman bishop has been built[2]. The writer of the Clementine Homilies, an adherent of the Petrine or Jewish party in the Church, bent on doing honour to his favourite Apostle, represents Clement as the disciple or successor of St Peter. In order to do this, he is obliged to throw the date of Clement farther back and thus to represent him as the kinsman not of Domitian, but of Tiberius. The forger of the Philippian Epistle writes at a later date when this fiction has been generally received as an accredited fact. Though himself a Pauline Christian, he is anxious to conciliate the Petrine faction and for this purpose represents this imaginary but now all-famous disciple of St Peter, as a fellow-labourer of St Paul. The whole epistle in fact is written up to this mention of Clement. The prætorium, the household of Cæsar, are both introduced to give an air of probability to the notice. In this criticism, unsubstantial as it is, one element of truth may be recognised. The Roman Clement, as he appears in his extant letter and as he may be discerned through the dim traditions of antiquity, is a man of large sympathies and comprehensive views, if not a successful reconciler, at all events a fit mediator between the extreme parties in the Church. The theory itself it will not be necessary to discuss seriously. The enormous difficulties which it involves will be apparent at once. But it may be worth while to call attention to the hollow basis on which it rests. Baur omits to notice that the Clement here mentioned appears as resident at Philippi and not at Rome: though on this point the supposed forger would have been scrupulously exact, as supplying the key to his whole meaning. To these speculations Schwegler[3], following up a hint thrown out by Baur, adds his own contribution. Euodia and Syntyche, he maintains, are not two women but two parties in the Church, the 'true yokefellow' being none other than St Peter himself. Were they the names of historical persons, he writes, it would give the passage 'an extremely strange character.' It may be inferred from this that he considers his own interpretation entirely simple and natural. Schwegler however stops short of explaining why the one party is called Euodia and the other Syntyche. It is left to a later and bolder critic to supply the deficiency. Volkmar[4] finds the solution in the Apostolic Constitutions, where it is stated that Euodius was made bishop of Antioch by St Peter and Ignatius by St Paul[5]. As Euodius is the Petrine bishop, so Euodia will represent the Petrine party. The names, he supposes, are adopted with a view to their significance. Euodia, 'taking the right path,' is a synonyme for orthodoxy, and therefore aptly describes the Jewish community: while Syntyche,

*Baur's theory.*

*Schwegler.*

*Volkmar.*

[1] *Paulus*, p. 469 sq.
[2] See above, p. 22.
[3] *Nachapost. Zeit.* II. p. 135.
[4] *Theolog. Jahrb.* XV. p. 311 sq. (1856), XVI. p. 147 sq. (1857). Graetz answers Volkmar by claiming Flavius Clemens as a proselyte to Judaism. His own speculations are equally extravagant: *Gesch. der Juden* IV. p. 435 (ed. 2), *Monatsschr. f. Gesch. u. Wiss. d. Judenth.* April 1869, p. 169.
[5] *Apost. Const.* vii. 46.

'the partner (consors),' is an equally fit designation of the later associated Gentile Church[1]. This last story completes the building thus piled by three successive hands. Meanwhile it will be obvious to all, that a writer could not more effectually have concealed his meaning and thereby frustrated his own designs, than by wearing the impenetrable veil of enigma thus ascribed to him. But indeed it is needless to waste time on this learned trifling, which might be overlooked if the interests indirectly involved were less serious. In dealing with such theories the bare statement is often the best refutation[2].

## Cæsar's Household.

THE mention of certain members of Cæsar's household at the close of the Philippian Epistle has given rise to much speculation and formed the groundwork of more than one capricious theory. It has been assumed that this phrase must designate persons of high rank and position, powerful minions of the court, great officers of state, or even blood relations of the emperor himself. On this assumption, maintained in a more or less exaggerated form, it has been inferred that some time must have elapsed between St Paul's arrival at Rome and the date of this epistle, to account for this unwonted triumph of the Gospel. And extreme critics have even taken the expression as the starting-point for an attack on the genuineness of the letter, charging the writer with an anachronism and supposing him to refer to Clemens and Domitilla, the kinsman and kinswoman of Domitian, who suffered for the faith at the close of the century[3]. *Baseless theories.*

All such inferences are built on a misconception of the meaning of the term. The 'domus' or 'familia Cæsaris' (represented by the Greek οἰκία Καίσαρος) includes the whole of the imperial household, the meanest slaves as well as the most powerful courtiers. On the character and constitution of this household we happen to possess more information than perhaps on any other department of social life in Rome. The inscriptions relating thereto are so numerous, that a separate section is assigned to them in all good collections. And almost every year is adding to these stores of information by fresh discoveries. In Rome itself, if we may judge by these inscriptions, the 'domus Augusta' must have formed no inconsiderable fraction of the whole population; but it comprised likewise all persons in the emperor's service, whether slaves or freemen, in Italy and even in the provinces. *Extent of the household.*

The monuments to which I have referred are chiefly sepulchral. Columbaria have been discovered from time to time, whose occupants be- *Sources of information.*

---

[1] When I wrote the above, I should not have thought it possible to outbid in extravagance the speculations mentioned in the text; but Hitzig, *Zur Kritik Paulinischer Briefe*, p. 7 sq. (1870), far exceeds them all. The refutation of Hilgenfeld, *Zeitschr.* 1871, p. 331 sq., was quite unnecessary.

[2] Other recent speculations relating to the history of the Roman Clement, more innocent but equally unsubstantial, will be found in Lagarde's introduction to his *Clementina*, p. (12) sq. (1865).

[3] See above, pp. 22, 170.

longed principally, if not solely, to this class. In 1726 one of these places of sepulture was exhumed on the Appian way. Its contents will appear from the title of a work published the following year, and giving an account of the discovery: *Monumentum sive Columbarium Libertorum et Servorum Liviæ Augustæ et Cæsarum*, etc., *ab A. F. Gorio*. More recent excavations have added to our knowledge on this subject. Since the year 1840 several other sepulchral dove-cotes, situated also near the Appian way, have been brought to light. Accounts of these, more or less complete, with copies of inscriptions will be found in Canina's *Prima Parte della Via Appia* I. p. 217 sq., in the *Dissertazioni della Pontificia Accademia Romana di Archeologia* XI. p. 317 sq. (1852), and in the *Monumenti ed Annali pubblicati dall' Instituto di Corrispondenza Archeologica nel* 1856 (a paper by Henzen). The occupants of these recently excavated columbaria again are almost all freedmen or slaves of the emperors. The frequency of the name Ti. Claudius suggests a date not earlier and not much later than the second and fourth Cæsars: and this date is confirmed by the mention of other members of the imperial family at this time, as Messalina, Octavia, Agrippina, Drusus, etc. Though here and there a name points to a later emperor, the great majority must be assigned to the reign of Nero or his immediate predecessors and successors, and thus the persons to whom they refer were mostly contemporaries of St Paul. Besides these special sources of information, a vast number of isolated inscriptions relating to the servants and dependents of the emperors have been discovered from time to time, and will be found in the general collections of Muratori, Gruter, Orelli, and others. By these means we obtain some insight into the names and offices of the 'household of Cæsar' at the date when the expression was used in the Epistle to the Philippians.

List of offices in the household.

The following list will give some idea of the number and variety of places which the 'domus Augusta' included: 'pædagogus puerorum, dispensator rationis privatæ, exactor tributorum, præpositus velariorum, procurator prægustatorum, præpositus auri escarii, procurator balnei, villicus hortorum, etc.; a lapidicinis, a pendice cedri, a frumentis, a commentariis equorum, a veste regia, a cura catellæ, ab argento potorio, a supellectile castrensi, a veste forensi, a libellis, a studiis, ab epistulis, a rationibus, a bibliotheca Latina Apollinis, a bibliotheca Græca Palatina, etc.; architectus, tabellarius, castellarius, chirurgus, ocularius, diætarchus, nomenclator, tesserarius, designator, vicarius, symphoniacus, musicarius, pedissequus, lecticarius, cocus, argentarius, sutor, cubicularius, triclinarius, ostiarius, ornator, unctor, etc.; tonstrix, sarcinatrix, obstetrix, etc.' This very imperfect list suggests a minute subdivision of offices. When we find several distinct functions in the single department of the wardrobe or the plate-chest, when even the 'tasters' form a separate class of servants under their own chief, the multitude and multiplicity thus exhibited forbid us to speculate on the exact office or rank which may have been held by these friends of St Paul. Least of all are we encouraged to assume that they were persons of great influence or distinguished rank. At the same time the connexion with Cæsar's household doubtless secured even to the lowest grades of slaves and freedmen substantial though undefined privileges and immunities, and conferred on them a certain social importance among their equals

Bearing on the reference in St Paul.

which made them value their position[1]. Hence we may account for the scrupulous care with which an office in the household, however mean, is always recorded on monumental inscriptions. At the time when St Paul wrote, the influence of the emperor's slaves and dependents had about reached its climax. The reigns of Claudius and Nero have been described as the saturnalia of the imperial freedmen[2].

Now, if I am right in supposing that the Epistle to the Philippians was written soon after St Paul's arrival in the metropolis, it would seem to follow that the members of Cæsar's household who sent their salutations to Philippi were earlier converts, who did not therefore owe their knowledge of the Gospel to St Paul's preaching in Rome[3]. Under any circumstances this supposition best explains the incidental character of the allusion. For St Paul obviously assumes that his distant correspondents know all about the persons thus referred to. If so, we are led to look for them in the long list of names saluted by St Paul some three years before in the Epistle to the Romans. *Members of the household were probably early converts.*

Nor is there any prior improbability in this supposition. The earliest converts in Rome would naturally be drawn from the classes of foreigners sojourning or permanently resident there[4], Greeks, Syrians, and especially Jews. Accordingly one of the persons thus saluted is described as a 'first-fruit of Asia'[5]. Aquila and Priscilla also, who are mentioned in this list, appear residing at one time at Corinth, at another at Ephesus[6]. Of several others again St Paul speaks as personal acquaintances, though he had not as yet visited Rome. Of these Mary bears a Jewish name[7], and others besides plainly belonged to the same race[8], though their names do not directly proclaim their origin. Now, though Greeks and Orientals formed a numerous and active portion of the general population of Rome, it was especially about the palace and the court that their numbers and influence were felt[9]. History reveals not Greeks only, of whom the Romans were a little less intolerant, but Syrians, Samaritans, Philistines[10], and Jews, *Foreigners named in the salutations sent to Rome. and four, about the court.*

---

[1] Plin. *N. H.* xiii. 5 'Marcelli Æserïni libertus sed qui se potentiæ causa Cæsaris libertis adoptasset,' Hist. Aug. *Pertinax* 8 'Reddidit præterea dominis eos qui se ex privatis domibus in aulam contulerant.'

[2] See Friedländer *Sittengeschichte Roms* i. pp. 65, 68 (ed. 2). In the 2nd chapter of this work much important information respecting the court of the early Cæsars is collected and arranged. The references in the last note are taken thence (p. 62).

[3] See above, pp. 19, 32.

[4] Seneca (*adv. Helv. Cons.* 6) says of the population of Rome at this time, 'Jube istos omnes ad nomen citari et unde domo quisque sit quære: videbis *majorem partem* esse quæ relictis sedibus suis venerit in maximam quidem et pulcherrimam urbem, non tamen suam.'

[5] Rom. xvi. 5 (the correct reading).

[6] Acts xviii. 2, 18, 26, 1 Cor. xvi. 19.

[7] Rom. xvi. 6. Probably Jewish, though not certainly, for the form is indecisive. The best mss read Maρίαν (not Μαριάμ), and 'Maria' is a good Latin name also.

[8] xvi. 7, 10, those whom St Paul calls his 'kinsmen' (comp. ix. 3).

[9] See above, p. 14, and comp. especially Friedländer i. p. 60 sq.

[10] Thallus a Samaritan under Tiberius (Joseph. *Ant.* xviii. 6. 4), and Apelles an Ascalonite under Caius (see below, p. 174), will serve as examples of these two minor races. Syrians and Jews very commonly rose to power at court. The case of the Jewish actor Aliturus mentioned above (p. 6) illustrates the influence of this latter people.

holding places of influence about the emperors at this time. And, for every one who succeeded in attaining to distinction, there must have been tens and hundreds of Orientals about the court who never emerged from obscurity. For, independently of other causes, the success of the few would draw around them crowds of their fellow-countrymen. Thus the household of the Cæsars would supply in the greatest abundance the material from which the conversions mentioned in the Epistle to the Romans would probably be wrought.

*Inference.*

Following this clue, it may be useful to consult the inscriptions with a view to ascertaining whether the information thence derived throws any additional light on the subject. And for this purpose I shall take in order those names in the salutations of the Epistle to the Romans which give promise of yielding a result.

*Amplias.*

1. AMPLIAS is a contraction of Ampliatus, which is read in some of the best copies. A common name in itself, it occurs several times in connexion with the imperial household. Thus AMPLIATUS . HILARI . AUGUSTOR . LIBERTI . SER . VILICUS (Grut. p. 62. 10). We meet with it also attached to the names ·Ti. Claudius' (Murat. p. 1249, 14, comp. p. 1150. 7). Again two persons bearing the name are mentioned in the inscriptions of columbaria specially appropriated to the household (*Acc. di Arch.* XI. pp. 359, 374). At a later date we read of one Ampliatus, a freedman of Hadrian (Grut. p. 591. 10).

*Urbanus.*

2. The name URBANUS is equally common with Ampliatus, and in the following inscriptions designates members of the household: TI . CLAUDI . URBANI . SER . MENSORIS . AEDIFICIORUM (Murat. p. 924. 8): CLAUDIAE . PHILETI . AUG . L . LIBERTAE . HEURESI . URBANUS . ET . SURUS . FRATRES . SORORI . PIISSIMAE (Murat. p. 996. 5): URBANUS . LYDES . AUG . L . DISPENS . INMUNIS . DAT . HERMAE . FRATRI . etc. (Murat. 920. 1): T . FLAVIUS . AUG . LIB . URBANUS (Grut. p. 589. 10). Accordingly the name C. Julius Urbanus is found more than once (Grut. p. 574. 1, p. 981. 3). On an inscription A.D. 115, Urbanus and Ampliatus occur next to each other in a list of imperial freedmen connected with the mint (Grut. p. 1070. 1).

*Stachys.*

3. The next name STACHYS is comparatively rare. Yet at least one person so called held an important office in the household near the time when St Paul wrote: STACHYS . MARCELLAE . MEDICUS, whose name occurs on the same monument with one TI . JULIUS . FIDES (Henzen in the *Instit. di Corrisp. Archeol.* 1856, p. 15, no. 44). Again in another inscription, where one Stachys is mentioned, and where the names of his relations, Julius, Julia, Claudia, are also given, we may safely infer some connexion with the court (Grut. p. 689. 1). Compare also Grut. p. 587. 2.

*Apelles.*

4. APELLES again is a name belonging to the imperial household. It was borne for instance by a famous tragic actor, a native of Ascalon, who at one time stood high in the favour of the emperor Caius, and is described as inheriting a national antipathy to the Jews (Philo *Leg. ad Cai.* p. 576 M; see Friedländer *Sittengesch. Roms* I. p. 98). One CL. APELLES again is mentioned as a member of the household (Orell. 2892) and the name TI. CLAUDIUS APELLA occurs in an inscription of the age of Vespasian (Grut. p. 240).

*Household*

5. ARISTOBULUS surnamed the younger, a grandson of Herod the Great, was educated in the metropolis, together with his brothers Agrippa and

Herod. While his two brothers became kings, the one of Judæa, the other of Chalcis, Aristobulus himself ended his days in a private station, and as it appears, in Rome (Joseph. *Bell. Jud.* ii. 11. 6). The date of his death is uncertain, but he was still living in the year 45 (*Antiq.* xx. 1. 2). The emperor Claudius, writing at this time, speaks of Aristobulus as entertaining most dutiful and friendly sentiments towards himself. When the slaves of a household passed into the hands of a new master, by cession or inheritance or confiscation, they continued to be designated by the name of their former proprietor. Thus a slave whom the emperor had inherited by the will of the Galatian king Amyntas is described as CAESARIS SER. AMYNTIANUS (Grut. p. 577. 5). In the same way in the imperial household we meet with Mæcenatiani, Agrippiani, Germaniciani, etc., where in like manner the names preserve the memory of their earlier masters[1]. Now it seems not improbable, considering the intimate relations between Claudius and Aristobulus, that at the death of the latter his servants, wholly or in part, should be transferred to the palace. In this case they would be designated *Aristobuliani*, for which I suppose St Paul's οἱ ἐκ τῶν 'Αριστοβούλου to be an equivalent. It is at least not an obvious phrase and demands explanation. And, as the household of Aristobulus would naturally be composed in a large measure of Jews, the Gospel would the more easily be introduced to their notice. Moreover it is worth observing that after saluting 'them of the household of Aristobulus,' St Paul immediately singles out one whom he designates his kinsman, i.e. his fellow-countryman[2], and whose name HERODION we might expect to find among the slaves or freedmen of a distinguished member of the Herodian family. This interpretation of the expression τοὺς ἐκ τῶν 'Αριστοβούλου will, I think, be confirmed by the salutation which follows.

6. For immediately after St Paul uses the same form of expression in speaking of the household of NARCISSUS. The name Narcissus indeed is common enough, and we meet with it several times where a connexion with the household seems probable, e.g. Ti. Claudius Narcissus (Murat. p. 1325. 5, comp. p. 1452. 8), Ti. Julius Narcissus (Murat. p. 1362. 2, 4). But here, as in the case of Aristobulus, the expression seems to point to some famous person of the name. And the powerful freedman Narcissus, whose wealth was proverbial (Juv. *Sat.* xiv. 329), whose influence with Claudius was unbounded, and who bore a chief part in the intrigues of this reign, alone satisfies this condition. He was put to death by Agrippina shortly after the accession of Nero (Tac. *Ann.* xiii. 1, Dion Cass. lx. 34), about three or four years before the Epistle to the Romans was written. As was usual in such cases, his household would most probably pass into the hands of the emperor, still however retaining the name of Narcissus. A member of this household apparently is commemorated in an extant inscription, TI . CLAUDIO . SP . F . NARCISSIANO (Murat. p. 1150. 4; comp. p. 902. 5). These Narcissiani I suppose to be designated by St Paul's οἱ ἐκ τῶν Ναρκίσσου.

7. In TRYPHÆNA and TRYPHOSA we may recognise two sisters or at least near relatives, for it was usual to designate members of the same

*Marginal notes:* of Aristobulus. — Household of Narcissus. — Tryphæna

---

[1] See *Ephemeris Epigraphica* II. p. 29.    [2] See above, p. 16, note 2.

family by derivatives of the same root. The name Tryphæna, though not common, was found in the imperial household at or about the time when St Paul wrote. On an inscription in the columbaria chiefly appropriated to the emperor's servants we read, D . M . TRYPHAENAE . VALERIA . TRYPHAE-NA . MATRI . B . M . F . ET . VALERIUS . FUTIANUS (*Acc. di Archeol.* XI. p. 375); where the direct connexion with the household is established by a neighbouring inscription, D . M . CLAUDIAE . AUG . LIB . NEREIDI . M . VALERIUS . FUTIANS (sic) . MATRI . CARISSIMAE (ib. p. 376). The names *Valerius, Valeria,* very frequently occur in connexion with *Claudius, Claudia,* the former having doubtless been introduced into the imperial household through the empress Messalina, a daughter of M. Valerius Messala[1]. The combination of these two gentile names fixes the date approximately. Another Valeria Tryphæna, if it be not the same, is mentioned elsewhere; Q . VALERIO . SALUTARI . AUG . PUTEOLIS . ET . CUMIS . ET VALERIAE . TRIFENAE . HEREDES (Grut. p. 481. 2). The name of one Claudia Tryphæna also is preserved : CLAUDIA . TRYPHAENA . FECIT . ASIATICAE . FILIAE . SUAE (Murat. p. 1150. 3).

and Tryphosa.    The name Tryphosa also, which occurs more frequently, is found several times in connexion with the household : AGRIAE . TRYPHOSAE . VESTIFICAE LIVIUS . THEONA . AB . EPISTULIS . GRAEC . SCRIBA . A . LIB . PONTIFICALIBUS . CONJUGI . SANCTISSIMAE . B.D.S.M. (Grut. p. 578. 6, comp. ib. p. 446. 6): DIS · MANIBUS . JULIAE . TRYPHOSAE . T. FLAVIUS . FORTUNATUS . CONJUGI etc. (Grut. p. 796. 3, comp. ib. p. 1133. 1). In another inscription again it is found connected with the name Valerius : VALERI . PRIMI . ET . JUN . TRYPHOSAE . VIVA . FEC . (Grut. p. 893. 2).

Rufus.    8. RUFUS is a very ordinary name, and would not have claimed notice here but for its occurrence in one of the Gospels. There seems no reason to doubt the tradition that St Mark wrote especially for the Romans ; and, if so, it is worth remarking that he alone of the evangelists describes Simon of Cyrene, as 'the father of Alexander and Rufus' (xv. 21). A person of this name therefore seems to have held a prominent place among the Roman Christians ; and thus there is at least fair ground for identifying the Rufus of St Paul with the Rufus of St Mark. The inscriptions exhibit several members of the household bearing the names Rufus and Alexander, but this fact is of no value where both names are so common.

Hermes.    9. Of the group which follows, HERMES is among the commonest slave-names. In the household alone probably not less than a score of persons might be counted up from the inscriptions, who bore this name at or about

Hermas.    the time when St Paul wrote. HERMAS again, being a contraction of several different names, such as Hermagoras, Hermeros, Hermodorus, Hermogenes, etc., though not quite so common as the former, is still very frequent.

Patrobas.    The remaining three are rare. Yet PATROBAS, an abbreviated form of Patrobius, was borne by a wealthy and powerful freedman of Nero, who was put to death by Galba (Tac. *Hist.* i. 49, ii. 95). But though the infrequency of the name would suggest his identity with the person saluted by St Paul, his character accords ill with the profession of a disciple of

---

[1] This inscription will serve as an illustration; VALERIA . HILARIA . NUTRIX . OCTAVIAE . CAESARIS . AUGUSTI . REQUIESCIT . CUM . TI . CLAUDIO . FRUCTO .

VIRO (Orelli, 4492). This Octavia is the unhappy daughter of Claudius and Messalina, who was afterwards married to Nero. See also Clem. Rom. § 59 (note).

Christ, unless history has done him a cruel wrong. The Patrobas of St Paul
however might well have been a dependent of this powerful freedman. To
some member of the household, possibly to this notorious Patrobius, the
following inscription refers: TI . CL . AUG . L . PATROBIUS (Grut. p. 610. 3),
where doubtless 'Patrobius' is correctly read for 'Patronus': comp. Murat.
p. 1329. 3, TI . CLAUDIO . PATROBIO.

10.   PHILOLOGUS and JULIA appear to have been man and wife, or bro- *Philologus*
ther and sister. The latter name points to a dependent of the court. The *and Julia.*
former also occurs more than once in connexion with the imperial household : C . JULIO . C . L . PHILOLOGO (Murat. p. 1586. 3) : DAMA . LIVIAE . L . CAS .
PHOEBUS . PHILOLOGI (*Mon. Liv.* p. 168) : TI . CLAUDIUS . AUGUSTI . LIB . PHILO-
LOGUS . AB . EPISTOLIS (Murat. p. 2043. 2)[1] : TI . CLAUDIUS . AUGUSTI . LIB .
PHILOLOGUS . LIBERALIS (Grut. p. 630. 1).

11.   Immediately after Philologus and Julia are mentioned NEREUS and *Nereus*
his sister. For Nereus compare this inscription found at Ancyra ; EUTY- *and his*
CHUS . NEREI . CAESARIS . AUG . SER . VIL . FILIO (Murat. p. 899. 7).   The sister's *sister.*
name is not given, but one Nereis was a member of the household about
this time, as appears from an inscription already quoted (p. 176).

As the result of this investigation, we seem to have established a fair *General*
presumption, that among the salutations in the Epistle to the Romans some *result.*
members at least of the imperial household are included. The inscriptions
indeed cannot generally be taken to show more than the fact that the same
*names* occurred there. A very faint probability of the identity of persons
may in some instances be added, though even with the rarer names the
identification must be held highly precarious. But a combination, such as
Philologus and Julia, affords more solid ground for inference : and in other
cases, as in the household of Narcissus, the probable circumstances suggest
a connexion with the palace. If so, an explanation has been found of the
reference to members of Cæsar's household in the Philippian letter. At all
events this investigation will not have been useless, if it has shown that
the names and allusions at the close of the Roman Epistle are in keeping
with the circumstances of the metropolis in St Paul's day ; for thus it
will have supplied an answer to two forms of objection ; the one denying
the genuineness of the last two chapters of this letter, and the other
allowing their genuineness but detaching the salutations from the rest and
assigning them to another epistle[2].

[1] It has been supposed that the name Philologus was given by the master to the freedman mentioned in this inscription, as being appropriate to his office ; Friedländer, 1. pp. 89, 160. The following inscription may be alleged in support of this conjecture; PUDENS . M . LEPIDI . L . GRAMMATICUS . etc. ATTEIUS . PHILOLOGUS . DISCIPULUS (Grut. p. 653. 2). If so, some light is thrown on the probable occupation of the Philologus of St Paul.

[2] The doxology (Rom. xvi. 25, 26, 27) is found in some copies at the end of the 14th, in others at the end of the 16th chapter, and in others in both places, while others again omit it entirely. Moreover in Marcion's copy the last two chapters of the epistle were wanting. All these variations are easily explained by the hypothesis that the Epistle to the Romans was circulated at a very early date in two forms, the personal matter being omitted in the shorter. Baur however condemns the last two chapters as spurious (*Paulus* p. 398 sq.), though the mind of St Paul is apparent in almost every phrase. Other

less extravagant critics have found difficulties in one or two historical notices which these chapters contain: and Ewald, whose opinion always deserves consideration, solves these difficulties by severing xvi. 3—20 from the rest, and treating it as a fragment of a lost Epistle to the Ephesians (*Die Sendschreiben etc.* p. 428). By this means he explains the reference to Epænetus as the first-fruit of Asia (ver. 5 where 'Aσίας, not 'Aχαΐας, is the right reading), and accounts also for the presence of Aquila and Priscilla (ver. 3), who were found not long before at Ephesus (1 Cor. xvi. 19). This view is far preferable to the former, inasmuch as it recognises St Paul's authorship; but on the other hand it loses all support from the phenomena of the MSS, which require the two chapters to be treated as a whole, and lend no countenance to this arbitrary dissection. The novel theory started by Renan (*Saint Paul* p. lxxiii), who supposes that an editor has combined four copies of the same encyclical letter of St Paul, each addressed to a different church and having a different ending, has the same advantage over Baur's view, but is condemned by its own complexity. Nor in fact are the difficulties serious enough to justify any

such treatment. At a time when the court and city of Rome swarmed with Asiatics (Friedländer 1. p. 59 sq.), it is no surprise to encounter one Christian convert among the crowd. And again, as Rome was the head-quarters of Aquila and Priscilla, and they had been driven thence by an imperial edict (Acts xviii. 2), it is natural enough that they should have returned thither, as soon as it was convenient and safe to do so. The year which elapses between the two notices of this couple (1 Cor. xvi. 19; Rom. xvi. 3—5) allows ample time for them to transfer themselves from Ephesus to Rome, and for the Apostle to hear of their return to their old abode. The results of the investigation in the text (whatever other value it may have) seem sufficient to counterbalance any such difficulties, for it has been shown that the notices are in keeping with Rome, and the same degree of coincidence probably could not be established in the case of any other place. A fuller refutation of Renan will be found in the *Journal of Philology*, II. p. 264 sq. In this and a later article (*ib.* III. p. 193 sq.) I have suggested a theory to account for the documentary facts, more especially the varying position of the doxology.

# DISSERTATIONS.

# I.
## THE CHRISTIAN MINISTRY.

# II.
## ST PAUL AND SENECA.

## I.

## THE CHRISTIAN MINISTRY.

THE kingdom of Christ, not being a kingdom of this world, is Ideal of the Christian Church. not limited by the restrictions which fetter other societies, political or religious. It is in the fullest sense free, comprehensive, universal. It displays this character, not only in the acceptance of all comers who seek admission, irrespective of race or caste or sex, but also in the instruction and treatment of those who are already its members. It has no sacred days or seasons, no special sanctuaries, because every time and every place alike are holy. Above all it has no sacerdotal system. It interposes no sacrificial tribe or class between God and man, by whose intervention alone God is reconciled and man forgiven. Each individual member holds personal communion with the Divine Head. To Him immediately he is responsible, and from Him directly he obtains pardon and draws strength.

It is most important that we should keep this ideal definitely Necessary qualification. in view, and I have therefore stated it as broadly as possible. Yet the broad statement, if allowed to stand alone, would suggest a false impression, or at least would convey only a half truth. It must be evident that no society of men could hold together without officers, without rules, without institutions of any kind; and the Church of Christ is not exempt from this universal law. The conception in short is strictly an *ideal*, which we must ever hold before our eyes, The idea and the realization. which should inspire and interpret ecclesiastical polity, but which nevertheless cannot supersede the necessary wants of human society, and, if crudely and hastily applied, will lead only to signal failure. As appointed days and set places are indispensable to her efficiency, so also the Church could not fulfil the purposes for which she exists, without rulers and teachers, without a ministry of reconciliation, in short, without an order of men who may in some sense be designated a priesthood. In this respect the ethics of Christianity present an analogy to the politics. Here also the ideal conception and the actual realization are incommensurate and in a manner contradictory. The Gospel is contrasted with the Law, as the spirit with the letter. Its ethical principle is not a code of positive ordinances, but conformity to a perfect exemplar, incorporation into a divine life. The distinction is most important and eminently fertile in practical results. Yet no man would dare to live without laying down more or less definite rules for his own guidance, without yielding obedience to law in some sense; and those who discard or attempt to discard all such aids are often farthest from the attainment of Christian perfection.

This qualification is introduced here to deprecate any misunderstanding to which the opening statement, if left without compensation, would fairly be exposed. It will be time to enquire hereafter in what sense the Christian ministry may or may not be called a priesthood. But in attempting to investigate the historical development of this divine institution, no better starting-point suggested itself than the characteristic distinction of Christianity, as declared occasionally by the direct language but more frequently by the eloquent silence of the apostolic writings.

*Special characteristic of Christianity.*

For in this respect Christianity stands apart from all the older religions of the world. So far at least, the Mosaic dispensation did not differ from the religions of Egypt or Asia or Greece. Yet the sacerdotal system of the Old Testament possessed one important characteristic, which separated it from heathen priesthoods and which deserves especial notice. The priestly tribe held this peculiar relation to God only as the *representatives* of the whole nation. As *delegates* of the people, they offered sacrifice and made atonement. The whole community is regarded as 'a kingdom of priests,' 'a holy nation.' When the sons of Levi are set apart, their consecration is distinctly stated to be due under the divine guidance not to any inherent sanctity or to any caste privilege, but to an act of delegation on the part of the entire people. The Levites are, so to speak, ordained by the whole congregation. 'The

*TheJewish priesthood.*

children of Israel,' it is said, 'shall put their hands upon the Levites[1].' The nation thus deputes to a single tribe the priestly functions which belong properly to itself as a whole.

The Christian idea therefore was the restitution of this immediate and direct relation with God, which was partly suspended but not abolished by the appointment of a sacerdotal tribe. The Levitical priesthood, like the Mosaic law, had served its temporary purpose. The period of childhood had passed, and the Church of God was now arrived at mature age. The covenant people resumed their sacerdotal functions. But the privileges of the covenant were no longer confined to the limits of a single nation. Every member of the human family was *potentially* a member of the Church, and, as such, a priest of God.

*Its relation to the Christian priesthood.*

The influence of this idea on the moral and spiritual growth of the individual believer is too plain to require any comment; but its social effects may call for a passing remark. It will hardly be denied, I think, by those who have studied the history of modern civilization with attention, that this conception of the Christian Church has been mainly instrumental in the emancipation of the degraded and oppressed, in the removal of artificial barriers between class and class, and in the diffusion of a general philanthropy untrammelled by the fetters of party or race; in short, that to it mainly must be attributed the most important advantages which constitute the superiority of modern societies over ancient. Consciously or unconsciously, the idea of an universal priesthood, of the religious equality of all men, which, though not untaught before, was first embodied in the Church of Christ, has worked and is working untold blessings in political institutions and in social life. But the careful student will also observe that this idea has hitherto been very imperfectly apprehended; that throughout the history of the Church it has been struggling for recognition, at most times discerned in some of its aspects but at all times wholly ignored in others; and that therefore the actual results are a very inadequate measure of its efficacy, if only it could assume due prominence and were allowed free scope in action.

*Influence of the Christian ideal.*

This then is the Christian ideal; a holy season extending the

---

[1] Num. viii. 10.

whole year round—a temple confined only by the limits of the habitable world—a priesthood coextensive with the human race.

**Practical organization.** Strict loyalty to this conception was not held incompatible with practical measures of organization. As the Church grew in numbers, as new and heterogeneous elements were added, as the early fervour of devotion cooled and strange forms of disorder sprang up, it became necessary to provide for the emergency by fixed rules and definite officers. The community of goods, by which the infant Church had attempted to give effect to the idea of an universal brotherhood, must very soon have been abandoned under the pressure of circumstances. The celebration of the first day in the week **Fixed days and places of worship;** at once, the institution of annual festivals afterwards, were seen to be necessary to stimulate and direct the devotion of the believers. The appointment of definite places of meeting in the earliest days, the erection of special buildings for worship at a later date, were found indispensable to the working of the Church. But the Apostles never **but the idea kept in view.** lost sight of the idea in their teaching. They proclaimed loudly that 'God dwelleth not in temples made by hands.' They indignantly denounced those who 'observed days and months and seasons and years.' This language is not satisfied by supposing that they condemned only the temple-worship in the one case, that they reprobated only Jewish sabbaths and new moons in the other. It was against the false principle that they waged war ; the principle which exalted the means into an end, and gave an absolute intrinsic value to subordinate aids and expedients. These aids and expedients, for his own sake and for the good of the society to which he belonged, a Christian could not afford to hold lightly or neglect. But they were no part of the *essence* of God's message to man in the Gospel : they must not be allowed to obscure the idea of Christian worship.

**Appointment of a ministry.** So it was also with the Christian priesthood. For communicating instruction and for preserving public order, for conducting religious worship and for dispensing social charities, it became necessary to appoint special officers. But the priestly functions and privileges of the Christian people are never regarded as transferred or even delegated to these officers. They are called stewards or messengers of God, servants or ministers of the Church, and the like : but the sacerdotal title is never once conferred upon them. The only priests under the Gospel, designated as such in the New

Testament, are the saints, the members of the Christian brotherhood[1].

As individuals, all Christians are priests alike. As members of a corporation, they have their several and distinct offices. The similitude of the human body, where each limb or organ performs its own functions, and the health and growth of the whole frame are promoted by the harmonious but separate working of every part, was chosen by St Paul to represent the progress and operation of the Church. In two passages, written at two different stages in his apostolic career, he briefly sums up the offices in the Church with reference to this image. In the earlier[2] he enumerates 'first apostles, secondly prophets, thirdly teachers, then powers, then gifts of healing, helps, governments, kinds of tongues.' In the second passage[3] the list is briefer; 'some apostles, and some prophets, and some evangelists, and some pastors and teachers.' The earlier enumeration differs chiefly from the later in specifying distinctly certain miraculous powers, this being required by the Apostle's argument which is directed against an exaggerated estimate and abuse of such gifts. Neither list can have been intended to be exhaustive. In both alike the work of converting unbelievers and founding congregations holds the foremost place, while the permanent government and instruction of the several churches is kept in the background. This prominence was necessary in the earliest age of the Gospel. The apostles, prophets, evangelists, all range under the former head. But the permanent ministry, though lightly touched upon, is not forgotten; for under the designation of 'teachers, helps, governments' in the one passage, of 'pastors and teachers' in the other, these officers must be intended. Again in both passages alike it will be seen that great stress is laid on the work of the Spirit. The faculty of governing not less than the utterance of prophecy, the gift of healing not less than the gift of tongues, is an inspiration of the Holy

*Two passages in St Paul relating thereto.*

*They refer chiefly to the temporary ministry.*

---

[1] 1 Pet. ii. 5, 9, Apoc. i. 6, v. 10, xx. 6. The commentator Hilary has expressed this truth with much distinctness: 'In lege nascebantur sacerdotes ex genere Aaron Levitæ: nunc autem omnes ex genere sunt sacerdotali, dicente Petro Apostolo, Quia estis genus regale et sacerdotale etc.' (Ambrosiast. on Ephes. iv. 12). The whole passage, to which I shall have occasion to refer again, contains a singularly appreciative account of the relation of the ministry to the congregation.

[2] 1 Cor. xii. 28.

[3] Ephes. iv. 11.

Ghost. But on the other hand in both alike there is an entire silence about priestly functions : for the most exalted office in the Church, the highest gift of the Spirit, conveyed no sacerdotal right which was not enjoyed by the humblest member of the Christian community.

Growing importance of the permanent ministry. From the subordinate place, which it thus occupies in the notices of St Paul, the permanent ministry gradually emerged, as the Church assumed a more settled form, and the higher but temporary offices, such as the apostolate, fell away. This progressive growth and development of the ministry, until it arrived at its mature and normal state, it will be the object of the following pages to trace.

Definition of terms necessary. But before proceeding further, some definition of terms is necessary. On no subject has more serious error arisen from the confusion of language. The word ' priest' has two different senses. In the one it is a synonyme for presbyter or elder, and designates the minister who presides over and instructs a Christian congregation : in the other it is equivalent to the Latin sacerdos, the Greek ἱερεύς, or the Hebrew כהן, the offerer of sacrifices, who also performs other mediatorial offices between God and man. How the confusion between these two meanings has affected the history and theology of the Church, it will be instructive to consider in the sequel. At present it is sufficient to say that the word will be used throughout this essay, as it has been used hitherto, in the latter sense only, so that priestly will be equivalent to 'sacerdotal' or 'hieratic.' Etymologically indeed the other meaning is alone correct (for the words priest and presbyter are the same); but convenience will justify its restriction to this secondary and imported sense, since the English language supplies no other rendering of sacerdos or ἱερεύς. On the other hand, when the Christian elder is meant, the longer form ' presbyter' will be employed throughout.

'Priest' and 'presbyter.'

Different views on the origin of the threefold ministry. History seems to show decisively that before the middle of the second century each church or organized Christian community had its three orders of ministers, its bishop, its presbyters, and its deacons. On this point there cannot reasonably be two opinions. But at what time and under what circumstances this organization was matured, and to what extent our allegiance is due to it as an authoritative ordinance, are more difficult questions. Some have recognised in episcopacy an institution of divine origin, absolute and indispensable; others have represented it as destitute of all apostolic sanction and authority. Some again have sought for the archetype of the threefold ministry in the Aaronic priesthood; others in the arrangements of synagogue worship. In this clamour of antagonistic opinions history is obviously the sole upright, impartial referee; and the historical mode of treatment will therefore be strictly adhered to in the following investigation. The doctrine in this instance at all events is involved in the history[1].

St Luke's narrative represents the Twelve Apostles in the earliest days as the sole directors and administrators of the Church. For the financial business of the infant community, not less than for its spiritual guidance, they alone are responsible. This state of things could not last long. By the rapid accession of numbers, and still more by the admission of heterogeneous classes into the Church, the work became too vast and too various for them to discharge unaided. To relieve them from the increasing pressure, the inferior and less important functions passed successively into other hands: and thus each grade of the ministry, beginning from the lowest, was created in order.

*Ministry appointed to relieve the Apostles.*

1. The establishment of the diaconate came first. Complaints had reached the ears of the Apostles from an outlying portion of the community. The Hellenist widows had been overlooked in the daily distribution of food and alms. To remedy this neglect a new office was created. Seven men were appointed whose duty it was to superintend the public messes[2], and, as we may suppose, to provide in other ways for the bodily wants of the helpless poor. Thus relieved, the Twelve were enabled to devote themselves without interruption 'to prayer and to the ministry of the word.' The Apostles suggested the creation of this new office, but the persons were chosen by popular election and afterwards ordained by the Twelve with imposition of hands. Though the complaint came from the Hellenists, it must not be supposed that the ministrations of the

*1. DEA-CONS. Appoint-ment of the Seven.*

---

[1] The origin of the Christian ministry is ably investigated in Rothe's *Anfänge der Christlichen Kirche etc.* (1837), and Ritschl's *Entstehung der Altkatholischen Kirche* (2nd ed. 1857). These are the most important of the more recent works on the subject with which I am acquainted, and to both of them I wish to acknowledge my obligations, though in many respects I have arrived at results different from either.

[2] Acts vi. 2 διακονεῖν τραπέζαις.

Seven were confined to this class[1]. The object in creating this new office is stated to be not the partial but the entire relief of the Apostles from the serving of tables. This being the case, the appointment of Hellenists (for such they would appear to have been from their names[2]) is a token of the liberal and loving spirit which prompted the Hebrew members of the Church in the selection of persons to fill the office.

The Seven were deacons.

I have assumed that the office thus established represents the later diaconate; for though this point has been much disputed, I do not see how the identity of the two can reasonably be called in question[3]. If the word deacon does not occur in the passage, yet the corresponding verb and substantive, διακονεῖν and διακονία, are repeated more than once. The functions moreover are substantially those which devolved on the deacons of the earliest ages, and which still in theory, though not altogether in practice, form the primary duties of the office. Again, it seems clear from the emphasis with which St Luke dwells on the new institution, that he looks on the establishment of this office, not as an isolated incident, but as the initiation of a new order of things in the Church. It is in short one of those representative facts, of which the earlier part of his narrative is almost wholly made up. Lastly, the tradition of the identity of the two offices has been unanimous from the earliest times. Irenæus, the first writer who alludes to the appointment of the Seven, distinctly holds them to have been deacons[4]. The Roman Church some centuries later, though the presbytery had largely increased meanwhile, still restricted the number of deacons to seven, thus preserving the memory of the first institution of this office[5].

---

[1] So for instance Vitringa *de Synag.* III. 2. 5, p. 928 sq., and Mosheim *de Reb. Christ.* p. 119, followed by many later writers.

[2] This inference however is far from certain, since many Hebrews bore Greek names, e. g. the Apostles Andrew and Philip.

[3] It is maintained by Vitringa III. 2. 5, p. 920 sq., that the office of the Seven was different from the later diaconate. He quotes Chrysost. *Hom.* 14 *in Act.* (IX. p. 115, ed. Montf.) and Can. 10 of the Quinisextine Council (comp.

p. 189, note 1) as favouring his view. With strange perversity Böhmer (*Diss. Jur. Eccl.* p. 349 sq.) supposes them to be presbyters, and this account has been adopted even by Ritschl, p. 355 sq. According to another view the office of the Seven branched out into the two later orders of the diaconate and the presbyterate, Lange *Apost. Zeit.* II. i. p. 75.

[4] Iren. i. 26. 3, iii. 12. 10, iv. 15. 1.

[5] In the middle of the third century, when Cornelius writes to Fabius, Rome has 46 presbyters but only 7 deacons, Euseb. *H. E.* vi. 43; see Routh's *Rel.*

And in like manner a canon of the Council of Neocæsarea (A.D. 315) enacted that there should be no more than seven deacons in any city however great[1], alleging the apostolic model. This rule, it is true, was only partially observed; but the tradition was at all events so far respected, that the creation of an order of subdeacons was found necessary in order to remedy the inconvenience arising from the limitation[2].

The narrative in the Acts, if I mistake not, implies that the office thus created was entirely new. Some writers however have explained the incident as an extension to the Hellenists of an institution which already existed among the Hebrew Christians and is implied in the 'younger men' mentioned in an earlier part of St Luke's history[3]. This view seems not only to be groundless in itself, but also to contradict the general tenour of the narrative. It would appear moreover, that the institution was not merely new within the Christian Church, but novel absolutely. There is no reason for connecting it with any prototype existing in the Jewish community. The narrative offers no hint that it was either a continuation of the order of Levites or an adaptation of an office in the synagogue. The philanthropic purpose for which it was established presents no direct point of contact with the known duties of either. The Levite, whose function it was to keep the beasts for slaughter, to cleanse away the blood and offal of the sacrifices, to serve as porter at the temple gates, and to swell the chorus of sacred psalmody, bears no strong resemblance to the Christian deacon, whose ministrations lay among the widows and orphans, and whose time was almost wholly spent in works of charity. And again, the Chazan or attendant in the synagogue, whose duties were confined to the care of the building and the preparation for service, has more in common with the modern parish clerk than with the deacon in the infant Church of

*The office was a new institution*

*not borrowed from the Levitical order,*

*nor from the synagogue.*

---

Sacr. III. p. 23, with his note p. 61. Even in the fourth and fifth centuries the number of Roman deacons still remained constant: see Ambrosiast. on I Tim. iii. 13, Sozom. vii. 19 διάκονοι δὲ παρὰ Ῥωμαίοις εἰσέτι νῦν εἰσὶν ἑπτά... παρὰ δὲ τοῖς ἄλλοις ἀδιάφορος ὁ τούτων ἀριθμός.

[1] Concil. Neocæs. c. 14 (Routh Rel.

Sacr. IV. p. 185): see Bingham's Antiq. II. 20. 19. At the Quinisextine or 2nd Trullan council (A.D. 692) this Neocæsarean canon was refuted and rejected: see Hefele Consiliengesch. III. p. 304, and Vitringa p. 922.

[2] See Bingham III. I. 3.

[3] Acts v. 6, 10. This is the view of Mosheim de Reb. Christ. p. 114.

Christ[1]. It is therefore a baseless, though a very common, assumption that the Christian diaconate was copied from the arrangements of the synagogue. The Hebrew Chazan is not rendered by deacon in the Greek Testament; but a different word is used instead[2]. We may fairly presume that St Luke dwells at such length on the establishment of the diaconate, because he regards it as a novel creation.

Teaching only incidental to the office. Thus the work primarily assigned to the deacons was the relief of the poor. Their office was essentially a 'serving of tables,' as distinguished from the higher function of preaching and instruction. But partly from the circumstances of their position, partly from the personal character of those first appointed, the deacons at once assumed a prominence which is not indicated in the original creation of the office. Moving about freely among the poorer brethren and charged with the relief of their material wants, they would find opportunities of influence which were denied to the higher officers of the Church who necessarily kept themselves more aloof. The devout zeal of a Stephen or a Philip would turn these opportunities to the best account; and thus, without ceasing to be dispensers of alms, they became also ministers of the Word. The Apostles themselves had directed that the persons chosen should be not only 'men of honest report,' but also 'full of the Holy Ghost and wisdom' : and this careful foresight, to which the extended influence of the diaconate may be ascribed, proved also the security against its abuse. But still the work of teaching must be traced rather to the capacity of the individual officer than to the direct functions of the office. St Paul, writing thirty years later, and stating the requirements of the diaconate, lays the stress mainly on those qualifications which would be most important in persons moving about from house to house and entrusted with the distribution of alms. While he requires that they shall hold the mystery of the faith in a pure conscience, in other words, that they shall be sincere believers, he is not anxious, as in the case of the presbyters, to secure 'aptness to teach,' but demands especially that they shall be free from certain vicious habits, such as

[1] Vitringa (III. 2. 4, p. 914 sq., III. 2. 22, p. 1130 sq.) derives the Christian deacon from the Chazan of the synagogue. Among other objections to this view, the fact that as a rule there was only one Chazan to each synagogue must not be overlooked.

[2] ὑπηρέτης, Luke iv. 20.

a love of gossiping, and a greed of paltry gain, into which they might easily fall from the nature of their duties[1].

From the mother Church of Jerusalem the institution spread to Gentile Christian brotherhoods. By the 'helps[2]' in the First Epistle to the Corinthians (A.D. 57), and by the 'ministration[3]' in the Epistle to the Romans (A.D. 58), the diaconate solely or chiefly seems to be intended; but besides these incidental allusions, the latter epistle bears more significant testimony to the general extension of the office. The strict seclusion of the female sex in Greece and in some Oriental countries necessarily debarred them from the ministrations of men : and to meet the want thus felt, it was found necessary at an early date to admit women to the diaconate. A woman-deacon belonging to the Church of Cenchreæ is mentioned in the Epistle to the Romans[4]. As time advances, the diaconate becomes still more prominent. In the Philippian Church a few years later (about A.D. 62) the deacons take their rank after the presbyters, the two orders together constituting the recognised ministry of the Christian society there[5]. Again, passing over another interval of some years, we find St Paul in the First Epistle to Timothy (about A.D. 66) giving express directions as to the qualifications of men-deacons and women-deacons alike[6]. From the tenour of his language it seems clear that in the Christian communities of proconsular Asia at all events the institution was so common that ministerial organization would be considered incomplete without it. On the other hand we may perhaps infer from the instructions which he sends about the same time to Titus in Crete, that he did not consider it indispensable; for while he mentions having given direct orders to his delegate to appoint presbyters in every city, he is silent about a diaconate[7].

*Spread of the diaconate to Gentile churches.*

2. While the diaconate was thus an entirely new creation, called forth by a special emergency and developed by the progress of events, the early history of the presbyterate was different. If the sacred historian dwells at length on the institution of the lower office but is silent about the first beginnings of the higher, the explanation seems to be, that the latter had not the claim of novelty like the former.

*2. PRESBYTERS,*

---

[1] 1 Tim. iii. 8 sq.
[2] 1 Cor. xii. 28.
[3] Rom. xii. 7.
[4] Rom. xvi. 1.
[5] Phil. i. 1.
[6] 1 Tim. iii. 8 sq.
[7] Tit. i. 5 sq.

not a new office, The Christian Church in its earliest stage was regarded by the body of the Jewish people as nothing more than a new sect springing up by the side of the old. This was not unnatural: for the first disciples conformed to the religion of their fathers in all essential points, practising circumcision, observing the sabbaths, and attending the temple-worship. The sects in the Jewish commonwealth were not, properly speaking, nonconformists. They only superadded their own special organization to the established religion of their country, which but adopt-ed from the synagogue. for the most part they were careful to observe. The institution of synagogues was flexible enough to allow free scope for wide divergences of creed and practice. Different races as the Cyrenians and Alexandrians, different classes of society as the freedmen[1], perhaps also different sects as the Sadducees or the Essenes, each had or could have their own special synagogue[2], where they might indulge their peculiarities without hindrance. As soon as the expansion of the Church rendered some organization necessary, it would form a 'synagogue' of its own. The Christian congregations in Palestine long continued to be designated by this name[3], though the term 'ecclesia' took its place from the very first in heathen countries. With the synagogue itself they would naturally, if not necessarily, adopt the normal government of a synagogue, and a body of elders or presbyters would be chosen to direct the religious worship and partly also to watch over the temporal well-being of the society.

Occasion of its adoption. Hence the silence of St Luke. When he first mentions the presbyters, he introduces them without preface, as though the institution were a matter of course. But the moment of their introduction is significant. I have pointed out elsewhere[4] that the two persecutions, of which St Stephen and St James were respectively the chief victims, mark two important stages in the diffusion of the Gospel. Their connexion with the internal organization of the Church is not less remarkable. The first results directly from the establishment of

---

[1] Acts vi. 9.

[2] It is stated, that there were no less than 480 synagogues in Jerusalem. The number is doubtless greatly exaggerated, but must have been very considerable: see Vitringa prol. 4, p. 28, and I. 1. 14, p. 253.

[3] James ii. 2. Epiphanius (xxx. 18, p. 142) says of the Ebionites, συναγω-

γὴν οὗτοι καλοῦσι τὴν ἑαυτῶν ἐκκλησίαν, καὶ οὐχὶ ἐκκλησίαν. See also Hieron. *Epist.* cxii. 13 (I. p. 746, ed. Vall.) 'per totas orientis synagogas,' speaking of the Nazaræans; though his meaning is not altogether clear. Comp. *Test. xii Patr.* Benj. 11.

[4] See *Galatians* pp. 298, 303.

the lowest order in the ministry, the diaconate. To the second may probably be ascribed the adoption of the next higher grade, the presbytery. This later persecution was the signal for the dispersion of the Twelve on a wider mission. Since Jerusalem would no longer be their home as hitherto, it became necessary to provide for the permanent direction of the Church there; and for this purpose the usual government of the synagogue would be adopted. Now at all events for the first time we read of 'presbyters' in connexion with the Christian brotherhood at Jerusalem[1].

From this time forward all official communications with the mother Church are carried on through their intervention. To the presbyters Barnabas and Saul bear the alms contributed by the Gentile Churches[2]. The presbyters are persistently associated with the Apostles, in convening the congress, in the superscription of the decree, and in the general settlement of the dispute between the Jewish and Gentile Christians[3]. By the presbyters St Paul is received many years later on his last visit to Jerusalem, and to them he gives an account of his missionary labours and triumphs[4]. *Presbytery of Jerusalem.*

But the office was not confined to the mother Church alone. Jewish presbyteries existed already in all the principal cities of the dispersion, and Christian presbyteries would early occupy a not less wide area. On their very first missionary journey the Apostles Paul and Barnabas are described as appointing presbyters in every church[5]. The same rule was doubtless carried out in all the brotherhoods founded later; but it is mentioned here and here only, because the mode of procedure on this occasion would suffice as a type of the Apostles' dealings elsewhere under similar circumstances. *Extension of the office to Gentile Churches.*

The name of the presbyter then presents no difficulty. But what must be said of the term 'bishop'? It has been shown that in the apostolic writings the two are only different designations of one and the same office[6]. How and where was this second name originated? *Presbyters called also bishops,*

To the officers of Gentile Churches alone is the term applied, as a synonyme for presbyter. At Philippi[7], in Asia Minor[8], in Crete[9], *but only in Gentile Churches.*

[1] Acts xi. 30. On the sequence of events at this time see *Galatians* p. 124.
[2] Acts xi. 30.
[3] Acts xv. 2, 4, 6, 22, 23, xvi. 4.
[4] Acts xxi. 18.
[5] Acts xiv. 23.
[6] See above, p. 96 sq.
[7] Phil. i. 1.
[8] Acts xx. 28, 1 Tim. iii. 1, 2; comp. 1 Pet. ii. 25, v. 2.
[9] Tit. i. 7.

the presbyter is so called. In the next generation the title is employed in a letter written by the Greek Church of Rome to the Greek Church of Corinth[1]. Thus the word would seem to be especially Hellenic. Beyond this we are left to conjecture. But if we may assume that the directors of religious and social clubs among the heathen were commonly so called[2], it would naturally occur, if not to the Gentile Christians themselves, at all events to their heathen associates, as a fit designation for the presiding members of the new society. The infant Church of Christ, which appeared to the Jew as a synagogue, would be regarded by the heathen as a confraternity[3]. But whatever may have been the origin of the term, it did not altogether dispossess the earlier name 'presbyter,' which still held its place as a synonyme even in Gentile congregations[4]. And, when at length the term bishop was appropriated to a higher office in the Church, the latter became again, as it had been at first, the sole designation of the Christian elder[5].

Possible origin of the term.

The duties of the presbyters were twofold. They were both rulers and instructors of the congregation. This double function appears in St Paul's expression 'pastors and teachers'[6], where, as the form of the original seems to show, the two words describe the same office under different aspects. Though *government* was probably the first conception of the office, yet the work of *teaching* must have fallen to the presbyters from the very first and have assumed greater prominence as time went on. With the growth of the Church, the visits of the apostles and evangelists to any individual community must have become less and less frequent, so that the burden of instruction would be gradually transferred from these missionary preachers to the local officers of the congregation. Hence St Paul

Twofold duties of the presbyter.

The function of teaching.

---

[1] Clem. Rom. 42, 45.

[2] The evidence however is slight: see above p. 95, note 2. Some light is thrown on this subject by the fact that the Roman government seems first to have recognised the Christian brotherhoods in their corporate capacity, as burial clubs: see de Rossi *Rom. Sotterr.* I. p. 371.

[3] On these clubs or confraternities see Renan *Les Apôtres* p. 351 sq.; comp. *Saint Paul* p. 239.

[4] Acts xx. 17, 1 Tim. v. 17, Tit. i. 5, 1 Pet. v. 1, Clem. Rom. 21, 44.

[5] Other more general designations in the New Testament are οἱ προιστάμενοι (1 Thess. v. 12, Rom. xii. 8: comp. 1 Tim. v. 17), or οἱ ἡγούμενοι (Hebr. xiii. 7, 17, 24). For the former comp. Hermas *Vis.* ii. 4, Justin. *Apol.* i. 67 (ὁ προεστώς); for the latter, Clem. Rom. 1, 21, Hermas *Vis.* ii. 2, iii. 9 (οἱ προηγούμενοι).

[6] Ephes. iv. 11 τοὺς δὲ ποιμένας καὶ διδασκάλους. For ποιμαίνειν applied to the ἐπίσκοπος or πρεσβύτερος see Acts xx. 28, 1 Pet. v. 2; comp. 1 Pet. ii. 25.

in two passages, where he gives directions relating to bishops or presbyters, insists specially on the faculty of teaching as a qualification for the position[1]. Yet even here this work seems to be regarded rather as incidental to than as inherent in the office. In the one epistle he directs that double honour shall be paid to those presbyters who have ruled well, but *especially* to such as 'labour in word and doctrine[2],' as though one holding this office might decline the work of instruction. In the other, he closes the list of qualifications with the requirement that the bishop (or presbyter) hold fast the faithful word in accordance with the apostolic teaching, 'that he may be able both to exhort in the healthy doctrine and to confute gainsayers,' alleging as a reason the pernicious activity and growing numbers of the false teachers. Nevertheless there is no ground for supposing that the work of teaching and the work of governing pertained to separate members of the presbyteral college[3]. As each had his special gift, so would he devote himself more or less exclusively to the one or the other of these sacred functions.

3. It is clear then that at the close of the apostolic age, the two lower orders of the threefold ministry were firmly and widely established; but traces of the third and highest order, the episcopate properly so called, are few and indistinct.

For the opinion hazarded by Theodoret and adopted by many later writers[4], that the same officers in the Church who were first

3. Bishopa

The office not a continuation

[1] 1 Tim. iii. 2, Tit. i. 9.
[2] 1 Tim. v. 17 μάλιστα οἱ κοπιῶντες ἐν λόγῳ καὶ διδασκαλίᾳ. At a much later date we read of 'presbyteri doctores,' whence it may perhaps be inferred that even then the work of teaching was not absolutely indispensable to the presbyteral office; Act. Perp. et Fel. 13, Cyprian. Epist. 29: see Ritschl p. 352.
[3] The distinction of lay or ruling elders, and ministers proper or teaching elders, was laid down by Calvin and has been adopted as the constitution of several presbyterian Churches. This interpretation of St Paul's language is refuted by Rothe p. 224, Ritschl p. 352 sq., and Schaff Hist. of Apost. Ch. II. p. 312, besides older writers such as Vitringa and Mosheim.

[4] On 1 Tim. iii. 1, τοὺς δὲ νῦν καλουμένους ἐπισκόπους ἀποστόλους ὠνόμαζον· τοῦ δὲ χρόνου προϊόντος τὸ μὲν τῆς ἀποστολῆς ὄνομα τοῖς ἀληθῶς ἀποστόλοις κατέλιπον, τὸ δὲ τῆς ἐπισκοπῆς τοῖς πάλαι καλουμένοις ἀποστόλοις ἐπέθεσαν. See also his note on Phil. i. 1. Comp. Wordsworth Theoph. Angl. c. x, Blunt First Three Centuries p. 81. Theodoret, as usual, has borrowed from Theodore of Mopsuestia on 1 Tim. iii. 1, 'Qui vero nunc episcopi nominantur, illi tunc apostoli dicebantur...Beatis vero apostolis decedentibus, illi qui post illos ordinati sunt ... grave existimaverunt apostolorum sibi vindicare nuncupationem; diviserunt ergo ipsa nomina etc.' (Raban. Maur. VI. p. 604 D, ed. Migne). Theodore however makes a distinction between the two offices: nor does he,

of the apo-called apostles came afterwards to be designated bishops, is baseless.
stolate. If the two offices had been identical, the substitution of the one name for the other would have required some explanation. But in fact the functions of the Apostle and the bishop differed widely. The Apostle, like the prophet or the evangelist, held no *local* office. He was essentially, as his name denotes, a missionary, moving about from place to place, founding and confirming new brotherhoods. The only ground on which Theodoret builds his theory is a false interpretation of a passage in St Paul. At the opening of the Epistle to Philippi the presbyters (here called bishops) and deacons are saluted, while in the body of the letter one Epaphroditus is

Phil. ii. 25 mentioned as an 'apostle' of the Philippians. If 'apostle' here had
wrongly the meaning which is thus assigned to it, all the three orders of the
explained. ministry would be found at Philippi. But this interpretation will not stand. The true Apostle, like St Peter or St John, bears this title as the messenger, the delegate, of Christ Himself: while Epaphroditus is only so styled as the messenger of the Philippian brotherhood; and in the very next clause the expression is explained by the statement that he carried their alms to St Paul[1]. The use of the word here has a parallel in another passage[2], where messengers (or apostles) of the churches are mentioned. It is not therefore to the apostle that we must look for the prototype of the bishop. How far indeed and in what sense the bishop may be called a successor of the Apostles, will be a proper subject for consideration: but the succession at least does not consist in an identity of office.

The epis-        The history of the name itself suggests a different account of the
copate de-origin of the episcopate. If bishop was at first used as a synonyme
veloped
out of the for presbyter and afterwards came to designate the higher officer under
presby-whom the presbyters served, the episcopate properly so called
tery. would seem to have been developed from the subordinate office. In other words, the episcopate was formed not out of the apostolic order by localisation but out of the presbyteral by elevation: and the title, which originally was common to all, came at length to be appropriated to the chief among them[3].

---

like Theodoret, misinterpret Phil.ii.25. The commentator Hilary also, on Ephes. iv. 11, says 'apostoli episcopi sunt.'
    [1] See Phil. ii. 25, with the note.

[2] 2 Cor. viii. 23, see *Galatians* p. 96, note 3.
    [3] A parallel instance from Athenian institutions will illustrate this usage

If this account be true, we might expect to find in the mother St James Church of Jerusalem, which as the earliest founded would soonest was the earliest ripen into maturity, the first traces of this developed form of the bishop, ministry. Nor is this expectation disappointed. James the Lord's brother alone, within the period compassed by the apostolic writings, can claim to be regarded as a bishop in the later and more special sense of the term. In the language of St Paul he takes precedence even of the earliest and greatest preachers of the Gospel, St Peter and St John[1], where the affairs of the Jewish Church specially are concerned. In St Luke's narrative he appears as the local representative of the brotherhood in Jerusalem, presiding at the congress, whose decision he suggests and whose decree he appears to have framed[2], receiving the missionary preachers as they revisit the mother Church[3], acting generally as the referee in communications with foreign brotherhoods. The place assigned to him in the spurious Clementines, where he is represented as supreme arbiter over the Church universal in matters of doctrine, must be treated as a gross exaggeration. This kind of authority is nowhere conferred upon him in the apostolic writings: but his social and ecclesiastical position, as it appears in St Luke and St Paul, explains how the exaggeration was possible. And this position is the more remarkable if, as seems to have been the case, he was not one of the Twelve[4].

On the other hand, though especially prominent, he appears in the but yet Acts as a member of a body. When St Peter, after his escape from not isolated from his prison, is about to leave Jerusalem, he desires that his deliverance presbytery. shall be reported to 'James and the brethren[5].' When again St Paul on his last visit to the Holy City goes to see James, we are told that all the presbyters were present[6]. If in some passages St James is named by himself, in others he is omitted and the presbyters alone are mentioned[7]. From this it may be inferred that though

---

The ἐπιστάτης was chairman of a body of ten πρόεδροι, who themselves were appointed in turn by lot to serve from a larger body of fifty πρυτάνεις. Yet we find the ἐπιστάτης not only designated πρύτανις par excellence (Demosth. Timocr. § 157), but even addressed by this name in the presence of the other πρόεδροι (Thuc. vi. 14).

[1] Gal. ii. 9; see the note.
[2] Acts xv. 13 sq. St James speaks

last and apparently with some degree of authority (ἐγὼ κρίνω ver. 19). The decree is clearly framed on his recommendations, and some indecisive coincidences of style with his epistle have been pointed out.
[3] Acts xxi. 18; comp. xii. 17. See also Gal. i. 19, ii. 12.
[4] See Galatians p. 252 sq.
[5] Acts xii. 17.    [6] Acts xxi. 18.
[7] Acts xi. 30; comp. xv. 4, 23, xvi. 4.

holding a position superior to the rest, he was still considered as a member of the presbytery; that he was in fact the head or president of the college. What power this presidency conferred, how far it was recognised as an independent official position, and to what degree it was due to the ascendancy of his personal gifts, are questions which in the absence of direct information can only be answered by conjecture. But his close relationship with the Lord, his rare energy of character, and his rigid sanctity of life which won the respect even of the unconverted Jews[1], would react upon his office, and may perhaps have elevated it to a level which was not definitely contemplated in its origin.

No bishops as yet in the Gentile Churches. But while the episcopal office thus existed in the mother Church of Jerusalem from very early days, at least in a rudimentary form, the New Testament presents no distinct traces of such organization in the Gentile congregations. The government of the Gentile churches, as there represented, exhibits two successive stages of development tending in this direction; but the third stage, in which episcopacy definitely appears, still lies beyond the horizon.

Two stages of development:

(1) Occasional supervision by the Apostles themselves. (1) We have first of all the Apostles themselves exercising the superintendence of the churches under their care, sometimes in person and on the spot, sometimes at a distance by letter or by message. The imaginary picture drawn by St Paul, when he directs the punishment of the Corinthian offender, vividly represents his position in this respect. The members of the church are gathered together, the elders, we may suppose, being seated apart on a dais or tribune; he himself, as president, directs their deliberations, collects their votes, pronounces sentence on the guilty man[2]. How the absence of the apostolic president was actually supplied in this instance, we do not know. But a council was held; he did direct their verdict 'in spirit though not in person'; and 'the majority' condemned the offender[3]. In the same way St Peter, giving directions to the elders, claims a place among them. The title 'fellow-presbyter,' which he applies to himself[4], would doubtless recal to the memory of his readers the occasions when he himself had presided with the elders and guided their deliberations.

---

[1] See *Galatians* p. 365 sq.
[2] 1 Cor. v. 3 sq.

[3] 2 Cor. ii. 6 ἡ ἐπιτιμία αὕτη ἡ ὑπὸ τῶν πλειόνων.
[4] 1 Pet. v. 1.

(2) As the first stage then, the Apostles themselves were the superintendents of each individual church. But the wider spread of the Gospel would diminish the frequency of their visits and impair the efficiency of such supervision. In the second stage therefore we find them, at critical seasons and in important congregations, delegating some trustworthy disciple who should fix his abode in a given place for a time and direct the affairs of the church there. The Pastoral Epistles present this second stage to our view. It is the conception of a later age which represents Timothy as bishop of Ephesus and Titus as bishop of Crete[1]. St Paul's own language implies that the position which they held was temporary. In both cases their term of office is drawing to a close, when the Apostle writes[2]. But the conception is not altogether without foundation. With less permanence but perhaps greater authority, the position occupied by these apostolic delegates nevertheless fairly represents the functions of the bishop early in the second century. They were in fact the link between the Apostle whose superintendence was occasional and general and the bishop who exercised a permanent supervision over an individual congregation.

Beyond this second stage the notices in the apostolic writings do not carry us. The angels of the seven churches indeed are frequently alleged as an exception[3]. But neither does the name 'angel' itself suggest such an explanation[4], nor is this view in keeping with the highly figurative style of this wonderful book. Its sublime imagery

[1] Const. Apost. vii. 46, Euseb. H. E. iii. 4, and later writers.
[2] See 1 Tim. i. 3, iii. 14, 2 Tim. iv. 9, 21, Tit. i. 5, iii. 12.
[3] See for instance among recent writers Thiersch Gesch. der Apost. Kirche p. 278, Trench Epistles to the Seven Churches p. 47 sq., with others. This explanation is as old as the earliest commentators. Rothe supposes that the word anticipates the establishment of episcopacy, being a kind of prophetic symbol, p. 423 sq. Others again take the angel to designate the collective ministry, i.e. the whole body of priests and deacons. For various explanations see Schaff Hist. of Apost. Ch. ii. p. 223. Rothe (p. 426) supposes that Diotrephes ὁ φιλοπρωτεύων αὐτῶν (3 Joh. 9)

was a bishop. This cannot be pronounced impossible, but the language is far too indefinite to encourage such an inference.
[4] It is conceivable indeed that a bishop or chief pastor should be called an angel or messenger of God or of Christ (comp. Hag. i. 13, Mal. ii. 7), but he would hardly be styled an angel of the church over which he presides. See the parallel case of ἀπόστολος above, p. 196. Vitringa (ii. 9, p. 550), and others after him, explain ἄγγελος in the Apocalypse by the שׁלִיחַ, the messenger or deputy of the synagogue. These however were only inferior officers, and could not be compared to stars or made responsible for the well-being of the churches; see Rothe p. 504.

seems to be seriously impaired by this interpretation. On the other hand St John's own language gives the true key to the symbolism. 'The seven stars,' so it is explained, 'are the seven angels of the seven churches, and the seven candlesticks are the seven churches[1].' This contrast between the heavenly and the earthly fires—the star shining steadily by its own inherent eternal light, and the lamp flickering and uncertain, requiring to be fed with fuel and tended with care—

True explanation. cannot be devoid of meaning. The star is the suprasensual counterpart, the heavenly representative; the lamp, the earthly realisation, the outward embodiment. Whether the angel is here conceived as an actual person, the celestial guardian, or only as a personification, the idea or spirit of the church, it is unnecessary for my present purpose to consider. But whatever may be the exact conception, he is identified with and made responsible for it to a degree wholly unsuited to any human officer. Nothing is predicated of him, which may not be predicated of it. To him are imputed all its hopes, its fears, its graces, its shortcomings. He is punished with it, and he is rewarded with it. In one passage especially the language applied to the angel seems to exclude the common interpretation. In the message to Thyatira the angel is blamed, because he suffers himself to be led astray by 'his wife Jezebel[2].' In this image of Ahab's idolatrous queen some dangerous and immoral teaching must be personified; for it does violence alike to the general tenour and to the individual expressions in the passage to suppose that an actual woman is meant. Thus the symbolism of the passage is entirely in keeping. Nor again is this mode of representation new. The 'princes' in the prophecy of Daniel[3] present a very near if not an exact parallel to the angels of the Revelation. Here, as elsewhere, St John seems to adapt the imagery of this earliest apocalyptic book.

Indeed, if with most recent writers we adopt the early date of the Apocalypse of St John, it is scarcely possible that the episcopal organization should have been so mature when it was written. In this case probably not more than two or three years have elapsed from the date of the Pastoral Epistles[4], and this interval seems quite

---

[1] Rev. i. 20.
[2] Rev. ii. 20 τὴν γυναῖκά σου ᾿Ιεζάβελ. The word σου should probably be retained in the text: or at least, if not a correct reading, it seems to be a correct gloss.
[3] Dan. x. 13, 20, 21.
[4] The date of the Pastoral Epistles

insufficient to account for so great a change in the administration
of the Asiatic churches.

As late therefore as the year 70 no distinct signs of episcopal go- Episcopa-
vernment have hitherto appeared in Gentile Christendom. Yet unless blished in
we have recourse to a sweeping condemnation of received documents, Gentile
it seems vain to deny that early in the second century the episcopal before the
office was firmly and widely established. Thus during the last three close of the
decades of the first century, and consequently during the lifetime of century.
the latest surviving Apostle, this change must have been brought
about. But the circumstances under which it was effected are
shrouded in darkness; and various attempts have been made to read
the obscure enigma. Of several solutions offered one at least deserves
special notice. If Rothe's view cannot be accepted as final, its ex- Rothe's
amination will at least serve to bring out the conditions of the solution.
problem: and for this reason I shall state and discuss it as briefly
as possible[1]. For the words in which the theory is stated I am
myself responsible.

'The epoch to which we last adverted marks an important crisis Import-
in the history of Christianity. The Church was distracted and ance of the
dismayed by the growing dissensions between the Jewish and crisis.
Gentile brethren and by the menacing apparition of Gnostic heresy.
So long as its three most prominent leaders were living, there had
been some security against the extravagance of parties, some guarantee of harmonious combination among diverse churches. But St
Peter, St Paul, and St James, were carried away by death almost at
the same time and in the face of this great emergency. Another
blow too had fallen : the long-delayed judgment of God on the once
Holy City was delayed no more. With the overthrow of Jerusalem
the visible centre of the Church was removed. The keystone of the
fabric was withdrawn, and the whole edifice threatened with ruin.
There was a crying need for some organization which should cement
together the diverse elements of Christian society and preserve it
from disintegration.'

may be and probably is as late as A.D.
66 or 67; while the Apocalypse on
this hypothesis was written not later
than A.D. 70.
[1] See Rothe's *Anfänge etc.* pp. 354—
392. Rothe's account of the origin of

episcopacy is assailed (on grounds in
many respects differing from those
which I have urged) by Baur *Ursprung
des Episcopats* p. 39 sq., and Ritschl
p. 410 sq.

Origin of
the Catho-
lic Church. 'Out of this need the Catholic Church arose. Christendom had
hitherto existed as a number of distinct isolated congregations, drawn
in the same direction by a common faith and common sympathies,
accidentally linked one with another by the personal influence and
apostolic authority of their common teachers, but not bound together
in a harmonious whole by any permanent external organization.
Now at length this great result was brought about. The magnitude
of the change effected during this period may be measured by the
difference in the constitution and conception of the Christian Church
as presented in the Pastoral Epistles of St Paul and the letters of St
Ignatius respectively.'

Agency of
the surviv-
ing Apo-
stles. 'By whom then was the new constitution organized? To this
question only one answer can be given. This great work must be
ascribed to the surviving Apostles. St John especially, who built
up the speculative theology of the Church, was mainly instrumental
in completing its external constitution also; for Asia Minor was the
centre from which the new movement spread. St John however
was not the only Apostle or early disciple who lived in this province. St Philip is known to have settled in Hierapolis[1]. St
Andrew also seems to have dwelt in these parts[2]. The silence of
history clearly proclaims the fact which the voice of history but
faintly suggests. If we hear nothing more of the Apostles' missionary labours, it is because they had organized an united Church, to
which they had transferred the work of evangelization.'

Evidence
of a se-
cond Apo-
stolic
Council. 'Of such a combined effort on the part of the Apostles, resulting
in a definite ecclesiastical polity, in an united Catholic Church,
no direct account is preserved: but incidental notices are not wanting; and in the general paucity of information respecting the whole
period more than this was not to be expected[3].'

Hegesip-
pus. '(1) Eusebius relates that after the martyrdom of St James
and the fall of Jerusalem, the remaining Apostles and personal dis-

---

[1] Papias in Euseb. *H. E.* iii. 39;
Polycrates and Caius in Euseb. *H. E.*
iii. 21.

[2] Muratorian Canon (circ. 170 A.D.),
Routh *Rel. Sacr.* I. p. 394.

[3] Besides the evidence which I have
stated and discussed in the text, Rothe
also brings forward a fragment of the
*Prædicatio Pauli* (preserved in the tract

*de Baptismo Hæreticorum*, which is
included among Cyprian's works, app.
p. 30, ed. Fell; see *Galatians* p. 353
note), where the writer mentions a
meeting of St Peter and St Paul in
Rome. The main question however is
so slightly affected thereby, that I have
not thought it necessary to investigate
the value and bearing of this fragment.

ciples of the Lord, with his surviving relations, met together and after consultation unanimously appointed Symeon the son of Clopas to the vacant see[1]. It can hardly be doubted, that Eusebius in this passage quotes from the earlier historian Hegesippus, from whom he has derived the other incidents in the lives of James and Symeon : and we may well believe that this council discussed larger questions than the appointment of a single bishop, and that the constitution and prospects of the Church generally came under deliberation. It may have been on this occasion that the surviving Apostles partitioned out the world among them, and 'Asia was assigned to John[2].'

'(2) A fragment of Irenæus points in the same direction. Writing of the holy eucharist he says, 'They who have paid attention to the second ordinances of the Apostles know that the Lord appointed a new offering in the new covenant[3].' By these 'second ordinances' must be understood some later decrees or injunctions than those contained in the apostolic epistles : and these would naturally be framed and promulgated by such a council as the notice of Eusebius suggests.'

'(3) To the same effect St Clement of Rome writes, that the Apostles, having appointed elders in every church and foreseeing the disputes which would arise, 'afterwards added a codicil (supplementary direction) that if they should fall asleep, other approved men should succeed to their office[4].' Here the pronouns 'they,' 'their,' must refer, not to the first appointed presbyters, but to the Apostles themselves. Thus interpreted, the passage contains a distinct notice of the institution of bishops as successors of the Apostles ; while in the word 'afterwards' is involved an allusion to the later council to which the 'second ordinances' of Irenæus also refer[5].'

*Marginal notes:* Irenæus. Clement of Rome.

---

[1] Euseb. *H. E.* iii. 11.

[2] According to the tradition reported by Origen as quoted in Euseb. *H. E.* iii. 1.

[3] One of the Pfaffian fragments, no. xxxviii, p. 854 in Stieren's edition of Irenæus.

[4] Clem. Rom. § 44 κατέστησαν τοὺς προειρημένους (sc. πρεσβυτέρους) καὶ μεταξὺ†ἐπινομὴν†δεδώκασιν, ὅπως, ἐὰν κοιμηθῶσιν, διαδέξωνται ἕτεροι δεδοκιμασμένοι ἄνδρες τὴν λειτουργίαν αὐτῶν. The interpretation of the passage depends on

the persons intended in κοιμηθῶσιν and αὐτῶν (see the notes on the passage).

[5] A much more explicit though somewhat later authority may be quoted in favour of his view. The Ambrosian Hilary on Ephes. iv. 12, speaking of the change from the presbyteral to the episcopal form of government, says 'immutata est ratio, *prospiciente concilio*, ut non ordo etc.' If the reading be correct, I suppose he was thinking of the Apostolic Constitutions. See also the expression of St

'These notices seem to justify the conclusion that immediately
after the fall of Jerusalem a council of the apostles and first
teachers of the Gospel was held to deliberate on the crisis, and to
Results of frame measures for the well-being of the Church.  The centre of
the Coun-
cil. the system then organized was episcopacy, which at once secured the
compact and harmonious working of each individual congregation,
and as the link of communication between separate brotherhoods
formed the whole into one undivided Catholic Church.  Recom-
mended by this high authority, the new constitution was immediately and generally adopted.'

Value of        This theory, which is maintained with much ability and vigour,
Rothe's
theory. attracted considerable notice, as being a new defence of episcopacy
advanced by a member of a presbyterian Church.  On the other
hand, its intrinsic value seems to have been unduly depreciated; for,
if it fails to give a satisfactory solution, it has at least the merit of
stating the conditions of the problem with great distinctness, and of
pointing out the direction to be followed.  On this account it seemed
worthy of attention.

The evi-        It must indeed be confessed that the historical notices will not
dence ex-
amined. bear the weight of the inference built upon them.  (1) The account
Hegesip-
pus. of Hegesippus (for to Hegesippus the statement in Eusebius may
fairly be ascribed) confines the object of this gathering to the
appointment of a successor to St James.  If its deliberations had
exerted that vast and permanent influence on the future of the
Church which Rothe's theory supposes, it is scarcely possible that
this early historian should have been ignorant of the fact or knowing
it should have passed it over in silence.  (2) The genuineness of the
Irenæus. Pfaffian fragments of Irenæus must always remain doubtful[1].  Independently of the mystery which hangs over their publication, the very
passage quoted throws great suspicion on their authorship; for the expression in question[2] seems naturally to refer to the so called Apostolic
Constitutions, which have been swelled to their present size by the

---

Jerome on Tit. i. 5 (quoted below p.
206) 'in toto orbe decretum est.'
    [1] The controversial treatises on either
side are printed in Stieren's Irenæus II.
p. 381 sqq.  It is sufficient here to
state that shortly after the transcrip-
tion of these fragments by Pfaff, the
Turin MS from which they were taken

disappeared; so that there was no
means of testing the accuracy of the
transcriber or ascertaining the character of the MS.
    [2] The expression αἱ δεύτεραι τῶν ἀπο-
στόλων διατάξεις closely resembles the
language of these Constitutions; see
Hippol. p. 74, 82 (Lagarde).

accretions of successive generations, but can hardly have existed even in a rudimentary form in the age of Irenæus, or if existing have been regarded by him as genuine. If he had been acquainted with such later ordinances issued by the authority of an apostolic council, is it conceivable that in his great work on heresies he should have omitted to quote a sanction so unquestionable, where his main object is to show that the doctrine of the Catholic Church in his day represented the true teaching of the Apostles, and his main argument the fact that the Catholic bishops of his time derived their office by direct succession from the Apostles? (3) The passage in Clement. the epistle of St Clement cannot be correctly interpreted by Rothe: for his explanation, though elaborately defended, disregards the purpose of the letter. The Corinthian Church is disturbed by a spirit of insubordination. Presbyters, who have faithfully discharged their duties, have nevertheless been ruthlessly expelled from office. St Clement writes in the name of the Roman Church to correct these irregularities. He reminds the Corinthians that the presbyteral office was established by the Apostles, who not only themselves appointed elders, but also gave directions that the vacancies caused from time to time by death should be filled up by other men of character, thus providing for a succession in the ministry. Consequently in these unworthy feuds they were setting themselves in opposition to officers of repute either actually nominated by Apostles, or appointed by those so nominated in accordance with the apostolic injunctions. There is no mention of episcopacy, properly so called, throughout the epistle; for in the language of St Clement, 'bishop' and 'presbyter' are still synonymous terms[1]. Thus the pronouns 'they,' 'their,' refer naturally to the presbyters first appointed by the Apostles themselves. Whether (supposing the reading to be correct[2]) Rothe has rightly translated ἐπινομήν 'a codicil,' it is unnecessary to enquire, as the rendering does not materially affect the question.

Nor again does it appear that the rise of episcopacy was so Episcopasudden and so immediate, that an authoritative order issuing from cy not a sudden an apostolic council alone can explain the phenomenon. In the creation, mysterious period which comprises the last thirty years of the first

---

[1] See above, pp. 97, 98.

[2] The right reading is probably ἐπι-

μονήν; see the notes on the passage.

century, and on which history is almost wholly silent, episcopacy must, it is true, have been mainly developed. But before this period its beginnings may be traced, and after the close it is not yet fully matured. It seems vain to deny with Rothe[1] that the position of St James in the mother Church furnished the precedent and the pattern of the later episcopate. It appears equally mistaken to maintain, as this theory requires, that at the close of the first and the beginning of the second century the organization of all churches alike had arrived at the same stage of development and exhibited the episcopate in an equally perfect form.

but ma-
tured by
a critical
emergency

On the other hand, the emergency which consolidated the episcopal form of government is correctly and forcibly stated. It was remarked long ago by Jerome, that 'before factions were introduced into religion by the prompting of the devil,' the churches were governed by a council of elders, 'but as soon as each man began to consider those whom he had baptized to belong to himself and not to Christ, it was decided throughout the world that one elected from among the elders should be placed over the rest, so that the care of the church should devolve on him, and the seeds of schism be removed[2].' And again in another passage he writes to the same effect; 'When afterwards one presbyter was elected that he might be placed over the rest, this was done as a remedy against schism, that each man might not drag to himself and thus break up the Church of Christ[3].' To the dissensions of Jew and Gentile converts, and to the disputes of Gnostic false teachers, the development of episcopacy may be mainly ascribed.

and in
Asia Minor
under the
influence
of St John.

Nor again is Rothe probably wrong as to the authority mainly instrumental in effecting the change. Asia Minor was the adopted home of more than one Apostle after the fall of Jerusalem. Asia Minor too was the nurse, if not the mother, of episcopacy in the Gentile Churches. So important an institution, developed in a Christian community of which St John was the living centre and guide, could hardly have grown up without his sanction: and, as will be seen presently, early tradition very distinctly connects his name with the appointment of bishops in these parts.

But to the question how this change was brought about, a some-

---

[1] p. 264 sq.                           [3] Epist. cxlvi ad Evang. (I. p.
[2] On Tit. i. 5 (VII. p. 694, ed. Vall.).    1082).

what different answer must be given. We have seen that the needs of the Church and the ascendancy of his personal character placed St James at the head of the Christian brotherhood in Jerusalem. Though remaining a member of the presbyteral council, he was singled out from the rest and placed in a position of superior responsibility. His exact power it would be impossible, and it is unnecessary, to define. When therefore after the fall of the city St John with other surviving Apostles removed to Asia Minor and found there manifold irregularities and threatening symptoms of disruption, he would not unnaturally encourage an approach in these Gentile Churches to the same organization, which had been signally blessed, and proved effectual in holding together the mother Church amid dangers not less serious. The existence of a council or college necessarily supposes a presidency of some kind, whether this presidency be assumed by each member in turn, or lodged in the hands of a single person[1]. It was only necessary therefore for him to give permanence, definiteness, stability, to an office which already existed in germ. There is no reason however for supposing that any direct ordinance was issued to the churches. The evident utility and even pressing need of such an office, sanctioned by the most venerated name in Christendom, would be sufficient to secure its wide though gradual reception. Such a reception, it is true, supposes a substantial harmony and freedom of intercourse among the churches, which remained undisturbed by the troubles of the times; but the silence of history is not at all unfavourable to this supposition. In this way, during the historical blank which extends over half a century after the fall of Jerusalem, episcopacy was matured and the Catholic Church consolidated[2].

---

[1] The Ambrosian Hilary on Ephes. iv. 12 seems to say that the senior member was president; but this may be mere conjecture. The constitution of the synagogue does not aid materially in settling this question. In the New Testament at all events ἀρχισυνάγωγος is only another name for an *elder* of the synagogue (Mark v. 22, Acts xiii. 15, xviii. 8, 17; comp. Justin *Dial. c. Tryph.* § 137), and therefore corresponds not to the bishop but to the presbyter of the Christian Church. Sometimes however ἀρχισυνάγωγος ap-

pears to denote the president of the council of elders: see Vitringa II. 2. p. 586 sq., III. 1. p. 610 sq. The opinions of Vitringa must be received with caution, as his tendency to press the resemblance between the government of the Jewish synagogue and the Christian Church is strong. The real likeness consists in the council of presbyters; but the threefold order of the Christian ministry as a whole seems to have no counterpart in the synagogue.

[2] The expression 'Catholic Church' is found first in the Ignatian letter to

This view
supported
by the no-
tices of in-
dividual
churches.
At all events, when we come to trace the early history of the
office in the principal churches of Christendom in succession, we
shall find all the facts consistent with the account adopted here,
while some of them are hardly reconcileable with any other.  In
this review it will be convenient to commence with the mother
Church, and to take the others in order, as they are connected either
by neighbourhood or by political or religious sympathy.

JERUSA-
LEM.
1.  The Church of JERUSALEM, as I have already pointed out,
presents the earliest instance of a bishop.  A certain official pro-
St James. minence is assigned to James the Lord's brother, both in the Epistles of St Paul and in the Acts of the Apostles.  And the inference
drawn from the notices in the canonical Scriptures is borne out by
the tradition of the next ages.  As early as the middle of the second
century all parties concur in representing him as a bishop in the
strict sense of the term[1].  In this respect Catholic Christians and
Ebionite Christians hold the same language : the testimony of
Hegesippus on the one hand is matched by the testimony of the
Clementine writings on the other.  On his death, which is recorded
Symeon. as taking place immediately before the war of Vespasian, Symeon
was appointed in his place[2].  Hegesippus, who is our authority for
this statement, distinctly regards Symeon as holding the same office
with James, and no less distinctly calls him a bishop.  This same
historian also mentions the circumstance that one Thebuthis (apparently on this occasion), being disappointed of the bishopric, raised
a schism and attempted to corrupt the virgin purity of the Church
with false doctrine.  As Symeon died in the reign of Trajan at an
advanced age, it is not improbable that Hegesippus was born during
Later
bishops. his lifetime.  Of the successors of Symeon a complete list is preserved
by Eusebius[3].  The fact however that it comprises thirteen names
within a period of less than thirty years must throw suspicion on

the Smyrnæans § 8.  In the Martyrdom of Polycarp it occurs several
times, inscr. and §§ 8, 16, 19.  On its
meaning see Westcott Canon p. 28,
note (4th ed.).

[1] Hegesipp. in Euseb. H. E. ii. 23,
iv. 22 ; Clem. Hom. xi. 35, Ep. Petr.
init., and Ep. Clem. init. ; Clem.
Recogn. i. 43, 68, 73 ; Clem. Alex.
in Euseb. ii. 1 ; Const. Apost. v. 8, vi.
14, viii. 35, 46.

[2] Hegesipp. in Euseb. H. E. iv. 22.
[3] H. E. iv. 5.  The episcopate of
Justus the successor of Symeon commences about A.D. 108 : that of Marcus
the first Gentile bishop, A.D. 136.  Thus
thirteen bishops occupy only about
twenty-eight years.  Even after the
foundation of Ælia Capitolina the succession is very rapid.  In the period
from Marcus (A.D. 136) to Narcissus
(A.D. 190) we count fifteen bishops

its accuracy. A succession so rapid is hardly consistent with the known tenure of life offices in ordinary cases : and if the list be correct, the frequent changes must be attributed to the troubles and uncertainties of the times [1]. If Eusebius here also had derived his information from Hegesippus, it must at least have had some solid foundation in fact ; but even then the alternation between Jerusalem and Pella, and the possible confusion of the bishops with other prominent members of the presbytery, might introduce much error. It appears however that in this instance he was indebted to less trustworthy sources of information [2]. The statement that after the foundation of Aelia Capitolina (A.D. 136) Marcus presided over the mother Church, as its first Gentile bishop, need not be questioned ; and beyond this point it is unnecessary to carry the investigation [3].

Of other bishops in PALESTINE and the neighbourhood, before the latter half of the second century, no trustworthy notice is preserved, so far as I know. During the Roman episcopate of Victor however (about A.D. 190), we find three bishops, Theophilus of Cæsarea, Cassius of Tyre, and Clarus of Ptolemais, in conjunction with Narcissus of Jerusalem, writing an encyclical letter in favour of the western view in the Paschal controversy [4]. If indeed any reliance could be placed on the Clementine writings, the episcopate of Palestine was matured at a very early date : for St Peter is there represented as appointing bishops in every city which he visits, in Cæsarea, Tyre, Sidon, Berytus, Tripolis, and Laodicea [5]. And though the fictions of this theological romance have no direct historical value, it is

*Other sees in Palestine and neighbouring countries.*

---

The repetition of the same names however suggests that some conflict was going on during this interval.

[1] Parallels nevertheless may be found in the annals of the papacy. Thus from A.D. 882 to A.D. 904 there were thirteen popes: and in other times of trouble the succession has been almost as rapid.

[2] This may be inferred from a comparison of *H. E.* iv. 5 τοσοῦτον ἐξ ἐγγράφων παρείληφα with *H. E.* v. 12 αἱ τῶν αὐτόθι διαδοχαὶ περιέχουσι. His information was probably taken from a list kept at Jerusalem; but the case of the spurious correspondence with Abgarus

preserved in the archives of Edessa (*H. E.* i. 13) shows how treacherous such sources of information were.

[3] Narcissus, who became bishop of Jerusalem in 190 A.D., might well have preserved the memory of much earlier times. His successor Alexander, in whose favour he resigned A.D. 214, speaks of him as still living at the advanced age of 116 (Euseb. *H.E.* vi. 11).

[4] Euseb. *H.E.* v. 25.

[5] *Clem. Hom.* iii. 68 sq. (Cæsarea), vii. 5 (Tyre), vii. 8 (Sidon), vii. 12 (Berytus), xi. 36 (Tripolis), xx. 23 (Laodicea): comp. *Clem. Recogn.* iii. 65, 66, 74, vi. 15, x. 68.

hardly probable that the writer would have indulged in such statements, unless an early development of the episcopate in these parts
had invested his narrative with an air of probability. The institution would naturally spread from the Church of Jerusalem to the
more important communities in the neighbourhood, even without the
direct intervention of the Apostles.

**ANTIOCH.** 2. From the mother Church of the Hebrews we pass naturally
to the metropolis of Gentile Christendom. ANTIOCH is traditionally
**Evodius.** reported to have received its first bishop Evodius from St Peter[1].
The story may perhaps rest on some basis of truth, though no confidence
can be placed in this class of statements, unless they are known to
**Ignatius.** have been derived from some early authority. But of Ignatius, who
stands second in the traditional catalogue of Antiochene bishops,
we can speak with more confidence. He is designated a bishop by
very early authors, and he himself speaks as such. He writes to
one bishop, Polycarp; and he mentions several others. Again and
again he urges the duty of obedience to their bishops on his correspondents. And, lest it should be supposed that he uses the
term in its earlier sense as a synonyme for presbyter, he names
in conjunction the three orders of the ministry, the bishop, the
presbyter, and the deacons[2]. Altogether it is plain that he looks
upon the episcopal system as the one recognised and authoritative
form of government in all those churches with which he is most
directly concerned. It may be suggested indeed that he would
hardly have enforced the claims of episcopacy, unless it were an
object of attack, and its comparatively recent origin might therefore be inferred : but still some years would be required before it
could have assumed that mature and definite form which it has in
his letters. It seems impossible to decide, and it is needless to
investigate, the exact date of the epistles of St Ignatius : but we
cannot do wrong in placing them during the earliest years of the
**Later** second century. The immediate successor of Ignatius is reported
**bishops.** to have been Hero[3] : and from his time onward the list of
Antiochene bishops is complete[4]. If the authenticity of the list,

[1] *Const. Apost.* vii. 46, Euseb. *H.E.*
iii. 22.
[2] e.g. *Polyc.* 6. I single out this
passage from several which might be
alleged, because it is found in the
Syriac. See below, p. 234.
[3] Euseb. *H. E.* iii. 36.
[4] Euseb. *H. E.* iv. 20.

as a whole, is questionable, two bishops of Antioch at least during the second century, Theophilus and Serapion, are known as historical persons.

If the Clementine writings emanated, as seems probable, from Clemen-Syria or Palestine[1], this will be the proper place to state their attitude with regard to episcopacy. *tine writings.* Whether the opinions there advanced exhibit the recognised tenets of a sect or congregation, or the private views of the individual writer or writers, will probably never be ascertained ; but, whatever may be said on this point, these heretical books outstrip the most rigid orthodoxy in their reverence for the episcopal office. Monarchy is represented as necessary to the peace of the Church[2]. The bishop occupies the seat of Christ and must be honoured as the image of God[3]. And hence St Peter, as he moves from place to place, ordains bishops everywhere, as though this were the crowning act of his missionary labours[4]. The divergence of the Clementine doctrine from the tenets of Catholic Christianity only renders this phenomenon more remarkable, when we remember the very early date of these writings ; for the Homilies cannot well be placed later than the end, and should perhaps be placed before the middle of the second century.

3. We have hitherto been concerned only with the Greek Church of Syria. Of the early history of the SYRIAN CHURCH, *Syrian Church.* strictly so called, no trustworthy account is preserved. The documents which profess to give information respecting it are comparatively late : and while their violent anachronisms discredit them as a whole, it is impossible to separate the fabulous from the historic[5]. It should be remarked however, that they exhibit a high sacerdotal view of the episcopate as prevailing in these churches from the earliest times of which any record is preserved[6].

---

[1] See *Galatians* pp. 340 sq.

[2] *Clem. Hom.* iii. 62.

[3] *Clem. Hom.* iii. 62, 66, 70. See below, p. 238.

[4] See the references given above p. 209, note 5.

[5] *Ancient Syriac Documents* (ed. Cureton). The *Doctrine of Addai* has recently been published complete by Dr Phillips, London 1876. This work at all events must be old, for it was found by Eusebius in the archives of Edessa (*H. E.* i. 13) ; but it abounds

in gross anachronisms and probably is not earlier than the middle of the 3rd century: see Zahn *Gött. Gel. Anz.* 1877, p. 161 sq.

[6] See for instance pp. 13, 16, 18, 21, 23, 24, 26, 29, 30, 33, 34, 35, 42, 71 (Cureton). The succession to the episcopate is conferred by the 'Hand of Priesthood' through the Apostles, who received it from our Lord, and is derived ultimately from Moses and Aaron (p. 24).

ΛBIΛ MI-   4. ASIA MINOR follows next in order ; and here we find the
NOR.     widest and most unequivocal traces of episcopacy at an early date.
         Clement of Alexandria distinctly states that St John went about from
         city to city, his purpose being 'in some places to establish bishops, in
Activity of others to consolidate whole churches, in others again to appoint to
St John in
proconsu- the clerical office some one of those who had been signified by the
lar Asia. Spirit[1].' 'The sequence of bishops,' writes Tertullian in like manner
         of Asia Minor, 'traced back to its origin will be found to rest on
         the authority of John[2].' And a writer earlier than either speaks of
         St John's 'fellow-disciples and bishops[3]' as gathered about him. The
         conclusiveness even of such testimony might perhaps be doubted, if
         it were not supported by other more direct evidence. At the begin-
         ning of the second century the letters of Ignatius, even if we accept
         as genuine only the part contained in the Syriac, mention by name
Onesimus. two bishops in these parts, Onesimus of Ephesus and Polycarp of
Polycarp.
         Smyrna[4]. Of the former nothing more is known : the latter evi-
         dently writes as a bishop, for he distinguishes himself from his
         presbyters[5], and is expressly so called by other writers besides
         Ignatius. His pupil Irenæus says of him, that he had 'not
         only been instructed by Apostles and conversed with many who had
         seen Christ but had also been established by Apostles in Asia as
         bishop in the Church at Smyrna[6].' Polycrates also, a younger con-
         temporary of Polycarp and himself bishop of Ephesus, designates him
         by this title[7]; and again in the letter written by his own church
         and giving an account of his martyrdom he is styled 'bishop of
         the Church in Smyrna[8].' As Polycarp survived the middle of
         the second century, dying at a very advanced age (A.D. 155 or 156),
         the possibility of error on this point seems to be excluded : and
         indeed all historical evidence must be thrown aside as worthless, if
         testimony so strong can be disregarded.
Ignatian    It is probable however, that we should receive as genuine not
letters.
         only those portions of the Ignatian letters which are represented in

---

[1] *Quis Div. Salv.* 42 (p. 959).

[2] *Adv. Marc.* iv. 5.

[3] Muratorian Fragment, Routh *Rel. Sacr.* I. p. 394. Irenæus too, whose experience was drawn chiefly from Asia Minor, more than once speaks of bishops appointed by the Apostles, iii. 3. 1, v. 20. 1.

[4] *Polyc.* inscr., *Ephes.* 1.

[5] Polyc. *Phil.* init.

[6] Iren. iii. 3. 4. Comp. Tertull. *de Præscr.* 32.

[7] In Euseb. v. 24.

[8] *Mart. Polyc.* 16. Polycarp is called 'bishop of Smyrna' also in *Mart. Ignat. Ant.* 3.

the Syriac, but also the Greek text in its shorter form. Under any circumstances, this text can hardly have been made later than the middle of the second century[1], and its witness would still be highly valuable, even if it were a forgery. The staunch advocacy of the episcopate which distinguishes these writings is well known and will be considered hereafter. At present we are only concerned with the historical testimony which they bear to the wide extension and authoritative claims of the episcopal office. Besides Polycarp and Onesimus, mentioned in the Syriac, the writer names also Damas bishop of Magnesia[2] and Polybius bishop of Tralles[3]; and he urges on the Philadelphians also the duty of obedience to their bishop[4], though the name is not given. Under any circumstances it seems probable that these were not fictitious personages, for, even if he were a forger, he would be anxious to give an air of reality to his writings : but whether or not we regard his testimony as indirectly affecting the age of Ignatius, for his own time at least it must be regarded as valid.

But the evidence is not confined to the persons and the churches already mentioned. Papias, who was a friend of Polycarp and had conversed with personal disciples of the Lord, is commonly designated bishop of Hierapolis[5]; and we learn from a younger contemporary Serapion[6], that Claudius Apollinaris, known as a writer against the Montanists, also held this see in the reign of M. Aurelius. Again Sagaris the martyr, who seems to have perished in the early years of M. Aurelius, about A.D. 165[7], is designated bishop of Laodicea by an author writing towards the close of the same century, who also alludes to Melito the contemporary of Sagaris as holding the see of Sardis[8]. The authority just quoted, Polycrates of Ephesus, who flourished in the last decade of the century, says moreover that he had had seven relations bishops before him, himself being the eighth, and that he followed their tradition[9]. When he wrote he had been 'sixty-five years in the Lord'; so that even if this period

*Marginal notes:* Bishops of Hierapolis. Sagaris. Melito. Polycrates and his relations.

---

[1] See below, p. 234, note.
[2] *Magn.* 2.
[3] *Trall.* 1.
[4] *Philad.* 1.
[5] Euseb. *H. E.* iii. 36.
[6] In Euseb. *H. E.* v. 19.
[7] On the authority of his contemporary Melito in Euseb. *H. E.* iv. 26 :

see *Colossians* p. 63.
[8] Polycrates in Euseb. *H. E.* v. 24. Melito's office may be inferred from the contrast implied in περιμένων τὴν ἀπὸ τῶν οὐρανῶν ἐπισκοπήν.
[9] In Euseb. *H. E.* v. 24. See *Galatians* p. 362 note.

date from the time of his birth and not of his conversion or baptism, he must have been born scarcely a quarter of a century after the death of the last surviving Apostle, whose latest years were spent in the very Church over which Polycrates himself presided. It appears moreover from his language that none of these relations to whom he refers were surviving when he wrote.

Thus the evidence for the early and wide extension of episcopacy throughout proconsular Asia, the scene of St John's latest labours, may be considered irrefragable. And when we pass to other districts of Asia Minor, examples are not wanting, though these are neither so early nor so frequent. Marcion a native of Sinope is related to have been the son of a Christian bishop[1]: and Marcion himself had elaborated his theological system before the middle of the second century. Again, a bishop of Eumenia, Thraseas by name, is stated by Polycrates to have been martyred and buried at Smyrna[2]; and, as he is mentioned in connexion with Polycarp, it may fairly be supposed that the two suffered in the same persecution. Dionysius of Corinth moreover, writing to Amastris and the other churches of Pontus (about A.D. 170), mentions Palmas the bishop of this city[3]: and when the Paschal controversy breaks out afresh under Victor of Rome, we find this same Palmas putting his signature first to a circular letter, as the senior of the bishops of Pontus[4]. An anonymous writer also, who took part in the Montanist controversy, speaks of two bishops of repute, Zoticus of Comana and Julianus of Apamea, as having resisted the impostures of the false prophetesses[5]. But indeed the frequent notices of encyclical letters written and synods held towards the close of the second century are a much more powerful testimony to the wide extension of episcopacy throughout the provinces of Asia Minor than the incidental mention of individual names. On one such occasion Polycrates speaks of the 'crowds' of bishops whom he had summoned to confer with him on the Paschal question[6].

5. As we turn from Asia Minor to MACEDONIA and GREECE, the evidence becomes fainter and scantier. This circumstance is no

*Marginal notes:* Bishops in other parts of Asia Minor. Episcopal synods. MACEDONIA and GREECE.

---

[1] [Tertull.] *adv. omn. hæres.* 6.
[2] In Euseb. *H. E.* v. 24.
[3] In Euseb. *H. E.* iv. 23.
[4] Euseb. *H. E.* v. 23.
[5] In Euseb. *H. E.* v. 16. As Ap-

amea on the Mæander is mentioned at the end of the chapter, probably this is the place meant.
[6] In Euseb. *H. E.* v. 24 πολλὰ πλήθη.

doubt due partly to the fact that these churches were much less active and important during the second century than the Christian communities of Asia Minor, but the phenomena cannot perhaps be wholly explained by this consideration. When Tertullian in one of his rhetorical flights challenges the heretical teachers to consult the apostolic churches, where 'the very sees of the Apostles still preside,' adding, 'If Achaia is nearest to you, then you have Corinth ; if you are not far from Macedonia, you have Philippi, you have the Thessalonians ; if you can reach Asia, you have Ephesus[1]': his main argument was doubtless just, and even the language would commend itself to its own age, for episcopacy was the only form of government known or remembered in the church when he wrote : but a careful investigation scarcely allows, and certainly does not encourage us, to place Corinth and Philippi and Thessalonica in the same category with Ephesus as regards episcopacy. The term 'apostolic see' was appropriate to the latter ; but so far as we know, it cannot be strictly applied to the former. During the early years of the second century, when episcopacy was firmly established in the principal churches of Asia Minor, Polycarp sends a letter to the Philippians. He writes in the name of himself and his presbyters ; he gives advice to the Philippians respecting the obligations and the authority of presbyters and deacons ; he is minute in his instructions respecting one individual presbyter, Valens by name, who had been guilty of some crime ; but throughout the letter he never once refers to their bishop ; and indeed its whole tone is hardly consistent with the supposition that they had any chief officer holding the same prominent position at Philippi which he himself held at Smyrna. We are thus led to the inference that episcopacy did not exist at all among the Philippians at this time, or existed only in an elementary form, so that the bishop was a mere president of the presbyteral council. At Thessalonica indeed, according to a tradition mentioned by Origen[2], the same Caius whom St Paul describes as his host at Corinth was afterwards appointed bishop ; but with so common a name the possibilities of error are great, even if the testimony were earlier in date and expressed in more distinct terms. When from Macedonia we pass to Achaia, the same phenomena present

*Later development of episcopacy.*

*Philippi.*

*Thessalonica.*

[1] Tertull. *de Præscr.* 37.

[2] On Rom. xvi. 23 ; 'Fertur sane

traditione majorum ' (IV. p. 86, ed. Delarue).

themselves. At the close of the first century Clement writes to Corinth, as at the beginning of the second century Polycarp writes to Philippi. As in the latter epistle, so in the former, there is no allusion to the episcopal office : yet the main subject of Clement's letter is the expulsion and ill treatment of certain presbyters, whose authority he maintains as holding an office instituted by and handed down from the Apostles themselves. If Corinth however was without a bishop in the strict sense at the close of the first century, she cannot long have remained so. When some fifty years later Hegesippus stayed here on his way to Rome, Primus was bishop of this Church; and it is clear moreover from this writer's language that Primus had been preceded by several occupants of the see[1]. Indeed the order of his narrative, so far as we can piece it together from the broken fragments preserved in Eusebius, might suggest the inference, not at all improbable in itself, that episcopacy had been established at Corinth as a corrective of the dissensions and feuds which had called forth Clement's letter[2]. Again Dionysius, one of the immediate successors of Primus, was the writer of several letters of which fragments are extant[3]; and at the close of the century we meet with a later bishop of Corinth, Bacchyllus, who takes an active part in the Paschal controversy[4]. When from Corinth we pass on to Athens, a very early instance of a bishop confronts us, on authority which seems at first sight good. Eusebius represents Dionysius of Corinth, who wrote apparently about the year 170, as stating that his namesake the Areopagite, 'having been brought to the faith by the Apostle Paul according to the account in the Acts, was the first to be entrusted with the bishopric (or supervision) of the diocese (in the language of those times, the parish) of the Athenians[5].' Now, if we could be sure that Eusebius was

---

[1] In Euseb. *H. E.* iv. 22, καὶ ἐπέμενεν ἡ ἐκκλησία ἡ Κορινθίων ἐν τῷ ὀρθῷ λόγῳ μέχρι Πρίμου ἐπισκοπεύοντος ἐν Κορίνθῳ κ.τ.λ. A little later he speaks of ἑκάστη διαδοχή, referring apparently to Corinth among other churches.

[2] Hegesippus mentioned the feuds in the Church of Corinth during the reign of Domitian, which had occasioned the writing of this letter (*H. E.* iii. 16); and then after some account of Clement's epistle (μετά τινα περὶ τῆς Κλή-

μεντος πρὸς Κορινθίους ἐπιστολῆς αὐτῷ εἰρημένα, *H. E.* iv. 22) he continued in the words which are quoted in the last note (ἐπιλέγοντος ταῦτα, Καὶ ἐπέμενεν ἡ ἐκκλησία κ.τ.λ.). On the probable tenor of Hegesippus' work see below, p. 220.

[3] The fragments of Dionysius are found in Euseb. *H. E.* iv. 23. See also Routh *Rel. Sacr.* 1. p. 177 sq.

[4] Euseb. *H. E.* v. 22, 23.

[5] In Euseb. *H. E.* iv. 23.

here reporting the exact words of Dionysius, the testimony though not conclusive would be entitled to great deference. In this case the easiest solution would be, that this ancient writer had not unnaturally confounded the earlier and later usage of the word bishop. But it seems not improbable that Eusebius (for he does not profess to be giving a direct quotation) has unintentionally paraphrased and interpreted the statement of Dionysius by the light of later ecclesiastical usages. However Athens, like Corinth, did not long remain without a bishop. The same Dionysius, writing to the Athenians, reminds them how, after the martyrdom of Publius their ruler (τὸν προεστῶτα), Quadratus becoming bishop sustained the courage and stimulated the faith of the Athenian brotherhood[1]. If, as seems more probable than not, this was the famous Quadratus who presented his apology to Hadrian during that emperor's visit to Athens, the existence of episcopacy in this city is thrown back early in the century; even though Quadratus were not already bishop when Hadrian paid his visit.

6. The same writer, from whom we learn these particulars about episcopacy at Athens, also furnishes information on the Church in CRETE. He writes letters to two different communities in this island, the one to Gortyna commending Philip who held this see, the other to the Cnossians offering words of advice to their bishop Pinytus[1]. The first was author of a treatise against Marcion[2]: the latter wrote a reply to Dionysius, of which Eusebius has preserved a brief notice[3].

7. Of episcopacy in THRACE, and indeed of the Thracian Church generally, we read nothing till the close of the second century, when one Ælius Publius Julius bishop of Debeltum, a colony in this province, signs an encyclical letter[3]. The existence of a see at a place so unimportant implies the wide spread of episcopacy in these regions.

8. As we turn to ROME, we are confronted by a far more perplexing problem than any encountered hitherto. The attempt to decipher the early history of episcopacy here seems almost hopeless, where the evidence is at once scanty and conflicting. It has been

CRETE. THRACE. ROME.

[1] Euseb. H. E. iv. 23.
[2] Euseb. H. E. iv. 25.
[3] Euseb. H. E. v. 19. The combination of three gentile names in 'Ælius Publius Julius' is possible at this late epoch; but, being a gross violation of Roman usage, suggests the suspicion that the signatures of three distinct persons have got confused. The error however, if error it be, does not affect the inference in the text.

The prevailing spirit not monarchical. often assumed that in the metropolis of the world, the seat of imperial rule, the spirit which dominated in the State must by natural predisposition and sympathy have infused itself into the Church also, so that a monarchical form of government would be developed more rapidly here than in other parts of Christendom. This supposition seems to overlook the fact that the influences which prevailed in the early church of the metropolis were more Greek than Roman[1], and that therefore the tendency would be rather towards individual liberty than towards compact and rigorous government. But indeed such presumptions, however attractive and specious, are valueless against the slightest evidence of facts. And the most trustworthy sources of information which we possess do not countenance the idea.

Bearing of Clement's epistle. The earliest authentic document bearing on the subject is the Epistle from the Romans to the Corinthians, probably written in the last decade of the first century. I have already considered the bearing of this letter on episcopacy in the Church of Corinth, and it is now time to ask what light it throws on the same institution at Rome. Now we cannot hesitate to accept the universal testimony of antiquity that it was written by Clement, the reputed bishop of Rome : and it is therefore the more surprising that, if he held this high office, the writer should not only not distinguish himself in any way from the rest of the church (as Polycarp does for instance), but that even his name should be suppressed[2]. It is still more important to observe that, though he has occasion to speak of the ministry as an institution of the Apostles, he mentions only two orders and is silent about the episcopal office. Moreover he still uses the word 'bishop' in the older sense in which it occurs in the apostolic writings, as a synonyme for presbyter[3], and it may be argued that the recognition of the episcopate as a higher and distinct office would oblige the adoption of a special name and therefore must have synchronized roughly with the separation of meaning between 'bishop' and 'presbyter.' Again not many years after the date of Clement's

Testimony of Ignatius letter, St Ignatius on his way to martyrdom writes to the Romans. Though this saint is the recognised champion of episcopacy, though the remaining six of the Ignatian letters all contain direct injunctions of obedience to bishops, in this epistle alone there is no allu-

---

[1] See above, p. 20 sq.    [2] See *S. Clement of Rome* p. 252 sq. *Appendix.*
[3] See above, p. 96 sq.

sion to the episcopal office as existing among his correspondents. The lapse of a few years carries us from the letters of Ignatius to the and Shepherd of Hermas. And here the indications are equivocal. Hermas receives directions in a vision to impart the revelation to the presbyters and also to make two copies, the one for Clement who shall communicate with the foreign churches (such being his duty), the other for Grapte who shall instruct the widows. Hermas himself is charged to 'read it to this city with the elders who preside over the church¹.' Elsewhere mention is made of the 'rulers' of the church².

And again, in an enumeration of the faithful officers of the churches past and present, he speaks of the 'apostles and bishops and teachers and deacons³.' Here most probably the word 'bishop' is used in its later sense, and the presbyters are designated by the term 'teachers.' Yet this interpretation cannot be regarded as certain, for the 'bishops and teachers' in Hermas, like the 'pastors and teachers' in St Paul, might possibly refer to the one presbyteral office in its twofold aspect. Other passages in which Hermas uses the same terms are indecisive. Thus he speaks of 'apostles and teachers who preached to the whole world and taught with reverence and purity the word of the Lord⁴'; of 'deacons who exercised their diaconate ill and plundered the life (τὴν ζωήν) of widows and orphans⁵'; of 'hospitable bishops who at all times received the servants of God into their homes cheerfully and without hypocrisy,' 'who protected the bereaved and the widows in their ministrations without ceasing⁶.' From these passages it seems impossible to arrive at a safe conclusion respecting the ministry at the time when Hermas wrote. In other places he condemns the false prophet 'who, seeming to have the Spirit, exalts himself and would fain have the first seat⁷'; or he warns 'those who rule over the church and those who hold the chief-seat,' bidding them give up their dissensions and live at peace among themselves⁸; or he de-

---

¹ *Vis.* ii. + γράψεις οὖν δύο βιβλιδάρια ‧ καὶ πέμψεις ἐν Κλήμεντι καὶ ἐν Γραπτῇ. πέμψει οὖν Κλήμης εἰς τὰς ἔξω πόλεις‧ ἐκείνῳ γὰρ ἐπιτέτραπται‧ Γραπτὴ δὲ νουθετήσει τὰς χήρας καὶ τοὺς ὀρφανούς‧ σὺ δὲ ἀναγνώσεις εἰς ταύτην τὴν πόλιν μετὰ τῶν πρεσβυτέρων τῶν προϊσταμένων τῆς ἐκκλησίας.

² *Vis.* ii. 2, iii. 9.

³ *Vis.* iii. 5.

⁴ *Sim.* ix. 25.

⁵ *Sim.* ix. 26.

⁶ *Sim.* ix. 27.

⁷ *Mand.* xi.

⁸ *Vis.* iii. 9 ὑμῖν λέγω τοῖς προηγουμένοις τῆς ἐκκλησίας καὶ τοῖς πρωτοκαθεδρίταις, κ.τ.λ. For the form πρωτοκαθεδρίτης see the note on συνδιδασκαλίταις, Ignat. *Ephes.* 3.

220   THE CHRISTIAN MINISTRY.

**Unwar-
ranted
inference.**

nounces those who have 'emulation one with another for the first place or for some honour[1].' If we could accept the suggestion that in this last class of passages the writer condemns the ambition which aimed at transforming the presbyterian into the episcopal form of government[2], we should have arrived at a solution of the difficulty : but the rebukes are couched in the most general terms and apply at least as well to the ambitious pursuit of existing offices as to the arrogant assertion of a hitherto unrecognized power[3]. This clue failing us, the notices in the Shepherd are in themselves too vague to lead to any result. Were it not known that the writer's own brother was bishop of Rome, we should be at a loss what to say about the constitution of the Roman Church in his day[4].

But while the testimony of these early writers appears at first sight and on the whole unfavourable to the existence of episcopacy in Rome when they wrote, the impression needs to be corrected by important considerations on the other side. Hegesippus, who visited Rome about the middle of the second century during the papacy of Anicetus, has left it on record that he drew up a list of the Roman bishops to his own time[5]. As the list is not preserved, we can only conjecture its contents; but if we may judge from the sentence immediately following, in which he praises the orthodoxy of this and other churches under each succession, his object was probably to show that the teachings of the Apostles had been carefully preserved and handed down, and he would therefore trace the episcopal succession back to apostolic times[6]. Such at all events is the aim and method of Irenæus who, writing somewhat later than Hegesippus and combating Gnostic heresies, appeals especially to the bishops of Rome, as depositaries of the apostolic tradition[7]. The list of Irenæus commences

**Testimony of Hege-sippus**

**and of Ire-næus.**

---

[1] *Sim.* viii. 7.

[2] So Ritschl pp. 403, 535.

[3] Comp. Matt. xxiii. 6, etc. When Irenæus wrote, episcopacy was certainly a venerable institution: yet his language closely resembles the reproachful expressions of Hermas: 'Contumeliis agunt reliquos et principalis consessionis (MSS concessionis) tumore elati sunt' (iv. 26. 3).

[4] See above, p. 168, note 9, and *S. Clement of Rome* p. 316, *Appendix.*

[5] In Euseb. *H. E.* iv. 22.

[6] The words of Hegesippus ἐν ἑκάστῃ διαδοχῇ καὶ ἐν ἑκάστῃ πόλει κ.τ.λ. have a parallel in those of Irenæus (iii. 3. 3) τῇ αὐτῇ τάξει καὶ τῇ αὐτῇ διδαχῇ (Lat. 'hac ordinatione et successione') ἥ τε ἀπὸ τῶν ἀποστόλων ἐν τῇ ἐκκλησίᾳ παράδοσις καὶ τὸ τῆς ἀληθείας κήρυγμα κατήντηκεν εἰς ἡμᾶς. May not Irenæus have derived his information from the διαδοχή of Roman bishops which Hegesippus drew up? See below, p. 240.

[7] Iren. iii. 3. 3.

with Linus, whom he identifies with the person of this name men- Lists of<br>Roman<br>bishops.
tioned by St Paul, and whom he states to have been 'entrusted with
the office of the bishopric' by the Apostles. The second in succession
is Anencletus of whom he relates nothing, the third Clemens whom
he describes as a hearer of the Apostles and as writer of the letter to
the Corinthians. The others in order are Evarestus, Alexander,
Xystus, Telesphorus, Hyginus, Pius, Anicetus, Soter, and Eleutherus during whose episcopacy Irenæus writes. Eusebius in different
works gives two lists, both agreeing in the order with Irenæus,
though not according with each other in the dates. Catalogues are
also found in writers later than Irenæus, transposing the sequence of
the earliest bishops, and adding the name Cletus or substituting it
for Anencletus[1]. These discrepancies may be explained by assuming
two distinct churches in Rome—a Jewish and a Gentile community
—in the first age ; or they may have arisen from a confusion of the
earlier and later senses of ἐπίσκοπος ; or the names may have been
transposed in the later lists owing to the influence of the *Clementine
Homilies,* in which romance Clement is represented as the immediate
disciple and successor of St Peter[2]. With the many possibilities of Linus,
error, no more can safely be assumed of LINUS and ANENCLETUS than A. D. 68.<br>Anencle-
that they held some prominent position in the Roman Church. But tus,
the reason for supposing CLEMENT to have been a bishop is as strong A. D. 80.<br>Clement,
as the universal tradition of the next ages can make it. Yet, while A. D. 92.
calling him a bishop, we need not suppose him to have attained the
same distinct isolated position of authority which was occupied by
his successors Eleutherus and Victor for instance at the close of the
second century, or even by his contemporaries Ignatius of Antioch
and Polycarp of Smyrna. He was rather the chief of the presbyters
than the chief over the presbyters. Only when thus limited, can the
episcopacy of St Clement be reconciled with the language of his own

[1] On this subject see Pearson's *Dis-
sertationes duæ de serie et successione
primorum Romæ episcoporum* in his
*Minor Theological Works* II. p. 296 sq.
(ed. Churton), and especially the recent
work of Lipsius *Chronologie der römischen Bischöfe,* Kiel 1869. The earliest
list which places Clement's name first
belongs to the age of Hippolytus. The
omission of his name in a recently
discovered Syriac list (*Ancient Syriac

Documents* p. 71) is doubtless due to
the fact that the names Cletus, Clemens, begin with the same letters. In
the margin I have for convenience
given the dates of the Roman bishops
from the Ecclesiastical History of Eusebius, without however attaching any
weight to them in the case of the
earlier names. See above, p. 169.
[2] See *Galatians* p. 329.

epistle or with the notice in his younger contemporary Hermas. At
the same time the allusion in the Shepherd, though inconsistent with
any exalted conception of his office, does assign to him as his special
province the duty of communicating with foreign churches[1], which in
the early ages was essentially the bishop's function, as may be seen
by the instances of Polycarp, of Dionysius, of Irenæus, and of Poly-

Evarestus, crates. Of the two succeeding bishops, EVARESTUS and ALEXANDER,
A.D. 100. no authentic notices are preserved. XYSTUS, who follows, is the re-
Alexander,
A.D. 109. puted author of a collection of proverbs, which a recent distinguished
Xystus,
A.D. 119. critic has not hesitated to accept as genuine[2]. He is also the earliest
of those Roman prelates whom Irenæus, writing to Victor in the
name of the Gallican Churches, mentions as having observed Easter
after the western reckoning and yet maintained peace with those
Telespho- who kept it otherwise[3]. The next two, TELESPHORUS and HYGINUS,
rus,
A.D. 128. are described in the same terms. The former is likewise distin-
Hyginus, guished as the sole martyr among the early bishops of the metro-
A.D. 139. polis[4]; the latter is mentioned as being in office when the peace of
the Roman Church was disturbed by the presence of the heretics
Pius, Valentinus and Cerdon[5]. With PIUS, the next in order, the office,
A.D. 142. if not the man, emerges into daylight. An anonymous writer, treating on the canon of Scripture, says that the Shepherd was written
by Hermas 'quite lately while his brother Pius held the see of the
Church of Rome[6].' This passage, written by a contemporary, be-
sides the testimony which it bears to the date and authorship of the
Shepherd (with which we are not here concerned), is valuable in its
bearing on this investigation ; for the use of the 'chair' or 'see' as
a recognised phrase points to a more or less prolonged existence
of episcopacy in Rome, when this writer lived. To Pius succeeds
Anicetus, ANICETUS. And now Rome becomes for the moment the centre of
A.D. 157. interest and activity in the Christian world[7]. During this episcopate
Hegesippus, visiting the metropolis for the purpose of ascertaining

---

[1] See above, p. 219, note 1
[2] Ewald, Gesch. des V. I. VII. p. 321
sq. On the other hand see Zeller
Philos. der Griechen III. 1. p. 601 note,
and Sänger in the Jüdische Zeitschrift
(1867) p. 29 sq. It has recently been
edited by Gildemeister, Sexti Senten-
tiæ, 1873.
[3] Iren. in Euseb. H. E. v. 24.

[4] Iren. iii. 3. 3. At least Irenæus
mentions him alone as a martyr. Later
stories confer the glory of martyrdom
on others also.
[5] Iren. iii. 4. 3.
[6] See above, p. 168, note 9, where the
passage is quoted.
[7] See Westcott Canon p. 191, ed. 4.

and recording the doctrines of the Roman Church, is welcomed by the bishop[1]. About the same time also another more illustrious visitor, Polycarp the venerable bishop of Smyrna, arrives in Rome to confer with the head of the Roman Church on the Paschal dispute[2] and there falls in with and denounces the heretic Marcion[3]. These facts are stated on contemporary authority. Of SOTER also, the next in succession, a contemporary record is preserved. Dionysius of Corinth, writing to the Romans, praises the zeal of their bishop, who in his fatherly care for the suffering poor and for the prisoners working in the mines had maintained and extended the hereditary fame of his church for zeal in all charitable and good works[4]. In ELEUTHERUS, who succeeds Soter, we have the earliest recorded instance of an archdeacon. When Hegesippus paid his visit to the metropolis, he found Eleutherus standing in this relation to the bishop Anicetus, and seems to have made his acquaintance while acting in this capacity[5]. Eleutherus however was a contemporary, not only of Hegesippus, but also of the great writers Irenæus and Tertullian[6], who speak of the episcopal succession in the churches generally, and in Rome especially, as the best safeguard for the transmission of the true faith from apostolic times[7]. With VICTOR, the successor of Eleutherus, a new era begins. Apparently the first Latin prelate who held the metropolitan see of Latin Christendom[8], he was moreover the first Roman bishop who is known to have had intimate

Soter,
A. D. 168.

Eleutherus,
A. D. 177.

Victor,
A. D. 189.

---

[1] Hegesipp. in Euseb. *H. E.* iv. 22.

[2] Iren. in Euseb. *H. E.* v. 24.

[3] Iren. iii. 3. 4; comp. iii. 4. 4.

[4] In Euseb. *H. E.* iv. 23.

[5] In Euseb. *H. E.* iv. 22 μέχρις Ἀνικήτου οὗ διάκονος ἦν Ἐλεύθερος.

[6] He is mentioned by Irenæus iii. 3. 3 νῦν δωδεκάτῳ τόπῳ τὸν τῆς ἐπισκοπῆς ἀπὸ τῶν ἀποστόλων κατέχει κλῆρον Ἐλεύθερος, and by Tertullian, *Præscr.* 30 'sub episcopatu Eleutheri benedicti.'

[7] Iren. iii. 3. 2, Tertull. *de Præscr.* 32, 36, *adv. Marc.* iv. 5.

[8] All the predecessors of Victor bear Greek names with two exceptions, Clemens and Pius; and even these appear not to have been Latin. Clement writes in Greek, and his style is wholly unlike what might be expected from a Roman. Hermas, the brother of Pius, not only employs the Greek language

in writing, but bears a Greek name also. It is worth observing also that Tertullian (*de Præscr.* 30), speaking of the episcopate of Eleutherus, designates the church of the metropolis not 'ecclesia Romana,' but 'ecclesia Romanensis,' i.e. not the Church *of* Rome, but the Church *in* Rome. The transition from a Greek to a Latin Church was of course gradual; but, if a definite epoch must be named, the episcopate of Victor serves better than any other. The two immediate successors of Victor, Zephyrinus (202—219) and Callistus (219—223), bear Greek names, and it may be inferred from the account in Hippolytus that they were Greeks; but from this time forward the Roman bishops, with scarcely an exception, seem to have been Latins.

relations with the imperial court[1], and the first also who advanced those claims to universal dominion which his successors in later ages have always consistently and often successfully maintained[2]. ' I hear,' writes Tertullian scornfully, 'that an edict has gone forth, aye and that a peremptory edict ; the chief pontiff, forsooth, I mean the bishop of bishops, has issued his commands[3].' At the end of the first century the Roman Church was swayed by the mild and peaceful counsels of the presbyter-bishop Clement ; the close of the second witnessed the autocratic pretensions of the haughty pope Victor, the prototype of a Hildebrand or an Innocent.

GAUL.

9. The Churches of GAUL were closely connected with and probably descended from the Churches of Asia Minor. If so, the episcopal form of government would probably be coeval with the foundation of Christian brotherhoods in this country. It is true we do not meet with any earlier bishop than the immediate predecessor of Irenæus at Lyons, the aged Pothinus, of whose martyrdom an account is given in the letter of the Gallican Churches[4]. But this is also the first distinct historical notice of any kind relating to Christianity in Gaul.

AFRICA.

10. AFRICA again was evangelized from Rome at a comparatively late date. Of the African Church before the close of the second century, when a flood of light is suddenly thrown upon it by the writings of Tertullian, we know absolutely nothing. But we need not doubt that this father represents the traditions and sentiments of his church, when he lays stress on episcopacy as an apostolic institution and on the episcopate as the depositary of pure Christian doctrine. If we may judge by the large number of prelates assembled in the African councils of a later generation, it would appear that the extension of the episcopate was far more rapid here than in most parts of Christendom[5].

---

[1] Hippol. *Hær.* ix. 12, pp. 287, 288.

[2] See the account of his attitude in the Paschal controversy, Euseb. *H. E.* v. 24.

[3] Tertull. *de Pudic.* 1. The bishop here mentioned will be either Victor or Zephyrinus; and the passage points to the assumption of extraordinary titles by the Roman bishops about this time. See also Cyprian in the opening of the *Concil. Carth.* p. 158 (ed. Fell) ' neque

enim quisquam nostrum episcopum se episcoporum constituit etc.,' doubtless in allusion to the arrogance of the Roman prelates.

[4] The Epistle of the Gallican Churches in Euseb. *H. E.* v. 1.

[5] At the African council convoked by Cyprian about 50 years later, the opinions of as many as 87 bishops are recorded ; and allusion is made in one of his letters (*Epist.* 59) to a council

11. The Church of ALEXANDRIA, on the other hand, was pro- ALEXAN-
bably founded in apostolic times[1]. Nor is there any reason to doubt DRIA.
the tradition which connects it with the name of St Mark, though the
authorities for the statement are comparatively recent. Nevertheless of its early history we have no authentic record. Eusebius
indeed gives a list of bishops beginning with St Mark, which here, as
in the case of the Roman see, is accompanied by dates[2]; but from
what source he derived his information, is unknown. The first contemporary notice of church officers in Alexandria is found in a
heathen writer. The emperor Hadrian, writing to the consul Servi- Hadrian's
anus, thus describes the state of religion in this city : ' I have become letter.
perfectly familiar with Egypt, which you praised to me ; it is fickle,
uncertain, blown about by every gust of rumour. Those who worship
Serapis are Christians, and those are devoted to Serapis who call
themselves bishops of Christ. There is no ruler of a synagogue there,
no Samaritan, no Christian presbyter, who is not an astrologer, a
soothsayer, a quack. The patriarch himself whenever he comes to
Egypt is compelled by some to worship Serapis, by others to worship
Christ[3].' In this letter, which seems to have been written in the

held before his time, when 90 bishops
assembled. For a list of the African
bishoprics at this time see Münter
*Primord. Eccl. Afric.* p. 31 sq. The
enormous number of African bishops a
few centuries later would seem incredible, were it not reported on the best
authority. Dupin (Optat. Milev. p. lix)
counts up as many as 690 African sees:
compare also the Notitia in Ruinart's
Victor Vitensis p. 117 sq., with the
notes p. 215 sq. These last references
I owe to Gibbon, c. xxxvii and c. xli.
[1] Independently of the tradition relating to St Mark, this may be inferred
from extant canonical and uncanonical
writings which appear to have emanated
from Alexandria. The Epistle to the
Hebrews, even if we may not ascribe
it to the learned Alexandrian Apollos
(Acts xviii. 24), at least bears obvious
marks of Alexandrian culture. The so-
called Epistle of Barnabas again, which
may have been written as early as the
reign of Vespasian and can hardly date
later than Nerva, must be referred to
the Alex. drian school of theology.

[2] Euseb. *H. E.* ii. 24, iii. 14, etc.
See Clinton's *Fasti Romani* ii. p. 544.
[3] Preserved in Vopiscus *Vit. Saturn.*
8. The Jewish patriarch (who resided
at Tiberias) is doubtless intended ; for
it would be no hardship to the Christian
bishop of Alexandria to be ' compelled
to worship Christ.' Otherwise the anachronism involved in such a title would
alone have sufficed to condemn the letter as spurious. Yet Salmasius, Casau-
bon, and the older commentators generally, agree in the supposition that the
bishop of Alexandria is styled patriarch
here. The manner in which the document is stated by Vopiscus to have
been preserved ('Hadriani epistolam ex
libris Phlegontis liberti ejus proditam ')
is favourable to its genuineness ; nor
does the mention of Verus as the emperor's 'son' in another part of the
letter present any real chronological
difficulty. Hadrian paid his visit to
Egypt in the autumn of 130, but the
letter is not stated to have been written
there. The date of the third consul-
ship of Servianus is A.D. 134, and the

year 134, Hadrian shows more knowledge of Jewish ecclesiastical
polity than of Christian : but, apparently without knowing the exact
value of terms, he seems to distinguish the bishop and the presbyter
in the Christian community[1]. From the age of Hadrian to the age
of Clement no contemporary or nearly contemporary notices are
found, bearing on the government of the Alexandrian Church. The
language of Clement is significant; he speaks sometimes of two
orders of the ministry, the presbyters and deacons[2]; sometimes of
three, the bishops, presbyters, and deacons[3]. Thus it would appear
that even as late as the close of the second century the bishop of
Alexandria was regarded as distinct and yet not distinct from the
presbytery[4]. And the language of Clement is further illustrated by
the fact, which will have to be considered at length presently, that
at Alexandria the bishop was nominated and apparently ordained by
the twelve presbyters out of their own number[5]. The episcopal
office in this Church during the second century gives no presage of
the world-wide influence to which under the prouder name of patriarchate it was destined in later ages to attain. The Alexandrian
succession, in which history is hitherto most interested, is not the
succession of the bishops but of the heads of the catechetical school.

Clement of
Alexan-
dria.

---

account of Spartianus (*Ver.* 3) easily
admits of the adoption of Verus before
or during this year, though Clinton
(*Fast. Rom.* I. p. 124) places it as late
as A.D. 135. Gregorovius (*Kaiser Hadrian* p. 71) suggests that 'filium meum'
may have been added by Phlegon or by
some one else. The prominence of the
Christians in this letter is not surprising,
when we remember how Hadrian interested himself in their tenets on another
occasion (at Athens). This document
is considered genuine by such opposite
authorities as Tillemont (*Hist. des Emp.*
II. p. 265) and Gregorovius (l. c. p. 41),
and may be accepted without hesitation.

[1] At this time there appears to have
been only one bishop in Egypt (see
below, p. 232). But Hadrian, who would
have heard of numerous bishops elsewhere, and perhaps had no very precise
knowledge of the Egyptian Church,
might well indulge in this rhetorical
flourish. At all events he seems to

mean different offices, when speaking
of the bishop and the presbyter.

[2] *Strom.* vii. 1 (p. 830, Potter) ὁμοίως
δὲ καὶ κατὰ τὴν ἐκκλησίαν, τὴν μὲν βελ-
τιωτικὴν οἱ πρεσβύτεροι σώζουσιν εἰκόνα,
τὴν ὑπηρετικὴν δὲ οἱ διάκονοι.

[3] *Strom.* vi. 13 (p. 793) αἱ ἐνταῦθα
κατὰ τὴν ἐκκλησίαν προκοπαί, ἐπισκόπων,
πρεσβυτέρων, διακόνων, μιμήματα οἶμαι
ἀγγελικῆς δόξης, *Strom.* iii. 12 (p. 552),
*Pæd.* iii. 12 (see the next note): see
Kaye's *Clement of Alexandria* p. 463 sq.

[4] Yet in one passage he, like Irenæus
(see above p. 98), betrays his ignorance
that in the language of the new Testament bishop and presbyter are synonymes ; see *Pæd.* iii. 12 (p. 309) μυρίαι
δὲ ὅσαι ὑποθῆκαι εἰς πρόσωπα ἐκλεκτὰ
διατείνουσαι ἐγγεγράφαται ταῖς βίβλοις
ταῖς ἁγίαις, αἱ μὲν πρεσβυτέροις αἱ
δὲ ἐπισκόποις αἱ δὲ διακόνοις, ἄλλαι
χήραις κ.τ.λ.

[5] See below, p. 231.

The first bishop of Alexandria, of whom any distinct incident is recorded on trustworthy authority, was a contemporary of Origen.

The notices thus collected[1] present a large body of evidence establishing the fact of the early and extensive adoption of episcopacy in the Christian Church. The investigation however would not be complete, unless attention were called to such indirect testimony as is furnished by the tacit assumptions of writers living towards and at the close of the second century. Episcopacy is so inseparably interwoven with all the traditions and beliefs of men like Irenæus and Tertullian, that they betray no knowledge of a time when it was not. Even Irenæus, the earlier of these, who was certainly born and probably had grown up before the middle of the century, seems to be wholly ignorant that the word bishop had passed from a lower to a higher value since the apostolic times[2]. Nor is it important only to observe the positive though indirect testimony which they afford. Their silence suggests a strong negative presumption, that while every other point of doctrine or practice was eagerly canvassed, the form of Church government alone scarcely came under discussion.

Inferences. The general prevalence of episcopacy.

But these notices, besides establishing the general prevalence of episcopacy, also throw considerable light on its origin. They indicate that the solution suggested by the history of the word 'bishop' and its transference from the lower to the higher office is the true solution, and that the episcopate was created out of the presbytery. They show that this creation was not so much an isolated act as a progressive development, not advancing everywhere at an uniform rate but exhibiting at one and the same time different stages of growth in different churches. They seem to hint also that, so far as this development was affected at all by national temper and characteristics, it was slower where the prevailing influences were more purely Greek, as at Corinth and Philippi and Rome, and more rapid where an oriental spirit predominated, as at Jerusalem and Antioch

Gradual and uneven development of the office.

---

[1] In this sketch of the episcopate in the different churches I have not thought it necessary to carry the lists later than the second century. Nor (except in a very few cases) has any testimony been accepted, unless the writer himself flourished before the close of this century. The Apostolic Constitutions would add several names to the list; but this evidence is not trustworthy, though in many cases the statements doubtless rested on some traditional basis.

[2] See above, p. 98. The same is true of Clement of Alexandria: see p. 226, note 4.

and Ephesus. Above all, they establish this result clearly, that its maturer forms are seen first in those regions where the latest surviving Apostles (more especially St John) fixed their abode, and at a time when its prevalence cannot be dissociated from their influence or their sanction.

Original relation of the two offices not forgotten.

The original relation of the bishop to the presbyter, which this investigation reveals, was not forgotten even after the lapse of centuries. Though set over the presbyters, he was still regarded as in some sense one of them. Irenæus indicates this position of the episcopate very clearly. In his language a presbyter is never designated a bishop, while on the other hand he very frequently speaks of a bishop as a presbyter. In other words, though he views the episcopate as a distinct office from the presbytery, he does not regard it as a distinct order in the same sense in which the diaconate is a distinct order. Thus, arguing against the heretics he says, 'But when again we appeal against them to that tradition which is derived from the Apostles, which is preserved in the churches by successions of *presbyters*, they place themselves in opposition to it, saying that they, being wiser not only than the *presbyters* but even than the Apostles, have discovered the genuine truth[1].' Yet just below, after again mentioning the apostolic tradition, he adds, 'We are able to enumerate those who have been appointed by the Apostles *bishops* in the churches and their successors down to our own time[2]'; and still further, after saying that it would take up too much space if he were to trace the succession in all the churches, he declares that he will confound his opponents by singling out the ancient and renowned Church of Rome founded by the Apostles Peter and Paul and will point out the tradition handed down to his own time 'by the succession of *bishops*,' after which he gives a list from Linus to Eleutherus[3]. So again in another passage he writes, 'Therefore obedience ought to be rendered to the *presbyters* who are in the churches, who have the succession from the Apostles as we have shown, who with the succession of the *episcopate* have also received the sure grace of truth according to the pleasure of the Father'; after which he mentions some 'who are believed by many to be *presbyters*, but serve their own lusts and are elated with the

A bishop still called a presbyter by Irenæus

---

[1] Iren. iii. 2. 2.
[2] Iren. iii. 3. 2, 3.

Iren. iii. 3. 1.

pomp of the *chief seat*,' and bids his readers shun these and seek
such as 'together with the rank of the *presbytery* show their speech
sound and their conversation void of offence,' adding of these
latter, 'Such *presbyters* the Church nurtures and rears, concerning
whom also the prophet saith, "I will give thy rulers in peace and
thy *bishops* in righteousness¹"'. Thus also writing to Victor of
Rome in the name of the Gallican churches, he says, 'It was not so
observed by the *presbyters* before Soter, who ruled the Church which
thou now guidest, we mean Anicetus and Pius, Hyginus and Telesphorus and Xystus².' And the same estimate of the office appears
in Clement of Alexandria : for, while he speaks elsewhere of the
three offices in the ministry, mentioning them by name, he in one
passage puts forward a twofold division, the presbyters whose duty
it is to *improve*, and the deacons whose duty it is to *serve*, the
Church³. The functions of the bishop and presbyter are thus regarded as substantially the same in kind, though different in degree,
while the functions of the diaconate are separate from both. More
than a century and a half later, this view is put forward with the
greatest distinctness by the most learned and most illustrious of
the Latin fathers. 'There is one ordination,' writes the commentator Hilary, ' of the bishop and the presbyter ; for either is a priest,
but the bishop is first. Every bishop is a presbyter, but every presbyter is not a bishop : for he is bishop who is first among the pres-
byters⁴.' The language of St Jerome to the same effect has been
quoted above⁵. To the passages there given may be added the following : 'This has been said to show that with the ancients presbyters were the same as bishops : but gradually all the responsibility

*and Cle-
ment of
Alexan-
dria.*

*Testimony
of Ambro-
siaster,*

*Jerome,*

---

¹ Iren. iv. 26. 2, 3, 4, 5.
² In Euseb. *H. E.* v. 24. In other
places Irenæus apparently uses πρεσβύτεροι to denote antiquity and not office,
as in the letter to Florinus, Euseb.
*H. E.* v. 20 οἱ πρὸ ἡμῶν πρεσβύτεροι
οἱ καὶ τοῖς ἀποστόλοις συμφοιτήσαντες
(comp. ii. 22. 5); in which sense the
word occurs also in Papias (Euseb. *H.E.*
iii. 39; see *Contemporary Review*, Aug.
1875, p. 379 sq.); but the passages quoted in the text are decisive, nor is there
any reason (as Rothe assumes, p. 414
sq.) why the usage of Irenæus should

throughout be uniform in this matter.
³ See the passage quoted above, p.
226, note 2. So also in the anecdote of
St John (*Quis div. salv.* 42, p. 959) we
read τῷ καθεστῶτι προσβλέψας ἐπισκόπῳ, but immediately afterwards ὁ
δὲ πρεσβύτερος ἀναλαβών κ.τ.λ., and
then again ἄγε δή, ἔφη, ὦ ἐπίσκοπε,
of the same person. Thus he too, like
Irenæus, regards the bishop as a presbyter, though the converse would not
be true.
⁴ Ambrosiast. on 1 Tim. iii. 10.
⁵ See p. 98.

was deferred to a single person, that the thickets of heresies might be rooted out. Therefore, as presbyters know that by *the custom of the Church* they are subject to him who shall have been set over them, so let bishops also be aware that they are superior to presbyters *more owing to custom than to any actual ordinance of the Lord*, etc. : Let us see therefore what sort of person ought to be ordained pres-

**and Augustine.** byter or bishop[1].' In the same spirit too the great Augustine writing to Jerome says, 'Although according to titles of honour which *the practice of the Church has now made valid*, the episcopate is greater than the presbytery, yet in many things Augustine is less than Jerome[2].' To these fathers this view seemed to be an obvious deduction from the identity of the terms 'bishop' and 'presbyter' in the apostolic writings; nor indeed, when they wrote, had usage

**Bishops styled themselves fellow-presbyters.** entirely effaced the original connexion between the two offices. Even in the fourth and fifth centuries, when the independence and power of the episcopate had reached its maximum, it was still customary for a bishop in writing to a presbyter to address him as 'fellow-presbyter[3],' thus bearing testimony to a substantial identity of order. Nor does it appear that this view was ever questioned until the era of the Reformation. In the western Church at all events it carried the sanction of the highest ecclesiastical authorities and was maintained even by popes and councils[4].

Nor was it only in the *language* of the later Church that the memory of this fact was preserved. Even in her practice indications might here and there be traced, which pointed to a time when

**The bishop of Alexandria chosen and** the bishop was still only the chief member of the presbytery. The case of the Alexandrian Church, which has already been mentioned casually, deserves special notice. St Jerome, after denouncing the audacity of certain persons who 'would give to deacons the prece-

---

[1] On Tit. i. 5 (VII. p. 696).

[2] *Epist.* lxxxii. 33 (II. p. 202, ed. Ben.).

[3] So for instance Cyprian, *Epist.* 14, writes 'compresbyteri nostri Donatus et Fortunatus'; and addressing Cornelius bishop of Rome (*Epist.* 45) he says 'cum ad me talia de te et compresbyteris tecum considentibus scripta venissent.' Compare also *Epist.* 44, 45, 71, 76. Augustine writes to Jerome in the same terms, and in fact this seems to have been the recognised form of ad-

dress. See the *Quæst. Vet. et Nov. Test.* ci (in Augustin. *Op.* III. P. 2, p. 93) 'Quid est enim episcopus nisi primus presbyter, hoc est summus sacerdos? Denique non aliter quam compresbyteros hic vocat et consacerdotes suos. Numquid et ministros condiaconos suos dicit episcopus?', where the writer is arguing against the arrogance of the Roman deacons. See above, p. 96.

[4] See the references collected by Gieseler I. p. 105 sq.

dence over presbyters, that is over bishops,' and alleging scriptural created by
proofs of the identity of the two, gives the following fact in illus- the pres-<br>bytery.
tration: 'At Alexandria, from Mark the Evangelist down to the
times of the bishops Heraclas (A.D. 233—249) and Dionysius (A.D.
249—265), the presbyters always nominated as bishop one chosen
out of their own body and placed in a higher grade : just as if an
army were to appoint a general, or deacons were to choose from
their own body one whom they knew to be diligent and call him
archdeacon'.' Though the direct statement of this father refers only
to the *appointment* of the bishop, still it may be inferred that the
function of the presbyters extended also to the *consecration*. And
this inference is borne out by other evidence. 'In Egypt,' writes
an older contemporary of St Jerome, the commentator Hilary, 'the
presbyters seal (i.e. ordain or consecrate), if the bishop be not present[2].' This however might refer only to the ordination of presbyters, and not to the consecration of a bishop. But even the latter
is supported by direct evidence, which though comparatively late
deserves consideration, inasmuch as it comes from one who was himself a patriarch of Alexandria. Eutychius, who held the patriarchal Testimony
see from A.D. 933 to A.D. 940, writes as follows : 'The Evangelist of Euty-<br>chius.
Mark appointed along with the patriarch Hananias twelve presbyters
who should remain with the patriarch, to the end that, when the
patriarchate was vacant, they might choose one of the twelve presbyters, on whose head the remaining eleven laying their hands should
bless him and create him patriarch.' The vacant place in the presbytery was then to be filled up, that the number twelve might be
constant[3]. 'This custom,' adds this writer, 'did not cease till the
time of Alexander (A.D. 313—326), patriarch of Alexandria. He
however forbad that henceforth the presbyters should create the
patriarch, and decreed that on the death of the patriarch the bishops

---

[1] *Epist.* cxlvi *ad Evang.* (I. p. 1082).
[2] Ambrosiast. on Ephes. iv. 12. So
too in the *Quæst. Vet. et Nov. Test.* ci
(falsely ascribed to St Augustine), August. *Op.* III. P. 2, p. 93, 'Nam in
Alexandria et per totam Ægyptum,
si desit episcopus, consecrat (v. l. con-
signat) presbyter.'
[3] Eutychii Patr. Alexandr. *Annales* I.
p. 331 (Pococke, Oxon. 1656). The in-

ferences in the text are resisted by Abra-
ham Ecchellensis *Eutychius vindicatus*
p. 22 sq. (in answer to Selden the translator of Eutychius), and by Le Quien
*Oriens Christianus* II. p. 342, who urge
all that can be said on the opposite side.
The authority of a writer so inaccurate
asEutychius,ifit had been unsupported,
would have had no weight; but, as we
have seen, this is not the case.

should meet to ordain the (new) patriarch, etc.[1]' It is clear from this passage that Eutychius considered the functions of nomination and ordination to rest with the same persons.

If this view however be correct, the practice of the Alexandrian Church was exceptional; for at this time the formal act of the bishop was considered generally necessary to give validity to ordination. Nor is the exception difficult to account for. At the close of the second century, when every considerable church in Europe and Asia appears to have had its bishop, the only representative of the episcopal order in Egypt was the bishop of Alexandria. It was Demetrius first (A.D. 190—233), as Eutychius informs us[2], who appointed three other bishops, to which number his successor Heraclas (A.D. 233—249) added twenty more. This extension of episcopacy to the provincial towns of Egypt paved the way for a change in the mode of appointing and ordaining the patriarch of Alexandria. But before this time it was a matter of convenience and almost of necessity that the Alexandrian presbyters should themselves ordain their chief.

Increase of the Egyptian episcopate.

Nor is it only in Alexandria that we meet with this peculiarity. Where the same urgent reason existed, the same exceptional practice seems to have been tolerated. A decree of the Council of Ancyra (A.D. 314) ordains that ' it be not allowed to country-bishops (χωρεπισκόποις) to ordain presbyters or deacons, nor even to city-presbyters, except permission be given in each parish by the bishop in writing[3].' Thus while restraining the existing license, the framers

Decree of the Council of Ancyra.

---

[1] Between Dionysius and Alexander four bishops of Alexandria intervene, Maximus (A.D. 265), Theonas (A.D. 283), Peter I (A.D. 301), and Achillas (A.D. 312). It will therefore be seen that there is a considerable discrepancy between the accounts of Jerome and Eutychius as to the time when the change was effected. But we may reasonably conjecture (with Ritschl, p. 432) that the transition from the old state of things to the new would be the result of a prolonged conflict between the Alexandrian presbytery who had hitherto held these functions, and the bishops of the recently created Egyptian sees to whom it was proposed to transfer them.

Somewhat later one Ischyras was

deprived of his orders by an Alexandrian synod, because he had been ordained by a presbyter only: Athan. *Apol. c. Arian.* 75 (I. p. 152). From this time at all events the Alexandrian Church insisted as strictly as any other on episcopal ordination.

[2] Eutych. *Ann.* l. c. p. 332. Heraclas, we are informed on the same authority (p. 335), was the first Alexandrian prelate who bore the title of patriarch; this designation being equivalent to metropolitan or bishop of bishops.

[3] *Concil. Ancyr.* can. 13 (Routh *Rel. Sacr.* IV. p. 121) χωρεπισκόποις μὴ ἐξεῖναι πρεσβυτέρους ἢ διακόνους χειροτονεῖν, ἀλλὰ [μὴν] μηδὲ πρεσβυτέροις πόλεως

of the decree still allow very considerable latitude. And it is especially important to observe that they lay more stress on episcopal sanction than on episcopal ordination. Provided that the former is secured, they are content to dispense with the latter.

As a general rule however, even those writers who maintain a substantial identity in the offices of the bishop and presbyter reserve the power of ordaining to the former[1]. This distinction in fact may be regarded as a settled maxim of Church polity in the fourth and later centuries. And when Aerius maintained the equality of the bishop and presbyter and denied the necessity of episcopal ordina- *Ordination confined to the bishops.*

---

χωρὶς τοῦ ἐπιτραπῆναι ὑπὸ τοῦ ἐπισκόπου μετὰ γραμμάτων ἐν ἑκάστῃ παροικίᾳ.
The various readings and interpretations of this canon will be found in Routh's note, p. 144 sq. Routh himself reads ἀλλὰ μὴν μηδὲ πρεσβυτέρους πόλεως, making πρεσβυτέρους πόλεως the object of χειροτονεῖν, but to this there is a twofold objection: (1) he necessarily understands the former πρεσβυτέρους to mean πρεσβυτέρους χώρας, though this is not expressed: (2) he interprets ἀλλὰ μὴν μηδὲ 'much less,' a sense which μηδέ seems to exclude and which is not borne out by his examples.

The name and office of the χωρεπί-σκοπος appear to be reliques of the time when ἐπίσκοπος and πρεσβύτερος were synonymes. While the large cities had their college of presbyters, for the villages a single πρεσβύτερος (or ἐπίσκοπος) would suffice; but from his isolated position he would be tempted, even if he were not obliged, to perform on his own responsibility certain acts which in the city would only be performed by the bishop properly so called, or at least would not be performed without his consent. Out of this position the office of the later χωρεπίσκοπος would gradually be developed; but the rate of progression would not be uniform, and the regulations affecting it would be determined by the circumstances of the particular locality. Hence, at a later date, it seems in some places to have been presbyteral, in others episcopal. In the Ancyran canon just quoted a

chorepiscopus is evidently placed below the city presbytery; but in other notices he occupies a higher position. For the conflicting accounts of the χωρεπίσκοπος see Bingham II. xiv.

Baur's account of the origin of the episcopate supposes that each Christian congregation was presided over, not by a college of presbyters, but by a single πρεσβύτερος or ἐπίσκοπος, i.e. that the constitution of the Church was from the first monarchical: see *Pastoralbriefe* p. 81 sq., *Ursprung des Episcopats* p. 84 sq. This view is inconsistent alike with the analogy of the synagogue and with the notices in the apostolic and early ecclesiastical writings. But the practice which he considers to have been the general rule would probably hold in small country congregations, where a college of presbyters would be unnecessary as well as impossible.

[1] St Jerome himself (*Epist.* cxlvi), in the context of the passage in which he maintains the identity of the two orders and alleges the tradition of the Alexandrian Church (see above, p. 231), adds, 'Quid enim facit *excepta ordinatione* episcopus quod presbyter non faciat?' So also *Const. Apost.* viii. 28 ἐπίσκοπος χειροθετεῖ χειροτονεῖ...πρεσβύ-τερος χειροθετεῖ οὐ χειροτονεῖ, Chrysost. *Hom.* xi on 1 Tim. iii. 8 τῇ χειροτονίᾳ μόνῃ ὑπερβεβήκασι καὶ τούτῳ μόνον δο-κοῦσι πλεονεκτεῖν πρεσβυτέρους. See Bingham II. iii. 5, 6, 7, for other references.

tion, his opinion was condemned as heretical, and is stigmatized as 'frantic' by Epiphanius[1].

It has been seen that the institution of an episcopate must be placed as far back as the closing years of the first century, and that it cannot, without violence to historical testimony, be dissevered from the name of St John.  But it has been seen also that the earliest bishops did not hold the same independent position of supremacy which was and is occupied by their later representatives.  It will therefore be instructive to trace the successive stages by which the power of the office was developed during the second and third centuries.  Though something must be attributed to the frailty of human pride and love of power, it will nevertheless appear that the pressing needs of the Church were mainly instrumental in bringing about the result, and that this development of the episcopal office was a providential safeguard amid the confusion of speculative opinion, the distracting effects of persecution, and the growing anarchy of social life, which threatened not only the extension but the very existence of the Church of Christ.  Ambition of office in a society where prominence of rank involved prominence of risk was at least no vulgar and selfish passion.

*Causes of the development of episcopacy.*

This development will be conveniently connected with three great names, each separated from the other by an interval of more than half a century, and each marking a distinct stage in its progress. Ignatius, Irenæus, and Cyprian, represent three successive advances towards the supremacy which was ultimately attained.

*Three names connected with its progress.*

1.  IGNATIUS of Antioch is commonly recognized as the staunchest advocate of episcopacy in the early ages.  Even, though we should refuse to accept as genuine any portions which are not contained in the Syriac Version[2], this view would nevertheless be amply justified.  Confining our attention for the moment to the Syriac letters we find that to this father the chief value of episcopacy lies in the fact that it constitutes a visible *centre of unity* in the con-

*1. Ignatius.*

*The Syriac Version.*

---

[1] *Hæres.* lxxv. 3; comp. Augustine *Hæres.* § 53. See Wordsworth *Theoph. Angl.* c. x.

[2] In the earlier editions of this work I assumed that the Syriac Version published by Cureton represented the Epistles of Ignatius in their original form.  I am now convinced that this is only an abridgment and that the shorter Greek form is genuine; but for the sake of argument I have kept the two apart in the text.  I hope before long to give reasons for this change of opinion in my edition of this father.

gregation. He seems in the development of the office to keep in view The bishop regarded as a centre of unity. the same purpose which we may suppose to have influenced the last surviving Apostles in its institution. The withdrawal of the autho-ritative preachers of the Gospel, the personal disciples of the Lord, had severed one bond of union. The destruction of the original abode of Christendom, the scene of the life and passion of the Saviour and of the earliest triumphs of the Church, had removed another. Thus de-prived at once of the personal and the local ties which had hitherto bound individual to individual and church to church, the Christian brotherhood was threatened with schism, disunion, dissolution. 'Vindicate thine office with all diligence,' writes Ignatius to the bishop of Smyrna, 'in things temporal as well as spiritual. Have a care of unity, than which nothing is better[1].' 'The crisis requires thee, as the pilot requires the winds or the storm-tossed mariner a haven, so as to attain unto God[2].' 'Let not those who seem to be plausible and teach falsehoods dismay thee; but stand thou firm as an anvil under the hammer: 'tis the part of a great athlete to be bruised and to conquer[3].' 'Let nothing be done without thy con-sent, and do thou nothing without the consent of God[4].' He adds directions also, that those who decide on a life of virginity shall dis-close their intention to the bishop only, and those who marry shall obtain his consent to their union, that 'their marriage may be accord-ing to the Lord and not according to lust[5].' And turning from the bishop to the people he adds, 'Give heed to your bishop, that God also may give heed to you. I give my life for those who are obedient to the bishop, to presbyters, to deacons. With them may I have my portion in the presence of God[6].' Writing to the Ephesians also he says that in receiving their bishop Onesimus he is receiving their whole body, and he charges them to love him, and one and all to be in his likeness[7], adding, 'Since love does not permit me to be silent, therefore I have been forward in exhorting you to conform to the will of God[8].'

From these passages it will be seen that St Ignatius values the episcopate chiefly as a security for good discipline and harmonious

---

[1] Polyc. 1.
[2] Polyc. 2.
[3] Polyc. 3.
[4] Polyc. 4.

[5] Polyc. 5.
[6] Polyc. 6.
[7] Ephes. 1.
[8] Ephes. 3.

The Greek
letters. working in the Church. And, when we pass from the Syriac letters to the Short Greek, the standing ground is still unchanged.
At the same time, though the point of view is unaltered, the Greek
letters contain far stronger expressions than are found in the
Syriac. Throughout the whole range of Christian literature, no
more uncompromising advocacy of the episcopate can be found
than appears in these writings. This championship indeed is
extended to the two lower orders of the ministry [1], more espe-
Their ex-  cially to the presbyters [2]. But it is when asserting the claims of the
travagant
exaltation  episcopal office to obedience and respect, that the language is strained
of the
episcopate.  to the utmost. 'The bishops established in the farthest parts of
the world are in the counsels of Jesus Christ [3].' 'Every one whom
the Master of the house sendeth to govern His own household we
ought to receive, as Him that sent him ; clearly therefore we ought
to regard the bishop as the Lord Himself [4].' Those 'live a life after
Christ,' who ' obey the bishop as Jesus Christ [5].' 'It is good to know
God and the bishop; he that honoureth the bishop is honoured of
God; he that doeth anything without the knowledge of the bishop
serveth the devil [6].' He that obeys his bishop, obeys 'not him, but
the Father of Jesus Christ, the Bishop of all.' On the other hand,
he that practises hypocrisy towards his bishop, 'not only deceiveth
the visible one, but cheateth the Unseen [7].' 'As many as are of God
and of Jesus Christ, are with the bishop [8].' Those are approved
who are 'inseparate [from God], from Jesus Christ, and from the
bishop, and from the ordinances of the Apostles [9].' 'Do ye all,' says
this writer again, 'follow the bishop, as Jesus Christ followed the
Father [10].' The Ephesians are commended accordingly, because they
are so united with their bishop 'as the Church with Jesus Christ
and as Jesus Christ with the Father.' 'If,' it is added, 'the prayer
of one or two hath so much power, how much more the prayer of the
bishop and of the whole Church [11].' 'Wherever the bishop may
appear, there let the multitude be, just as where Jesus Christ may

---

[1] *Magn.* 13, *Trall.* 3, 7, *Philad.* 4, 7,
*Smyrn.* 8, 12.
[2] *Ephes.* 2, 20, *Magn.* 2, 6, *Trall.* 13.
[3] *Ephes.* 3.
[4] *Ephes.* 6.
[5] *Trall.* 2.

[6] *Smyrn.* 9.
[7] *Magn.* 3.
[8] *Philad.* 3.
[9] *Trall.* 7.
[10] *Smyrn.* 8, comp. *Magn.* 7.
[11] *Ephes.* 5.

be, there is the universal Church[1].' Therefore 'let no man do anything pertaining to the Church without the bishop[2].' 'It is not allowable either to baptize or to hold a love-feast without the bishop: but whatsoever he may approve, this also is well pleasing to God, that everything which is done may be safe and valid[3].' 'Unity of God,' according to this writer, consists in harmonious co-operation with the bishop[4].

And yet with all this extravagant exaltation of the episcopal office, the presbyters are not put out of sight. They form a council[5], a 'worthy spiritual coronal[6]' round the bishop. It is the duty of every individual, but especially of them, 'to refresh the bishop unto the honour of the Father and of Jesus Christ and of the Apostles[7].' They stand in the same relation to him, 'as the chords to the lyre[8].' If the bishop occupies the place of God or of Jesus Christ, the presbyters are as the Apostles, as the council of God[9]. If obedience is due to the bishop as the grace of God, it is due to the presbytery as the law of Jesus Christ[10]. *The presbytery however not forgotten.*

It need hardly be remarked how subversive of the true spirit of Christianity, in the negation of individual freedom and the consequent suppression of direct responsibility to God in Christ, is the crushing despotism with which this language, if taken literally, would invest the episcopal office. It is more important to bear in mind the extenuating fact, that the needs and distractions of the age seemed to call for a greater concentration of authority in the episcopate; and we might well be surprised, if at a great crisis the defence of an all-important institution were expressed in words carefully weighed and guarded. *Considerations suggested by this language.*

Strangely enough, not many years after Ignatius thus asserted the claims of the episcopate as a safeguard of orthodoxy, another writer used the same instrument to advance a very different form of Chistianity. The organization, which is thus employed to consolidate and advance the Catholic Church, might *The same views advanced in the interests of Ebionism.*

---

[1] *Smyrn.* 8.

[2] *ib.*; comp. *Magn.* 4, *Philad.* 7.

[3] *Smyrn.* 8.

[4] *Polyc.* 8 ἐν ἑνότητι Θεοῦ καὶ ἐπισκόπου (v. l. ἐπισκοπῇ): comp. *Philad.* 3, 8.

[5] The word πρεσβυτέριον, which occurs 1 Tim. iv. 14, is very frequent in the Ignatian Epistles.

[6] *Magn.* 13.

[7] *Trall.* 12.

[8] *Ephes.* 4; comp. the metaphor in *Philad.* 1.

[9] *Trall.* 2, 3, *Magn.* 6, *Smyrn.* 8.

[10] *Magn.* 2.

serve equally well to establish a compact Ebionite community. I
have already mentioned the author of the Clementine Homilies as
a staunch advocate of episcopacy[1]. His view of the sanctions and
privileges of the office does not differ materially from that of
Ignatius. 'The multitude of the faithful,' he says, 'must obey
a single person, that so it may be able to continue in harmony.' Monarchy is a necessary condition of peace; this may be
seen from the aspect of the world around : at present there are many
kings, and the result is discord and war ; in the world to come God
has appointed one King only, that 'by reason of monarchy an inde-
structible peace may be established : therefore all ought to follow
some one person as guide, preferring him in honour as the image of
God ; and this guide must show the way that leadeth to the Holy
City[2].' Accordingly he delights to speak of the bishop as occupying
the place or the seat of Christ[3]. Every insult, he says, and every
honour offered to a bishop is carried to Christ and from Christ is
taken up to the presence of the Father ; and thus it is requited
manifold[4]. Similarly another writer of the Clementine cycle, if he
be not the same, compares Christ to the captain, the bishop to the
mate, and the presbyters to the sailors, while the lower orders and
the laity have each their proper place in the ship of the Church[5].

Monta-
nism, a
reaction
against
this extra-
vagance.
It is no surprise that such extravagant claims should not have
been allowed to pass unchallenged. In opposition to the lofty
hierarchical pretensions thus advanced on the one hand in the
Ignatian letters on behalf of Catholicism and on the other by
the Clementine writer in the interests of Ebionism, a strong spiritual-
ist reaction set in. If in its mental aspect the heresy of Montanus
must be regarded as a protest against the speculative subtleties
of Gnosticism, on its practical side it was equally a rebound from
the aggressive tyranny of hierarchical assumption. Montanus taught
that the true succession of the Spirit, the authorized channel of
Divine grace, must be sought not in the hierarchical but in the prophetic order. For a rigid outward system he substituted the free
inward impulse. Wildly fanatical as were its manifestations, this
reaction nevertheless issued from a true instinct which rebelled

[1] See above, p. 209.
[2] *Clem. Hom.* iii. 61, 62.
[3] ib. iii. 60, 66, 70.
[4] ib. iii. 66, 70.
[5] ib. Ep. Clem. 15.

against the oppressive yoke of external tradition and did battle for the freedom of the individual spirit. Montanus was excommunicated and Montanism died out; but though dead, it yet spake; for a portion of its better spirit was infused into the Catholic Church, which it leavened and refreshed and invigorated.

2. IRENÆUS followed Ignatius after an interval of about two generations. With the altered circumstances of the Church, the aspect of the episcopal office has also undergone a change. The religious atmosphere is now charged with heretical speculations of all kinds. Amidst the competition of rival teachers, all eagerly bidding for support, the perplexed believer asks for some decisive test by which he may try the claims of the disputants. To this question Irenæus supplies an answer. 'If you wish,' he argues, 'to ascertain the doctrine of the Apostles, apply to the Church of the Apostles. In the succession of bishops tracing their descent from the primitive age and appointed by the Apostles themselves, you have a guarantee for the transmission of the pure faith, which no isolated, upstart, self-constituted teacher can furnish. There is the Church of Rome for instance, whose episcopal pedigree is perfect in all its links, and whose earliest bishops, Linus and Clement, associated with the Apostles themselves: there is the Church of Smyrna again, whose bishop Polycarp, the disciple of St John, died only the other day [1].' Thus the episcopate is regarded now not so much as the *centre of ecclesiastical unity* but rather as the *depositary of apostolic tradition*.

*2. IRENÆUS.*

*The bishop the depositary of primitive truth.*

This view is not peculiar to Irenæus. It seems to have been advanced earlier by Hegesippus, for in a detached fragment he lays stress on the succession of the bishops at Rome and at Corinth, adding that in each church and in each succession the pure faith was preserved [2]; so that he seems here to be controverting that ' gnosis falsely so called' which elsewhere he denounces [3]. It is distinctly maintained by Tertullian, the younger contemporary of Irenæus, who refers, if not with the same frequency, at least with equal emphasis, to the tradition of the apostolic churches as preserved by the succession of the episcopate [4].

*The same view held by Hegesippus and Tertullian.*

---

[1] See especially iii. cc. 2, 3, 4, iv. 26. p. 220.
[2] sq., iv. 32. 1, v. præf., v. 20. 1, 2.   [3] Euseb. *H. E.* iii. 32.
[2] In Euseb. *H. E.* iv. 22. See above,   [4] Tertull. *de Præscr.* 32.

3. CY-
PRIAN.

3. As two generations intervened between Ignatius and Irenæus, so the same period roughly speaking separates Irenæus from
CYPRIAN. If with Ignatius the bishop is the centre of Christian
unity, if with Irenæus he is the depositary of the apostolic tradition,
with Cyprian he is the *absolute vicegerent of Christ* in things
spiritual. In mere strength of language indeed it would be difficult
to surpass Ignatius, who lived about a century and a half earlier
With the single exception of the sacerdotal view of the ministry which
had grown up meanwhile, Cyprian puts forward no assumption which
this father had not advanced either literally or substantially long
before. This one exception however is all important, for it raised
the sanctions of the episcopate to a higher level and put new force
into old titles of respect. Theoretically therefore it may be said
that Cyprian took his stand on the combination of the ecclesiastical authority as asserted by Ignatius with the sacerdotal claim
which had been developed in the half century just past. But
the real influence which he exercised in the elevation of the episcopate consisted not in the novelty of his theoretical views, but in his
practical energy and success. The absolute supremacy of the bishop
had remained hitherto a lofty title or at least a vague ill-defined
assumption: it became through his exertions a substantial and patent
and world-wide fact. The first prelate whose force of character
vibrated throughout the whole of Christendom, he was driven not
less by the circumstances of his position than by his own tempe-
rament and conviction to throw all his energy into this scale. And
the permanent result was much vaster than he could have anticipated beforehand or realized after the fact. Forced into the episcopate against his will, he raised it to a position of absolute independence, from which it has never since been deposed. The two
great controversies in which Cyprian engaged, though immediately
arising out of questions of discipline, combined from opposite sides
to consolidate and enhance the power of the bishops[1].

The first question of dispute concerned the treatment of such
as had lapsed during the recent persecution under Decius. Cyprian

*Margin notes:*

The bishop the vicegerent of Christ.

Influence of Cyprian on the epi-scopate.

First con-troversy.

---

[1] The influence of Cyprian on the
episcopate is ably stated in two vigorous articles by Kayser entitled *Cyprien
ou l'Autonomie de l'Épiscopat* in the
*Revue de Théologie* xv. pp. 138 sq., 242
sq. (1857). See also Rettberg *Thascius
Cäcilius Cyprianus* p. 367 sq., Huther
*Cyprian's Lehre von der Kirche* p. 59
sq. For Cyprian's work generally see
*Smith's Dict. of Christ. Biogr.* s. v.

found himself on this occasion doing battle for the episcopate against a twofold opposition, against the confessors who claimed the right of absolving and restoring these fallen brethren, and against his own presbyters who in the absence of their bishop supported the claims of the confessors. From his retirement he launched his shafts against this combined array, where an aristocracy of moral influence was leagued with an aristocracy of official position. With signal determination and courage in pursuing his aim, and with not less sagacity and address in discerning the means for carrying it out, Cyprian had on this occasion the further advantage, that he was defending the cause of order and right. He succeeded moreover in enlisting in his cause the rulers of the most powerful church in Christendom. The Roman clergy declared for the bishop and against the presbyters of Carthage. Of Cyprian's sincerity no reasonable question can be entertained. In maintaining the authority of his office he believed himself to be fighting his Master's battle, and he sought success as the only safeguard of the integrity of the Church of Christ. In this lofty and disinterested spirit, and with these advantages of position, he entered upon the contest.

*Treatment of the lapsed.*

It is unnecessary for my purpose to follow out the conflict in detail : to show how ultimately the positions of the two combatants were shifted, so that from maintaining discipline against the champions of too great laxity Cyprian found himself protecting the fallen against the advocates of too great severity ; to trace the progress of the schism and the attempt to establish a rival episcopate ; or to unravel the entanglements of the Novatian controversy and lay open the intricate relations between Rome and Carthage[1]. It is sufficient to say that Cyprian's victory was complete. He triumphed over the confessors, triumphed over his own presbyters, triumphed over the schismatic bishop and his party. It was the most signal success hitherto achieved for the episcopate, because the battle had been fought and the victory won on this definite issue. The absolute supremacy of the episcopal office was thus established against the two antagonists from which it had most to fear, against a recognised aris-

*Power of the bishop in his own church defined.*

---

[1] The intricacy of the whole proceeding is a strong evidence of the genuineness of the letters and other documents which contain the account of the controversy. The situations of the antago- nists, varying and even interchanged with the change of circumstances, are very natural, but very unlike the invention of a forger who has a distinct side to maintain.

tocracy of ecclesiastical office and an irregular but not less powerful aristocracy of moral weight.

The position of the bishop with respect to the individual church over which he ruled was thus defined by the first contest in which Cyprian engaged. The second conflict resulted in determining his relation to the Church universal. The schism which had grown up during the first conflict created the difficulty which gave occasion to the second. A question arose whether baptism by heretics and schismatics should be held valid or not. Stephen the Roman bishop, pleading the immemorial custom of his church, recognised its validity. Cyprian insisted on rebaptism in such cases. Hitherto the bishop of Carthage had acted in cordial harmony with Rome : but now there was a collision. Stephen, inheriting the haughty temper and aggressive policy of his earlier predecessor Victor, excommunicated those who differed from the Roman usage in this matter. These arrogant assumptions were directly met by Cyprian. He summoned first one and then another synod of African bishops, who declared in his favour. He had on his side also the churches of Asia Minor, which had been included in Stephen's edict of excommunication. Thus the bolt hurled by Stephen fell innocuous, and the churches of Africa and Asia retained their practice. The principle asserted in the struggle was not unimportant. As in the former conflict Cyprian had maintained the independent supremacy of the bishop over the officers and members of his own congregation, so now he contended successfully for his immunity from any interference from without. At a later period indeed Rome carried the victory, but the immediate result of this controversy was to establish the independence and enhance the power of the episcopate. Moreover this struggle had the further and not less important consequence of defining and exhibiting the relations of the episcopate to the Church in another way. As the individual bishop had been pronounced indispensable to the existence of the individual community, so the episcopal order was now put forward as the absolute indefeasible representative of the universal Church. Synods of bishops indeed had been held frequently before ; but under Cyprian's guidance they assumed a prominence which threw all existing precedents into the shade. A 'one undivided episcopate' was his watchword. The unity of the Church, he maintained, consists in the

*Second contro-versy. Re-baptism of heretics.*

*Relations of the bishops to the Universal Church defined.*

unanimity of the bishops[1]. In this controversy, as in the former, he acted throughout on the principle, distinctly asserted, that the existence of the episcopal office was not a matter of practical advantage or ecclesiastical rule or even of apostolic sanction, but an absolute incontrovertible decree of God. The triumph of Cyprian therefore was the triumph of this principle.

The greatness of Cyprian's influence on the episcopate is indeed due to this fact, that with him the statement of the principle precedes and necessitates the practical measures. Of the sharpness and distinctness of his sacerdotal views it will be time to speak presently; but of his conception of the episcopal office generally thus much may be said here, that he regards the bishop as exclusively the representative of God to the congregation and hardly, if at all, as the representative of the congregation before God. The bishop is the indispensable channel of divine grace, the indispensable bond of Christian brotherhood. The episcopate is not so much the roof as the foundation-stone of the ecclesiastical edifice; not so much the legitimate development as the primary condition of a church[2]. The bishop is appointed directly by God, is responsible directly to God, is inspired directly from God[3]. This last point deserves especial notice. Though in words he frequently defers to the established usage of consulting the presbyters and even the laity in the appointment of officers and in other matters affecting the well-being of the community, yet he only makes the concession to nullify it immediately. He pleads a direct official inspiration[4] which enables him

*Cyprian's view of the episcopate.*

[1] De Unit. Eccl. 2 'Quam unitatem firmiter tenere et vindicare debemus maxime episcopi qui in ecclesia praesidemus, ut episcopatum quoque ipsum unum atque indivisum probemus'; and again 'Episcopatus unus est, cujus a singulis in solidum pars tenetur: ecclesia quoque una est etc.' So again he argues (Epist. 43) that, as there is one Church, there must be only 'unum altare et unum sacerdotium (i.e. one episcopate)'. Comp. also Epist. 46, 55, 67.

[2] Epist. 66 'Scire debes episcopum in ecclesia esse et ecclesiam in episcopo, et si quis cum episcopo non sit, in ecclesia non esse'; Epist. 33 'Ut ecclesia super episcopos constituatur et omnis actus ecclesiae per eosdem praepositos

gubernetur.' Hence the expression 'nec episcopum nec ecclesiam cogitans,' Epist. 41; hence also 'honor episcopi' is associated not only with 'ecclesiae ratio' (Epist. 33) but even with 'timor dei' (Epist. 15). Compare also the language (Epist. 59) 'Nec ecclesia istic cuiquam clauditur nec episcopus alicui denegatur', and again (Epist. 43) 'Soli cum episcopis non sint, qui contra episcopos rebellarunt.'

[3] See esp. Epist. 3, 43, 55, 59, 73, and above all 66 (Ad Pupianum).

[4] Epist. 38 'Expectanda non sunt testimonia humana, cum praecedunt divina suffragia'; Epist. 39 'Non humana suffragatione sed divina dignatione conjunctum'; Epist. 40 'Ad-

to dispense with ecclesiastical custom and to act on his own responsibility. Though the presbyters may still have retained the shadow of a controlling power over the acts of the bishop, though the courtesy of language by which they were recognised as fellow-presbyters[1] was not laid aside, yet for all practical ends the independent supremacy of the episcopate was completely established by the principles and the measures of Cyprian.

The power of the bishops a question of practical convenience,

In the investigation just concluded I have endeavoured to trace the changes in the relative position of the first and second orders of the ministry, by which the power was gradually concentrated in the hands of the former. Such a development involves no new principle and must be regarded chiefly in its practical bearings. It is plainly competent for the Church at any given time to entrust a particular office with larger powers, as the emergency may require. And, though the grounds on which the independent authority of the episcopate was at times defended may have been false or exaggerated, no reasonable objection can be taken to later forms of ecclesiastical polity because the measure of power accorded to the bishop does not remain exactly the same as in the Church of the subapostolic ages. Nay, to many thoughtful and dispassionate minds even the gigantic power wielded by the popes during the middle ages will appear justifiable in itself (though they will repudiate the false pretensions on which it was founded, and the false opinions which were associated with it), since only by such a providential concentration of authority could the Church, humanly speaking, have

and unconnected with sacerdotalism.

braved the storms of those ages of anarchy and violence. Now however it is my purpose to investigate the origin and growth of a new principle, which is nowhere enunciated in the New Testament, but which notwithstanding has worked its way into general recognition and seriously modified the character of later Christianity. The progress of the *sacerdotal* view of the ministry is one of the most striking and important phenomena in the history of the Church.

No sacerdotalism in the New Testament.

It has been pointed out already that the sacerdotal functions and privileges, which alone are mentioned in the apostolic writings, pertain to all believers alike and do not refer solely or specially to the

monitos nos et instructos sciatis dignatione divina ut Numidicus presbyter adscribatur presbyterorum etc.
[1] See above p. 230, note 3.

ministerial office. If to this statement it be objected that the inference is built upon the *silence* of the Apostles and Evangelists, and that such reasoning is always precarious, the reply is that an exclusive sacerdotalism (as the word is commonly understood)[1] contradicts the general tenour of the Gospel. But indeed the strength or weakness of an argument drawn from silence depends wholly on the circumstance under which the silence is maintained. And in this case it cannot be considered devoid of weight. In the Pastoral Epistles for instance, which are largely occupied with questions relating to the Christian ministry, it seems scarcely possible that this aspect should have been overlooked, if it had any place in St Paul's teaching. The Apostle discusses at length the requirements, the responsibilities, the sanctions, of the ministerial office : he regards the presbyter as an example, as a teacher, as a philanthropist, as a ruler. How then, it may well be asked, are the sacerdotal functions, the sacerdotal privileges, of the office wholly set aside ? If these claims were recognised by him at all, they must necessarily have taken a foremost place. The same argument again applies with not less force to those passages in the Epistles to the Corinthians, where St Paul asserts his apostolic authority against his detractors. Nevertheless, so entirely had the primitive conception of the Christian Church been supplanted by this sacerdotal view of the ministry, before the northern races were converted to the Gospel, and the dialects derived from the Latin took the place of the ancient tongue, that the languages of modern Europe very generally supply only one word to represent alike the priest of the Jewish or heathen ceremonial and the presbyter of the Christian ministry[2].

*Its rapid spread at a later date.*

---

[1] In speaking of sacerdotalism, I assume the term to have essentially the same force as when applied to the Jewish priesthood. In a certain sense (to be considered hereafter) all officers appointed to minister 'for men in things pertaining to God' may be called priests; and sacerdotal phraseology, when first applied to the Christian ministry, may have borne this innocent meaning. But at a later date it was certainly so used as to imply a substantial identity of character with the Jewish priesthood, i.e. to designate the Christian minister as one who offers sacrifices and makes atonement for the sins of others.

[2] It is a significant fact that in those languages which have only one word to express the two ideas, this word etymologically represents 'presbyterus' and not 'sacerdos,' e.g. the French *prêtre*, the German *priester*, and the English *priest;* thus showing that the sacerdotal idea was imported and not original. In the Italian, where two words *prete* and *sacerdote* exist side by side, there is no marked difference in usage, except that *prete* is the more common. If the latter brings out the sacerdotal idea more prominently, the former is also applied

For, though no distinct traces of sacerdotalism are visible in the ages immediately after the Apostles, yet having once taken root in the Church it shot up rapidly into maturity. Towards the close of the second century we discern the first germs appearing above the surface : yet, shortly after the middle of the third, the plant has all but attained its full growth. The origin of this idea, the progress of its development, and the conditions favourable to its spread, will be considered in the present section of this essay.

Distinction of the clergy from the laity A separation of orders, it is true, appeared at a much earlier date, and was in some sense involved in the appointment of a special ministry. This, and not more than this, was originally contained in the distinction of clergy and laity. If the sacerdotal view of the ministry engrafted itself on this distinction, it nevertheless was not necessarily implied or even indirectly suggested thereby.

not derived from the Levitical priesthood. The term 'clerus,' as a designation of the ministerial office, did not owing to any existing associations convey the idea of sacerdotal functions. The word is not used of the Aaronic priesthood in any special sense which would explain its transference to the Christian ministry. It is indeed said of the Levites, that they have no 'clerus' in the land, the Lord Himself being their 'clerus'[1]. But the Jewish priesthood is never described conversely as the special ' clerus' of Jehovah : while on the other hand the metaphor thus inverted is more than once applied to the whole Israelite people[2]. Up to this point therefore the analogy of Old Testament usage would

to Jewish and Heathen priests and therefore distinctly involves this idea. Wiclif's version of the New Testament naturally conforms to the Vulgate, in which it seems to be the rule to translate πρεσβύτεροι by 'presbyteri' (in Wiclif 'preestes') where it obviously denotes the second order in the ministry (e.g. Acts xiv. 23, 1 Tim. v. 17, 19, Tit. i. 5, James v. 14), and by 'seniores' (in Wiclif 'eldres' or 'elder men') in other passages: but if so, this rule is not always successfully applied (e.g. Acts xi. 30, xxi. 18, 1 Pet. v. 1). A doubt about the meaning may explain the anomaly that the word is translated 'presbyteri,' 'preestes,' Acts xv. 2, and 'seniores,' 'elder men,' Acts xv. 4, 6, 22, xvi. 4; though the persons intended are the same. In Acts xx. 17, it is

rendered in Wiclif's version 'the grettist men of birthe,' a misunderstanding of the Vulgate 'majores natu.' The English versions of the reformers and the reformed Church from Tyndale downward translate πρεσβύτεροι uniformly by 'elders.'

[1] Deut. x. 9, xviii. 1, 2; comp. Num. xxvi. 62, Deut. xii. 12, xiv. 27, 29, Josh. xiv. 3. Jerome (Epist. lii. 5, 1. p. 258) says, 'Propterea vocantur clerici, vel quia de sorte sunt Domini, vel quia ipse Dominus sors, id est pars, clericorum est.' The former explanation would be reasonable, if it were supported by the language of the Old Testament: the latter is plainly inadequate.

[2] Deut. iv. 20 εἶναι αὐτῷ λαὸν ἔγκληρον: comp. ix. 29 οὗτοι λαός σου καὶ κλῆρός σου.

have suggested 'clerus' as a name rather for the entire body of the faithful than for the ministry specially or exclusively. Nor do other references to the clerus or lot in connexion with the Levitical priesthood countenance its special application. The tithes, it is true, were assigned to the sons of Levi as their 'clerus'[1]; but in this there is nothing distinctive, and in fact the word is employed much more prominently in describing the lands allotted to the whole people. Again the courses of priests and Levites selected to conduct the temple-service were appointed by lot[2]; but the mode adopted in distributing a particular set of duties is far too special to have supplied a distinctive name for the whole order. If indeed it were an established fact that the Aaronic priesthood at the time of the Christian era commonly bore the name of 'clergy,' we might be driven to explain the designation in this or in some similar way; but apparently no evidence of any such usage exists[3], and it is therefore needless to cast about for an explanation of a fact which itself is only conjectural. The origin of the term clergy, as applied to the Christian ministry, must be sought elsewhere.

And the record of the earliest appointment made by the Christian Church after the Ascension of the Lord seems to supply the clue. Exhorting the assembled brethren to elect a successor in place of Judas, St Peter tells them that the traitor 'had been numbered among them and had received the *lot* (κλῆρον) of the ministry': while in the account of the subsequent proceedings it is recorded that the Apostles 'distributed *lots*' to the brethren, and that 'the *lot* fell on Matthias and he was added to the eleven Apostles[4].' The following therefore seems to be the sequence of meanings, by which the word κλῆρος arrived at this peculiar sense: (1) the lot by which the office was assigned; (2) the office thus assigned by lot; (3) the body of persons holding the office. The first two senses are illustrated by the passages quoted from the

*Origin of 'Clerus' as a name for the Christian ministry.*

---

[1] Num. xviii. 21, 24, 26.
[2] 1 Chron. xxiv. 5, 7, 31, xxv. 8, 9.
[3] On the other hand λαὸς is used of the people, as contrasted either with the rulers or with the priests. From this latter contrast comes λαϊκός, 'laic' or 'profane,' and λαϊκόω 'to profane'; which, though not found in the LXX, occur frequently in the versions of Aquila, Symmachus, and Theodotion

(λαϊκός, 1 Sam. xxi. 4, Ezek. xlviii. 15; λαϊκόω, Deut. xx. 6, xxviii. 30, Ruth i. 12, Ezek. vii. 22); comp. Clem. Rom. 40.
[4] Acts i. 17 ἔλαχεν τὸν κλῆρον, 26 ἔδωκαν κλήρους αὐτοῖς καὶ ἔπεσεν ὁ κλῆρος ἐπὶ Ματθίαν. In ver. 25 κλῆρον is a false reading. The use of the word in 1 Pet. v. 3 κατακυριεύοντες τῶν κλήρων (i.e. of the flocks assigned to them) does not illustrate this meaning.

Acts; and from the second to the third the transition is easy and natural. It must not be supposed however that the mode of appointing officers by lot prevailed generally in the early Church. Besides the case of Matthias no other instance is recorded in the New Testament; nor is this procedure likely to have been commonly adopted. But just as in the passage quoted the word is used to describe the office of Judas, though Judas was certainly not selected by lot, so generally from signifying one special mode of appointment to office it got to signify office in the Church generally[1]. If this account of the application of 'clerus' to the Christian ministry be correct, we should expect to find it illustrated by a corresponding progress in the actual usage of the word. And this is in fact the case. The sense 'clerical appointment or office' chronologically precedes the sense 'clergy'. The former meaning occurs several times in Irenæus. He speaks of Hyginus as 'holding the ninth clerus of the episcopal succession from the Apostles[2]'; and of Eleutherus in like manner he says, 'He now occupies the clerus of the episcopate in the tenth place from the Apostles[3].' On the other hand the earliest instance of 'clerus', meaning clergy, seems to occur in Tertullian[4], who belongs to the next generation.

No sacerdotal idea conveyed by the term. It will thus be seen that the use of 'clerus' to denote the ministry cannot be traced to the Jewish priesthood, and is therefore wholly unconnected with any sacerdotal views. The term does indeed recognise the clergy as an order distinct from the laity; but this is a mere question of ecclesiastical rule or polity, and

---

[1] See Clem. Alex. *Quis div. salv.* 42, where κληροῦν is 'to appoint to the ministry'; and Iren. iii. 3. 3 κληροῦσθαι τὴν ἐπισκοπήν. A similar extension of meaning is seen in this same word κλῆρος applied to land. Signifying originally a piece of ground assigned by lot, it gets to mean landed property generally, whether obtained by assignment or by inheritance or in any other way.

[2] Iren. i. 27. 1.

[3] Iren. iii. 3. 3. In this passage however, as in the preceding, the word is explained by a qualifying genitive. In Hippol. *Hær.* ix. 12 (p. 290), ἤρξαντο ἐπίσκοποι καὶ πρεσβύτεροι καὶ διάκονοι δίγαμοι καὶ τρίγαμοι καθίστασθαι εἰς κλή-

ρους, it is used absolutely of 'clerical offices.' The Epistle of the Gallican Churches (Euseb. *H. E.* v. 1) speaks more than once of the κλῆρος τῶν μαρτύρων, i.e. the order or rank of martyrs: comp. *Test. xii Patr.* Levi 8. See Ritschl p. 390 sq., to whom I am indebted for several of the passages which are quoted in this investigation.

[4] e.g. *de Monog.* 12 'Unde enim episcopi et clerus?' and again 'Extollimur et inflamur adversus clerum.' Perhaps however earlier instances may have escaped notice. In Clem. Alex. *Qui div. salv.* 42 the word seems not to be used in this sense.

involves no doctrinal bearings. The origin of sacerdotal phraseology and ideas must be sought elsewhere.

Attention has been already directed to the absence of any appeal to sacerdotal claims in the Pastoral Epistles. The silence of the apostolic fathers deserves also to be noticed. Though the genuine letters of all three may be truly said to hinge on questions relating to the ministry, no distinct traces of this influence are visible. St Clement, as the representative of the Roman Church, writes to the Christian brotherhood at Corinth, offering friendly counsel in their disputes and rebuking their factious and unworthy conduct towards certain presbyters whom, though blameless, they had ejected from office. He appeals to motives of Christian love, to principles of Christian order. He adduces a large number of examples from biblical history condemnatory of jealousy and insubordination. He urges that men, who had been appointed directly by the Apostles or by persons themselves so appointed, ought to have received better treatment. Dwelling at great length on the subject, he nevertheless advances no sacerdotal claims or immunities on behalf of the ejected ministers. He does, it is true, adduce the Aaronic priesthood and the Temple service as showing that God has appointed set persons and set places and will have all things done in order. He had before illustrated this lesson by the subordination of ranks in an army, and by the relation of the different members of the human body: he had insisted on the duties of the strong towards the weak, of the rich towards the poor, of the wise towards the ignorant, and so forth: he had enforced the appeal by reminding his readers of the utter feebleness and insignificance of man in the sight of God, as represented in the Scriptures of the Old Testament; and then follows the passage which contains the allusion in question: 'He hath not commanded (the offerings and ministrations) to be performed at random or in disorder, but at fixed times and seasons; and where and through whom He willeth them to be performed, He hath ordained by His supreme will. They therefore who make their offerings at the appointed seasons are acceptable and blessed, since following the ordinances of the Master they do not go wrong. For to the high priest peculiar services are entrusted, and the priests have their peculiar office assigned to them, and on Levites peculiar ministrations are imposed:

*Silence of the apostolic fathers on sacerdotalism.*

*Clement.*

*Import of his comparison with the Aaronic priesthood.*

the layman is bound by lay ordinances. Let each of you, brethren, in his own rank give thanks to God, retaining a good conscience, not transgressing the appointed rule of his service (λειτουργίας) etc.'' Here it is clear that in St Clement's conception the sanction possessed in common by the Aaronic priesthood and the Christian ministry is not the sacerdotal consecration, but the divinely appointed order. He passes over in silence the numerous passages in the Old Testament which enjoin obedience to the priests; while the only sentence (§ 42) which he puts forward as anticipating and enforcing the authority of the Christian ministry is a misquoted and misinterpreted verse from Isaiah; 'I will establish their overseers (bishops) in righteousness and their ministers (deacons) in faith[2]'. Again a little later he mentions in illustration the murmuring of the Israelites which was rebuked by the budding of Aaron's rod[3]. But here too he makes it clear how far he considers the analogy to extend. He calls the sedition in the one case 'jealousy concerning the priesthood', in the other strife concerning the honour of the episcopate[4]. He keeps the names and the offices distinct. The significance of this fact will be felt at once by comparing his language with the expressions used by any later writer, such as Cyprian, who was penetrated with the spirit of sacerdotalism[5].

Ignatius.     Of St Ignatius, as the champion of episcopacy, much has been said already. It is sufficient to add here, that he never regards the ministry as a sacerdotal office. This is equally true, whether we accept as genuine the whole of the seven letters in the short Greek, or only those portions contained in the Syriac version. While these

[1] Clem.Rom. 40,41. Neander (*Church History*, I. p. 272 note, Bohn's translation) conjectures that this passage is an 'interpolation from a hierarchical interest,' and Dean Milman (*Hist. of Christianity*, III. p. 259) says that it is 'rejected by all judicious and impartial scholars.' At the risk of forfeiting all claim to judiciousness and impartiality one may venture to demur to this arbitrary criticism. Indeed the recent discovery of a second independent MS and of a Syriac Version, both containing the suspected passage, may be regarded as decisive on this point.

[2] Is. lx. 17, where the A. V. correctly renders the original, 'I will also

make thy officers (lit. magistrates) peace and thine exactors (i.e. task-masters) righteousness'; i.e. there shall be no tyranny or oppression. The LXX departs from the original, and Clement has altered the LXX. By this double divergence a reference to the two orders of the ministry is obtained.

[3] Clem. Rom. 43.

[4] Contrast § 43 ζήλου ἐμπεσόντος περὶ τῆς ἱερωσύνης with § 44 ἔρις ἔσται ἐπὶ τοῦ ὀνόματος τῆς ἐπισκοπῆς. The common feature which connects the two offices together is stated in the words, § 43 ἵνα μὴ ἀκαταστασία γένηται.

[5] See below p. 259.

letters teem with passages enjoining the strictest obedience to bishops, while their language is frequently so strong as to sound almost profane, this father never once appeals to sacerdotal claims[1], though such an appeal would have made his case more than doubly strong. If it be ever safe to take the sentiments of an individual writer as expressing the belief of his age, we may infer from the silence which pervades these letters, that the sacerdotal view of the ministry had not yet found its way into the Christian Church.

When we pass on to the third apostolic father, the same phenomenon is repeated. Polycarp, like Clement and Ignatius, occupies Polycarp. much space in discussing the duties and the claims of Christian ministers. He takes occasion especially to give his correspondents advice as to a certain presbyter who had disgraced his office by a grave offence[2]. Yet he again knows nothing, or at least says nothing, of any sacerdotal privileges which claimed respect, or of any sacerdotal sanctity which has been violated.

Justin Martyr writes about a generation later. He speaks at Justin length and with emphasis on the eucharistic offerings. Here at least Martyr we might expect to find sacerdotal views of the Christian ministry propounded. Yet this is far from being the case. He does indeed lay stress on sacerdotal functions, but these belong to the whole body of the Church, and are not in any way the exclusive right of the clergy. 'So we,' he writes, when arguing against Trypho the Jew, maintains 'who through the name of Jesus have believed as one man in God an universal priesthood. the maker of the universe, having divested ourselves of our filthy garments, that is our sins, through the name of His first-born Son, and having been refined (πυρωθέντες) by the word of His calling, are the true high-priestly race of God, as God Himself also beareth witness, saying that in every place among the Gentiles are men offering sacrifices well-pleasing unto Him and pure (Mal. i. 11). Yet God

---

[1] Some passages are quoted in Greenwood *Cathedra Petri* 1. p. 73 as tending in this direction, e.g. *Philad.* 9 καλοὶ καὶ οἱ ἱερεῖς, κρεῖσσον δὲ ὁ ἀρχιερεύς κ.τ.λ. But rightly interpreted they do not favour this view. In the passage quoted for instance, the writer seems to be maintaining the superiority of the new covenant, as represented by the great High-Priest (ἀρχιερεύς) in and

through whom the whole Church has access to God, over the old dispensation of the Levitical priesthood (ἱερεῖς). If this interpretation be correct, the passage echoes the teaching of the Epistle to the Hebrews, and is opposed to exclusive sacerdotalism. On the meaning of θυσιαστήριον in the Ignatian Epistles see below p. 265, note 2.

[2] See above p. 63 sq.

doth not receive sacrifices from any one, except through His priests. Therefore God anticipating all sacrifices through this name, which Jesus Christ ordained to be offered, I mean those offered by the Christians in every region of the earth with ($\grave{\epsilon}\pi\grave{\iota}$) the thanksgiving (the eucharist) of the bread and of the cup, beareth witness that they are well-pleasing to Him; but the sacrifices offered by you and through those your priests he rejecteth, saying, "And your sacrifices I will not accept from your hands etc. (Mal. i. 10)"[1].' The whole Christian people therefore (such is Justin's conception) have not only taken the place of the Aaronic priesthood, but have become a nation of *high-priests*, being made one with the great High-Priest of the new covenant and presenting their eucharistic offerings in His name.

Irenæus Another generation leads us from Justin Martyr to Irenæus. When Irenæus writes, the second century is very far advanced. Yet still the silence which has accompanied us hitherto remains unbroken. And here again it is important to observe that Irenæus, if he held the sacerdotal view, had every motive for urging it, since the importance and authority of the episcopate occupy a large space in his teaching. Nevertheless he not only withholds this title as a special designation of the Christian ministry, but advances an entirely different view of the priestly office. He recognises only the priesthood of moral holiness, the priesthood of apostolic self-denial. Thus commenting on the reference made by our Lord to the incident in David's life where the king and his followers eat the shew-bread, 'which it is not lawful to eat save for the priests alone,' Irenæus remarks[2]; 'He excuseth His disciples by the words of the law, and signifieth that it is lawful for priests to act freely. For David had been called to be a priest in the sight of God, although Saul carried on a persecution against him; for all just men belong to the sacerdotal order[3]. Now all apostles of the Lord are priests, for they inherit neither lands nor houses here, but ever attend on the altar and on God': 'Who are they', he goes on, 'that have left father and

*acknow-ledges only a moral priesthood.*

---

[1] *Dial. c. Tryph.* c. 116, 117, p. 344.

[2] *Hær.* iv. 8. 3.

[3] This sentence is cited by John Damascene and Antonius πᾶς βασιλεὺς δίκαιος ἱερατικὴν ἔχει τάξιν; but the words were quoted doubtless from memory by the one writer and borrowed by the other from him. βασιλεὺς is not represented in the Latin and does not suit the context. The close conformity of their quotations from the Ignatian letters is a sufficient proof that these two writers are not independent authorities; see the passages in Cureton's *Corp. Ignat.* p. 180 sq.

mother and have renounced all their kindred for the sake of the word of God and His covenant, but the disciples of the Lord? Of these Moses saith again, "But they shall have no inheritance; for the Lord Himself shall be their inheritance"; and again, "The priests, the Levites, in the whole tribe of Levi shall have no part nor inheritance with Israel: the first-fruits (fructificationes) of the Lord are their inheritance; they shall eat them." For this reason also Paul saith, "I require not the gift, but I require the fruit." The disciples of the Lord, he would say, were allowed when hungry to take food of the seeds (they had sown): for "The labourer is worthy of his food." ' Again, striking upon the same topic in a later passage and commenting on the words of Jeremiah (xxxi. 14), "I will intoxicate the soul of the priests the sons of Levi, and my people shall be filled with my good things," he adds, 'we have shown in a former book, that all disciples of the Lord are priests and Levites: who also profaned the Sabbath in the temple and are blameless.' Thus Irenæus too recognises the whole body of the faithful under the new dispensation as the counterparts of the sons of Levi under the old. The position of the Apostles and Evangelists has not yet been abandoned.

A few years later, but still before the close of the century, Poly-crates of Ephesus writes to Victor of Rome. Incidentally he speaks of St John as 'having been made a priest' and 'wearing the mitre'[2], and this might seem to be a distinct expression of sacerdotal views, for the 'mitre' to which he alludes is doubtless the tiara of the Jewish high-priest. But it may very reasonably be questioned if this is the correct meaning of the passage. Whether St John did actually wear this decoration of the high-priestly office, or whether Polycrates has mistaken a symbolical expression in some earlier writer for an actual fact, or whether lastly his language itself should be treated as a violent metaphor, I have had occasion to discuss elsewhere[3]. But in any case the notice is explained by the language of St John himself, who regards the whole body of believers as high-priests of the new covenant[4]; and it is certain that the contemporaries of Poly-

Explana-tion of a passage in Poly-crates.

---

[1] *Hær.* v. 34. 3.

[2] In Euseb. *H. E.* v. 24 ὃς ἐγενήθη ἱερεὺς τὸ πέταλον πεφορεκώς. Comp. Tertull. *adv. Jud.* 14 'exornatus podere et mitra', *Test. xii Patr.* Levi 8 ἀνα-στὰς ἐνδύσαι τὴν στολὴν τῆς ἱερατείας... τὸν ποδήρη τῆς ἀληθείας καὶ τὸ πέταλον

τῆς πίστεως κ.τ.λ. See also, as an illus-tration of the metaphor, Tertull. *Monog.* 12 'Cum ad peræquationem disciplinæ sacerdotalis provocamur, *deponimus in fulas.*'

[3] See *Galatians* p. 362 note.

[4] Rev. ii. 17; see the commentators.

crates still continued to hold similar language[1]. As a figurative expression or as a literal fact, the notice points to St John as the veteran teacher, the chief representative, of a pontifical race. On the other hand, it is possible that this was not the sense which Polycrates himself attached to the figure or the fact: and if so, we have here perhaps the earliest passage in any extant Christian writing where the sacerdotal view of the ministry is distinctly put forward.

**Clement of Alexandria.** Clement of Alexandria was a contemporary of Polycrates. Though his extant writings are considerable in extent and though they are largely occupied with questions of Christian ethics and social life, the ministry does not hold a prominent place in them. In the few passages where he mentions it, he does not betray any tendency to sacerdotal or even to hierarchical views. The bias of his mind indeed lay in an opposite direction. He would be much more inclined to maintain an aristocracy of intellectual contemplation than of sacerdotal office. And in Alexandria generally, as we have seen, the development of the hierarchy was slower than in other churches. How far he is from maintaining a sacerdotal view of the ministry and how substantially he coincides with Irenæus in this respect, **His 'gnostic' priesthood.** will appear from the following passage. 'It is possible for men even now, by exercising themselves in the commandments of the Lord and by living a perfect gnostic life in obedience to the Gospel, to be inscribed in the roll of the Apostles. Such men are genuine presbyters of the Church and true deacons of the will of God, if they practise and teach the things of the Lord, being not indeed ordained by men nor considered righteous because they are presbyters, but enrolled in the presbytery because they are righteous: and though here on earth they may not be honoured with a chief seat, yet shall they sit on the four and twenty thrones judging the people[2].' It is quite consistent with this truly spiritual view, that he should elsewhere recognise the presbyter, the deacon, and the layman, as distinct orders[3]. But on the other hand he never uses the words 'priest,' 'priestly,' 'priesthood,' of the Christian ministry. In one passage indeed he contrasts laity and priesthood, but without any such reference. Speaking of the veil of the temple and as-

---

[1] So Justin in the words already quoted (p. 250), *Dial. c. Tryph.* § 116 ἀρχιερατικὸν τὸ ἀληθινὸν γένος ἐσμὲν τοῦ Θεοῦ. See also the passage of Origen

quoted below p. 257.
[2] *Strom.* vi. 13, p. 793.
[3] *Strom.* iii. 90, p. 552.

signing to it a symbolical meaning, he describes it as 'a barrier against laic unbelief,' behind which 'the priestly ministration is hidden[1].' Here the laymen and the priests are respectively those who reject and those who appropriate the spiritual mysteries of the Gospel. Accordingly in the context St Clement, following up the hint thrown out in the Epistle to the Hebrews, gives a spiritual meaning to all the furniture of the holy place.

His younger contemporary Tertullian is the first to assert direct sacerdotal claims on behalf of the Christian ministry. Of the heretics he complains that they impose sacerdotal functions on laymen[2]. 'The right of giving baptism,' he says elsewhere, 'belongs to the chief priest (summus sacerdos), that is, the bishop[3].' 'No woman,' he asserts, 'ought to teach, baptize, celebrate the eucharist, or arrogate to herself the performance of any duty pertaining to males, much less of the sacerdotal office[4].' And generally he uses the words sacerdos, sacerdotium, sacerdotalis, of the Christian ministry. It seems plain moreover from his mode of speaking, that such language was not peculiar to himself but passed current in the churches among which he moved. Yet he himself supplies the true counterpoise to this special sacerdotalism in his strong assertion of the universal priesthood of all true believers. 'We should be foolish,' so he writes when arguing against second marriages, 'to suppose that a latitude is allowed to laymen which is denied to priests. Are not we laymen also priests? It is written, "He hath also made us a kingdom and priests to God and His Father." It is the authority of the Church which makes a difference between the order (the clergy) and the people—this authority and the consecration of their rank by the assignment of special benches to the clergy. Thus where there is no bench of clergy, you present the eucharistic offerings and baptize and are your own sole priest. For where three are gathered together, there is a church, even though they be laymen. Therefore if you exercise the rights of a priest in cases of necessity, it is your duty also to observe the discipline enjoined on a priest, where of necessity you exercise the rights of a priest[5].' And in another treatise he

*(marginal notes:)* Tertullian holds a sacerdotal view of the ministry, yet qualifies it by his assertion of an universal priesthood.

---

[1] *Strom.* v. 33 sq., p. 665 sq. Bp. Kaye (*Clement of Alexandria* p. 464) incorrectly adduces this passage as an express mention of 'the distinction between the clergy and laity.'

[2] *de Præscr. Hær.* 41 'Nam et laicis sacerdotalia munera injungunt.'

[3] *de Baptismo* 17.

[4] *de Virg. vel.* 9.

[5] *de Exh. Cast.* 7. See Kaye's *Tertul-*

writes in bitter irony, 'When we begin to exalt and inflame our-selves against the clergy, then we are all one; then we are all priests, because "He made us priests to God and His Father": but when we are required to submit ourselves equally to the priestly discipline, we throw off our fillets and are no longer equal[1].' These passages, it is true, occur in treatises probably written after Ter-tullian had become wholly or in part a Montanist: but this con-sideration is of little consequence, for they bear witness to the fact that the scriptural doctrine of an universal priesthood was common ground to himself and his opponents, and had not yet been obscured by the sacerdotal view of the Christian ministry[2].

Sacerdotal language in Hippo-lytus. An incidental expression in Hippolytus serves to show that a few years later than Tertullian sacerdotal terms were commonly used to designate the different orders of the clergy. 'We,' says the zealous bishop of Portus, 'being successors of the Apostles and partaking of the same grace both of *high-priesthood* and of teaching and accounted guardians of the Church, do not close our eyes drowsily or tacitly suppress the true word, etc.[3]'

Origen in-terprets the priest-hood spiri-tually, The march of sacerdotal ideas was probably slower at Alexandria than at Carthage or Rome. Though belonging to the next gene-ration, Origen's views are hardly so advanced as those of Tertul-lian. In the temple of the Church, he says, there are two sanc-tuaries : the heavenly, accessible only to Jesus Christ, our great High-Priest; the earthly, open to all priests of the new covenant, that is, to all faithful believers. For Christians are a sacerdotal race and therefore have access to the outer sanctuary. There they must present their offerings, their holocausts of love and self-denial. From this outer sanctuary our High-Priest takes the fire, as He enters the Holy of Holies to offer incense to the Father (see

---

*lian* p. 211, whose interpretation of 'honor per ordinis consessum sanctifi-catus' I have adopted.

[1] *de Monog.* 12. I have taken the reading 'impares' for 'pares,' as re-quired by the context.

[2] Tertullian regards Christ, our great High-Priest, as the counterpart under the new dispensation of the priest under the old, and so interprets the text 'Show thyself to the priest'; *adv. Marc.*

iv. 9, *adv. Jud.* 14. Again, he uses 'sacerdos' in a moral sense, *de Spectac.* 16 'sacerdotes pacis,' *de Cult. Fem.* ii. 12 'sacerdotes pudicitiæ,' *ad Uxor.* i. 6 (comp. 7) 'virginitatis et viduitatis sacerdotia.' On the other hand in *de Pall.* 4 he seems to compare the Chris-tian minister with the heathen priests, but too much stress must not be laid on a rhetorical image.

[3] *Hær.* prooem. p. 3.

Lev. xvi. 12)[1]. Very many professed Christians, he writes else-where (I am here abridging his words), occupied chiefly with the concerns of this world and dedicating few of their actions to God, are represented by the tribes, who merely present their tithes and first-fruits. On the other hand 'those who are devoted to the divine word, and are dedicated sincerely to the sole worship of God, may not unreasonably be called priests and Levites according to the differ-ence in this respect of their impulses tending thereto.' Lastly 'those who excel the men of their own generation perchance will be high-priests.' They are only high-priests however after the order of Aaron, our Lord Himself being High-Priest after the order of Mel-chisedek[2]. Again in a third place he says, 'The Apostles and they that are made like unto the Apostles, being priests after the order of the great High-Priest, having received the knowledge of the worship of God and being instructed by the Spirit, know for what sins they ought to offer sacrifices, etc.[3].' In all these passages Origen has taken spiritual enlightenment and not sacerdotal office to be the Christian counterpart to the Aaronic priesthood. Elsewhere how-ever he makes use of sacerdotal terms to describe the ministry of the Church[4]; and in one place distinguishes the priests and the Levites as representing the presbyters and deacons respectively[5]. *but applies sacerdotal terms to the minis-try.*

Hitherto the sacerdotal view of the Christian ministry has not been held apart from a distinct recognition of the sacerdotal func-tions of the whole Christian body. The minister is thus regarded as a priest, because he is the mouthpiece, the representative, of a priestly race. Such appears to be the conception of Tertullian, who speaks of the clergy as separate from the laity only because the *The priest-hood of the ministry springs from the priesthood*

---

[1] *Hom. ix in Lev.* 9, 10 (II. p. 243 Delarue).

[2] *In Joann.* i. § 3 (IV. p. 3).

[3] *de Orat.* 28 (I. p. 255). See also *Hom. iv in Num.* 3 (II. p. 283).

[4] *Hom. v in Lev.* 4 (II. p. 208 sq.) 'Discant sacerdotes Domini qui eccle-siis præsunt,' and also ib. *Hom.* ii. 4 (II.p.191)'Cum non erubescit sacerdoti Domini indicare peccatum suum et quærere medicinam' (he quotes James v. 14 in illustration). But *Hom. x in Num.* 1, 2 (II. p. 302), quoted by Rede-penning (*Origenes* II. p. 417), hardly

bears this sense, for the 'pontifex' ap-plies to our Lord; and it is clear from *Hom. in Ps.* xxxvii. § 6 (II. p. 688) that in Origen's opinion the confessor to the penitent need not be an ordained minister. The passages in Rede-penning's *Origenes* bearing on this subject are I. p. 357, II. pp. 250, 417, 436 sq.

[5] *Hom. xii in Jerem.* 3 (III. p. 196) 'If any one therefore among these priests (I mean us the presbyters) or among these Levites who stand about the people (I mean the deacons) etc.'

of the congregation. Church in the exercise of her prerogative has for convenience entrusted to them the performance of certain sacerdotal functions belonging properly to the whole congregation, and of Origen, who, giving a moral and spiritual interpretation to the sacerdotal office, considers the priesthood of the clergy to differ from the priesthood of the laity only in degree, in so far as the former devote their time and their thoughts more entirely to God than the latter. So long as this important aspect is kept in view, so long as the priesthood of the ministry is regarded as springing from the priesthood of the whole body, the teaching of the Apostles has not been directly violated. But still it was not a safe nomenclature which assigned the terms sacerdos, ἱερεύς, and the like, to the ministry, as a *special* designation. The appearance of this phenomenon marks the period of transition from the universal sacerdotalism of the New Testament to the particular sacerdotalism of a later age.

Cyprian the champion of undisguised sacerdotalism.    If Tertullian and Origen are still hovering on the border, Cyprian has boldly transferred himself into the new domain. It is not only that he uses the terms sacerdos, sacerdotium, sacerdotalis, of the ministry with a frequency hitherto without parallel. But he treats all the passages in the Old Testament which refer to the privileges, the sanctions, the duties, and the responsibilities of the Aaronic priesthood, as applying to the officers of the Christian Church. His opponents are profane and sacrilegious; they have passed sentence of death on themselves by disobeying the command of the Lord in Deuteronomy to 'hear the priest[1]'; they have forgotten the injunction of Solomon to honour and reverence God's priests[2]; they have despised the example of St Paul who regretted that he 'did not know it was the high priest[3]'; they have been guilty of the sin of Korah, Dathan, and Abiram[4]. These passages are urged again and again. They are urged moreover, as applying not by parity of reasoning, not by analogy of circumstance, but as absolute and immediate and unquestionable. As Cyprian crowned the edifice of episcopal power, so also was he the first to put forward without relief or disguise these sacer-

---

[1] Deut. xvii. 12; see *Epist.* 3, 4, 43, 59, 66.
[2] Though the words are ascribed to Solomon, the quotation comes from Ecclus. vii. 29, 31; see *Epist.* 3.

[3] Acts xxiii. 4; see *Epist.* 3, 59, 66.
[4] *De Unit. Eccl.* p. 83 (Fell), *Epist.* 3, 67, 69, 73.

dotal assumptions; and so uncompromising was the tone in which he asserted them, that nothing was left to his successors but to enforce his principles and reiterate his language[1].

After thus tracing the gradual departure from the Apostolic teaching in the encroachment of the sacerdotal on the pastoral and ministerial view of the clergy, it will be instructive to investigate the causes to which this divergence from primitive truth may be ascribed. To the question whether the change was due to Jewish or Gentile influences, opposite answers have been given. To some it has appeared as a reproduction of the Aaronic priesthood, due to Pharisaic tendencies, such as we find among St Paul's converts in Galatia and at Corinth, still lingering in the Church: to others, as imported into Christianity by the ever increasing mass of heathen converts who were incapable of shaking off their sacerdotal prejudices and appreciating the free spirit of the Gospel. The latter view seems correct in the main, but requires some modification.

*Were sacerdotal views due to Jewish or Gentile influences?*

At all events so far as the evidence of extant writings goes, there is no reason for supposing that sacerdotalism was especially rife among the Jewish converts. The Testaments of the Twelve Patriarchs may be taken to represent one phase of Judaic Christianity; the Clementine writings exhibit another. In both alike there is an entire absence of sacerdotal views of the ministry. The former work indeed dwells at length on our Lord's office, as the descendant and heir of Levi [2], and alludes more than once to his institution of a new priesthood; but this priesthood is spiritual and comprehensive. Christ Himself is the High priest[3], and the sacerdotal office is described as being 'after the type of the Gentiles, extending to all the Gentiles [4].' On the Christian ministry the writer is silent. In the Clementine Homilies the case is somewhat different, but the inference is still more obvious. Though the episcopate is regarded as the backbone of the Church, though the claims of the ministry are urged with great distinctness, no appeal is ever made to priestly sanctity as the ground

*The earliest Jewish Christian writings contain no traces of sacerdotalism.*

[1] The sacerdotal language in the *Apostolical Constitutions* is hardly less strong, while it is more systematic; but their date is uncertain and cannot well be placed earlier than Cyprian.

[2] See *Galatians* p. 319.

[3] Ruben 6, Symeon 7, Levi 18.

[4] Levi 8.

of this exalted estimate[1]. Indeed the hold of the Levitical priest-hood on the mind of the pious Jew must have been materially weakened at the Christian era by the development of the synagogue organization on the one hand, and by the ever growing influence of the learned and literary classes, the scribes and rabbis, on the other. The points on which the Judaizers of the apostolic age insist are the rite of circumcision, the distinction of meats, the observance of sabbaths, and the like. The necessity of a priest-hood was not, or at least is not known to have been, part of their programme. Among the Essene Jews especially, who went so far as to repudiate the temple sacrifices, no great importance could have been attached to the Aaronic priesthood[2]: and after the Apostolic ages at all events, the most active Judaizers of the Dispersion seem to have belonged to the Essene type. But indeed the overwhelming argument against ascribing the growth of sacerdotal views to Jewish influence lies in the fact, that there is a singular absence of distinct sacerdotalism during the first century and a half, when alone on any showing Judaism was powerful enough to impress itself on the belief of the Church at large.

Sacerdotalism was due to Gentile influences, It is therefore to Gentile feeling that this development must be ascribed. For the heathen, familiar with auguries, lustrations, sacrifices, and depending on the intervention of some priest for all the manifold religious rites of the state, the club, and the family, the sacerdotal functions must have occupied a far larger space in the affairs of every day life, than for the Jew of the Dispersion who of necessity dispensed and had no scruple at dispensing with priestly ministrations from one year's end to the other. With this presumption drawn from probability the evidence of fact accords. In Latin Christendom, as represented by the Church of Carthage, the germs of the sacerdotal idea appear first and soonest ripen to maturity. If we could satisfy ourselves of the early date of the Ancient Syriac Documents lately published, we should have discovered another centre from which this idea

---

[1] See the next note.

[2] See *Galatians* pp. 323, 326, *Colossians* pp. 89, 371. In the syzygies of the Clementine Homilies (ii. 16, 33) Aaron is opposed to Moses, the high-priest to the lawgiver, as the bad to the good, the false to the true, like Cain to Abel, Ishmael to Isaac, etc. In the Recognitions the estimate of the high-priest's position is still unfavourable (i. 46, 48). Compare the statement in Justin, *Dial. c Tryph.* 117.

was propagated. And so far their testimony may perhaps be accepted. Syria was at least a soil where such a plant would thrive and luxuriate. In no country of the civilized world was sacerdotal authority among the heathen greater. The most important centres of Syrian Christianity, Antioch and Emesa, were also the cradles of strongly-marked sacerdotal religions which at different times made their influence felt throughout the Roman empire[1]. This being so, it is a significant fact that the first instance of the term 'priest', applied to a Christian minister, occurs in a heathen writer. At least I have not found any example of this application earlier than Lucian[2].

But though the spirit, which imported the idea into the Church of Christ and sustained it there, was chiefly due to Gentile education, yet its form was almost as certainly derived from the Old Testament. And this is the modification which needs to be made in the statement, in itself substantially true, that sacerdotalism must be traced to the influence of Heathen rather than of Jewish converts.

*but sought support in Old Testament analogies.*

In the Apostolic writings we find the terms ' offering ', ' sacrifice ', applied to certain conditions and actions of the Christian life. These sacrifices or offerings are described as spiritual[3]; they consist of praise[4], of faith[5], of almsgiving[6], of the devotion of the body[7], of the conversion of unbelievers[8], and the like. Thus whatever is dedicated to God's service may be included under this metaphor. In one passage also the image is so far extended, that the Apostolic writer speaks of an *altar*[9] pertaining to the spiritual service of the Christian Church. If on this noble Scriptural language a false superstructure has been reared, we have here only one instance out of many, where the truth has been impaired by transferring statements from the region of metaphor to the region of fact.

*(1) Metaphor of 'sacrifices.'*

These ' sacrifices' were very frequently the acts not of the

---

[1] The worship of the Syrian goddess of Antioch was among the most popular of oriental superstitions under the earlier Cæsars; the rites of the Sungod of Emesa became fashionable under Elagabalus.

[2] *de Mort. Peregr.* 11 τὴν θαυμαστὴν σοφίαν τῶν Χριστιανῶν ἐξέμαθε περὶ τὴν Παλαιστίνην τοῖς ἱερεῦσι καὶ γραμματεῦσιν αὐτῶν ξυγγενόμενος.

[3] 1 Pet. ii. 5.
[4] Heb. xiii. 15.
[5] Phil. ii. 17.
[6] Acts xxiv. 17, Phil. iv. 18; comp. Heb. xiii. 16.
[7] Rom. xii. 1.
[8] Rom. xv. 16.
[9] Heb. xiii. 10. See below p. 265, note 2.

individual Christian, but of the whole congregation. Such for
instance were the offerings of public prayer and thanksgiving, or the
collection of alms on the first day of the week, or the contribution
of food for the agape, and the like. In such cases the congregation

**Offerings presented by the ministers.** was represented by its minister, who thus acted as its mouthpiece
and was said to 'present the offerings' to God. So the expression
is used in the Epistle of St Clement of Rome[1]. But in itself it
involves no sacerdotal view. This ancient father regards the sacrifice or offering as the act of the whole Church performed through
its presbyters. The minister is a priest in the same sense only
in which each individual member of the congregation is a priest.
When St Clement denounces those who usurp the functions of the
presbyters, he reprobates their conduct not as an act of sacrilege
but as a violation of order. He views the presbytery as an Apostolic
ordinance, not as a sacerdotal caste.

Thus when this father speaks of the presbytery as 'presenting
the offerings,' he uses an expression which, if not directly scriptural,
is at least accordant with the tenour of Scripture. But from such
language the transition to sacerdotal views was easy, where the
sacerdotal spirit was rife. From being the act of the whole congregation, the sacrifice came to be regarded as the act of the minister
who officiated on its behalf.

**Special reference of the metaphor to the eucharist.** And this transition was moreover facilitated by the growing
tendency to apply the terms 'sacrifice' and 'offering' exclusively or
chiefly to the eucharistic service. It may be doubted whether, even as
used by St Clement, the expression may not have a special reference
to this chief act of Christian dedication[2]. It is quite certain that

---

[1] Clem. Rom. 44 τοὺς ἀμέμπτως καὶ
ὁσίως προσενεγκόντας τὰ δῶρα. What
sort of offerings are meant, may be
gathered from other passages in Clement's Epistle; e.g. § 35 θυσία αἰνέσεως
δοξάσει με, § 52 θῦσον τῷ Θεῷ θυσίαν
αἰνέσεως καὶ ἀπόδος τῷ ὑψίστῳ τὰς εὐχάς
σου, § 36 εὕρομεν τὸ σωτήριον ἡμῶν
Ἰησοῦν Χριστὸν τὸν ἀρχιερέα τῶν προσ-
φορῶν ἡμῶν τὸν προστάτην καὶ βοηθὸν
τῆς ἀσθενείας ἡμῶν, and § 41 ἕκαστος
ὑμῶν, ἀδελφοί, ἐν τῷ ἰδίῳ τάγματι εὐχαριστείτω τῷ Θεῷ ἐν ἀγαθῇ συνειδήσει
ὑπάρχων, μὴ παρεκβαίνων τὸν ὡρισμένον
τῆς λειτουργίας αὐτοῦ κανόνα. Compare

especially Heb. xiii. 10, 15, 16, ἔχομεν
θυσιαστήριον ἐξ οὗ φαγεῖν οὐκ ἔχουσιν
[ἐξουσίαν] οἱ τῇ σκηνῇ λατρεύοντες...Δι'
αὐτοῦ οὖν ἀναφέρωμεν θυσίαν αἰνέσεως
διὰ παντὸς τῷ Θεῷ, τουτέστιν, καρπὸν
χειλέων ὁμολογούντων τῷ ὀνόματι αὐτοῦ·
τῆς δὲ εὐποιΐας καὶ κοινωνίας μὴ ἐπιλαν-
θάνεσθε, τοιαύταις γὰρ θυσίαις εὐαρεσ-
τεῖται ὁ Θεός.

The doctrine of the early Church respecting 'sacrifice' is investigated by
Höfling die Lehre der ältesten Kirche
vom Opfer (Erlangen 1851).

[2] On the whole however the language
of the Epistle to the Hebrews quoted

writers belonging to the generations next following, Justin Martyr and Irenæus for instance [1], employ the terms very frequently with this reference. We may here reserve the question in what sense the celebration of the Lord's supper may or may not be truly called a sacrifice. The point to be noticed at present is this; that the offering of the eucharist, being regarded as the one special act of sacrifice and appearing externally to the eye as the act of the officiating minister, might well lead to the minister being called a priest and then being thought a priest in some exclusive sense, where the religious bias was in this direction and as soon as the true position of the minister as the representative of the congregation was lost sight of.

But besides the metaphor or the analogy of the sacrifice, there was another point of resemblance also between the Jewish priesthood and the Christian ministry, which favoured the sacerdotal view of the latter. As soon as the episcopate and presbytery ceased to be regarded as sub-orders and were looked upon as distinct orders, the correspondence of the threefold ministry with the three ranks of the Levitical priesthood could not fail to suggest itself. The solitary bishop represented the solitary high-priest; the principal acts of Christian sacrifice were performed by the presbyters, as the principal acts of Jewish sacrifice by the priests; and the attendant ministrations were assigned in the one case to the deacon, as in the other to the Levite. Thus the analogy seemed complete. To this correspondence however there was one grave impediment. The only

*(2) Analogy of the three orders and the Levitical priesthood.*

in the last note seems to be the best exponent of St Clement's meaning, as he very frequently follows this Apostolic writer. If εὐχαριστείτω has any special reference to the holy eucharist, as it may have, δῶρα will nevertheless be the alms and prayers and thanksgivings which accompanied the celebration of it. Compare *Const. Apost.* ii. 25 αἱ τότε θυσίαι νῦν εὐχαὶ καὶ δεήσεις καὶ εὐχαριστίαι, αἱ τότε ἀπαρχαὶ καὶ δεκάται καὶ ἀφαιρέματα καὶ δῶρα νῦν προσφοραὶ αἱ διὰ τῶν ὁσίων ἐπισκόπων προσφερόμεναι Κυρίῳ κ.τ.λ., § 27 προσήκει οὖν καὶ ὑμᾶς, ἀδελφοί, τὰς θυσίας ὑμῶν ἤτοι προσφορὰς τῷ ἐπισκόπῳ προσφέρειν ὡς ἀρχιερεῖ κ.τ.λ., § 34 τοὺς

καρποὺς ὑμῶν καὶ τὰ ἔργα τῶν χειρῶν ὑμῶν εἰς εὐλογίαν ὑμῶν προσφέροντες αὐτῷ (sc. τῷ ἐπισκόπῳ)...τὰ δῶρα ὑμῶν διδόντες αὐτῷ ὡς ἱερεῖ Θεοῦ, § 53 δῶρον δέ ἐστι Θεῷ ἡ ἑκάστου προσευχὴ καὶ εὐχαριστία: comp. also § 35. These passages are quoted in Höfling, p. 27 sq.

[1] The chief passages in these fathers relating to Christian oblations are, Justin. *Apol.* i. 13 (p. 60), i. 65, 66, 67 (p. 97 sq.), *Dial.* 28, 29 (p. 246), 41 (p. 259 sq.), 116, 117 (p. 344 sq.), Iren. *Hær.* iv. cc. 17, 18, 19, v. 2. 3, [*Fragm.* 38, Stieren]. The place occupied by the eucharistic elements in their view of sacrifice will only be appreciated by reading the passages continuously.

High Priest under the Gospel recognised by the apostolic writings, is our Lord Himself. Accordingly in the Christian remains of the ages next succeeding this title is reserved as by right to Him[1]; and though belonging to various schools, all writers alike abstain from applying it to the bishop. Yet the scruple was at length set aside. When it had become usual to speak of the presbyters as 'sacerdotes', the designation of 'pontifex' or 'summus sacerdos' for the bishop was far too convenient and too appropriate to be neglected.

Thus the analogy of the sacrifices and the correspondence of the threefold order supplied the material on which the sacerdotal feeling worked. And in this way, by the union of Gentile sentiment with the ordinances of the Old Dispensation, the doctrine of an exclusive priesthood found its way into the Church of Christ.

*Question suggested.* How far is the language of the later Church justifiable? Can the Christian ministry be called a priesthood in any sense? and if so, in what sense? The historical investigation, which has suggested this question as its proper corollary, has also supplied the means of answering it.

*Silence of the Apostolic writers.* Though different interpretations may be put upon the fact that the sacred writers throughout refrain from applying sacerdotal terms to the Christian ministry, I think it must be taken to signify this much at least, that this ministry, if a priesthood at all, is a priesthood of a type essentially different from the Jewish. Otherwise we shall be perplexed to explain why the earliest Christian teachers should have abstained from using those terms which alone would adequately express to their hearers the one most important aspect of the ministerial office. It is often said in reply, that we have here a question not of words, but of things. This is undeniable: but words express things; and the silence of the Apostles still requires an explanation.

*Epistle to the Hebrews;* However the interpretation of this fact is not far to seek. The Epistle to the Hebrews speaks at great length on priests and sacrifices in their Jewish and their Christian bearing. It is plain from this epistle, as it may be gathered also from other notices Jewish

---

[1] See Clem. Rom. 36, 58, Polyc. *Phil.* 12, Ignat. *Philad.* 9, *Test. xii*     *Patr.* Rub. 6, Sym. 7, etc., *Clem. Recogn.* i. 48.

and Heathen, that the one prominent idea of the priestly office at its doctrinal teaching,
this time was the function of *offering sacrifice* and thereby making
atonement. Now this Apostolic writer teaches that all sacrifices
had been consummated in the one Sacrifice, all priesthoods absorbed
in the one Priest. The offering had been made once for all : and,
as there were no more victims, there could be no more priests[1]. All
former priesthoods had borne witness to the necessity of a human
mediator, and this sentiment had its satisfaction in the Person and
Office of the Son of Man. All past sacrifices had proclaimed the
need of an atoning death, and had their antitype, their realisation,
their annulment, in the Cross of Christ. This explicit statement
supplements and interprets the silence elsewhere noticed in the
Apostolic writings.

Strictly accordant too with the general tenour of his argument and spiritual analogies.
is the language used throughout by the writer of this epistle. He
speaks of Christian sacrifices, of a Christian altar ; but the sacrifices
are praise and thanksgiving and well-doing, the altar is apparently the Cross of Christ[2]. If the Christian ministry were a

---

[1] The epistle deals mainly with the office of Christ as the antitype of the *High Priest* offering the *annual* sacrifice of atonement: and it has been urged that there is still room for a sacrificial priesthood under the High Priest. The whole argument however is equally applicable to the inferior priests: and in one passage at least it is directly so applied (x. 11, 12), ' And every priest standeth daily (καθ' ἡμέραν) ministering and offering the same sacrifices, etc.'; where the v.l. ἀρχιερεὺς for ἱερεὺς seems to have arisen from the desire to bring the verse into more exact conformity with what has gone before. This passage, it should be remembered, is the summing up and generalisation of the previous argument.

[2] It is surprising that some should have interpreted θυσιαστήριον in Heb. xiii. 10 of the Lord's table. There may be a doubt as to the exact significance of the term in this passage, but an actual altar is plainly not intended. This is shown by the context both before and after: e.g. ver. 9 the opposition of χάρις and βρώματα, ver. 15 the

contrast implied in the mention of θυσία αἰνέσεως and καρπὸς χειλέων, and ver. 16 the naming εὐποιία καὶ κοινωνία as the kind of sacrifice with which God is well pleased. In my former editions I interpreted the θυσιαστήριον of the congregation assembled for worship, having been led to this interpretation by the Christian phraseology of succeeding ages. So Clem. Alex. *Strom.* vii. 6, p. 848, ἔστι γοῦν τὸ παρ' ἡμῖν θυσιαστήριον ἐνταῦθα τὸ ἐπίγειον τὸ ἄθροισμα τῶν ταῖς εὐχαῖς ἀνακειμένων. The use of the word in Ignatius also, though less obvious, appears to be substantially the same, *Ephes.* 5, *Trall.* 7, *Philad.* 4 (but in *Magn.* 7 it seems to be a metaphor for our Lord Himself); see Höfling *Opfer* etc. p. 32 sq. Similarly too Polycarp (§ 4) speaks of the body of widows as θυσιαστήριον Θεοῦ. But I have since been convinced that the context points to the Cross of Christ spiritually regarded, as the true interpretation.

[Since my first edition appeared, a wholly different interpretation of the passage has been advocated by more

sacerdotal office, if the holy eucharist were a sacerdotal act, ·in the same sense in which the Jewish priesthood and the Jewish sacrifice were sacerdotal, then his argument is faulty and his language misleading. Though dwelling at great length on the Christian coun-terparts to the Jewish priest, the Jewish altar, the Jewish sacri fice, he omits to mention the one office, the one place, the one act, which on this showing would be their truest and liveliest coun-terparts in the every-day worship of the Church of Christ. He has rejected these, and he has chosen instead moral and spiritual analo-gies for all these sacred types[1]. Thus in what he has said and in what he has left unsaid alike, his language points to one and the same result.

Christian ministers are priests in another sense;

If therefore the sacerdotal office be understood to imply the offering of sacrifices, then the Epistle to the Hebrews leaves no place for a Christian priesthood. If on the other hand the word be taken in a wider and looser acceptation, it cannot well be withheld from the ministry of the Church of Christ. Only in this case the meaning of the term should be clearly apprehended: and it might have been

than one writer. It is maintained that ἔχομεν θυσιαστήριον should be understood 'we Jews have an altar,' and that the writer of the epistle is here bringing an example from the Old Dispensation itself (the sin-offering on the day of atonement) in which the sacrifices were not eaten. This inter-pretation is attractive, but it seems to me inadequate to explain the *whole* context (though it suits parts well enough), and is ill adapted to indi-vidual expressions (e.g. θυσιαστήριον where θυσία would be expected, and οἱ τῇ σκηνῇ λατρεύοντες which thus becomes needlessly emphatic), not to mention that the first person plural and the present tense ἔχομεν seem unnatural where the author and his readers are spoken of, not as actual Christians, but as former Jews. In fact the analogy of the sacrifice on the day of atonement appears not to be introduced till the next verse, ὧν γὰρ εἰσφέρεται ζώων κ.τ.λ.]

Some interpreters again, from a com-parison of 1 Cor. ix. 13 with 1 Cor. x. 18, have inferred that St Paul recog-nises the designation of the Lord's table as an altar. On the contrary it is a speaking fact, that in both pas-sages he avoids using this term of the Lord's table, though the language of the context might readily have sug-gested it to him, if he had considered it appropriate. Nor does the argu-ment in either case require or en-courage such an inference. In 1 Cor. ix. 13, 14, the Apostle writes 'Know ye not that they which wait at the altar are partakers with the altar? Even so hath the Lord ordained that they which preach the gospel should live of the gospel.' The point of resem-blance in the two cases is the holding a sacred office; but the ministering on the altar is predicated only of the former. So also in 1 Cor. x. 18 sq., the *altar* is named as common to Jews and Heathens, but the *table* only as common to Christians and Heathens; i.e. the holy eucharist is a banquet but it is not a sacrifice (in the Jewish or Heathen sense of sacrifice).

[1] For the passages see above, pp. 261, 262.

better if the later Christian vocabulary had conformed to the silence of the Apostolic writers, so that the possibility of confusion would have been avoided.

According to this broader meaning, the priest may be defined as one who represents God to man and man to God. It is moreover indispensable that he should be called by God, for no man 'taketh this honour to himself.' The Christian ministry satisfies both these conditions.

Of the fulfilment of the latter the only evidence within our cognisance is the fact that the minister is called according to a divinely appointed order. If the preceding investigation be substantially correct, the three-fold ministry can be traced to Apostolic direction; and short of an express statement we can possess no better assurance of a Divine appointment or at least a Divine sanction. If the facts do not allow us to unchurch other Christian communities differently organized, they may at least justify our jealous adhesion to a polity derived from this source. *as having a divine appointment,*

And while the mode of appointment satisfies the one condition, the nature of the office itself satisfies the other; for it exhibits the doubly representative character which is there laid down.

The Christian minister is God's ambassador to men: he is charged with the ministry of reconciliation; he unfolds the will of heaven; he declares in God's name the terms on which pardon is offered; and he pronounces in God's name the absolution of the penitent. This last mentioned function has been thought to invest the ministry with a distinctly sacerdotal character. Yet it is very closely connected with the magisterial and pastoral duties of the office, and is only priestly in the same sense in which they are priestly. As empowered to declare the conditions of God's grace, he is empowered also to proclaim the consequences of their acceptance. But throughout his office is representative and not vicarial[1]. He does not interpose between God and man in such a way that direct communion with God is superseded on the one hand, or that his own mediation becomes indispensable on the other. *as representing God to man.*

Again the Christian minister is the representative of man to God—of the congregation primarily, of the individual indirectly *and as representing man to God.*

---

[1] The distinction is made in Maurice's *Kingdom of Christ* II. p. 116.

a member of the congregation. The alms, the prayers, the thanks-givings of the community are offered through him. Some represen-tation is as necessary in the Church as it is in a popular govern-ment: and the nature of the representation is not affected by the fact that the form of the ministry has been handed down from Apostolic times and may well be presumed to have a Divine sanction. For here again it must be borne in mind that the minister's function is *representative* without being *vicarial*. He is a priest, as the mouthpiece, the delegate, of a priestly race. His acts are not his own, but the acts of the congregation. Hence too it will follow that, viewed on this side as on the other, his function cannot be absolute and indispensable. It may be a general rule, it may be under ordinary circumstances a practically universal law, that the highest acts of congregational worship shall be performed through the principal officers of the congregation. But an emergency may arise when the spirit and not the letter must decide. The Christian ideal will then interpose and interpret our duty. The higher ordinance of the universal priesthood will overrule all special limitations. The layman will assume functions which are otherwise restricted to the ordained minister[1].

The preva-lence of sacerdotal-ism con-sidered.
Yet it would be vain to deny that a very different conception prevailed for many centuries in the Church of Christ. The Apo-stolic ideal was set forth, and within a few generations forgotten. The vision was only for a time and then vanished. A strictly sacerdotal view of the ministry superseded the broader and more spiritual conception of their priestly functions. From being the representatives, the ambassadors, of God, they came to be regarded His vicars. Nor is this the only instance where a false conception has seemed to maintain a long-lived domination over the Church. For some centuries the idea of the Holy Roman Empire enthralled the minds of men. For a still longer period the idea of the Holy Roman See held undisturbed sway over Western Christendom. To those who take a comprehensive view of the progress of Christianity, even these more lasting obscurations of the truth will present no serious difficulty. They will not suffer themselves to be blinded

---

[1] For the opinion of the early Church on this subject see especially the passage of Tertullian quoted above, p. 256.

thereby to the true nobility of Ecclesiastical History : they will not fail to see that, even in the seasons of her deepest degradation, the Church was still the regenerator of society, the upholder of right principle against selfish interest, the visible witness of the Invisible God; they will thankfully confess that, notwithstanding the pride and selfishness and dishonour of individual rulers, notwithstanding the imperfections and errors of special institutions and developments, yet in her continuous history the Divine promise has been signally realised, ' Lo I am with you always, even unto the end of the world.'

# ST PAUL AND SENECA.

Seneca traditionally accounted a Christian.

THE earliest of the Latin fathers, Tertullian, writing about a century and a half after the death of Seneca, speaks of this philosopher as 'often our own[1].' Some two hundred years later St Jerome, having occasion to quote him, omits the qualifying adverb and calls him broadly 'our own Seneca[2].' Living midway between these two writers, Lactantius points out several coincidences with the teaching of the Gospel in the writings of Seneca, whom nevertheless he styles 'the most determined of the Roman Stoics[3].' From the age of St Jerome, Seneca was commonly regarded as standing on the very threshold of the Christian Church, even if he had not actually passed within its portals. In one Ecclesiastical Council at least, held at Tours in the year 567, his authority is quoted with a deference generally accorded only to fathers of the Church[4]. And even to the present day in the marionette plays of his native Spain St Seneca takes his place by the side of St Peter and St Paul in the representations of our Lord's passion[5].

Comparing the language of Tertullian and Jerome, we are able to measure the growth of this idea in the interval of time which separates the two. One important impulse however, which it received meanwhile, must not be overlooked. When St Jerome wrote,

---

[1] Tertull. *de Anim.* 20 'Seneca sæpe noster.'

[2] *Adv. Jovin.* i. 49 (II. p. 318) 'Scripserunt Aristoteles et Plutarchus et noster Seneca de matrimonio libros etc.'

[3] *Div. Inst.* i. 5 'Annæus Seneca qui ex Romanis vel acerrimus Stoicus

fuit' : comp. ii. 9, vi. 24, etc.

[4] Labbæi *Concilia* v. p. 856 (Paris, 1671) 'Sicut ait Seneca pessimum in eo vitium esse qui in id quo insanit cæteros putat furere.' See Fleury *Saint Paul et Sénèque* I. p. 14.

[5] So Fleury states, I. p. 289.

the Christianity of Seneca seemed to be established on a sounder basis than mere critical inference.  A correspondence, purporting to have passed between the heathen philosopher and the Apostle of the Gentiles, was then in general circulation; and, without either affirming or denying its genuineness, this father was thereby induced to give a place to Seneca in his catalogue of Christian writers[1].  If the letters of Paul and Seneca, which have come down to us, are the same with those read by him (and there is no sufficient reason for doubting the identity[2]), it is strange that he could for a moment have entertained the question of their authenticity.  The poverty of thought and style, the errors in chronology and history, and the whole conception of the relative positions of the Stoic philosopher and the Christian Apostle, betray clearly the hand of a forger.  Yet this correspondence has without doubt been mainly instrumental in fixing the belief on the mind of the later Church, as it was even sufficient to induce some hesitation in St Jerome himself.  How far the known history and the extant writings of either favour this idea, it will be the object of the present essay to examine.  The enquiry into the historical connexion between these two great contemporaries will naturally expand into an investigation of the relations, whether of coincidence or of contrast, between the systems of which they were the respective exponents.  And, as Stoicism was the only philosophy which could even pretend to rival Christianity in the earlier ages of the Church, such an investigation ought not to be uninstructive[3].

Like all the later systems of Greek philosophy, Stoicism was the offspring of despair.  Of despair in religion : for the old mythologies had ceased to command the belief or influence the conduct of men.  Of despair in politics : for the Macedonian conquest had broken the independence of the Hellenic states and stamped out the last sparks of corporate life.  Of despair even in philosophy itself : for the older

[1] *Vir. Illustr.* 12 'Quem non ponerem in catalogo sanctorum, nisi me illæ epistolæ provocarent quæ leguntur a plurimis, Pauli ad Senecam et Senecæ ad Paulum.'<br>[2] See the note at the end of this dissertation.<br>[3] In the sketch, which I have given, of the relation of Stoicism to the circumstances of the time and to other

earlier and contemporary systems of philosophy, I am greatly indebted to the account in Zeller's *Philosophie der Griechen* Th. III. Abth. 1 *Die nach-aristotelische Philosophie* (2nd ed. 1865), which it is impossible to praise too highly. See also the instructive essay of Sir A. Grant on 'The Ancient Stoics' in his edition of *Aristotle's Ethics* I. p. 243 sq. (2nd ed.).

thinkers, though they devoted their lives to forging a golden chain which should link earth to heaven, appeared now to have spent their strength in weaving ropes of sand. The sublime intuitions of Plato had been found too vague and unsubstantial, and the subtle analyses of Aristotle too hard and cold, to satisfy the natural craving of man for some guidance which should teach him how to live and to die.

Greece prepared for new systems of philosophy.

Thus the soil of Greece had been prepared by the uprootal of past interests and associations for fresh developments of religious and philosophic thought. When political life became impossible, the moral faculties of man were turned inward upon himself and concentrated on the discipline of the individual soul. When speculation had been cast aside as barren and unprofitable, the search was directed towards some practical rule or rules which might take its place. When the gods of Hellas had been deposed and dishonoured, some new powers must be created or discovered to occupy their vacant throne.

Coincidences and contrasts of the Epicurean and Stoic philosophies.

Stimulated by the same need, Epicurus and Zeno strove in different ways to solve the problem which the perplexities of their age presented. Both alike, avoiding philosophy in the proper sense of the term, concentrated their energies on ethics : but the one took happiness, the other virtue, as his supreme good, and made it the starting point of his ethical teaching. Both alike contrasted with the older masters in building their systems on the needs of the individual and not of the state : but the one strove to satisfy the cravings of man, as a being intended by nature for social life, by laying stress on the claims and privileges of friendship, the other by expanding his sphere of duty and representing him as a citizen of the world or even of the universe. Both alike paid a certain respect to the waning beliefs of their day : but the one without denying the existence of the gods banished them from all concern in the affairs of men, while the other, transforming and utilising the creations of Hellenic mythology, identified them with the powers of the physical world. Both alike took conformity to nature as their guiding maxim : but nature with the one was interpreted to mean the equable balance of all the impulses and faculties of man, with the other the absolute supremacy of the reason, as the ruling principle of his being. And lastly ; both alike sought refuge from the turmoil and confusion of the age in the inward calm and composure of the soul. If Serenity (ἀταραξία) was the supreme virtue of the one, her twin sister Passionlessness (ἀπαθία) was the sovereign principle of the other.

These two later developments of Greek philosophy both took root and grew to maturity in Greek soil. But, while the seed of the one was strictly Hellenic, the other was derived from an Oriental stock. Epicurus was a Greek of the Greeks, a child of Athenian parents. Zeno on the other hand, a native of Citium, a Phœnician colony in Crete, was probably of Shemitic race, for he is commonly styled 'the Phœnician¹.' Babylon, Tyre, Sidon, Carthage, reared some of his most illustrious successors. Cilicia, Phrygia, Rhodes, were the homes of others. Not a single Stoic of any name was a native of Greece proper².

*Oriental origin of Stoicism.*

To Eastern affinities Stoicism was without doubt largely indebted for the features which distinguished it from other schools of Greek philosophy. To this fact may be ascribed the intense moral earnestness which was its most honourable characteristic. If the later philosophers generally, as distinguished from the earlier, busied themselves with ethics rather than metaphysics, with the Stoics this was the one absorbing passion. The contrast between the light reckless gaiety of the Hellenic spirit and the stern, unbending, almost fanatical moralism of the followers of Zeno is as complete as could well be imagined. The ever active conscience which is the glory, and the proud self-consciousness which is the reproach, of the Stoic school are alike alien to the temper of ancient Greece. Stoicism breathes rather the religious atmosphere of the East, which fostered on the one hand the inspired devotion of a David or an Isaiah, and on the other the self-mortification and self-righteousness of an Egyptian therapeute or an Indian fakir. A recent writer, to whom we are indebted for a highly appreciative account of the Stoic school, describes this new phase of Greek philosophy, which we have been reviewing and of which Stoicism was the truest exponent, as 'the transition to *modernism*³.' It might with greater truth be described as the contact of Oriental influences with the world of classical thought.

*Its moral earnestness derived thence.*

¹ See Diog. Laert. vii. 3, where rates addresses him τί φεύγεις, ὦ Φοινίκιον; comp. § 15 Φοίνισσαν; § 25 ᾽οινικικῶς; § 30 εἰ δὲ πάτρα Φοίνισσα, τίς φθόνος. We are told also § 7 ἀντεποιοῦντο δ᾽ αὐτοῦ καὶ οἱ ἐν Σιδῶνι Κιτιεῖς.

So again ii. 114 Ζήνωνα τὸν Φοίνικα.
² See below, pp. 299, 303.
³ Grant, *l. c.* p. 243. Sir A. Grant however fully recognises the eastern element in Stoicism (p. 246).

Stoicism was in fact the earliest offspring of the union between the religious consciousness of the East and the intellectual culture of the West. The recognition of the claims of the individual soul, the sense of personal responsibility, the habit of judicial introspection, in short the subjective view of ethics, were in no sense new, for they are known to have held sway over the mind of the chosen people from the earliest dawn of their history as a nation. But now for the first time they presented themselves at the doors of Western civilization and demanded admission. The occasion was eminently favourable. The conquests of Alexander, which rendered the fusion of the East and West for the first time possible, also evoked the moral need which they had thus supplied the means of satisfying. By the overthrow of the state the importance of the individual was enhanced. In the failure of political relations, men were thrown back on their inward resources and led to examine their moral wants and to educate their moral faculties.

It was in this way that the Eastern origin of Stoicism combined with the circumstances and requirements of the age to give it an exclusively *ethical* character. The Stoics did, it is true, pay some little attention to physical questions : and one or two leading representatives of the school also contributed towards the systematic treatment of logic. But consciously and expressly they held these branches of study to be valueless except in their bearing on moral questions. Representing philosophy under the image of a field, they compared physics to the trees, ethics to the fruit for which the trees exist, and logic to the wall or fence which protects the enclosure[1]. Or again, adopting another comparison, they likened logic to the shell of an egg, physics to the white, and ethics to the yolk[2]. As the fundamental maxim of Stoical ethics was conformity to nature, and as therefore it was of signal importance to ascertain man's rela-

---

[1] Diog. Laert. vii. 40, Philo *de Agric.* 3, p. 302 M. See also *de Mut. Nom.* § 10, p. 589 M, where Philo after giving this comparison says οὕτως οὖν ἔφασαν καὶ ἐν φιλοσοφίᾳ δεῖν τήν τε φυσικὴν καὶ λογικὴν πραγματείαν ἐπὶ τὴν ἠθικὴν ἀναφέρεσθαι κ.τ.λ.

[2] Sext. Emp. vii. 17. On the other hand Diog. Laert. *l.c.* makes ethics the white and physics the yolk. See Zeller *l.c.* p. 57, and Ritter and Preller *Hist.*

*Phil.* § 396. But this is a matter of little moment ; for, whichever form of the metaphor be adopted, the ethical bearing of physics is put prominently forward. Indeed as ancient naturalists were not agreed about the respective functions of the yolk and the white, the application of the metaphor must have been influenced by this uncertainty. The inferiority of logic appears in all the comparisons.

tion to the world around, it might have been supposed that the study of physics would have made great progress in the hands of Zeno's disciples. But, pursuing it for the most part without any love for the study itself and pursuing it moreover only to support certain foregone ethical conclusions, they instituted few independent researches and discovered no hidden truths. To logic they assigned a still meaner part. The place which it occupies in the images already mentioned *and depreciation of logic.* clearly points to their conception of its functions. It was not so much a means of arriving at truth, as an expedient for protecting truth already attained from external assaults. An extreme representative of the school went so far as to say that 'Of subjects of philosophical investigation some pertain to us, some have no relation to us, and some are beyond us : ethical questions belong to the first class ; dialectics to the second, for they contribute nothing towards the amendment of life ; and physics to the third, for they are beyond the reach of knowledge and are profitless withal[1].' This was the genuine spirit of the school[2], though other adherents were more guarded in their statements. Physical science is conversant in *experiment*; logical science in *argumentation*. But the Stoic was impatient alike of the one and the other ; for he was essentially a philosopher of *intuitions*.

And here again the Oriental spirit manifested itself. The Greek *Prophetic spirit of the school.* moralist was a reasoner : the Oriental for the most part, whether inspired or uninspired, a prophet. Though they might clothe their systems of morality in a dialectical garb, the Stoic teachers belonged essentially to this latter class. Even Chrysippus, the great logician and controversialist of the sect, is reported to have told his master Cleanthes, that 'he only wanted the doctrines, and would himself find out the proofs[3].' This saying has been condemned as 'betraying a want of earnestness as to the truth[4]'; but I can hardly think that it ought to be regarded in this light. Flippant though it would appear at first sight, it may well express the intense faith in intuition, or what I have called the prophetic[5] spirit, which distinguishes the

---

[1] Ariston in Diog. Laert. vii. 160, Stob. *Flor.* lxxx. 7. See Zeller *l.c.* p. 50.

[2] 'Quicquid legeris *ad mores* statim referas,' says Seneca *Ep. Mor.* lxxxix. See the whole of the preceding epistle

[3] Diog. Laert. vii. 179 πολλάκις ἔλεγε μόνης τῆς τῶν δογμάτων διδασκαλίας χρήζειν τὰς δ' ἀποδείξεις αὐτὸς εὑρήσειν.

[4] Grant *l.c.* p. 253.

[5] Perhaps the use of this term needs some apology ; but I could not find

school. Like the other Stoics, Chrysippus had no belief in argumentation, but welcomed the highest truths as intuitively apprehended.
Logic was to him, as to them, only the egg-shell which protected the
germ of future life, the fence which guarded the fruitful garden. As
a useful weapon of defence against assailants and nothing more, it
was regarded by the most perfect master of the science which the
school produced. The doctrines did not derive their validity from
logical reasoning : they were absolute and self-contained. Once stated,
they must commend themselves to the innate faculty, when not
clouded by ignoble prejudices of education or degrading habits of life.

Parallel to Christianity in the westward progress of Stoicism.
But though the germ of Stoicism was derived from the East, its
systematic development and its practical successes were attained by
transplantation into a western soil. In this respect its career, as it
travelled westward, presents a rough but instructive parallel to the
progress of the Christian Church. The fundamental ideas, derived
from Oriental parentage, were reduced to a system and placed on an
Influence of Greece intellectual basis by the instrumentality of Greek thought. The
schools of Athens and of Tarsus did for Stoicism the same work
which was accomplished for the doctrines of the Gospel by the con-
troversial writings of the Greek fathers and the authoritative decrees
of the Greek councils. Zeno and Chrysippus and Panætius are the
counterparts of an Origen, an Athanasius, or a Basil. But, while the
systematic expositions of the Stoic tenets were directly or indirectly
the products of Hellenic thought and were matured on Greek soil,
and of Rome. the scene of its greatest practical manifestations was elsewhere. It
must be allowed that the Roman representatives of the school were
very inadequate exponents of the Stoic philosophy regarded as a speculative system : but just as Latin Christianity adopted from her
Greek sister the creeds which she herself was incapable of framing,
and built thereupon an edifice of moral influence and social organization far more stately and enduring, so also when naturalised in its
Latin home Stoicism became a motive power in the world, and exhibited those practical results to which its renown is chiefly due.
This comparison is instituted between movements hardly comparable

a better. I meant to express by it the characteristic of enunciating moral truths as authoritative, independently of processes of reasoning. The Stoic, being a pantheist and having no dis- tinct belief in a personal God, was not a prophet in the ordinary sense, but only as being the exponent of his own inner consciousness, which was his su- preme authority.

in their character or their effects; and it necessarily stops short of the incorporation of the Teutonic nations. But the distinctive feature of Christianity as a Divine revelation and of the Church as a Divine institution does not exempt them from the ordinary laws of progress : and the contrasts between the doctrines of the Porch and the Gospel, to which I shall have to call attention later, are rendered only the more instructive by observing this parallelism in their outward career.

It is this latest or Roman period of Stoic philosophy which has chiefly attracted attention, not only because its practical influence then became most manifest, but also because this stage of its history alone is adequately illustrated by extant writings of the school. On the Christian student moreover it has a special claim; for he will learn an instructive lesson in the conflicts or coincidences of Stoicism with the doctrines of the Gospel and the progress of the Church. And of this stage in its history Seneca is without doubt the most striking representative. *Attention directed to the Roman period.*

Seneca was strictly a contemporary of St Paul. Born probably within a few years of each other, the Christian Apostle and the Stoic philosopher both died about the same time and both fell victims of the same tyrant's rage. Here, it would have seemed, the parallelism must end. One might indeed indulge in an interesting speculation whether Seneca, like so many other Stoics, had not Shemitic blood in his veins. The whole district from which he came was thickly populated with Phœnician settlers either from the mother country or from her great African colony. The name of his native province Bætica, the name of his native city Corduba, are both said to be Phœnician. Even his own name, though commonly derived from the Latin, may perhaps have a Shemitic origin; for it is borne by a Jew of Palestine early in the second century[1]. This however is thrown out merely as a conjecture. Otherwise the Stoic philosopher from the extreme West and the Christian Apostle from the extreme East of the Roman dominions would seem very unlikely to present any features in common. The one a wealthy courtier and statesman settled in the metropolis, the other a poor and homeless *Seneca* *contrasted with St Paul.*

---

[1] The name Σεννεκᾶς or Σενεκᾶς occurs in the list of the early bishops of Jerusalem, Euseb. *H. E.* iv. 5. The word is usually connected with 'senex.' Curtius *Griech. Etym.* § 428.

preacher wandering in distant provinces, they were separated not less by the manifold influences of daily life than by the circum-

Coinci-
dences of
thought
and lan-
guage.

stances of their birth and early education. Yet the coincidences of thought and even of language between the two are at first sight so striking, that many writers have been at a loss to account for them, except on the supposition of personal intercourse, if not of direct plagiarism[1]. The inference indeed appears unnecessary: but the facts are remarkable enough to challenge investigation, and I propose now to consider their bearing.

Though general resemblances of sentiment and teaching will carry less weight, as compared with the more special coincidences of language and illustration, yet the data would be incomplete without taking the former into account[2]. Thus we might imagine ourselves

[1] The connection of St Paul and Seneca has been a favourite subject with French writers. The most elaborate of recent works is A. Fleury's *Saint Paul et Sénèque* (Paris 1853), in which the author attempts to show that Seneca was a disciple of St Paul. It is interesting and full of materials, but extravagant and unsatisfactory. Far more critical is C. Aubertin's *Étude Critique sur les rapports supposés entre Sénèque et Saint Paul* (Paris 1857), which appears intended as an answer to Fleury. Aubertin shows that many of the parallels are fallacious, and that many others prove nothing, since the same sentiments occur in earlier writers. At the same time he fails to account for other more striking coincidences. It must be added also that he is sometimes very careless in his statements. For instance (p. 186) he fixes an epoch by coupling together the names of Celsus and Julian, though they are separated by nearly two centuries. Fleury's opinion is combated also in Baur's articles *Seneca und Paulus*, republished in *Drei Abhandlungen etc.* p. 377 sq. (ed. Zeller, 1876). Among other recent French works in which Seneca's obligations to Christianity are maintained, may be named those of Troplong, *De l'influence du Christianisme sur le droit civil des Romains* p. 76 (Paris 1843), and C. Schmidt *Essai historique sur la société civile dans le monde Romain et sur sa transformation*

*par le Christianisme* (Paris 1853). The opposite view is taken by C. Martha *Les Moralistes sous l'Empire Romain* (2ᵐᵉ ed. Paris 1866). *Le Stoicisme à Rome*, by P. Montée (Paris, 1865), is a readable little book, but does not throw any fresh light on the subject. *Seekers after God*, a popular and instructive work by the Rev. F. W. Farrar, appeared about the same time as my first edition. Still later are the discussions of G. Boissier *La Religion Romaine* II. p. 52 sq. (Paris, 1874) and K. Franke *Stoicismus u. Christenthum* (Breslau, 1876). The older literature of the subject will be found in Fleury I. p. 2 sq. In reading through Seneca I have been able to add some striking coincidences to those collected by Fleury and others, while at the same time I have rejected a vast number as insufficient or illusory.

[2] No account is here taken of certain direct reproductions of Christian teaching which some writers have found in Seneca. Thus the doctrine of the Trinity is supposed to be enunciated by these words 'Quisquis formator universi fuit, sive ille *Deus* est *potens omnium*, sive incorporalis *ratio* ingentium operum artifex, sive *divinus spiritus* per omnia maxima ac minima æquali intentione diffusus, sive fatum et inmutabilis causarum inter se cohærentium series' (*ad Helv. matr.* 8). Fleury (I. p. 97), who holds this view, significantly ends his quotation with 'diffusus,' omit-

listening to a Christian divine, when we read in the pages of
Seneca that 'God made the world because He is good,' and that Goodness
'as the good never grudges anything good, He therefore made every- of God.
thing the best possible[1].' Yet if we are tempted to draw a hasty
inference from this parallel, we are checked by remembering that it is
a quotation from Plato. Again Seneca maintains that 'in worshipping Relation
the gods, the first thing is to believe in the gods,' and that 'he who of man to
has copied them has worshipped them adequately[2]'; and on this duty God.
of imitating the gods he insists frequently and emphatically[3]. But
here too his sentiment is common to Plato and many other of the
older philosophers. 'No man,' he says elsewhere, 'is good without
God[4].' 'Between good men and the gods there exists a friendship—
a friendship do I say? nay, rather a relationship and a resemblance[5]';
and using still stronger language he speaks of men as the children of
God[6]. But here again he is treading in the footsteps of the older
Stoic teachers, and his very language is anticipated in the words quoted
by St Paul from Cleanthes or Aratus, 'We too His offspring are[7].'

From the recognition of God's fatherly relation to man im- Fatherly
portant consequences flow. In almost Apostolic language Seneca chastise-
describes the trials and sufferings of good men as the chastisements God.
of a wise and beneficent parent: 'God has a fatherly mind towards
good men and loves them stoutly; and, saith He, Let them be
harassed with toils, with pains, with losses, that they may gather
true strength[8].' 'Those therefore whom God approves, whom He

ting the clause 'sive fatum, etc.' Thus
again some writers have found an allusion to the Christian sacraments in
Seneca's language, 'Ad hoc sacramen-
tum adacti sumus ferre mortalia,' de Vit.
beat. 15 (comp. Ep. Mor. lxv). Such
criticisms are mere plays on words and
do not even deserve credit for ingenuity.
On the other hand Seneca does mention
the doctrine of guardian angels or demons; 'Sepone in praesentia quae qui-
busdam placent, unicuique nostrum
paedagogum dari deum,' Ep. Mor. cx;
but, as Aubertin shows (p. 284 sq.), this
was a tenet common to many earlier
philosophers; and in the very passage
quoted Seneca himself adds, 'Ita tamen
hoc seponas volo, ut memineris majores
nostros, qui crediderunt, Stoicos fuisse,

singulis enim et Genium et Junonem
dederunt.' See Zeller p. 297 sq.
[1] Ep. Mor. lxv. 10.
[2] Ep. Mor. xcv. 50.
[3] de Vit. beat. 15 'Habebit illud
in animo vetus praeceptum: deum se-
quere'; de Benef. iv. 25 'Propositum
est nobis secundum rerum naturam vivere et deorum exemplum sequi'; ib.
i. 1 'Hos sequamur duces quantum
humana imbecillitas patitur'; Ep. Mor.
cxxiv. 23 'Animus emendatus ac purus,
aemulator dei.'
[4] Ep. Mor. xli; comp. lxxiii.
[5] de Prov. 1; comp. Nat. Quaest. prol.
etc.
[6] de Prov. 1, de Benef. ii. 29.
[7] Acts xvii. 28.
[8] de Prov. 2.

loves, them He hardens, He chastises, He disciplines[1].' Hence the 'sweet uses of adversity' find in him an eloquent exponent. 'Nothing,' he says, quoting his friend Demetrius, 'seems to me more unhappy than the man whom no adversity has ever befallen[2].' 'The life free from care and from any buffetings of fortune is a dead sea[3].' Hence too it follows that resignation under adversity becomes a plain duty. 'It is best to endure what you cannot mend, and without murmuring to attend upon God, by whose ordering all things come to pass. He is a bad soldier who follows his captain complaining[4].'

The indwelling spirit of God. Still more strikingly Christian is his language, when he speaks of God, who 'is near us, is with us, is within,' of 'a holy spirit residing in us, the guardian and observer of our good and evil deeds[5].' 'By what other name,' he asks, 'can we call an upright and good and great mind except (a) god lodging in a human body[6]?' The spark of a heavenly flame has alighted on the hearts of men[7]. They are associates with, are members of God. The mind came from God and yearns towards God[8].

From this doctrine of the abiding presence of a divine spirit the practical inferences are not less weighty. 'So live with men, as if God saw you; so speak with God, as if men heard you[9].' 'What profits it, if any matter is kept secret from men? nothing is hidden from God[10].' 'The gods are witnesses of everything[11].'

Universal dominion of sin. But even more remarkable perhaps, than this devoutness of tone in which the duties of man to God arising out of his filial relation are set forth, is the energy of Seneca's language, when he paints the internal struggle of the human soul and prescribes the discipline needed for its release. The soul is bound in a prison-house, is weighed down by a heavy burden[12]. Life is a continual warfare[13].

---

[1] de Prov. 4; comp. ib. § 1.
[2] de Prov. 3.
[3] Ep. Mor. lxvii. This again is a saying of Demetrius.
[4] Ep. Mor. cvii; comp. ib. lxxvi.
[5] Ep. Mor. xli; comp. ib. lxxiii.
[6] Ep. Mor. xxxi. The want of the definite article in Latin leaves the exact meaning uncertain; but this uncertainty is suited to the vagueness of Stoic theology. In Ep. Mor. xli Seneca quotes the words 'Quis deus, incertum est; habitat Deus' (Virg. Æn. viii. 352), and applies them to this inward monitor.
[7] de Otio 5.
[8] Ep. Mor. xcii.
[9] Ep. Mor. x.
[10] Ep. Mor. lxxxiii; comp. Fragm. 14 (in Lactant. vi. 24).
[11] Ep. Mor. cii.
[12] Ad Helv. matr. 11, Ep. Mor. lxv, cii.
[13] See below, p. 287, note 9.

From the terrors of this struggle none escape unscathed. The Apostolic doctrine that all have sinned has an apparent counterpart in the teaching of Seneca; 'We shall ever be obliged to pronounce the same sentence upon ourselves, that we are evil, that we have been evil, and (I will add it unwillingly) that we shall be evil[1].' 'Every vice exists in every man, though every vice is not prominent in each[2].' 'If we would be upright judges of all things, let us first persuade ourselves of this, that not one of us is without fault[3].' 'These are vices of mankind and not of the times. No age has been free from fault[4].' 'Capital punishment is appointed for all, and this by a most righteous ordinance[5].' 'No one will be found who can acquit himself; and any man calling himself innocent has regard to the witness, not to his own conscience[6].' 'Every day, every hour,' he exclaims,' 'shows us our nothingness, and reminds us by some new token, when we forget our frailty[7].' Thus Seneca, in common with the Stoic school generally, lays great stress on the office of the conscience, as 'making cowards of us all.' 'It reproaches them,' he says, 'and shows them to themselves[8].' 'The first and greatest punishment of sinners is the fact of having sinned[9].' 'The beginning of safety is the knowledge of sin.' 'I think this,' he adds, 'an admirable saying of Epicurus[10].'

*Office of the conscience.*

Hence also follows the duty of strict self-examination. 'As far as thou canst, accuse thyself, try thyself: discharge the office, first of a prosecutor, then of a judge, lastly of an intercessor[11].' Accordingly he relates at some length how, on lying down to rest every night, he follows the example of Sextius and reviews his shortcomings during the day: 'When the light is removed out of sight, and my wife, who is by this time aware of my practice, is now silent, I pass the whole

*Self-examination and confession.*

---

[1] *de Benef*, i. 10.
[2] *de Benef.* iv. 27.
[3] *de Ira* ii. 28; comp. *ad Polyb.* 11, *Ep. Mor.* xlii..
[4] *Ep. Mor.* xcvii.
[5] *Qu. Nat.* ii. 59.
[6] *de Ira* i. 14.
[7] *Ep. Mor.* ci.
[8] *Ep. Mor.* xcvii. 15.
[9] *ib.* 14.
[10] *Ep. Mor.* xxviii. 9 'Initium est salutis notitia peccati.' For convenience I have translated *peccatum* here

as elsewhere by 'sin'; but it will be evident at once that in a saying of Epicurus, whose gods were indifferent to the doings of men, the associations connected with the word must be very different. See the remarks below, p. 296. Fleury (I. p. 111) is eloquent on this coincidence, but omits to mention that it occurs in a saying of Epicurus. His argument crumbles into dust before our eyes, when the light of this fact is admitted.
[11] *ib.* 10.

of my day under examination, and I review my deeds and words. I hide nothing from myself, I pass over nothing[1].' Similarly he describes the good man as one who 'has opened out his conscience to the gods, and always lives as if in public, fearing himself more than others[2].' In the same spirit too he enlarges on the advantage of having a faithful friend, 'a ready heart into which your every secret can be safely deposited, whose privity you need fear less than your own[3]'; and urges again and again the duty of meditation and self-converse[4], quoting on this head the saying of Epicurus, 'Then retire within thyself most, when thou art forced to be in a crowd[5].'

Duties towards others. Nor, when we pass from the duty of individual self-discipline to the social relations of man, does the Stoic philosophy, as represented by Seneca, hold a less lofty tone. He acknowledges in almost Scriptural language the obligation of breaking bread with the hungry[6]. 'You must live for another,' he writes, 'if you would live for yourself[7].' 'For what purpose do I get myself a friend?' he exclaims with all the extravagance of Stoic self-renunciation, 'That I may have one for whom I can die, one whom I can follow into exile, one whom I can shield from death at the cost of my own life[8].' 'I will so live,' he says elsewhere, 'as if I knew that I was born for others, and will give thanks to nature on this score[9].'

Moreover these duties of humanity extend to all classes and ranks in the social scale. The slave has claims equally with the freeman, the base-born equally with the noble. 'They are slaves, you urge; nay, they are men. They are slaves; nay, they are comrades. They are slaves; nay, they are humble friends. They are slaves; nay, they are fellow-slaves, if you reflect that fortune has the same power over both.' 'Let some of them,' he adds, 'dine with you, because they are worthy; others, that they may become worthy.' 'He is a slave, you say. Yet perchance he is free in spirit. He is a slave. Will this harm him? Show me who is not.

[1] de Ira iii. 36.
[2] de Benef. vii. 1.
[3] de Tranq. Anim. 7. Comp. Ep. Mor. xi.
[4] Ep. Mor. vii 'Recede in teipsum quantum potes,' de Otio 28 (1) 'Proderit tamen per se ipsum secedere; meliores erimus singuli': comp. ad Marc. 23.

[5] Ep. Mor. xxv.
[6] Ep. Mor. xcv 'Cum esuriente panem suum dividat': comp. Is. lviii. 7 (Vulg.) 'Frange esurienti panem tuum, Ezek. xviii. 7, 16.
[7] Ep. Mor. xlviii.
[8] Ep. Mor. ix.
[9] de Vit. beat. 20: comp. de Otio 30 (3).

One is a slave to lust, another to avarice, a third to ambition, all
alike to fear[1].'

But the moral teaching of Seneca will be brought out more *Parallels to the Sermon on the Mount*
clearly, while at the same time the conditions of the problem before
us will be better understood, by collecting the parallels, which are
scattered up and down his writings, to the sentiments and images
in the Sermon on the Mount.

'The mind, unless it is pure and holy, comprehends not God[2].' *Matt. v. 8.*

'A man is a robber even before he stains his hands; for he is *v. 21 sq.*
already armed to slay, and has the desire to spoil and to kill[3].'

'The deed will not be upright, unless the will be upright[4].'

'Cast out whatsoever things rend thy heart: nay, if they could *v. 29.*
not be extracted otherwise, thou shouldst have plucked out thy
heart itself with them[5].'

'What will the wise man do when he is buffeted (colaphis per- *v. 39.*
cussus)? He will do as Cato did when he was smitten on the
mouth. He did not burst into a passion, did not avenge himself.
did not even forgive it, but denied its having been done[6].'

'I will be agreeable to friends, gentle and yielding to enemies[7].' *v. 44.*

'Give aid even to enemies[8].'

'Let us follow the gods as leaders, so far as human weakness *v. 45.*
allows: let us give our good services and not lend them on usury...
How many are unworthy of the light: and yet the day arises...
This is characteristic of a great and good mind, to pursue not the
fruits of a kind deed but the deeds themselves[9].' 'We propose
to ourselves...to follow the example of the gods...See what great

---

[1] *Ep. Mor.* xlvii. 15, 17.

[2] *Ep. Mor.* lxxxvii. 21.

[3] *de Benef.* v. 14. So also *de Const. Sap.* 7 he teaches that the sin consists in the intent, not the act, and instances adultery, theft, and murder.

[4] *Ep. Mor.* lvii 'Actio recta non erit, nisi recta fuerit voluntas,' *de Benef.* v. 19 'Mens spectanda est dantis.'

[5] *Ep. Mor.* li. 13.

[6] *de Const. Sap.* 14.

[7] *de Vit. beat.* 20 'Ero amicis jucundus, inimicis mitis et facilis.'

[8] *de Otio* 28 (1) 'Non desinemus communi bono operam dare, adjuvare singulos, opem ferre etiam inimicis miti

(*v.l.* senili) manu' : comp. also *de Benef.* v. 1 (fin.), vii. 31, *de Ira* i. 14. Such however is not always Seneca's tone with regard to enemies: comp. *Ep. Mor.* lxxxi 'Hoc certe, inquis, justitiæ convenit, suum cuique reddere, beneficio gratiam, injuriæ talionem aut certe malam gratiam. Verum erit istud, cum alius injuriam fecerit, alius beneficium dederit etc.' This passage shows that Seneca's doctrine was a very feeble and imperfect recognition of the Christian maxim 'Love your enemies.'

[9] *de Benef.* i. 1. See the whole context.

things they bring to pass daily, what great gifts they bestow, with what abundant fruits they fill the earth.. with what suddenly falling showers they soften the ground...All these things they do without reward, without any advantage accruing to themselves...Let us be

[Luke vi. 35.] ashamed to hold out any benefit for sale: we find the gods giving gratuitously. If you imitate the gods, confer benefits even on the unthankful : for the sun rises even on the wicked, and the seas are open to pirates[1].'

vi. 3 sq. 'One ought so to give that another may receive. It is not giving or receiving to transfer to the right hand from the left[2].' 'This is the law of a good deed between two: the one ought at once to forget that it was conferred, the other never to forget that it was received[3].'

vi. 10. ' Let whatsoever has been pleasing to God, be pleasing to man[4].'

vi. 16. ' Do not, like those whose desire is not to make progress but to be seen, do anything to attract notice in your demeanour or mode of life. Avoid a rough exterior and unshorn hair and a carelessly kept beard and professed hatred of money and a bed laid on the ground and whatever else affects ambitious display by a perverse path...Let everything within us be unlike, but let our outward appearance (frons) resemble the common people[5].'

vi. 19. 'Apply thyself rather to the true riches. It is shameful to depend for a happy life on silver and gold[6].' ' Let thy good deeds be invested like a treasure deep-buried in the ground, which thou canst not bring to light, except it be necessary[7].'

vii. 3 sq. 'Do ye mark the pimples of others, being covered with countless ulcers ? This is as if a man should mock at the moles or warts on the most beautiful persons, when he himself is devoured by a fierce scab[8].'

---

[1] de Benef. iv. 25, 26. See the context. Compare also de Benef. vii. 31.

[2] de Benef. v. 8.

[3] de Benef. ii. 10.

[4] Ep. Mor. lxxiv. 20.

[5] Ep. Mor. v. 1, 2. Other writers are equally severe on the insincere professors of Stoic principles. 'Like their Jewish counterpart, the Pharisees, they were formal, austere, pretentious, and not unfrequently hyprocritical'; Grant p. 281. Of the villain P. Egnatius Tacitus writes (Ann. xvi 32), 'Auctori- tatem Stoicæ sectæ præferebat habitu et ore ad exprimendam imaginem honesti exercitus.' Egnatius, like so many other Stoics, was an Oriental, a native of Beyrout (Juv. iii. 116). If the philosopher's busts may be trusted, the language of Tacitus would well describe Seneca's own appearance: but probably with him this austerity was not affected.

[6] Ep. Mor. cx. 18.

[7] de Vit. beat. 24.

[8] de Vit. beat. 27.

'Expect from others what you have done to another[1].'  'Let us vii. 12,
so give as we would wish to receive[2].'

'Therefore good things cannot spring of evil...good does not vii. 16, 17.
grow of evil, any more than a fig of an olive tree. The fruits correspond to the seed[3].'

'Not otherwise than some rock standing alone in a shallow vii. 26.
sea, which the waves cease not from whichever side they are
driven to beat upon, and yet do not either stir it from its place,
etc....Seek some soft and yielding material in which to fix your
darts[4].'

Nor are these coincidences of thought and imagery confined to Other co-
the Sermon on the Mount. If our Lord compares the hypocritical incidences
Pharisees to whited walls, and contrasts the scrupulously clean with our Lord's lan-
outside of the cup and platter with the inward corruption, Seneca guage.
also adopts the same images : 'Within is no good : if thou shouldest
see them, not where they are exposed to view but where they
are concealed, they are miserable, filthy, vile, adorned without like
their own walls...Then it appears how much real foulness beneath
the surface this borrowed glitter has concealed[5].'  If our Lord
declares that the branches must perish unless they abide in the
vine, the language of Seneca presents an eminently instructive
parallel : 'As the leaves cannot flourish by themselves, but want
a branch wherein they may grow and whence they may draw sap,
so those precepts wither if they are alone : they need to be
grafted in a sect[6].'  Again the parables of the sower, of the mustard-
seed, of the debtor forgiven, of the talents placed out at usury,
of the rich fool, have all their echoes in the writings of the Roman
Stoic : 'Words must be sown like seed which, though it be small,
yet when it has found a suitable place unfolds its strength and
from being the least spreads into the largest growth...They are few
things which are spoken : yet if the mind has received them well,
they gain strength and grow. The same, I say, is the case with
precepts as with seeds. They produce much and yet they are
scanty[7].'  'Divine seeds are sown in human bodies. If a good

---

[1] *Ep. Mor.* xciv. 43. This is a quotation.
[2] *de Benef.* ii. 1.
[3] *Ep. Mor.* lxxxvii. 24, 25.
[4] *de Vit. beat.* 27.

[5] *de Provid.* 6.
[6] *Ep. Mor.* xcv. 59. See the remarks
below, p. 326, on this parallel.
[7] *Ep. Mor.* xxxviii. 2.

husbandman receives them, they spring up like their origin...; if a bad one, they are killed as by barren and marshy ground, and then weeds are produced in place of grain[1].' 'We have received our good things as a loan. The use and advantage are ours, and the duration thereof the Divine disposer of his own bounty regulates. We ought to have in readiness what He has given us for an uncertain period, and to restore it, when summoned to do so, without complaint. He is the worst debtor, who reproaches his creditor[2].' 'As the money-lender does not summon some creditors whom he knows to be bankrupt...So I will openly and persistently pass over some ungrateful persons nor demand any benefit from them in turn[3].' 'O how great is the madness of those who embark on distant hopes : I will buy, I will build, I will lend out, 1 will demand payment, I will bear honours : then at length I will resign my old age wearied and sated to rest. Believe me, all things are uncertain even to the prosperous. No man ought to promise himself anything out of the future. Even what we hold slips through our hands, and fortune assails the very hour on which we are pressing[4].' If our Master declares that 'it is more blessed to give than to receive,' the Stoic philosopher tells his readers that he 'would rather not receive benefits, than not confer them[5],' and that 'it is more wretched to the good man to do an injury than to receive one[6].' If our Lord reminds His hearers of the Scriptural warning 'I will have mercy and not sacrifice,' if He commends the poor widow's mite thrown into the treasury as a richer gift than the most lavish offerings of the wealthy, if His whole life is a comment on the prophet's declaration to the Jews that God 'cannot away with their sabbaths and new moons,' so also Seneca writes: 'Not even in victims, though they be fat and their brows glitter with gold, is honour paid to the gods, but in the pious and upright intent of the worshippers[7].' The gods are 'worshipped not by the wholesale slaughter of fat carcasses of bulls nor by votive offerings of gold or silver, nor by money poured into their treasuries, but by the pious and upright intent[8].' 'Let us

---

[1] *Ep. Mor.* lxxiii. 16.
[2] *Ad Marc.* 10.
[3] *de Benef.* v. 21.
[4] *Ep. Mor.* ci. 4.
[5] *de Benef.* i. 1.
[6] *Ep. Mor.* xcv. 52: comp. *de Benef.* iv. 12, vii. 31, 32.
[7] *de Benef.* i. 6.
[8] *Ep. Mor.* cxv. 5.

forbid any one to light lamps on sabbath-days, since the gods do not want light, and even men take no pleasure in smoke...he worships God, who knows Him[1].' And lastly, if the dying prayer of the Redeemer is 'Father, forgive them, for they know not what they do,' some have discovered a striking counterpart (I can only see a mean caricature) of this expression of triumphant self-sacrifice in the language of Seneca : 'There is no reason why thou shouldest be angry: pardon them; they are all mad[2].'

Nor are the coincidences confined to the Gospel narratives. The writings of Seneca present several points of resemblance also to the Apostolic Epistles. The declaration of St John that 'perfect love casteth out fear[3]' has its echo in the philosopher's words, 'Love cannot be mingled with fear[4].' The metaphor of St Peter, also, ' Girding up the loins of your mind be watchful and hope[5],' reappears in the same connexion in Seneca, ' Let the mind stand ready-girt, and let it never fear what is necessary but ever expect what is uncertain[6].' And again, if St James rebukes the presumption of those who say, ' To-day or to-morrow we will go into such a city, when they ought to say, If the Lord will, we shall live and do this or that[7],' Seneca in a similar spirit says that the wise man will ' never promise himself anything on the security of fortune, but will say, I will sail unless anything happen, and, I will become prætor unless anything happen, and, My business will turn out well for me unless anything happen[8].'

The coincidences with St Paul are even more numerous and not less striking. It is not only that Seneca, like the Apostle of the Gentiles, compares life to a warfare[9], or describes the struggle after good as a ' contest with the flesh[10],' or speaks of this present

*Margin notes:* Coincidences with the Apostolic Epistles, and especially with St Paul.

---

[1] *Ep. Mor.* xcv. 47.
[2] *de Benef.* v. 17. See the remarks below, p. 297.
[3] 1 Joh. iv. 18.
[4] *Ep. Mor.* xlvii. 18.
[5] 1 Pet. i. 13.
[6] *ad Polyb.* 11 'In procinctu stet animus etc.'
[7] James iv. 13.
[8] *de Tranq. Anim.* 13.
[9] *Ep. Mor.* xcvi 'Vivere, Lucili, militare est'; *ib.* li 'Nobis quoque militandum est et quidem genere militiæ

quo numquam quies, numquam otium, datur'; *ib.* lxv 'Hoc quod vivit stipendium putat'; *ib.* cxx. 12 'Civem se esse universi et militem credens.' The comparison is at least as old as the Book of Job, vii. 1.
[10] *ad Marc.* 24 'Omne illi cum hac carne grave certamen est.' The flesh is not unfrequently used for the carnal desires and repulsions, e. g. *Ep. Mor.* lxxiv 'Non est summa felicitatis nostræ in carne ponenda.' This use of σάρξ has been traced to Epicurus.

existence as a pilgrimage in a strange land and of our mortal bodies as tabernacles of the soul[1]. Though some of these metaphors are more Oriental than Greek or Roman, they are too common to suggest any immediate historical connexion. It is more to the purpose to note special coincidences of thought and diction. The hateful flattery, first of Claudius and then of Nero, to which the expressions are prostituted by Seneca, does not conceal the resemblance of the following passages to the language of St Paul where they occur in a truer and nobler application. Of the former emperor he writes to a friend at court, 'In him are all things and he is instead of all things to thee[2]': to the latter he says, 'The gentleness of thy spirit will spread by degrees through the whole body of the empire, and all things will be formed after thy likeness: health passes from the head to all the members[3].' Nor are still closer parallels wanting. Thus, while St Paul professes that he will 'gladly spend and be spent' for his Corinthian converts, Seneca repeats the same striking expression, 'Good men toil, they spend and are spent[4].' While the Apostle declares that 'unto the pure all things are pure, but unto the defiled and unbelieving nothing is pure,' it is the Roman philosopher's dictum that 'the evil man turns all things to evil[5].' While St Paul in a well-remembered passage compares and contrasts the training for the mortal and the immortal crown, a strikingly similar use is made of the same comparison in the following words of Seneca; 'What blows do athletes receive in their face, what blows all over their body. Yet they bear all the torture from thirst of glory. Let us also overcome all things, for our reward is not a crown or a palm branch or the trumpeter proclaiming silence for the announcement of our name, but virtue and strength of mind and peace acquired ever after[6].'

The coincidence will be further illustrated by the following

*(margin notes)* 2 Cor. xii. 15.　Tit. i. 15.　1 Cor. ix. 25.

---

[1] *Ep. Mor.* cxx 'Nec domum esse hoc corpus sed hospitium et quidem breve hospitium,' and again 'Magnus animus...nihil horum quae circa sunt suum judicat, sed ut commodatis utitur peregrinus et properans.' So also *Ep. Mor.* cii. 24 'Quicquid circa te jacet rerum tamquam hospitalis loci sarcinas specta.' In this last letter (§ 23) he speaks of advancing age as a 'ripening to another birth (in alium maturesci-

mus partum),' and designates death by the term since consecrated in the language of the Christian Church, as the birth-day of eternity: 'Dies iste, quem tamquam supremum reformidas, æterni natalis est' (§ 26).

[2] *ad Polyb.* 7.
[3] *de Clem.* ii. 2.
[4] *de Provid.* 5.
[5] *Ep. Mor.* xcviii. 3.
[6] *Ep. Mor.* lxxviii. 16.

passages of Seneca, to which the corresponding references in St Paul are given in the margin.

'They consecrate the holy and immortal and inviolable gods in motionless matter of the vilest kind : they clothe them with the forms of men, and beasts, and fishes[1].' Rom. i. 23.

'They are even enamoured of their own ill deeds, which is the last ill of all : and then is their wretchedness complete, when shameful things not only delight them but are even approved by them[2].' Rom. i. 28, 32.

'The tyrant is angry with the homicide, and the sacrilegious man punishes thefts[3].' Rom. ii. 21, 22.

'Hope is the name for an uncertain good[4].' Rom. viii. 24.

'Pertinacious goodness overcomes evil men[5].' Rom. xii. 21.

'I have a better and a surer light whereby I can discern the true from the false. The mind discovers the good of the mind[6].' 1 Cor. ii. 11.

'Let us use them, let us not boast of them : and let us use them sparingly, as a loan deposited with us, which will soon depart[7].' 1 Cor. vii. 31.

'To obey God is liberty[8].' 2 Cor. iii. 17.

'Not only corrected but transfigured[9].' 2 Cor. iii. 18.

'A man is not yet wise, unless his mind is transfigured into those things which he has learnt[10].'

'What is man? A cracked vessel which will break at the least fall[11].' 2 Cor. iv. 7.

'This is salutary ; not to associate with those unlike ourselves and having different desires[12].' 2 Cor. vi. 14.

'That gift is far more welcome which is given with a ready than that which is given with a full hand[13].' 2 Cor. ix. 7. (Prov. xxii. 9.)

'Gather up and preserve the time[14].' Eph. v. 16.

'I confess that love of our own body is natural to us[15].' Eph. v. 28, 29.

---

[1] de Superst. (Fragm. 31) in August. Civ. Dei vi. 10.
[2] Ep. Mor. xxxix. 6.
[3] de Ira ii. 28.
[4] Ep. Mor. x. § 2.
[5] de Benef. vii. 31.
[6] de Vit. beat. 2.
[7] Ep. Mor. lxxiv. 18.
[8] de Vit. beat. 15. Compare the language of our Liturgy, 'Whose service is perfect freedom.' Elsewhere (Ep. Mor. viii) he quotes a saying of Epicurus, 'Thou must be the slave of philosophy, that true liberty may fall to thy lot.'
[9] Ep. Mor. vi. 1.
[10] Ep. Mor. xciv. 48.
[11] ad Marc. 11. So Ps. xxxi. 14 'I am become like a broken vessel.'
[12] Ep. Mor. xxxii. 2.
[13] de Benef. i. 7.
[14] Ep. Mor. i. 1. So also he speaks elsewhere (de Brev. Vit. 1) of 'investing' time (conlocaretur).
[15] Ep. Mor. xiv. 1. The word used for love is 'caritas.'

Col. ii. 22.   'Which comes or passes away very quickly, destined to perish in the very using (in ipso usu sui periturum)[1].'

1 Tim.ii.9.   'Neither jewels nor pearls turned thee aside[2].'

1 Tim.iv.8.   'I reflect how many exercise their bodies, how few their minds[3].' 'It is a foolish occupation to exercise the muscles of the arms.... Return quickly from the body to the mind: exercise this, night and day[4].'

1 Tim.v.6.   'Do these men fear death, into which while living they have buried themselves[5]?' 'He is sick: nay, he is dead[6].'

2 Tim. iii. 7.   'They live ill, who are always learning to live[7].' 'How long wilt thou learn? begin to teach[8].'

In the opening sentences of our Burial Service two passages
1 Tim. vi. 7.   of Scripture are combined: 'We brought nothing into this world
Job i. 21.   and it is certain we can carry nothing out. The Lord gave and the Lord hath taken away: blessed be the name of the Lord.' Both passages have parallels in Seneca: 'Non licet plus efferre quam intuleris[9];' 'Abstulit (fortuna) sed dedit[10].'

In the speech on the Areopagus again, which was addressed partly to a Stoic audience, we should naturally expect to find parallels. The following passages justify this expectation.

Acts xvii. 24 sq.   'The whole world is the temple of the immortal gods[11].' 'Temples are not to be built to God of stones piled on high: He must be consecrated in the heart of each man[12].'

xvii. 25.   'God wants not ministers. How so? He Himself ministereth to the human race. He is at hand everywhere and to all men[13].'

xvii. 27.   'God is near thee: He is with thee; He is within[14].'

xvii. 29.   'Thou shalt not form Him of silver and gold: a true likeness of God cannot be moulded of this material[15].'

The first impression from these parallels   The first impression made by this series of parallels is striking. They seem to show a general coincidence in the fundamental principles of theology and the leading maxims in ethics: they exhibit moreover special resemblances in imagery and expression, which, it

---

1  de Vit. beat. 7.
2  ad Helv. matr. 16.
3  Ep. Mor. lxxx. 2.
4  Ep. Mor. xv. 2, 5.
5  Ep. Mor. cxxii. 3.
6  de Brev. Vit. 12.
7  Ep. Mor. xxiii. 9.
8  Ep. Mor. xxxiii. 9.
9  Ep. Mor. cii. 25.
10  Ep. Mor. lxiii. 7.
11  de Benef. vii. 7.
12  Fragm. 123, in Lactant. Div. Inst. vi. 25.
13  Ep. Mor. xcv. 47.
14  Ep. Mor. xli. 1.
15  Ep. Mor. xxxi. 11.

would seem, cannot be explained as the result of accident, but must needs to be modified.
point to some historical connexion.

Nevertheless a nearer examination very materially diminishes the force of this impression. In many cases, where the parallels are most close, the theory of a direct historical connexion is impossible; in many others it can be shown to be quite unnecessary; while in not a few instances the resemblance, however striking, must be condemned as illusory and fallacious. After deductions made on all these heads, we shall still have to consider whether the remaining coincidences are such as to require or to suggest this mode of solution.

1. In investigating the reasonableness of explaining coinci- Difficulty of establishing the relative chronology.
dences between two different authors by direct obligation on the one hand or the other, the dates of the several writings are obviously a most important element in the decision. In the present instance the relative chronology is involved in considerable difficulty. It is roughly true that the literary activity of Seneca comprises about the same period over which (with such exceptions as the Gospel and Epistles of St John) the writings of the Apostles and Evangelists extend. But in some cases of parallelism it is difficult, and in others wholly impossible, to say which writing can claim priority of time. If the Epistles of St Paul may for the most part be dated within narrow limits, this is not the case with the Gospels : and on the other hand the chronology of Seneca's writings is with some few exceptions vague and uncertain. In many cases The priority sometimes belongs to Seneca.
however it seems impossible that the Stoic philosopher can have derived his thoughts or his language from the New Testament. Though the most numerous and most striking parallels are found in his latest writings, yet some coincidences occur in works which must be assigned to his earlier years, and these were composed certainly before the first Gospels could have been circulated in Rome, and perhaps before they were even written. Again several strong resemblances occur in Seneca to those books of the New Testament which were written after his death. Thus the passage which dwells on the fatherly chastisement of God [1] presents a coincidence, as remarkable as any, to the language of the Epistle to the Hebrews. Thus again in tracing the portrait of the perfect man (which has been

---

[1] See above, p. 279 sq. Compare 11, 12, which is quoted there.
Hebrews xii. 5 sq.. and see Prov. iii·

thought to reflect many features of the life of Christ, delineated in the Gospels) he describes him as 'shining like a light in the darkness[1]'; an expression which at once recalls the language applied to the Divine Word in the prologue of St John's Gospel. And again in the series of parallels given above many resemblances will have been noticed to the Pastoral Epistles, which can hardly have been written before Seneca's death. These facts, if they do not prove much, are at least so far valid as to show that the simple theory of direct borrowing from the Apostolic writings will not meet all the facts of the case.

Seneca's obligations to previous writers.

2. Again; it is not sufficient to examine Seneca's writings by themselves, but we must enquire how far he was anticipated by the older philosophers in those brilliant flashes of theological truth or of ethical sentiment, which from time to time dazzle us in his writings. If after all they should prove to be only lights reflected from the noblest thoughts and sayings of former days, or at best old fires rekindled and fanned into a brighter flame, we have found a solution more simple and natural, than if we were to ascribe them to direct intercourse with Christian teachers or immediate acquaintance with Christian writings. We shall not cease in this case to regard them as true promptings of the Word of God which was from the beginning, bright rays of the Divine Light which 'was in the world' though 'the world knew it not,' which 'shineth in the darkness' though 'the darkness comprehended it not': but we shall no longer confound them with the direct effulgence of the same Word made flesh, the Shechinah at length tabernacled among men, 'whose glory we beheld, the glory as of the only-begotten of the Father.'

And this is manifestly the solution of many coincidences which have been adduced above. Though Seneca was essentially a Stoic, yet he read widely and borrowed freely from all existing schools of philosophy[2]. To the Pythagoreans and the Platonists he is largely indebted; and even of Epicurus, the founder of the rival school, he speaks with the deepest respect[3]. It will have been noticed that several of the most striking passages cited above are direct quo-

---

[1] *Ep. Mor.* cxx. 13 'Non aliter quam in tenebris lumen effulsit.'

[2] See what he says of himself, *de Vit. beat.* 3, *de Otio* 2 (29).

[3] *de Vit. beat.* 13 'In ea quidem ipsa sententia sum, invitis hoc nostris popularibus dicam, sancta Epicurum et recta præcipere et, si propius accesseris, tristia': comp. *Ep. Mor.* ii. 5, vi. 6, viii. 8, xx. 9.

tations from earlier writers, and therefore can have no immediate connexion with Christian ethics. The sentiment for instance, which approaches most nearly to the Christian maxim 'Love your enemies,' is avowedly based on the teaching of his Stoic predecessors[1].

And where this is not the case, recent research has shown that (with some exceptions) passages not only as profound in feeling and truthful in sentiment, but often very similar in expression and not less striking in their resemblance to the Apostolic writings, can be produced from the older philosophers and poets of Greece and Rome[2]. Parallels as striking found in earlier authors.

One instance will suffice. Seneca's picture of the perfect man has been already mentioned as reflecting some features of the 'Son of Man' delineated in the Gospels. Yet the earlier portrait drawn by Plato in its minute touches reproduces the likeness with a fidelity so striking, that the chronological impossibility alone has rescued him from the charge of plagiarism : 'Though doing no wrong,' Socrates is represented saying, 'he will have the greatest reputation for wrong-doing,' 'he will go forward immovable even to death, appearing to be unjust throughout life but being just,' 'he will be scourged,' 'last of all after suffering every kind of evil he will be crucified (ἀνασχινδυλευθήσεται)[3].' Not unnaturally Clement of Alexandria, quoting this passage, describes Plato as 'all but foretelling the dispensation of salvation[4].'

3. Lastly: the proverbial suspicion which attaches to statistics ought to be extended to coincidences of language, for they may be, and often are, equally fallacious. An expression or a maxim, which detached from its context offers a striking resemblance to the theology or the ethics of the Gospel, is found to have a wholly different bearing when considered in its proper relations. Many coincidence are fallacious.

This consideration is especially important in the case before us. Stoicism and Christianity are founded on widely different theological conceptions ; and the ethical teaching of the two in many respects presents a direct contrast. St Jerome was led astray either by his ignorance of philosophy or by his partiality for a stern asceticism, Stoicism and Christianity are opposed.

---

[1] de Otio 1 (28). See above, p. 283, note 8. See also Schneider Christliche Klänge p. 327 sq.

[2] Such parallels are produced from older writers by Aubertin (Sénèque et Saint Paul), who has worked out this line of argument. See also the large collection of passages in R. Schneider Christliche Klänge aus den Griechischen und Römischen Klassikern(Gotha,1865).

[3] Plato Resp. ii. pp. 361, 362. See Aubertin p. 254 sq.

[4] Strom. v. 14 μονονουχὶ προφητεύων τὴν σωτήριον οἰκονομίαν.

when he said that 'the Stoic dogmas in very many points coincide with our own[1].' It is in the doctrines of the Platonist and the Pythagorean that the truer resemblances to the teaching of the Bible are to be sought. It was not the Porch but the Academy that so many famous teachers, like Justin Martyr and Augustine, found to be the vestibule to the Church of Christ. Again and again the Platonic philosophy comes in contact with the Gospel; but Stoicism moves in another line, running parallel indeed and impressive by its parallelism, but for this very reason precluded from any approximation. Only when he deserts the Stoic platform, does Seneca really approach the level of Christianity. Struck by their beauty, he adopts and embodies the maxims of other schools: but they betray their foreign origin, and refuse to be incorporated into his system.

Seneca was a true Stoic.

For on the whole Lactantius was right, when he called Seneca a most determined follower of the Stoics[2]. It can only excite our marvel that any one, after reading a few pages of this writer, should entertain a suspicion of his having been in any sense a Christian. If the superficial colouring is not seldom deceptive, we cannot penetrate skindeep without encountering some rigid and inflexible dogma of the Stoic school. In his fundamental principles he is a disciple of Zeno; and, being a disciple of Zeno, he could not possibly be a disciple of Christ.

His pantheistic materialism.

Interpreted by this fact, those passages which at first sight strike us by their resemblance to the language of the Apostles and Evangelists assume a wholly different meaning. The basis of Stoic theology is gross materialism, though it is more or less relieved and compensated in different writers of the school by a vague mysticism. The supreme God of the Stoic had no existence distinct from external nature. Seneca himself identifies Him with fate, with necessity, with nature, with the world as a living whole[3]. The different elements of the universe, such as the planetary bodies, were inferior

---

[1] Hieron. Comm. in Isai. IV. c. 11 'Stoici qui nostro dogmati in plerisque concordant' (Op. IV. p. 159, Vallarsi).

[2] See above, p. 270.

[3] See especially de Benef. IV. 7, 8 'Natura, inquit, hoc mihi præstat. Non intelligis te, cum hoc dicis, mutare nomen deo? quid enim aliud est natura quam deus et divina ratio toti mundo partibusque ejus inserta?...Hunc eundem et fatum si dixeris, non mentieris... Sic nunc naturam voca, fatum, fortunam, omnia ejusdem dei nomina sunt varie utentis sua potestate'; de Vit. beat. 8 'Mundus cuncta complectens rectorque universi deus.' Occasionally a more personal conception of deity appears: e. g. ad Helv. Matr. 8.

gods, members of the Universal Being[1]. With a bold consistency the Stoic assigned a corporeal existence even to moral abstractions. Here also Seneca manifests his adherence to the tenets of his school. Courage, prudence, reverence, cheerfulness, wisdom, he says, are all bodily substances, for otherwise they could not affect bodies, as they manifestly do[2].

Viewed by the light of this material pantheism, the injunction to be 'followers of God' cannot mean the same to him as it does even to the Platonic philosopher, still less to the Christian Apostle. In Stoic phraseology 'imitation of God' signifies nothing deeper than a due recognition of physical laws on the part of man, and a conformity thereto in his own actions. It is merely a synonyme for the favourite Stoic formula of 'accordance with nature.' This may be a useful precept; but so interpreted the expression is emptied of its religious significance. In fact to follow the world and to follow God are equivalent phrases with Seneca[3]. Again in like manner, the lesson drawn from the rain and the sunshine freely bestowed upon all[4], though in form it coincides so nearly with the language of the Gospel, loses its theological meaning and becomes merely an appeal to a physical fact, when interpreted by Stoic doctrine.

*His language must be interpreted by his tenets.*

Hence also language, which must strike the ear of a Christian as shocking blasphemy, was consistent and natural on the lips of a Stoic. Seneca quotes with approbation the saying of his revered Sextius, that Jupiter is not better than a good man; he is richer, but riches do not constitute superior goodness; he is longer-lived, but greater longevity does not ensure greater happiness[5]. 'The good man,' he says elsewhere, 'differs from God only in length of time[6].' 'He is like God, excepting his mortality[7].' In the same spirit an earlier Stoic, Chrysippus, had boldly argued that the wise man is as useful to Zeus, as Zeus is to the wise man[8]. Such language is the legitimate consequence of Stoic pantheism.

*Consistent blasphemies in speaking of God.*

---

[1] de Clem. i. 8.
[2] Ep. Mor. cvi: comp. Ep. Mor. cxvii.
[3] de Ira ii. 16 'Quid est autem cur hominem ad tam infelicia exempla revoces, cum habeas mundum deumque, quem ex omnibus animalibus ut solus imitetur, solus intellegit.'
[4] See the passages quoted above, p. 283 sq.

[5] Ep. Mor. lxxiii. 12, 13.
[6] de Prov. 1.
[7] de Const. Sap. 8: comp. Ep. Mor. xxxi 'Par deo surges.' Nay, in one respect good men excel God, 'Ille extra patientiam malorum est, vos supra patientiam,' de Prov. 6.
[8] Plut. adv. Stoic. 33 (Op. Mor. p. 1078).

He has no consciousness of sin.    Hence also the Stoic, so long as he was true to the tenets of his school, could have no real consciousness of sin.   Only where there is a distinct belief in a personal God, can this consciousness find a resting-place.   Seneca and Tertullian might use the same word *peccatum*, but its value and significance to the two writers cannot be compared. The Christian Apostle and the Stoic philosopher alike can say, and do say, that 'All men have erred[1]'; but the moral key in which the saying is pitched is wholly different.   With Seneca error or sin is nothing more than the failure in attaining to the ideal of the perfect man which he sets before him, the running counter to the law of the universe in which he finds himself placed.   He does not view it as an offence done to the will of an all-holy all-righteous Being, an unfilial act of defiance towards a loving and gracious Father.   The Stoic conception of error or sin is not referred at all to the idea of God[2].   His pantheism had so obscured the personality of the Divine Being, that such reference was, if not impossible, at least unnatural.

Meaning of the holy spirit in Seneca.    And the influence of this pantheism necessarily pervades the Stoic vocabulary.   The 'Sacer spiritus' of Seneca may be translated literally by the Holy Spirit, the πνεῦμα ἅγιον, of Scriptural language; but it signifies something quite different.   His declaration, that we are 'members of God,' is in words almost identical with certain expressions of the Apostle ; but its meaning has nothing in common. Both the one and the other are modes of stating the Stoic dogma, that the Universe is one great animal pervaded by one soul or principle of life, and that into men, as fractions of this whole, as limbs of this body, is transfused a portion of the universal spirit[3].   It is almost purely a physical conception, and has no strictly theological value.

His moral teaching has all the repulsive features of Stoicism.    Again, though the sterner colours of Stoic morality are frequently toned down in Seneca, still the foundation of his ethical system betrays the repulsive features of his school.   His fundamental maxim is not to guide and train nature, but to *overcome* it[4].   The passions and affections are not to be directed, but to be crushed.   The wise man, he says, will be clement and gentle, but he will not feel pity, for only old women and girls will be moved by

---

[1]  See the passages quoted above, p. 284.
[2]  See the remarks of Baur *l. c.* p. 190 sq., on this subject.
[3]  Compare the well-known passage in Virgil, *Æn.* vi. 726 'Spiritus intus alit totamque infusa per artus mens agitat molem et magno se corpore miscet.'
[4]  *de Brev. Vit.* 14 'Hominis naturam cum Stoicis vincere.'

tears; he will not pardon, for pardon is the remission of a deserved penalty; he will be strictly and inexorably just[1].

It is obvious that this tone leaves no place for repentance, for forgiveness, for restitution, on which the theological ethics of the Gospel are built. The very passage[2], which has often been quoted as a parallel to the Saviour's dying words, 'Father, forgive them, for they know not what they do,' really stands in direct contrast to the spirit of those words : for it is not dictated by tenderness and love, but expresses a contemptuous pity, if not a withering scorn.

In the same spirit Seneca commits himself to the impassive calm which forms the moral ideal of his school[3]. He has no sympathy with a righteous indignation, which Aristotle called 'the spur of virtue'; for it would disturb the serenity of the mind[4]. He could only have regarded with a lofty disdain (unless for the moment the man triumphed over the philosopher) the grand outburst of passionate sympathy which in the Apostle of the Gentiles has wrung a tribute of admiration even from unbelievers, 'Who is weak, and I am not weak? Who is offended, and I burn not[5]?' He would neither have appreciated nor respected the spirit which dictated those touching words, 'I say the truth...I lie not...I have great heaviness and continual sorrow of heart...for my brethren, my kinsmen according to the flesh[6].' He must have spurned the precept which bids the Christian 'rejoice with them that do rejoice, and weep with them that weep[7],' as giving the direct lie to a sovereign maxim of Stoic philosophy. To the consistent disciple of Zeno the agony of Gethsemane could not have appeared, as to the Christian it ever will appear, the most sublime spectacle of moral sympathy, the proper consummation of a Divine life: for insensibility to the sorrows and sufferings of others was the only passport to perfection, as conceived in the Stoic ideal.

These considerations will have shown that many even of the most obvious parallels in Seneca's language are really no parallels at

*Marginal note:* Its impassiveness contrasts with the ethics of theGospel.

---

[1] de Clem. ii. 5—7, where he makes a curious attempt to vindicate the Stoics.

[2] It is quoted above, p. 287.

[3] Ep. Mor. lxxiv. 30 'Non adfligitur sapiens liberorum amissione, non amicorum : eodem enim animo fert illorum mortem quo suam exspectat. Non

magis hanc timet quam illam dolet... Inhonesta est omnis trepidatio et sollicitudo.' And see especially Ep. Mor. cxvi.

[4] de Ira iii. 3.

[5] 2 Cor. xi. 29.

[6] Rom. ix. 1, 2, 3.

[7] Rom. xii. 15.

Inconsist-
encies of
Seneca
and of Sto-
icism.

all. They will have served moreover to reveal the wide gulf which separates him from Christianity. It must be added however, that his humanity frequently triumphs over his philosophy; that he often writes with a kindliness and a sympathy which, if little creditable to his consistency, is highly honourable to his heart. In this respect however he does not stand alone. Stoicism is in fact the most incongruous, the most self-contradictory, of all philosophic systems. With a gross and material pantheism it unites the most vivid expressions of the fatherly love and providence of God: with the sheerest fatalism it combines the most exaggerated statements of the independence and self-sufficiency of the human soul : with the hardest and most uncompromising isolation of the individual it proclaims the most expansive view of his relations to all around. The inconsistencies of Stoicism were a favourite taunt with the teachers of rival schools[1]. The human heart in fact refused to be silenced by the dictation of a rigorous and artificial system, and was constantly bursting its philosophical fetters.

Coinci-
dences
still re-
main to be
explained.

But after all allowance made for the considerations just urged, some facts remain which still require explanation. It appears that the Christian parallels in Seneca's writings become more frequent as he advances in life[2]. It is not less true that they are much more striking and more numerous than in the other great Stoics of the Roman period, Epictetus and M. Aurelius; for though in character these later writers approached much nearer to the Christian ideal than the minister of Nero, though their fundamental doctrines are as little inconsistent with Christian theology and ethics as his, yet the closer resemblances of sentiment and expression, which alone would suggest any direct obligations to Christianity, are, I believe, decidedly more frequent in Seneca[3]. Lastly : after all deductions made, a class of coincidences still remains, of which the expression

---

[1] See for instance the treatise of Plutarch de Repugnantiis Stoicorum (Op. Mor. p. 1033 sq.).

[2] Among his more Christian works are the de Providentia, de Otio, de Vita beata, de Beneficiis, and the Epistolæ Morales; among his less Christian, the de Constantia Sapientis and de Ira. In some cases the date is uncertain; but what I have said in the text will, I think, be found substantially true.

[3] I have read Epictetus and M. Aurelius through with a view to such coincidences, and believe the statement in the text to be correct. Several of the more remarkable parallels in the former writer occur in the passages quoted below, p. 314 sq., and seem to warrant the belief that he was acquainted with the language of the Gospel.

'spend and be spent' may be taken as a type[1], and which can hardly be considered accidental. If any historical connexion (direct or indirect) can be traced with a fair degree of probability, we may reasonably look to this for the solution of such coincidences. I shall content myself here with stating the different ways in which such a connexion was possible or probable, without venturing to affirm what was actually the case, for the data are not sufficient to justify any definite theory.

Historical connexion.

1. The fact already mentioned is not unimportant, that the principal Stoic teachers all came from the East, and that therefore their language and thought must in a greater or less degree have borne the stamp of their Oriental origin. We advance a step further towards the object of our search, if we remember that the most famous of them were not only Oriental but Shemitic. Babylonia, Phœnicia, Syria, Palestine, are their homes. One comes from Scythopolis, a second from Apamea, a third from Ascalon, a fourth from Ptolemais, two others from Hierapolis, besides several from Tyre and Sidon or their colonies, such as Citium and Carthage[2]. What religious systems they had the opportunity of studying, and how far they were indebted to any of these, it is impossible to say. But it would indeed be strange if, living on the confines and even within the borders of the home of Judaism, the Stoic teachers escaped all influence from the One religion which, it would seem, must have attracted the attention of the thoughtful and earnest mind, which even then was making rapid progress through the Roman Empire, and which afterwards through the Gospel has made itself far

(1) The Eastern origin of Stoicism.

Its possible obligations to Judaism.

---

[1] See above p. 288. Aubertin has attacked this very instance (p. 360 sq.), but without success. He only shows (what did not need showing) that 'impendere' is used elsewhere in this same sense. The important feature in the coincidence is the combination of the active and passive voices.

[2] I have noted down the following homes of more or less distinguished Stoic teachers from the East; *Seleucia*, Diogenes (p. 41); *Epiphania*, Euphrates (p. 613); *Scythopolis*, Basilides (p. 614); *Ascalon*, Antibius, Eubius (p. 615); *Hierapolis in Syria* (?), Serapio (p. 612), Publius (p. 615); *Tyre*, Antipater, Apollonius (p. 520); *Sidon*, Zeno (p. 36).

Boethus? (p. 40); *Ptolemais*, Diogenes (p. 43); *Apamea in Syria*, Posidonius (p. 509); *Citium*, Zeno (p. 27), Persæus (p. 34); *Carthage*, Herillus (p. 33); *Cyrene*, Eratosthenes (p. 39). The Cilician Stoics are enumerated below p. 303. Of the other famous teachers belonging to the School, Cleanthes came from Assos (p. 31), Ariston from Chios (p. 32), Dionysius from Heraclea (p. 35), Sphærus from Bosporus (p. 35), Panætius from Rhodes (p. 500), Epictetus from Hierapolis in Phrygia (p. 660). The references are to the pages of Zeller's work, where the authorities for the statements will be found.

more widely felt than any other throughout the civilised world. I have already ventured to ascribe the intense moral earnestness of the Stoics to their Eastern origin. It would be no extravagant assumption that they also owed some ethical maxims and some theological terms (though certainly not their main doctrines) directly or indirectly to the flourishing Jewish schools of their age, founded on the teaching of the Old Testament. The exaggerations of the early Christian fathers, who set down all the loftier sentiments of the Greek philosophers as plagiarisms from the lawgiver or the prophets, have cast suspicion on any such affiliation : but we should not allow ourselves to be blinded by reactionary prejudices to the possibilities or rather the probabilities in the case before us.

(2) Seneca's possible knowledge of Christianity.

2. The consideration which I have just advanced will explain many coincidences : but we may proceed a step further. Is it impossible, or rather is it improbable, that Seneca was acquainted with the teaching of the Gospel in some rudimentary form ? His silence about Christianity proves nothing, because it proves too much. If an appreciable part of the lower population of Rome had become Christians some few years before Seneca's death[1], if the Gospel claimed converts within the very palace walls[2], if a few (probably not more than a few) even in the higher grades of society, like Pomponia Græcina[3], had adopted the new faith, his acquaintance with its main facts is at least a very tenable supposition. If his own account may be trusted, he made a practice of dining with his slaves and engaging them in familiar conversation[4]; so that the avenues of information open to him were manifold[5]. His acquaintance with any written documents of Christianity is less probable ; but of the oral Gospel, as repeated from the lips of slaves and others, he might at least have had an accidental and fragmentary knowledge. This supposition would explain the coincidences with the Sermon on the Mount and with the parables of our Lord, if they are clear and numerous enough to demand an explanation.

(3) His supposed

3. But the legend goes beyond this, and connects Seneca directly

---

[1] See above, p. 17 sq., 25 sq.
[2] Phil. iv. 22; see p. 171 sq.
[3] See above, p. 21.
[4] Ep. Mor. xlvii.
[5] An early inscription at Ostia (de Rossi Bull. de Archeol. Crist. 1867, p.

6, quoted by Friedländer, III. p. 535) mentions one M. Anneus Paulus Petrus, obviously a Christian. Was he descended from some freedman of Seneca's house?

with St Paul. The Stoic philosopher is supposed to be included connexion with St among the 'members of Cæsar's household' mentioned in one of the Paul. Apostle's letters from Rome. The legend itself however has no value as independent evidence. The coincidences noted above would suggest it, and the forged correspondence would fix and substantiate it. We are therefore thrown back on the probabilities of the case; and it must be confessed that, when we examine the Apostle's history with a view to tracing a historical connexion, the result is not very encouraging. St Paul, it is true, when at Corinth, was brought before Seneca's brother Gallio, to whom the philosopher dedicates Gallio. more than one work and of whom he speaks in tenderly affectionate language[1]; but Gallio, who 'cared for none of these things,' to whom the questions at issue between St Paul and his accusers were merely idle and frivolous disputes about obscure national customs[2], would be little likely to bestow a serious thought upon a case apparently so unimportant, still less likely to communicate his experiences to his brother in Rome. Again it may be urged that as St Paul on his arrival in Rome was delivered to Burrus the prefect of the prætorian guards[3], the intimate friend Burrus. of Seneca, it might be expected that some communication between the Apostle and the philosopher would be established in this way. Yet, if we reflect that the prætorian prefect must yearly have been receiving hundreds of prisoners from the different provinces, that St Paul himself was only one of several committed to his guardian- ship at the same time, that the interview of this supreme magistrate with any individual prisoner must have been purely formal, that from his position and character Burrus was little likely to discrimi- nate between St Paul's case and any other, and finally that he appears to have died not very long after the Apostle's arrival in Rome[4], we shall see very little cause to lay stress on such a supposi- tion. Lastly; it is said that, when St Paul was brought before Nero Nero. for trial, Seneca must have been present as the emperor's adviser, and being present must have interested himself in the religious opinions of so remarkable a prisoner. But here again we have only

---

[1] *Nat. Qu.* iv. præf. § 10 'Gallionem fratrem meum quem nemo non parum amat, etiam qui amare plus non potest,' and again § 11 'Nemo mortalium uni tam dulcis est, quam hic omnibus':

comp. *Ep. Mor.* civ 'domini mei Gal. lionis.'
[2] Acts xviii. 14, 45.
[3] See above, p. 7 sq.
[4] See above, pp. 5, 8, 39.

a series of assumptions more or less probable. It is not known under what circumstances and in whose presence such a trial would take place; it is very far from certain that St Paul's case came on before Seneca had retired from the court; and it is questionable whether amid the formalities of the trial there would have been the opportunity, even if there were the will, to enter into questions of religious or philosophical interest. On the whole therefore it must be confessed that no great stress can be laid on the direct historical links which might connect Seneca with the Apostle of the Gentiles.

Summary of results.

I have hitherto investigated the historical circumstances which might explain any coincidences of language or thought as arising out of obligations on the part of Seneca or of his Stoic predecessors. It has been seen that the teachers of this school generally were in all likelihood indebted to Oriental, if not to Jewish, sources for their religious vocabulary; that Seneca himself not improbably had a vague and partial acquaintance with Christianity, though he was certainly anything but a Christian himself; and that his personal intercourse with the Apostle of the Gentiles, though not substantiated, is at least not an impossibility. How far the coincidences may be ascribed to one or other of these causes, I shall not attempt to discriminate : but there is also another aspect of the question which must not be put out of sight. In some instances at least, if any obligation exist at all, it cannot be on the side of the philosopher, for the chronology resists this inference: and for these cases some other solution must be found.

Stoicism, like Alexandrian Judaism, a preparation for the Gospel.

As the speculations of Alexandrian Judaism had elaborated a new and important theological vocabulary, so also to the language of Stoicism, which itself likewise had sprung from the union of the religious sentiment of the East with the philosophical thought of the West, was due an equally remarkable development of moral terms and images. To the Gospel, which was announced to the world in 'the fulness of time,' both the one and the other paid their tribute. As St John (nor St John alone) adopted the terms of Alexandrian theosophy as the least inadequate to express the highest doctrines of Christianity, so St Paul (nor St Paul alone) found in the ethical language of the Stoics expressions more fit than he could find elsewhere to describe in certain aspects the duties and privileges, the struggles and the triumphs, of the Christian life. But though the words and symbols remained substantially the same, yet in their application they became instinct with new force and meaning. This change in either case they owed to their being placed in relation to the central fact of Christianity, the Incarnation of the Son. The Alexandrian terms, expressing the attributes and operations of the Divine Word, which in their origin had a purely metaphysical bearing, were translated into the sphere of practical theology, when God had descended among men to lift up men to God. The Stoic expressions, describing the independence of the individual spirit, the subjugation of the unruly passions, the universal empire of a triumphant self-control, the cosmopolitan relations of the wise man, were quickened into new life, when an unfailing source of strength and a boundless hope of victory had been revealed in the Gospel, when all men were proclaimed to be brothers, and each and every man united with God in Christ.

It is difficult to estimate, and perhaps not very easy to overrate, the extent to which Stoic philosophy had leavened the moral vocabulary of the civilised world at the time of the Christian era. To take a single instance; the most important of moral terms, the crowning triumph of ethical nomenclature, συνείδησις, conscientia, the internal, absolute, supreme judge of individual action, if not struck in the mint of the Stoics, at all events became current coin through their influence. To a great extent therefore the general diffusion of Stoic language would lead to its adoption by the first teachers of Christianity; while at the same time in St Paul's own case personal circumstances might have led to a closer acquaintance with the diction of this school.

*Wide influence of the ethical language of Stoicism.*

Tarsus, the birth-place and constant home of St Paul, was at this time a most important, if not the foremost, seat of Greek learning. Of all the philosophical schools, the Stoic was the most numerously and ably represented at this great centre. Its geographical position, as a half-way house, had doubtless some influence in recommending it to a philosophy which had its birth-place in the East and grew into maturity in the West. At all events we may count up six or more[1]

*Stoicism at Tarsus.*

---

[1] Strabo (xiv. 13, 14. p. 673 sq.) mentions five by name, Antipater, Archedemus, Nestor, Athenodorus sur- named Cordylion, and Athenodorus son of Sandon. To these may be added Zeno (Zeller, p. 40: Diog. Laert. vii.

well-known Stoic teachers whose home was at Tarsus, besides Chrysippus and Aratus who came from the neighbouring Soli[1], and three others who resided at Mallos, also a Cilician town[2]. If St Paul's early education was Jewish, he was at least instructed by the most liberal teacher of the day, who, unlike his stricter countrymen and contemporaries, had no dread of Greek learning; and during his repeated and lengthened sojourns in Tarsus, he must have come in contact with Stoic maxims and dogmas. But indeed it is not mere conjecture, that St Paul had some acquaintance with the teachers or the writings of this school. The speech on the Areopagus, addressed partly to Stoics, shows a clear appreciation of the elements of truth contained in their philosophy, and a studied coincidence with their modes of expression[3]. Its one quotation moreover is taken from a Stoic writing, the hymn of Cleanthes, the noblest expression of heathen devotion which Greek literature has preserved to us[4].

And I think we may find occasionally also in St Paul's epistles sufficiently distinct traces of the influence of Stoic diction. A few instances are set down in the notes to this epistle. Many more might be gathered from his other letters, especially the Pastoral Epistles. But I will content myself with giving two broad examples, where the characteristic common-places of Stoic morality seem to be adopted and transfigured in the language of the Christian Apostle.

1. The portrait of the wise man, the ideal of Stoic aspiration, has very distinct and peculiar features—so peculiar that they presented an easy butt for the ridicule of antagonists. It is his prominent characteristic that he is sufficient in himself, that he wants

*St Paul's acquaintance with Stoic teaching.*

*Two instances given.*

*1. The portrait of the wise man.*

---

35 enumerates eight of the name), and Heracleides (Zeller, p. 43). Of Athenodorus son of Sandon, Strabo adds ὅν καὶ Κανανίτην φασὶν ἀπὸ κώμης τινός. If Strabo's explanation of Κανανίτης be correct, the coincidence with a surname of one of the Twelve Apostles is accidental. But one is tempted to suspect that the word had a Shemitic origin.

[1] The fathers of both these famous men appear to have migrated from Tarsus. For Chrysippus see Strabo xiv. 8, p. 671; of Aratus we are told that Asclepiades Ταρσέα φησὶν αὐτὸν γεγονέναι ἀλλ᾽ οὐ Σολέα (Arati Opera II. p. 429 ed. Buhle).

[2] Crates (Zeller, p. 42), the two Procluses (ib. p. 615).
[3] See above, p. 290.
[4] Acts xvii. 28. The words in Cleanthes are ἐκ σοῦ γὰρ γένος ἐσμέν. The quotation of St Paul agrees exactly with a half-line in Aratus another Stoic poet, connected with his native Tarsus, τοῦ γὰρ καὶ γένος ἐσμέν. Since the Apostle introduces the words as quoted from *some* of their own poets, he would seem to have both passages in view. By οἱ καθ᾽ ὑμᾶς ποιηταί he probably means the poets belonging to the same school as his Stoic audience.

nothing, that he possesses everything. This topic is expanded with a fervour and energy which often oversteps the proper bounds of Stoic calm. The wise man alone is free: he alone is happy: he alone is beautiful. He and he only possesses absolute wealth. He is the true king and the true priest[1].

Now may we not say that this image has suggested many expressions to the Apostle of the Gentiles? 'Even now are ye full,' he exclaims in impassioned irony to the Corinthians, 'even now are ye rich, even now are ye made kings without us': 'we are fools for Christ, but ye are wise in Christ: we are weak, but ye are strong: ye are glorious, but we are dishonoured.' 'All things are yours,' he says elsewhere, 'all things are yours, and ye are Christ's, and Christ is God's.' So too he describes himself and the other Apostles, 'As being grieved, yet always rejoicing; as beggars, yet making many rich; as having nothing, and yet possessing all things.' 'In every thing at every time having every self-sufficiency (αὐτάρκειαν)...in every thing being enriched.' 'I have learnt,' he says again, 'in whatsoever circumstances I am, to be self-sufficing. I have all strength in Him that giveth me power. I have all things to the full and to overflowing.'   1 Cor. iv. 8.   1Cor.iv.10.   1 Cor. iii. 22, 23.   2 Cor. vi. 10.   2 Cor. ix. 8, 11.   Phil. iv 11, 13, 18.

If the coincidence of imagery in these passages is remarkable, the contrast of sentiment is not less striking. This universal dominion, this boundless inheritance, is promised alike by the Stoic philosopher to the wise man and by the Christian Apostle to the believer. But the one must attain it by self-isolation, the other by incorporation. The essential requisite in the former case is a proud independence; in the latter an entire reliance on, and intimate union with, an unseen power. It is ἐν τῷ ἐνδυναμοῦντι that the faithful becomes all-sufficient, all-powerful; it is ἐν Χριστῷ that he is crowned a king and consecrated a priest. All things are his, but they are only his, in so far as he is Christ's and because Christ is God's. Here and here only the Apostle found the realisation of the proud ideal which the chief philosophers of his native Tarsus had sketched in such bold outline and painted in these brilliant colours.  Coincidence and contrast with Stoicism in St Paul's conception.

2. The instance just given relates to the development of the individual man. The example which I shall next take expresses  2. The cosmopolitan

---

[1] See esp. Seneca de Benef. vii. 3, 4, 6, 10, Ep. Mor. ix. Compare Zeller p. 231. The ridicule of Horace (Sat. i. 3. 124 sq.) will be remembered. See also the passages from Plutarch quoted in Orelli's Excursus (ii. p. 67).

his widest relations to others. The cosmopolitan tenets of the Stoics have been already mentioned. They grew out of the history of one age and were interpreted by the history of another. Negatively they were suggested by the hopeless state of politics under the successors of Alexander. Positively they were realised, or rather represented, by the condition of the world under the Roman Empire[1]. In the age of the Seleucids and Ptolemies, when the old national barriers had been overthrown, and petty states with all their interests and ambitions had crumbled into the dust, the longing eye of the Greek philosopher wandered over the ruinous waste, until his range of view expanded to the ideal of a world-wide state, which for the first time became a possibility to his intellectual vision, when it became also a want to his social instincts. A few generations passed, and the wide extension of the Roman Empire, the far-reaching protectorate of the Roman franchise[2], seemed to give a definite meaning, a concrete form, in some sense a local habitation, to this idea which the Stoic philosopher of Greece had meanwhile transmitted to the Stoic moralist of Rome.

The language of Seneca well illustrates the nature of this cosmopolitan ideal. 'All this, which thou seest, in which are comprised things human and divine, is one. We are members of a vast body. Nature made us kin, when she produced us from the same things and to the same ends[3].' 'I will look upon all lands as belonging to me, and my own lands as belonging to all. I will so live as if I knew that I am born for others, and on this account I will give thanks to nature...She gave me alone to all men and all men to me alone[4].' 'I well know that the world is my country and the gods its rulers; that they stand above me and about me, the censors of my deeds and words[5].' 'Seeing that we assigned to the wise man

---

[1] Plutarch (*Op. Mor.* p. 329 B) says that Alexander himself realised this ideal of a world-wide polity, which Zeno only delineated as a dream or a phantom (ὥσπερ ὄναρ ἢ εἴδωλον ἀνατυπωσά-μενος). If Plutarch's statement be correct that Alexander looked upon himself as entrusted with a divine mission to 'reconcile the whole world,' he certainly had the conception in his mind; but his actual work was only the beginning of the end, and the realisation of the idea (so far as it was destined to be realised) was reserved for the Romans. 'Fecisti patriam diversis gentibus unam,' 'Urbem fecisti quod prius orbis erat,' says a later poet addressing the emperor of his day; Rutil. *de Red.* i. 63, 66.

[2] See Cicero *pro Balb.* 13, Verr. v. 57, 65.

[3] *Ep. Mor.* xcv. 52.

[4] *de Vit. beat.* 20.

[5] *ibid.*

a commonwealth worthy of him, I mean the world, he is not beyond the borders of his commonwealth, even though he has gone into retirement. Nay, perhaps he has left one corner of it and passed into a larger and ampler region; and raised above the heavens he understands (at length) how lowly he was seated when he mounted the chair of state or the bench of justice[1].' 'Let us embrace in our thoughts two commonwealths, the one vast and truly named common, in which are comprised gods and men, in which we look not to this corner or to that, but we measure the boundaries of our state with the sun; the other, to which the circumstances of our birth have assigned us[2].' 'Virtue is barred to none : she is open to all, she receives all, she invites all, gentlefolk, freedmen, slaves, kings, exiles alike[3].' 'Nature bids me assist *men ;* and whether they be bond or free, whether gentlefolk or freedmen, whether they enjoy liberty as a right or as a friendly gift, what matter ? Wherever a *man* is, there is room for doing good[4].' 'This mind may belong as well to a Roman knight, as to a freedman, as to a slave : for what is a Roman knight or a freedman or a slave ? Names which had their origin in ambition or injustice[5].'

Did St Paul speak quite independently of this Stoic imagery, when the vision of a nobler polity rose before him, the revelation of a city not made with hands, eternal in the heavens ? Is there not a strange coincidence in his language—a coincidence only the more striking because it clothes an idea in many respects very different ? 'Our citizenship is in heaven.' 'God raised us with Him, and seated us with Him in the heavenly places in Christ Jesus.' 'Therefore ye are no more strangers and sojourners, but fellow-citizens with the saints and members of God's household.' 'Fulfil your duties as citizens worthily of the Gospel of Christ.' 'We being many are one body in Christ, and members one of another.' 'For as the body is one and hath many members, and all the members of the body being many are one body, so also is Christ : for we all are baptized in one Spirit into one body, whether Jews or Greeks, whether bond or free. Ye are the body of Christ

*Its Christian counterpart in the heavenly citizenship of St Paul.*

*Phil. iii. 20.*
*Ephes. ii. 6.*

*Ephes. ii.*
*19.*

*Phil. i. 27.*

*Rom. xii.*
*5.*
*1 Cor. xii.*
*12, 13, 27.*

*[Ephes. iv.*
*25, v. 30.]*

---

[1] *Ep. Mor.* lxviii.
[2] *de Otio* 4 (31). 'Glaubt man hier nicht,' asks Zeller (p. 275), 'fast Augustin De Civitate Dei zu hören?'

[3] *de Benef.* iii. 18.
[4] *de Vit. beat.* 24.
[5] *Ep. Mor.* xxxi. 11.

Gal. iii. 28. and members in particular.' 'There is neither Jew nor **Greek**;
there is neither bond nor free; there is no male and female: for ye
Col. iii. 11. all are one in Christ Jesus.' 'Not Greek and Jew, circumcision and
uncircumcision, barbarian, Scythian, bond, free: but Christ is all
things and in all[1].'

Here again, though the images are the same, the idea is transfigured and glorified. At length the bond of coherence, the missing
principle of universal brotherhood, has been found. As in the
former case, so here the magic words ἐν Χριστῷ have produced the
change and realised the conception. A living soul has been breathed
into the marble statue by Christianity; and thus from the 'much
admired polity of Zeno[2]' arises the Civitas Dei of St Augustine.

Summary.   It has been the aim of the investigation just concluded to point
out how far the coincidences between Seneca and St Paul are real,
and how far fallacious; to show that these coincidences may in some
cases be explained by the natural and independent development of
religious thought, while in others a historical connexion seems to be
required; and to indicate generally the different ways in which this
historical connexion was probable or possible, without however attempting to decide by which of several channels the resemblance in
each individual instance was derived.

Christiani-  In conclusion it may be useful to pass from the special connexion
ty and
Stoicism between St Paul and Seneca to the more general relation between
compared. Christianity and Stoicism, and to compare them very briefly in their
principles, their operations, and their results. Stoicism has died
out, having produced during its short lifetime only very transient

---

[1] *Ecce Homo* p. 136 'The city of God,
of which the Stoics doubtfully and
feebly spoke, was now set up before the
eyes of men. It was no unsubstantial
city such as we fancy in the clouds, no
invisible pattern such as Plato thought
might be laid up in heaven, but a visible
corporation whose members met together to eat bread and drink wine, and into which they were initiated by bodily
immersion in water. Here the Gentile
met the Jew whom he had been accus-
tomed to regard as an enemy of the
human race: the Roman met the lying
Greek sophist, the Syrian slave, the

gladiator born beside the Danube. In
brotherhood they met, the natural birth
and kindred of each forgotten, the baptism alone remembered in which they
have been born again to God and to
each other.' See the whole context.

[2] Plut. *Op. Mor.* p. 329 ἡ πολὺ θαυ-
μαζομένη πολιτεία τοῦ τὴν Στωϊκὴν αἵρεσιν καταβαλομένου Ζήνωνος. It is remarkable that this ideal is described in
the context under a scriptural image,
εἷς δὲ βίος ᾖ καὶ κόσμος, ὥσπερ ἀγέλης συν-
νόμου νομῷ κοινῷ συντρεφομένης: comp.
Joh. x. 16 καὶ γενήσεται μία ποίμνη, εἷς
ποιμήν.

and partial effects; Christianity has become the dominant religion of the civilised world, and leavened society through its whole mass. The very coincidences, on which we have been dwelling so long, throw into relief the contrast between the failure of the one and the triumph of the other, and stimulate enquiry into the causes of this difference.

To some it may seem sufficient to reply that the one is a mere human philosophy, the other a Divine revelation. But this answer shelves without solving the problem; for it is equivalent to saying that the one is partial, defective, and fallacious, while the other is absolutely true. The question therefore, to which an answer is sought, may be stated thus : What are those theological and ethical principles, ignored or denied by Stoicism, and enforced by the Gospel, in which the Divine power of the latter lies, and to which it owes its empire over the hearts and actions of men? This is a very wide subject of discussion; and I shall only attempt to indicate a few more striking points of contrast. Yet even when treated thus imperfectly, such an investigation ought not to be useless. In an age when the distinctive characteristics of Christianity are regarded as a stumblingblock by a few, and more or less consciously ignored as of little moment by others, it is a matter of vast importance to enquire whether the secret of its strength does or does not lie in these; and the points at issue cannot be better suggested, than by comparing it with an abstract system of philosophy so imposing as the Stoic.

*The question at issue stated.*

Indeed our first wonder is, that from a system so rigorous and unflinching in its principles and so heroic in its proportions the direct results should have been marvellously little. It produced, or at least it attracted, a few isolated great men : but on the life of the masses, and on the policy of states, it was almost wholly powerless.

*Meagre results of Stoicism.*

Of the founder and his immediate successors not very much is known ; but we are warranted in believing that they were men of earnest aspirations, of rare self-denial, and for the most part (though the grossness of their language seems hardly reconcilable with this view[1]) of moral and upright lives. Zeno himself indeed cannot be

*The older Stoics.*

---

[1] It is impossible to speak with any confidence on this point. The language held by Zeno and Chrysippus was grossly licentious, and might be taken to show that they viewed with indifference and even complacency the most hateful forms of heathen impurity (see Plutarch *Op. Mor.* p. 1044, *Clem. Hom.* v. 18, Sext. Emp. *Pyrrh.* iii. 200 sq.). But it is due to the known character

set down to the credit of the school. He made the philosophy and
was not made by it. But Cleanthes was directly moulded by the
influence of his master's teaching : and for calm perseverance, for
rigorous self-discipline, and for unwavering devotion to a noble
ideal, few characters in the history of Greek philosophy are comparable to him. Yet Cleanthes, like Zeno, died a suicide. The example, not less than the precept, of the first teachers of the sect
created a fatal passion for self-murder, which was the most indelible,
if not the darkest, blot on Stoic morality.

Stoicism in Rome.     It was not however among the Greeks, to whose national temper
the genius of Stoicism was alien, that this school achieved its proud-
est triumphs. The stern and practical spirit of the Romans offered
a more congenial sphere for its influence. And here again it is
worth observing, that their principal instructors were almost all East-
erns. Posidonius for instance, the familiar friend of many famous
Its obliga-tions to the East.     Romans and the most influential missionary of Stoic doctrine in
Rome, was a native of the Syrian Apamea. From this time forward
it became a common custom for the Roman noble to maintain in
his house some eminent philosopher, as the instructor of his children
and the religious director of himself and his family [1] ; and in this
capacity we meet with several Oriental Stoics. Thus Cato the
younger had at different times two professors of this sect domesti-
cated in his household, both of Eastern origin, Antipater of Tyre
Cato the younger.     and Athenodorus of Tarsus [2]. In Cato himself, whom his contemporaries regarded as the 'most perfect Stoic [3],' and in whom the sect
at large would probably have recognised its most illustrious representative, we have a signal example alike of the virtues and of the

and teaching of these men, that we
should put the most favourable construction on such expressions ; and they
may perhaps be regarded as theoretical
extravagances of language, illustrating
the Stoic doctrine that externals are
indifferent (see Zeller, p. 261 sq.). Yet
this mode of speaking must have been
highly dangerous to morals ; and the
danger would only be increased by the
fact that such language was held by
men whose characters were justly admired in other respects.

[1] Seneca ad Marc. 4 'Consol [atori se]
Areo philosopho viri sui præbuit et mul-

tum eam rem profuisse sibi confessa est,'
where he is speaking of Livia after the
death of her son Drusus. This philosopher is represented as using the following words in his reply to her: 'Ego
adsiduus viri tui comes, cui non tantum
quæ in publicum emittuntur nota, sed
omnes sunt secretiores animorum ves-
trorum motus.' For another allusion
to these domestic chaplains of heathendom see de Tranq. Anim. 14 'Proseque-
batur illum philosophus suus.'

[2] Plutarch Vit. Cat. 4, 10, 16.
[3] Cicero Brut. xxxi, Parad. proœm. 2.

defects of the school. Honest, earnest, and courageous even to death, His excellences and defects.
but hard, stolid, impracticable, and almost inhuman, he paralysed
the higher qualities of his nature by his unamiable philosophy, so
that they were rendered almost useless to his generation and country.
A recent Roman historian has described him as 'one of the most
melancholy phenomena in an age so abounding in political carica-
tures.' 'There was more nobility,' he writes bitterly, 'and above
all more judgment in the death of Cato than there had been in his
life.' 'It only elevates the tragic significance of his death that he
was himself a fool[1].' Exaggerated as this language may be, it is
yet not wholly without truth; and, were the direct social and political results of Cato's life alone to be regarded, his career must be
pronounced a failure. But in fact his importance lies, not in what
he did, but in what he was. It was a vast gain to humanity, that
in an age of worldly self-seeking, of crooked and fraudulent policy,
of scepticism and infidelity to all right principle, one man held his
ground, stern, unbending, upright to the last. Such a man may
fail, as Cato failed, in all the practical aims of life : but he has left
a valuable legacy to after ages in the staunch assertion of principle;
he has bequeathed to them a fructifying estate, not the less productive because its richest harvests must be reaped by generations yet
unborn. Cato was the true type of Stoicism in its striking excellence, as in its hopeless weakness. The later Roman Stoics are Later Roman Stoics.
feeble copies, more or less conscious, of Cato. Like him, they were
hard, impracticable, perverse, studiously antagonistic to the prevailing spirit or the dominant power of their age : but, like him also,
they were living protests, when protests were most needed, against
the dishonesty and corruption of the times; and their fearless demeanour was felt as a standing reproach alike to the profligate despotism of the ruler and to the mean and cringing flattery of the subject. Yet it is mournful to reflect how much greater might have
been the influence of men like Thrasea Pætus and Helvidius Priscus
on their generation, if their strict integrity had been allied to a more
sympathetic creed.

In these men however there was an earnest singleness of purpose, which may condone many faults. Unhappily the same cannot
be said of Seneca. We may reject as calumnies the grosser charges Seneca.

---

[1] Mommsen's *History of Rome*, IV. pp. 156, 448 sq. (Eng. trans.).

with which the malignity of his enemies has laden his memory; but
enough remains in the admissions of his admirers, and more than
enough in the testimony of his own writings, to forfeit his character
His faults. as a high-minded and sincere man.  No words are too strong to
condemn the baseness of one who could overwhelm the emperor
Claudius, while living, with the most fulsome and slavish flattery,
and then, when his ashes were scarcely cold, turn upon him and
poison his memory with the venom of malicious satire[1].  From this
charge there is no escape; for his extant writings convict him.
We may well refuse to believe, as his enemies asserted, that he coun-
selled the murder of Agrippina; but it seems that he was in some
way implicated with the matricide, and it is quite certain that he
connived at other iniquities of his imperial pupil.  We may indignantly repudiate, as we are probably justified in doing, the grave
charges of moral profligacy which were brought against him in his
lifetime and after his death; but the man who, while condemning,
can describe at length the grossest forms of impurity (as Seneca does
occasionally) had surely no very sensitive shrinking from sins 'of
which it is a shame even to speak.'  We may demur to accepting
the account of his enemies, that his wealth was amassed by fraud
and violence; but there is no doubt that, while preaching a lofty
indifference to worldly advantages, he consented to be enriched by a
profligate and unscrupulous tyrant, and that the enormous property
thus accumulated exposed him to the reproaches of his contemporaries.  A portrait which combines all these features will command
no great respect.  Yet, notwithstanding a somewhat obtrusive rhetoric, there is in Seneca's writings an earnestness of purpose, a
yearning after moral perfection, and a constant reference to an ideal
standard, which cannot be mere affectation.  He seems to have been
a rigorous ascetic in early life, and to the last to have maintained a
severe self-discipline.  Such at least is his own statement; nor is
it unsupported by less partial testimony[2].

For all this inconsistency however we must blame not the creed
but the man.  He would probably have been much worse, if his

---

[1] The treatise *ad Polybium de Conso-*
*latione* would be disgraceful, if it stood
alone; but contrasted with the *Ludus
de Morte Claudii* it become odious. To
complete his shame, he was the author

of the extravagant panegyric pronounced by Nero over his predecessor (Tac.
*Ann.* xiii. 3).

[2] See *Ep. Mor.* lxxxvii. 2, cviii. 14;
comp. Tac. *Ann.* xiv. 53, xv. 45, 63.

philosophy had not held up to him a stern ideal for imitation. His own
Is it genuine or affected humility—a palliative or an aggravation confes-
of his offence—that he himself confesses how far he falls short of this weakness.
ideal? To those taunting enemies of philosophy, who pointing to his
luxury and wealth ask 'Why do you speak more bravely than you
live?', he replies: 'I will add to your reproaches just now, and
I will bring more charges against myself than you think. For the
present I give you this answer: I am not wise, and (to feed your
malevolence) I shall not be wise. Therefore require of me, not that
I should equal the best men, but that I should be better than the
bad. It is enough for me daily to diminish my vices in some degree and to chide my errors.' 'These things,' he adds, 'I say not
in my own defence, for I am sunk deep in all vices, but in defence
of him who has made some progress[1].' 'The wise man,' he writes
apologetically, 'does not think himself unworthy of any advantages
of fortune. He does not love riches but he prefers them. He
receives them not into his soul but into his house. Nor does he
spurn them when he has them in his possession, but retains them
and desires ampler material for his virtue to be furnished thereby[2].'
'I am not now speaking to you of myself,' he writes to Lucilius,
'for I fall far short of a moderate, not to say a perfect man, but
of one over whom fortune has lost her power[3].' Seneca, more than
any man, must have felt the truth of the saying, 'How hardly shall
they that have riches enter into the kingdom of God[4].'

From Seneca it is refreshing to turn to Epictetus. The lame Epictetus.
slave of Epaphroditus is a far nobler type of Stoic discipline than the
wealthy courtier of Epaphroditus' master. Here at all events, we
feel instinctively that we have to do with genuine earnestness. His
motto 'bear and forbear[5]' inspires his discourses throughout, as it
appears also to have been the guide of his life. But more striking still
is the spirit of piety which pervades his thoughts. 'When ye have
shut the doors,' he says, 'and have made all dark within, remem-

---

[1] de Vit. beat. 17; comp. ad Helv.
Matr. 5.
[2] de Vit. beat. 21.
[3] Ep. Mor. lvii. 3.
[4] The account of Seneca in Martha's
Moralistes p. 1 sq. is well worth reading,
though the idea of the spiritual direc-

tion in the letters to Lucilius seems
exaggerated. I wish I could take as
favourable a view of Seneca's character
as this writer does.
[5] ἀνέχου καὶ ἀπέχου, Aul. Gell. xvii.
19, where the words are explained.

Expres-
sions of
piety in his
writings.

ber never to say that ye are alone, for ye are not; but God is within and so is your angel (δαίμων); and what need of light have these to see what ye do? To this God ye also ought to swear allegiance, as soldiers do to Cæsar[1].' 'If we had sense, ought we to do anything else both in public and in private but praise and honour the divine being (τὸ θεῖον) and recount his favours?......What then? Since ye, the many, are blinded, should there not be some one to fill this station and to sing for all men the hymn to God? For what else can I, a lame old man, do but sing hymns to God? Nay, if I were a nightingale, I had done the work of a nightingale; if a swan, the work of a swan. So being what I am, a rational creature, I must sing hymns to God. This is my task, and I perform it; nor will I ever desert this post, so far as it is vouchsafed me: and you I exhort to join in this same song[2].' 'How then dost thou appear? As a witness called by God: *Come thou and bear witness to me...* What witness dost thou bear to God? *I am in wretched plight, O Lord, and I am miserable; no one cares for me, no one gives me anything; all men blame me, all men speak ill of me.* Wilt thou bear this witness, and disgrace the calling wherewith He hath called thee, for that He honoured thee and held thee worthy to be brought forward as a witness in this great cause[3]?' 'When thou goest to visit any great person, remember that Another also above seeth what is done, and that thou oughtest to please Him rather than this one[4].' 'Thou art an offshoot (ἀπόσπασμα) of God; thou hast some part of Him in thyself. Why therefore dost thou not perceive thy noble birth? Why dost thou not know whence thou art come? Thou bearest God about with thee, wretched man, and thou dost not perceive it. Thinkest thou that I mean some god of silver or gold, without thee? Within thyself thou bearest Him, and thou dost not feel that thou art defiling Him with thy impure thoughts and thy filthy deeds. If

---

[1] *Diss.* i. 14. 13 sq.; comp. Matt. xxii. 21.

[2] *Diss.* i. 16. 15 sq.

[3] *Diss.* i. 29. 46 sq. The words τὴν κλῆσιν ἣν κέκληκεν appear from the context to refer to citing witnesses, but they recall a familiar expression of St Paul; 1 Cor. vii. 20, Ephes. iv. 1, comp. 2 Tim. i. 9. The address Κύριε, used in prayer to God, is frequent in Epic-

tetus, but does not occur (so far as I am aware) in any heathen writing before the Apostolic times. Sometimes we find Κύριε ὁ Θεός, and once he writes Κύριε ἐλέησον (ii. 7. 12). It is worth noting that all the three cities where Epictetus is known to have lived—Hierapolis, Rome, Nicopolis—occur in the history of St Paul.

[4] *Diss.* i. 30. 1.

an image of God were present, thou wouldest not dare to do any of these things which thou doest: but, God Himself being present within thee, and overlooking and overhearing all, thou art not ashamed to think and to do these things, O man, insensible of thine own nature, and visited with the wrath of God[1].' 'Remember that thou art a son. What profession is due to this character? To consider all that belongs to Him as belonging to a father, to obey Him in all things, never to complain of Him to any one, nor to say or do anything hurtful to Him, to yield and give way to Him in all things, working with Him to the utmost of thy power[2].' 'Dare to look up to God and say, Use me henceforth whereunto thou wilt, I consent unto Thee, I am Thine. I shrink from nothing that seemeth good to Thee. Lead me where Thou wilt: clothe me with what garments Thou wilt. Wouldest Thou that I should be in office or out of office, should live at home or in exile, should be rich or poor? I will defend Thee for all these things before men[3].' 'These (vices) thou canst not cast out otherwise than by looking to God alone, by setting thine affections (προσπεπονθότα) on Him alone, by being consecrated to His commands[4].' 'When thou hast heard these words, O young man, go thy way and say to thyself, It is not Epictetus who has told me these things (for whence did *he* come by them?), but some kind God speaking through him. For it would never have entered into the heart of Epictetus to say these things, seeing it is not his wont to speak (so) to any man. Come then, let us obey God, lest God's wrath fall upon us (ἵνα μὴ θεοχόλωτοι ὦμεν[5]).' 'Thus much I can tell thee now, that he, who setteth his hand to so great a matter without God, calls down God's wrath and does but desire to behave himself unseemly in public. For neither in a well-ordered household does any one come forward and say to himself *I must be steward*. Else the master, observing him and seeing him giving his orders insolently, drags him off to be scourged. So it happens also in this great city (of the world); for here too there is a householder, who ordereth everything[6].' 'The cynic (i. e.

---

[1] *Diss.* ii. 8. 11 sq. We are reminded of the surname θεοφόρος, borne by a Christian contemporary of Epictetus; see the notes on Ignat. *Ephes.* inscr., 9.

[2] *Diss.* ii. 10. 7.

[3] *Diss.* ii. 16. 42.

[4] *Diss.* ii. 16. 46.

[5] *Diss.* iii. 1. 36 sq.

[6] *Diss.* iii. 22. 2 sq. The passage bears a strong resemblance to our Lord's parable in Matt. xxiv. 45 sq., Luke xii. 41 sq. The expressions, ὁ

the true philosopher) ought to know that he is sent a messenger from God to men, to show them concerning good and evil[1].' ' He must be wholly given without distraction to the service of God, free to converse with mankind, not tied down by private duties, nor entangled in relations, which if he transgresses, he will no longer keep the character of a noble and good man, and if he observes, he will fail in his part as the messenger and watchman and herald of the gods[2].'

Improved tone of Stoic theology.

The genuine piety of these passages is a remarkable contrast to the arrogance and blasphemy in which the older Stoics sometimes indulged and which even Seneca repeats with approval[3]. Stoic theology, as represented by Epictetus, is fast wiping away its reproach; but in so doing it has almost ceased to be Stoic. The pantheistic creed, which identifies God with the world, is kept in the background; and by this subordination greater room is left for the expansion of true reverence. On the other hand (to pass over graver defects in his system) he has not yet emancipated himself from the austerity and isolation of Stoical ethics. There still remains a hardness and want of sympathy about his moral teaching, which betrays its parentage. But enough has been said to account for the fact that the remains of Epictetus have found a place in the library of the Church, and that the most pious and thoughtful Christian divines have listened with admiration to his devout utterances[4].

οἰκονόμος, ὁ κύριος, ὁ οἰκοδεσπότης, occur in both the philosopher and the Evangelists. Moreover the word ἔτεμεν in Epictetus corresponds to διχοτομήσει in the Gospels, and in both words the difficulty of interpretation is the same. I can hardly believe that so strange a coincidence is quite accidental. Combined with the numerous parallels in Seneca's writings collected above (p. 281 sq.), it favours the supposition that our Lord's discourses in some form or other were early known to heathen writers. For other coincidences more or less close see i. 9. 19, i. 25. 10, i. 29. 31, iii. 21. 16, iii. 22. 35, iv. 1. 79 (ἂν δ' ἀγγαρεία ᾖ κ.τ.λ., comp. Matt. v. 41), iv. 8. 36.

[1] Diss. iii. 22, 23.
[2] Diss. iii. 22. 69. I have only been able to give short extracts, but the

whole passage should be read. Epictetus appears throughout to be treading in the footsteps of St Paul. His words, ἀπερίσπαστον εἶναι δεῖ ὅλον πρὸς τῇ διακονίᾳ τοῦ Θεοῦ, correspond to the Apostle's expression, εὐπάρεδρον τῷ Κυρίῳ ἀπερισπάστως (1 Cor. vii. 35), and the reason given for remaining unmarried is the same. Another close coincidence with St Paul is ὃ μὲν θέλει οὐ ποιεῖ (ii. 26. 1). Again such phrases as νομίμως ἀθλεῖν (iii. 10. 8), γράμματα συστατικά (ii. 3. 1), ταῦτα μελέτα (iv. 1. 170), οὐκ εἰμὶ ἐλεύθερος; (iii. 22. 48), recall the Apostle's language. Other Scriptural expressions also occur, such as Θεοῦ ζηλωτής (ii. 14. 13), τροφὴ στερεωτέρα (ii. 16, 39), etc.

[3] See above p. 295.
[4] 'Epictetus seems as if he had come after or before his time; too late for

As Epictetus gives a higher tone to the theology of the school, M. Aureli-
so the writings of M. Aurelius manifest an improvement in its us.
ethical teaching. The manifold opportunities of his position would
cherish in an emperor naturally humane and sensitive wider sympathies, than were possible to a lame old man born and bred a slave,
whom cruel treatment had estranged from his kind and who was Improved
still further isolated by his bodily infirmity. At all events it is in tone of
Stoic
this point, and perhaps in this alone, that the meditations of M. morality.
Aurelius impress us more favourably than the discourses of Epictetus. As a conscious witness of God and a stern preacher of righteousness, the Phrygian slave holds a higher place : but as a kindly
philanthropist, conscientiously alive to the claims of all men far and
near, the Roman emperor commands deeper respect. In him, for the
first and last time in the history of the school, the cosmopolitan
sympathies, with which the Stoic invested his wise man, become
more than a mere empty form of rhetoric. His natural disposition
softened the harsher features of Stoical ethics. The brooding melancholy and the almost feminine tenderness, which appear in his meditations, are a marked contrast to the hard outlines in the por-
traiture of the older Stoics. Cato was the most perfect type of the
school : but M. Aurelius was the better man, because he was the worse
Stoic. Altogether there is a true beauty and nobleness of character in
this emperor, which the accidents of his position throw into stronger
relief. Beset by all the temptations which unlimited power could
create, and sorely tried in the most intimate and sacred relations of
life—with a profligate wife and an inhuman son—he neither sullied
nor hardened his heart, but remained pure and upright and amiable
to the end, the model of a conscientious if not a wise ruler, and the
best type which heathendom could give of a high-minded gentleman.
With all this it is a more than 'tragical fact,' that his justice and his Persecu-
humanity alike broke down in one essential point, and that by his tion of the
Christians

philosophy, too early for religion. We
are tempted continually to apply to his
system the hackneyed phrase: It is all
very magnificent, but it is not philosophy—it is too one-sided and careless of
knowledge for its own sake; and it is
not religion—it is inadequate and wants
a basis. Yet for all this, as long as
men appreciate elevated thought, in

direct and genuine language, about
human duties and human improvement,
Epictetus will have much to teach those
who know more than he did both of
philosophy and religion. It is no wonder that he kindled the enthusiasm of
Pascal or fed the thought of Butler.'
*Saturday Review*, Vol. xxii. p. 580.

bigotry or through his connivance the Christians suffered more widely
and cruelly during his reign than at any other epoch in the first
century and a half of their existence[1]. Moreover the inherent and
vital defects of the school, after all the modifications it had undergone and despite the amiable character of its latest representative,
are still patent. 'The Stoicism of M. Aurelius gives many of the
moral precepts of the Gospel, but without their foundation, which
can find no place in his system. It is impossible to read his re-
flections without emotion, but they have no creative energy. They
are the last strain of a dying creed[2].'

References
to Christi-
anity in
Epictetus
and M. Au-
relius.
It is interesting to note the language in which these two latest
and noblest representatives of Stoicism refer to the Christians. Once
and once only is the now numerous and rapidly growing sect mentioned by either philosopher, and in each case dismissed curtly with
an expression of contempt. 'Is it possible,' asks Epictetus, 'that a
man may be so disposed under these circumstances from madness, or
from habit like the Galileans, and can no one learn by reason and
demonstration that God has made all things which are in the world[3]?'
'This readiness to die,' writes M. Aurelius, 'should follow from individual judgment, not from sheer obstinacy as with the Christians,
but after due consideration and with dignity and without scenic display (ἀτραγῴδως), so as to convince others also[4].' The justice of such
contemptuous allusions may be tested by the simple and touching
narrative of the deaths of this very emperor's victims, of the Gallic
martyrs at Vienne and Lyons: and the appeal may confidently be
made to the impartial judgment of mankind to decide whether
there was more scenic display or more genuine obstinacy in their
last moments, than in the much vaunted suicide of Cato and Cato's
imitators.

[1] Martha, *Moralistes* p. 212, attempts
to defend M. Aurelius against this
charge; but the evidence of a wide
persecution is irresistible. For the motives which might lead M. Aurelius,
both as a ruler and as a philosopher, to
sanction these cruelties, see Zeller *Marcus Aurelius Antoninus* in his *Vorträge*
p. 101 sq. If it were established that
this emperor had intimate relations with
a Jewish rabbi, as has been recently

maintained (*M. Aurelius Antoninus als
Freund u. Zeitgenosse des Rabbi Jehuda
ha-Nasi* by A. Bodek, Leipzig 1868),
he would have an additional motive
for his treatment of the Christians;
but, to say the least, the identification
of the emperor is very uncertain.
[2] Westcott in Smith's *Dictionary of
the Bible* II. p. 857, s. v. *Philosophy*.
[3] *Diss.* iv. 7. 6.
[4] M. Anton. xi. 3.

I have spoken of Epictetus and M. Aurelius as Stoics, for so they regarded themselves; nor indeed could they be assigned to any other school of philosophy. But their teaching belongs to a type, which in many respects would hardly have been recognised by Zeno or Chrysippus. Stoicism during the Roman period had been first attaching to itself, and then assimilating, diverse foreign elements, Platonic, Pythagorean, even Jewish and Christian. In Seneca these appear side by side, but distinct; in Epictetus and M. Aurelius they are more or less fused and blended. Roman Stoicism in fact presents to us not a picture with clear and definite outlines, but a dissolving view. It becomes more and more eclectic. The materialism of its earlier theology gradually recedes; and the mystical element appears in the foreground[1]. At length Stoicism fades away; and a new eclectic system, in which mysticism has still greater predominance, emerges and takes its place. Stoicism has fought the battle of heathen philosophy against the Gospel, and been vanquished. Under the banner of Neoplatonism, and with weapons forged in the armoury of Christianity itself, the contest is renewed. But the day of heathendom is past. This new champion also retires from the conflict in confusion, and the Gospel remains in possession of the field.

In this attempt to sketch the progress and results of this school, I have not travelled beyond a few great names. Nor has any injustice been done to it by this course, for Stoicism has no other history, except the history of its leaders. It consisted of isolated individuals, but it never attracted the masses or formed a community. It was a staff of professors without classes. This sterility must have been due to some inherent vicious principles: and I propose now to consider its chief defects, drawing out the contrast with Christianity at the same time.

1. The fundamental and invincible error of Stoic philosophy was its theological creed. Though frequently disguised in devout language which the most sincere believer in a personal God might have welcomed as expressing his loftiest aspirations, its theology was nevertheless, as dogmatically expounded by its ablest teachers, nothing better than a pantheistic materialism. This inconsistency between the philosophic doctrine and the religious phraseology of

---

[1] On the approximation of the later Stoics, and more especially of M. Aure- lius, to Neoplatonism, see Zeller's *Nach- aristotelische Philosophie* II. p. 201 sq.

the Stoics is a remarkable feature, which perhaps may be best explained by its mixed origin. The theological language would be derived in great measure from Eastern (I venture to think from Jewish) affinities, while the philosophical dogma was the product of Hellenized thought. Heathen devotion seldom or never soars

**Hymn of Cleanthes.** higher than in the sublime hymn of Cleanthes. 'Thine offspring are we,' so he addresses the Supreme Being, 'therefore will I hymn Thy praises and sing Thy might for ever. Thee all this universe which rolls about the earth obeys, wheresoever Thou dost guide it, and gladly owns Thy sway.' 'No work on earth is wrought apart from Thee, nor through the vast heavenly sphere, nor in the sea, save only the deeds which bad men in their folly do.' 'Unhappy they, who ever craving the possession of good things, yet have no eyes or ears for the universal law of God, by wise obedience whereunto they might lead a noble life.' 'Do Thou, Father, banish fell ignorance from our soul, and grant us wisdom, whereon relying Thou rulest all things with justice, that being honoured, we with honour may requite Thee, as beseemeth mortal man : since neither men nor gods have any nobler task than duly to praise the universal law for

**Contradiction between Stoic dogma and Stoic hymnology.** aye[1].' If these words might be accepted in their first and obvious meaning, we could hardly wish for any more sublime and devout expression of the relations of the creature to his Creator and Father. But a reference to the doctrinal teaching of the school dispels the splendid illusion. Stoic dogma empties Stoic hymnology of half its sublimity and more than half its devoutness. This Father in heaven, we learn, is no personal Being, all righteous and all holy, of whose loving care the purest love of an earthly parent is but a shadowy counterfeit. He—or It—is only another name for nature, for necessity, for fate, for the universe. Just in proportion as the theological doctrine of the school is realised, does its liturgical language appear forced and unnatural. Terms derived from human relationships are confessedly very feeble and inadequate at best to express the person and attributes of God; but only a mind prepared by an artificial training could use such language as I have quoted with the meaning which it is intended to bear. To simple people it would be impossible to address fate or necessity or universal

---

[1] *Fragm. Philos. Græc.* i. p. 151 (ed. Mullach).

nature, as a Father, or to express towards it feelings of filial obedience and love.

And with the belief in a Personal Being, as has been already remarked, the sense of sin also will stand or fall[1]. Where this belief is absent, error or wrong-doing may be condemned from two points of view, irrespective of its consequences and on grounds of independent morality. It may be regarded as a defiance of the law of our being, or it may be deprecated as a violation of the principles of beauty and propriety implanted in the mind. In other words it may be condemned either from *physical* or from *æsthetic* considerations. The former aspect is especially common with the Stoics, for indeed conformity with nature is the groundwork of Stoical ethics. The latter appears occasionally, though this point of view is characteristic rather of the Academy than of the Porch. These are important subsidiary aids to ethical teaching, and should not be neglected : but the consciousness of sin, as sin, is distinct from both. It is only possible where there is a clear sense of a personal relation to a Personal Being, whom we are bound to love and obey, whose will must be the law of our lives and should be the joy of our hearts. Here again the Stoic's language is treacherous. He can talk of sin, just as he can talk of God his Father. But so long as he is true to his dogma, he uses terms here, as before, in a non-natural sense. Only so far as he deserts the theological standing-ground of his school (and there is much of this happy inconsistency in the great Stoic teachers), does he attain to such an apprehension of the ' exceeding sinfulness of sin' as enables him to probe the depths of the human conscience.

2. When we turn from the theology to the ethics of the Stoical school, we find defects not less vital in its teaching. Here again Stoicism presents in itself a startling and irreconcilable contradiction. The fundamental Stoic maxim of conformity to nature, though involving great difficulties in its practical application, might at all events have afforded a starting-point for a reasonable ethical code. Yet it is hardly too much to say that no system of morals, which the wit of man has ever devised, assumes an attitude so fiercely defiant of nature as this. It is mere folly to maintain that pain and privation are no evils. The paradox must defeat its own

*Margin notes:*
No consciousness of sin.

2. Defects in Stoical ethics.

Defiance of nature.

[1] See above, p. 296.

ends. True religion, like true philosophy, concedes the point, and sets itself to counteract, to reduce, to minimise them. Our Lord 'divides himself at once from the ascetic and the Stoic. They had said, Make yourselves independent of bodily comforts: he says, Ye have need of these things[1].' Christianity itself also preaches an αὐτάρκεια, a moral independence, but its preaching starts from a due recognition of the facts of human life.

Want of sympathy.

And, while Stoicism is thus paradoxical towards the individual, its view of the mutual relations between man and man is a still greater outrage on humanity. 'In every age the Christian temper has shivered at the touch of Stoic apathy[2].' Pity, anger, love—all the most powerful social impulses of our nature—are ignored by the Stoic, or at least recognised only to be crushed. There is no attempt to chasten or to guide these affections : they must simply be rooted out. The Stoic ideal is stern, impassive, immovable. As a natural consequence, the genuine Stoic is isolated and selfish : he feels no sympathy with others, and therefore he excites no sympathy in others. Any wide extension of Stoicism was thus rendered impossible by its inherent repulsiveness. It took a firm hold on a few solitary spirits, but it was wholly powerless with the masses.

Stoicism exclusive and not proselytizing.

Nor indeed can it be said in this respect to have failed in its aim. The true Stoic was too self-contained, too indifferent to the condition of others, to concern himself whether the tenets of his school made many proselytes or few. He wrapped himself up in his self-conceit, declared the world to be mad, and gave himself no more trouble about the matter. His avowal of cosmopolitan principles, his tenet of religious equality, became inoperative, because the springs of sympathy, which alone could make them effective, had been frozen at their source. Where enthusiasm is a weakness and love a delusion, such professions must necessarily be empty verbiage. The temper of Stoicism was essentially aristocratic and exclusive in religion, as it was in politics. While professing the largest comprehension, it was practically the narrowest of all philosophical castes.

3. No distinct belief in man's immortality.

3. Though older philosophers had speculated on the immortality of the soul, and though the belief had been encouraged by some schools of moralists as supplying a most powerful motive for well-doing, yet still it remained for the heathen a vague theory, unascer-

---

[1] *Ecce Homo* p. 116.          [2] *Ecce Homo* p. 119.

tained and unascertainable. To the Christian alone, when he accepted the fact of Christ's resurrection, did it become an established and incontrovertible truth. Stoicism does not escape the vagueness which overclouds all mere philosophical speculation on this subject. On one point alone were the professors of this school agreed. An *eternal* existence of the human soul was out of the question. At the great periodic conflagration, when the universe should be fused and the manifold organizations dissolved into chaos, the souls of men must necessarily be involved in the common destruction[1]. But within this limit much diversity of opinion prevailed. Some maintained a longer, some a shorter, duration of the soul. Cleanthes said that all men would continue to exist till the conflagration; Chrysippus confined even this limited immortality to the wise[2]. The language of Seneca on this point is both timid and capricious. 'If there be any sense or feeling after death' is his cautious hypothesis, frequently repeated[3]. 'I was pleasantly engaged,' he writes to his friend Lucilius, 'in enquiring about the eternity of souls, or rather, I should say, in trusting. For I was ready to trust myself to the opinions of great men, who avow rather than prove so very acceptable a thing. I was surrendering myself to this great hope, I was beginning to be weary of myself, to despise the remaining fragments of a broken life, as though I were destined to pass away into that illimitable time, and into the possession of eternity; when I was suddenly aroused by the receipt of your letter, and this beautiful dream vanished[4].' When again he would console the bereaved mourner, he has no better words of comfort to offer than these: 'Why do I waste away with fond regret for one who either is happy or does not exist at all? It is envy to bewail him if he is happy, and madness if he does not exist[5].' 'Bear in mind that no evils affect the dead; that the circumstances which make the lower world terrible to us are an idle story.' 'Death is the release and end of all pains.' 'Death is neither a good nor an evil: for that only can be good or evil which

*Marginal notes:* Diversity of opinion among the Stoics. Seneca's inconsistency and vagueness

---

[1] See e.g. Seneca *ad Marc.* 26, *ad Polyb.* 1. (20).

[2] Diog. Laert. vii. 157.

[3] *De Brev. Vit.* 18, *ad Polyb.* 5, 9, *Ep. Mor.* xxiv. 18, lxv. 24, lxxi. 16. Tertullian (*de Resurr. Carn.* 1, *de Anim.* 42) quotes Seneca as saying 'Omnia post mortem finiri, etiam ipsam.'

[4] *Ep. Mor.* cii. 2; comp. *Ep. Mor.* cxvii. 6 'Cum animarum æternitatem disserimus, non leve momentum apud nos habet consensus hominum aut ti mentium inferos aut colentium.'

[5] *Ad Polyb.* 9.

is something.' 'Fortune can retain no hold, where nature has given
a release : nor can one be wretched, who does not exist at all[1].'
Afterwards indeed he speaks in a more cheerful strain : 'Eternal rest
awaits him leaving this murky and troubled (earth) and migrating to
the pure and liquid (sky)[2]' : but such expressions must be qualified
by what has gone before. Again in this same treatise, as in other
places[3], he promises after death an enlarged sphere of knowledge
and a limitless field of calm and pure contemplation. But the promise which he gives in one sentence is often modified or retracted
in the next ; and even where the prospects held out are the brightest,
it is not always clear whether he contemplates a continuance of conscious individual existence, or merely the absorption into Universal
Being and the impersonal participation in its beauty and order[4].
The views of Epictetus and M. Aurelius are even more cloudy and
cheerless than those of Seneca. Immortality, properly so called, has
no place in their philosophies.

**Import-
ance of the
doctrine to
Christian-
ity.** Gibbon, in his well-known chapter on the origin and growth
of Christianity, singles out the promise of eternal life as among
the chief causes which promoted its diffusion. Overlooking much
that is offensive in the tone of his remarks, we need not hesitate
to accept the statement as substantially true. It is indeed more
than questionable whether (as Gibbon implies) the growth of the
Church was directly due to the inducements of the offer ; for (looking
only to self-interest) it has a repulsive as well as an attractive side :
but without doubt it added enormously to the moral power of the
Gospel in commending it to the hearts and consciences of men.
Deterring, stimulating, reassuring, purifying and exalting the inward
and outward life, 'the power of Christ's resurrection' extends over
the whole domain of Christian ethics.

**Its indif-
ference to
Stoicism.** On the other hand it was a matter of indifference to the Stoic
whether he doubted or believed or denied the immortality of man ;
for the doctrine was wholly external to his creed, and nothing

[1] *Ad Marc.* 19 ; comp. *Ep. Mor.*
xxxvi. 10 'Mors nullum habet incommodum: esse enim debet aliquis, cujus
sit incommodum,' with the context.

[2] *Ad Marc.* 24.

[3] Comp. e.g. *Ep. Mor.* lxxix. 12,
lxxxvi. 1, cii. 22, 28 sq.

[4] Holzherr *Der Philosoph I. Annæus*

*Seneca* II. p. 58 sq. (1859) endeavours
to show that Seneca is throughout consistent with himself and follows the
Platonists rather than the Stoics in his
doctrine of the immortality of the soul.
I do not see how it is possible, after
reading the treatise *ad Marciam*, to acquit him of inconsistency.

could be lost or gained by the decision. Not life but death was the constant subject of his meditations. His religious director was summoned to his side, not to prepare him for eternity, but to teach him how to die[1]. This defect alone would have rendered Stoicism utterly powerless with the masses of men : for the enormous demands which it made on the faith and self-denial of its adherents could not be sustained without the sanction and support of such a belief. The Epicurean motto, 'Let us eat and drink, for to-morrow Conse-we die,' base though it was, had at least this recommendation, that quent pa-radoxes the conclusion did seem to follow from the premisses : but the moral and per-plexities of teaching of the Stoic was practically summed up in the paralogism, Stoicism. 'Let us neither eat nor drink, for to-morrow we die,' where no wit of man could bridge over the gulf between the premisses and the conclusion. A belief in man's immortality might have saved the Stoic from many intellectual paradoxes and much practical perplexity : but then it would have made him other than a Stoic. He had a profound sense of the reign of moral order in the universe. Herein he was right. But the postulate of man's immortality alone reconciles this belief with many facts of actual experience ; and, refusing to extend his views beyond the present life, he was obliged to misstate or deny these facts in order to save his thesis[2]. He staunchly maintained the inherent quality of actions as good or bad (irrespective of their consequences), and he has deserved the gratitude of mankind as the champion of a morality of principles. But he falsely supposed himself bound in consequence to deny any force to the utilitarian aspect of ethics, as though it were irreconcilable with his own doctrine ; and so he was led into the wildest paradoxes, calling good evil and evil good. The meeting-point of these two distinct lines of view is beyond the grave, and he refused to carry his range of vision so far. It was inconsistent with his tenets to hold out the hope of a future life as an incentive to well-doing and a dissuasive from sin ; for he wholly ignored the idea of retribution.

---

[1] Socrates (or Plato) said that true philosophers οὐδὲν ἄλλο αὐτοὶ ἐπιτηδεύ-ουσιν ἢ ἀποθνήσκειν τε καὶ τεθνάναι (Phædo 64 A). The Stoic, by accepting the ἀποθνήσκειν and forgetting the τεθνάναι, robbed the saying of its virtue.

[2] Butler argues from the fact that

'the divine government which we experience ourselves under in the present state, taken alone, is allowed not to be the perfection of moral government.' The Stoic denied what the Christian philosopher assumes, and contradicted experience by maintaining that it is perfect, taken alone.

So far, there was more substantial truth and greater moral power in the crude and gross conceptions of an afterworld embodied in the popular mythology which was held up to scorn by him, than in the imposing philosophy which he himself had devised to supplant them.

**4. Absence of a historical basis.**

4. Attention was directed above to an instructive parallel which Seneca's language presents to our Lord's image of the vine and the branches[1]. Precepts, writes the philosopher, wither unless they are grafted in a sect. By this confession Seneca virtually abandons the position of self-isolation and self-sufficiency, which the Stoic assumes. He felt vaguely the want of some historical basis, some bond of social union, in short some principle of cohesion, which should give force and vitality to his ethical teaching. No mere abstract philosophy has influenced or can influence permanently large masses of men. A Bible and a Church—

**A sacred record and a religious community necessary.**

a sacred record and a religious community—are primary conditions of extensive and abiding success. An isolated spirit here and there may have dispensed with such aids; but, as a social power, as a continuous agency, mere doctrine, however imposing, will for the most part be ineffective without such a support.

So far we have been speaking of conditions of success which were wanting indeed to Stoicism, but which nevertheless are not peculiar to Christianity. All creeds, which have secured any wide and lasting allegiance, have had their sacred books and their religious organi-

**Christianity centres in a Person.**

zation. But our Lord's language, of which Seneca's image is a partial though unconscious echo, points to the one distinguishing feature of Christianity. It is not a record nor a community, but a Person, whence the sap spreads to the branches and ripens into the rich clusters. I have already alluded to Gibbon's account of the causes which combined to promote the spread of the Church. It will seem strange to any one who has at all felt the spirit of the Gospel, that a writer, enumerating the forces to which the dissemination and predominance of Christianity were due, should omit all

**Christ the source of the moral power of Christianity.**

mention of the Christ. One might have thought it impossible to study with common attention the records of the Apostles and martyrs of the first ages or of the saints and heroes of the later Church, without seeing that the consciousness of personal union with

---

[1] See above, p. 285.

Him, the belief in His abiding presence, was the mainspring of their actions and the fountain of all their strength. This is not a preconceived theory of what should have happened, but a bare statement of what stands recorded on the pages of history. In all ages and under all circumstances, the Christian life has ever radiated from this central fire. Whether we take St Peter or St Paul, St Francis of Assisi or John Wesley, whether Athanasius or Augustine, Anselm or Luther, whether Boniface or Francis Xavier, here has been the impulse of their activity and the secret of their moral power. Their lives have illustrated the parable of the vine and the branches.

It is this which differentiates Christianity from all other religions, and still more from all abstract systems of philosophy. Those who assume the entire aim and substance of the Gospel to have been the inculcation of moral precepts, and who therefore rest its claims solely or chiefly on the purity of its ethical code, often find themselves sorely perplexed, when they stumble upon some noble and true utterance of Jewish or Heathen antiquity before the coming of Christ. A maxim of a Stoic philosopher or a Rabbinical schoolman, a saying of Plato or Confucius, startles them by its resemblance to the teaching of the Gospel. Such perplexity is founded on a twofold error. On the one hand they have not realised the truth that the same Divine Power was teaching mankind before He was made flesh : while on the other they have failed to see what is involved in this incarnation and its sequel. To those who have felt how much is implied in St John's description of the pre-incarnate Word as the life and light of men ; to those who allow the force of Tertullian's appeal to the 'witness of a soul naturally Christian' ; to those who have sounded the depths of Augustine's bold saying, that what we now call the Christian religion existed from the dawn of the human race, though it only began to be named Christian when Christ came in the flesh[1] ; to those who can respond to the sentiment of the old English poem,

> 'Many man for Cristes love
> Was martired in Romayne,
> Er any Cristendom was knowe there
> Or any cros honoured' ;

it cannot be a surprise to find such flashes of divine truth in men

*Distinctive feature of Christianity.*

*Not a moral code*

---

[1] *Retract.* i. 13.

who lived before the coming of our Lord or were placed beyond
the reach of the Gospel. The significance of Christ's moral precepts
does not lose but gain by the admission : for we learn to view Him
no longer as one wholly apart from our race, but recognising in His
teaching old truths which 'in manhood darkly join,' we shall only be
the more prompt to

> 'Yield all blessing to the name
> Of Him that made them current coin.'

but a prin-<br>ciple of life<br>centred in<br>a Person. But the mere ethical teaching, however important, is the least
important, because the least distinctive part of Christianity.    If
there be any meaning in the saying that Christ appeared to 'bring
life and immortality to light,' if the stedfast convictions of St Peter
and St Paul and St John were not a delusion, and their lives not
built upon a lie, then obviously a deeper principle is involved.    The
moral teaching and the moral example of our Lord will ever have
the highest value in their own province ; but the core of the Gospel
does not lie here.    Its distinctive character is, that in revealing a
Person it reveals also a principle of life—the union with God in
Christ, apprehended by faith in the present and assured to us hereafter by the Resurrection.    This Stoicism could not give ; and therefore its dogmas and precepts were barren.    Its noblest branches
bore neither flowers nor fruit, because there was no parent stem
from which they could draw fresh sap.

## The Letters of Paul and Seneca.

THE spurious correspondence between the Apostle and the philosopher to which reference is made in the preceding essay, consists of fourteen letters, the 1st, 3rd, 5th, 7th, 9th, 11th, 12th, and 13th written in the name of Seneca, and the 2nd, 4th, 6th, 8th, 10th, and 14th of St Paul. In the address of the 6th the name of Lucilius is added to that of Seneca, and in the same way in the address of the 7th Theophilus is named along with St Paul. *The correspondence described.*

I have not thought it worth while to reprint these letters, as they may be read conveniently in the recent edition of Seneca's works by F. Haase (III. p. 476 sq.) included in Teubner's series, and are to be found likewise in several older editions of this author. They have been printed lately also in Fleury's *St Paul et Sénèque* (II. p. 300 sq.) and in Aubertin's *Sénèque et St Paul* (p. 409 sq.), and still more recently in an article by Kraus, entitled *Der Briefwechsel Pauli mit Seneca*, in the *Theologische Quartalschrift* XLIX. p. 601 (1867). *Editions of the letters.*

The great popularity of this correspondence in the ages before the Reformation is shown by the large number of extant MSS. Fleury, making use of the common catalogues, has enumerated about sixty; and probably a careful search would largely increase the number. The majority, as is usual in such cases, belong to the thirteenth, fourteenth, and fifteenth centuries, but two at least are as early as the ninth. Haase used some fresh collations, from which however he complains that little was to be got (p. xxii); and Fleury also collated three MSS from Paris and one from Toulouse. Haase directed attention to the two most ancient, Ambrosianus C. 90 and Argentoratensis C. VI. 5, both belonging to the ninth century (which had not yet been examined), but had no opportunity of collating them himself. Collations from these (together with another later Strassburg MS, Argentoratensis C. VI. 7) were afterwards used by Kraus for his text, which is thus constructed of better materials than any other. But after all, it remains in an unsatisfactory state, which the worthlessness of the letters themselves may well excuse. *The MSS and collations.*

This correspondence was probably forged in the fourth century, either to recommend Seneca to Christian readers or to recommend Christianity to students of Seneca. In favour of this view may be urged the fact that in several MSS these spurious letters precede the genuine works of Seneca[1]. Nor does any other motive seem consistent with the letters themselves; for they have no doctrinal bearing at all, and no historical interest of *Probable motive of the forgery.*

---

[1] As for instance Argent. C. vi. 5 described by Kraus. So in Burn. 251 (British Museum), which I have examined, they are included in a collection of genuine and spurious works of Seneca, being themselves preceded by the notice of Jerome and followed by the first of the epistles to Lucilius. It is not uncommon to find them immediately before the genuine epistles.

sufficient importance to account for the forgery. They are made up chiefly of an interchange of compliments between the Apostle and the philosopher; and the only historical thread which can be said to run through them is the endeavour of Seneca to gain the ear of Nero for the writings of St Paul.

Reference to the letters by Jerome,

It is commonly said that St Jerome, who first mentions these letters, had no suspicion that they were spurious. This statement however is exaggerated, for he does not commit himself to any opinion at all about their genuineness. He merely says, that he 'should not have given a place to Seneca in a catalogue of saints, unless challenged to do so by those letters of Paul to Seneca and from Seneca to Paul which are read by very many persons' (*de Vir. Ill.* 12 'nisi me illæ epistolæ provocarent quæ leguntur a plurimis'). When it is remembered how slight an excuse serves to bring other names into his list, such as Philo, Josephus, and Justus Tiberiensis, we cannot lay any stress on the vague language which he uses in this case. The more probable inference is that he did not deliberately accept them as genuine. Indeed, if he had so accepted them, his profound silence about them elsewhere would be wholly inexplicable.

Augustine,

St Augustine, as generally happens in questions of historical criticism, repeats the language of Jerome and perhaps had not seen the letters (*Epist.* cliii. 14 'Seneca cujus quædam ad Paulum apostolum leguntur

and later writers.

epistolæ[1]'). Throughout the middle ages they are mentioned or quoted, most frequently as genuine, but occasionally with an expression of doubt, until the revival of learning, when the light of criticism rapidly dispelled the illusion[2].

These letters a manifest forgery.

As they are now universally allowed to be spurious, it will be unnecessary to state at length the grounds of their condemnation. It is sufficient to say that the letters are inane and unworthy throughout; that the style of either correspondent is unlike his genuine writings; that the relations between the two, as there represented, are highly improbable; and lastly, that the chronological notices (which however are absent in some important MSS) are wrong in almost every instance. Thus, independently of the unbroken silence of three centuries and a half about this correspondence, internal evidence alone is sufficient to condemn them hopelessly.

Yet the writer is not ignorant nor wholly careless.

Yet the writer is not an ignorant man. He has read part of Seneca and is aware of the philosopher's relations with Lucilius; he is acquainted with the story of Castor and Pollux appearing to one Vatinius (or Vatienus); he can talk glibly of the gardens of Sallust; he is acquainted with the character of Caligula whom he properly calls Gaius Cæsar; he is even aware of the Jewish sympathies of the empress Poppæa and makes her regard St Paul as a renegade[3]; and lastly, he seems to have had before him some account of the Neronian fire and persecution[4] which is no

---

[1] Another passage quoted above, p. 29, note 2, in which Augustine remarks on Seneca's silence about the Christians, is inconsistent with a conviction of the genuineness of these letters.

[2] See Fleury I. p. 269 sq. for a catena of references.

[3] *Ep.* 5 'Indignatio dominæ, quod a ritu et secta veteri recesseris et [te] aliorsum converteris'; comp. *Ep.* 8, where however the reading is doubtful.

[4] Yet there must be some mistake in the numbers, which appear too small.

longer extant, for he speaks of 'Christians and Jews' being punished as the authors of the conflagration and mentions that 'a hundred and thirty-two houses and six insulæ were burnt in six days.'

Moreover I believe he attempts, though he succeeds ill in the attempt, to make a difference in the styles of Seneca and St Paul, the writing of the latter being more ponderous. Unfortunately he betrays himself by representing Seneca as referring more than once to St Paul's bad style; and in one letter the philosopher mentions sending the Apostle a book *de Copia Verborum*, obviously for the purpose of improving his Latin.

I mention these facts, because they bear upon a theory maintained by some modern critics[1], that these letters are not the same with those to which Jerome and Augustine refer ; that they had before them a genuine correspondence between St Paul and Seneca, which has since perished; and that the extant epistles were forged later (say about the ninth century), being suggested by the notices in these fathers and invented in consequence to supply their place. The only specious arguments advanced in favour of this view, so far as I know, are these: (1) A man like Jerome could not possibly have believed the extant correspondence to be genuine, for the forgery is transparent ; (2) The *de Copia Verborum* is a third title to a work otherwise known as *de Formula Honestæ Vitæ* or *de Quatuor Virtutibus*, written by Martinus Bragensis or Dumiensis († circ. A.D. 580), but ascribed in many MSS to Seneca. Sufficient time therefore must have elapsed since this date to allow the false title and false ascription to take the place of the true and to be generally circulated and recognised[2].

To both these arguments a ready answer may be given : (1) There is no reason to suppose that Jerome did believe the correspondence to be genuine, as I have already shown. He would hardly have spoken so vaguely, if he had accepted them as genuine or even inclined to this belief. (2) A much better account can be given of the false title and ascription of Martin's treatise, if we suppose that they arose out of the allusion in the letters, than on the converse hypothesis that they were prior to and suggested this allusion. This Martin, whose works appear to have had a very large circulation in the middle ages, wrote on kindred subjects and seems occasionally to have abridged and adapted Seneca's writings. For this reason his works were commonly bound up with those of Seneca, and in some instances came to be ascribed to the Stoic philosopher. This is the case at all events with the *de Moribus*, as well as the *de Quatuor Virtutibus*, and perhaps other spurious treatises bearing the name of Seneca may be assigned to the same author. A copy of the *de Quatuor Virtutibus*, either designedly abridged or accidentally mutilated, and on this account wanting the title, was bound up so as to precede or follow the correspondence of Paul and Seneca[3]; and, as Seneca in one of these

*Marginal notes:*

Theory of some modern critics.

The arguments for this view stated

and answered.

Martinus Bragensis

Account of *de Copia Verborum*.

---

[1] An account of these views will be found in Fleury II. p. 225 sq. He himself holds that the letters read by these fathers were not the same with our correspondence, but questions whether those letters were genuine.

[2] This argument is urged by Fleury

II. p. 267 sq. The *de Formula Honestæ Vitæ* is printed in Haase's edition of Seneca (III. p. 468) together with other spurious works.

[3] It is found in some extant MSS (e.g. Flor. Pl. xlv. Cod. iv) immediately before the letters, and it may perhaps

letters mentions sending the *de Copia Verborum*, a later transcriber assumed that the neighbouring treatise must be the work in question, and without reflecting gave it this title[1]. Whether the forger of the correspondence invented an imaginary title, or whether a standard work bearing this name, either by Seneca himself or by some one else, was in general circulation when he wrote, we have no means of deciding ; but the motive in the allusion is clearly the improvement of St Paul's Latin, of which Seneca more than once complains. On the other hand the *de Quatuor Virtutibus* is, as its name implies, a treatise on the cardinal virtues. An allusion to this treatise therefore would be meaningless; nor indeed has any reasonable explanation been given, how it got the title *de Copia Verborum*, on the supposition that this title was prior to the allusion in the correspondence and was not itself suggested thereby, for it is wholly alien to the subject of the treatise.

Direct reasons against this theory.
But other strong and (as it seems to me) convincing arguments may be brought against this theory : (1) Extant MSS of the correspondence date from the ninth century, and in these the text is already in a corrupt state. (2) The historical knowledge which the letters show could hardly have

occur in some others immediately after them. [Since the first edition appeared, in which this conjecture was hazarded, I have found the treatise immediately after the letters, Bodl. *Laud. Misc.* 383, fol. 77 a, where it is anonymous.]

[1] The work, when complete, consists of (1) A dedication in Martin's name to Miro king of Gallicia, in which he mentions the title of the book *Formula Vitæ Honestæ ;* (2) A short paragraph enumerating the four cardinal virtues ; (3) A discussion of these several virtues and the measure to be observed in each. In the MSS, so far as I have learnt from personal inspection and from notices in other writers, it is found in three different forms ; (1) Complete (e. g. Cambridge Univ. Libr. Dd. xv. 21; Bodl. *Laud. Misc.* 444, fol. 146), in which case there is no possibility of mistaking its authorship ; (2) Without the dedicatory preface, so that it begins *Quatuor virtutum species* etc. In this form it is generally entitled *de Quatuor Virtutibus* and ascribed to Seneca. So it is for instance in three British Museum MSS, *Burn.* 251 fol. 33 a (XIIIth cent.; the treatise being mutilated at the end and concluding ' In has ergo maculas prudentia immensurata perducet'), *Burn.* 360, fol. 35 a (XIVth cent.?), and *Harl.* 233 (XIIIth or XIVth cent.? ; where how-

ever the general title is wanting and the treatise has the special heading *Seneca de prudentia*). The transcriber of *Arund.* 249 (XVth cent.) also gives it in this form, but is aware of the true author, for the heading is *Incipit tractatus libri honeste vite editus a Martino episcopo Qui a multis intitulatur de quatuor virtutibus et attribuitur Senece;* but he ends it *Explicit tractatus de quatuor virtutibus Annei Senece Cordubensis,* as he doubtless found it in the copy which he transcribed. In Bodl. *Laud. Lat.* 86, fol. 58 a, where it occurs in this form, it is ascribed to its right author; while again in Bodl. *Laud. Misc.* 280, fol. 117 a, it is anonymous. These MSS I have examined. (3) It occurs without either the dedicatory preface or the general paragraph on the four virtues, and some extraneous matter is added at the end. Only in this form, so far as I can discover, does it bear the strange title *de Verborum Copia.* So in one of the Gale MSS at Trinity College Cambridge (o. 3. 31) it begins '*Senece de quatuor virtutibus primo*(?) *de prudentia.* Quisquis prudentiam...' and ends '... jactura que per negligentiam fit. *Explicit liber Senece de verborum copia* '; and the MS described by Haase (III. p. xxii) belongs to the same type. These facts accord with the account of the title which I have suggested in the text.

been possessed, or turned to such account, by a writer later than the fourth or fifth century. (3) Jerome quotes obliquely a passage from the letters, and this passage is found in the extant correspondence. To this it is replied, that the forger, taking the notice of Jerome as his starting-point, would necessarily insert the quotation to give colour to his forgery. But I think it may be assumed in this case that the pseudo-Seneca would have preserved the words of Jerome accurately or nearly so; whereas, though the sense is the same, the difference in form is considerable[1]. It may be added also that the sentiment is in entire keeping with the pervading tone of the letters, and has no appearance of being introduced for a distinct purpose. (4) It is wholly inconceivable that a genuine correspondence of the Apostle could have escaped notice for three centuries and a half; and not less inconceivable that, having once been brought to light at the end of the fourth and beginning of the fifth century, it should again have fallen into oblivion and been suffered to disappear. This theory therefore may be confidently rejected.

---

[1] The reference in St Jerome is ' (Seneca) optare se dicit ejus esse loci apud suos, cujus sit Paulus apud Christianos.' The words stand in the letters (no. 11), '[Uti] nam qui meus, tuus apud te locus, qui tuus, velim ut meus.'

# INDEX.

## Additional Note on the Christian Ministry.

As a full treatment of the information contained in the recently published *Doctrine of the Twelve Apostles* would have required more extensive additions to the Essay on the Christian Ministry than the time at my disposal allowed, I have thought it best to leave the Essay itself unaltered, and to add a few remarks here relating to the new discovery. This course was the less difficult, because this newly discovered work seems to me in almost every respect to confirm the view which I have taken, and any alterations which I might have to make would be chiefly in the way of elucidation and supplement.

The date of the *Didache* has been variously fixed. The first editor Bryennios placed it about A.D. 120—160. Among the advocates of a late date are Harnack (*Texte u. Untersuchungen* II. ii. p. 63 sq.), who assigns it to the period between A.D. 135 (or 140) and A.D. 165, and Hilgenfeld, who places it after the rise of the Montanist controversy. On the other hand Zahn (*Forsch. zur Gesch. d. Kanons* III. p. 319) considers that it cannot have been written later than A.D. 120; Spence (*Teaching of the Twelve Apostles* p. 139) gives the probable limits as A.D. 70 and A.D. 106; Schaff (*Teaching of the Twelve Apostles*, p. 122) places it between A.D. 90 and A.D. 100, as a rough approximation; and Funk (*Theolog. Quartalschr.* 1884, p. 381 sq.) assigns it to the last quarter of the first century; while Sabatier (*La Didachè* p. 165) would even date it as early as A.D. 50, before St Paul's great missionary journeys were undertaken.

For myself, I see no reason to depart from the rough limits (A.D. 80—A.D. 110), which I assigned to it in a paper read at the *Carlisle Church Congress* (*Official Report*, p. 230 sq.; see also *Expositor*, Jan. 1885, p. 1 sq.), though it might possibly have been written a few years earlier or later. In that paper I spoke of Alexandria as not improbably the place of writing, on the ground that it is quoted by, or contains matter in common with, more than one Alexandrian writer. But to this view, which has been generally maintained, a very serious and (it appears to me now) almost insuperable objection has been urged. The writer (§ 9) speaks of the corn from which the eucharistic bread is made as having been 'scattered upon the mountains (διεσκορπισμένον ἐπάνω ὀρέων) and gathered together' into one. This is the last expression which would have occurred to any one writing in the Delta of the Nile, though natural enough in Palestine or Syria. Yet it is obviously quite incidental and unpremeditated.

The main reasons for the early date are, besides the archaic simplicity of the whole document, the two facts that the Eucharist is still part of a meal and connected with the Agape (an arrangement which at all events did not survive the persecution of Trajan in Bithynia, even if it lasted so long) and that there is no trace of the episcopal office as distinct from the presbyteral (a phenomenon which points to the first rather than the second century).

Moreover the picture, which it presents of the temporary and the permanent ministry working side by side—the latter encroaching upon the former—is the same which I have set forth (p. 185 sq.) as characteristic of the later decades of the Apostolic age; and even Harnack allows (p. 101) that the aspect of Church organization which it exhibits closely resembles the representations in the First Epistle to the Corinthians—more closely (he thinks) even than those in the Epistle to the Ephesians. The permanent ministry is represented in the *Didache* by 'Apostles' and 'prophets'; the temporary by 'bishops' and 'deacons'. But we are told (§ 15) that the latter (the 'bishops' and 'deacons') 'likewise minister the ministration of the prophets and teachers' (λειτουργοῦσι καὶ αὐτοὶ τὴν λειτουργίαν τῶν προφητῶν καὶ διδασκάλων). This is an illustration of what I have said (p. 194) as to the gradual transference of the function of teaching from the missionary preachers to the local officers of the congregations. It is possible indeed that the term 'Apostle' in the *Didache* has a wider range than I have assigned to it elsewhere (*Galatians* p. 97 sq.), where following the language of S. Paul it is laid down as a necessary qualification of an 'Apostle' that he should 'have seen the Lord,' and should be in some sense a witness of the Resurrection. But in Syria and Palestine at all events, about the years (say) A.D. 80—90, there must have been not a few who possessed this qualification, as there certainly were several even in proconsular Asia. If for instance this work emanated from the neighbourhood of Pella, whither the Christian community retired before the siege of Jerusalem by Titus, this more restricted sense of the term 'Apostle' would create no difficulty.

The discussion of the original form of the Ignatian Epistles, to which I have referred in a note (p. 234) to this Essay on the Christian Ministry, will be found in my new work on the Epistles of S. Ignatius and S. Polycarp, (*Apostolic Fathers* Part 2, I. p. 267 sq.) which will appear, I hope, nearly simultaneously with this edition.